White Collar Crime

ASPEN CASEBOOK SERIES

White Collar Crime Law, Procedure, Theory, Practice

Michael L. Seigel
University of Florida Research Foundation Professor of Law
Director, Criminal Justice Center
Fredric G. Levin College of Law

Wolters Kluwer
Law & Business

Published by Wolters Kluwer Law & Business in New York.

Wolters Kluwer Law & Business serves customers worldwide with CCH, Aspen Publishers, and Kluwer Law International products. (www.wolterskluwerlb.com)

To contact Customer Service, e-mail customer.service@wolterskluwer.com, call 1-800-234-1660, fax 1-800-901-9075, or mail correspondence to:

Wolters Kluwer Law & Business
Attn: Order Department
PO Box 990
Frederick, MD 21705

Printed in the United States of America.

1 2 3 4 5 6 7 8 9 0

ISBN 978-0-7355-9651-1

Library of Congress Cataloging-in-Publication Data

Seigel, Michael L.
White collar crime : law, procedure, theory, practice / Michael Seigel.
p. cm. — (Aspen casebook series)
Includes bibliographical references and index.
ISBN 978-0-7355-9651-1
1. White collar crimes — United States. 2. White collar crimes — United States — Cases. I. Title.

KF9350.S42 2011
345.73′0268 — dc23

2011040474

About Wolters Kluwer Law & Business

Wolters Kluwer Law & Business is a leading global provider of intelligent information and digital solutions for legal and business professionals in key specialty areas, and respected educational resources for professors and law students. Wolters Kluwer Law & Business connects legal and business professionals as well as those in the education market with timely, specialized authoritative content and information-enabled solutions to support success through productivity, accuracy and mobility.

Serving customers worldwide, Wolters Kluwer Law & Business products include those under the Aspen Publishers, CCH, Kluwer Law International, Loislaw, Best Case, ftwilliam.com and MediRegs family of products.

CCH products have been a trusted resource since 1913, and are highly regarded resources for legal, securities, antitrust and trade regulation, government contracting, banking, pension, payroll, employment and labor, and healthcare reimbursement and compliance professionals.

Aspen Publishers products provide essential information to attorneys, business professionals and law students. Written by preeminent authorities, the product line offers analytical and practical information in a range of specialty practice areas from securities law and intellectual property to mergers and acquisitions and pension/benefits. Aspen's trusted legal education resources provide professors and students with high-quality, up-to-date and effective resources for successful instruction and study in all areas of the law.

Kluwer Law International products provide the global business community with reliable international legal information in English. Legal practitioners, corporate counsel and business executives around the world rely on Kluwer Law journals, looseleafs, books, and electronic products for comprehensive information in many areas of international legal practice.

Loislaw is a comprehensive online legal research product providing legal content to law firm practitioners of various specializations. Loislaw provides attorneys with the ability to quickly and efficiently find the necessary legal information they need, when and where they need it, by facilitating access to primary law as well as state-specific law, records, forms and treatises.

Best Case Solutions is the leading bankruptcy software product to the bankruptcy industry. It provides software and workflow tools to flawlessly streamline petition preparation and the electronic filing process, while timely incorporating ever-changing court requirements.

ftwilliam.com offers employee benefits professionals the highest quality plan documents (retirement, welfare and non-qualified) and government forms (5500/PBGC, 1099 and IRS) software at highly competitive prices.

MediRegs products provide integrated health care compliance content and software solutions for professionals in healthcare, higher education and life sciences, including professionals in accounting, law and consulting.

Wolters Kluwer Law & Business, a division of Wolters Kluwer, is headquartered in New York. Wolters Kluwer is a market-leading global information services company focused on professionals.

Summary of Contents

Contents

chapter 5

chapter 6

chapter 8

chapter 9

chapter 10

chapter 11

chapter 12

chapter 13

chapter 14

Preface

The twenty-first century has been rocked time and again by unprecedented white collar scandals, from Enron's collapse, to Bernard Madoff's $50 billion Ponzi scheme, to, most recently, the fraud (and bad practices) in the real estate investment market that brought the entire U.S. economy to its knees. The federal government has reacted by devoting an ever-increasing quantity of resources to the problem through agencies that include the U.S. Department of Justice, the Federal Bureau of Investigation, and the U.S. Securities and Exchange Commission. At this point, there can be no doubt that the investigation and prosecution of white collar crime is a permanent fixture in our society.

Accordingly, the study of white collar crime will be a staple in U.S. law schools for the foreseeable future. Such courses are relevant not only to those students interested in a career in criminal law, but to the much larger body of students who are interested in working in the corporate environment. The line between regulatory infractions and criminal acts in the white collar world is very thin; every competent corporate lawyer needs to understand just where the courts have drawn it. Thus, a course in White Collar Crime is as much a successor in the curriculum to Corporations and Securities Regulation as it is to Criminal Law and Procedure.

Goals of this Text

This book is designed to accomplish a number of objectives simultaneously. First, it reflects the *present* state of white collar criminal prosecution, not the past. For instance, the book discards some topics traditionally found in other books on the subject—such as the study of racketeering and money laundering—because white collar prosecutors no longer make wide-scale use of these crimes. On the other hand, the book features an extensive chapter on securities fraud and separate chapters on bank fraud, sentencing, and parallel proceedings—because these are critical areas where most of the real-life action is taking place today. It contains also a far-reaching discussion of "honest services fraud," a very hot topic addressed (but not resolved) by the U.S. Supreme Court in its 2009-2010 term. Additionally, the book integrates the recent Sarbanes-Oxley and Dodd-Frank Acts into the text and materials.

Second, as its title suggests, the book puts an emphasis on white collar theory, most of which comes from writings in sociology, economics, and law. The book asks the big questions, including:

(1) What is white collar crime anyway?
(2) What motivates white collar criminals?
(3) How does society best deter white collar crime, and is it appropriate to use the criminal law to do so?
(4) Do white collar defendants receive better treatment in the criminal justice system compared to their blue collar counterparts and, if so, why?

Third, the book is written from a practical and strategic point of view. Learning the law is not enough; rather, effective lawyers must learn how to use the law to their advantage. Many of the notes and questions that follow the excerpted materials reflect this practical bent.

Fourth, the book features a unique balance between law and procedure. Some white collar casebooks contain no procedure whatsoever; others feature so much procedure that these materials dwarf the books' presentation of criminal law doctrine. This book is carefully balanced. Although it is weighted in favor of white collar criminal law, two chapters (Chapters 11 and 12) are devoted to procedural issues—one written from the prosecutor's perspective and the other from the defense point of view. In concert with the book's practical orientation, these chapters focus on how lawyers on both sides of the isle use procedure as both a shield and a sword to the extent the law allows. Neither is intended to be comprehensive, as in-depth criminal procedure is the subject of other courses in the typical law school curriculum.

Pedagogy

This volume provides a multifaceted approach to the teaching of white collar crime. To a large degree, it features the time-honored format of presenting excerpts from cases and other sources followed by two or more notes or questions designed to provide additional context and intellectual stimulation. The cases vary from old chestnuts to recent holdings; many of the latter involve defendants with whom students should be familiar. All of the cases have been edited to preserve enough factual material to enhance students' understanding of the business world—which is critical to their understanding of white collar crime. Fruitful and interesting classes could be centered on this material alone. However, the book also accommodates those who prefer to teach using a problem-oriented approach. Each chapter contains one or more problems that are designed to facilitate coverage of most, if not all, of the key material in that chapter or unit. Many of these problems are based on real cases, which connects students to reality and provides them with the ability to check their reasoning against that of a sitting judge.

Personal Acknowledgments

A project of this magnitude cannot be undertaken and completed by one person. Thus, I would like to thank the many individuals who provided me with essential support and assistance. At the top of the list are my many wonderful research assistants from the University of Florida Levin College of Law, set out in alphabetical order. First, thanks go to Senior Research Assistants Tiffany Cummins, Kathryn Kimball, Allison Sirica, and Alicia Taylor; next, to Research Assistants Elizabeth Manno, Nell Robinson, Chelsea Shea, Leigh Anne Siddle, Niklas Stubbendorf, Kara Wick, Jennifer White, and Jennie Zilner. I also offer my gratitude to Aspen Publisher Carol McGeehan, for believing in the proposal of a first-time casebook author; Aspen Managing Editor John Devins, for graciously shepherding me and my work through the publication process; Troy Froebe, for editing the copy; Stetson University College of Law student Morgan Vasigh for some freelance proofreading; and Mary (Meg) Daniels, for creating the Index and Table of Statutes. Any errors that remain are mine alone.

I am most indebted, of course, to my family—not necessarily because of their overwhelming support of this particular project (my wife: "You're kidding—you have to work another weekend, dear?"; my daughters: "Are you *still* writing that same book, Dad?"), but because they are the constant sources of sunshine in my life.

MLS
Gainesville, Florida
October 2011

Acknowledgments

The author would like to acknowledge the authors, publishers, and copyright holders of the following publications for permission to reproduce excerpts from the works listed below:

Arlen, Jennifer, The Potentially Perverse Effects of Corporate Criminal Liability, 23 Journal of Legal Studies 833 (1994). Copyright © 1994 by the University of Chicago, The Journal of Legal Studies. Reprinted by permission of University of Chicago Press: Journals Division.

Bucy, Pamela H., et. al., Why Do They Do It?: The Motives, Mores, and Character of White Collar Criminals, 82 St. John's Law Review 401, 401-13 (2009). Copyright © 2009 St. John's Law Review Ass'n. Reprinted by permission of St. John's Law Review Ass'n.

Cohn, Stuart R., Securities Counseling for Small and Emerging Companies, Section 1.4 (Sept. 2007). Copyright © 2006-2011 Thomas Reuters. Reprinted by permission of Thomson Reuters.

Coleman, James William, The Criminal Elite: Understanding White-Collar Crime, 187-93 (5th ed. 2002). Copyright © 2002 by Worth Publishers. Used with the permission of Worth Publishers.

Credit Crisis-The Essentials Overview, from The New York Times, Sept. 22 © 2009 The New York Times. All rights reserved. Used by permission and protected by the Copyright Laws of the United States. The printing, copying, redistribution, or retransmission of this Content without express written permission is prohibited. Reprinted by permission of PARS International Corp.: The New York Times.

Cullen, Francis T., William J. Maakestad, & Gray Caender, Corporate Crime Under Attack 351-53 (1987). Copyright © 1987 by Elsevier. Reprinted by permission of Elsevier, Francis T. Cullen, William J. Maakestad, and Gray Cavender.

Discovery and Access to Evidence, 37 Georgetown Law Journal Annual Review of Criminal Procedure 334 (2008). Copyright © 2008 by Georgetown University and The Georgetown Law Journal. Reprinted by permission of Georgetown Law CLE.

Filip, Mark, U.S. Department of Justice, Office of the Deputy Attorney General Memorandum: Principles of Federal Prosecution of Business Organizations (Aug. 28, 2008).

Fitzpatrick, Robert B., PLLC, ABA Section of Labor and Employment Law Federal Labor Standards Legislation Committee 2011 Midwinter Meeting Report: Subcommittee on the Sarbanes-Oxley Act of 2002, Mar. 31-Apr. 2, 2011.

Copyright © 2011 by the American Bar Association. Reprinted with permission by American Bar Association.

Green, Stewart P., The Concept of White Collar Crime in Law and Legal Theory, 8 Buffalo Criminal Law Review 1, 11-34 (2004). Reprinted by permission of Copyright Clearance Center.

Hirsch, Travis & Michael Gottfredson, Causes of White Collar Crime, 25 Criminology 949, 949-71 (1987). Reprinted by permission of American Society of Criminology.

Holderman, Judge James F. & Charles B. Redfern, Preindictment Prosecutorial Conduct in the Federal System Revisited, 96 Journal of Criminal Law and Criminology 527 (2006). Reprinted by special permission of Northwestern University School of Law, The Journal of Criminal Law and Criminology.

Investigations and Police Practices, 37 Georgetown Law Journal Annual Review of Criminal Procedure 133 (2008). Reprinted by permission of Georgetown Law CLE.

Kim, Sung Hui, Naked Self-Interest? Why the Legal Profession Resists Gatekeeping, 63 Florida Law Review 129 (2011). Reprinted by permission of University of Florida Law Review.

Leland, Hayne E., Insider Trading: Should It Be Prohibited?, 100 Journal of Political Economy 859 (1992). Copyright © 1992 by University of Chicago. Reprinted by permission of University of Chicago Press.

Lenzer, Robert, Bernie Madoff's $50 Billion Ponzi Scheme, *available at* http://www.forbes.com/2008/12/12/madoff-ponzi-hedge-pf-ii-in_rl_1212croesus_inl.html. Reprinted by Permissions of Forbes Media LLC © 2010.

Mann, Kenneth, Defending White Collar Crime, A Portrait of Attorneys at Work, Yale University Press 1985. Reprinted by permission of Yale University Press.

Manne, Henry, Insider Trading: Hayek, Virtual Markets, and the Dog that did not Bark, 31 Journal of Corporation Law 167 (2005). Reprinted by permission of Henry Manne.

Marmaro, Richard & John W. Crumpacker, Government Procurement: The Ever-Expanding Scope of Liability and Methods of Damage Control, 161 Practising Law Institute/Criminal Law 371 (1991). Reprinted by permission of Richard Marmaro and John Crumpacker.

Moberly, Richard E., Sarbanes-Oxley's Structural Model to Encourage Corporate Whistleblowers, 2006 Brigham Young University Law Review 1107 (2006). Reprinted by permission of Brigham Young University Law Review and Richard Moberly.

Mohanty, Sarita, Sarbanes-Oxley: Can One Model Fit All?, 12 The New England Journal of International & Comparative Law 246, 249 (2006). Reprinted by permission of The New England Journal of International & Comparative Law.

O'Sullivan, Julie R., The Last Straw: The Department of Justice's Privilege Waiver Policy and the Death of Adversarial Justice in Criminal Investigations of Corporations, 57 DePaul Law Review 329 (2008). Reprinted by permission of DePaul Law Review and Julie R. O'Sullivan.

Pankratz, Howard, Exxon-Mobil Pleads Guilty to Bird-Treaty Violations, The Denver Post, Aug. 13, 2009, *available at* http://www.denverpost.com/business/ci_13052849. Reprinted by permission of The Denver Post.

Press Release, United States Attorney's Office for the Southern District of Florida, Miami-Dade Police Officers Charged with Obstruction of Justice and Perjury (Feb. 12, 2010).

Reilly, Ryan J., Ted Stevens Prosecutor Felt "Scapegoated" During Misconduct Investigation, Sept. 28, 2010, *available at* tpmmuckraker.talkingpointsmemo.com. Copyright © TPM Media LLC. All rights reserved. Reprinted by permission of Talking Points Memo.

Ribstein, Larry E., Market v. Regulatory Responses to Corporate Fraud: A Critique of the Sarbanes Oxley Act of 2002, 28 Journal of Corporation Law 1 (2002). Reprinted by permission of Larry Ribstein.

Samuelson, Robert J., A Crowded Field in a Race for Distinction, Washington Post, Nov. 5, 2003, p. 14A. From St. Petersburg Times, © Nov. 5, 2003 St. Petersburg Times. All rights reserved. Used by permission and protected by the Copyright Laws of the United States. The printing, copying, redistribution, or retransmission of the Material without express written consent is prohibited. Reprinted by permission of PARS International Corp.

Seigel, Michael L. & Christopher Slobogin, Prosecuting Martha: Federal Prosecutorial Power and the Need for a Law of Counts, 109 Penn State Law Review 1107 (2005). Reprinted by permission of Penn State Law Review, Michael Seigel, and Christopher Slobogin.

Seigel, Michael L., Corporate America Fights Back: The Battle Over Waiver of the Attorney-Client Privilege, 49 Boston College Law Review 1, 10-13, 21-22 (2008). Reprinted by permission of Boston College Law Review.

Sutherland, Edwin H., White-Collar Criminality, 5 American Psychological Review 1, 1-5, 8-10 (1940).

Thomson Reuters Westlaw Criminal Practice Manual Database, Part II, Investigation. Chapter 11: Joint Defense Agreements, *updated* Mar. 2011. Reprinted by permission of Thomson Reuters.

United States Attorney Manual, Coordination of Criminal and Civil Fraud Against the Government Cases, Title 9, Section 42.010 (2011).

Unites States Attorney Manual, Multi-District (Global) Agreement Requests, Title 9, Section 27.641 (2011).

United States Attorney Manual, Title 9, Section 69.200: Criminal Resource Manual at 1751 (2011).

United States Department of Justice, Office of Public Affairs, GlaxoSmithKline to Plead Guilty & Pay $750 Million to Resolve Criminal and Civil Liability Regarding Manufacturing Deficiencies at Puerto Rico Plant (Oct. 26, 2010).

Wright, Richard A. & David O. Friedrichs, White-Collar Crime in the Criminal Justice Curriculum, 1 Journal of Criminal Justice 95, 98 (1991). Copyright © 1991 by Taylor & Francis, Ltd. Reprinted by permission of Taylor & Francis, Ltd.

White Collar Crime

chapter 1

What Is White Collar Crime and Who Commits It?

I. PROLOGUE

White Collar Crime is all around us: a daily event happening in virtually every part of the country, every sector of the economy, and every government entity in the United States and abroad. This section is designed to give you a sampling of some recent white collar cases to provide you with a flavor of what you are about to study. You can find more examples at the book's Web site, or simply pick up (or click on) the business section of any major U.S. newspaper for a sampling of more current prosecutions and investigations.

ROBERT LENZNER, BERNIE MADOFF'S $50 BILLION PONZI SCHEME

forbes.com, Dec. 12, 2008[1]

The shocking revelation that prominent investment manager Bernard Madoff's hedge fund, Ascot Partners, was a giant scam will intensify redemptions from scores of other hedge funds that will be forced to liquidate holdings and increase downward pressure on stock prices.

This additional negative influence on the market, together with liquidations by mutual funds facing redemptions and endowments facing the need for liquidity, are three significant barriers for optimism about the direction of stock prices in the near term.

The arrest of the 70-year-old Madoff, widely considered to have the magic touch as an investor, is another serious black eye for the hedge fund industry and all non-transparent investment vehicles. Investors across the New York area have

1. http://www.forbes.com/2008/12/12/madoff-ponzi-hedge-pf-ii-in_rl_1212croesus_inl.html.

clamored to be in Ascot because of the stability of double-digit returns and the reports of serious wealth creation. The scandal is bound to reveal the inner workings of the hedge fund industry, whereby intermediary feeders bring in their clients and take fees for putting clients with an investment manager.

If Madoff hadn't faced $7 billion in redemptions, this Ponzi scheme might not have been discovered. What's astonishing is that he got away with it for so long with nobody discovering it. What his four family members in Ascot knew is a puzzle that everyone wants answered, but one thing is certain: It's virtually impossible to have returns like Madoff reported, and it should have been a major warning signal.

Aside from the impact on stocks overall, the exposure of fraud on a massive scale is also devastating to individuals who trusted Madoff with their fortunes and to non-profit organizations like Yeshiva University, which counted on Madoff's purported secret trading system to help operate its institutions. Sterling Equities, the investment vehicle of the Wilpon family, which owns the New York Mets baseball team, had $300 million reportedly invested in Ascot. So did some wealthy investors who had money in related hedge funds who were never informed of ties to Ascot. Another private bank executive placed $10 million from a client just two weeks ago. He knew of another family that had $100 million with Madoff. A woman in California told us that she had lost everything with Madoff and another hedge fund.

Everyone in New York wants to know how Madoff could have pulled off this Ponzi scheme whereby these new investment funds were apparently used to pay double-digit returns to some of the older investors. A charitable account that operates institutions in Israel received a 12% return recently. Other individual investors report that they got nothing.

Ascot's monthly reports are voluminous, showing many transactions in and out of the market every day. Madoff was supposed to have some "black box" model that signaled when to buy and when to sell. He was one of the most active traders in the marketplace, and his annual returns in these short-term trades were mainly ordinary income, which made Ascot attractive mostly to tax free institutions like foundations, hospitals and religious groups. After many years of returns in the range of 12% to 15%, in recent times the profits have been in the high single digits at times.

If indeed, $50 billion was lost, as apparently Madoff claims, it is the largest such fraud in history, and one that might even shame the conman whose name is attached to this brand of deception. In 1920, Charles Ponzi, an Italian immigrant, began advertising that he could make a 50% return for investors in only 45 days. Incredibly, Ponzi began taking in money from all over New England and New Jersey. By July of 1920, he was making millions as people mortgaged their homes and invested their life savings. As with all frauds, he was discovered to have a jail record and was indicted on 86 counts of fraud. Some tens of millions of dollars were invested with him.

Other fraudsters have made inglorious names for themselves. In March of 1932, Ivar Kreuger, a Swedish businessman who had cooked the books of his match manufacturing business and forged $142 million of bonds, shot himself in the head. It was reported that he may have burned through $400 million of investor money by falsifying the accounts of 400 separate companies.

Until Madoff came along, the Equity Funding scandal may have been the largest fraud in dollar terms in U.S. history. A publicly held company whose shares traded on the New York Stock Exchange, the top executives falsified 64,000 insurance policies that were used to report revenues of $2 billion. The company also sold $25 million in counterfeit bonds and had missing assets of $100 million. Three auditors and high ranking executives served prison terms.

Expect Madoff to be one of the first jailed investors of the 2008 market meltdown. Hopefully, there will be others.

UNITED STATES ATTORNEY'S OFFICE FOR THE SOUTHERN DISTRICT OF FLORIDA, PRESS RELEASE: MIAMI-DADE POLICE OFFICERS CHARGED WITH OBSTRUCTION OF JUSTICE AND PERJURY

Feb. 12, 2010

Jeffrey H. Sloman, United States Attorney for the Southern District of Florida, John V. Gillies, Special Agent in Charge, Federal Bureau of Investigation, Miami Field Office, and James K. Loftus, Director, Miami-Dade Police Department, announced that a federal grand jury returned an Indictment against three Miami-Dade Police Department officers in connection with their involvement in a conspiracy to obstruct justice, make false statements, and commit perjury in a federal criminal case.

The Indictment charges Officers Jorge Luis Gonzalez, 27, and Alkibiades Dodge, 37, and Sergeant Waell Majed Farraj, 33, with conspiracy to make false statements, obstruct justice, and commit perjury, in violation of Title 18, United States Code, Section 371, making false statements to a federal agent, in violation of Title 18, United States Code, Section 1001, and obstruction of justice, in violation of Title 18, United States Code, Section 1503. In addition, Officer Gonzalez and Sergeant Farraj are charged with committing perjury in their sworn testimony before a United States District Judge, in violation of Title 18, United States Code, Section 1623(a).

The charges in the Indictment arise out of the actions of these three defendants in connection with the arrest and subsequent federal prosecution of an individual ("P.M.") on a firearms possession charge. As alleged in the Indictment, the three defendants made false statements, and wrote and used Miami-Dade Police Department documents containing false statements, concerning the circumstances surrounding the stop and search of a vehicle in which P.M. was a passenger. The defendants then allegedly provided this false information and these documents to an agent of the federal Bureau of Alcohol, Tobacco, Firearms, and Explosives on the evening of the stop and seizure, and P.M. was arrested by federal authorities.

After P.M. was charged federally, all three defendants allegedly perpetuated the obstruction of justice scheme, and Gonzalez and Farraj committed perjury by testifying to the same false account while under oath at a hearing before the presiding judge, United States District Judge Cecilia M. Altonaga. This material false sworn testimony was given in a suppression hearing which Judge Altonaga was conducting to determine whether the firearm seized from the vehicle, and the statements made by P.M., would be admissible against P.M. in his trial. When the criminal conduct of these three officers was uncovered, the government then dismissed the case against P.M.

U.S. Attorney Jeffrey H. Sloman said, "Our system of justice is based on the integrity and truthfulness of every witness that testifies in court. Law enforcement officers, like any other witnesses, are sworn to tell the truth. When any witness lies under oath or conspires to obstruct justice, our system of justice is undermined. The damage is twofold when it is a police officer who lies or obstructs justice: it not only weakens the public's faith in our legal system, but also shakes the public's confidence in police officers who are sworn to uphold the laws. As prosecutors and law enforcement officers, it is our responsibility to safeguard the integrity of the legal system."

John V. Gilles, Special Agent in Charge of the FBI's Miami Office, added, "A police officer's integrity is never negotiable. It is the backbone of every law enforcement agency and a department will not be successful if it doesn't have the trust of the people it serves. We are fortunate to have a professional, well-respected organization such as the Miami-Dade County Police Department. Unfortunately, a few police officers have betrayed the oath they took and will be held accountable for their actions, losing not only their jobs but their reputations. The FBI will continue to work with our partners to root out those officers who have not lived up to the high ethical standards law enforcement officers are proud to uphold." . . .

An Indictment is only an accusation and a defendant is presumed innocent until and unless proven guilty.

HOWARD PANKRATZ, EXXON-MOBIL PLEADS GUILTY TO BIRD-TREATY VIOLATIONS

Denv. Post, Aug. 13, 2009[2]

Exxon-Mobil Corp. has pleaded guilty in Denver to violating the federal Migratory Bird Treaty Act in five states, including Colorado, the U.S. Justice Department announced today.

The charges stem from the deaths of about 85 protected birds—including waterfowl, hawks and owls—at Exxon-Mobil drilling and production facilities in Colorado, Wyoming, Oklahoma, Texas and Kansas between 2004 and 2009.

According to the charges and other information presented in court, most of the birds died after exposure to hydrocarbons in uncovered natural-gas well reserve pits and wastewater-storage facilities.

The company agreed late Wednesday to pay fines and community-service payments totaling $600,000 and will implement an environmental-compliance plan over the next three years aimed at preventing bird deaths on the company's facilities in the affected states.

2. http://www.denverpost.com/business/ci_13052849.

According to the Justice Department, Exxon-Mobil has already spent more than $2.5 million to begin implementation of the program.

The $400,000 in fines will be deposited into the federally-administered North American Wetlands Conservation Fund. The $200,000 community service payments will be made to a nonprofit waterfowl-rehabilitation foundation in Colorado and the congressionally-chartered National Fish and Wildlife Foundation.

"The environmental compliance plan that Exxon-Mobil has agreed to in this multi-district plea agreement is an important step in protecting migratory birds in five states," said John Cruden, acting assistant attorney general for the Justice Department's Environment and Natural Resources Division.

The Migratory Bird Treaty Act was enacted in 1918.

The Justice Department noted that migratory birds often land on open wastewater ponds at oil and gas facilities and become coated with, or swallow, fatal amounts of hydrocarbons discharged into the water during drilling or production operations.

Such deaths can be prevented by scrubbing the water of contaminants before discharge, removing the ponds, or placing netting or plastic "bird balls" over the water to prevent contact.

DEPARTMENT OF JUSTICE OFFICE OF PUBLIC AFFAIRS, PRESS RELEASE: GLAXOSMITHKLINE TO PLEAD GUILTY & PAY $750 MILLION TO RESOLVE CRIMINAL AND CIVIL LIABILITY REGARDING MANUFACTURING DEFICIENCIES AT PUERTO RICO PLANT

Oct. 26, 2010

BOSTON—SB Pharmco Puerto Rico Inc., a subsidiary of GlaxoSmithKline, PLC (GSK), has agreed to plead guilty to charges relating to the manufacture and distribution of certain adulterated drugs made at GSK's now-closed Cidra, Puerto Rico, manufacturing facility, the Justice Department announced today. The resolution includes a criminal fine and forfeiture totaling $150 million and a civil settlement under the False Claims Act and related state claims for $600 million.

The drugs, manufactured at the plant between 2001and 2005, are Kytril, Bactroban, Paxil CR and Avandamet. Kytril is a sterile anti-nausea medication. Bactroban is a topical anti-infection ointment commonly used to treat skin infections. Paxil CR is the controlled release formulation of the popular anti-depressant drug, Paxil, and Avandamet is a combination Type II diabetes drug.

The Food, Drug and Cosmetic Act (FDCA) prohibits the introduction or delivery for introduction into interstate commerce of any drug that is adulterated. Under the FDCA, a drug is deemed adulterated if the methods used in, or the facilities or controls used for, its manufacturing, processing, packing or holding did not conform to or were not operated or administered in conformity with current good manufacturing practice to assure that such drug met the requirements as to safety and had the identity and strength, and met the quality and purity characteristics, which it purported or was represented to possess.

The criminal information filed today alleges that SB Pharmco's manufacturing operations failed to ensure that Kytril and Bactroban finished products were free of contamination from microorganisms. The criminal information further alleges that SB Pharmco's manufacturing process caused Paxil CR two-layer tablets to split. The splitting, which the company itself called a "critical defect," caused the potential distribution of tablets that did not have any therapeutic effect and tablets that did not contain any controlled release mechanism.

The criminal information also alleges that Avandamet tablets manufactured by SB Pharmco did not always have the Food and Drug Administration (FDA)-approved mix of active ingredients, and, as a result, potentially contained too much or too little of the ingredient with the therapeutic effect. Finally, the criminal information alleges that SB Pharmco's Cidra facility suffered from longstanding problems of product mix-ups, which caused tablets of one drug type and strength to be commingled with tablets of another drug type and/or strength in the same bottle.

SB Pharmco has agreed to plead guilty to a criminal felony for releasing into interstate commerce adulterated Kytril, Bactroban, Paxil CR and Avandamet, in violation of the FDCA. Under the plea agreement, the company will pay a criminal fine of $150 million, which includes forfeiting assets of $10 million. The guilty plea and sentence is not final until accepted by the U.S. District Court in Boston.

Under the civil settlement, GSK has agreed to pay an additional $600 million to the federal government and the states to resolve claims that it caused false claims to be submitted to government health care programs for certain quantities of adulterated Kytril, Bactroban, Paxil CR and Avandamet. The United States contends that GSK sold certain batches, lots or portions of lots of drugs, the strength of which differed materially from, or the purity or quality of which fell materially below, the strength, purity or quality specified in the drugs' FDA applications or related documents. GSK thereby knowingly caused false and/or fraudulent claims to be submitted to, or caused purchases by, Medicaid and the other federal health care programs.

The federal share of the civil settlement amount is $436,440,000, and GSK will pay up to $163,560,000 to states that participate in the agreement.

"Adulterated drugs undermine the integrity of the FDA's approval process, can introduce substandard or ineffective drugs on to the market and, in the worst cases, can potentially put patients' health at risk," said Tony West, Assistant Attorney General for the Civil Division of the Department of Justice. "We will continue to work with our law enforcement partners to hold pharmaceutical companies accountable for this type of conduct and protect taxpayers from fraud, waste, and abuse." . . .

The civil settlement resolves one lawsuit filed in federal court in the District of Massachusetts under the qui tam, or whistleblower, provisions of the False Claims Act, which allow private citizens to bring civil actions on behalf of the United States and share in any recovery. As part of today's resolution, the whistleblower—Cheryl Eckard—will receive approximately $96 million from the federal share of the settlement amount.

The criminal case is being prosecuted by the U.S. Attorney's Office for the District of Massachusetts and the Department of Justice's Office of Consumer Litigation. The civil settlement was negotiated by the U.S. Attorney's Office for the

District of Massachusetts and the Civil Division's Commercial Litigation Branch. The HHS Office of Counsel to the Inspector General, the Center for Medicare and Medicaid Services, FDA's Office of Chief Counsel, and the National Association of Medicaid Control Units provided assistance.

The case was investigated by agents from the FBI, the Department of Veterans Affairs, Office of the Inspector General, HHS-IG, the FDA's Office of Criminal Investigations, the Defense Criminal Investigative Service and the Office of the Inspector General for the Office of Personnel Management.

This settlement is part of the government's emphasis on combating health care fraud. One of the most powerful tools in that effort is the False Claims Act, which the Justice Department has used to recover approximately $4.2 billion since January 2009 in cases involving fraud against federal health care programs. The Justice Department's total recoveries in False Claims Act cases since January 2009 have topped $5.4 billion.

II. DEFINING WHITE COLLAR CRIME

The brief and random survey of recently reported crimes set out in Part I, above, obscures a serious underlying problem: What, exactly, is white collar crime? As we shall see, that question is much more difficult to answer than one might think. Nevertheless, it is important to seek an answer, for it makes little sense to undertake the study of an area of law without any conception of its common themes, characteristics, and parameters.

We start by reading the memorialization of a speech delivered by Edwin Sutherland, an American sociologist, in which he coined the term "white collar crime."

EDWIN H. SUTHERLAND, WHITE-COLLAR CRIMINALITY

5 Am. Psychol. Rev. 1, 1-5 (Feb. 1940)

The criminal statistics show unequivocally that crime, *as popularly conceived and officially measured*, has a high incidence in the lower class and a low incidence in the upper class; less than two percent of the persons committed to prisons in a year belong to the upper class. These statistics refer to criminals handled by the police, the criminal and juvenile courts, and the prisons, and to such crimes as murder, assault, burglary, robbery, larceny, sex offenses, and drunkenness, but exclude traffic violations.

The criminologists have used the case histories and criminal statistics derived from these agencies of criminal justice as their principal data. From them, they have derived general theories of criminal behavior. These theories are that, since crime is concentrated in the lower class, it is caused by poverty or by personal and social characteristics believed to be associated statistically with poverty, including feeblemindedness, psychopathic deviations, slum neighborhoods, and "deteriorated" families. . . .

The thesis of this paper is that the conception and explanations of crime which have just been described are misleading and incorrect, that crime is in fact not closely correlated with poverty or with the psychopathic and sociopathic conditions associated with poverty, and that an adequate explanation of criminal behavior must proceed along quite different lines. The conventional explanations are invalid principally because they are derived from biased samples. The samples are biased in that they have not included vast areas of criminal behavior of persons not in the lower class. One of these neglected areas is the criminal behavior of business and professional men, which will be analyzed in this paper.

The "robber barons" of the last half of the nineteenth century were white-collar criminals, as practically everyone now agrees. Their attitudes are illustrated by these statements: Colonel Vanderbilt asked, "You don't suppose you can run a railroad in accordance with the statutes, do you?" A.B. Stickney, a railroad president, said to sixteen other railroad presidents in the home of J.P. Morgan in 1890, "I have the utmost respect for you gentlemen, individually, but as railroad presidents I wouldn't trust you with my watch out of my sight." Charles Francis Adams said, "The difficulty in railroad management . . . lies in the covetousness, want of good faith, and low moral tone of railway managers, in the complete absence of any high standard of commercial honesty." . . .

White-collar criminality in business is expressed most frequently in the form of misrepresentation in financial statements of corporations, manipulation in the stock exchange, commercial bribery, bribery of public officials directly or indirectly in order to secure favorable contracts and legislation, misrepresentation in advertising and salesmanship, embezzlement and misapplication of funds, short weights and measures and misgrading of commodities, tax frauds, misapplication of funds in receiverships and bankruptcies. These are what Al Capone called "the legitimate rackets." These and many others are found in abundance in the business world.

In the medical profession, which is here used as an example because it is probably less criminalistic than some other professions, are found illegal sale of alcohol and narcotics, abortion, illegal services to underworld criminals, fraudulent reports and testimony in accident cases, extreme cases of unnecessary treatment, fake specialists, restriction of competition, and fee-splitting. Fee-splitting is a violation of a specific law in many states and a violation of the conditions of admission to the practice of medicine in all. The physician who participates in fee-splitting tends to send his patients to the surgeon who will give him the largest fee rather than to the surgeon who will do the best work. It has been reported that two thirds of the surgeons in New York City split fees, and that more than one half of the physicians in a central western city who answered a questionnaire on this point favored fee-splitting.

These varied types of white-collar crimes in business and the professions consist principally of violation of delegated or implied trust, and many of them can be reduced to two categories: misrepresentation of asset values and duplicity in the manipulation of power. The first is approximately the same as fraud or swindling; the second is similar to the double-cross. The latter is illustrated by the corporation director who, acting on inside information, purchases land which the corporation will need and sells it at a fantastic profit to his corporation. The principle of this duplicity is that the offender holds two antagonistic positions, one of which is a position of trust, which is violated, generally by misapplication of funds, in the interest of the other position. A football coach, permitted to referee a game in which his own team was playing, would illustrate this antagonism of positions. Such situations cannot be completely avoided in a complicated business structure, but many concerns make a practice of assuming such antagonistic functions and regularly violating the trust thus delegated to them. When compelled by law to make a separation of their functions, they make a nominal separation and continue by subterfuge to maintain the two positions. . . .

The financial cost of white-collar crime is probably several times as great as the financial cost of all the crimes which are customarily regarded as the "crime problem." An officer of a chain grocery store in one year embezzled $600,000, which was six times as much as the annual losses from five hundred burglaries and robberies of the stores in that chain. Public enemies numbered one to six secured $130,000 by burglary and robbery in 1938, while the sum stolen by [one particular white collar criminal] is estimated at $250,000,000, or nearly two thousand times as much. *The New York Times* in 1931 reported four cases of embezzlement in the United States with a loss of more than a million dollars each and a combined loss of nine million dollars. Although a million-dollar burglar or robber is practically unheard of, these million-dollar embezzlers are small-fry among white-collar criminals. The estimated loss to investors in one investment trust from 1929 to 1935 was $580,000,000, due primarily to the fact that 75 percent of the values in the portfolio were in securities of affiliated companies, although it advertised the importance of diversification in investments and its expert services in selecting safe securities. In Chicago, the claim was made six years ago that householders had lost $54,000,000 in two years during the administration of a city sealer who granted immunity from inspection to stores which provided Christmas baskets for his constituents.

The financial loss from white-collar crime, great as it is, is less important than the damage to social relations. White-collar crimes violate trust and therefore create distrust, which lowers social morale and produces social disorganization on a large scale. Other crimes produce relatively little effect on social institutions or social organization. White-collar crime is real crime.

STEWART P. GREEN, THE CONCEPT OF WHITE COLLAR CRIME IN LAW AND LEGAL THEORY

8 Buff. Crim. L. Rev. 1, 11-34 (2004)

[L]et us assume that, at least in the limited context of law and legal theory, the term "white collar crime" should refer neither to non-criminalized, deviant behavior, nor to crimes committed by offenders holding particular kinds of jobs or enjoying a particular social status. Instead, let us use "white collar crime" to refer exclusively to a category of criminal offenses that reflects some particular group of legal or moral characteristics.

Not surprisingly, this is the approach taken by various lawyers and law enforcement officials interested in formulating a standard definition of white collar crime. For example, in 1970, U.S. Department of Justice official Herbert Edlehertz described white collar crime as "an illegal act or series of illegal acts committed by nonphysical means and by concealment or guile, to obtain money or property, or to obtain business advantage." Nineteen years later, the FBI defined white collar crime as

> those illegal acts which are characterized by deceit, concealment, or violation of trust and which are not dependent upon the application or threat of physical force or violence. Individuals and organizations commit these acts to obtain money, property, or services; to avoid the payment or loss of money or services; or to secure personal or business advantage. One of the most influential formulations has been offered by the U.S. Department of Justice, Bureau of Justice Statistics, which defines white collar crime as:
>
>> [n]onviolent crime for financial gain committed by means of deception by persons whose occupational status is entrepreneurial, professional or semi-professional and utilizing their special occupational skills and opportunities; also, nonviolent crimes for financial gain utilizing deception and committed by anyone having special technical and professional knowledge of business and government, irrespective of the person's occupation.

From the perspective of legal analysis, an act-focused definitional approach such as these is much preferable to [an] actor-focused approach. . . . Nevertheless, each of the particular definitions offered presents significant problems: First, it is unclear what it means to commit a crime by "nonphysical" means, since it is generally assumed that every crime commission requires, at a minimum, a physical act. Nor is it clear even what is meant for a crime to be "nonviolent." For example, would the release of toxic chemicals into a public water source in violation of the Clean Water Act, or the sale of adulterated drugs in violation of the Federal Food, Drug, and Cosmetic Act, qualify as such?

Second, there is virtually no explanation for why the definition of white collar crime should be limited to those offenses committed for the purpose of obtaining "money," "property," or "services," or to secure "financial gain" or "business advantage." To the extent that such an approach would exclude many cases of presumptively core white collar offenses such as perjury, bribery, and obstruction of justice; and at the same time include presumptively non-white collar offenses such as larceny, robbery, and embezzlement, it would seem to require some justification. Indeed, this may explain why some scholars now prefer the term "economic" or "business" crime to "white collar crime."

Third, and even more problematic, is the unexplained use of the terms "deception," "concealment," "guile," and "violation of trust." Even if the meaning of such terms were not highly contested (as it is), one could not help but wonder whether this limited list of moral wrongs would fully capture the moral content of white collar offenses such as insider trading, tax evasion, extortion, blackmail, obstruction of justice, and many regulatory and intellectual property crimes. . . .

[T]he moral content of criminal offenses can be divided into three basic elements: Culpability reflects the mental element with which an offense is committed, such as intent, knowledge, or belief. Harmfulness reflects the degree to which a criminal act causes, or risks causing, harm to others or self. And moral wrongfulness involves the way in which the criminal act entails a violation of moral norms. Following this approach, then, one way to determine which offenses should be included within the category of white collar crime would be to ask whether—in terms of culpability, harmfulness, and wrongfulness—a particular offense "resembles" other offenses within that category. . . .

I would argue that white collar crime does differ from non-white collar crime in all three of the dimensions identified: First, the harms that white collar crimes cause (think, for example, of bribery, tax evasion, and insider trading) tend to be more diffuse and aggregative than in the case of conventional crime; and it is often harder to say who (or what, in the case of governmental institutions or corporations) has been victimized, and how. Second, white collar crime tends to involve certain distinctive forms of moral wrongfulness: not only deception and breach of trust, but also cheating, exploitation, coercion, promise-breaking, and disobedience. Third, white collar offenses frequently reflect a distinctive role for mens rea: They either require no mens rea at all (as is the case with many regulatory offenses), or make proof of mens rea so important that conduct performed without it not only fails to expose the actor to criminal liability, but may not be regarded as wrongful at all.

My point, of course, is not that all white collar offenses (and only such offenses) exhibit such qualities. If we expect to find some fixed and universally-agreed-upon collection of necessary and sufficient conditions that define the category of white collar crime across all disciplines, we are bound to be disappointed. Nevertheless, I believe that it would be a mistake to give up on the term entirely. Provided that we recognize its context-specific, family-resemblance-like-quality, "white collar crime" remains for the legal theorist a term both powerfully evocative and ultimately indispensable.

RICHARD A. WRIGHT & DAVID O. FRIEDRICHS, WHITE-COLLAR CRIME IN THE CRIMINAL JUSTICE CURRICULUM

1 J. Crim. Just. 95, 98 (1991)

For our purposes, "white-collar" crime is conceived of most appropriately as a heuristic or residual term that can serve as a point of departure for studying an array of demonstrably harmful activities, motivated by finance-related or power-related objectives and carried out by individuals, organizations, and institutions enjoying a generally respectable status, in the overall context (or behind the facade) of a legitimate administrative or occupational (finance-related) pursuit. It encompasses governmental (e.g., corruption), corporate (e.g., antitrust), and occupational (e.g., medical fraud) activities. White-collar crime most typically involves the violation of some form of trust; an absence of direct force or violence, or the threat of force or violence; an carried out over an extended period of time rather than a single, isolated incident; some form of collusion or cooperation; multiple victims or organizational victims; and offenders who do not regard themselves primarily as criminals, and who typically have a legitimate master status.

Ultimately, then, "white-collar crime" is a relativistic term. Some offenses (e.g., corporate price-fixing) can be cited as classic examples of a white-collar crime. Other offenses (e.g., the frauds perpetrated by "shady" businesses) are viewed somewhat more marginally as white-collar crime. Some specific individuals and organizations may occupy a gray area between white-collar crime and other forms of crime, such as organized crime.

NOTES AND QUESTIONS

1. Sutherland, a sociologist, is considered the "father" of white collar crime. He was writing at a time when sociology and the related social science of criminology were new fields attempting to gain respectability compared to the "hard" sciences, such as biology and physics. He was disturbed by the fact that, at that time, all of the theories concerning the causes of crime focused on poverty and lower-class upbringing, which of course did not explain the robber barons and other criminals of the upper classes. His was a clarion call to social scientists to better comport their theory with known observation.
2. The U.S. Department of Justice (DOJ), as quoted in the Green piece, has a much more practical reason for distinguishing white collar crime from street crime. DOJ is the law enforcement agency with the primary responsibility to combat white collar crime in the United States. It must give content to the definition to determine how to deploy its limited resources and to set up objective measures of success and failure in the battle against such crime.
3. Green criticizes many of the descriptors of white collar crime suggested by others as being too vague. What are these descriptors? What are the characteristics of white collar crime put forward by Green? Are they any less vague?
4. For a thorough discussion of the composition and characteristics of white collar crime, see TERRY L. LEAP, DISHONEST DOLLARS 53-95 (2007).

III. DEFINING WHITE COLLAR CRIMINALS

EDWIN H. SUTHERLAND, WHITE-COLLAR CRIMINALITY

5 Am. Psychol. Rev. 1, 4, 8-10 (Feb. 1940)

Perhaps it should be repeated that "white-collar" (upper) and "lower" classes merely designate persons of high and low socioeconomic status. Income and amount of money involved in the crime are not the sole criteria. Many persons of "low" socioeconomic status are "white-collar" criminals in the sense that they are well-dressed, well-educated, and have high incomes, but "white-collar" as used in this paper means "respected," "socially accepted and approved," "looked up to." Some people in this class may not be well-dressed or well-educated, nor have high incomes, although the "upper" usually exceed the "lower" classes in these respects as well as in social status. . . .

The crimes of the upper class either result in no official action at all, or result in suits for damages in civil courts, or are handled by inspectors, and by administrative boards or commissions, with penal sanctions in the form of warnings, orders to cease and desist, occasionally the loss of a license, and only in extreme cases by fines or prison sentences. Thus, the white-collar criminals are segregated administratively from other criminals, and largely as a consequence of this are not regarded as real criminals by themselves, the general public, or the criminologists.

This difference in the implementation of the criminal law is due principally to the difference in the social position of the two types of offenders. Judge Woodward, when imposing sentence upon the officials of the H.O. Stone and Company, bankrupt real estate firm in Chicago, who had been convicted in 1933 of the use of the mails to defraud, said to them, "You are men of affairs, of experience, of refinement and culture, of excellent reputation and standing in the business and social world." That statement might be used as a general characterization of white-collar criminals for they are oriented basically to legitimate and respectable careers. Because of their social status they have a loud voice in determining what goes into the statutes and how the criminal law as it affects themselves is implemented and administered. . . . The statement of Daniel Drew, a pious old fraud, describes the criminal law with some accuracy, "Law is like a cobweb; it's made for flies and the smaller kinds of insects, so to speak, but lets the big bumblebees break through. When technicalities of the law stood in my way, I have always been able to brush them aside easy as anything."

The preceding analysis should be regarded neither as an assertion that all efforts to influence legislation and its administration are reprehensible nor as a particularistic interpretation of the criminal law. It means only that the upper class has greater influence in moulding the criminal law and its administration to its own interests than does the lower class. The privileged position of white-collar criminals before the law results to a slight extent from bribery and political pressures, principally from the respect in which they are held and without special effort on their part. The most powerful group in medieval society secured relative immunity by "benefit of clergy," and now our most powerful groups secure relative immunity by "benefit of business or profession."

JAMES WILLIAM COLEMAN, THE CRIMINAL ELITE: UNDERSTANDING WHITE-COLLAR CRIME

187-188 (5th ed. 2002)

Taken as a group, the conflicting conclusions of these studies provide scant evidence for the proposition that white-collar criminals have significant psychological differences from other white-collar workers. However, it would be unwise to disregard the personality factor completely, pending the arrival of more conclusive data. It is easy to imagine how personality differences could lead one executive to embrace criminal activities, and another similarly placed executive to reject them. It seems likely, however, that a particular personality orientation will facilitate criminal activities in one occupational situation and discourage them in another, so that no single set of characteristics is conducive to crime in all situations. For example, nonconformists might well be more likely to become involved in an occupational crime directed against an employer but less likely to go along with organizational crimes demanded by their employer. A strict conformist could be expected to show the opposite tendencies.

Stanton Wheeler's work on the motivation of white-collar criminals illustrates the way in which psychological variables can operate in conjunction with situational factors. The beginning of Wheeler's investigation is a question that has long puzzled both the general public and many criminologists as well: "Why do people who are already extremely wealthy individuals risk involvement in white collar crimes, when the money they make can add little or nothing to their already lavish standard of living?" Certainly, such behavior runs counter to the expectations of classical economic theory. Wheeler answers this question in terms of personality. Such individuals are, he claims, "risk seekers" who derive a high degree of satisfaction from increasing their wealth regardless of the actual utility of those gains. These people are characterized by "greed as a personality trait: people who want even more, the more they already have." In contrast, Wheeler argues that other white-collar criminals are motivated by a very different drive—the "fear of falling" and losing some of the wealth and status they have already achieved.

However, the overall impact of personality on the problem of white-collar crime is still open to question for at least two important reasons. First, because the culture of industrial capitalism tends to encourage values, attitudes, and personality structures conducive to white-collar crime, there are always a large number of people with the needed characteristics. Moreover, the operation of the corporate system and the competitive struggles of small business give such individuals a far greater chance of reaching key decision-making positions. As Willem Bonger put it way back in 1905, "As always it is the environment that is the cause of the crimes taking place; it is the individual differences which explain in part who is the one to commit them." Another limitation on the value of personality variables in explaining white-collar crime is the fact that the structural demands in many occupational positions virtually force their occupants to violate the law, regardless of their personal desires or characteristics. For example, when J. Scott Armstrong asked business students to play the role of board members of a pharmaceutical company and presented them with a problem faced by an actual company—a very profitable drug was found to be dangerous to the public—79 percent of the students made the same decision as the real company's management did. They not only refused to withdraw the drug from the market, but they undertook legal and political maneuvers to prevent the government from banning it.

IV. CAUSES OF WHITE COLLAR CRIME

EDWIN H. SUTHERLAND, WHITE-COLLAR CRIMINALITY

5 Am. Psychol. Rev. 1, 9-10 (Feb. 1940)

The hypothesis which is here suggested as a substitute for the conventional theories is that white-collar criminality, just as other systematic criminality, is learned; that it is learned in direct or indirect association with those who already practice the behavior; and that those who learn this criminal behavior are segregated from frequent and intimate contacts with law-abiding behavior. Whether a person becomes a criminal or not is determined largely by the comparative frequency and intimacy of his contacts with the two types of behavior. This may be called the process of differential association. It is a genetic explanation both of white-collar criminality and lower class criminality. Those who become white-collar criminals generally start their careers in good neighborhoods and good homes, graduate from colleges with some idealism, and with little selection on their part, get into particular business situations in which criminality is practically a folkway and are inducted into that system of behavior just as into any other folkway. The lower class criminals generally start their careers in deteriorated neighborhoods and families, find delinquents at hand from whom they acquire the attitudes toward, and techniques of, crime through association with delinquents and in partial segregation from law-abiding people. The essentials of the process are the same for the two classes of criminals. This is not entirely a process of assimilation, for inventions are frequently made, perhaps more frequently in white-collar crime than in lower class crime. The inventive geniuses for the lower class criminals are generally professional criminals, while the inventive geniuses for many kinds of white-collar crime are generally lawyers.

A second general process is social disorganization in the community. Differential association culminates in crime because the community is not organized solidly against that behavior. The law is pressing in one direction, and other forces are pressing in the opposite direction. In business, the "rules of the game" conflict with the legal rules. A business man who wants to obey the law is driven by his competitors to adopt their methods. This is well illustrated by the persistence of commercial bribery in spite of the strenuous efforts of business organizations to eliminate it. Groups and individuals are individuated; they are more concerned with their specialized group or individual interests than with the larger welfare. Consequently, it is not possible for the community to present a solid front in opposition to crime. . . .

JAMES WILLIAM COLEMAN, THE CRIMINAL ELITE: UNDERSTANDING WHITE-COLLAR CRIME

188-193 (5th ed. 2002)

Whether or not the personality of the offender is considered important, conventional wisdom offers an even more popular explanation of the motivation for white-collar crime. White-collar criminals break the law, according to this view, because it is the easiest way for them to make a lot of money. Robert Lane found that the business and government officials he studied saw the desire for financial gain as the principal cause of white-collar crime: "Most businessmen and most responsible government officers, at least from the sample interviewed, believe that businessmen run afoul of the law for economic reasons—they may want to 'make a fast buck.'" Those who are familiar with criminological theory will recognize these views as an unknowing restatement of the principles of the classical criminology created in the late eighteenth and early nineteenth centuries by Cesare Beccaria and Jeremy Bentham and carried on by its more modern descendants, such as those promoting rational choice theory. According to this perspective, people violate the law because, after evaluating their situation, they believe some criminal activity will bring them more pleasure and less pain than the other courses of action available to them.

The longevity of this kind of explanation is not hard to understand. Although it may not provide a very convincing account of the reasons a woman would murder her husband in a fit of rage, it is highly persuasive when applied to rational, calculating crimes. But Lane's formulation is too narrow, for although the desire to get rich quick is certainly a motivating factor in many white-collar crimes, other kinds of financial motivations are often equally important. Many white-collar offenders are driven by the fear that they will lose what they already have rather than by the desire for more. For example, when David Weisburd and his colleagues examined the statements of a sample of convicted white-collar criminals made in their presentence information reports, they found that this "fear of falling" was a central motivating force for a large group of offenders. Such offenders would have been "reasonably happy with the place they have achieved through conventional means if only they could keep that place. But the fate of organizational success and failure, or the changing nature of the economy in their line of work, may put them at least temporarily under great financial pressure, where they risk losing the lifestyle that they have achieved.... The motivation for their crime is not selfish ego gratification, but rather the *fear of falling*—of losing what they have worked so hard to gain." Of course, the desire to make more money and the desire to protect what one already has are two closely related aspects of the same phenomenon, which may be termed *financial self-interest.*

But the numerous case studies we have examined make it clear that financial self-interest, even in its most general sense, is only part of a larger motivational complex that is deeply ingrained in white-collar workers. Along with the desire for great wealth goes the desire to prove oneself by "winning" the competitive struggles that play such a prominent role in our economic system, and this desire to be "a winner" provides another powerful motivation for white-collar crime....

The definition of wealth and success as the central goals of human activity is part of what may be termed the culture of competition, which is particularly strong in social systems based on industrial capitalism. This culture of competition defines the competitive struggle for personal gain as a positive, rather than a negative or selfish, activity. Competition is seen not only to build the character and endurance of the competitors... but also to produce the maximum economic value for society as a whole. Not surprisingly, the competitive economic struggles typical of industrial capitalism are seen by and large as a fair battle in which the most capable and the hardest-working individuals emerge victorious. This belief in turn becomes an important legitimation for social inequality, as it implies that the poor deserve their inferior position because they are lazy or incompetent. The winners, on the other hand, are admired for the ability and drive that made them successful. . . .

But neither the desire for wealth and success nor the fear of failure can account for all the motivations behind white-collar crimes. Some of these crimes are clearly rooted in the offenders' efforts to live up to the expectations of the significant others in their occupational world. This is particularly true of the various functionaries who, out of an unreflective sense of obedience, carry out their superiors' orders to commit some illegal act, as well as the members of occupational subcultures who go along with illegal activities in order to win the acceptance and support of their peers. In such cases, the offenders often ignore the larger society's condemnation of their crimes and accept their occupational associates' definition of such actions as acceptable and even necessary behavior. . . .

Another more fundamental problem with Sutherland's theory is his insistence that the construction of personal reality is entirely a product of one's associations with others. Sutherland felt that individuals automatically adopt the definitions of those with whom they have the greatest frequency, duration, and intensity of association. But if that were true, how could those definitions ever change? For that matter, how could they have originated in the first place? . . .

Despite these objections, it still seems fair to say that most of our attitudes, values, and definitions are learned from others. But that doesn't explain the origins of those ideas. To do so, we must look for their structural causes.

Anthropological studies of the few remaining foraging societies where people live primarily from hunting and collecting edible plants indicate that their people are generally not acquisitive or competitive. Most of those societies are, moreover, strongly egalitarian, with no social classes or even much in the way of permanent political leadership. The enormous differences between foraging societies and the industrial societies with which we are familiar can be traced to their relationship to the environment and the economic system it creates. The cooperative, egalitarian ethos of most foraging societies can be attributed, at least in part, to the fact that such societies produce little surplus wealth. Thus, the economic base cannot support the system of status competition based on the accumulation of wealth that is found in the industrial societies. Significantly, the Indians living along what is now the northwestern coast of the United States and Canada, whose fishing activities generated a more substantial surplus, were in some important respects less egalitarian and more competitive than other foraging peoples. . . .

The culture of competition that plays such an important role in white-collar crime is rooted in the structure of the industrial economy. Most obviously, the enormous surplus wealth generated through industrial production provides a vast store of material goods to be competed for—a condition largely absent from foraging societies. A second key factor is the displacement of the open sharing of reciprocal exchange with the calculated self-interest of market exchange. Of course, reciprocal exchange still persists in industrial capitalism, particularly among relatives and close friends, but market exchange is the dominant mode, and that mode of exchange fosters a very different kind of personal outlook from that found among foragers. Market exchange is inevitably tied to the notion of profit and loss: The gain of one trading partner often comes at the expense of the other. Thus, as production for market replaces production for immediate consumption, competition and the quest for personal gain replace the more cooperative sentiments fostered in reciprocal exchange. In addition, the use of money provides an objective, impersonal standard by which to measure profit and loss in industrial society, thus further reinforcing the spirit of competition and the goal of the personal acquisition of wealth.

TRAVIS HIRSCH & MICHAEL GOTTFREDSON, CAUSES OF WHITE COLLAR CRIME

25 Criminology 949, 949-971 (1987)

The explicit thesis of this paper is that the distinction between white-collar crime and crime in general should be viewed in the same way as distinctions between any particular type of crime and crime in general, that the usefulness of the distinction for some purposes has been illegitimately generalized to areas where it is inapplicable and therefore inappropriate. . . . [T]he desire to control white-collar criminals should not be confused with the conclusion that they are products of unique causal processes. In fact, our general theory of crime accounts for the frequency and distribution of white-collar crime at the same time it accounts for the frequency and distribution of all other forms of crime, whether they be rape, vandalism, or simple assault. . . .

A major problem facing scholars who study white-collar crime is to determine the claims or assertions implicit in the concept. On its face, the term assumes that white-collar crimes are indeed crimes, that people of high social standing commit real crimes, that the crimes they commit differ from common crimes, that the causes of their law breaking differ from those affecting other people, and that the official response to white-collar crime is different from the official response to common crime. (Not obvious from the term itself, but nonetheless commonly encountered in connection with it, is the view that white-collar crime is actually more serious or more dangerous or more detrimental to social or civic values than is ordinary crime.)

At first glance, these assertions do not seem particularly problematic or unreasonable. On reflection, however, it turns out that the concept of "church crime" would permit the same conclusions. The crimes committed by church leaders are undoubtedly real or true crimes, crimes that differ from nonchurch crimes (that is, theft of nontaxable contributions is only possible in a nonprofit organization); the reasons for their crimes may be particular to their culture or economic situation; and, of course, the legal system may respond more leniently or severely to church crime than to crime in other systems.

So, what appears to be a straightforward or useful concept turns out to be a potential source of considerable complexity. If we did not know that "white-collar crime" arose as a reaction to the idea that crime is concentrated in the lower class, there would be nothing to distinguish it from other ways of reminding us that crime may be found in all groups, even in the low rate categories of its causes (for example, intact-home crime; valedictorian crime; female crime; elderly crime; small-town crime). The question is: does the concept of white-collar crime have virtues or uses that distinguish it from the countless alternative ways of classifying crimes by the characteristics of their perpetrators? . . .

We have been developing a general theory of crime designed to account for the distribution of all forms of criminal behavior. This emerging theory starts from a distinction between crimes as events and criminality as a characteristic of people. Whereas traditional positivistic theories begin by looking at offenders, we begin by looking at crime. We conclude that criminal events have properties that must be taken into account in devising explanations of them. That is, there are features of criminal events themselves that are capable of falsifying traditional theories that derive their dependent variable from ordinary disciplinary perspectives. For example, as we have seen, crimes have in common features that make those engaging in any one of them extremely likely to engage in others as well. These common features are not money, success, or peer approval. They are therefore inconsistent with most theories of crime and must be identified by a valid theory of crime. On inspection, most theories of crime assume that offenders specialize in types of crime (an expectation that has found its way into the white-collar crime literature); that they have careers in crime that progress, develop, or change over time; and that each type of crime has its own motives. These assumptions are contrary to the evidence.

Crime. Because the evidence suggests that the essential properties of crimes are not money, success, reduction of frustration, or peer approval (as one or another modern theory would have us believe) and because versatility in offenders is an established empirical fact, all crimes must share other common properties that make them appealing to potential offenders.

A concept of crime that will reveal attractive properties common to diverse acts presupposes a concept of human nature. In our view, the concept of human nature that best organizes the data is that found in the classical assumption that human behavior is motivated by the self-interested pursuit of pleasure and the avoidance of pain. Crimes are events in which force or fraud are used to satisfy self-interest, where self-interest refers to the enhancement of pleasure and the avoidance of pain. Features of events that enhance their pleasure or minimize their pain will be implicated in their causation. To be maximally pleasurable, events should take place immediately; pleasure is therefore enhanced by the *rapidity* with which it is obtained. Force and fraud can often produce more rapid results than alternative means; they are therefore useful in the pursuit of self-interest. To be maximally pleasurable, events should be *certain* in outcome; force and fraud can provide more certain benefit than alternative means, particularly when the benefit sought is short-term and the long-term consequences of the act are of little concern. To be maximally pleasurable, events should require *minimal effort*; force and fraud can provide benefit with less effort than alternative means, especially when the benefit also has the properties of rapidity and certainty.

White-collar crimes satisfy these defining conditions. They provide relatively quick, relatively certain benefit, with minimal effort. Crimes, including white-collar crimes, therefore require no motivation or pressure that is not present in any other form of human behavior. . . .

Criminality. Our conception of the essential features of *crime* provides the basis of a theory of *criminality.* Criminality is the tendency of individuals to pursue short-term gratification in the most direct way with little consideration for the long-term consequences of their acts. (Indicators of such a tendency include impulsivity, aggression, activity level, and lack of concern for the opinion of others.) People high on this tendency are relatively unable or unwilling to delay gratification; they are relatively indifferent to punishment and to the interests of others. As a consequence, they tend to be impulsive, active, and risk-taking.

Work demonstrating consistency in behavior over substantial periods of time is consistent with the concept of criminality as we use it here. For example, it is established that differences in the tendency toward aggression persist from childhood to adulthood; likewise, the evidence is strong that differences in the tendency toward delinquency and crime persist over the same period

Such tendencies do not lead ineluctably to crime, regardless of the setting in which the individual is located. As indicated, crimes require physical opportunity and immunity from immediate punishment in addition to individual tendencies. Also, many noncriminal acts have the capacity to provide the benefits of crime and are therefore attractive to those with high levels of "criminality"—for example, drug, alcohol, and cigarette use, sex, divorce, job quitting, and fast cars. To complicate things further, these tendencies often affect the settings in which the individuals possessing them are located—for example, the amount of education they attain, the kind of job they have, whether they marry and stay married.

Application of the General Theory to White-Collar Crime. The characteristics described above have implications for the likelihood of criminal acts, but they also have implications for selection into the occupational structure. Ordinary occupations require people to be in a particular place at a particular time. They also require educational persistence, willingness and ability to defer to the interests of others, and attention to conventional appearance. These occupational requirements tend to be inconsistent with the traits comprising criminality. White-collar occupations therefore tend to demand characteristics inconsistent with high levels of criminality. In other words, selection processes inherent to the high end of the occupational structure tend to recruit people with relatively low propensity to crime.

Our theory therefore predicts a relatively low rate of offending among white-collar workers, contrary to the now standard view in the literature (for example, Reiman, 1979; Sutherland, 1983). The standard view is based on misleading statistics about the extent of white-collar offending. For one thing, white-collar researchers often take *organizations* as the unit of analysis and do not adjust for their size and complexity when making comparisons with blue-collar *individuals.* For another, the reference period for the organization is often much longer than that applied to individuals. As a consequence, the white-collar crime literature often compares the number of crimes committed by an organization with many thousands of employees over a period of many years with those committed by single individuals in a single year. . . .

PAMELA H. BUCY ET AL., WHY DO THEY DO IT?: THE MOTIVES, MORES, AND CHARACTER OF WHITE COLLAR CRIMINALS

82 St. John's L. Rev. 401, 401-413 (2009)

Why do talented, bright, highly educated, successful people, who have "made it," risk it all by lying, stealing, and cheating, especially when what they're stealing is not much compared to what they have? The simple answer is, "because they can." This Article looks at the more complex answer. Based upon extensive interviews with seasoned prosecutors and accomplished defense counsel, we explore the views and perceptions traditionally held about white collar criminals. . . .

Statistical studies indicate that white collar crime occurs quite frequently. For example, according to the Association of Certified Fraud Examiners ("CFE"), fraud accounts for 6% of corporate losses in America annually, totaling an estimated $660 billion each year. Small businesses of less than 100 employees appear to be more frequent targets of white collar crime, with 46% of frauds being committed at these companies. The largest corporations experience the smallest percentage of fraud schemes, though on average fraud in these companies costs more than schemes in much smaller companies.

II. Study Results

A. White Collar Criminals: "Leaders" and "Followers"? . . .

Most of the study participants (77.8%) agreed that white collar criminals fall into categories of either "leaders" or "followers." One-fourth of these respondents provided caveats to their responses, for example, by identifying a third category as those who "retaliate" either by becoming whistleblowers or by agreeing to testify for the government in exchange for complete immunity, a reduced charge, or a reduced sentence. Another example would be those who wander unknowingly into white collar crime schemes, never realizing they are violating the law. Some participants pointed out that the line between "leaders" and "followers" becomes blurred depending on the nature of the investigation and the charges brought against the criminal, and that followers may morph or graduate at some point into principals. . . .

B. Motives for Committing White Collar Crimes

1. Motives of "Leaders"

Greed was the most commonly cited reason by study participants as to why "leaders" engage in white collar criminal acts. Money, financial gain, and greed were cited by almost every participant in the study as the motive for committing crime with some listing this as the sole motivator and others including it among top reasons. Beyond greed, participants noted opportunity, a sense of entitlement, arrogance, competitiveness, and rationalization as motivating factors. Some participants thought that "leaders" are often motivated by fear of failure or of losing one's job or lifestyle. With such fear, desperation kicks in and overrides the individual's inner moral compass. Other participants thought that white collar criminals cut ethical corners because of pressure from above to meet particular financial goals. In so doing, these actors either convince themselves that the act is not really criminal or they believe their actions are a common practice in their field, and, therefore, they will not or should not get in trouble. Interestingly, less than 5% of the study participants expressed the view that white collar criminals commit crimes because they are "amoral" or "evil." . . .

2. Motives of "Followers"

Compared to the nearly unanimous view of our study participants that "leaders" engage in white collar crimes because of greed, there was less consensus among study participants about the motives of "followers." Four different themes emerged from our interviews. One view was that "followers" are non-assertive, "weak" people who trail behind someone else, even into criminal schemes. The second view was that followers are "convinced of the rightness of their cause." If they have any doubts, they believe that no harm can come to them because they are following a leader whom they trust—or fear. Followers tend to be naïve and unaware of what is really happening, or they are simply taken in by the personal charisma of the leader and are intensely loyal to that person. The third view was that followers engage in criminal acts to make more money and because they desire a "piece of the action." They want to increase their status or receive a promotion, and they believe that if they curry favor with the "leader," they will achieve their ambitions. These followers believe that criminal acts are the only way to compete. The fourth view was that the followers are motivated by fear of losing their job or of physical harm.

C. Personality Traits of White Collar Criminals

1. Personalities of "Leaders"

The study participants who thought that white collar criminals fall into two groups consistently described "leaders" as "Type A" personalities: intelligent, arrogant, cunning, successful, greedy, prone to take risks, aggressive, narcissistic, determined, and charismatic. Only fifteen percent of study participants ventured to describe common demographic traits and without exception these participants stated that white collar criminals are most often men, not women, and that "leaders" tend to be white, upper-middle class, and well-educated people. . . .

2. Personalities of "Followers"

This question received the fewest number of responses from our study participants with almost half (44.5%) of the participants either opting out of this question or reporting that they had not observed a typical personality type among followers. Those who did respond, however, were consistent, describing "followers" as less confident, less aggressive, less ambitious, passive, subservient, dominated, gullible, prone to blindly follow others, and less likely to accept responsibility for their own actions. In the view of these study participants, followers tend to view their actions as less culpable since they are only doing what the "leader" asks.

ROBERT J. SAMUELSON, A CROWDED FIELD IN A RACE FOR DISTINCTION

Wash. Post, Nov. 5, 2003, at 14A

Ours is an era of excess. It's everywhere—in my case, just around the corner. Someone is building a three-floor "mansion." An architect friend estimates the floor area at about 6,600 square feet, roughly triple the size of a median new home (2,100 square feet in 2002). The surrounding homes now look like shacks next to their new neighbor. The question about this home is not why people spend so much to build something so oversized but what are they going to do with all the space. A similar question applies to Dick Grasso, the former head of the New York Stock Exchange, and his $140-million pay package. What is he going to do with all the money?

The answer is that the excess itself is the point. We Americans are constantly grasping for symbols of superiority: something to show everyone that we've done better than those around us. In an ever-richer society, the pursuit of these badges of success has become progressively harder because yesterday's accepted markers of distinction have become today's mass merchandise. You have to build a home three times what you need just to make sure everyone receives the message. You have to negotiate a lavish pay package to guarantee that people take notice.

Becoming a millionaire once signified great wealth. No more. Millionaires are too ordinary. In 2001, almost 200,000 Americans reported income of $1 million or more, says the Internal Revenue Service. By wealth, the figures are even larger. From 1989 to 2001, the share of Americans whose net worth (assets minus liabilities) exceeds $1 million rose from 3 percent to 7 percent, says the Federal Reserve. That's 7 million households.

It's not enough to be a millionaire if the idea is to have stuff that most of your pals don't—to set yourself apart. It is this impulse, and not simply greed, that ignited the feverish competition among corporate executives for outlandish compensation packages, including Grasso's. The search for exclusivity is made more exhausting because the spread of wealth has reduced the power of yesterday's status symbols.

In 1980, only 4.5 percent of Americans bought "luxury" cars—mainly Cadillacs and Lincolns, says J.D. Power and Associates, a market research firm. In 2003, "luxury" vehicles (including Lexuses, other new brands and Mercedeses and BMWs) account for 10.5 percent of sales. It's not just cars. A book by Michael Silverstein and Neil Fiske, *Trading Up—The New American Luxury*, shows how middle-income Americans pay premium prices for furniture, wines and other goods that convey taste and achievement. Renovated kitchens are popular. A typical makeover runs $58,000, say Silverstein and Fiske, with granite countertops alone costing $15,000.

With the trappings of success so common, the race for distinction grows more frustrating. Competition intensifies for things that seem naturally scarce—say, prestigious college degrees. There's a stampede to get into Ivy League schools and their kin. Harvard receives about 20,000 applications for 1,600 spots; Amherst, 5,200 for 400 openings. New status symbols emerge for those with stupendous sums. The *Washington Post* reports that the very wealthy are buying small ownership shares of professional sports teams, mainly for the prestige value. Nancy House, 54, of San Francisco bought a 1 percent interest in the Giants, citing the "coolness factor" that included—said the *Post*—"fourth row seats, mingling with players in spring training, jetting with the team in its Boeing 767."

Paradoxically, the engine of American excess is the preoccupation with equality. In a society that supposedly provides everyone an equal chance, people want to show that they've made the most of their chance. Silverstein and Fiske interview Jake, a $50,000-a-year construction worker, an avid golfer who has spent $3,000 to buy an elite set of titanium-tipped Callaway golf clubs. Says Jake: "The real reason I bought them is that they make me feel rich. You can run the biggest company in the world . . . but you can't buy any better clubs that these. When I kick your butt on the course, I feel good. I feel equal."

A democratic society constantly destroys preserves of privilege. Yesterday, golf clubs; tomorrow, the Ivy League. Even the status of a Harvard degree is eroding. Popular demand for more prestigious schools is increasing the supply of prestigious schools. Colleges improve; the publication of rankings raises reputations.

Keeping up with the Rockefellers and Gateses is a stressful and often self-defeating struggle. Grasso got his money and lost his reputation. But the quest is deeply rooted in the culture. In 25 years, all the homes in my neighborhood—which now seem normal and adequate—will have been demolished for bigger replacements that will then seem normal and adequate. People will need something else to impress. It will drive them to excess.

NOTES AND QUESTIONS

1. In 1940, Sutherland's claims that "crimes of the upper class" result at most in civil or administrative sanctions and that "white collar criminals are segregated administratively from other criminals, and largely as a consequence of this are not regarded as criminals by themselves, the general public, or the criminologists" rang true. Do these claims strike you as true today? Consider the case of Bernie Madoff. Do you think that he is regarded as a criminal by all concerned? Nevertheless, the alleged special treatment white collar criminals receive at all levels of the criminal justice system is a recurrent theme throughout this volume.
2. For an excellent study of white collar crime focusing on the comparison of white collar versus street career criminals, see DAVID WEISBURD & ELIN WARING, WHITE-COLLAR CRIME AND CRIMINAL CAREERS (Cambridge University Press 2001).
3. James Coleman sees capitalism—what he calls market exchange—as the structural basis for the cultural competition that is at the root of white collar crime. Do you agree that capitalism is the problem? If Coleman is correct, does that mean that there is no white collar crime in socialist economies, or is it simply of a different nature?
4. What is Hirsch and Gottfredson's "general theory of crime"? How does it impact their view of white collar versus street crime? Is it so general as to

lack explanatory power? Are they correct that white collar crime is overstated in the literature, or is Bucy more accurate when she says that white collar crime occurs "quite frequently"? Six hundred billion dollars of annual fraud (estimated by the Association of Certified Fraud Examiners and cited by Bucy) is hardly trivial, is it?

5. Does Bucy's division of white collar criminals into leaders and followers comport with common sense? Does it tie in with the theory that white collar crime is motivated by greed, on the one hand, and "fear of falling," on the other? If so, how should it impact policy making in the white collar arena?
6. Samuelson's explanation for white collar crime is an interesting one. In essence, no matter how rich we are, we compare ourselves to our peers, some of whom will inevitably be even richer. Thus, even a multi-millionaire feels "relatively poor." Do you think this is true? Do you find yourself looking at your friends' possessions and occasionally feeling envious, even though you are perfectly well off? Is there any counter to this phenomenon?

chapter 2

Criminal Liability in the Corporate (Collective Entity) Setting

I. CORPORATE CRIMINAL LIABILITY

One of the most important—and perplexing—issues in white collar crime is whether a collective entity, such as a corporation, can and should be held liable for a violation of the criminal law. Although we shall see that, in the United States, this question was resolved in the *New York Central* case more than 100 years ago, it is nevertheless hotly debated in other countries around the world.[1] Some legal commentators believe that without a corpus (literally, a body) to throw in prison, criminal law cannot function on a legal or metaphysical plane. Others argue that holding a company liable for the sins of a few of its agents violates the fundamental Kantian premise that society may not punish an individual who is not personally culpable. Yet other opponents of corporate criminal liability claim as an empirical matter that if civil and administrative penalties are high enough, criminal liability is simply redundant. On the other hand, many law professors and jurists (including this author) take the opposite point of view. The arguments for and against criminal liability for collective entities is explored in detail in the materials that follow.

1. For example, Brazil has it only for certain environmental crimes; it's new in France. *See* Kevin A. Gaynor & Thomas Bartman, *Criminal Enforcement of Environmental Laws*, 10 COLO. J. INT'L ENVTL. L. & POL'Y 39, 92 (1999) (discussing Brazil's criminal punishment of corporations responsible for pollution and regulatory crimes, and environmental damage to plants and wildlife; penalties include restriction of rights, fines, and imprisonment); *see generally* Leonard Orland & Charles Cachera, *Corporate Crime and Punishment in France: Criminal Responsibility of Legal Entities (Personnes Morales) Under the New French Criminal Code (Nouveau Code Penal*, 11 CONN. J. INT'L L. 111, 112 (1995) (discussing the 1994 imposition of criminal liability on French companies and foreign corporations with establishments in France).

A. Constitutionality

NEW YORK CENTRAL & HUDSON RIVER RAILROAD v. UNITED STATES

212 U.S. 481 (1909)

Mr. Justice DAY delivered the opinion of the Court.

[New York Central & Hudson River Railroad Company and Fred L. Pomeroy, its assistant traffic manager, were convicted for paying rebates to the American Sugar Refining Company, among others. The railroad paid American Sugar a rebate of between 3 and 5 cents for each 100 pounds of sugar shipped between New York and Detroit for a specified period of time. This made New York Central's effective shipping rates lower than those allowed by the Elkins Act, which regulated interstate commerce.]

Numerous objections and exceptions were taken at every stage of the trial to the validity of the indictment and the proceedings thereunder. The principal attack in this court is upon the constitutional validity of certain features of the Elkins act. That act, among other things, provides:

> (1) That anything done or omitted to be done by a corporation common carrier subject to the act to regulate commerce, and the acts amendatory thereof, which, if done or omitted to be done by any director or officer thereof, or any receiver, trustee, lessee, agent, or person acting for or employed by such corporation, would constitute a misdemeanor under said acts, or under this act, shall also be held to be a misdemeanor committed by such corporation; and, upon conviction thereof, it shall be subject to like penalties as are prescribed in said acts, or by this act, with reference to such persons, except as such penalties are herein changed.
>
> In construing and enforcing the provisions of this section, the act, omission, or failure of any officer, agent, or other person acting for or employed by any common carrier, acting within the scope of his employment, shall, in every case, be also deemed to be the act, omission, or failure of such carrier, as well as that of the person.

It is contended that these provisions of the law are unconstitutional because Congress has no authority to impute to a corporation the commission of criminal offenses, or to subject a corporation to a criminal prosecution by reason of the things charged. The argument is that to thus punish the corporation is in reality to punish the innocent stockholders, and to deprive them of their property without opportunity to be heard, consequently without due process of law. And it is further contended that these provisions of the statute deprive the corporation of the presumption of innocence—a presumption which is part of due process in criminal prosecutions. It is urged that, as there is no authority shown by the board of directors or the stockholders for the criminal acts of the agents of the company, in contracting for and giving rebates, they could not be lawfully charged against the corporation. As no action of the board of directors could legally authorize a crime, and as, indeed, the stockholders could not do so, the arguments come to this: that, owing to the nature and character of its organization and the extent of its power and authority, a corporation cannot commit a crime of the nature charged in this case.

Some of the earlier writers on common law held the law to be that a corporation could not commit a crime. It is said to have been held by Lord Chief Justice Holt that "a corporation is not indictable, although the particular members of it are." In Blackstone's Commentaries, chapter 18, §12, we find it stated: "A corporation cannot commit treason, or felony, or other crime in its corporate capacity, though its members may, in their distinct individual capacities." The modern authority, universally, so far as we know, is the other way. In considering the subject, Bishop's New Criminal Law, §417, devotes a chapter to the capacity of corporations to commit crime, and states the law to be: "Since a corporation acts by its officers and agents, their purposes, motives, and intent are just as much those of the corporation as are the things done. If, for example, the invisible, intangible essence or air which we term a corporation can level mountains, fill up valleys, lay down iron tracks, and run railroad cars on them, it can intend to do it, and can act therein as well viciously as virtuously." Without citing the state cases holding the same view, we may note Telegram Newspaper Co. v. Com. 172 Mass. 294 (Sup. Ct. Mass. 1899), in which it was held that a corporation was subject to punishment for criminal contempt; and the court, speaking by Mr. Chief Justice Field, said: "We think that a corporation may be liable criminally for certain offenses of which a specific intent may be a necessary element. There is no more difficulty in imputing to a corporation a specific intent in criminal proceedings than in civil. A corporation cannot be arrested and imprisoned in either civil or criminal proceedings, but its property may be taken either as compensation for a private wrong or as punishment for a public wrong." It is held in England that corporations may be criminally prosecuted for acts of misfeasance as well as nonfeasance.

It is now well established that, in actions for tort, the corporation may be held responsible for damages for the acts of its agent within the scope of his employment. . . . And this is the rule when the act is done by the agent in the course of his employment, although done wantonly or recklessly or against the express orders of the principal. In such cases the liability is not imputed because the principal actually participates in the malice or fraud, but because the act is done for the benefit of the principal, while the agent is acting within the scope of his employment in the business of the principal, and justice requires that the latter shall be held responsible for damages to the individual who has suffered by such conduct. . . .

We see no valid objection in law, and every reason in public policy, why the corporation, which profits by the transaction, and can only act through its agents and officers, shall be held punishable by fine because of the knowledge and intent of its agents to whom it has entrusted authority to act in the subject-matter of making and fixing rates of transportation, and whose knowledge and purposes may well be attributed to the corporation for which the agents act. While the law should have regard to the rights of all, and to those of corporations no less than to those of individuals, it cannot shut its eyes to the fact that the great majority of business transactions in modern times are conducted through these bodies, and particularly that interstate commerce is almost entirely in their hands, and to give them immunity from all punishment because of the old and exploded doctrine that a corporation cannot commit a crime would virtually take away the only means of effectually controlling the subject-matter and correcting the abuses aimed at. . . .

We find no error in the proceedings of the Circuit Court, and its judgment is affirmed.

Mr. Justice MOODY took no part in this case.

B. Policy Considerations

MARK FILIP, U.S. DEPARTMENT OF JUSTICE, OFFICE OF THE DEPUTY ATTORNEY GENERAL, MEMORANDUM: PRINCIPLES OF FEDERAL PROSECUTION OF BUSINESS ORGANIZATIONS

Aug. 28, 2008

9-28.100 Duties of the Federal Prosecutor and Duties of Corporate Leaders

The prosecution of corporate crime is a high priority for the Department of Justice. By investigating allegations of wrongdoing and by bringing charges where appropriate for criminal misconduct, the Department promotes critical public interests. These interests include, to take just a few examples: (1) protecting the integrity of our free economic and capital markets; (2) protecting consumers, investors, and business entities that compete only through lawful means; and (3) protecting the American people from misconduct that would violate criminal laws safeguarding the environment.

In this regard, federal prosecutors and corporate leaders typically share common goals. For example, directors and officers owe a fiduciary duty to a corporation's shareholders, the corporation's true owners, and they owe duties of honest dealing to the investing public in connection with the corporation's regulatory filings and public statements. The faithful execution of these duties by corporate leadership serves the same values in promoting public trust and confidence that our criminal cases are designed to serve.

A prosecutor's duty to enforce the law requires the investigation and prosecution of criminal wrongdoing if it is discovered. In carrying out this mission with the diligence and resolve necessary to vindicate the important public interests discussed above, prosecutors should be mindful of the common cause we share with responsible corporate leaders. Prosecutors should also be mindful that confidence in the Department is affected both by the results we achieve and by the real and perceived ways in which we achieve them. Thus, the manner in which we do our job as prosecutors—the professionalism we demonstrate, our willingness to secure the facts in a manner that encourages corporate compliance and self-regulation, and also our appreciation that corporate prosecutions can potentially harm blameless investors, employees, and others—affects public perception of our mission. Federal prosecutors recognize that they must maintain public confidence in the way in which they exercise their charging discretion. This endeavor requires the thoughtful analysis of all facts and circumstances presented in a given case. As always professionalism and civility play an important part in the Department's discharge of its responsibilities in all areas, including the area of corporate investigations and prosecutions.

9-28.200 General Considerations of Corporate Liability

A. General Principle: Corporations should not be treated leniently because of their artificial nature nor should they be subject to harsher treatment. Vigorous enforcement of the criminal laws against corporate wrongdoers, where appropriate, results in great benefits for law enforcement and the public, particularly in the area of white collar crime. Indicting corporations for wrongdoing enables the government to be a force for positive change of corporate culture, and a force to prevent, discover, and punish serious crimes.

B. Comment: In all cases involving corporate wrongdoing, prosecutors should consider the factors discussed further below. In doing so, prosecutors should be aware of the public benefits that may flow from indicting a corporation in appropriate cases. For instance, corporations are likely to take immediate remedial steps when one is indicted for criminal misconduct that is pervasive throughout a particular industry, and thus an indictment can provide a unique opportunity for deterrence on a massive scale. In addition, a corporate indictment may result in specific deterrence by changing the culture of the indicted corporation and the behavior of its employees. Finally, certain crimes that carry with them a substantial risk of great public harm—e.g., environmental crimes or sweeping financial frauds—may be committed by a business entity, and there may therefore be a substantial federal interest in indicting a corporation under such circumstance....

Where a decision is made to charge a corporation, it does not necessarily follow that individual directors, officers, employees, or shareholders should not also be charged. Prosecution of a corporation is not a substitute for the prosecution of criminally culpable individuals within or without the corporation. Because a corporation can act only through individuals, imposition of individual criminal liability may provide the strongest deterrent against future corporate wrongdoing. Only rarely should provable individual culpability not be pursued, particularly if it relates to high-level corporate officers, even in the face of an offer of a corporate guilty plea or some other disposition of the charges against the corporation.

MICHAEL L. SEIGEL, CORPORATE AMERICA FIGHTS BACK: THE BATTLE OVER WAIVER OF THE ATTORNEY-CLIENT PRIVILEGE

49 B.C. L. Rev. 1, 10-13, 21-22 (2008)

Setting aside for a moment . . . factors bearing on cooperation, if . . . other factors line up the right way, prosecution (or at least the threat of prosecution) of the corporate entity is in the public's interest. Specifically, if (1) the criminality was serious, pervasive, and high-reaching, (2) criminal prosecution would not unduly harm investors and consumers, and (3) other remedies are either unavailable or insufficient, then corporate criminal liability furthers a number of critical social goods.

As an initial matter, corporate culpability achieves significant additional deterrence, specific and general, beyond that achieved solely by the prosecution of individuals. Specifically, corporate liability deters corporate officers from creating an atmosphere in which mid- and lower-level employees know that criminal conduct is either tolerated or encouraged, but which shields the officers themselves from liability. High-level management can generate this situation in a number of ways; one method is to set sales or other targets so high that they cannot be met through legal means and then fire or demote employees who fail to meet these unrealistic targets. Employees quickly understand what they need to do to keep their jobs and get promoted, while management hides behind a veil of plausible deniability. Later, if criminal proceedings are initiated and lower-level employees get caught, management can point to the fact that it never sanctioned criminal activity and was not aware of its existence. It can go even further and throw a couple of minor employees to the prosecution wolves, claiming that they were rogues and that their termination (and prosecution) has cured the problem. Meanwhile, the managers—the true rogues—continue their way up the sleazy corporate ladder.

Entity prosecution helps to reverse this equation. If managers obliquely encourage widespread criminality and the entity gets caught, prosecution of the corporation means that the entity will pay a price. It will suffer a loss of reputation and perhaps even lost revenues, monetary penalties, and debarment. Harm to the corporation means harm to the officers. They may lose their jobs or at least suffer monetary losses such as a reduction in the value of their stock portfolios and perhaps the loss of future salary increases or bonuses. Certainly, their professional reputations will be forever tainted. Given these prospects, preventing—as opposed to encouraging—criminality within the corporation looks to the officers like the better path to choose.

Of course, nothing deters a white collar criminal more than the prospect of serving time in prison. Thus, for deterrence purposes, prosecutors place an emphasis on having both tools at their disposal: individual liability, when it can be proved, and corporate liability as a vital complement to it.

Corporate liability also plays an important role in the area of victim restitution. Often, white collar prosecutions involve millions—even hundreds of millions or billions—of dollars of fraud. Convicted individuals rarely have at their disposal anything near the amount of money necessary to pay restitution to the victims of the crime. The corporate entity, however, is a potential deep pocket. Given that the risk of corporate criminality is priced into the market, it is not unfair to make the entity (and thus its shareholders) responsible for repaying the victims, if possible.

In addition, the threat of criminal liability gives corporations an incentive to set up compliance programs with real teeth in them. Absent criminal liability, the decision whether to comply with the law is simply a matter of dollars and cents: is compliance more or less costly than the cost of fines and penalties (multiplied by the risk of getting caught)? Criminal liability, with its negative stigma, raises the stakes to a higher level, and one much more difficult to measure. It is hard to estimate in advance the degree to which a criminal conviction will harm a corporation's bottom line; indeed, in the very rare case, criminal conviction can effectively be a "death penalty." The resultant uncertainty undoubtedly makes corporate officers much more risk adverse, increasing the attractiveness of implementing procedures and hiring experts to assure legal and regulatory compliance.

Finally, the threat of entity liability provides prosecutors with leverage to encourage the corporation to cooperate with the investigation. . . . When a collective entity decides to be cooperative, the balance of power shifts dramatically. No longer foes, the corporation and the government can team up to unmask the individuals who were at the center of the criminal activity, thereby getting to the heart of the matter quickly and efficiently. . . . With company cooperation, the successful completion of a complex white collar prosecution, including resolution of corporate as well as all individual charges, could very well be reduced from a matter of years to a matter of months. This huge efficiency gain represents a significant public good. Far more white collar criminal behavior can be attacked with the same amount of resources devoted to the effort.

The efficiency argument is equally strong even when prosecutors erroneously target an innocent company. The fastest way a company can convince government agents of its innocence is to share all pertinent information with them so that they can draw this conclusion themselves.

JENNIFER ARLEN, THE POTENTIALLY PERVERSE EFFECTS OF CORPORATE CRIMINAL LIABILITY

23 J. Legal Stud. 833 (1994)

Some scholars, recognizing the agency cost nature of corporate crime, argue that corporate criminal liability is best analyzed as a substitute for direct criminal liability of the agent. In this view, corporate liability is simply an indirect means of sanctioning wrongful agents, on the assumption that corporations subject to criminal liability will in turn sanction the wrongful agents, either by seeking indemnification or by reducing the agents' wages. Corporate criminal liability accordingly is warranted when corporations are better able to sanction agents than is the state. Should this be the case, this view holds that a corporation should be strictly liable for its agents' crimes and subject to a fine equal to H/p. The corporation will in turn impose this liability on the wrongful agent in each case, producing efficient deterrence. Corporate criminal liability is not justifiable, however, when the state is as capable as the corporation of sanctioning the wrongful agent directly—as often is the case.

Corporate criminal liability may indeed sometimes deter crime by inducing corporations to sanction their agents for wrongful acts. But corporate liability also has another effect. Many corporate crimes—such as securities fraud, government procurement fraud, and some environmental crimes—cannot be readily detected by the government. Corporations often are better positioned to detect such crimes and determine which agents committed them. In these circumstances, corporate criminal liability may affect corporate expenditures on detecting and investigating crimes committed by their employees, here described as "enforcement costs."

Should vicarious criminal liability increase corporate enforcement expenditures, it magnifies the deterrent effect of direct agent liability by increasing the probability that wrongful agents will be detected and sanctioned. Should it have the opposite effect, however, corporate crime will increase. The deterrent effect of vicarious criminal liability therefore depends on the effect of vicarious liability on corporate enforcement expenditures.

Recognizing the influence of corporate enforcement expenditures, this article demonstrates, dramatically changes the analysis of corporate criminal liability. Previous analysis suggests that increased corporate liability necessarily reduces crime. Introducing corporate enforcement costs, however, reveals that increased corporate liability does not necessarily reduce corporate crime and, indeed, may result in increased crime. The existing legal regime governing many crimes is best approximated as a rule of "pure strict vicarious liability," under which the fine imposed for a particular crime is fixed, in that it does not vary precisely with the level of corporate enforcement expenditures. This regime of strict vicarious liability presents corporations contemplating enforcement expenditures with conflicting, potentially perverse, incentives. On the one hand, increased enforcement expenditures reduce the number of agents who commit crimes by increasing the probability of detection and thus each agent's expected cost of crime. On the other hand, these expenditures also increase the probability that the government will detect those crimes that are committed, thereby increasing the corporation's expected criminal liability for those crimes. If the expected cost to the corporation of the resulting increase in its expected criminal liability exceeds the expected benefit to the corporation of the reduction in the number of crimes, a corporation subject to strict vicarious liability will not respond by increasing its enforcement expenditures because additional enforcement would only increase the firm's expected criminal liability. In fact, in some circumstances a corporation subject to vicarious liability may spend less on enforcement than it would absent vicarious liability. Moreover, even when strict vicarious liability can induce efficient enforcement, the conflicting incentives it creates affect the efficient fine: to induce efficient enforcement, the fixed fine must exceed the net social cost of crime divided by the efficient probability of detection. These results call into question both the current trend toward increased corporate criminal liability and much of the accepted wisdom regarding strict vicarious criminal liability. This analysis also may be relevant to administrative sanctions against corporations and to vicarious civil liability, including employer liability for sexual harassment under Title VII.

In theory, the perverse incentives created by strict vicarious criminal liability can be eliminated by employing a variable fine equal to the net social cost of crime divided by the actual probability of detection (given the corporation's expenditures on enforcement). This rule would eliminate the perverse incentives otherwise present under strict vicarious liability because any increase in the probability of detection occasioned by corporate enforcement expenditures would result in an equivalent decrease in the fine imposed. Implementing this rule, however, would require a dramatic change in the current law. In particular, it would require us to abandon the goal of imposing relatively fixed fines for each type of crime—a goal that permeates the U.S. Sentencing Guidelines—in favor of a rule under which the corporate criminal fine could not be determined until after the crime was committed and investigated since only then could the corporation's precise expenditures on enforcement be determined. Perhaps more important, the precise calculations required for this rule—if feasible—would be very costly.

Accordingly, alternative rules to strict vicarious criminal liability warrant consideration. Three such rules are considered briefly in the present analysis: (1) mitigation rules, under which the fine is reduced (but not eliminated) if the firm's enforcement is efficient; (2) a "negligence" rule, under which the firm bears no liability if it incurs efficient enforcement; and (3) a modified "evidentiary privilege" (akin to use immunity) under which any information disclosed by the corporation can be used to prosecute the wrongful agents but cannot be used against the corporation in criminal or civil litigation. . . .

FRANCIS T. CULLEN, WILLIAM J. MAAKESTAD & GARY CAVENDER, CORPORATE CRIME UNDER ATTACK

351-353 (1987)

Corporate Criminals or Criminal Corporations?

Students of corporate social control have asked increasingly whether individual executives or corporate entities should be the object of criminal sanctions. Is it best to speak about "corporate criminals" or "criminal corporations"? The most common answer is that the preferred statutory scheme provides both individual and entity liability; the appropriateness of each is to be determined case by case by the prosecutor. Accordingly, a wide range of methods, apart from the traditional practice of fining businesses, have been proposed or tried to penalize corporate entities more effectively: mandatory community service, managerial intervention, government contract proscription, equity fines, and especially formal publicity.

Some critics, however, have argued against the application of criminal sanctions to corporate entities, primarily on two grounds. First, they challenge the deterrent effect of the sanction essentially because "corporations don't commit crimes, people do"; second, they question the retributive function because corporate criminal sanctions may actually punish innocent shareholders (by reducing the value of their shares) and consumers (by increasing the costs of goods and services). Although a detailed analysis of each objection is beyond the scope of this chapter, a few comments are in order, particularly because the Pinto prosecution—along with other important cases like the E.F. Hutton prosecution—involved corporate rather than individual defendants. We suggest that, in many instances, sanctioning the corporation is the most prudent and equitable policy, and thus that prosecutors' options should not be confined to imposing individual criminal liability.

The critics' first objection—that people, not corporations, commit crimes—ignores the reality that the labyrinthian structure of many modern corporations often makes it extremely difficult to pinpoint individual responsibility for specific decisions. Even in cases where employees who carried out criminal activities can be identified, controversial questions remain. John S. Martin, a former U.S. Attorney who actively prosecuted corporate and white-collar crime cases, comments that when individual offenders can be identified they "often turn out to be lower-level corporate employees who never made a lot of money, who never benefited personally from the transaction, and who acted with either the real or mistaken belief that if they did not commit the acts in question their jobs might be in jeopardy." Further, says Martin, "they may have believed that their superior was aware [of] and approved of the crime, but could not honestly testify to a specific conversation or other act of the superior that would support an indictment of the superior." Thus a thorough investigation may well lead a prosecutor to conclude that indictments against individuals simply cannot be justified, even though the corporation benefitted from a clear violation of a criminal statute. Such a result would disserve the deterrent function.

The existence of corporate criminal liability also provides an incentive for top officers to supervise middle- and lower-level management more closely. Individual liability, in the absence of corporate liability, encourages just the opposite: top executives may take the attitude of "don't tell me, I don't want to know." In the words of Peter Jones, former chief legal counsel at Levi Strauss, "a fundamental law of organizational physics is that bad news does not flow upstream." Only when directives come from the upper echelon of the corporation "will busy executives feel enough pressure to prevent activities that seriously threaten public health and safety." For a similar reason, proponents of the conservative "Chicago School" of law and economic thought advocate corporate rather than individual sanctioning: a firm's control mechanisms will be more efficient than the state's in deterring misconduct by its agents and will bring about adequate compliance with legal standards as long as the costs of punishment outweigh the potential benefits.

The second objection—that the cost of corporate criminal fines is actually borne by innocent shareholders and consumers—also seems unfounded. With regard to shareholders, whether individual or institutional, incidents of corporate criminal behavior may give the owners the right to redress the diminution of their interest by filing a derivative suit against individual officers and/or members of the board of directors. Although the cost and the uncertainty of winning such a suit may be high, shareholders must regard this cost as one of the risks incurred when they invest in securities. Just as shareholders may occasionally be enriched unjustly through undetected misbehavior by their company, it is only fair to expect them to bear a part of the burden on those occasions when illegality is discovered and duly sanctioned.

Finally, it is simplistic, if not untenable, to argue that corporate criminal fines will simply be passed on to the consuming public through higher prices. Stephen Yoder, among others, notes that in such instances, our economic system allows consumers to exert a type of indirect, collective control. If we assume that competition exists in the offending corporation's industry, the firm cannot simply decide to raise its prices to absorb the fine or the costs related to the litigation. If it does so, it risks becoming less competitive and suffering such concomitant problems as decreased profits, difficulty in securing debt and equity financing, curtailed expansion, and the loss of investors to more law-abiding corporations.

NOTES AND QUESTIONS

1. The main argument put forward in *New York Central* supporting the position that corporate criminal liability offends the Constitution appears to be that it punishes innocent shareholders without due process of law. How does Justice Day respond to this issue? Does he ever directly engage it?
2. Cullen et al. address the contention that corporate criminal enforcement hurts innocent shareholders by arguing that (1) shareholders can recover losses through derivative suits and (2) shareholders occasionally are unjustly enriched by criminal activity, therefore "it is only fair to expect them to bear a part of the burden on those occasions when illegality . . . is duly sanctioned." Is this a satisfactory response? In a publicly traded company, is it likely that the *same* shareholders who are enriched will also be the ones to pay?
3. Seigel and Cullen et al. argue that corporate criminal liability leverages the government's prosecutorial power by providing incentives to corporate officers to fight rather than foster internal crime. What are the main points in their arguments? Arlen, on the other hand, contends that corporate criminal liability is a form of strict liability that can have the perverse incentive of increasing corporate criminal behavior. How, exactly, does she think this takes place? Who's got the better argument?
4. Can corporate criminal liability cause more shareholder oversight of a corporation's actions? Or is shareholder power too diffuse to expect such an outcome except in the most extraordinary circumstances?

Not directly discussed in these excerpts is the question whether criminal liability is simply an extension of civil liability (into the territory of heftier fines) or whether it is different in kind. The behavior of corporate officers in recent times suggests the latter. Fines—even serious ones—are seen as the "cost of doing business." They are not embarrassing, just harmful to the short-term bottom line. By way of contrast, no officer wants his or her company to be labeled a "convicted felon." Right or wrong, this designation can have a serious impact on a company's good will, and a drop in good will could very well mean a drop—perhaps even a precipitous one—in the company's market value. This unpredictable and potentially devastating consequence of criminal prosecution causes many corporate boards (especially post-Enron) to avoid a corporate conviction at nearly all costs. *Cf.* United States v. Stein, 435 F. Supp. 2d 330 (2006) (holding that accounting firm KPMG's extreme conduct intended to satisfy the government and avoid prosecution violated its employees' constitutional rights) (reprinted *infra* p. 573).

Problem 2-1

Assume you are an international expert in white collar crime. The Minister of Finance for Country *X* hires you to provide expert advice. Country *X* has a population of

45 million persons. It is characterized by a robust economy that is rapidly transitioning from Third-World to First-World status. It has had an active stock market for about two decades and is fast approaching the point where more than 50 percent of its GDP will be attributable to the corporate sector. Up until now, Country *X* has never imposed criminal liability on a corporation on the theory that there is no corpus to incarcerate. The Minister of Finance asks you to advise her on the pros and cons of overturning this policy. She wants to know if imposing corporate criminal liability will lead to a measurable reduction in crime, which is presently rampant in the white collar community. She specifically wants you to address the societal conditions necessary for such liability to be effective, assuming it can be effective at all.

What advice would you give to the Minister and why?

C. When Is a Corporation Criminally Liable for the Acts of Its Agents?

Once a society determines that corporations can and should be held criminally liable, the next question it faces is, "Under what circumstances?" One possibility is that a corporation would not be able to commit a crime unless the crime's statutory definition unambiguously provided for liability of this sort. Some countries have taken this approach, but not the United States. Here, corporations are potentially liable for any criminal offense committable by a human being. This raises the ultimate question: Given that a corporation is a mere legal fiction, exactly when should it bear responsibility for the acts of one or more of its agents?

1. Respondeat Superior Doctrine

STANDARD OIL v. UNITED STATES
307 F.2d 120 (C.A. Tex. 1962)

[With the help of employees from Standard Oil and Pasotex, both corporations, Thompson Oil (a third corporation) was able, in effect, to steal Standard Oil's product and run it through Pasotex pipelines. This was a violation of the federal Connally Hot Oil Act, which, among other things, forbids the transportation in interstate commerce of contraband oil. *See* 15 U.S.C. §715. The Standard Oil and Pasotex employees were compensated by Thompson for their part in the scheme. Standard Oil and Pasotex were indicted and convicted of violating the Act along with others, and appealed.]

John R. Brown, Circuit Judge.

This appeal by two corporate defendants, from fines imposed on judgments of conviction under the Connally Hot Oil Act, raises this basic question. May a corporate employer be held liable for a crime committed by employees who, although ostensibly acting in the performance of their duties, were really cooperating with a third person in the accomplishment of a criminal purpose for the benefit of that third person, and whose acts not only did not benefit the employer, but in some instances, at least, result in a theft of its property? . . .

The corporations can be found guilty . . . only if the evidence shows that each, acting through its human agents, deliberately did these acts, that is, with the corporation "knowing" that they were being done for it. Inquiry along this line brings us face-to-face with the everyday problem of imputing knowledge to a corporation.

As these defendants here are the first to acknowledge, several things afford no insulation from corporate knowledge. Thus, no contention is made that "knowledge" can be acquired only through supervisory or executive personnel. On the contrary, while status of the actor in the corporate hierarchy might well have decisive significance in determining the question we later discuss concerning the intention to benefit the corporation, the corporation may be criminally bound by the acts of subordinate, even menial, employees. . . . Likewise, no contention is, or can at this late date, be made that mere violation of instructions would shield the corporation from criminal responsibility for actions which its agents have taken for it.

There results are certainly not startling. They are a part of the law of respondeat superior and accepted as established principles in civil tort situations. They are a recognition that law as a useful tool must accommodate pure theoretical logic to the demands of common sense. Consequently, while it was perhaps long in coming, it is now almost ancient law that despite these conceptual, logical difficulties, a corporation acting through human agents has the legal capacity to do wrong as well as right. It is a logical paradox that this creature of the law—the corporate entity—is created by law with the power to violate law. Nevertheless this has been the holding in the federal system since 1909 when the Court decided *New York Central.* Of course those theoretic difficulties had for a time plagued the law in civil liabilities as well, but by applying usual principles of agency, the law had long recognized that the corporation would have a civil responsibility for injuries or wrongs done by those acting in the course and scope of their employment. Indeed, in going "only a step farther" to hold the corporation criminally liable for "the act of the agent (done) while exercising the authority delegated to him" was merely "applying the principle governing civil liability." *New York Central* at 494.

In the very context of this decisive holding of criminal liability, those governing principles of civil liability were made equally clear. Civil liability is imposed on the corporation, the Court said, "when the act is done by the agent in the course of his employment, although done wantonly or recklessly or against the express orders of the principal. In such cases the liability is not imputed because the principal actually participates in the malice or fraud, but because the act is done for the benefit of the principal, while the agent is acting within the scope of his employment in the business of the principal."

And even more recently the Court, in recognizing that Congress has the power to "personify the company" and thereby charge a partnership entity with criminal liability, spelled out that it was "through the doctrine of respondeat superior" that "corporations and other impersonal entities can be guilty of "knowing" or "willful" violations of regulatory statutes." *United States v. A. & P. Trucking Co.*, 358 U.S. 121 (1958). And again the rationale is couched in the familiar concepts of civil tort law of (1) a purpose to benefit the corporation and (2) an act by an agent in line of his duties. "The treasury of the business may not with impunity obtain the fruits of violations which are committed knowingly by agents of the entity in the scope of their employment." *Id.* at 126.

Of course the defendants do not contend, nor could they, that criminal accountability and actual benefit are equated. There have been many cases, and there may well be others in the future, in which the corporation is criminally liable even though no benefit has been received in fact. But while benefit is not essential in terms of result, the purpose to benefit the corporation is decisive in terms of equating the agent's action with that of the corporation. For it is an elementary principle of agency that "an act of a servant is not within the scope of employment if it is done with no intention to perform it as a part of or incident to a service on account of which he is employed." Restatement of the Law of Agency (2d) §235.

It is for this reason that the simple "function" test applied by the District Court—while obviously a factor of relevance—is alone insufficient upon which to rest convictions here. Thus the taking in or paying out of money by a bank teller, while certainly one of his regular functions, would hardly cast the corporation for criminal liability if in such "handling" the faithless employee was pocketing the funds as an embezzler or handing them over to a confederate under some ruse. . . .

[B]enefit is evidential in determining the purpose and motive for which the agent does the act in question. If it is done with a view of furthering the master's business, of doing something for the master, then the expectation or hope of a benefit, whether direct or indirect, makes the act that of the principal. The act is no less the principal's if from such intended conduct either no benefit accrues, a benefit is undiscernible, or, for that matter, the result turns out to be adverse.

On the facts of this record, only the most hypercritical, artificial view would find any benefit intended by the actions of [the employees of Standard Oil and Pasotex]. . . .

As to all counts, therefore, the judgments of conviction as to the corporate defendants must be reversed and rendered in favor of the appellants.

Reversed and rendered.

UNITED STATES v. SINGH

518 F.3d 236 (4th Cir. 2008)

King, Circuit Judge:

These appeals arise from a criminal proceeding in the Northern District of West Virginia in which defendants [Singh, "Dan" Patel, and Jalaram, Inc.] were convicted by jury of a total of fourteen offenses, including conspiracy to violate the Mann Act, in contravention of 18 U.S.C. §371 [and] ten counts of violating the Mann Act, in contravention of 18 U.S.C. §2422(a). . . .

Each of the fourteen offenses of conviction arose from the Defendants' involvement in an interstate prostitution scheme. . . .

From 2000 to 2003, a prostitution ring known as the "Gold Club" operated out of the Economy Inn and Scottish Inn motels in Martinsburg, West Virginia. The

Gold Club was operated by Susan Powell, who has pleaded guilty to a federal tax offense and who testified at trial on behalf of the Government. During the Gold Club's two-and-one-half years of operation, Powell employed approximately fifty prostitutes, using as many as nine motel rooms per day on peak days, and four or five rooms on average days. All together, the Gold Club received proceeds from its operations that totalled more than $670,000. Powell recruited female prostitutes for the Gold Club from West Virginia and the neighboring states of Maryland and Virginia by advertising in newspapers in the three states. Each of the out-of-state prostitutes who testified acknowledged that, when she travelled to work in West Virginia, she did so for the purpose of engaging in prostitution.

The Gold Club began operating out of the Martinsburg Economy Inn in approximately March 2000. . . . In 2001, Powell decided to transfer the Gold Club's operations from the Economy Inn to a new location. . . . Powell visited the Scottish Inn [a motel in Martinsburg owned by Jalaram, Inc.] to discuss moving the Gold Club's operations there. Suresh Patel [President of closely-held Jalaram, Inc.] was present, identified himself as the Scottish Inn's owner, and talked with Powell about the Gold Club. Powell explained to Suresh that she ran an "adult entertainment company" and was looking for rooms to rent for that purpose. Suresh advised Powell that she should address the issue with [Dan] Patel, the Inn's manager, and scheduled a meeting between Powell and [Dan] Patel for the next day. . . . As a result, Powell moved the Gold Club's operations to the Scottish Inn. . . .

Powell ran the Gold Club's operations at the Scottish Inn as she had at the Economy Inn. She communicated with the prostitutes through the Inns switchboard and discussed their appointments with [Dan] Patel. Like Singh at the Economy Inn, Patel would monitor the Gold Club's customers at the Scottish Inn to ensure that the prostitutes paid for their rooms after their first customer. The prostitutes paid for their rooms at the Scottish Inn as they had at the Economy Inn: using $40 of the receipts from the first daily customer to pay for a room for the balance of the day.

As the manager of the Scottish Inn, Patel was responsible for its daily operations. He registered guests, accepted room rental payments, and cleaned rooms after they had been occupied. In carrying out these duties, Patel and his wife lived and worked at the Scottish Inn seven days a week, twenty-four hours a day. Suresh Patel, the Inn's owner, visited the Scottish Inn a few times each month. . . .

The Gold Club operated out of the Scottish Inn for about six months in late 2001 and early 2002. . . . Patel may well have kept for himself a substantial portion of the cash payments he received from the prostitutes for the Scottish Inn rooms. During the period the Gold Club operated at the Scottish Inn, however, Jalaram[, Inc.] received a minimum of $700 from the Gold Club's operations. The prosecution contends that, under the evidence, the payments actually received by Jalaram were several times that amount. . . .

[T]he Government maintains that the district court erred in granting a new trial to Jalaram on its convictions on the Mann Act conspiracy and Mann Act counts. . . .

In its August 1 Order, the district court concluded that "the evidence adduced at trial does not support the jury's finding that Dan Patel was acting in furtherance of the corporation." Prior to issuing that Order, at the status conference of July 22, 2005, the court observed that "something of an independent contractor exception should have occurred," because the evidence showed that "Patel was acting on his own behalf [and] not for the benefit of the corporation Jalaram." As a result, the court, by its August 1 Order, awarded Jalaram a new trial on its convictions.

We have recognized that "a corporation is liable for the criminal acts of its employees and agents done within the scope of their employment with the intent to benefit the corporation." Mylan Labs., Inc. v. Akzo, N.V., 2 F.3d 56, 63 (4th Cir. 1993). The appropriate "scope of employment" of such an employee or agent has been defined to include all those acts falling within the employee's or agent's general line of work, when they are motivated—at least in part—by an intent to benefit the corporate employer.

In this situation, the district court apparently perceived that the evidence failed to establish Jalaram's corporate criminal liability based on the conduct of Patel. The court also perceived that, but for instructional error, Jalaram would have been acquitted. In so ruling, the court erred, first, in determining, that the evidence was insufficient to sustain the finding of corporate criminal liability against Jalaram, and, second, in concluding that instructional error had occurred. As explained above, a corporate accused is liable for the criminal acts of its "employees and agents" acting "within the scope of their employment" for the "benefit [of] the corporation," and such liability arises if the employee or agent has acted for his own benefit as well as that of his employer.

Under the evidence, viewed in the light most favorable to the prosecution, the court erred in failing to recognize that [Dan] Patel, as manager of the Scottish Inn, was an agent of Jalaram, and was acting within the scope of that relationship when he rented rooms to the Gold Club's prostitutes. The court also misperceived the importance of the fact that Powell first spoke with Jalaram's President, Suresh Patel, about moving the Gold Club's operations to the Scottish Inn. . . . The evidence demonstrates that [Dan] Patel thereafter received funds from the Gold Club prostitutes with the intent—at least in part—of benefitting Jalaram. Jalaram received, by its own admission, at least $700 from the Gold Club's prostitution enterprise. And the jury was entitled to find, under the evidence, that such receipts substantially exceeded that sum. In these circumstances, the evidence of Jalaram's corporate criminal liability did not at all weigh heavily against the verdict as to Jalaram, but was wholly sufficient to support it.

Moreover, contrary to the district court's conclusion that it erred in instructing the jury, the instructions properly explained the controlling legal principles on the issue of corporate criminal liability. In this regard, the jury was instructed on three important legal points:

> A corporation may be responsible for the actions of its agents done or made within the scope of their authority;
>
> The term "scope of employment" refers to acts on the corporation's behalf in performance of an agent's general line of work. To be acting within the scope of his employment, those acts must be motivated, at least in part, by an intent to benefit the corporation; and an agent may act for his own benefit while also acting for the benefit of the corporation.

As a result, the court made an error of law—thereby abusing its discretion—in concluding, during the July 22, 2005 status conference, that an independent contractor instruction should have been given to the jury.[20] . . . The court further abused its discretion by relying on the perceived instructional error to award a new trial to Jalaram in the face of trial evidence that fully supported (rather than weighed heavily against) the jury's verdict. The award of a new trial to Jalaram is thus vacated and the verdict is reinstated on the Mann Act conspiracy and Mann Act counts against Jalaram. We remand on those convictions for the appropriate sentencing proceedings.

NOTES AND QUESTIONS

1. *Standard Oil* states the classic respondeat superior test for the criminal liability of a collective entity for an act of its agent. *Singh* makes clear just how far this liability goes—not only can a relatively low-level manager of a corporation create vicarious liability under the respondeat superior test, but he can do so even when he is acting mostly in his own interests. An alternative test, originally proposed in 1957 by the American Law Institute in its Model Penal Code, limits corporate liability to situations where "the commission of the offense was authorized, requested, commanded, performed or recklessly tolerated by the board of directors or by a high managerial agent acting in behalf of the corporation within the scope of his office or employment." MPC §2.07(1)(c). This has become known as the "high managerial agent" rule. The drafters of the MPC believed that only agents in high positions could truly act or speak for the corporate entity. Although accepted in a few states, *see, e.g.*, State v. Chapman Dodge Center, Inc., 428 So. 2d 413 (La. 1983); State v. Christy Pontiac-GMC, Inc., 354 N.W. 2d 17 (Minn. 1984), this doctrine has had little influence overall. More to the point, it has had no influence in the federal courts, where most corporate crime is prosecuted.

20. Because of our disposition of the corporate criminal liability issue, we need not reach and dispose of the Government's alternative contention that, from a legal standpoint, there is no independent contractor exception to corporate criminal liability. We note, however, that the Government makes a compelling argument in that regard, asserting that

> the leading treatises recognize, for purposes of imposing criminal liability, [that] "a court may be unconcerned with technical distinctions between agents and independent contractors." 1 Brickey, Corporate Criminal Liability §3:05, at 104 (2d ed. 1991) ("The lines of reasoning used to support imposition of corporate liability for criminal misconduct of subordinate employees have also been advanced to impose liability on a corporation for acts of those who are not, strictly speaking, its employees."); *see also* 2 LaFave, *supra*, §13.5(c), at 390-91 (describing limits on corporate criminal liability, but making no mention of an independent contractor defense). The rule "prevent[s] corporations from avoiding liability by simply contracting-out the more risky elements of their business." Joseph S. Hall, Corporate Criminal Liability, 35 Am. Crim. L. Rev. 549, 553 (1998).

2. What are the pros and cons of the respondeat superior versus the high managerial agent tests?
3. Note that courts have approved the use of the respondeat superior doctrine even when the corporation is, to some extent, a victim of the crime. For example, in United States v. Sun Diamond Growers of America, 138 F.3d 961 (D.C. Cir. 1998), the defendant corporation employed a lobbyist who had the job of courting Secretary of Agriculture Mike Espy. When Espy asked the lobbyist to provide his brother with campaign funds, the lobbyist did so by defrauding Sun Diamond itself. Nevertheless, the court held:

   > The facts in the record, however—that [the employee] hid the illegal contribution scheme from others at the company and used company funds to accomplish it—do not preclude a valid finding that he undertook the scheme to benefit Sun-Diamond. Part of [his] job was to cultivate his, and Sun-Diamond's, relationship with Secretary Espy. By responding to the Secretary's request to help his brother, [the employee] may have been acting out of pure friendship, but the jury was entitled to conclude that he was acting instead, or also, with an intent (however befuddled) to further the interests of his employer. The scheme came at some cost to Sun-Diamond but it also promised some benefit.

   Id. at 970.
4. The doctrine of respondeat superior applies not just to corporations but in all collective entity settings, such as labor unions, *see* United Mine Workers v. Coronado Coal Co. 259 U.S. 344 (1922), and partnerships, *see* People v. Lessoff & Berger, 608 N.Y.S. 54 (1994).

Problem 2-2

Marlene is a cashier for the national retail chain, Best Deal, Inc. She is a computer whiz, and she figures out how to overcharge customers by adding an extra 2 percent in tax to each bill, which does not show up on the company's internal receipt. (If a customer happens to catch the discrepancy, she blames it on an isolated computer error and refunds that customer's money.)

a. Assume first that, at the end of the day, Marlene removes the excess 2 percent from her cash drawer and pockets it herself. Is Best Deal liable for her theft under the respondeat superior rule?
b. Assume now that Marlene has learned that Best Deal promotes cashiers based, in part, on their daily cash register receipts. As a result, Marlene decides that it is in her overall best interest to split the stolen money with her employer so she can get "credit" for some of it. She re-rigs the computer to split the surreptitiously collected 2 percent 50-50 with Best Deal. Is Best Deal liable for her theft under the respondeat superior rule?
c. Best Deal argues that, when committing theft, Marlene was working outside the scope of her employment, and that the respondeat superior rule should therefore not apply. Evaluate this argument.

d. Best deal argues that Marlene's theft from customers, once exposed, caused the company tremendous embarrassment. Therefore, her conduct was certainly not for the benefit of the company. Evaluate this argument.

2. Due Diligence

UNITED STATES v. HILTON HOTELS CORP.

467 F.2d 1000 (9th Cir.), cert. denied, 409 U.S. 1125 (1973)

BROWNING, Circuit Judge:

This is an appeal from a conviction under an indictment charging a violation of section 1 of the Sherman Act, 15 U.S.C. §1.

Operators of hotels, restaurants, hotel and restaurant supply companies, and other businesses in Portland, Oregon, organized an association to attract conventions to their city. To finance the association, members were asked to make contributions in predetermined amounts. Companies selling supplies to hotels were asked to contribute an amount equal to one per cent of their sales to hotel members. To aid collections, hotel members, including appellant, agreed to give preferential treatment to suppliers who paid their assessments, and to curtail purchases from those who did not. . . .

Appellant's president testified that it would be contrary to the policy of the corporation for the manager of one of its hotels to condition purchases upon payment of a contribution to a local association by the supplier. The manager of appellant's Portland hotel and his assistant testified that it was the hotel's policy to purchase supplies solely on the basis of price, quality, and service. They also testified that on two occasions they told the hotel's purchasing agent that he was to take no part in the boycott. The purchasing agent confirmed the receipt of these instructions, but admitted that, despite them, he had threatened a supplier with loss of the hotel's business unless the supplier paid the association assessment. He testified that he violated his instructions because of anger and personal pique toward the individual representing the supplier.

Based upon this testimony, appellant requested certain instructions bearing upon the criminal liability of a corporation for the unauthorized acts of its agents. These requests were rejected by the trial court. The court instructed the jury that a corporation is liable for the acts and statements of its agents "within the scope of their employment," defined to mean "in the corporation's behalf in performance of the agent's general line of work," including "not only that which has been authorized by the corporation, but also that which outsiders could reasonably assume the agent would have authority to do." The court added:

> "A corporation is responsible for acts and statements of its agents, done or made within the scope of their employment, even though their conduct may be contrary to their actual instructions or contrary to the corporation's stated policies."

Appellant objects only to the court's concluding statement.

Congress may constitutionally impose criminal liability upon a business entity for acts or omissions of its agents within the scope of their employment. Such liability may attach without proof that the conduct was within the agent's actual authority, and even though it may have been contrary to express instructions.

The intention to impose such liability is sometimes express, but it may also be implied. The text of the Sherman Act does not expressly resolve the issue. For the reasons that follow, however, we think the construction of the Act that best achieves its purpose is that a corporation is liable for acts of its agents within the scope of their authority even when done against company orders. . . .

The breadth and critical character of the public interests protected by the Sherman Act, and the gravity of the threat to those interests that led to the enactment of the statute, support a construction holding business organizations accountable, as a general rule, for violations of the Act by their employees in the course of their businesses. In enacting the Sherman Act, "Congress was passing drastic legislation to remedy a threatening danger to the public welfare. . . ." United Mine Workers v. Coronado Coal Co., 259 U.S. 344, 392 (1922). The statute "was designed to be a comprehensive charter of economic liberty aimed at preserving free and unfettered competition as the rule of trade. It rests on the premise that the unrestrained interaction of competitive forces will yield the best allocation of our economic resources, the lowest prices, the highest quality and the greatest material progress, while at the same time providing an environment conducive to the preservation of our democratic political and social institutions." Northern Pacific Ry. v. United States, 356 U.S. 1, 4 (1956).

With such important public interests at stake, it is reasonable to assume that Congress intended to impose liability upon business entities for the acts of those to whom they choose to delegate the conduct of their affairs, thus stimulating a maximum effort by owners and managers to assure adherence by such agents to the requirements of the Act. . . .

Because of the nature of Sherman Act offenses and the context in which they normally occur, the factors that militate against allowing a corporation to disown the criminal acts of its agents apply with special force to Sherman Act violations.

Sherman Act violations are commercial offenses. They are usually motivated by a desire to enhance profits. They commonly involve large, complex, and highly decentralized corporate business enterprises, and intricate business processes, practices, and arrangements. More often than not they also involve basic policy decisions, and must be implemented over an extended period of time.

Complex business structures, characterized by decentralization and delegation of authority, commonly adopted by corporations for business purposes, make it difficult to identify the particular corporate agents responsible for Sherman Act violations. At the same time, it is generally true that high management officials, for whose conduct the corporate directors and stockholders are the most clearly responsible, are likely to have participated in the policy decisions underlying Sherman Act violations, or at least to have become aware of them.

Violations of the Sherman Act are a likely consequence of the pressure to maximize profits that is commonly imposed by corporate owners upon managing agents and, in turn, upon lesser employees. In the face of that pressure, generalized directions to obey the Sherman Act, with the probable effect of foregoing profits, are the least likely to be taken seriously. And if a violation of the Sherman Act occurs, the corporation, and not the individual agents, will have realized the profits from the illegal activity.

In sum, identification of the particular agents responsible for a Sherman Act violation is especially difficult, and their conviction and punishment is peculiarly ineffective as a deterrent. At the same time, conviction and punishment of the business entity itself is likely to be both appropriate and effective.

For these reasons we conclude that as a general rule a corporation is liable under the Sherman Act for the acts of its agents in the scope of their employment, even though contrary to general corporate policy and express instructions to the agent.

Thus the general policy statements of appellant's president were no defense. Nor was it enough that appellant's manager told the purchasing agent that he was not to participate in the boycott. The purchasing agent was authorized to buy all of appellant's supplies. Purchases were made on the basis of specifications, but the purchasing agent exercised complete authority as to source. He was in a unique position to add the corporation's buying power to the force of the boycott. Appellant could not gain exculpation by issuing general instructions without undertaking to enforce those instructions by means commensurate with the obvious risks. . . .

Affirmed.

UNITED STATES v. BEUSCH

596 F.2d 871 (9th Cir. 1979)

James M. Carter, Circuit Judge:

Deak & Company of California (Deak), headquartered in San Francisco, is a wholly-owned subsidiary of Deak and Co. of New York, the largest foreign currency exchange dealer in the world. *Beusch* was Vice-President and the senior corporate officer of Deak located in San Francisco. Deak was convicted of 377 misdemeanor violations of the Bank Secrecy Act, 31 U.S.C. §§1058 & 1101, for failure to report receipt of currency in an amount exceeding $5,000 from outside the United States. *Beusch* . . . was likewise convicted of the 377 misdemeanors. . . . [Among other things,] Deak [appeals from its convictions, claiming that] one of the jury instructions given constituted reversible error. . . .

For reasons discussed more fully below, we affirm the convictions of Deak. . . .

The facts show that in 1972, Beusch initiated contact between Deak and two Filipinos Gimenez and Lai Man who began sending large amounts of currency to the United States for further disbursal throughout the world. Between 1972 and 1976, approximately $11 million were sent and disbursed. None of the money shipments was reported to the Treasury Department as required by certain provisions of the Bank Secrecy Act, 31 U.S.C. §1101.

Sometime in the Spring of 1976, customs agents in Hawaii inadvertently discovered currency in a package sent from the Phillippines to Deak's offices in San Francisco. Suspicions were aroused when customs, postal, and courier records revealed that in the recent past, many similar packages had been sent from the same source to the same address, but Treasury records showed no §1101 reports.

A search warrant was issued and executed in May, 1976, at Deak's offices in San Francisco. Incriminating ledgers, files and packages of money were discovered there. Convictions and these appeals followed. . . .

Deak's . . . contention is that one of the instructions given to the jury prior to its deliberation was erroneous because, in effect, it imposed strict liability on Deak for Beusch's acts in spite of the requirement of specific intent found in 31 U.S.C. §1058 . . . . The challenged instruction reads as follows:

> "A corporation may be responsible for the acts of its agents done or made within the scope of its authority, even though the agent's conduct may be contrary to the corporation's actual instruction or contrary to the corporation's stated policies."

We have examined all of the instructions related to vicarious responsibility and find that, read in context,[7] the challenged instruction does not mean what Deak says it means. It does not impose strict liability on Deak without proof of intent. Rather, it suggests that a corporation may be liable for acts of its employees done contrary to express instructions and policies, but that the existence of such instructions and policies may be considered in determining whether the employee in fact acted to benefit the corporation. Merely stating or publishing such instructions and policies without diligently enforcing them is not enough to place the acts of an employee who violates them outside the scope of his employment. It is a question of fact whether measures taken to enforce corporate policy in this area will adequately insulate the corporation against such acts, and we see no reason to disturb the jury's finding in this regard. The instruction given the jury, read in context, is a proper statement of the law. . . .

AFFIRMED in part, REVERSED in part, and REMANDED for further proceedings consistent with this opinion.

[Opinion of Bright, Circuit Judge, concurring in part and dissenting in part, is omitted.]

7. The other relevant instructions were as follows, and appear in the order in which they were given:

> "The acts of a corporate agent or corporation's employee are within the scope of his authority if those acts are done on the corporation's behalf or for its benefit in the performance of the agent's general duties.
>
> "Acts included within the scope of the agent's authority are not only those that have been specifically authorized by the corporation but also those which a reasonable person would reasonably assume such an agent or employee [had] the authority to do
>
> . . . (The challenged instruction). . . .
>
> "You may, however, consider the corporate policies and instructions as one of the circumstances along with any other circumstances that you find to be significant in determining what the authority of the agent actually was and whether the agent was acting on behalf of the corporation.
>
> "In order to be acting within the scope of his authority, the employee must be found to be acting on behalf of the corporation with the purpose of benefiting the corporation or serving some corporate purpose."

NOTES AND QUESTIONS

1. To what extent is due diligence a defense to a charge of corporate criminal liability? Why is the standard so tilted in favor of the prosecution?
2. Note that although the court's analysis in *Hilton Hotels* is at times specific to the Sherman Act, its holding has not been limited in this fashion. Rather, its rule has been applied across the board to all criminal statutes.
3. Is the trial court's jury instruction in *Beusch* the same as the one in *Hilton Hotels*? If not, how are they different? Which is the better doctrine?
4. If you were a lawyer advising the CEO of a company, would you advise him to implement a strong regulatory compliance program? What factors would you suggest that he take into account?

3. Limitations on Prosecutorial Discretion

As we have just seen, the respondeat superior doctrine is incredibly broad. Under the right conditions, a multi-billion dollar international conglomerate can be held criminally liable for one employee's rogue act even if the act violates express company policy. Not surprisingly, as the Department of Justice started to indict corporations on a routine basis in the 1990s, the Attorney General determined that a set of guidelines was needed to help prosecutors exercise this tremendous power wisely. The AG also wanted to promote uniformity in the use of corporate criminal liability throughout the country. Excerpts from these guidelines follow, in their most up-to-date form.

MARK FILIP, U.S. DEPARTMENT OF JUSTICE, OFFICE OF THE DEPUTY ATTORNEY GENERAL, MEMORANDUM: PRINCIPLES OF FEDERAL PROSECUTION OF BUSINESS ORGANIZATIONS

Aug. 28, 2008 (Excerpts)

9-28.300 Factors to Be Considered

A. General Principle:

1. Generally, prosecutors apply the same factors in determining whether to charge a corporation as they do with respect to individuals. *See* USAM 9-27.220 et seq.[2] Thus, the prosecutor must weigh all of the factors normally considered in the sound exercise of prosecutorial judgment: the sufficiency of the evidence; the likelihood of success at trial; the

2. [This is a reference to the United States Attorneys' Manual, which can be found online at http://www.justice.gov/usao/eousa/foia_reading_room/usam/—Eds.]

probable deterrent, rehabilitative, and other consequences of conviction; and the adequacy of noncriminal approaches. *See id.* However, due to the nature of the corporate "person," some additional factors are present. In conducting an investigation, determining whether to bring charges, and negotiating plea or other agreements, prosecutors should consider the following factors in reaching a decision as to the proper treatment of a corporate target;

2. the nature and seriousness of the offense, including the risk of harm to the public, and applicable policies and priorities, if any, governing the prosecution of corporations for particular categories of crime (*see* USAM 9-28.400);
3. the pervasiveness of wrongdoing within the corporation, including the complicity in, or the condoning of, the wrongdoing by corporate management (*see* USAM 9-28.500);
4. the corporation's history of similar misconduct, including prior criminal, civil, and regulatory enforcement actions against it (*see* USAM 9-28.600);
5. the corporation's timely and voluntary disclosure of wrongdoing and its willingness to cooperate in the investigation of its agents (*see* USAM 9-28.700);
6. the existence and effectiveness of the corporation's pre-existing compliance program (*see* USAM 9-28.800);
7. the corporation's remedial actions, including any efforts to implement an effective corporate compliance program or to improve an existing one, to replace responsible management, to discipline or terminate wrongdoers, to pay restitution, and to cooperate with the relevant government agencies (*see* USAM 9-28.900);
8. collateral consequences, including whether there is disproportionate harm to shareholders, pension holders, employees, and others not proven personally culpable, as well as impact on the public arising from the prosecution (*see* USAM 9-28.1000);
9. the adequacy of the prosecution of individuals responsible for the corporation's malfeasance; and
10. the adequacy of remedies such as civil or regulatory enforcement actions (*see* USAM 9-28.1100).

9-28.400 Special Policy Concerns

General Principle: The nature and seriousness of the crime, including the risk of harm to the public from the criminal misconduct, are obviously primary factors in determining whether to charge a corporation. In addition, corporate conduct, particularly that of national and multi-national corporations, necessarily intersects with federal economic, tax, and criminal law enforcement policies. In applying these Principles, prosecutors must consider the practices and policies of the appropriate Division of the Department, and must comply with those policies to the extent required by the facts presented.

9-28.500 Pervasiveness of Wrongdoing Within the Corporation

General Principle: A corporation can only act through natural persons, and it is therefore held responsible for the acts of such persons fairly attributable to it. Charging a corporation for even minor misconduct may be appropriate where the wrongdoing was pervasive and was undertaken by a large number of employees, or by all the employees in a particular role within the corporation, or was condoned by upper management. On the other hand, it may not be appropriate to impose liability upon a corporation, particularly one with a robust compliance program in place, under a strict respondeat superior theory for the single isolated act of a rogue employee. There is, of course, a wide spectrum between these two extremes, and a prosecutor should exercise sound discretion in evaluating the pervasiveness of wrongdoing within a corporation.

9-28.600 The Corporation's Past History

General Principle: Prosecutors may consider a corporation's history of similar conduct, including prior criminal, civil, and regulatory enforcement actions against it, in determining whether to bring criminal charges and how best to resolve cases.

9-28.700 The Value of Cooperation

General Principle: In determining whether to charge a corporation and how to resolve corporate criminal cases, the corporation's timely and voluntary disclosure of wrongdoing and its cooperation with the government's investigation may be relevant factors. In gauging the extent of the corporation's cooperation, the prosecutor may consider, among other things, whether the corporation made a voluntary and timely disclosure, and the corporation's willingness to provide relevant information and evidence and identify relevant actors within and outside the corporation, including senior executives.

Cooperation is a potential mitigating factor, by which a corporation—just like any other subject of a criminal investigation—can gain credit in a case that otherwise is appropriate for indictment and prosecution. Of course, the decision not to cooperate by a corporation (or individual) is not itself evidence of misconduct, at least where the lack of cooperation does not involve criminal misconduct or demonstrate consciousness of guilt (e.g., suborning perjury or false statements, or refusing to comply with lawful discovery requests). Thus, failure to cooperate, in and of itself, does not support or require the filing of charges with respect to a corporation any more than with respect to an individual.

9-28.800 Corporate Compliance Programs

General Principle: Compliance programs are established by corporate management to prevent and detect misconduct and to ensure that corporate activities are conducted in accordance with applicable criminal and civil laws, regulations, and rules. The Department encourages such corporate self-policing, including voluntary disclosures to the government of any problems that a corporation discovers on its own. However, the existence of a compliance program is not sufficient, in and of itself, to justify not charging a corporation for criminal misconduct undertaken by its officers, directors, employees, or agents. In addition, the nature of some crimes, e.g., antitrust violations, may be such that national law enforcement policies mandate prosecutions of corporations notwithstanding the existence of a compliance program.

9-28.900 Restitution and Remediation

General Principle: Although neither a corporation nor an individual target may avoid prosecution merely by paying a sum of money, a prosecutor may consider the corporation's willingness to make restitution and steps already taken to do so. A prosecutor may also consider other remedial actions, such as improving an existing compliance program or disciplining wrongdoers, in determining whether to charge the corporation and how to resolve corporate criminal cases.

9-28.1000 Collateral Consequences

General Principle: Prosecutors may consider the collateral consequences of a corporate criminal conviction or indictment in determining whether to charge the corporation with a criminal offense and how to resolve corporate criminal cases.

9-28.1100 Other Civil or Regulatory Alternatives

General Principle: Non-criminal alternatives to prosecution often exist and prosecutors may consider whether such sanctions would adequately deter, punish, and rehabilitate a corporation that has engaged in wrongful conduct. In evaluating the adequacy of non-criminal alternatives to prosecution—e.g., civil or regulatory enforcement actions—the prosecutor may consider all relevant factors, including:

the sanctions available under the alternative means of disposition;

the likelihood that an effective sanction will be imposed; and

the effect of non-criminal disposition on federal law enforcement interests.

NOTES AND QUESTIONS

1. What are the advantages of a system whereby the charging decision rests almost entirely within the discretion of the prosecutor? What are the disadvantages? How can DOJ enforce its guidelines vis-à-vis its line prosecutors? Or is that simply impossible? Are there other forces at play that will hold federal prosecutors' exercise of power in check? Note that internal DOJ guidelines are *not* enforceable in any fashion by a third party, including a criminal defendant.
2. Most of the factors set out in the guidelines, such as the seriousness of the crime and its pervasiveness throughout the organization, are non-controversial. However, as we shall see in Chapter 12, one factor originally listed—the extent to which a corporation waived attorney-client privilege in the context of cooperation—brought on a firestorm of protest from

organizations such as the American Chamber of Commerce and the American Bar Association. It is notable that the most recent version of the guidelines no longer mentions attorney-client privilege at all.

4. Collective Entity Mens Rea

As can be inferred from *Standard Oil* and the other cases set out above, ascribing mens rea to a collective entity is in most situations a simple proposition: If any agent commits a criminal act on behalf of the entity, the mens rea of the agent is imputed to the entity itself. But on rare occasions the situation is not that simple—there may not be any one agent in the entity with the complete mens rea required to commit the crime. What then?

UNITED STATES v. BANK OF NEW ENGLAND, N.A.

821 F.2d 844 (1st Cir.), cert. denied, 484 U.S. 943 (1987)

Bownes, Circuit Judge.

The Bank of New England appeals a jury verdict convicting it of thirty-one violations of the Currency Transaction Reporting Act (the Act). 31 U.S.C. §§5311-22 (1982). Department of Treasury regulations promulgated under the Act require banks to file Currency Transaction Reports (CTRs) within fifteen days of customer currency transactions exceeding $10,000. The Act imposes felony liability when a bank willfully fails to file such reports "as part of a pattern of illegal activity involving transactions of more than $100,000 in a twelve-month period. . . ." 31 U.S.C. §5322(b).

I. The Issues

The Bank was found guilty of having failed to file CTRs on cash withdrawals made by James McDonough. It is undisputed that on thirty-one separate occasions between May 1983 and July 1984, McDonough withdrew from the Prudential Branch of the Bank more than $10,000 in cash by using multiple checks—each one individually under $10,000—presented simultaneously to a single bank teller. The Bank contends that . . . the trial judge's instructions on willfulness were fatally flawed, and that, in any event, the evidence did not suffice to show that it willfully failed to file CTRs on McDonough's transactions. . . .

The Bank had been named in a federal grand jury indictment which was returned on October 15, 1985. Count One of the indictment alleged that between May 1983 and May 1985, James McDonough, the Bank, and Carol Orlandella and Patricia Murphy—both of whom were former head tellers with the Bank's Prudential Branch—unlawfully conspired to conceal from the IRS thirty-six of McDonough's currency transactions. The trial court directed a verdict of acquittal on this count. Defendants Murphy and Orlandella were found not guilty of charges that they individually aided and abetted the failure to file CTRs on McDonough's transactions.

The bulk of the indictment alleged that the Bank, as principal, and McDonough, as an aider and abettor, willfully failed to file CTRs on thirty-six occasions between

May 1983 and July 1984. Five counts were dismissed because, on those occasions, McDonough received cashier's checks from the Bank, rather than currency. McDonough was acquitted of all charges against him. The Bank was found guilty on the thirty-one remaining counts. We affirm.

II. The Reportability of McDonough's Transactions

. . . In the instant case, McDonough's practice was to visit the same branch of the same bank on only one occasion in a single day. He simultaneously would present to a single bank teller two to four checks, all made payable to cash, for varying amounts under $10,000 which, when added together, equaled a sum greater than $10,000. In return, the same bank teller would transfer to him in a single motion a wad of cash totaling more than $10,000.

We have no trouble categorizing such conduct as a single physical transfer of currency in excess of $10,000 from the Bank to McDonough. We, therefore, conclude that the language of the regulations itself gave the Bank fair warning that McDonough's transactions were reportable. . . .

IV. Willfulness of the Bank's Conduct

A. The Trial Court's Instruction on Willfulness

Criminal liability under 31 U.S.C. §5322 only attaches when a financial institution "willfully" violates the CTR filing requirement. A finding of willfulness under the Reporting Act must be supported by "proof of the defendant's knowledge of the reporting requirements and his specific intent to commit the crime." United States v. Hernando Ospina, 798 F.2d 1570, 1580 (11th Cir. 1986). Willfulness can rarely be proven by direct evidence, since it is a state of mind; it is usually established by drawing reasonable inferences from the available facts.

The Bank contends that the trial court's instructions on knowledge and specific intent effectively relieved the government of its responsibility to prove that the Bank acted willfully. The trial judge began her instructions on this element by outlining generally the concepts of knowledge and willfulness:

> Knowingly simply means voluntarily and intentionally. It's designed to exclude a failure that is done by mistake or accident, or for some other innocent reason. Willfully means voluntarily, intentionally, and with a specific intent to disregard, to disobey the law, with a bad purpose to violate the law.

The trial judge properly instructed the jury that it could infer knowledge if a defendant consciously avoided learning about the reporting requirements. The court then focused on the kind of proof that would establish the Bank's knowledge of its filing obligations. The judge instructed that the knowledge of individual employees acting within the scope of their employment is imputed to the Bank. She told the jury that "if any employee knew that multiple checks would require the filing of reports, the bank knew it, provided the employee knew it within the scope of his employment. . . ."

The trial judge then focused on the issue of "collective knowledge":

> In addition, however, you have to look at the bank as an institution. As such, its knowledge is the sum of the knowledge of all of the employees. That is, the bank's knowledge is the totality of what all of the employees know within the scope of their employment. So, if Employee A knows one facet of the currency reporting requirement, B knows another facet of it, and C a third facet of it, the bank knows them all. So if you find that an employee within the scope of his employment knew that CTRs had to be filed, even if multiple checks are used, the bank is deemed to know it. The bank is also deemed to know it if each of several employees knew a part of that requirement and the sum of what the separate employees knew amounted to knowledge that such a requirement existed.

After discussing the two modes of establishing knowledge—via either knowledge of one of its individual employees or the aggregate knowledge of all its employees—the trial judge turned to the issue of specific intent:

> There is a similar double business with respect to the concept of willfulness with respect to the bank. In deciding whether the bank acted willfully, again you have to look first at the conduct of all employees and officers, and, second, at what the bank did or did not do as an institution. The bank is deemed to have acted willfully if one of its employees in the scope of his employment acted willfully. So, if you find that an employee willfully failed to do what was necessary to file these reports, then that is deemed to be the act of the bank, and the bank is deemed to have willfully failed to file. . . .
>
> Alternatively, the bank as an institution has certain responsibilities; as an organization, it has certain responsibilities. And you will have to determine whether the bank as an organization consciously avoided learning about and observing CTR requirements. The Government to prove the bank guilty on this theory, has to show that its failure to file was the result of some flagrant organizational indifference. In this connection, you should look at the evidence as to the bank's effort, if any, to inform its employees of the law; its effort to check on their compliance; its response to various bits of information that it got in August and September of '84 and February of '85; its policies, and how it carried out its stated policies. . . .
>
> If you find that the Government has proven with respect to any transaction either that an employee within the scope of his employment willfully failed to file a required report or that the bank was flagrantly indifferent to its obligations, then you may find that the bank has willfully failed to file the required reports.

The Bank contends that the trial court's instructions regarding knowledge were defective because they eliminated the requirement that it be proven that the Bank violated a known legal duty. It avers that the knowledge instruction invited the jury to convict the Bank for negligently maintaining a poor communications network that prevented the consolidation of the information held by its various employees. The Bank argues that it is error to find that a corporation possesses a particular item of knowledge if one part of the corporation has half the information making up the item, and another part of the entity has the other half.

A collective knowledge instruction is entirely appropriate in the context of corporate criminal liability. The acts of a corporation are, after all, simply the acts of all of its employees operating within the scope of their employment. The law on corporate criminal liability reflects this. Similarly, the knowledge obtained by corporate employees acting within the scope of their employment is imputed to the corporation. Corporations compartmentalize knowledge, subdividing the elements of specific duties and operations into smaller components. The aggregate of those components constitutes the corporation's knowledge of a particular operation. It is irrelevant whether employees administering one component of an operation know the specific activities of employees administering another aspect of the operation:

> [A] corporation cannot plead innocence by asserting that the information obtained by several employees was not acquired by any one individual who then would have comprehended its full import. Rather the corporation is considered to have acquired the collective knowledge of its employees and is held responsible for their failure to act accordingly.

United States v. T.I.M.E.-D.C., Inc., 381 F. Supp. 730, 734 (1974). Since the Bank had the compartmentalized structure common to all large corporations, the court's collective knowledge instruction was not only proper but necessary.

Nor do we find any defects in the trial court's instructions on specific intent. The court told the jury that the concept of willfulness entails a voluntary, intentional, and bad purpose to disobey the law. Her instructions on this element, when viewed as a whole, directed the jury not to convict for accidental, mistaken or inadvertent acts or omissions. It is urged that the court erroneously charged that willfulness could be found via flagrant indifference by the Bank toward its reporting obligations. With respect to federal regulatory statutes, the Supreme Court has endorsed defining willfulness, in both civil and criminal contexts, as "a disregard for the governing statute and an indifference to its requirements." Trans World Airlines, Inc. v. Thurston, 469 U.S. 111 (1985). Accordingly, we find no error in the court's instruction on willfulness.

B. Evidence of Willfulness

The Bank asserts that the evidence did not suffice to show that it had willfully failed to comply with the Act's reporting requirements. We review the evidence in the light most favorable to the government.

As already discussed, the language of the Treasury regulations itself gave notice that cash withdrawals over $10,000 were reportable, regardless of the number of checks used. Primary responsibility for CTR compliance in the Bank's branch offices was assigned to head tellers and branch managers. Head tellers Orlandella and Murphy, who knew of the nature of McDonough's transactions, also knew of the CTR filing obligations imposed by the Bank. The jury heard testimony from former bank teller Simona Wong, who stated that she knew McDonough's transactions were reportable, and that the source of her knowledge was head teller Murphy.

Even if some Bank personnel mistakenly regarded McDonough as engaging in multiple transactions, there was convincing evidence that the Bank knew that his withdrawals were reportable. An internal memo sent in May 1983 by project coordinator Jayne Brady to all branch managers and head tellers stated that "'[r]eportable transactions are expanded to include multiple transactions which aggregate more than $10,000 in any *one day*.' This includes deposits or withdrawals by a customer to or from more than one account." (Emphasis in original.) The Prudential Branch Manual instructed that if Bank personnel know that a customer has engaged in multiple transactions totaling $10,000 or more, then such transactions should be regarded as a single transaction. In addition, since 1980, the instructions on the back of CTR forms have directed that reports be filed on multiple transactions which aggregate to over $10,000. Finally, a Bank auditor discussed with Orlandella and Murphy, the Bank's obligation to report a customer's multiple transactions in a single day which amount to more than $10,000. We do not suggest that these evidentiary items in themselves legally bound the Bank to report McDonough's transactions; it is the language of the regulations that impose such a duty. This evidence, however, proved that the Bank had ample knowledge that transactions like McDonough's came within the purview of the Act.

Regarding the Bank's specific intent to violate the reporting obligation, Simona Wong testified that head teller Patricia Murphy knew that McDonough's transactions were reportable, but, on one occasion, deliberately chose not to file a CTR on him because he was "a good customer." In addition, the jury heard testimony that bank employees regarded McDonough's transactions as unusual, speculated that he was a bookie, and suspected that he was structuring his transactions to avoid the Act's reporting requirements. An internal Bank memo, written after an investigation of the McDonough transactions, concluded that a "person managing the branch would have to have known that something strange was going on." Given the suspicions aroused by McDonough's banking practices and the abundance of information indicating that his transactions were reportable, the jury could have concluded that the failure by Bank personnel to, at least, inquire about the reportability of McDonough's transactions constituted flagrant indifference to the obligations imposed by the Act.

We hold that the evidence was sufficient for a finding of willfulness. . . .

Affirmed.

NOTES AND QUESTIONS

1. Enforcement of CTR requirements fall within the jurisdiction of the Department of the Treasury, which also enforces the Internal Revenue Code. Consequently, for criminal purposes, the mens rea term "willfulness" has been given the same definition in both contexts. From your reading of *Bank of New England*, what is this definition? Note that it is not the same definition as that assigned to the identical term when it is used in connection with securities fraud, *infra* Chapter 6.

2. Willfulness in the CTR and tax realm has a strong "mistake of law" defense built into it. The prosecution must overcome a defendant's claim that he "did not [act with] a specific intent to disregard [or] disobey the law, with a bad purpose to violate the law." Typically, ignorance or mistake of law is not a defense to a criminal act. Why is that not true in this arena? What is the mistake of law defense designed to do?
3. Why did the prosecution ask for, and the trial court give, instructions on the collective knowledge and flagrant organizational indifference doctrines in the first place? Didn't these instructions merely serve to complicate the case unnecessarily? Why wasn't the bank vicariously liable for the acts of the head tellers, who clearly knew what the CTR requirements were and who also knew that, on some occasions, the requirements were not being enforced with respect to McDonough?
4. What does it mean to "know something within the scope of one's employment"? If someone in the company knows something, why isn't that alone sufficient to impute the knowledge to the company itself, regardless of whether the knowledge is within the scope of the individual's employment?
5. Does *Bank of New England* go too far in the application of corporate criminal liability? Does the resultant doctrine amount to holding an organization criminally liable for mere recklessness or negligence, as the Bank suggested?

Problem 2-3

Abigail is the CEO of State Bank. She is on a three-week vacation on Tahiti with her husband, Bob, and her four small children. While on the beach, she reads in the international edition of the *Wall Street Journal* that the Department of Treasury has just issued guidelines regarding when multiple transactions on the same day by the same bank customer will require the filing of a CTR. She makes a mental note to discuss this issue with her CFO when she returns from vacation, but forgets about it and never does. It turns out that State Bank fails to comply with the new interpretation and is prosecuted, in part on the theory that, as soon as Abigail read the piece in the *WSJ*, she "knew" the new CTR requirements on behalf of the bank. The bank moves to dismiss the indictment on the grounds that Abigail never knew this fact "within the scope of her employment." Who's right?

II. PERSONAL LIABILITY IN THE COLLECTIVE ENTITY SETTING

Having completed our examination of corporate liability for the acts of its agents, we now turn to the flip side of the equation, that is, to the study of the extent to which corporate agents are liable for crimes committed in the context of the workplace. You may be surprised to learn that the fundamental principle you learned in your basic Criminal Law course—that an individual is not guilty of a crime unless he possesses the requisite mens rea at the same time he engages in the prohibited actus reus—is at least stretched, if not occasionally abandoned, in the collective entity setting.

A. Basic Principle

UNITED STATES v. WISE

370 U.S. 405 (1962)

Mr. Chief Justice WARREN delivered the opinion of the Court.

A grand jury returned an indictment charging the National Dairy Products Corporation with engaging "in a combination and conspiracy to eliminate price competition in the sale of milk in the Greater Kansas City market in unreasonable restraint of trade and commerce, in violation of Section 1" of the Sherman Act, 15 U.S.C. §1. Two counts incorporated by reference the alleged illegal acts of the corporation and named the appellee as codefendant. In a bill of particulars the Government charged that the appellee had "been acting solely in his capacity as an officer, director, or agent who authorized, ordered, or did some of the acts" constituting the violation. The appellee moved for a dismissal on the ground that the indictment, as particularized by the bill, failed to charge a crime. According to appellee, the Sherman Act does not apply to corporate officers acting in a representative capacity; he contends that the statute exclusively applicable to these officers is §14 of the Clayton Act, 15 U.S.C. §24. Over the Government's opposition the dismissal was ordered by the district judge. An appeal was perfected pursuant to 18 U.S.C. §3731 and we noted probable jurisdiction.

Although the Sherman Act has been in existence for over 70 years and although corporate officers have been indicted under that Act for almost as long this question is one of first impression for this Court. The impetus for raising this issue at such a late date comes from the fact that in 1955 the Congress raised the penalty provision in the Sherman Act from \$5,000 to \$50,000 without making a corresponding increase in the \$5,000 penalty found in the Clayton Act.

Section 1 of the Sherman Act imposes criminal sanctions upon "every person" who violates that provision, 15 U.S.C. §1. The Government contends that a corporate officer is obviously a "person" within the Act. The appellee, however, distinguishes between a corporate officer who represents his corporation and one who acts on his own account. In the latter case the appellee agrees that the Sherman Act applies. But, when the officer is acting solely for his corporation, the appellee contends that he is no longer a "person" within the Act. The rationale for this distinction is that the activities of an officer, however illegal and culpable, are chargeable to the corporation as the principal but not to the individual who perpetrates them.

No substantial support for such an artificial interpretation of a seemingly clear statute is provided by the legislative history. The most that can be said for the appellee's position is that the Reagan Bill, an unsuccessful competitor of the Sherman Bill, specifically included corporate officers in its penal section while the Sherman Bill had no penal section at one time. The penal provision of the Reagan Bill was offered as an amendment to the Sherman Bill, and the Senate Committee on the Judiciary then redrafted and resubmitted a bill in the form which became the Sherman Act. That Act outlawed certain acts by "persons," and there is nothing to indicate that the Congress intended to restrict the meaning as applied to corporate officers.

The appellee points to §8 of the Sherman Act which defines "person" "to include corporations and associations." He argues that, since corporations are included within the term, individual corporate officers are thereby excluded. This is a non sequitur. The mere fact that the term is given a broad construction does not alter its basic meaning, and no such inference can be drawn from the express inclusion of corporations as "persons." The reason for this inclusion is readily understandable. The doctrine of corporate criminal responsibility for the acts of the officers was not well established in 1890. *See New York Central*. . . . Therefore, we attribute no significance to the specific inclusion of corporations in the definition of "persons" in determining whether a corporate officer is within the term.

We have found no case between 1890 and 1914 in which a corporate officer successfully secured the dismissal of an indictment or the reversal of a conviction on the ground that he was not a "person" within the Sherman Act when he acted solely as a representative of the corporation. . . .

Based upon the foregoing, we hold that a corporate officer is subject to prosecution under §1 of the Sherman Act whenever he knowingly participates in effecting the illegal contract, combination, or conspiracy—be he one who authorizes, orders, or helps perpetrate the crime—regardless of whether he is acting in a representative capacity. It follows that the District Court erred when it dismissed the indictment against the appellee. The case is reversed and remanded for proceedings consistent with this opinion.

Reversed and remanded.

Mr. Justice FRANKFURTER took no part in the consideration or decision of this case.

[Opinion of Mr. Justice Harlan, concurring, is omitted.]

B. Aiding and Abetting

1. 18 U.S.C. §2(a)

UNITED STATES v. BROWN & TOBEY

925 F.2d 1182 (9th Cir. 1991)

FLETCHER, Circuit Judge:

Defendants Brown and Tobey appeal their jury convictions for conspiracy to suppress competition for billboard sites in violation of the Sherman Anti-Trust Act, 15 U.S.C. §1 (1988). We affirm.

Facts

Appellant Brown is senior vice president for public affairs in a division of Gannett Company, Inc. that includes fifteen separate billboard advertising companies. One of these companies is Gannett Outdoor Company, Inc. of Southern California, an original defendant in this case and the descendant of a company that Brown's father founded in the early 1930s. Brown himself started working part-time in the family company in 1954, and in late 1968 or early 1969 he became the company's president and chief operating officer. He left the billboard advertising business in 1973, but returned two years later to become president and chief executive officer of the company. In 1984 he was promoted from these positions to his current, national management position. Gannett Outdoor Company, Inc. of Southern California and its predecessors will be referred to collectively as "Gannett."

Appellant Tobey is a senior executive in Foster & Kleiser Corp. ("F & K"), a subsidiary of Metromedia, Inc. and the other original defendant in this case. F & K has been a dominant force in the billboard advertising business since the 1920s, when it controlled a monopolistic share of billboard sites in California and three other western states. Tobey joined F & K as a lease representative in 1963, and worked his way into management. In 1971 he became vice-president and executive vice-president in charge of public relations, and in 1984 he assumed control of F & K's leasing department.

Gannett and F & K are the two largest billboard advertising companies in California and have been dominant for some time. In 1964 they entered into a written agreement, a portion of which provided that the companies would refrain from bidding on each other's former leaseholds for a period of one year after the space was lost or abandoned by the lessee-company. To implement this "one-year rule," the agreement established a notification procedure whereby each company would send written notice to the other when it either leased a new billboard site or removed a billboard from an existing site. Although this explicit written agreement was terminated sometime in 1969 and the notification procedures abandoned, the one-year rule was honored by both companies for fifteen more years.

On December 12, 1988, the government filed a one-count felony information against both companies and against appellants Brown and Tobey, charging them with conspiring to restrain trade in violation of the Sherman Anti-Trust Act, 15 U.S.C. §1 (1988). The information alleged that the defendants participated in an ongoing conspiracy to suppress competition for billboard sites from 1964 until 1984. Gannett and Metromedia, F & K's corporate parent, entered pleas of nolo contendere, and F & K was dismissed in conjunction with Metromedia's plea, but the case against Brown and Tobey went to trial.

Much testimony was presented at trial regarding the agreement and appellants' participation in it. Joseph Cubiero, a subordinate of Brown's, testified that the agreement was in effect from 1975 until sometime in 1984. He also testified that Brown confronted him at least a half dozen times about "violations" of the no-compete aspects of the agreement and informed him that such transgressions would make Brown's life miserable in negotiating with F & K on other issues. Cubiero also testified that when he approached Brown in 1984 regarding investigation of the companies, Brown simply stated that he had terminated the agreement.

Witnesses gave similar testimony about Tobey's involvement. Cubiero testified that Tobey complained about violations of the agreement to appellant Brown. Bart Browne, a subordinate of Tobey's at F & K, testified that he informed Tobey of violations of the agreement and urged him to contact Gannett to resolve the problem. He also testified that Tobey contacted Cubiero at Gannett and, after conversing with him, decided that "all deals are off." Tobey then asked Browne to inform other F & K employees. Finally, Drake Kennedy, the president of a competing billboard company, testified that Tobey stated that if Cubiero would not honor the agreement, he would not do so either.

At the conclusion of the trial, the jury convicted both Brown and Tobey. They now appeal.

Discussion

Brown and Tobey raise seven issues on appeal [including] . . . whether the jury instruction on appellants' liability for the illegal conduct of their subordinates was proper . . . and . . . whether the evidence was sufficient to support the appellants' convictions. . . .

The district court instructed the jury that appellants could be held criminally liable for the illegal actions of subordinates if they knowingly authorized or consented to such behavior.[14] Appellants timely objected to the instruction; they argue that it erroneously permitted the jury to convict them for merely knowing about the illegal conduct of others and failing to stop it, even if they were not wrongdoers themselves. . . .

[W]e reject appellants' premise that the instructions in this case allowed conviction based on mere knowledge of the wrongdoing of others. The charge asked the jury to determine whether the appellants knowingly consented to their subordinates' participation in the conspiracy. Further instructions defined "knowingly" as "voluntarily and intentionally", and defined "participating knowingly" as "encouraging, advising or assisting for the purpose of furthering the conspiracy." These instructions and definitions adequately reflect the standard established in *Wise*. . . .

The convictions of Brown and Tobey are AFFIRMED.

NOTES AND QUESTIONS

1. The jury instruction at issue stated that Brown and Tobey could be found criminally liable if they merely consented to the participation of their subordinates in the anticompetitive conspiracy. Although the court tries to dress up this instruction with one about "participating knowingly," most observers interpret its holding to be that consent is sufficient actus reus to cause a supervisor to become criminally liable for the acts of his

14. The relevant jury instructions read as follows:

> Defendants Hal Brown, Jr. and Michael F. Tobey were officials of Gannett and Foster & Kleiser with subordinate employees under their supervision during the time of their alleged involvement in the conspiracy charged in the Information. To find the defendant liable for the acts of the subordinate as distinguished from his own acts, you must find beyond a reasonable doubt that the defendant knew of the existence of the conspiracy and knowingly authorized[,] ordered or consented to the participation of a subordinate in that conspiracy. A company official who knowingly participates in the conspiracy in this manner is liable to the same extent as any other member of the conspiracy.

subordinates. Is mere consent to the criminal activity of others adequate actus reus in other contexts? Consider the case of three friends on their way to the local mall for innocent clothes shopping. The driver of the car tells the others that she is taking a small detour to "do a little drug deal" before they get to the mall. The friends are not happy about it, but they consent to the stop. They both wait in the car while their friend does her business. They never have anything to do with the drugs.

Are the passengers liable for drug dealing, or even a conspiracy to deal drugs, as a result of their consent? If not, why should a supervisor in a company be liable for merely consenting to the criminal activity of his subordinates? Is it because the supervisor, simply by means of his position, can't help but aid and abet the criminal activity he fails to stop?

2. From a factual standpoint, this is an easy case, isn't it? Brown and Tobey both personally participated in the criminal activity, making it effectively impossible for them to argue a successful innocent bystander defense. Could the court have decided the case on the alternative ground that, even assuming a flaw in the trial court's instruction on supervisor liability, it would have been harmless? Should it have?

UNITED STATES v. BROWN & MEADOWS

151 F.3d 476 (6th Cir. 1998)

RYAN, Circuit Judge. . . .

This case centers on the misuse of public housing funds by employees of the Detroit Housing Department, or DHD, in connection with the "Section 8 housing" program. . . .

Under the program, qualifying tenants pay a portion of their income to a private landlord, and in order to meet market-level rents, the [Public Housing Authority, here DHD] makes additional "assistance payments" to the landlord with the federal funds it receives from HUD. *See* 42 U.S.C. §§1437a(a), 1437f(b), (c), and (o).

To participate in the Section 8 program, would-be recipients must apply to the local PHA, which determines eligibility based on a number of financial and family-status factors. The PHA also evaluates applicants with respect to three federal preferences, given to (1) families who occupy substandard housing; (2) families who are involuntarily displaced; and (3) families who are paying more than 50% of their income for rent. *See* 24 C.F.R. §§882.219, 887.157.

If an applicant is selected to participate in the Section 8 program, the local PHA issues the family a "certificate" or a "voucher," either of which entitles them to benefits. . . . Once a PHA issues a certificate or a voucher, the recipient may use it to pay the rent for any apartment he or she chooses so long as the landlord participates in the Section 8 program. The recipient gives the certificate or voucher to the landlord, who in turn presents it to the PHA, which in turn pays the balance of the rent; HUD then reimburses the PHA. . . .

At issue in this case is the intermediate step between an application and the issuance of Section 8 subsidies: that is, the selection of a particular applicant for receipt of a certificate or voucher. The government takes the position that the applicable regulations require the DHD to place those applicants who qualify on a waiting list, and to select applicants in a particular order. The theory of its prosecution is that Brown and Meadows ignored this regulatory requirement, instead giving benefits to people based on improper and impermissible considerations. The government further asserts that in signing and issuing the certificates or vouchers, the defendants represented that the PHA had determined a recipient's "eligibility," and that the definition of "eligible" necessarily includes a representation that the recipient came off of a waiting list. Since the recipients in question did *not* come off of a waiting list—which fact is not contested by the defendants—the government contends that the defendants, in representing the applicants' eligibility, made a false statement in violation of 18 U.S.C. §1001.

B. Actions of Brown and Meadows

The defendants, Brown and Meadows, were both employees of the DHD; they were also, to use Meadows's phrasing, "personal friends." Meadows was a "housing eligibility investigator," and her job responsibilities were to "process individuals for the Section 8 program, verifying income, verifying identity, birth certificates, that type of thing," as well as to arrange for housing inspections and to draft leases. Meadows's personnel file contained a certificate dated October 1991 showing that she had satisfied the training requirements for her position; no evidence was presented, however, as to what the precise training requirements were.

Brown, on the other hand, was appointed by Mayor Coleman Young in October 1992 to be superintendent of housing operations and maintenance. As superintendent, Brown was responsible for the management and maintenance of all of Detroit's public housing properties. In March 1993, Brown received a new assignment, and assumed the duties of administering the Section 8 program.

It is undisputed that the DHD was in a state of chaos and mismanagement long before the events at issue here. In June 1991, HUD began investigating the Section 8 program in Detroit, and in January 1993, HUD decided to provide assistance to the DHD in order to allow Detroit to continue administering the program. The alternative was for HUD to take the program over itself. There was testimony at trial that HUD directed its attention to the DHD's outdated and improper waiting-list format. . . .

As . . . part of the effort to remedy the problems with the waiting list, the DHD's employees, including Brown, were shown various training videotapes and provided with pamphlets and booklets. There is no evidence, however, that Meadows ever saw videos or received pamphlets; further, the witness who testified about this training never actually testified that the training materials discussed the use of a waiting list. It is clear, however, that Brown requested and received a manual of relevant regulations, some of which . . . refer to the use of waiting lists. Further, although there was no evidence about the specific content of the discussions, there *was* evidence that Brown discussed waiting lists with a HUD representative about six times. Finally, it is undisputed that there was a sign on the exterior door to the DHD office informing that the "Section 8 Housing waiting list is closed," and that no further applications were being accepted. . . .

Between January 1993 and June 1994, the DHD was under orders from HUD to freeze rental activity and not issue any certificates or vouchers. These orders were disregarded by Brown, who continued both to add names to the waiting list and to issue certificates and vouchers. It is clear that Brown was the only employee with authority to issue certificates and vouchers; Meadows had no such authority.

. . . It is readily apparent [from the record]—and there is no dispute on this point—that a number of certificates and vouchers were improperly issued to people who would not have been selected from the waiting list in the absence of impermissible considerations. Some certificates and vouchers were issued as favors to political cronies; some were issued to friends and family members of Meadows; some were issued to people legitimately on the waiting list but not actually entitled to receive certificates or vouchers, as an attempt by Brown to dispel suspicion. And it is undisputed that some were issued as a result of bribes. In early 1994, Brown was introduced to Maxine Floyd, who paid a series of bribes to Brown in order to obtain his assistance in finding Section 8 housing for senior citizens on whose behalf Floyd was acting; in return, Brown instructed that certificates or vouchers be issued.

Four of the housing vouchers for which Brown and Meadows were indicted were issued to friends and family members of defendant Meadows. One voucher was issued in September 1993 to Joya Craighead, who had been a friend of Meadows for 16 years. Craighead testified that she spoke with Meadows about her need for housing, but Meadows "didn't tell [her] anything in regards to what [she] should do." Craighead later went to the DHD, spoke with Brown, and about three weeks later, was "processed into the program," receiving a voucher signed by Brown. Craighead testified that Meadows did not work on her application. Craighead also testified that she asked Brown for help in finding housing for her niece, Tamika Craighead; Joya and Tamika met at Brown's house, along with Meadows, and Brown told her he "would look into it"; there is no evidence that Meadows, although present, took part in the conversation. Joya Craighead also testified that while she was "sure" she talked to Meadows regarding Tamika's entry into the Section 8 program, Meadows simply told her that Joya would have to speak directly with Brown. Tamika received a voucher in April 1994, which voucher was signed by Brown.

Finally, Meadows's mother, Deloris Meadows, received a voucher in September 1993, and her sister, Yvette Johnson, received a voucher in December 1993. Defendant Meadows brought her mother the necessary papers to sign and then handled the application process; with respect to her sister, Meadows instructed her to meet with Brown, and someone else filled out the paperwork. Both vouchers were signed by Brown. . . .

Meadows [argues] that she lacked the necessary *mens rea*. She contends that she was inadequately trained, and ignorant of the existence or function of the Section 8 waiting list; the DHD was completely chaotic and disorganized, and no employee, including Meadows, knew what was expected. This is a traditional sufficiency-of-the-evidence challenge, and its proponent necessarily carries a heavy burden. . . .

[A] defendant can be guilty of violating 18 U.S.C. §1001 as a principal even if the evidence does not show that she herself actually made false statements, so long as the evidence shows that she aided, abetted, counseled, induced, or procured the commission of the fraud, or, alternatively, caused the false statements to be made. . . .

In United States v. Martin, 920 F.2d 345, 348 (6th Cir. 1990), this court affirmed a conviction under 18 U.S.C. §2, explaining that "[t]o be found guilty of the crime of aiding and abetting a criminal venture, a defendant must associate himself with the venture in a manner whereby he participates in it as something that he wishes to bring about and seeks by his acts to make succeed." And in United States v. Horton, 847 F.2d 313, 322 (6th Cir. 1988), the court indicated that in order to be guilty under 18 U.S.C. §2, a defendant must "willfully participate in the commission of a crime. . . . Participation is willful if done voluntarily and intentionally and with the specific intent to do something which the law forbids or with the specific intent to fail to do something which the law requires to be done, that is to say, with bad purpose either to disobey or disregard the law." It is clear that to be guilty under 18 U.S.C. §2, there must be evidence "'that the defendant shared in the criminal intent of the principal.'" Thus, "to convict a person accused of making a false statement, the government must prove not only that the statement was false, but that the accused knew it to be false. . . ."

Bearing these principles in mind, we conclude that Meadows's convictions on Counts 47 through 50 should be reversed for two reasons: first, she lacked the necessary specific intent, and second, in all but one instance, she failed to engage in the type of affirmative conduct necessary to aid or abet the commission of the §1001 violation.

We note that the government's brief largely fails to respond to Meadows's argument that she lacked the necessary *mens rea*. But we have reviewed every single page of the transcript that the government says supports the proposition that Meadows was aware of the existence of a waiting list and the requirement that people be selected from that list, and conclude that while there is evidence of the former—because there was a sign on the door of the DHD stating that the waiting list was closed—there is no evidence whatsoever that she had any understanding of the waiting list's function or purpose or proper use. Her listed job duties did not refer to the waiting list, and there was no evidence that she was trained with respect to the waiting list. The director prior to Brown, under whom Meadows had worked, had treated the waiting list in a casual fashion, at one point making an offer at a staff meeting to allow every staff member to put one favorite client on the list. Finally, this is not the type of *mala in se* offense that would lead a reasonable person to infer that Meadows *must* have known she was breaking the law; the friends and relatives that received benefits were all income-eligible, and in that sense, qualified to receive the benefits.

An alternative reason for reversing three of Meadows's four §1001 counts is that there is no evidence she played any sort of active role in the predicate offenses, necessary to support an aiding-and-abetting conviction. Except in the case of her mother, to whom Meadows brought the necessary paperwork, there was no evidence that Meadows helped in the preparation of the documentation or submission of it to HUD. At most, there is evidence that Meadows may have known about the applications, but that is not equivalent to knowledge even that the representation of eligibility was being made. Her participation, in every instance except that of her mother, was not the kind of participation that can give rise to liability for aiding and abetting the *filing* of the documents because there simply was no evidence that she did any act to bring the §1001 offenses about, or make them succeed. . . .

We will therefore reverse in full the judgment of conviction with respect to Meadows. . . .

[Opinion of Gilman, J., concurring in part and dissenting in part, omitted.]

NOTES AND QUESTIONS

1. Excuse me? Aiding and abetting liability under 18 U.S.C. §2(a) requires proof that the defendant "in some sort associate[d] himself with the venture, that he participate[d] in it as in something that he wishe[d] to bring about, that he [sought] by his action to make it succeed." Nye & Nissen v. United States, 336 U.S. 613, 619 (1949) (quoting United States v. Peoni, 100 F.2d 401, 402 (2d Cir. 1938) (internal quotation marks omitted)). In this case, four of the individuals who "jumped the line" were family and friends of Meadows. Isn't the court wrong in failing to defer to the jury's apparent conclusion that this was not a coincidence, but evidence that Meadows had, at minimum, *encouraged* her "boyfriend" to provide favorable treatment to people about whom she cared? That would surely be sufficient actus reus, wouldn't it? Moreover, wasn't the jury entitled to conclude that, unless Meadows was severely mentally challenged, she had to know that the wait list existed for *some* reason and that folks who had not followed the rules regarding getting onto the wait list were not eligible for Section 8 vouchers?
2. Note the court's inconsistency in the paragraph describing the mens rea required for the commission of an offense through the operation of 18 U.S.C. §2(a). (The paragraph starts out by citing to the *Martin* case.) In the beginning, the court appears to be describing a "purpose" mens rea as that term is defined by the MPC ("he wishes to bring about" the illegal outcome). Then, the court cites to cases requiring willfulness, which it interprets as supplying the defendant with a mistake of law defense. Finally, it states that, when applying aiding and abetting to the crime of false statements, the government must prove not only that the statement was false, but that the accused knew it to be false. This is a simple knowledge requirement, which is the mens rea of the underlying offense. Which of these is the correct standard?
3. Why was the court so sympathetic to Meadows?

2. 18 U.S.C. §2(b)

UNITED STATES v. WALSER

3 F.3d 380 (11th Cir. 1993)

DUBINA, Circuit Judge:

This appeal presents a novel question: can one who intentionally causes an innocent party to commit perjury unwittingly be held liable as a principal under 18 U.S.C. §2? This question arises from Virginia Nell Walser's ("Walser") appeal from her convictions for perjury and aiding and abetting, in violation of 18 U.S.C. §§1623 and 2(b), and making false and fraudulent statements to a government agency or department, in violation of 18 U.S.C. §1001. For the reasons that follow, we affirm.

I. Facts

Walser and her husband farmed in Marion, Alabama. In 1989 a federal grand jury indicted them for defrauding the Federal Crop Insurance Corporation ("FCIC") and the Southern Crop Insurance Corporation ("SCIC") by submitting fraudulent crop insurance claims.[1] The government had alleged that the Walsers failed to report all the soybeans they produced on acreage insured by the SCIC. Specifically, the government claimed that Walser and her husband surreptitiously grew approximately 4,980 bushels of insured soybeans and sold them under another name. Thus, the government contended, the Walsers were overpaid on their subsequent crop loss claims because they grew and sold more soybeans than were reported to the SCIC.

At trial, the Walsers defended by claiming that those 4,980 bushels of soybeans were an uninsured crop derived from another farm. They contended that Walser notified the SCIC of these uninsured beans through a document known as an SCI-013 form, entitled Statement of Facts ("SCI-013"). The SCI-013 is a standard form used for all correspondence with the SCIC.

Walser called Richmond Morrow ("Morrow"), an FCIC claims specialist, as a defense witness. Pursuant to a subpoena, Morrow brought certain documents from his file to the trial. Two were admitted into evidence. The first was a letter dated July 14, 1986, from Walser to Morrow at the FCIC. It stated as follows:

> Dear Mr. Morrow,
>
> I am sending you a copy of the SCI-013 Statement of Facts that I have attached to my 1986 acreage report. My crop insurance is with reinsurance, but due to the confussion [sic] in 1985 soybean production I wanted a copy of this statement, that was attached to my acreage report, on record with you in your office.
>
> Sincerely,
>
> /s/Virginia N. Walser

1. The FCIC is an agency of the United States Department of Agriculture that provides crop insurance to farmers. Farmers pay premiums and, if a loss is suffered, collect from the premium pool. The SCIC is a private company that sells and services crop insurance for the FCIC.

The second document was the SCI-013 form referred to in Walser's letter. Entitled "Southern Crop Insurance Agency, Incorporated, Statement of Facts" and also dated July 14, 1986, it stated as follows:

> I have broadcast approximately 300 acres of soybeans on the Bob Rees place, ASCS farm number 024. These soybeans will not be covered by crop insurance. So there will not be a confussion [sic] or mix up between the production of soybeans covered by crop insurance and the production on farm 024, I am attaching a copy of this statement to my acreage report.

The SCI-013 form sent to Morrow thus purported to show that the 4,980 bushels of soybeans at issue were not insured beans harvested from Walser's farm, but were uninsured beans planted on a farm owned by a man named Bob Rees.

A jury acquitted Walser and her husband of all charges.

After the trial, special agent William Doles ("Agent Doles") of the Office of the Inspector General ("OIG"), United States Department of Agriculture ("USDA"), examined the SCI-013 form. He noticed that the name of the printer, AAA Printing & Graphics ("AAA"), appeared at the bottom of the form. Agent Doles contacted AAA and learned that AAA did not print and deliver the SCI-013 form to the SCIC until July 22, 1986, one week *after* the July 14, 1986 date used by Walser on the form sent to Morrow. It thus appeared that Walser prepared and back-dated a false document.

A second federal grand jury returned a three-count indictment against Walser based on this and other evidence of alleged false statements. Count I charged Walser with perjury and aiding and abetting by knowingly and willfully causing Morrow to present false evidence under oath, in violation of 18 U.S.C. §§1623 and 2(b). . . .

A jury found Walser guilty on all counts. The district court sentenced her to concurrent terms of twenty-seven months imprisonment, followed by a three-year term of supervised release. This appeal followed. . . .

At the 1992 trial Agent Doles testified that he examined all official FCIC and SCIC files pertaining to Walser before her first trial and found no mention of the uninsured soybeans purportedly planted on Bob Rees' farm. He further examined Walser's 1986 soybean acreage reports and, contrary to Walser's statement in her letter to Morrow, found no copy of the SCI-013 attached to them. Those acreage reports were dated July 14, 1986, the same date used by Walser when she created the SCI-013 form and the accompanying letter. Each acreage report was marked on the reverse side: "Received July 28, 1986." The SCI-013 form retrieved from Morrow's files had no date stamp. Agent Doles testified that he did not examine Morrow's files because Morrow, as an FCIC official, was not authorized to maintain official SCIC files. In sum, Agent Doles testified that neither Walser's 1986 acreage reports nor any other document in the FCIC or SCIC official files indicated that Walser informed the SCIC of uninsured soybeans.

Morrow testified that Walser sent him the SCI-013 and the accompanying letter, although he could not recall when he received them. He noted that it was unusual for him to have SCIC documents because he worked for the federal government and the SCIC was a private organization. He kept the documents, however, because he routinely filed all correspondence. He further testified that after Walser subpoenaed the documents in his file she called Morrow to ensure he possessed the subpoenaed documents. Morrow told her that he did. Walser then explained that Morrow need not give the OIG a copy of the SCI-013 because it had one already. Morrow testified that he felt tricked by Walser because he now knew the SCI-013 Walser sent him to be false and back-dated.

Robert Hagan ("Hagan"), the owner of AAA, testified that the SCIC ordered 5,000 SCI-013 Statement of Fact forms on July 10, 1986. Prior to this order, another printing company printed the forms. The old forms did not identify the printer. AAA delivered the first 500 forms on July 22 and the remainder on July 28. No AAA forms were printed or delivered prior to July 14, 1986. . . .

II. Analysis

The government does not contend that Walser knowingly used false information under oath. Rather, it argues that Walser aided and abetted the commission of perjury, and thus, via operation of 18 U.S.C. §2(b), is liable as a principal. Walser argues that her conviction under 18 U.S.C. §1623 cannot be based upon application of the aiding and abetting provision of §2(b) because she was never placed under oath in regard to the offenses alleged in Count I of the indictment. Thus, she claims, she had no legal capacity to commit the crime of perjury. Alternatively, she argues that the district court erred by denying her motions for a judgment of acquittal under Count I. . . .

[A]n individual is criminally culpable for causing an intermediary to commit a criminal act even though the intermediary has no criminal intent and is innocent of the substantive crime. In United States v. Tobon-Builes, 706 F.2d 1092 (11th Cir. 1983), the defendant, Oscar de J. Tobon-Builes ("Tobon-Builes"), knowingly caused several banks not to file Currency Transaction Reports for transactions exceeding $10,000 as required by law. Tobon-Builes was indicted for the substantive offense of willfully concealing and causing to be concealed, by trick, scheme, or device, material facts within the jurisdiction of the Department of Treasury of the United States in violation of 18 U.S.C. §1001. He was also charged with aiding and abetting in violation of §2. A jury convicted him. On appeal, Tobon-Builes argued that his conviction was improper because, unlike a bank, he had no legal duty to report currency transactions above $10,000. Thus, he argued, his legal incapacity to commit the crime of concealment—based on his lack of a duty to report currency transactions exceeding $10,000—freed him from culpability.

We affirmed his conviction, noting that courts have interpreted §2(b) to find that a person

> who is incapable of committing a substantive criminal offense if he acted alone may nevertheless be liable as a principal where he willfully causes the prohibited conduct . . . to be committed by intermediaries . . . who have the capacity to commit the substantive criminal offense but who lack the criminal intent to be guilty of that offense.

Id. at 1100. . . .

As noted by the Sixth Circuit and cited by the *Tobon-Builes* court:

> It is but to quote the hornbook to say that in every crime there must exist a union or joint operation of act, or failure to act, and intent. However, this is far from

> suggesting that the essential element of criminal intent must always reside in the person who does the forbidden act. Indeed, the latter may act without any criminal intent whatever, while the mens rea—"willfulness"—may reside in a person wholly incapable of committing the forbidden act. When such is the case, as at bar, the "joint operation of act and intent" prerequisite to commission of the crime is provided by the person who willfully causes the innocent actor to commit the illegal act. And in such a case, of course, only the person who willfully causes the forbidden act to be done is guilty of the crime.

Id. at 1101 (quoting United States v. Lester, 363 F.2d 68 (6th Cir. 1966), *cert. denied*, 385 U.S. 1002 (1967)).

Walser knew the document she sent to Morrow was false and back-dated. Indeed, the SCI-013 form she used had not even been printed or delivered by the date she purportedly wrote it. By falsifying and back-dating the SCI-013, then introducing it at trial through the innocent testimony of Morrow, Walser knowingly caused a fraudulent document to be entered into evidence during a court proceeding. Morrow lacked the criminal intent to commit perjury. As a witness under oath, he merely had the capacity to commit perjury. Section 2, however, operates to unite Morrow's capacity to commit perjury with Walser's intent that perjury be committed. Walser, as the crime's instigator and malefactor, adopted Morrow's capacity to commit perjury, including his status as a witness under oath. She is thus liable as a principal. . . . For the foregoing reasons, we affirm Walser's perjury conviction. . . .

NOTES AND QUESTIONS

1. What is the difference between the operation of 18 U.S.C. §§2(a) and 2(b)?
2. Though just a "simple" farmer, Walzer turned out to be quite the criminal mastermind. For example, she sent the false letter and SCI-013 form to Morrow at the FCIC, but not to the SCIC. Why? Did her scheme work as planned? But for the "unfortunate" fact that the paper she used for her backdated documents had been printed after the fact, might she have gotten away with her crime?
3. When 18 U.S.C. §2 says that an aider and abettor is punishable as a principal, it simply means that, for purposes of liability, federal criminal law does not distinguish between the two. This is not to say, however, that the two are treated the same when it comes to punishment. Following a long tradition in the common law, the federal sentencing guidelines take a defendant's "role in the offense" into account in calculating the defendant's sentence. Note, as well, that the term "aider and abettor" does not correlate with the defendant's relative culpability level. Sometimes the aider and abettor is merely a helper of the principal and thus less culpable; but sometimes he is the driving force for the crime, as when an individual hires someone else to commit murder on his behalf. In such cases, he is more culpable than the principal.
4. Aiding and abetting is not itself a crime; rather, it is simply a method of committing some other criminal offense. As such, aiding and abetting

need not be mentioned in an indictment for the prosecutor to rely on the theory when arguing her case against the defendant. If it is mentioned in the indictment, it is typically referenced by a simple statement at the end of a charge that defendant's conduct was "in violation of 18 U.S.C. §[substantive count] and 18 U.S.C. §2." In light of the aforementioned doctrine, why do you think prosecutors bother to list §2 at all?

C. Responsible Corporate Officer Doctrine

UNITED STATES v. DOTTERWEICH
320 U.S. 277 (1943)

Mr. Justice FRANKFURTER delivered the opinion of the Court.

This was a prosecution begun by two informations, consolidated for trial, charging Buffalo Pharmacal Company, Inc., and Dotterweich, its president and general manager, with violations of . . . the Federal Food, Drug, and Cosmetic Act. The Company, a jobber in drugs, purchased them from their manufacturers and shipped them, repacked under its own label, in interstate commerce. . . . The informations were based on §301 of that Act, 21 U.S.C. §331 . . . which prohibits "The introduction or delivery for introduction into interstate commerce of any drug that is adulterated or misbranded." "Any person" violating this provision is . . . made "guilty of a misdemeanor." Three counts went to the jury—two, for shipping misbranded drugs in interstate commerce, and a third, for so shipping an adulterated drug. The jury disagreed as to the corporation and found Dotterweich guilty on all three counts. . . .

The Food and Drugs Act of 1906 was an exertion by Congress of its power to keep impure and adulterated food and drugs out of the channels of commerce. By the Act of 1938, Congress extended the range of its control over illicit and noxious articles and stiffened the penalties for disobedience. The purposes of this legislation thus touch phases of the lives and health of people which, in the circumstances of modern industrialism, are largely beyond self-protection. Regard for these purposes should infuse construction of the legislation if it is to be treated as a working instrument of government and not merely as a collection of English words. The prosecution to which Dotterweich was subjected is based on a now familiar type of legislation whereby penalties serve as effective means of regulation. Such legislation dispenses with the conventional requirement for criminal conduct—awareness of some wrongdoing. In the interest of the larger good it puts the burden of acting at hazard upon a person otherwise innocent but standing in responsible relation to a public danger. And so it is clear that shipments like those now in issue are "punished by the statute if the article is misbranded (or adulterated), and that the article may be misbranded (or adulterated) without any conscious fraud at all. It was natural enough to throw this risk on shippers with regard to the identity of their wares."

Whether an accused shares responsibility in the business process resulting in unlawful distribution depends on the evidence produced at the trial and its submission—assuming the evidence warrants it—to the jury under appropriate guidance. The offense is committed . . . by all who do have such a responsible share in the furtherance of the transaction which the statute outlaws, namely, to put into the stream of interstate commerce adulterated or misbranded drugs. Hardship there doubtless may be under a statute which thus penalizes the transaction though consciousness of wrongdoing be totally wanting. Balancing relative hardships, Congress has preferred to place it upon those who have at least the opportunity of informing themselves of the existence of conditions imposed for the protection of consumers before sharing in illicit commerce, rather than to throw the hazard on the innocent public who are wholly helpless.

It would be too treacherous to define or even to indicate by way of illustration the class of employees which stands in such a responsible relation. To attempt a formula embracing the variety of conduct whereby persons may responsibly contribute in furthering a transaction forbidden by an Act of Congress, to wit, to send illicit goods across state lines, would be mischievous futility. In such matters the good sense of prosecutors, the wise guidance of trial judges, and the ultimate judgment of juries must be trusted. Our system of criminal justice necessarily depends on conscience and circumspection in prosecuting officers, even when the consequences are far more drastic than they are under the provision of law before us. For present purpose it suffices to say that in what the defense characterized as "a very fair charge" the District Court properly left the question of the responsibility of Dotterweich for the shipment to the jury, and there was sufficient evidence to support its verdict.

Judgment reversed.

Mr. Justice MURPHY, dissenting. . . .

It is a fundamental principle of Anglo-Saxon jurisprudence that guilt is personal and that it ought not lightly to be imputed to a citizen who, like the respondent, has no evil intention or consciousness of wrongdoing. It may be proper to charge him with responsibility to the corporation and the stockholders for negligence and mismanagement. But in the absence of clear statutory authorization it is inconsistent with established canons of criminal law to rest liability on an act in which the accused did not participate and of which he had no personal knowledge. Before we place the stigma of a criminal conviction upon any such citizen the legislative mandate must be clear and unambiguous. Accordingly that which Chief Justice Marshall has called "the tenderness of the law for the rights of individuals" entitles each person, regardless of economic or social status, to an unequivocal warning from the legislature as to whether he is within the class of persons subject to vicarious liability. Congress cannot be deemed to have intended to punish anyone who is not "plainly and unmistakably" within the confines of the statute.

Moreover, the fact that individual liability of corporate officers may be consistent with the policy and purpose of a public health and welfare measure does not authorize this Court to impose such liability where Congress has not clearly intended or actually done so. Congress alone has the power to define a crime and to specify the offenders. It is not our function to supply any deficiencies in these respects, no matter how grave the consequences. Statutory policy and purpose are not constitutional substitutes for the requirement that the legislature specify with reasonable certainty those individuals it desires to place under the interdict of the Act. . . .

UNITED STATES v. PARK
421 U.S. 658 (1975)

Mr. Chief Justice Burger delivered the opinion of the Court.

We granted certiorari to consider whether the jury instructions in the prosecution of a corporate officer under [21 U.S.C. §331(k) of the Federal Food, Drug, and Cosmetic Act] were appropriate under United States v. Dotterweich, 320 U.S. 277 (1943).

Acme Markets, Inc., is a national retail food chain with approximately 36,000 employees, 874 retail outlets, 12 general warehouses, and four special warehouses. Its headquarters, including the office of the president, respondent Park, who is chief executive officer of the corporation, are located in Philadelphia, Pa. In a five-count information filed in the United States District Court for the District of Maryland, the Government charged Acme and respondent with violations of the Federal Food, Drug and Cosmetic Act. Each count of the information alleged that the defendants had received food that had been shipped in interstate commerce and that, while the food was being held for sale in Acme's Baltimore warehouse following shipment in interstate commerce, they caused it to be held in a building accessible to rodents and to be exposed to contamination by rodents. These acts were alleged to have resulted in the food's being adulterated within the meaning of 21 U.S.C. §§342(a)(3) and (4), in violation of 21 U.S.C. §331(k).

Acme pleaded guilty to each count of the information. Respondent pleaded not guilty. The evidence at trial demonstrated that in April 1970 the Food and Drug Administration (FDA) advised respondent by letter of insanitary conditions in Acme's Philadelphia warehouse. In 1971 the FDA found that similar conditions existed in the firm's Baltimore warehouse. An FDA consumer safety officer testified concerning evidence of rodent infestation and other insanitary conditions discovered during a 12-day inspection of the Baltimore warehouse in November and December 1971. He also related that a second inspection of the warehouse had been conducted in March 1972. On that occasion the inspectors found that there had been improvement in the sanitary conditions, but that "there was still evidence of rodent activity in the building and in the warehouses and we found some rodent-contaminated lots of food items."

The Government also presented testimony by the Chief of Compliance of the FDA's Baltimore office, who informed respondent by letter of the conditions at the Baltimore warehouse after the first inspection. There was testimony by Acme's Baltimore division vice president, who had responded to the letter on behalf of Acme and respondent and who described the steps taken to remedy the insanitary conditions discovered by both inspections. The Government's final witness, Acme's vice president for legal affairs and assistant secretary, identified respondent as the president and chief executive officer of the company and read a bylaw prescribing the duties of the chief executive officer. He testified that respondent functioned by delegating "normal operating duties," including sanitation, but that he retained "certain things, which are the big, broad, principles of the operation of the company," and had "the responsibility of seeing that they all work together."

At the close of the Government's case in chief, respondent moved for a judgment of acquittal on the ground that "the evidence in chief has shown that

Mr. Park is not personally concerned in this Food and Drug violation." The trial judge denied the motion, stating that *Dotterweich* was controlling.

Respondent was the only defense witness. He testified that, although all of Acme's employees were in a sense under his general direction, the company had an "organizational structure for responsibilities for certain functions" according to which different phases of its operation were "assigned to individuals who, in turn, have staff and departments under them." He identified those individuals responsible for sanitation, and related that upon receipt of the January 1972 FDA letter, he had conferred with the vice president for legal affairs, who informed him that the Baltimore division vice president "was investigating the situation immediately and would be taking corrective action and would be preparing a summary of the corrective action to reply to the letter." Respondent stated that he did not "believe there was anything (he) could have done more constructively than what (he) found was being done."

On cross-examination, respondent conceded that providing sanitary conditions for food offered for sale to the public was something that he was "responsible for in the entire operation of the company," and he stated that it was one of many phases of the company that he assigned to "dependable subordinates." Respondent was asked about and, over the objections of his counsel, admitted receiving, the April 1970 letter addressed to him from the FDA regarding insanitary conditions at Acme's Philadelphia warehouse. He acknowledged that, with the exception of the division vice president, the same individuals had responsibility for sanitation in both Baltimore and Philadelphia. Finally, in response to questions concerning the Philadelphia and Baltimore incidents, respondent admitted that the Baltimore problem indicated the system for handling sanitation "wasn't working perfectly" and that as Acme's chief executive officer he was responsible for "any result which occurs in our company."

At the close of the evidence, respondent's renewed motion for a judgment of acquittal was denied. The relevant portion of the trial judge's instructions to the jury challenged by respondent is set out in the margin.[9] Respondent's counsel objected

9. "In order to find the Defendant guilty on any count of the Information, you must find beyond a reasonable doubt on each count. . . .

"Thirdly, that John R. Park held a position of authority in the operation of the business of Acme Markets, Incorporated.

"However, you need not concern yourselves with the first two elements of the case. The main issue for your determination is only with the third element, whether the Defendant held a position of authority and responsibility in the business of Acme Markets.

"The statute makes individuals, as well as corporations, liable for violations. An individual is liable if it is clear, beyond a reasonable doubt, that the elements of the adulteration of the food as to travel in interstate commerce are present. As I have instructed you in this case, they are, and that the individual had a responsible relation to the situation, even though he may not have participated personally.

"The individual is or could be liable under the statute, even if he did not consciously do wrong. However, the fact that the Defendant is pres(id)ent and is a chief executive officer of the Acme Markets does not require a finding of guilt. Though, he need not have personally participated in the situation, he must have had a responsible relationship to the issue. The issue is, in this case, whether the Defendant, John R. Park, by virtue of his position in the company, had a position of authority and responsibility in the situation out of which these charges arose."

to the instructions on the ground that they failed fairly to reflect our decision in *Dotterweich*, and to define "responsible relationship." The trial judge overruled the objection. The jury found respondent guilty on all counts of the information, and he was subsequently sentenced to pay a fine of $50 on each count. . . .

We granted certiorari because of an apparent conflict among the Courts of Appeals with respect to the standard of liability of corporate officers under the Federal Food, Drug, and Cosmetic Act as construed in *Dotterweich*, and because of the importance of the question to the Government's enforcement program. We reverse. . . .

The rule [set out in *Dotterweich*] that corporate employees who have "a responsible share in the furtherance of the transaction which the statute outlaws" are subject to the criminal provisions of the Act was not formulated in a vacuum. *Cf.* Morissette v. United States, 342 U.S. 246, 258, (1952). Cases under the Federal Food and Drugs Act of 1906 reflected the view both that knowledge or intent were not required to be proved in prosecutions under its criminal provisions, and that responsible corporate agents could be subjected to the liability thereby imposed. Moreover, the principle had been recognized that a corporate agent, through whose act, default, or omission the corporation committed a crime, was himself guilty individually of that crime. The principle had been applied whether or not the crime required "consciousness of wrongdoing," and it had been applied not only to those corporate agents who themselves committed the criminal act, but also to those who by virtue of their managerial positions or other similar relation to the actor could be deemed responsible for its commission.

In the latter class of cases, the liability of managerial officers did not depend on their knowledge of, or personal participation in, the act made criminal by the statute. Rather, where the statute under which they were prosecuted dispensed with "consciousness of wrongdoing," an omission or failure to act was deemed a sufficient basis for a responsible corporate agent's liability. It was enough in such cases that, by virtue of the relationship he bore to the corporation, the agent had the power to prevent the act complained of. . . .

Dotterweich and the cases which have followed reveal that in providing sanctions which reach and touch the individuals who execute the corporate mission—and this is by no means necessarily confined to a single corporate agent or employee—the Act imposes not only a positive duty to seek out and remedy violations when they occur but also, and primarily, a duty to implement measures that will insure that violations will not occur. The requirements of foresight and vigilance imposed on responsible corporate agents are beyond question demanding, and perhaps onerous, but they are no more stringent than the public has a right to expect of those who voluntarily assume positions of authority in business enterprises whose services and products affect the health and well-being of the public that supports them.

The Act does not . . . make criminal liability turn on "awareness of some wrongdoing" or "conscious fraud." The duty imposed by Congress on responsible corporate agents is, we emphasize, one that requires the highest standard of foresight and vigilance, but the Act, in its criminal aspect, does not require that which is objectively impossible. The theory upon which responsible corporate agents are held criminally accountable for "causing" violations of the Act permits a claim that a defendant was "powerless" to prevent or correct the violation to "be raised defensively at a trial on the merits." If such a claim is made, the defendant has the burden of coming forward with evidence, but this does not alter the Government's ultimate burden of proving beyond a reasonable doubt the defendant's guilt, including his power, in light of the duty imposed by the Act, to prevent or correct the prohibited condition. Congress has seen fit to enforce the accountability of responsible corporate agents dealing with products which may affect the health of consumers by penal sanctions cast in rigorous terms, and the obligation of the courts is to give them effect so long as they do not violate the Constitution.

III

We cannot agree with the Court of Appeals that it was incumbent upon the District Court to instruct the jury that the Government had the burden of establishing "wrongful action" in the sense in which the Court of Appeals used that phrase. The concept of a "responsible relationship" to, or a "responsible share" in, a violation of the Act indeed imports some measure of blameworthiness; but it is equally clear that the Government establishes a prima facie case when it introduces evidence sufficient to warrant a finding by the trier of the facts that the defendant had, by reason of his position in the corporation, responsibility and authority either to prevent in the first instance, or promptly to correct, the violation complained of, and that he failed to do so. The failure thus to fulfill the duty imposed by the interaction of the corporate agent's authority and the statute furnishes a sufficient causal link. The considerations which prompted the imposition of this duty, and the scope of the duty, provide the measure of culpability.

Turning to the jury charge in this case, it is of course arguable that isolated parts can be read as intimating that a finding of guilt could be predicated solely on respondent's corporate position. But this is not the way we review jury instructions, because "a single instruction to a jury may not be judged in artificial isolation, but must be viewed in the context of the overall charge." . . . Reading the entire charge satisfies us that the jury's attention was adequately focused on the issue of respondent's authority with respect to the conditions that formed the basis of the alleged violations. Viewed as a whole, the charge did not permit the jury to find guilt solely on the basis of respondent's position in the corporation; rather, it fairly advised the jury that to find guilt it must find respondent "had a responsible relation to the situation," and "by virtue of his position . . . had . . . authority and responsibility" to deal with the situation. The situation referred to could only be "food . . . held in unsanitary conditions in a warehouse with the result that it consisted, in part, of filth or . . . may have been contaminated with filth." . . .

We conclude that, viewed as a whole and in the context of the trial, the charge was not misleading and contained an adequate statement of the law to guide the jury's determination. Although it would have been better to give an instruction more precisely relating the legal issue to the facts of the case, we cannot say that the failure to provide the amplification requested by respondent was an abuse of discretion. . . . Finally, we note that there was no request for an instruction that the Government was required to prove beyond a reasonable doubt that respondent was not without the power or capacity to affect the conditions which founded the charges in the information. In light of the evidence adduced at trial, we find no basis to conclude that the failure of the trial court to give such an instruction sua sponte was plain error or a defect affecting substantial rights. Fed. Rule Crim. Proc. 52(b). . . .

Reversed.

Mr. Justice STEWART, with whom Mr. Justice MARSHALL and Mr. Justice POWELL join, dissenting.

Although agreeing with much of what is said in the Court's opinion, I dissent from the opinion and judgment, because the jury instructions in this case were not consistent with the law as the Court today expounds it.

As I understand the Court's opinion, it holds that in order to sustain a conviction under §301(k) of the Federal Food, Drug, and Cosmetic Act the prosecution must at least show that by reason of an individual's corporate position and responsibilities, he had a duty to use care to maintain the physical integrity of the corporation's food products. A jury may then draw the inference that when the good is found to be in such condition as to violate the statute's prohibitions, that condition was "caused" by a breach of the standard of care imposed upon the responsible official. This is the language of negligence, and I agree with it. . . .

To affirm this conviction, however, the Court must approve the instructions given to the members of the jury who were entrusted with determining whether the respondent was innocent or guilty. Those instructions did not conform to the standards that the Court itself sets out today.

The trial judge instructed the jury to find Park guilty if it found beyond a reasonable doubt that Park "had a responsible relation to the situation. . . . The issue is, in this case, whether the Defendant, John R. Park, by virtue of his position in the company, had a position of authority and responsibility in the situation out of which these charges arose." Requiring, as it did, a verdict of guilty upon a finding of "responsibility," this instruction standing alone could have been construed as a direction to convict if the jury found Park "responsible" for the condition in the sense that his position as chief executive officer gave him formal responsibility within the structure of the corporation. But the trial judge went on specifically to caution the jury not to attach such a meaning to his instruction, saying that "the fact that the Defendant is pres(id)ent and is a chief executive officer of the Acme Markets does not require a finding of guilt." "Responsibility" as used by the trial judge therefore had whatever meaning the jury in its unguided discretion chose to give it.

The instructions, therefore, expressed nothing more than a tautology. They told the jury: "You must find the defendant guilty if you find that he is to be held accountable for this adulterated food." In other words: "You must find the defendant guilty if you conclude that he is guilty." The trial judge recognized the infirmities in these instructions, but he reluctantly concluded that he was required to give such a charge under *Dotterweich* which, he thought, in declining to define "responsible relation" had declined to specify the minimum standard of liability for criminal guilt. . . .

NOTES AND QUESTIONS

1. In Morissette v. United States, 342 U.S. 246 (1952), the Supreme Court explained that the "responsible corporate officer" doctrine is a rare application of strict liability—i.e., the imposition of guilt with no mens rea—in the criminal arena. Thus, the Court concluded that it is limited to cases involving "public welfare offenses." These are mala prohibitum offenses enacted by Congress primarily in the context of overarching regulatory schemes designed to protect innocent members of the public from the new and ever-increasing dangers of the industrial revolution.
2. In addition to being regulatory in nature, a crime must meet two further requirements before courts will consider it to be a public welfare offense. First, Congress must have indicated its desire to impose strict liability by failing to provide a mens rea element in the statute itself. Second, the maximum jail term for violating the offense cannot be too high—at most two or so years. If it is much higher than that, courts will reason that Congress could not possibly have meant to impose serious criminal penalties without proof of culpability, and they will read a mens rea requirement into the statute.
3. What defenses are left to an individual accused under the responsible corporate officer doctrine? If the government had indicted Acme's Vice President for Marketing along with Park, would he have had a valid defense?
4. What does it mean to be "powerless to prevent or correct" the violation? Would Park have been able to make such a claim if he had been given a new trial? What if the cost of cleaning up all of Acme's warehouses to a standard of perfection would have been so high putting Acme into bankruptcy? What if it were only possible (with 1970s technology) to rid warehouses of rats by using so much poison as to create the possibility of contaminating the food?
5. Assume that Park's orders had been followed and that the Baltimore warehouse was spotless the day before the government inspection, but that night some disgruntled employees broke in and spread rat droppings around to get Acme in trouble? Would that create a valid defense for Park?

D. Responsible Corporate Officer Doctrine: Outer Limits

UNITED STATES v. FREED

189 Fed. Appx. 888, 2006 U.S. App. LEXIS 17716 (11th Cir. 2006)
NOT FOR PUBLICATION

PER CURIAM:

Susan L. Freed appeals her convictions of the misdemeanor offenses of use of National Forest lands without a required special use permit, 16 U.S.C. §551; 36 C.F.R. §261.10(k), and construction and maintenance of improvements on National Forest Lands, 16 U.S.C. §551; 36 C.F.R. §261.10(a). We affirm.

I. Background

Freed is the incorporator and a trustee of Enota Mission Trust, which owns Enota, a campground located in the Chattahoochee National Forest. In 1999, Forest Service Ranger David Kuykendall discovered blaze marks and vegetation damage on trails in the National Forest leading to Enota and an old logging road between the Appalachian Trail and the Enota property. In addition, vegetation around the Joel Branch waterfall had been cut apparently to allow a better view of the falls. Kuykendall also discovered that an old dam and water system on Gurley Creek had been repaired. Fresh boards had been placed in the dam to hold water, and PVC pipe had been used to replace the cast iron piping of the water system. The water system carried water from Gurley Creek onto the Enota property. On another visit, Kuykendall observed a bridge that had been constructed on National Forest property.

In response to Kuykendall's findings, the District Ranger sent Freed two letters that informed Freed that the improvements observed by Kuykendall around Enota on National Forest land and the construction and maintenance of trails were in violation of Forest Service regulations and illegal. One letter stated, "All improvements made by your staff to the old . . . [w]ater tank, pipeline, and dam on National Forest land must be removed within 30 days of this date. No additional repair, maintenance, or use of these facilities will be allowed." Approximately one month later, no improvements had been removed from the water system.

In 2001, Kuykendall and another ranger returned to the area surrounding Enota. The rangers removed boards out of the dam, a section of pipe out of the waterline, and a valve. On a visit approximately one year later, rangers observed that someone had replaced the boards and piping and that water was flowing through the pipe to Enota.

In 2002, two undercover Forest Service officers visited Enota. Officer Phillip Greene spent the night and part of a day at Enota while Agent Jenny Davis walked the property. Greene observed repairs to the dam and water system, two log bridges that had been constructed on national forest land, and unauthorized trails that had been maintained. Davis also observed the repairs to the water system and recently cut vegetation and work on national forest land. Following her observations, Davis spoke with Freed about the unauthorized work and improvements and issued Freed citations for the violations she observed. The citations were eventually dropped.

In August 2004, Davis returned to Enota and observed that the dam was still in place, water was passing through the pipes, and a trail near Gurley Creek was still being maintained although there did not appear to be any fresh cutting. Freed was then served with the citations that are the subject of this appeal.

After a trial before a magistrate judge, at which Freed testified in her defense, the Magistrate Judge found Freed guilty of two violations: (1) use of national forest land without a special use authorization relating to the operation of the water system on Gurley Creek; and (2) construction and maintenance of improvements on National Forest land relating to improvements made to trails leading from Enota to waterfalls on National Forest land and the construction of two bridges on National Forest land. The Magistrate Judge found Freed guilty as a responsible corporate agent of Enota Mission Trust. On appeal, the district court affirmed the convictions.

* * *

III. Discussion

. . . Freed erroneously argues that the magistrate judge and district court clearly erred by concluding that she was guilty of trail maintenance on the date charged in the citation and by failing to address the testimony of witnesses who stated that Freed told employees not to perform maintenance on National Forest land. Evidence was presented at trial of trail maintenance on unauthorized trails from 1999 to August 2004. It was not clearly erroneous for the magistrate judge and district court to conclude that a violation occurred on or about July 30, 2004, the date of the citation. Evidence was presented, moreover, that the kind of maintenance performed on the trails required tools, time, and labor. Given the proximity of Enota to trails and Freed's residence at Enota since 2002 as the manager, it was not clearly erroneous to conclude that Enota was responsible for the damage to the National Forest. The court also did not clearly err when it concluded that Freed lived at Enota from 2002 to 2004, and was regarded as responsible for the actions of Enota.

Freed also argues that the district court committed three legal errors. First, Freed argues that the district court erroneously concluded that the offenses of which Freed was convicted were strict liability offenses. This argument fails.

Neither the forest service regulations of which Freed was convicted nor the enabling statute contain an element of *mens rea.* See 36 C.F.R. §261.10; 16 U.S.C. §551. Although proof of a guilty mind is generally required, certain regulatory or public welfare offenses may carry strict liability. United States v. Balint, 258 U.S. 250, 251-53 (1922). To determine whether an offense is one for which no proof of *mens rea* is required, we consider [a number of factors], including whether the statute involves a matter of policy, whether the standard imposed by the statute is reasonable, whether the penalty is small, whether a conviction would gravely affect the reputation of the individual, whether the crime was cognizable at common law, and whether the congressional purpose would be supported by the lack of an intent requirement. When we consider the regulation at issue in this appeal in the light of these factors, we conclude that the magistrate judge and district court correctly held that intent was not a necessary element.

The Forest Service regulations reflect the national policy to care and protect national forest land. The requirement that individuals receive permits before modifying the national forest is reasonable, the penalty imposed is small—a violation of the regulation is a misdemeanor offense that carries a minimal fine and sentence—and a conviction would not have a grave effect on the reputation of an individual convicted of the offense. We are supported in this conclusion by the decisions of at least two other circuits. . . .

Second, Freed erroneously argues that the district court mistakenly applied vicarious liability principles to find her guilty of the offenses. Freed contends that the responsible corporate officer doctrine applies only to public health and safety regulations concerning "dangerous or deleterious devices or products or obnoxious waste materials." This argument fails. The doctrine applies when a corporation is liable for an offense because "the only way in which a corporation can act is through the individuals who act on its behalf." *Dotterweich*, 320 U.S. at 281. To impose liability, the government must produce "evidence sufficient to warrant a finding by the trier of the facts that the defendant had, by reason of his position in the corporation, responsibility and authority either to prevent in the first instance, or promptly to correct, the violation complained of, and that he failed to do so." *Park*, 421 U.S. at 673-74. The government provided sufficient evidence that Freed was in a position of responsibility with regard to Enota. It was not error for the magistrate judge and district court to hold Freed liable as a responsible corporate officer.

Finally, Freed argues that the district court erroneously held that Freed could be guilty for failure to act. This argument fails. A responsible corporate officer can be held liable for failure to act precisely because that individual had the power to prevent the violation, and the finding of the district court that Freed was in a position to prevent the violations that occurred was not clearly erroneous. . . . Freed's convictions are AFFIRMED.

NOTES AND QUESTIONS

1. Do the misdemeanor offenses in *Freed* truly meet the requirements of a public welfare offense? What is different between a food and drug offense and one involving the disturbance of a National Forest?
2. If it was reasonable to conclude from the circumstantial evidence that Freed knew her employees were fixing the dam and improving the trail, was there any reason to invoke the responsible corporate officer doctrine in this case? On the other hand, if Freed was not aware of the conduct of her employees, what exactly is her actus reus? In other words, what did she fail to do?

UNITED STATES v. IVERSON

162 F.3d 1015 (9th Cir. 1998)

GRABER, Circuit Judge:

A jury convicted defendant of four counts of violating federal water pollution law, as embodied in the Clean Water Act (CWA), the Washington Administrative Code (WAC), and the City of Olympia's Municipal Code (Olympia code). The jury also convicted defendant of one count of conspiring to violate the WAC or the CWA.

Defendant was a founder of CH2O, Inc., and served as the company's President and Chairman of the Board. CH2O blends chemicals to create numerous products, including acid cleaners and heavy-duty alkaline compounds. The company ships the blended chemicals to its customers in drums.

CH2O asked its customers to return the drums so that it could reuse them. Although customers returned the drums, they often did not clean them sufficiently.

Thus, the drums still contained chemical residue. Before CH2O could reuse the drums, it had to remove that residue.

To remove the residue, CH2O instituted a drum-cleaning operation, which in turn generated wastewater. In the early to mid-1980s, defendant approached the manager of the local sewer authority to see whether the sewer authority would accept the company's wastewater. The sewer authority refused, because the wastewater "did not meet the parameters we had set for accepting industrial waste. It had too high of a metal content." Thereafter, defendant and the general manager of CH2O made two other attempts to convince the sewer authority to accept the wastewater. Both times, it refused.

Beginning in about 1985, defendant personally discharged the wastewater and ordered employees of CH2O to discharge the wastewater in three places: (1) on the plant's property, (2) through a sewer drain at an apartment complex that defendant owned, and (3) through a sewer drain at defendant's home. (The plant did not have sewer access.) Those discharges continued until about 1988, when CH2O hired Bill Brady.

Brady initially paid a waste disposal company to dispose of the wastewater. Those efforts cost the company thousands of dollars each month. Beginning in late 1991, CH2O stopped its drum-cleaning operation and, instead, shipped the drums to a professional outside contractor for cleaning.

In April 1992, CH2O fired Brady. Around that same time, defendant bought a warehouse in Olympia. Unlike the CH2O plant, the warehouse had sewer access. After the purchase, CH2O restarted its drum-cleaning operation at the warehouse and disposed of its wastewater through the sewer. CH2O obtained neither a permit nor permission to make these discharges. The drum-cleaning operation continued until the summer of 1995, when CH2O learned that it was under investigation for discharging pollutants into the sewer.

A few months before CH2O restarted its drum-cleaning operation, defendant announced his "official" retirement from CH2O. Thereafter, he continued to receive money from CH2O, to conduct business at the company's facilities, and to give orders to employees. Moreover, the company continued to list him as the president in documents that it filed with the state, and the employee who was responsible for running the day-to-day aspects of the drum-cleaning operation testified that he reported to defendant.

During the four years of the operation at the warehouse, defendant was sometimes present when drums were cleaned. During those occasions, defendant was close enough to see and smell the waste.

In some instances, defendant informed employees that he had obtained a permit for the drum-cleaning operation and that the operation was on the "up and up." At other times, however, defendant told employees that, if they got caught, the company would receive only a slap on the wrist. . . .

B. "Responsible Corporate Officer" Liability

The district court instructed the jury that it could find defendant liable under the CWA as a "responsible corporate officer" if it found, beyond a reasonable doubt:

1. That the defendant had knowledge of the fact that pollutants were being discharged to the sewer system by employees of CH2O, Inc.;
2. That the defendant had the authority and capacity to prevent the discharge of pollutants to the sewer system; and
3. That the defendant failed to prevent the on-going discharge of pollutants to the sewer system.

Defendant argues that the district court misinterpreted the scope of "responsible corporate officer" liability. Specifically, defendant suggests that a corporate officer is "responsible" only when the officer in fact exercises control over the activity causing the discharge or has an express corporate duty to oversee the activity. We have not previously interpreted the scope of "responsible corporate officer" liability under the CWA. We do so now and reject defendant's narrow interpretation.

"When interpreting a statute, this court looks first to the words that Congress used." The CWA holds criminally liable "any person who . . . knowingly violates" its provisions. See 33 U.S.C. §1319(c)(2). The CWA defines the term "person" to include "any responsible corporate officer." See 33 U.S.C. §1319(c)(6) ("For the purpose of this subsection, the term 'person' means, in addition to the definition contained in section 1362(5) of this title, any responsible corporate officer."). However, the CWA does not define the term "responsible corporate officer."

When a statute does not define a term, we generally interpret that term by employing the ordinary, contemporary, and common meaning of the words that Congress used. . . . As pertinent here, the word "responsible" means "answerable" or "involving a degree of accountability." *Webster's Third New Int'l Dictionary* 1935 (unabridged ed. 1993). Using that meaning, "any corporate officer" who is "answerable" or "accountable" for the unlawful discharge is liable under the CWA.

The history of the "responsible corporate officer" liability supports the foregoing construction. The "responsible corporate officer" doctrine originated in a Supreme Court case interpreting the Federal Food, Drug, and Cosmetic Act (FFDCA), *United States v. Dotterweich*. . . .

Because Congress used a similar definition of the term "person" in the CWA, we can presume that Congress intended that the principles of *Dotterweich* apply under the CWA. . . . Under *Dotterweich*, whether defendant had sufficient "responsibility" over the discharges to be criminally liable would be a question for the jury.

After Congress initially enacted the CWA in 1972, the Supreme Court further defined the scope of the "responsible corporate officer" doctrine under the FFDCA [in] *Park*. [In that case,] a corporate president argued that he could not be "responsible" under *Dotterweich*, because he had delegated decision-making control over the activity in question to a subordinate. The Court rejected that argument. . . .

The question for the jury is whether the corporate officer had "authority with respect to the conditions that formed the basis of the alleged violations." *Id.* at 674. The Court did not, however, require the corporate officer actually to exercise any authority over the activity.

In 1987, after the Supreme Court decided *Park*, Congress revised and replaced the criminal provisions of the CWA. (Most importantly, Congress made a violation of the CWA a felony, rather than a misdemeanor.) In replacing the criminal provisions of the CWA, Congress made no changes to its "responsible corporate officer" provision. That being so, we can presume that Congress intended for *Park*'s refinement of the "responsible corporate officer" doctrine to apply under the CWA.

Moreover, this court has interpreted similar terms in other statutes consistently with the Court's decision in *Park*. For example, the Internal Revenue Code (IRC) holds liable any "person required to collect, truthfully account for, and pay over any tax" under the IRC. 26 U.S.C. §6672(a). The IRC defines "person" to include any "officer . . . under a duty to perform the act in respect of which the violation occurs." 26 U.S.C. §6671(b). This court consistently has interpreted the term "person" to include corporate officers with authority to pay taxes, whether or not they exercise that authority. . . .

Taken together, the wording of the CWA, the Supreme Court's interpretations of the "responsible corporate officer" doctrine, and this court's interpretation of similar statutory requirements establish the contours of the "responsible corporate officer" doctrine under the CWA. Under the CWA, a person is a "responsible corporate officer" if the person has authority to exercise control over the corporation's activity that is causing the discharges. There is no requirement that the officer in fact exercise such authority or that the corporation expressly vest a duty in the officer to oversee the activity.

NOTES AND QUESTIONS

1. The responsible corporate officer doctrine seems to have taken on a life of its own. Recall that it was originally created by the Supreme Court to impose *strict liability* on corporate officers in public welfare offenses. Is the CWA a strict liability statute?
2. What did Congress accomplish by using the term "responsible corporate officer" in the CWA? It certainly did not need the doctrine for the purpose of expanding the statute's mens rea requirement: If *any* person acts knowingly in violation of the CWA, he is liable regardless of whether he is a responsible corporate officer or not. Instead, it appears that Congress used the term to make responsible corporate officers liable for certain omissions, that is, for the failure to prevent the commission of a CWA offense by subordinates in the corporation. This is the interpretation given to the CWA by the trial court, isn't it?
3. Think back to the *Brown & Tobey* case, *supra* p. 60. *Brown & Tobey* held that a supervisor can be liable for aiding and abetting the commission of a crime by his subordinates merely by consenting to their illegal activity. In light of that holding, was it necessary for Congress to transform the meaning of "responsible corporate officer" in the CWA to accomplish its goal? In any event, is it a good idea for the same legal phrase to have different meanings in different contexts?

chapter 3

Conspiracy

I. INTRODUCTION

The essence of conspiracy is the agreement between two or more persons to commit a criminal offense. The theory behind the crime is that, when multiple persons join up to form a criminal enterprise, they can carry out a more complex crime than any one of them could accomplish on his own. Additionally, members of a conspiracy are more likely to commit multiple crimes in the course of accomplishing their joint objective, and to continue their criminal ventures even after the initial objective has been achieved. Finally, conspiracies create special dangers through the operation of peer pressure and "groupthink"; while an individual might decide not to go through with the commission of a contemplated crime, the train tends to be much more difficult to derail once other individuals are on board.

Conspiracy has been aptly labeled the "darling" of the prosecutor's nursery. Rarely is a federal white collar criminal indictment brought that does not have a conspiracy charge as its first count. There are a variety of important reasons for this.

First, conspiracy is an inchoate offense, meaning that the crime is complete before any actual harm takes place. Under 18 U.S.C. §371, the granddaddy of federal conspiracy statutes, a conspiracy is chargeable once the agreement is made and any one of the co-conspirators carries out an "overt act" in furtherance of the conspiratorial plan. This overt act need not itself be criminal, and can be as simple and routine as placing a phone call or driving to a location for a meeting.

Second, by charging a group of defendants in one indictment as co-conspirators, the prosecution is typically able to try them together under Federal Rule of Criminal Procedure 8(b). This, of course, saves a lot of prosecutorial resources. It also has another, less talked about, advantage. Although the judge will instruct the jury at the end of trial to consider the case of each defendant separately, this is likely to be an impossible task. Evidence against one defendant will naturally spill over into the case against the others. Thus, it is to the prosecutor's advantage to try the "little guys" along side the "mastermind." Defense attorneys, of course, routinely move for severance in an attempt to secure separate trials for their clients. Typically, however, judicial efficiency trumps the "minimal" and unavoidable prejudice of joinder.

Third, Federal Rule of Evidence 801(d)(2)(E) declares as "not hearsay" the statements of one conspirator offered against his co-conspirators if the statement was made during the course and in furtherance of the conspiracy. Technically, conspiracy need not be charged to take advantage of this rule but, in actual practice, judges are much more likely to allow the use of co-conspirator statements when the charge is in the indictment. Rule 801(d)(2)(E) represents a huge evidentiary advantage for the prosecution in a multidefendant case.

Fourth, through a conspiracy charge, the prosecutor can make her indictment "speak." All other charges in the indictment must be direct and to the point (or suffer a defense motion to strike the surplusage), but a conspiracy charge can be written to delineate the prosecution's version of the crime. Indeed, if the crime is complex and the participants extensive, the conspiracy charge can contain separate sections explaining the background of the situation and listing a who's who of the players involved. It can then tell the story of the alleged crime, typically in chronological order, with as much detail as the prosecutor deems appropriate. (The limiting factor is that the prosecutor would not want to put particulars in the indictment that she could not prove at trial, as this would inevitably be called to the attention of the jury by defense counsel.) At its conclusion, the conspiracy charge specifies the object(s) of the conspiracy and lists a whole litany of overt acts.

Through the use of a "speaking indictment," the prosecutor attains two specific strategic benefits. Ethical rules (*see, e.g.*, ABA Model Rules of Professional Conduct 3.6 & 3.8) and Department of Justice guidelines prohibit the prosecutor from making public comments about the case beyond what is already in the public record. The speaking indictment enables the prosecutor to tell the pubic what the case is about by relating in press statements and at press conferences what the "grand jury charged" in the indictment. Additionally, the indictment is given to the jury for use during deliberations. A well-written conspiracy count provides the jury with a roadmap through the prosecution's version of the facts, which the prosecutor hopes will lead it down the path to conviction.

Finally, a conspiracy is properly venued in any jurisdiction in which any overt act of the conspiracy took place. This gives prosecutors a great deal of discretion in deciding where to bring charges. For the Department of Justice as a whole, this is a plus, as it allows the higher-ups (typically the Deputy Attorney General) to strategize about where a major multistate case ought to be brought. For individual U.S. Attorney's Offices, however, this legal rule causes more headaches than anything else, as it is the source of much infighting among offices.

Conspiracy doctrine has many interesting features, the most important of which are covered in this chapter.

II. THE PLURALITY REQUIREMENT

UNITED STATES v. STEVENS

909 F.2d 431 (11th Cir. 1990)

Roney, Senior Circuit Judge.

In this criminal conspiracy case, we hold that a sole stockholder who completely controls a corporation and is the sole actor in performance of corporate activities, cannot be guilty of a criminal conspiracy with that corporation in the absence of another human actor. We therefore reverse the conspiracy conviction of defendant Gary S. Stevens. . . . The indictment alleged the following scheme: Stevens formed four separate corporations in the state of Florida for the purpose of performing government contract work. The corporations entered into a government contract with the U.S. Navy to build an automated storage and retrieval system at the Portsmouth Naval Shipyard in Kittery, Maine. The contract provided for periodic progress payments from the Government as designated aspects of the project were completed.

Stevens was the sole shareholder of these corporations and exercised sole control over them. He was also the only agent of the corporations who executed forms relating to these contracts. Stevens misrepresented that certain work had been performed in several requests for progress payments. Stevens applied for both personal and commercial loans at several federally insured banks, duplicitously listing as security the income derived from this contract.

The jury focused on the issue, presented by this appeal, concerning the alleged conspiracy between Stevens and his corporations. During deliberations, it submitted several written questions to the district court, including the following:

> CAN A PERSON CONSPIRE WITH HIS OWN CORPORATION, REALIZING THAT HE IS THE PRIMARY (ONLY) AGENT OF HIS OWN CORPORATION?
>
> CAN WE HAVE A DEFINITION OF CONSPIRACY AS IT APPLIES TO WHOLLY OWNED CORPORATION?

The district court judge responded in writing that a person was legally able to conspire with his wholly owned corporation, and that the general definition of conspiracy applies to both humans and corporations.

Although a conspiracy under 18 U.S.C.A. §371 requires an agreement between two or more persons, we have held that a corporation may be held criminally liable under §371 when conspiring with its officers or employees. In so holding, we rejected the "single entity" theory that all agents of a corporation engaging in corporate conduct form a single, collective legal person—that is, the corporation—and that the acts of each agent constitute the acts of the corporation. The single entity theory shielded intracorporate associations of individuals from conspiracy liability on the rationale that a corporation cannot conspire with itself any more than a private individual can.

Distinguishing the antitrust context in which the single entity theory first arose, this Court decided that in the context of a criminal conspiracy to defraud the

Government, the single entity theory contravened "the underlying purpose that led to the creation of the fiction of corporate personification. It originated to broaden the scope of corporate responsibility; we will not use it to shield individuals or corporations from criminal liability." United States v. Hartley, 678 F.2d 961, 972 (11th Cir. 1982) (citing *United States v. Wise*, Harlan, J., concurring).

Hartley makes two important holdings in the field of intracorporate conspiracy. *First*, it holds that a group of conspirators cannot escape conspiracy responsibility merely because they all act on behalf of a corporation. *Second, Hartley* holds that liability for a conspiracy may be imputed to the corporation itself on a respondeat superior theory.

The [corporate] fiction was never intended to prohibit the imposition of criminal liability by allowing a corporation or its agents to hide behind the identity of the other. We decline to expand the fiction only to limit corporate responsibility in the context of the criminal conspiracy now before us. . . .

> In these situations, the action by an incorporated collection of individuals creates the "group danger" at which conspiracy liability is aimed, and the view of the corporation as a single legal actor becomes a fiction without a purpose.

678 F.2d at 970. . . .

In this case, we confront a different situation: there is only one human actor, acting for himself and for the corporate entity which he controls. In the great majority of reported decisions involving intracorporate conspiracies under §371, there were multiple human conspirators in addition to the corporate coconspirator. Some cases have expressly indicated that multiple actors must be involved.

The argument that a single human actor can be convicted of conspiracy under §371 under the circumstances of this case flies in the face of the traditional justification for criminal conspiracies. Conspiracy is a crime separate from the substantive criminal offense which is the purpose of the conspiracy. This separate punishment is targeted not at the substantive offenses themselves, but at the danger posed to society by combinations of individuals acting in concert.

This settled principle derives from the reason of things in dealing with socially reprehensible conduct: collective criminal agreement—partnership in crime—presents a greater potential threat to the public than individual derelicts. Concerted action both increases the likelihood that the criminal object will be successfully attained and decreases the probability that the individuals involved will depart from their path of criminality. Group association for criminal purposes often, if not normally, makes possible the attainment of ends more complex than those which one criminal could accomplish. Nor is the danger of a conspiratorial group limited to the particular end toward which it has embarked. Combination in crime makes more likely the commission of crimes unrelated to the original purpose for which the group was formed. In sum, the danger which a conspiracy generates is not confined to the substantive offense which is the immediate aim of the enterprise.

The threat posed to society by these combinations arises from the creative interaction of two autonomous minds. It is for this reason that the essence of a conspiracy is an *agreement*. The societal threat is of a different quality when one human simply uses the corporate mechanism to carry out his crime. The danger from agreement does not arise.

Even if it can be said that Stevens made up his mind as an individual to pursue fraudulent ends and at the same time made up the "minds" of his corporations to pursue these same ends, this case lacks any interaction between multiple autonomous actors. The basis for punishing Stevens for the separate offense of conspiracy, in addition to the substantive offenses he committed, is not present in this case.

Although it takes three incorporators to form a corporation in Florida, the Government does not assert that the incorporators, other than Stevens, were in any way involved in the criminal objective.

We accordingly reverse Stevens's conviction for conspiracy under §371. . . .

MCANDREW v. LOCKHEED MARTIN CORPORATION

206 F.3d 1031 (11th Cir. 2000)

MARCUS, Circuit Judge:

This case raises the discrete question of the applicability of the intracorporate conspiracy doctrine to claims arising under 42 U.S.C. §1985(2) and alleging a conspiracy among corporate officers and the corporation itself to deter by force, intimidation, or threat, an individual from testifying in a court of the United States. These allegations plainly describe criminal conduct in violation of 18 U.S.C. §1512 and a criminal conspiracy in violation of 18 U.S.C. §371. Accordingly, we hold that just as the intracorporate conspiracy doctrine cannot shield a criminal conspiracy from prosecution under the federal criminal code, the doctrine cannot shield the same conspiracy, alleging the same criminal wrongdoing, from civil liability arising under 42 U.S.C. §1985(2). Therefore, we reverse the district court's order dismissing McAndrew's §1985(2) claim as barred by the intracorporate conspiracy doctrine and remand for further proceedings consistent with this opinion.

I.

The facts of this case are straightforward. In 1993, the United States Department of Justice was investigating Lockheed's sale of three C-130 aircraft to the Arab Republic of Egypt for possible violations of the Foreign Corrupt Practices Act, 10 U.S.C. §2409 *et seq.* Robert McAndrew had served as Lockheed's Director of International Marketing since 1989 and was responsible for negotiating the sale of aircraft to foreign nations.

In the fall of 1993, McAndrew and more than 30 other Lockheed employees were subpoenaed to testify before a federal grand jury. McAndrew alleges that on the morning he was scheduled to appear before the grand jury, June 21, 1994, he received a phone call from T.A. Graham, Vice President of Business Development at Lockheed (and McAndrew's immediate supervisor). During the course of the conversation Graham supposedly expressed his dissatisfaction to McAndrew about McAndrew's appearance before the grand jury, and told him specifically that "the company was very unhappy with [McAndrew's] decision to testify." Indeed, the complaint alleges that Graham made clear to McAndrew that "it would not be in his best interest to testify." McAndrew explained that he had no choice about testifying, that he had been under subpoena since October, 1993, and that he had been ordered by the court to give testimony. McAndrew told Graham, according to the complaint, that McAndrew had to appear and answer truthfully whatever questions were posed to him. Plaintiff alleged that Graham was in Mexico when he called McAndrew and that Graham made it clear by his words that he was not only expressing his own personal sentiments, but was also speaking for Lockheed.

On June 21, 1994, under compulsion of subpoena and a separate court order, McAndrew appeared and testified before the grand jury regarding his knowledge of the sale of aircraft to Egypt. Two days later, McAndrew alleged, he received another call from Graham during which Graham told McAndrew that he, and Defendants A. Goldfarb (Vice President for Administration) and T.F. Powell (Vice President of Human Resources) were discussing what to do about McAndrew. Graham allegedly told McAndrew to take a couple of days off. Thereafter, according to the complaint, on June 28, 1994, Graham fired McAndrew by reading him the following statement: "The company has decided to end our relationship. This is due to your performance in International Marketing."

In June 1996, McAndrew sued Lockheed and five senior management employees—Graham, Powell, Goldfarb, J.A. Blackwell (Lockheed's Aeronautical Senior President and Chief Executive Officer), and J.S. McLellan (President of Lockheed Martin Aeronautical System Company, a division of Lockheed Martin)—alleging that they conspired to prevent him from testifying and then retaliated against him by firing him after he testified in violation of [inter alia] 42 U.S.C. §§1985(2). . . .

The district court . . . dismissed the complaint in its entirety. In doing so, the court held . . . that McAndrew's §1985(2) claim was barred by the intracorporate conspiracy doctrine. . . . McAndrew appealed. . . .

II.

The only issue before us is whether the intracorporate conspiracy doctrine applies to and bars a claim arising under Title 42 U.S.C. §1985(2), alleging a criminal conspiracy among a corporation and its employees to prevent by force, intimidation, or threat, an individual from testifying in a federal court. We hold that it does not. This outcome flows from the long-established conclusion that the intracorporate conspiracy doctrine does not apply to criminal conspiracies. Because a §1985(2) claim alleging a conspiracy to deter a person by force, intimidation, or threat from testifying in a federal court proceeding squarely and unambiguously alleges a criminal conspiracy in violation of 18 U.S.C. §§371, 1512, the intracorporate conspiracy doctrine does not apply and, therefore, cannot shield the Defendants from civil liability.

The intracorporate conspiracy doctrine holds that acts of corporate agents are attributed to the corporation itself, thereby negating the multiplicity of actors necessary for the formation of a conspiracy. Simply put, under the doctrine, a corporation cannot conspire with its employees, and its employees, when acting in the scope of their employment, cannot conspire among themselves. The doctrine is based on the nature of a conspiracy and the legal conception of a corporation. It is by now axiomatic that a conspiracy requires a meeting of the minds between two or more persons to accomplish a common and unlawful plan. . . . However, under basic agency principles, the acts of a corporation's agents are considered to be those of a single legal actor. Therefore, just as it is not legally possible for an individual person to conspire with himself, it is not possible for a single legal entity consisting of the corporation and its agents to conspire with itself. . . .

Not surprisingly, the intracorporate conspiracy doctrine first developed in the anti-trust context where it seemed particularly logical to conclude that a single corporation could not conspire with itself to restrain trade in the way imagined by Section 1 of the Sherman Antitrust Act. As the former Fifth Circuit explained in *Nelson Radio*, while a single corporation could act in violation of Section 2 of the Sherman Act—which prohibits attempts to monopolize—it could not *alone* form a contract, combination, or conspiracy in restraint of trade so as to violate Section 1 of the Act. . . . To hold otherwise would render Section 2 of the Act meaningless. . . .

We have long recognized an exception to the applicability of the intracorporate conspiracy doctrine for intracorporate criminal conspiracies arising under 18 U.S.C. §371 of the federal criminal code. In *Hartley*, we refused to apply the intracorporate conspiracy doctrine to shield from liability members of the same corporation who were accused of a criminal conspiracy. We considered an alleged conspiracy between a private food manufacturing company and government inspectors to bypass the government's food inspection guidelines. While we recognized that the conspiracy alleged did not require an analysis of the intracorporate conspiracy doctrine because it involved government inspectors who were not part of the corporation, we noted that "the provocative nature of the issue compels us to rule on its application to the facts of this case." We followed former Fifth Circuit precedent in holding that the intracorporate conspiracy doctrine does not apply to alleged intracorporate criminal conspiracies. . . .

The First, Sixth, Eighth, and Ninth Circuits have all ruled similarly. . . .

The rationale supporting the idea that the intracorporate conspiracy doctrine cannot shield corporate employees and corporations accused of criminal conspiracies is simple enough. As we explained in *Hartley*, the original purpose of the corporate entity fiction was to *expand* rather than shrink corporate responsibility by making a corporation answer for the negligent acts of its agents. The fiction was never intended to prohibit the imposition of criminal liability by allowing a corporation or its agents to hide behind the identity of the other. As the Fifth Circuit emphasized in *Dussouy*, in situations where a criminal conspiracy is alleged "the action by an incorporated collection of individuals creates the 'group danger' at which conspiracy liability is aimed, and the view of the corporation as a single legal actor becomes a fiction without a purpose." . . .

Simply put, we conclude that the criminal conspiracy exception to the intracorporate conspiracy doctrine applies regardless of whether the criminal conspiracy arises under 18 U.S.C. §371 or under 42 U.S.C. §1985. Because a claim, such as McAndrew's, alleging an intracorporate conspiracy to deter a person from testifying in a court of law by force, intimidation, or threat, necessarily alleges a criminal conspiracy, the intracorporate conspiracy doctrine cannot apply. Accordingly, we reverse the district court's order of dismissal on this issue and remand for further proceedings consistent with this opinion.

NOTES AND QUESTIONS

1. According to *Stevens*, can a corporate officer conspire with his corporation? Under what circumstances?
2. Explain the "intracorporate conspiracy doctrine." Why does it apply in price-fixing cases but nowhere else?

Problem 3-1

Traction Corporation, a supplier of tanks to the U.S. Deparment of Defense, obtains the tread mechanism for its vehicles from military part supplier Harbuton, Inc. Pursuant to a current contract, Traction is required to deliver 100 new tanks to DOD six months from now. The company has subcontracted with Harbuton for the necessary tread mechanisms.

Bob Peters and Joyce Schultz, employees of Harbuton, create a timeline and conclude that, with all of the DOD-required testing and inspections, it will be impossible to manufacture the treads on time. They relay this conclusion to the CEO of Harbuton, MaryJane Perculo. She, in turn, calls Mark Neejam, the CEO of Traction, to discuss their options.

After brainstorming, Neejam and Perculo decide that their only realistic course of action is to falsify the inspection stickers in a manner that will go undetected by DOD. Perculo calls in Peters and Schultz and instructs them on the falsification process, which they carry out. Neejam speaks to Jorge Gonzalez, his chief of compliance, to clue him in and make sure that the treads pass through Traction's internal inspection system.

Gonzalez is immediately uncomfortable with the plan. After consulting with his attorney, he speaks to the FBI and agrees to wear a wire and surreptitiously record incriminating conversations with the others, which he then does.

The falsification begins. After obtaining five tanks built without appropriate testing, the FBI and DOD shut down the allegedly illegal enterprise. They bring the case to the local U.S. Attorney's Office.

You are the Assistant U.S. Attorney (AUSA) tasked with the job of drafting the conspiracy charges(s) for the indictment. The other charges, presumably including making false statements to the United States in violation of 18 U.S.C. §1001, are being drafted by your colleague.

A. Is the plurality requirement met? Which "autonomous human minds" are involved in the agreement to falsify the inspection stickers?
B. Can Traction Corporation be charged with conspiracy? Under what theory? How about Harbuton? Does it matter that, given Gonzalez's cooperation with federal officials from the outset, the only person at Harbuton who agrees to the illicit activity is Neejam?

C. Can you charge Traction Corporation and Harbuton, Inc. with conspiring with each other to make false statements to the federal government? Can you charge the corporations with conspiring with the humans (their respective agents) to violate §1001? Assuming both are viable options, what are the pros and cons of choosing to do it one way or the other?

III. MENS REA AND THE OBJECT OFFENSE

Before reading the cases that follow, make sure to take a close look at the most commonly used federal conspiracy statute, 18 U.S.C. §371. Note that the statute describes two different means by which the offense of conspiracy can be committed. One is by agreeing with another person "to commit any offense against the United States," that is, by agreeing to commit any federal criminal offense. The second is by agreeing "to defraud the United States, or any agency thereof in any manner or for any purpose." This is often referred to as the "defraud clause" of the conspiracy statute.

UNITED STATES v. GRICCO

277 F.3d 339 (3d Cir. 2002)

ALITO, Circuit Judge.

Appellants Anthony Gricco and Michael McCardell were convicted of conspiracy to defraud the United States, tax evasion, and making false tax returns. All of the charges related to the conspirators' failure to report on their personal income tax returns money that had been stolen from airport parking facilities. We affirm the appellants' convictions. . . .

I.

From 1990 to 1994, Anthony Gricco was the regional manager for private companies that contracted with the Philadelphia Parking Authority to operate the parking facilities at the Philadelphia International Airport. Gricco was responsible for the general operation of the facilities, including the hiring of employees and the collection of parking fees. Michael McCardell, Gricco's brother-in-law, was Gricco's chief assistant. McCardell oversaw the day-to-day activities of the tollbooths and picked up money from the cashiers at the end of their shifts.

The parking facilities at the airport used automated ticket machines as well as cashiers. Upon entering a lot, a customer would take a ticket from a machine. The date and time would be printed on the ticket and encoded in the magnetic strip on the back. To leave the lot, the customer would drive to a tollbooth and the ticket would be put into another machine. This machine would read the date and time of issuance, calculate the length of time that the customer had parked in the lot, and display the parking fee owed. The customer would then pay the cashier in the tollbooth. . . .

In early 1990, Gricco, McCardell, and others made a plan to steal money by substituting customers' real tickets with replacement tickets showing false dates and times of entry. A customer who had parked in the lot for a long period of time would have a real ticket reflecting a high parking fee. On leaving the lot, the customer would pay this fee to the cashier. However, instead of inserting the real ticket into the ticket-reading machine, a cashier participating in the scheme would insert a replacement ticket, and the machine would calculate the parking fee based on the false date and time stamped on the replacement ticket. This replacement ticket would indicate that the customer had parked for only a short period of time, and thus the parking fee would be much lower. The thieves would pocket the difference between the amount paid by the customer and the amount of the fee shown on the replacement tickets. . . .

The leading participants in the scheme did not report their unlawful income on their federal income tax returns. Gricco kept his money in a safe, loaned cash to others and received repayments in the form of checks or money orders, gave cash to family members, and placed real estate under his family members' names. Through a real estate broker named Ludwig Cappozi, Gricco purchased several properties for cash. Capozzi also engaged in real estate transactions with McCardell's wife, who used cash to purchase properties under both her own and McCardell's name.

The cashiers involved in the scheme also failed to report their unlawful income on their income tax returns. They did not deposit their embezzled funds into banks for fear of being detected by the Internal Revenue Service. Gricco cautioned some cashiers not to put their money in banks, and he advised Flannery and Million to invest in real estate through Capozzi. . . .

In April 1999, a federal grand jury returned an indictment against Gricco, McCardell, Million, and Flannery for conspiracy to defraud the United States by obstructing the lawful function of the Internal Revenue Service in the collection of federal income taxes, in violation of 18 U.S.C. §371; tax evasion, in violation of 26 U.S.C. §7201; and making false federal income tax returns, in violation of 26 U.S.C. §7206(1). Prior to trial, Million and Flannery pleaded guilty and agreed to testify for the prosecution. Gricco and McCardell proceeded to trial. . . .

The jury found Gricco and McCardell guilty on all counts. . . . Gricco and McCardell appealed.

II.

The appellants contend that their convictions for conspiracy are not supported by sufficient evidence. The appellants were convicted for a so-called "Klein" conspiracy[1]—a conspiracy to defraud the United States by obstructing the lawful function of the Internal Revenue Service in assessing and collecting federal income taxes.

In order for a Klein conspiracy to exist, an agreed-upon objective must be to impede the IRS. This need not be the sole or even a major objective of the conspiracy.

1. *See* United States v. Klein, 247 F.2d 908 (2d Cir. 1957).

In addition, impeding the IRS need not be an objective that is sought as an end in itself: an intent to hide unlawful income from the IRS in order to conceal an underlying crime is enough. Moreover, in a Klein conspiracy case, as in other conspiracy prosecutions, the objectives of the conspiracy may sometimes be inferred from the conduct of the participants. In the end, however, the evidence must be sufficient to prove beyond a reasonable doubt that impeding the IRS was one of the conspiracy's objects and not merely a foreseeable consequence or collateral effect. *See* United States v. Goldberg, 105 F.3d 770, 774 (1st Cir. 1997) ("[M]ere collateral effects of jointly agreed-to activity, even if generally foreseeable, are not mechanically to be treated as an object of the conspiracy.") United States v. Adkinson, 158 F.3d 1147, 1154 (11th Cir. 1998) (The government must "prove that there was an agreement whose purpose was to impede the IRS (the conspiracy), and that each defendant knowingly participated in that conspiracy."). In determining whether the evidence is sufficient, we must of course view the proof in the light most favorable to the verdict and ask whether any rational jury could have found that the government met its burden. In this case, the government contends that the evidence is sufficient to meet this standard and relies chiefly on three categories of circumstantial proof.

First, the government relies on evidence that Gricco, McCardell, and other participants in the scheme did not report their illicit income. This evidence of parallel individual conduct has some probative value for present purposes, but it is plainly not enough by itself to show an agreed-upon objective to impede the IRS. It would not be at all surprising if all of these participants independently reached the conclusion that it would be best not to report their illicit income—either because they feared attracting investigative attention or because they simply wanted to keep the money that they would have been required to pay in taxes if the extra income had been reported. . . .

Second, the government points to evidence that Gricco and Capozzi, the real estate broker who assisted him in purchasing property, structured various financial transactions so as to avoid the filing of currency transaction reports. In addition, the government notes that on one occasion Gricco told Million never to "put any large sums of money in the bank, to be careful with that, especially anything over $10,000 because that would generate a report the bank would send to the IRS." This proof has some probative significance for present purposes because Gricco's desire to avoid the filing of currency transaction reports could have stemmed from a fear that such reports would interfere with his plan to evade the payment of taxes on the illicit income. . . .

The government's best evidence against Gricco is testimony that he told various participants not to deposit their illicit income in a bank but instead to purchase safes for their homes. These individuals testified that they followed this advice because they did not want to attract the attention of the IRS. It is likely that a person who acquires illegal cash and places that cash in a home safe, rather than a bank, will not report the cash as income on his or her tax returns. Accordingly, a rational jury could infer that Gricco knew that the participants to whom he gave this advice would, in all likelihood, not pay tax on their illicit income.

The difficult question is whether a rational jury could go further and find that Gricco not only foresaw that this would occur but actually intended for it to occur. Although the question is close, we conclude that the evidence, viewed as a whole, could persuade a rational jury to make such a finding. A rational jury could conclude that, if participants in the embezzlement scheme had reported their illicit income, this might have sparked an investigation that might have ultimately led to Gricco. Thus, not only did Gricco have strong grounds to foresee that the participants he advised would not report their illegal income, but a rational jury could conclude that he had also a reason to desire this result and that the result was something that he specifically intended. Viewing all of the evidence against Gricco together, we hold that it is sufficient to support his conspiracy conviction.

We reach the same conclusion respecting McCardell. McCardell admitted that Gricco told him to purchase a safe and that he did so. A rational jury could infer that McCardell agreed upon the objective of not reporting or paying taxes on the illicit income because to do so would have created a risk of discovery. We cannot say that the evidence against McCardell is insufficient as a matter of law.

IX.

In sum, we affirm the appellants' convictions. . . .

McKee, Circuit Judge, concurring in part and dissenting in part:

I concur with the majority in all aspects of its opinion except for my colleagues' conclusion that there was sufficient evidence to convict McCardell of a Klein conspiracy. In United States v. Alston, 77 F.3d 713 (3d Cir. 1995), we held:

> A Klein conspiracy is comprised of three elements: (1) the existence of an agreement, (2) an overt act by one of the conspirators in furtherance of the agreement's objectives, and (3) an intent on the part of the conspirators to agree, as well as to defraud the United States.

Id. at 720 n.17). Although a defendant's failure to report income can be an overt act in furtherance of a Klein conspiracy, the government must "still prove there was an *agreement* whose purpose was to impede the IRS (the conspiracy), and that each defendant knowingly participated in that conspiracy." Of course, where there is no direct evidence "of an agreement by all for each to evade his income taxes," the government can rely on circumstantial proof. . . .

McCardell argues that the government never produced any evidence that he spoke to, or agreed with, anyone about evading federal income taxes. Significantly, the government appears to concede that point. Its recitation of the evidence that McCardell was a Klein conspirator amounts to the following: (1) he told Million that he was concerned about alerting the IRS by exchanging large quantities of old $100 bills for new ones at a bank; (2) he did not report the stolen money on his federal tax returns; (3) he deposited small sums of cash to avoid generating a currency transaction report ("CTR"); (4) he purchased real estate; (5) he used Capozzi to purchase real estate and to launder the stolen money; and (6) he purchased a safe at Gricco's direction.

I agree that the evidence is sufficient to allow a rational jury to conclude that McCardell did all of these things to avoid paying taxes, and to avoid detection; and not just to hide the proceeds of the theft. However, as noted, a Klein conspiracy requires more. That crime is not established if the evidence implies only separate purposes to evade taxes. On the contrary, the evidence must "support an inference that each alleged tax evader . . . knew of the others' tax evasion" and "that they agreed to do so." I do not believe that a jury could reasonably conclude that this evidence proves that McCardell knew of anyone else's tax evasion, much less that he agreed with anyone else to evade the payment of income taxes. . . .

Accordingly, I respectfully dissent from the majority's decision insofar as it affirms McCardell's conviction for a Klein conspiracy.

UNITED STATES v. LICCIARDI

30 F.3d 1127 (9th Cir. 1994)

NOONAN, Circuit Judge:

Michael Licciardi appeals his conviction under 18 U.S.C. §371 of conspiracy to defraud the United States by obstructing the functions of the Bureau of Alcohol, Tobacco and Firearms (the BATF); of two convictions under 18 U.S.C. §1341 of mail fraud; and of his conviction under 18 U.S.C. §1001 of making a false statement. This case involves an effort of the government to extend substantially the scope of the general conspiracy statute. Despite disagreeing with one major theory of the government, we affirm Licciardi's conviction for conspiracy and his conviction on the other counts. . . .

Licciardi was charged with a conspiracy [lasting from January 1987 to April 1989] whose "object" was to "defraud the United States and its agency, the BATF, by obstructing, impairing and defeating the lawful function of the BATF to assure the integrity and varietal designations of wine through examination and analysis of records maintained honestly and accurately and free from deceit, trickery, fraud and dishonesty, in violation of Title 18 U.S.C. §371."

In Subsection b of the same count the "object of the conspiracy" was said to be the use of the mails to obtain money from Delicato Vineyards (Delicato) and other wine producers by fraud in violation of 18 U.S.C. §§1341 and 2 and to conduct financial transactions involving the concealment of the proceeds of unlawful activity in violation of 18 U.S.C. §1956(a)(1).

In addition to this section of the indictment entitled "Object of the Conspiracy" was a section called "Purpose of the Conspiracy," which stated: "The purpose of the conspiracy was to obtain a higher price for defendant's grapes than those grapes would otherwise have commanded in the market place by misrepresenting the variety and appellation of origin of grapes being sold. . . ."

At the trial Licciardi was found guilty of conspiracy under Count 1. . . . The district court denied his motion for a new trial [and] sentenced him to 51 months' imprisonment.

Facts

As the government prevailed at trial we take the facts established by testimony from the government's point of view:

Licciardi was a partner with his father in a grape brokerage business, Corvette Company (Corvette). Corvette bought grapes from the growers and sold them, almost exclusively, to Delicato; almost 90 percent of Delicato's purchases from brokers was from Corvette. During the crush in the fall of the year, Licciardi had 24-hour access to Delicato, including the areas where the grapes were received, weighed and dumped into the crushers. During this period Licciardi occupied an office at Delicato's from which he scheduled and supervised deliveries of grapes from Corvette. His position gave him the opportunity for the deceitful transactions set out here.

During the mid-80s there was a rise in the price of Zinfandel grapes, and between 1985-1988 the price rose from $100 per ton to $900 per ton. At the same time the price of similar-looking grapes such as Mission, Grenache, Barbera, and Valdepenas remained constant at approximately $150-200 per ton.

In 1987, before the harvest, Licciardi agreed with Nick Bavaro, a wine grower, for Bavaro to deliver grapes to Delicato without field tags. A field tag is a document prepared in the field at the time the grapes are harvested. It contains the name and address of the grape grower, the grape variety, the date, the name of the trucking company providing the grapes and the license number of the trucks. The field tag is taken to the winery by the truck driver with the load of grapes. The winery then uses the information on the field tags to prepare the California Department of Food and Agriculture Weighmaster Certificate. The winery uses the field tag and the certificate to file reports required by the BATF.

Bavaro and Licciardi arranged for grapes to be delivered at hours when the state inspector was not present. Deliveries were, for example, at two, three or four a.m. In 1987, according to Bavaro, he delivered between 1,400 and 1,500 tons of Carignane, Grenache and Valdepena grapes selling at approximately $150-175 per ton. They were represented to Delicato as Zinfandel grapes selling at $500 a ton. The difference in price between what was actually sold and what was charged was $420,000. In 1988, according to Bavaro, he delivered about 225 tons of Grenache or Riesling grapes selling at $175-$200 per ton, represented as Zinfandel grapes worth $1,000 a ton.

In addition to his deal with Bavaro, Licciardi in 1987 entered into an agreement with Gary Alfieri by which Licciardi would arrange to mix Valdepenas grapes with Zinfandel grapes coming from Alfieri's mother's property. . . .

Mens Rea

On appeal, Licciardi argues that there was no evidence that he had an intention to defraud the United States. It is true that the general conspiracy statute has been given a very broad meaning so that "defraud" extends beyond its common law usage and includes interference [with] or obstruction of a lawful governmental function "by deceit, craft or treachery or at least by means that are dishonest." Hammerschmidt v. United States, 265 U.S. 182, 188 (1923). If all the government had to prove was that Licciardi had used dishonest means and that these means had the effect of impairing a function of the BATF, the government would easily have prevailed. Under 27 U.S.C. §205(e) it is unlawful for a winery to sell in interstate commerce wine unless it is packaged in conformity with regulations prescribed by the Treasury with respect to labeling which will provide the consumer "with adequate information as to the identity and quality of the product." The Treasury has prescribed such regulations in 27 C.F.R. §§4.20 & 20. The BATF has the function of enforcing these standards. 27 C.F.R. §1. Licciardi's dishonest methods would have had the effect of preventing Delicato from complying with the regulations and would have therefore prevented the BATF from enforcing the regulations.

The difficulty for the government is Licciardi's *mens rea* for commission of the federal crime. *Mens rea* is, of course, a fundamental requirement of our criminal jurisprudence. In the case of a charge of conspiracy to violate [a] federal statute the government "must prove at least the degree of criminal intent necessary for the substantive offense itself." United States v. Feola, 420 U.S. 671, 686 (1975). This requirement has been the rule for at least a century.

Much of the reason for insisting on *mens rea* is to prevent "ostensibly innocuous conduct" from unwittingly becoming criminal. *See* Staples v. United States, 114 S. Ct. 1793 (1994). It will be observed that Licciardi was far from innocent morally or in terms of the law of California. But the question is whether he was innocent of any design to commit a federal crime. On this point evidence was required. . . .

[R]ecently the United States indicted and convicted two businessmen of defrauding the United States in violation of 18 U.S.C. §371 for their fraud on Seminole Electric Cooperative, Inc. in connection with a Seminole project guaranteed by the Rural Electrification Administration (REA). The theory of the government was that the fraud on Seminole impaired the lawful functions of the REA in running its guarantee loan program and that consequently the United States was defrauded. Undoubtedly, the REA's functions were impeded. Undoubtedly also, the conspiracy statute covers conspiracies to defraud the United States in "any manner for any purpose," putting no limits as to the methods used to defraud the United States. Tanner v. United States, 483 U.S. 107, 129 (1987). But the Supreme Court held that a conspiracy criminalized by § 371 is "most importantly" defined by the "*target* of the conspiracy." *Id.* at 130 (emphasis in original). The government's theory, the Court unanimously held, had "not even an arguable basis in the plain language of §371." *Id.* at 131. Consequently, the Court held that the government had failed to prove its case.

By the same standard, the Court in *Tanner* held that the conspiracy conviction could be upheld if, on remand, the court of appeals found that there was sufficient evidence to establish that the defendants had conspired to cause Seminole to make misrepresentations to the REA. In that event the defendants would have had the requisite *mens rea* of defrauding the United States, using an intermediary to accomplish their fraud.

Under this consistent construction for a century of §371, the government has failed to prove its case against Licciardi for conspiracy to defraud the United States by impairing the functions of the BATF. That the incidental effects of Licciardi's actions would have been to impair the functions of the BATF does not confer upon him the *mens rea* of accomplishing that object.

It might have been easy for the government to establish that Licciardi was familiar with the federal regulations on the labelling of wine and that it was a necessary part of his plan of deceit that Delicato provide information to the government that would frustrate these regulations. But we cannot speculate as to what the government might have proved when it did not make the effort to show that Licciardi had "conspired to cause" Delicato to provide false information to the BATF. Because this kind of proof was not offered, the basis suggested in *Tanner* for upholding the conviction of the Seminole defendants is lacking. . . .

The government has a second string to its bow. . . . If there is sufficient evidence of a second object of the charged conspiracy, we cannot set aside the jury verdict. The government says nothing on this appeal about the charged objective of Licciardi conducting financial transactions to conceal unlawful activities. The government does, however, refer to the charged objective of the conspiracy to obtain money from Delicato by fraudulent representations in violation of 18 U.S.C. §§1341 & -2. The government points to the mail fraud counts on which Licciardi was convicted.

In 1987, the first year of the conspiracy, Licciardi arranged with Alfieri for the establishment of a post office box in the name of a fictitious company, intending to use the mails to keep his fraud secret. In 1988, a check representing the proceeds of one of the fraudulent transactions was sent through the mails to this post office box and at Licciardi's direction recovered from this box. These facts established that Licciardi had the requisite *mens rea* to commit mail fraud. His conviction of conspiracy must be sustained. . . .

Accordingly, the judgments of convictions are AFFIRMED. The case is REMANDED for resentencing in accordance with this opinion.

FLETCHER, J. . . .

I concur in Judge Noonan's opinion except as I express my disagreements below. . . .

II

I disagree with the majority's conclusion that "the absence of mens rea" requires reversal of the conspiracy conviction under the first of the government's two conspiracy theories.

To understand my point, it is important to keep in mind that 18 U.S.C. §371 consists of both an "offense" clause and a "defraud" clause: it criminalizes both conspiracies "to commit any offense against the United States" and conspiracies "to defraud the United States or any agency thereof." The offense clause is premised on a conspiracy to commit a predicate act that violates a statute other than the conspiracy statute; the defraud clause involves a violation of the conspiracy statute itself. Count 1 included a charge under both clauses. Judge Noonan would affirm the conspiracy conviction under the offense clause, on the basis that Licciardi conspired to commit mail fraud; a conviction under the defraud clause, according to the majority, cannot stand. My focus is on the charge under the defraud clause. . . .

The Supreme Court case which addresses conspiracy charges brought under the defraud clause is Tanner v. United States, 483 U.S. 107 (1987). I disagree with the majority's reading of that case. The majority emphasizes *Tanner*'s statement that a conspiracy criminalized by §371 is "most importantly" defined by the "target of the conspiracy." The majority derives from the latter phrase the conclusion that a person whose conspiratorial acts have the effect of defrauding the federal government escapes §371 liability unless he knew that his acts would have the effect of defrauding the government. In fact, however, the Supreme Court's disposition in *Tanner* indicates just the opposite.

In *Tanner*, the prosecution tried to link the defendants' deceptive acts to an effect on the federal government in two distinct ways. The Court rejected the first way, but accepted the second. The government's first argument, which the Court disposed of in that part of the opinion on which the majority relies, was that a fraud on a private corporation which receives government funding *is* a fraud on the government. In dismissing that argument, the Court pointed out that such a "sweeping interpretation of §371 . . . would [i]n effect substitut[e] 'anyone receiving federal assistance and supervision' for the phrase 'the United States or any agency thereof.'" 483 U.S. at 132.

The prosecution's second argument was encapsulated in the language of the indictment, which the *Tanner* Court quoted:

> "It was further a part of the conspiracy that the defendants would and did cause [a third person] to falsely state and represent to the [government] that a [government]-approved competitive bidding procedure had been followed. . . ."

483 U.S. at 132. The Court *accepted* this method of connecting the conspiracy to the defrauding of the government, and remanded the case to the Eleventh Circuit for a determination of whether "the evidence presented at trial was sufficient to establish that petitioners conspired to cause [the third person] to make misrepresentations to [the government]."

The evidence in this case was sufficient to establish just such a conspiracy. There is no question but that Licciardi conspired with Bavaro, Alfieri and others to provide false field tags, and that Delicato passed these on to the BATF in compliance with its reporting obligations. This linkage between the conspiracy and the government—in which the defendant directly manipulated a third person and caused that person to *make a false statement to the government*—appears to be precisely what the *Tanner* Court held *would* be sufficient to uphold a §371 conviction. And it is entirely distinct from the linkage which was rejected by *Tanner*—where the fraud perpetrated on a private person may have some impact on the government simply because the government has a fiscal relationship with the private person. . . .

Because the conviction can be affirmed on the basis of a conspiracy under the defraud clause, I would not reach the question of whether a conviction based on conspiracy to violate the mail fraud statute could be affirmed in this case. I am not suggesting that it cannot be affirmed on that basis, but I am uncomfortable relying on a theory eschewed by the government.

[Dissent by Reinhardt, J. omitted.]

NOTES AND QUESTIONS

1. What *is* the mens rea requirement of conspiracy? The *Licciardi* court quotes the *Feola* case for the proposition that "in the case of a charge of conspiracy to violate [a] federal statute the government 'must prove at least the degree of criminal intent necessary for the substantive offense itself.'" A classic California case, People v. Lauria, 251 Cal. App. 2d 471 (1967), determined that the mens rea necessary to commit the crime of conspiracy is twofold: First, it is knowledge of the illegal activity (or the plan to commit it) and, second, it is the intent (the Model Penal Code would say "purpose") to further that activity. (This is sometimes referred to as the "knowing participation" requirement.) After reading *Licciardi* and *Gricco*, which of these definitions is correct? Or could it be that they are both correct, i.e., that conspiracy has a dual mens rea requirement? *See* WAYNE R. LAFAVE, CRIMINAL LAW §12.2 (c) (4th ed. 2003). This may be why courts so often have difficulty articulating and applying conspiracy's mens rea requirement. *See id.*
2. In his concurrence in *Licciardi*, Judge Fletcher states that the case can be saved by interpreting the government's evidence as Licciardi agreeing with others to *cause* Delicato to defraud the BATF. Can a case be properly upheld on appeal on a theory never charged in the indictment and never argued to the jury?
3. Does the *Licciardi* court make a mountain out of a molehill? Given all of the facts of the case—Licciardi's experience in the business; the care he took in making sure the tags were removed from the grapes; his sneaking the grapes in during the dead of the night—wasn't it reasonable for the jury to infer that one of his objects was to impede BATF? If BATF's regulatory function had not been impeded, could Licciardi have carried out his plan for very long?
4. Can an individual aid and abet a crime without being a co-conspirator? Consider this hypothetical. Arthur, an accountant at a Fortune 500 Company, is asked by his boss to generate a "more positive" accounts receivable report. Arthur provides the false report solely to keep his job. He has no discussion with his boss about the uses to which the false report will be put in the future, though he knows it will form part of the company's accounting statement that will eventually be provided to the SEC. Assuming the false report is so used, has Arthur aided and abetted the crime of presenting false information to the SEC under 15 U.S.C. §78ff? Has he conspired to do so?
5. Can an individual conspire to commit a crime without aiding and abetting it?

IV. SINGLE VERSUS MULTIPLE CONSPIRACIES

UNITED STATES v. BERGER
224 F.3d 107 (2d Cir. 2000)

JOHN M. WALKER, Jr., Circuit Judge:

Defendants-appellants Kalmen Stern ("Stern"), David Goldstein ("Goldstein"), Jacob Elbaum ("Elbaum"), and Benjamin Berger ("Berger") appeal from the November 1999 judgments of conviction entered and sentences imposed by the district court upon jury verdicts of guilty. They raise a number of issues on appeal. First, and most importantly, the appellants allege that they were improperly convicted of the fraud conspiracy charged in the indictment because the evidence showed multiple conspiracies rather than a single conspiracy and this variance was substantially prejudicial. . . .

Background

The . . . appellants . . . [were charged in a redacted indictment] with conspiracy and substantive counts [including embezzlement, mail fraud, wire fraud, false statements, money laundering, filing a false tax return, and failing to file a tax return] based upon their participation in a massive conspiracy to defraud the Department of Education ("DOE"), the Department of Housing and Urban Development ("HUD"), the Small Business Administration ("SBA"), the Social Security Administration ("SSA"), and the Internal Revenue Service ("IRS"). . . .

The evidence at trial, taken in the light most favorable to the government following the jury verdict in its favor, revealed that the appellants—most of whom resided in New Square, a Hasidic Jewish community in Rockland County, New York—participated in a massive conspiracy to obtain by fraud millions of dollars in student financial aid, rental subsidies, social security benefits, and small business loans. All four appellants participated in a fraud upon the DOE, which formed the centerpiece of the government's case, but the government also proved that the conspirators or subsets of them victimized other agencies as well. They also concealed their income to increase the amounts they could obtain under federal subsidy programs and reduce their tax liability. The conspiracy involved a number of other participants, including major figures in the New Square Hasidic community. We now examine the scheme in greater detail.

First, the conspirators defrauded the DOE's Pell Grant Program by falsely enrolling thousands of New Square residents and others in schools offering mentor-based independent study programs. Many students never actually studied at these institutions, even though the conspirators prepared a paper record of their academic progress. Ultimately, most of the false students were enrolled at Toldos Yakov Yosef Seminary ("TYY"), an institution that purported to employ all four appellants and received over $11 million in Pell Grants but never existed except on paper. As part of the conspiracy, the conspirators made extensive efforts to deceive the

Accrediting Council for Continuing Education and Training ("ACCET") in order to gain accreditation for TYY so that the school could qualify for federal aid. . . .

Second, the conspirators defrauded HUD's Section 8 housing subsidy program. Elbaum and Stern failed to report to HUD payments they received from accounts controlled by Chaim Berger, thus fraudulently increasing the amount of Section 8 subsidies for which they could qualify as tenants. Benjamin Berger fraudulently obtained Section 8 rent payments as a landlord by disguising his ownership of property in New Square—placing it in Cheindel Bernat's name—and then depositing checks from HUD in an account he controlled in Bernat's name. In addition, Berger obtained greater subsidies as a Section 8 tenant in Spring Valley by failing to report the income he received as a shadow landlord.

Third, various conspirators, including Goldstein and Stern, participated in schemes to defraud the SSA and the SBA, the details of which are not relevant to this appeal. . . .

On January 25, 1999, after a two-and-a-half month trial, the jury returned verdicts of guilty against all the appellants on all counts. In November 1999, the district court sentenced the appellants to prison terms ranging from 30 to 78 months and ordered them to pay restitution ranging from about $500,000 to over $10 million. This appeal followed.

Discussion

I. The Conspiracy Charge

The appellants contend that: (1) the jury was erroneously instructed on the conspiracy charge; (2) the evidence proved multiple conspiracies rather than the single conspiracy charged; and (3) the variance was prejudicial and requires reversal. We conclude that the appellants were properly convicted of the single conspiracy charged in the redacted indictment.

First, the jury was properly instructed on the issue of single versus multiple conspiracies. In the basic charge, the district court fully covered the issue. When, during its deliberations, the jury requested a more detailed explanation of these issues, the court responded with the following supplemental instruction, which the appellants challenge here:

> First, you should consider whether the conspiracy charged in Count 1 existed. In doing so, you must consider whether two or more conspirators agreed to accomplish at least one of the illegal objects of the conspiracy. If you determine that two or more conspirators agreed to accomplish one of the illegal objects, then you may find that the conspiracy charged in Count 1 existed. If you determine that two or more conspirators agreed to accomplish more than one object of the conspiracy, then you must consider whether single or multiple conspiracies exist.
>
> * * *
>
> In order to prove a single conspiracy, the Government must prove that each alleged member agreed to participate in what he knew to be a collective venture directed toward a common goal. Even if the evidence shows that more than one conspiracy exists, you may still find that the conspiracy charged in Count 1 exists

> if it happens to be one of those conspiracies. But if you find the evidence proves that separate conspiracies exist, you must acquit unless you find unanimously and beyond a reasonable doubt that one of those conspiracies is the single conspiracy charged in Count 1.

The appellants claim that this instruction was erroneous because it: (1) essentially directed the jury to find that the single conspiracy charged in Count 1 existed as long as "two or more conspirators agreed to accomplish at least one of the illegal objects of the conspiracy"; and (2) failed to instruct the jury to acquit if it found multiple conspiracies. Given the jury's apparent difficulty distinguishing single from multiple conspiracies, the appellants argue, this instruction made it too easy for the jurors to find the single conspiracy charged in the indictment. We disagree.

The supplemental instruction was neither erroneous nor prejudicial. The district court was correct as a matter of law to charge that the government needed only to prove agreement on one of the objectives charged in the indictment in order to establish that a conspiracy existed. Of course, in order to obtain a conviction, the government also had to show that each defendant knowingly participated in a scheme to achieve this particular goal, but the district court made this clear in both its original and supplemental instructions.

The appellants stress that agreement on a single objective is insufficient where multiple conspiracies might exist, as here, but the district court adequately advised the jury of this possibility as well. The language of the instruction indicated that the jurors could, but were not required to, find that the single conspiracy charged in Count 1 existed if they found an agreement to accomplish one of the alleged criminal objectives. The district court instructed that if the jury found "that two or more conspirators agreed to accomplish more than one object of the conspiracy," then it must consider whether "single or multiple conspiracies exist," evaluating whether "each alleged member agreed to participate in what he knew to be a collective venture directed toward a common goal." In this way, the court focused the jury's attention on the need to consider the possibility of multiple conspiracies. The jurors could not reasonably have been left with the impression that a simple finding of agreement on a single objective was enough to find a single conspiracy if they found agreement to accomplish other objectives as well.

The district court further instructed the jurors that, if they found multiple conspiracies, they had to acquit the defendants unless they found "unanimously and beyond a reasonable doubt that one of those conspiracies is the single conspiracy charged in Count 1." This was correct as a matter of law, notwithstanding the appellants' argument to the contrary. Acquittal is not automatically required if the jury finds multiple conspiracies because the jury can plausibly decide that one of those conspiracies is the single conspiracy charged in the indictment, as the court instructed here. Therefore, a charge should not instruct that a jury must acquit whenever it finds multiple conspiracies; acquittal is required only if the jury finds that the charged conspiracy is not one of the conspiracies that has been proved. What the charge should stress is "'that there must be [a] finding of the single conspiracy charged and individual knowing participation by each individual in it.'" The original and supplemental charges in this case adequately emphasize these points. Accordingly, the district court did not err in declining to instruct the jury simply to acquit if it found multiple conspiracies. . . .

Second, . . . [w]e believe that the evidence, taken in the light most favorable to the government, supports the jury's finding of a single conspiracy: (1) all the schemes served the same overriding goal of underwriting the needs of New Square's community institutions; (2) the schemes were led by the same core group of community leaders, including Chaim Berger and several unindicted co-conspirators; (3) the schemes shared common participants, including the appellants; (4) the frauds were mutually interdependent (e.g., fraudulent documents from one scheme supported the frauds against other agencies); and (5) the conspirators used the same distinctive methods and means in their different frauds. These means and methods included the creation of sham organizations, the submission of fraudulent documentation to establish the eligibility of New Square residents and others to participate in public funding programs, the opening of special bank accounts to collect and conceal fraudulently obtained funds, and the use of nominee names, aliases, and religious organizations to conceal income. . . .

Accordingly, we affirm the district court's judgments against all four appellants in every respect.

NOTES AND QUESTIONS

1. The terminology surrounding the problem of charging and proving one or more conspiracies can be confusing. *Berger* addresses the question whether the prosecution charged one conspiracy when the evidence showed multiple, different, conspiracies. This is the problem of "duplictity." The opposite problem is when an indictment is "multiplicitous," meaning that the prosecutor has taken one conspiracy and improperly broken it up into separate conspiracy counts. Because a complex white collar conspiracy is almost always fluid over time in terms of the individuals involved, the methods employed, and the objectives sought, sorting out the multiplicity versus duplicity issues can be a daunting task. Doing so correctly is critical, however, not only because the charges must ultimately match the evidence, but also because the existence of multiple conspiracies will impact the issues of co-conspirator statements, joinder, and venue, at the very least.
2. If the prosecution in *Berger* had decided to charge multiple conspiracies—one, say, to defraud DOE, another to defraud HUD, and a third to defraud the IRS—would the indictment have been multiplicitous? Could it be reasonable for different observers to infer a single agreement or multiple agreements based on the same set of facts?
3. Note that the conspiracy count described in *Berger* is often referred to as a "multiple object conspiracy." If the evidence shows a single overarching agreement to commit multiple crimes, a multiple object conspiracy charge

is warranted. The jury is instructed that it must find unanimously that the defendants agreed to at least one of these object before it can return a guilty verdict on the conspiracy charge, *provided that* the object is the same for all of the guilty defendants.

4. Sometimes complex conspiracy counts are identified as "wheel" or "chain" conspiracies. Wheel conspiracies involve a central hub figure, whose associates are the spokes who know that they are working for the hub. In a chain conspiracy, on the other hand, several links lead linearly from a source, and although each link may not be aware of the entire chain, the links eventually lead back to the source. The seminal case on point is Kotteakos v. United States, 328 U.S. 750 (1946). Although the metaphors can be helpful in analyzing conspiracies for issues such as multiplicity, they do not change the fundamental requirement that a single conspiracy is measured by whether the various individuals agreed to accomplish a common illegal goal. They need not all interact nor know each other; on the other hand, they must form a common enterprise, not separate enterprises linked by a few common players. For an excellent discussion of these issues, see United States v. Perez, 489 F.2d 51 (1973) (holding that participants in various aspects of a widescale and ongoing insurance fraud scheme featuring multiple faked collisions were members of a single conspiracy); *see also* United States v. Glinton, 154 F.3d 1245 (11th Cir. 1998) (holding that participants in a drug conspiracy linked only by the fact that they had the same supplier were not members of a single conspiracy).
5. A defendant can be charged with conspiracy to defraud the United States and conspiracy to commit a crime based on the same agreement. *See Licciardi, supra.* But can a defendant be sentenced separately on each count? Similarly, can he be tried in succession for each alleged violation? There is a split in the circuits on this point. *Compare* United States v. Rigas, 584 F.3d 594 (3d Cir. 2010) (en banc) (holding that double jeopardy prohibits successive prosecutions and multiple punishments), *with* United States v. Ervasti, 201 F.3d 1029 (8th Cir. 2000) (opposite).

V. TERMINATION AND WITHDRAWAL

UNITED STATES v. HUGHES

191 F.3d 1317 (10th Cir. 1999), cert. denied, 537 U.S. 985 (2000)

MAGILL, Circuit Judge.

T. Robert Hughes and a business trust managed by Hughes appeal from their convictions on one count of conspiracy to defraud the government. On appeal, Hughes argues that the evidence at trial showed that both defendants withdrew from the conspiracy, and thus that their prosecution was barred by the statute of limitations. . . . We affirm.

I.

A. Conspiracy

Hughes, an attorney, was a longtime business associate of the late Thomas Rhoades. In February 1988 Rhoades and his business associate, Stephen Schluneger, furnished payment and performance bonds for a government contract entered into by Frank Minelli (Minelli contract) with the United States Army Corps of Engineers (Corps) for sandblasting and painting various locks and dams along the Arkansas River. As sureties, Rhoades and Schluneger were liable on the contract if Minelli defaulted.

Minelli did default, and the Corps demanded that Rhoades and Schluneger satisfy their obligations under the bonds. At the time of default, the amount remaining on the Minelli contract was approximately $1.69 million. Rhoades accepted a bid from Skyline Painting Inc. (Skyline) to complete the work for $1.2 million.

After accepting Skyline's bid, Rhoades and Schluneger informed the Corps that they wished to sign a Takeover Agreement. . . . The Takeover Agreement provided that Rhoades and Schluneger were not to be compensated for "any amount in excess of [their] total expenditures necessarily made in completing the work and discharging" their liability under the performance bond. Hughes reviewed a preliminary draft of the Takeover Agreement, and Rhoades and Schluneger eventually signed it on August 14, 1989.

After receiving the Skyline bid but before signing the Takeover Agreement, Rhoades and Schluneger entered into a series of other agreements, all prepared by Hughes and not disclosed to the Corps, which had the intent and effect of billing the government for more than Rhoades and Schluneger's actual costs and expenses. Essentially, their plan was to recover the difference remaining on the Minelli contract over and above the price of the Skyline bid.

The plan worked in the following manner. Rhoades and Schluneger initially had Skyline sign a subcontract which stated that Skyline would complete the work for $1.69 million. Skyline understood, however, that it was to receive only $1.2 million, and that the $490,000 difference was to be paid over time to Rhoades and Schluneger as finder's fees and engineering consulting fees. These "fees," however, were for work which was never done and were merely the device by which Rhoades and Schluneger were to obtain the money.

Under the subcontract with Skyline, Skyline included these sham fees in the progress reports it prepared and submitted to the Corps. Rhoades would receive the payments and make disbursements to Skyline. Skyline, pursuant to a second agreement prepared by Hughes, would pay a percentage of those payments to ARCO Business Services, Ltd. (ARCO Business Services), one of Hughes's business trusts. ARCO Business Services would then distribute funds to ARCO Properties, Ltd. (ARCO Properties), another Hughes business trust. ARCO Properties, pursuant to a third agreement prepared by Hughes, would distribute funds to Rhoades. Rhoades distributed part of the kickbacks to his wife and to Schluneger. Although Hughes did not receive any portion of the kickbacks directly, Rhoades agreed to discharge a debt Hughes owed him as compensation for his efforts in creating the scheme.

This scheme continued over the next three years. At some point, Skyline began experiencing financial problems and abandoned the project. On June 27, 1992, after Skyline abandoned the project, ARCO Business Services sent a letter to Rhoades. The letter was prepared and signed by Hughes as Trustee for ARCO Business Services. It stated that since Skyline had stopped work on the project, the contract was "in effect null and void. . . . ARCO does not intend to be involved in any legal process under such conditions and as of today does not intend to seek or claim further benefit of any kind." The letter further stated, "Thank you for your many efforts in this enterprise and *please convey ARCO's current position* and its appreciation for the various endeavors undertaken to all of the other concerned/involved parties . . . (emphasis added)."

The scheme was discovered when Schluneger and Rhoades subsequently defaulted on the contract. The jury convicted Rhoades, Schluneger, Hughes, ARCO Business Services, and ARCO Properties each on one count of conspiracy to defraud the government. By special verdict, the jury found that ARCO Business Services withdrew from the conspiracy in June 1992. The jury found that neither Hughes nor ARCO Properties withdrew from the conspiracy. Hughes and ARCO Properties moved for a judgment of acquittal or a new trial. The district court denied the motion. Hughes was subsequently sentenced to twenty-four months' imprisonment and three years' supervised release, and was ordered to pay $236,158 in restitution.

II.

A.

Hughes . . . argues that because the jury in this case found that ARCO Business Services withdrew from the conspiracy, no rational jury could have failed to find that found that both he and ARCO Properties also withdrew. Thus, he argues, the district court erred in denying his and ARCO Properties's motion for a new trial or a judgment of acquittal. We review the denial of a judgment of acquittal de novo and the denial of motion for a new trial for an abuse of discretion. In reviewing these motions, we view the evidence in the light most favorable to the government.

"In order to withdraw from a conspiracy an individual must take affirmative action, either by reporting to the authorities or by communicating his intentions to his coconspirators. Mere cessation of one's participation in a conspiracy is insufficient to demonstrate withdrawal. Since neither Hughes nor ARCO Properties disclosed the conspiracy to the authorities, Hughes and ARCO Properties can demonstrate withdrawal only if each took affirmative steps to communicate an intent to withdraw to the coconspirators.

The only evidence of withdrawal by any party in this case is the June 1992 letter from ARCO Business Services. This letter, on ARCO Business Services letterhead, was from "ARCO BUSINESS SERVICES, LTD." and signed by Hughes as trustee. This letter does not establish an affirmative act of withdrawal by ARCO Properties, and there is no other evidence of an intent to withdraw by ARCO Properties.

Nor does the letter establish an affirmative act of withdrawal by Hughes. The letter was signed by Hughes in his capacity as trustee, not individually. The letter stated that ARCO "does not intend to seek or claim further benefit of any kind," asks to whom "ARCO should send any notice of its position," and requests that Rhoades "convey ARCO's current position . . . to all of the other concerned/involved parties. . . ." The letter does not refer at all to Hughes individually or to his continued involvement in the Skyline project. The fact that the jury found that Hughes's company, ARCO [Business Services], withdrew does not dictate a finding that Hughes as trustee also withdrew. . . .

We conclude, therefore, that the district court did not err in denying Hughes and ARCO Properties's motion for a new trial or judgment of acquittal. . . .

IV.

For the foregoing reasons, we AFFIRM the decision of the district court.

NOTES AND QUESTIONS

1. Generally speaking, to be effective, a conspirator's decision to withdraw must be clearly communicated to all of his co-conspirators. With this in mind, was the wording of ARCO Business Services' letter to Skyline—drafted by attorney Hughes—a matter of chance?
2. Why didn't Hughes write a similar letter personally and on behalf of ARCO Properties?
3. In the white collar context, it is not unusual for an individual participating in criminal activity within a company—i.e., a co-conspirator—to resign his position to take a new job with another firm for reasons completely unrelated to the criminal enterprise. His resignation letter, of course, will make no specific mention of the conspiracy, but it will affirmatively sever his ties with his criminal compatriots. Is such a letter sufficient to be prima facie evidence of withdrawal? At least one court has answered this question in the affirmative. *See* United States v. Steele, 685 F.2d 793 (3d Cir.), *cert denied*, 459 U.S. 908 (1982).

UNITED STATES v. RECIO
537 U.S. 270 (2003)

Justice Breyer delivered the opinion of the Court.

We here consider the validity of a Ninth Circuit rule that a conspiracy ends automatically when the object of the conspiracy becomes impossible to achieve—when, for example, the Government frustrates a drug conspiracy's objective by seizing the drugs that its members have agreed to distribute. In our view, conspiracy law does not contain any such "automatic termination" rule.

I

In United States v. Cruz, 127 F.3d 791, 795 (9th Cir. 1997), the Ninth Circuit . . . wrote that a conspiracy terminates when "'there is affirmative evidence of abandonment, withdrawal, disavowal *or defeat of the object of the conspiracy*'" (emphasis added). It considered the conviction of an individual who, the Government had charged, joined a conspiracy (to distribute drugs) after the Government had seized the drugs in question. The Circuit found that the Government's seizure of the drugs guaranteed the "defeat" of the conspiracy's objective, namely, drug distribution. The Circuit held that the conspiracy had terminated with that "defeat," *i.e.*, when the Government seized the drugs. Hence the individual, who had joined the conspiracy after that point, could not be convicted as a conspiracy member.

In this case the lower courts applied the *Cruz* rule to similar facts: On November 18, 1997, police stopped a truck in Nevada. They found, and seized, a large stash of illegal drugs. With the help of the truck's two drivers, they set up a sting. The Government took the truck to the drivers' destination, a mall in Idaho. The drivers paged a contact and described the truck's location. The contact said that he would call someone to get the truck. And three hours later, the two defendants, Francisco Jimenez Recio and Adrian Lopez-Meza, appeared in a car. Jimenez Recio drove away in the truck; Lopez-Meza drove the car away in a similar direction. Police stopped both vehicles and arrested both men.

A federal grand jury indicted Jimenez Recio, Lopez-Meza, and the two original truck drivers, charging them with having conspired, together and with others, to possess and to distribute unlawful drugs. A jury convicted all four. . . .

Jimenez Recio and Lopez-Meza appealed. They pointed out that, given *Cruz*, the jury had to find that they had joined the conspiracy before the Nevada stop, and they claimed that the evidence was insufficient at both trials to warrant any such jury finding. The Ninth Circuit panel, by a vote of 2 to 1, agreed. . . .

The Government sought certiorari. . . .

II

In *Cruz*, the Ninth Circuit held that a conspiracy continues "'until there is affirmative evidence of abandonment, withdrawal, disavowal or defeat of the object of the conspiracy.'" The critical portion of this statement is the last segment, that a conspiracy ends once there has been "'defeat of [its] object.'" The Circuit's holdings make clear that the phrase means that the conspiracy ends through "defeat" when the Government intervenes, making the conspiracy's goals impossible to achieve, even if the conspirators do not know that the Government has intervened and are totally unaware that the conspiracy is bound to fail. In our view, this statement of the law is incorrect. A conspiracy does not automatically terminate simply because the Government, unbeknownst to some of the conspirators, has "defeated" the conspiracy's "object."

Two basic considerations convince us that this is the proper view of the law. First, the Ninth Circuit's rule is inconsistent with our own understanding of basic conspiracy law. . . . Where police have frustrated a conspiracy's specific objective but conspirators (unaware of that fact) have neither abandoned the conspiracy nor withdrawn, [all of the] special conspiracy-related dangers remain. So too remains the essence of the conspiracy—the agreement to commit the crime. That being so, the Government's defeat of the conspiracy's objective will not necessarily and automatically terminate the conspiracy.

Second, the view we endorse today is the view of almost all courts and commentators but for the Ninth Circuit. No other Federal Court of Appeals has adopted the Ninth Circuit's rule. Three have explicitly rejected it. . . .

In tracing the origins of the statement of conspiracy law upon which the *Cruz* panel relied, we have found a 1982 Ninth Circuit case, United States v. Bloch, 696 F.2d 1213 (9th Cir. 1982), in which the court, referring to an earlier case, United States v. Krasn, 614 F.2d 1229 (9th Cir. 1980), changed the language of the traditional conspiracy termination rule. *Krasn* said that a conspiracy is "'presumed to continue unless there is affirmative evidence that *the defendant* abandoned, withdrew from, or disavowed the conspiracy *or defeated its purpose*'" (emphasis added). The *Bloch* panel changed the grammatical structure. It said that "a conspiracy is presumed to continue until *there is* . . . defeat of the purposes of the conspiracy" (emphasis added). Later Ninth Circuit cases apparently read the change to mean that a conspiracy terminates, not only when the *defendant* defeats its objective, but also when *someone else* defeats that objective, perhaps the police. . . . But, since the Circuit's earlier cases nowhere give any reason for the critical change of language, they cannot help to justify it.

III

We conclude that the Ninth Circuit's conspiracy-termination law holding set forth in *Cruz* is erroneous in the manner discussed. We reverse the present judgment insofar as it relies upon that holding. Because Jimenez Recio and Lopez-Meza have raised other arguments not here considered, we remand the case, specifying that the Court of Appeals may consider those arguments, if they were properly raised.

The judgment of the Ninth Circuit is reversed, and the case is remanded for further proceedings consistent with this opinion.

It is so ordered.

[Opinion by Justice Stevens concurring in part and dissenting in part omitted.]

chapter 4

Mail and Wire Fraud

I. INTRODUCTION

The mail fraud statute, 18 U.S.C. §1341, is without doubt the granddaddy of all federal fraud statutes. Originally passed by Congress in 1872 to protect the U.S. mails from abuse, it has evolved over the years to become the main federal weapon to combat frauds of all kinds, with use of the mails as a mere jurisdictional element. Indeed, through a 1994 amendment, the crime no longer depends on the use of the U.S. Postal Service for jurisdiction at all, but can be invoked whenever a defendant "deposits or causes to be deposited any matter or thing whatever to be sent or delivered by a private commercial interstate carrier."* Today, courts struggle with the fact that nearly every fraudulent gambit, no matter how small or localized, can be converted into a federal case if the defendants contemplated using the mails as part of their scheme.

Wire fraud, 18 U.S.C. §1343, has the same substantive elements of mail fraud with the exception of the jurisdictional element. United States v. LaMacchia, 871 F. Supp. 535, 541 (D. Mass. 1994). To violate §1343, one must "transmit[], or cause[] to be transmitted by means of wire, radio, or television communication in interstate or foreign commerce, any writings, signs, signals, pictures, or sounds" for the purpose of executing a fraudulent scheme. Although the wire communication must actually travel in interstate or foreign commerce (unlike the mailing under §1341), the defendant need not be aware of this fact. United States v. Blassingame, 427 F.2d 329, 330 (2d Cir. 1970). In all other respects, the courts have held that mail and wire fraud are *in pari materia*; in other words, they are to be interpreted in an identical fashion, and precedent for one constitutes precedent for the other. *See, e.g.*, United States v. Oren, 893 F.2d 1057, 1060 (9th Cir. 1990); United States v. Giovengo, 637 F.2d 941, 944 (3d Cir. 1980).

*For an excellent account of the history of mail fraud, see Peter J. Henning, *Maybe It Should Just Be Called Federal Fraud: The Changing Nature of the Mail Fraud Statute*, 36 B.C. L. Rev. 435 (1995).

II. ELEMENTS AND INTENT TO DEFRAUD

UNITED STATES v. HAWKEY

148 F.3d 920 (8th Cir. 1998)

HEANEY, Circuit Judge.

Lester A. Hawkey, a sheriff in Minnehaha County, South Dakota, was charged in a forty-one count indictment for misusing funds belonging to the Minnehaha Sheriff's Department (MSD) and the Minnehaha County Sheriff and Deputies Association (MCSDA). A jury convicted Hawkey on all but two counts. On July 21, 1997, the district court sentenced Hawkey to forty-one months of imprisonment. On appeal, Hawkey challenges[, among other things,] the sufficiency of the evidence supporting his convictions....

I. Background

In 1988, Hawkey, on behalf of the MSD and the MCSDA, entered into an agreement with Wildwood Productions, a benefit concert promoter, to conduct annual benefit concerts each April. The proceeds of the annual concerts were purportedly intended to aid local youth programs. Prompted by Hawkey's representations, Wildwood's telemarketers solicited money from individuals and businesses in South Dakota and neighboring states for the purchase of tickets, donations, and/or to purchase advertising space in the concert program book. By United States mail, Wildwood sent statements or invoices to individuals and businesses who agreed to purchase tickets, advertise, or make donations. Individuals and businesses also sent their checks to either the MSD or MCSDA via the United States mail.

Wildwood's contracts with the MSD and MCSDA called for the establishment of two bank accounts. One account was to hold proceeds of ticket sales and the other was to hold the proceeds of advertisement sales. Shortly after the 1991 concert, Hawkey began using the concert accounts for a variety of personal and business expenses. While making some contributions to youth programs and charities, Hawkey spent a significant portion of the benefit concert proceeds for personal items. Hawkey also made deposits of business and personal funds to the concert account to replace depleted funds.

II. Sufficiency of the Evidence

... In Hawkey's challenge to the sufficiency of the evidence used to support his twenty-four count conviction for mail fraud, he argues that no one suffered any property loss and that there was no scheme or intent to defraud. Title 18 U.S.C. §1341 prohibits the use of the mails to execute "any scheme or artifice to defraud, or for obtaining money or property by means of false or fraudulent pretenses, representations, or promises." 18 U.S.C. §1341. Accordingly, to obtain a conviction for mail fraud under §1341, the government must prove "(1) the existence of a scheme to defraud, [(2) intent to defraud, and (3)] the use of the mails . . . for purposes of executing the scheme." The scheme "need not be fraudulent on its face but must involve some sort of fraudulent [and material] misrepresentations or omissions...."

Hawkey argues that, because the businesses received their advertisements and ticket purchasers were able to attend the concerts, they were not deprived of money or property because they received what they paid for. We disagree. The record reveals that Hawkey solicited, or caused to be solicited, funds that were intended for charitable organizations; and, while some money was in fact paid to the charitable organizations, Hawkey converted most of the money for his own personal use. The businesses and concert-goers who responded to Hawkey's solicitations did not intend to merely purchase a ticket or advertising; they intended part of their payment as a contribution to a charitable organization. . . .

Hawkey contends that there was insufficient evidence to prove that he intended to defraud citizens responding to his solicitations. The jury was instructed that "to act with intent to defraud means to act knowingly and with the intent to deceive someone for the purpose of causing some financial loss . . . to another or bringing about some financial gain to oneself or another to the detriment of a third party." The jury found that Hawkey possessed the required intent to obtain personal gain from his misrepresentations and found him guilty of mail fraud. We conclude that this finding is supported by the record. . . .

For the foregoing reasons, we affirm the district court as to the sufficiency of the evidence supporting Hawkey's convictions. . . .

UNITED STATES v. EDWARDS

526 F.3d 747 (11th Cir. 2008)

Tjoflat, Circuit Judge:

This case involves a business that the defendant, Charles E. Edwards, claimed was legitimate. A Northern District of Georgia jury, however, found that Edwards was operating a Ponzi scheme and convicted him of wire fraud and related crimes.[1] Edwards now appeals his convictions. . . .

I.

A.

From its founding on June 7, 1994, through September 11, 2000, Charles E. Edwards was the Chairman of the Board and sole owner of ETS Payphones, Inc. ("ETS"), a privately owned Georgia corporation that provided management services to payphone owners. Edwards also controlled Payphone Systems Acquisitions, Inc. ("PSA"), a Delaware corporation that was a wholly owned subsidiary of ETS. Edwards and others often referred to these two companies—and others Edwards formed to support ETS's payphone program—collectively as ETS, and we do likewise.

1. "Generically, a Ponzi scheme is a phony investment plan in which monies paid by later investors are used to pay artificially high returns to the initial investors, with the goal of attracting more investors." United States v. Silvestri, 409 F.3d 1311, 1317 n.6 (11th Cir. 2005) (quotation omitted).

Edwards organized ETS to implement his idea of selling coin-operated payphones to investors who would then lease the phones back to Edwards for a guaranteed rate of return. Edwards discussed his idea with an acquaintance, Beverly Slater, who suggested that he use insurance agents, those selling life insurance, including annuities, to market the payphones. Edwards liked her suggestion and persuaded her to establish a network of independent insurance agents to sell the phones. She would serve as the distributor of the phones, purchasing them from ETS and selling them to the investors solicited by the insurance agents. . . .

Shortly after Edwards's sale and lease-back plan was up and running, Edwards formed PSA to deal with the distributors. The sale and lease-back of the payphones were handled as follows. The insurance agent, having found an investor, contacted the distributor, and the distributor sent the agent a five-year lease already executed by ETS, as lessee, for the investor to sign, as lessor. The lease identified the location for the payphone the investor was purchasing, specified the rent ETS would be paying the investor each month, spelled out ETS's responsibility for installing and servicing the phones, and contained a buy-back provision. The buy-back provision required ETS to purchase the payphone from the investor at the end of the lease for the same price the investor had paid for the phone. The provision also gave the investor the right to sell the payphone to ETS for that price at any time during the term of the five-year lease on 180 days notice to ETS.

If the investor agreed to this arrangement, the investor gave the insurance agent a check made out to the distributor for the price of the payphone. The agent then forwarded the check to the distributor, which deposited the check into its bank account. Once the investor's check cleared, the distributor deducted the sales commission, which was divided between it and the insurance agent, and wire transferred the net sale proceeds to PSA's bank account. On a regular basis, PSA wired funds from its account to ETS for operating expenses, lease payments, and buy-backs. PSA also wired funds to some 114 accounts designated by Edwards. Some of these accounts related to ETS's business, some were held by other business entities Edwards owned, and some accounts were held by Edwards for his and his wife's personal expenditures. . . .

The insurance agents touted the ETS payphone program as a highly profitable alternative to investing in annuities or other forms of life insurance. . . .

The revenues the payphones generated were insufficient to cover ETS's operating expenses, lease payments, and buy-back obligations. In short, Edwards's payphone business was never profitable. Because PSA paid its distributors and insurance agents commissions of up to 25% of the retail price of each phone sold, and ETS was contractually obligated to buy back every phone for the full price paid by the investor, ETS immediately owed each investor more money than it collected on the sale of the phone—a deficit that could only be overcome by operating the phones at a substantial profit. The revenues the payphones provided, however, were extremely inadequate; by 2000, ETS was operating its phones at a loss of $5 million a month. Nearly 90% of the installed payphones were unprofitable. This problem was compounded by the fact that ETS leased more payphones from investors than it actually placed into service, a gap that increased from 150 in October 1996 to 17,960 by September 11, 2000. ETS, therefore, always depended on the influx of money from new investors to sustain its payphone business. Moreover, if ETS suffered a "run on the bank"—a sudden invocation of the lease's buy-back provision by a significant number of investors—the company would have collapsed. Whenever ETS's board of directors met, ETS's mounting financial losses and the optimistic outlook ETS was portraying to the investors were discussed. According to Charles Bynum, ETS's Chief Operating Officer, Edwards attitude was that "we can't possibly let [investors] see what is really going on because if this money coming in from [new investors] ever stopped, the whole thing would crash." Edwards's attitude prevailed; the investors were kept in the dark. . . .

On March 30, 2000, Edwards sent a memo to all ETS employees stating that "profits were below expectations in 1999" and that the company had entered into a period of "drastic times for the Payphone Industry." Edwards kept this information from ETS's distributors and their insurance agents. The agents, having no reason to question ETS's financial viability, therefore kept touting ETS's program as a sound investment. Edwards also continued to paint a rosy picture of ETS's profitability for investors. In May 2000, he gave a group of prospective investors a tour of ETS's offices. At the completion of the tour, he told them that ETS had sales of $28 million the previous year, netted $8 million in profit, and planned to expand its business into Mexico and the Carribean.

By mid-2000, investors were cancelling their leases and triggering the buy-back provision at an increasing rate, causing significant cash flow problems for the company. Nevertheless, Edwards continued to woo investors with representations of ETS's prosperity. . . .

On September 11, 2000, ETS and PSA filed petitions or Chapter 11 bankruptcy relief in the United States Bankruptcy Court for the District of Delaware. During the two months prior to filing these petitions, PSA, at Edwards's direction, continued to sell payphones, taking in $22 million from investors. The sales ceased after the petitions were filed. As of September 11, ETS had 73,107 payphones under lease and was contractually obligated to buy back those phones at a total cost of $414,091,985. Edwards's investors lost millions, but Edwards faired quite well. He received more than $21 million from ETS and its subsidiaries in the form of salary, consulting fees, and interest free "loans" that he never repaid. He used this money to purchase "[e]verything from expensive cowboy boots to million-dollar homes."

B.

On June 8, 2004, a Northern District of Georgia grand jury indicted Edwards on fifty-seven counts of wire fraud, 18 U.S.C. §1343 [among other charges]. Edwards's trial began on September 12, 2005. The jury received the case in the afternoon of September 28 and returned its verdicts the next morning, finding Edwards guilty on all counts. . . .

D.

As his final challenge to his convictions, Edwards contends that the district court constructively amended the indictment in its instruction to the jury as to the definition of a "Ponzi scheme." The amendment, he submits, allowed the jury to convict him of wire fraud without finding that he acted with the intent to defraud. . . .

Conviction under the wire fraud statute requires that the defendant (1) intentionally participated in a scheme or artifice to defraud another person of money or property and (2) used or caused the use of interstate wires to execute the scheme or artifice. The first essential element of the offense, *mens rea*, was spelled out in the indictment thusly:

> Edwards did knowingly and willfully devise and intend to devise a scheme and artifice to defraud investors through the sale of coin-operated payphones and to obtain money from those investors by means of false and fraudulent pretenses and representations, and by omissions of material facts, well knowing and having reason to know that such pretenses and representations were and would be false and fraudulent when made and caused to be made and that said omissions were and would be material.

We now turn to the jury instruction at issue to determine whether it amended the indictment by effectively eliminating the *mens rea* element from the wire fraud offense. Referring to Counts One through Fifty-seven, the court informed the jury as follows:

> Title 18, United States Code, Section 1343 makes it a federal crime or offense for anyone to use interstate wire communications facilities in carrying out a scheme to defraud. The defendant can be found guilty of that offense only if all of the following facts are proved beyond a reasonable doubt. First, that the defendant knowingly devised or participated in a scheme to defraud or for obtaining money or property by means of false pretenses, representations, or promises. Second, that the false pretenses, representations, or promises related to a material fact. Third, that the defendant did so willfully and with the intent to defraud and, fourth, that the defendant transmitted or caused to be transmitted by wire in interstate commerce some communication for the purpose of executing the scheme to defraud.

The court then went on to expound upon the meaning of several key terms to help the jury better understand the elements of the wire fraud offense, beginning with "scheme to defraud":

> The term scheme to defraud includes any plan or course of action intended to deceive or cheat someone out of money or property by means of false or fraudulent pretenses, representations, or promises.
>
> Now, in this case the government alleges that the defendant operated a Ponzi scheme which defrauded investors. A Ponzi scheme is a fraudulent investment scheme in which "profits" to investors[ ] are not created by the success of the underlying business venture, but instead are derived fraudulently from capital contributions of other investors. In a typical Ponzi scheme a corporation operates and continue[s] to operate at a loss. The corporation gives the appearance of being profitable by obtaining new investors and using those investors to pay for the high returns promised to earlier investors.
>
> The effect of such a scheme is to put the corporation further and further into debt by incurring more and more liability, but to give the false appearance of profitability in order to obtain new investors.

Edwards argues that by defining a Ponzi scheme, the court constructively expanded the indictment by removing the element of criminal intent and allowing the jury to infer intent if it found that the ETS sale and lease-back program was a

Ponzi scheme. We disagree. To begin, the opening paragraph of the jury instruction clearly states that Edwards could only be found guilty if he possessed the "intent to defraud." What Edwards cites as offending language did not speak to the element of intent at all. Rather, the discussion of a Ponzi scheme merely served to define the particular type of "scheme to defraud" that Edwards was alleged to have perpetrated. Moreover, the court went on to reemphasize the *mens rea* requirement in defining what it meant to "act with an intent to defraud":

> Now, to act with "intent to defraud" means to act knowingly and with the specific intent to deceive or cheat someone, ordinarily for the purpose of causing some financial loss to another or bringing about financial gain to one's self. . . . What must be proved beyond a reasonable doubt is that the defendant, with the intent to defraud, knowingly and willfully devised, intended to devise, or participated in a scheme to defraud substantially the same as the one alleged in the indictment. . . .

As the jury instructions did not alter the *mens rea* element of the wire fraud offense, a constructive amendment did not occur. . . .

For the foregoing reasons, we AFFIRM Edwards's convictions. . . .

SO ORDERED.

NOTES AND QUESTIONS

1. What are the essential elements of the crime of mail fraud?
2. How do the courts define the *mens rea* of intent to defraud? Is this the same or different from the way they define intent to "defraud the United States" under the conspiracy statute, 18 U.S.C. §371?
3. Complicated schemes to defraud can often be described in different ways. Formulating a description includes identifying (1) the victim or victims (who is harmed by the fraud?); (2) the nature of the harm (have the victims been deprived of money, property, or something else?); (3) the perpetrators' methodology (what is the deception underlying the fraud?); and (4) the perpetrators. How a prosecutor conceptualizes the fraudulent scheme for the purpose of describing it in the indictment can often impact the resolution of critical issues in the case.
4. If the prosecution names the victims of the defendant's alleged fraud in the indictment, must the prosecution prove that the defendant specifically intended to defraud these victims? In United States v. Howard, 619 F.3d 723 (7th Cir. 2010), the court answered this question in the negative. It stated:

   > We have previously determined . . . that this type of "fraud does not include an element requiring a contemplated harm to a specific, identifiable victim." We have also addressed the particularity of the indictment, holding that specific victims need not be identified. United States v. Mizyed, 927 F.2d 979, 981 (7th Cir. 1991).
   >
   > By logical extension, we hold today that even if an indictment names particular victims, the government need not prove intent to harm those named victims. Although certainly the naming of First Marblehead and

> TERI in the superseding indictment was not good form, it was merely surplusage and did not raise the government's burden of proof. It is sufficient that the government in this case proved that Howard intended to defraud the scheme's victims, whomever they were, and such intent was established by examining the circumstances of the scheme itself, not by who was specifically named in the indictment.
>
> We also note that Howard's argument—that there was an improper variance between the indictment and what the government was required to prove at trial—is flawed for another reason. "A variance is fatal only when the defendant is prejudiced in [her] defense because [she] cannot anticipate from the indictment what evidence will be presented against [her] or [she] is exposed to double jeopardy." [That was not the case here.]

Do you agree with this analysis? Is it consistent with the definition of intent to defraud set out in *Hawkey*?

5. Assume you represent Edwards. What would your best factual defense be?

III. MATERIALITY

UNITED STATES v. SVETE

2009 WL 225254 (11th Cir. Feb. 2, 2009) (en banc)

PRYOR, Circuit Judge:

This appeal presents the question whether the crime of mail fraud, which prohibits "*any* scheme or artifice to defraud" by use of the mail, 18 U.S.C. §1341 (emphasis added), requires proof that the scheme be capable of deceiving a reasonably prudent person or whether schemes aimed at the gullible or improvident are also prohibited. . . .

I. Background

Svete, Girardot, and their agents were in the business of selling financial interests in viatical settlements, which are financial products based on agreements with persons (known as viators) who have terminal illnesses and sell their life insurance policies to third parties for less than the mature value of the policies to benefit from the proceeds while alive. Companies controlled by Svete obtained more than one hundred million dollars from more than 3000 investors, more than a third of whom were over the age of 65. Investors who purchased these financial interests from agents of Svete and Girardot testified at trial that the sales agents made false statements and provided them with literature that contained false statements about the life expectancies of viators, the status of the life insurance contracts, and the risks associated with the investments. . . .

Investors who purchased interests in the viatical settlements were required to sign contracts that acknowledged that the investors had not relied on any representations other than those contained in the contracts. The contracts also contained acknowledgments that the investors were sophisticated in financial matters and had sought or had access to professional advice and that the projected demise dates were only estimates. Several of the investors testified at trial that they did not read or did not understand the contracts and relied on the statements of the sales agents. . . .

As a defense to the charges of mail fraud, Svete and Girardot argued that a person of ordinary prudence and sophistication would have read the contracts and ignored the false statements by the sales agents. Svete and Girardot requested the following jury instruction based on that argument:

> To prove a fraud crime, the government must show that the defendant under consideration intended to devise or participate in a scheme reasonably calculated to deceive persons of ordinary prudence and comprehension. The person of ordinary prudence standard is an objective standard and is not directly related to the gullibility or level of knowledge and experience of any specific person or persons. For purposes of this offense, the government must prove that a reasonable person of average prudence and comprehension would have acted on the representation made by the defendant under consideration.

The district court rejected the requested jury instruction.

The district court instead gave the pattern jury instruction on mail fraud, which defines a "scheme to defraud" to include "any plan or course of action intended to deceive or cheat someone out of money or property by means of false or fraudulent pretenses, representations, or promises." As part of that instruction, the district court defined materiality: "A material fact is a fact that would be important to a reasonable person in deciding whether to engage or not to engage in a particular transaction. A fact is material if it has a natural tendency to influence or is capable of influencing the decision of the person or entity to whom or which it is addressed." The jury found the defendants guilty of mail fraud. . . .

III. Discussion

. . . Congress has never used any language that would limit the coverage of the mail fraud statute to schemes that would deceive only prudent persons. To the contrary, the sponsor of the original statute explained that its purpose was "to prevent the frauds which are mostly gotten up in the large cities . . . by thieves, forgers, and rapscallions generally, for the purpose of deceiving and fleecing the innocent people in the country" (remarks of Rep. Farnsworth during debate in the 40th Congress). When the statute was amended in 1889 to prohibit schemes to sell counterfeit money, the Senate report reiterated a concern for the ignorant and naive:

> A certain class of persons . . . send out circulars through the United States mails which appeal to the cupidity of the ignorant and hold out to the unfortunate the temptation to try to better their fortunes. . . . Farmers and country merchants and country postmasters are constantly plied with these circulars, . . . and plain as the fraud is upon its face, these men reap a golden harvest. The city papers frequently contain notices of the ignorant victims who venture to the cities and are relieved of their money; but there is no notice of the many smaller dupes who send their money through the mails in answer to these advertisements and pocket their losses. . . . This bill . . . will, if properly enforced, put an end to this infamous business.

S. Rep. No. 50-2566, at 2 (1889). . . .

In addition to this settled understanding of the broad reach of the prohibition of mail fraud, the Supreme Court recently held "that materiality of falsehood is an element of the federal . . . fraud statutes." Neder v. United States, 527 U.S. 1, 25 (1999). The Court invoked "the rule that Congress intends to incorporate the well-settled meaning of the common-law terms it uses" and explained that "at the time of the mail fraud statute's original enactment in 1872, and later when Congress enacted the wire fraud and bank fraud statutes, actionable 'fraud' had a well-settled meaning at common law." . . .

All the sources cited by the Supreme Court support the proposition that materiality may be proved without establishing that the misrepresentation was objectively reliable. Section 538 of the *Restatement (Second) of Torts* defines materiality, for example, and that definition, in subpart (b), includes misrepresentations that are aimed at recipients who would regard them as important even if a reasonable person would not:

The Restatement instructs that a matter is material if:

> "(a) a reasonable man would attach importance to its existence or nonexistence in determining his choice of action in the transaction in question; or
> (b) the maker of the representation knows or has reason to know that its recipient regards or is likely to regard the matter as important in determining his choice of action, although a reasonable man would not so regard it."

Neder, 527 U.S. at 22 n.5 (quoting *Restatement (Second) of Torts* §538, at 80). . . .

The objective reliability of a misrepresentation is sufficient to establish its materiality, but proof of objective reliability is not necessary to establish materiality if the defendant knows or should know that the victim is likely to regard the misrepresented facts as important. In the words of the *Restatement*, "[o]ne who practices upon another's known idiosyncrasies cannot complain if he is held liable when he is successful in what he is endeavoring to accomplish." "The focus of the language defining a scheme to defraud is on the violator, not the victim." United States v. Drake, 932 F.2d 861, 864 (10th Cir. 1991).

Because the focus of the mail fraud statute, like any criminal statute, is on the violator, the purpose of the element of materiality is to ensure that a defendant actually intended to create a scheme to defraud. Proof that a defendant created a scheme to deceive reasonable people is sufficient evidence that the defendant intended to deceive, but a defendant who intends to deceive the ignorant or gullible by preying on their infirmities is no less guilty. Either way, the defendant has criminal intent. . . .

[Concurring opinions omitted.]

NOTES AND QUESTIONS

1. Is the jury instruction approved by the Eleventh Circuit fully consistent with the *Restatement* definition set forth by the Supreme Court in *Neder*? Why or

why not? If not, could the Eleventh Circuit have upheld Svete's conviction while proposing a revision to the pattern jury instruction? If so, under what jurisprudential doctrine?

2. In the penultimate paragraph, the court says that a defendant is liable if he "knows or should know" that the victim will be deceived by the misrepresentation. Doesn't "know or should know" equate to the mens rea of negligence? Although negligence is the standard level of culpability in tort cases, is it appropriate in a criminal case?

PROBLEM 4-1

Regents Office Supply is a legitimate business that sells stationery supplies to more than 20,000 customers nationally through salesmen who solicit orders for merchandise by telephone. To secure new accounts, the agents falsely represented to potential customers that:

(a) the agent had been referred to the customer by a friend of the customer.
(b) the agent had been referred to customer firms by officers of such firms.
(c) the agent was a doctor, or other professional person, who had stationery to be disposed of.
(d) the agent was selling the stationery of a friend who had passed away and the customer's purchase would help to alleviate this difficult situation.

The false representations are made only as a preliminary part of the salesmen's solicitation. In addition, (1) the price and quality of the merchandise are always discussed honestly; (2) the price offered has been lower than the purchasing agent is or was paying at the time of the solicitation; (3) the goods can be returned if found to be unsatisfactory; and (4) when a complaint is made an additional discount is offered to induce the customer to keep the goods. Nevertheless, some solicited companies have complained to the Better Business Bureau about Regents' dishonest sales tactics.

Is Regents committing wire fraud? Why or why not? *See* United States v. Regents Office Supply Co., Inc., 421 F.2d 1174 (2d Cir. 1970).

IV. PROTECTED INTERESTS

As we have just seen, a key element of mail and wire fraud is the defendant's intent to deprive the victim of something through the use of deceit. Exactly what that "something" must be has been the subject of much litigation and debate over the last 50 years. Consider the following cases.

A. Money or Property

CARPENTER v. UNITED STATES
484 U.S. 19 (1987)

Justice WHITE delivered the opinion of the Court.

Petitioners Kenneth Felis and R. Foster Winans were convicted of violating §10(b) of the Securities Exchange Act of 1934, 15 U.S.C. §78j(b), and Rule 10b-5, 17 CFR §240.10b-5 (1987). They were also found guilty of violating the federal mail and wire fraud statutes, 18 U.S.C. §§1341, 1343, and were convicted for conspiracy under 18 U.S.C. §371. Petitioner David Carpenter, Winans' roommate, was convicted for aiding and abetting. With a minor exception, the Court of Appeals for the Second Circuit affirmed; we granted certiorari.

I.

In 1981, Winans became a reporter for the *Wall Street Journal* (the *Journal*) and in the summer of 1982 became one of the two writers of a daily column, "Heard on the Street." That column discussed selected stocks or groups of stocks, giving positive and negative information about those stocks and taking "a point of view with respect to investment in the stocks that it reviews." Winans regularly interviewed corporate executives to put together interesting perspectives on the stocks that would be highlighted in upcoming columns, but, at least for the columns at issue here, none contained corporate inside information or any "hold for release" information. Because of the "Heard" column's perceived quality and integrity, it had the potential of affecting the price of the stocks which it examined. The District Court concluded on the basis of testimony presented at trial that the "Heard" column "does have an impact on the market, difficult though it may be to quantify in any particular case."

The official policy and practice at the *Journal* was that prior to publication, the contents of the column were the *Journal*'s confidential information. Despite the rule, with which Winans was familiar, he entered into a scheme in October 1983 with Peter Brant and petitioner Felis, both connected with the Kidder Peabody brokerage firm in New York City, to give them advance information as to the timing and contents of the "Heard" column. This permitted Brant and Felis and another conspirator, David Clark, a client of Brant, to buy or sell based on the probable impact of the column on the market. Profits were to be shared. The conspirators agreed that the scheme would not affect the journalistic purity of the "Heard" column, and the District Court did not find that the contents of any of the articles were altered to further the profit potential of petitioners' stock-trading scheme. Over a 4-month period, the brokers made prepublication trades on the basis of information given them by Winans about the contents of some 27 "Heard" columns. The net profits from these trades were about $690,000.

In November 1983, correlations between the "Heard" articles and trading in the Clark and Felis accounts were noted at Kidder Peabody and inquiries began. Brant and Felis denied knowing anyone at the *Journal* and took steps to conceal the trades.

Later, the Securities and Exchange Commission began an investigation. Questions were met by denials both by the brokers at Kidder Peabody and by Winans at the *Journal*. As the investigation progressed, the conspirators quarreled, and on March 29, 1984, Winans and Carpenter went to the SEC and revealed the entire scheme. This indictment and a bench trial followed. Brant, who had pleaded guilty under a plea agreement, was a witness for the Government. . . .

In affirming the mail and wire fraud convictions, the Court of Appeals ruled that Winans had fraudulently misappropriated "property" within the meaning of the mail and wire fraud statutes and that its revelation had harmed the *Journal*. It was held as well that the use of the mail and wire services had a sufficient nexus with the scheme to satisfy §§1341 and 1343. The petition for certiorari challenged these conclusions.

The Court is evenly divided with respect to the convictions under the securities laws and for that reason affirms the judgment below on those counts. For the reasons that follow, we also affirm the judgment with respect to the mail and wire fraud convictions.

II.

Petitioners assert that their activities were not a scheme to defraud the *Journal* within the meaning of the mail and wire fraud statutes; and that in any event, they did not obtain any "money or property" from the *Journal*, which is a necessary element of the crime under our decision last Term in McNally v. United States, 483 U.S. 350 (1987). We are unpersuaded by either submission and address the latter first.

We held in *McNally* that the mail fraud statute does not reach "schemes to defraud citizens of their intangible rights to honest and impartial government," and that the statute is "limited in scope to the protection of property rights." Petitioners argue that the *Journal*'s interest in prepublication confidentiality for the "Heard" columns is no more than an intangible consideration outside the reach of §1341; nor does that law, it is urged, protect against mere injury to reputation. This is not a case like *McNally*, however. The *Journal*, as Winans' employer, was defrauded of much more than its contractual right to his honest and faithful service, an interest too ethereal in itself to fall within the protection of the mail fraud statute, which "had its origin in the desire to protect individual property rights." Here, the object of the scheme was to take the *Journal*'s confidential business information—the publication schedule and contents of the "Heard" column—and its intangible nature does not make it any less "property" protected by the mail and wire fraud statutes. *McNally* did not limit the scope of §1341 to tangible as distinguished from intangible property rights.

Both courts below expressly referred to the *Journal*'s interest in the confidentiality of the contents and timing of the "Heard" column as a property right, and we agree with that conclusion. Confidential business information has long been recognized as property. See Ruckelshaus v. Monsanto Co., 467 U.S. 986, 1001-1004 (1984); Board of Trade of Chicago v. Christie Grain & Stock Co., 198 U.S. 236, 250-251 (1905). "Confidential information acquired or compiled by a corporation in the course and conduct of its business is a species of property to which the corporation has the exclusive right and benefit, and which a court of equity will protect through the injunctive process or other appropriate remedy." 3 W. Fletcher, CYCLOPEDIA OF LAW OF PRIVATE CORPORATIONS §857.1, p. 260 (rev. ed. 1986) (footnote omitted). The *Journal* had a property right in keeping confidential and making exclusive use, prior to publication, of the schedule and contents of the "Heard" column. As the Court has observed before:

> "[N]ews matter, however little susceptible of ownership or dominion in the absolute sense, is stock in trade, to be gathered at the cost of enterprise, organization, skill, labor, and money, and to be distributed and sold to those who will pay money for it, as for any other merchandise." International News Service v. Associated Press, 248 U.S. 215, 236 (1918).

Petitioners' arguments that they did not interfere with the *Journal's* use of the information or did not publicize it and deprive the *Journal* of the first public use of it miss the point. The confidential information was generated from the business, and the business had a right to decide how to use it prior to disclosing it to the public. Petitioners cannot successfully contend based on *Associated Press* that a scheme to defraud requires a monetary loss, such as giving the information to a competitor; it is sufficient that the *Journal* has been deprived of its right to exclusive use of the information, for exclusivity is an important aspect of confidential business information and most private property for that matter.

We cannot accept petitioners' further argument that Winans' conduct in revealing prepublication information was no more than a violation of workplace rules and did not amount to fraudulent activity that is proscribed by the mail fraud statute. Sections 1341 and 1343 reach any scheme to deprive another of money or property by means of false or fraudulent pretenses, representations, or promises. As we observed last Term in *McNally*, the words "to defraud" in the mail fraud statute have the "common understanding" of "'wronging one in his property rights by dishonest methods or schemes,' and 'usually signify the deprivation of something of value by trick, deceit, chicane or overreaching.'" The concept of "fraud" includes the act of embezzlement, which is "'the fraudulent appropriation to one's own use of the money or goods entrusted to one's care by another.'"

We have little trouble in holding that the conspiracy here to trade on the *Journal's* confidential information is not outside the reach of the mail and wire fraud statutes, provided the other elements of the offenses are satisfied. The *Journal's* business information that it intended to be kept confidential was its property; the declaration to that effect in the employee manual merely removed any doubts on that score and made the finding of specific intent to defraud that much easier. Winans continued in the employ of the *Journal*, appropriating its confidential business information for his own use, all the while pretending to perform his duty of safeguarding it. In fact, he told his editors twice about leaks of confidential information not related to the stock-trading scheme, demonstrating both his knowledge that the *Journal* viewed information concerning the "Heard" column as confidential and his deceit as he played the role of a loyal employee. Furthermore, the District Court's conclusion that each of the petitioners acted with the required specific intent to defraud is strongly supported by the evidence.

Lastly, we reject the submission that using the wires and the mail to print and send the *Journal* to its customers did not satisfy the requirement that those mediums be used to execute the scheme at issue. The courts below were quite right in observing that circulation of the "Heard" column was not only anticipated but an essential part of the scheme. Had the column not been made available to *Journal* customers, there would have been no effect on stock prices and no likelihood of profiting from the information leaked by Winans.

The judgment below is

Affirmed.

UNITED STATES v. CZUBINSKI

106 F.3d 1069 (1st Cir. 1997)

TORRUELLA, Chief Judge.

Defendant-appellant Richard Czubinski ("Czubinski") appeals his jury conviction on nine counts of wire fraud, 18 U.S.C. §§1343. . . . [W]e reverse the conviction on the . . . ground that the trial evidence mustered by the government was insufficient to support a guilty verdict. . . .

Background

I. Pertinent Facts

. . . For all periods relevant to the acts giving rise to his conviction, the defendant Czubinski was employed as a Contact Representative in the Boston office of the Taxpayer Services Division of the Internal Revenue Service ("IRS"). To perform his official duties, which mainly involved answering questions from taxpayers regarding their returns, Czubinski routinely accessed information from one of the IRS's computer systems known as the Integrated Data Retrieval System ("IDRS"). Using a valid password given to Contact Representatives, certain search codes, and taxpayer social security numbers, Czubinski was able to retrieve, to his terminal screen in Boston, income tax return information regarding virtually any taxpayer—information that is permanently stored in the IDRS "master file" located in Martinsburg, West Virginia. In the period of Czubinski's employ, IRS rules plainly stated that employees with passwords and access codes were not permitted to access files on IDRS outside of the course of their official duties.

In 1992, Czubinski carried out numerous unauthorized searches of IDRS files. He knowingly disregarded IRS rules by looking at confidential information obtained by performing computer searches that were outside of the scope of his duties as a Contact Representative, including, but not limited to, the searches listed in the indictment. Audit trails performed by internal IRS auditors establish that Czubinski frequently made unauthorized accesses on IDRS in 1992. For example, Czubinski accessed information regarding: the tax returns of two individuals involved in the David Duke presidential campaign; the joint tax return of an assistant district attorney (who had been prosecuting Czubinski's father on an unrelated felony offense) and his wife; the tax return of Boston City Counselor

Jim Kelly's Campaign Committee (Kelly had defeated Czubinski in the previous election for the Counselor seat for District 2); the tax return of one of his brothers' instructors; the joint tax return of a Boston Housing Authority police officer, who was involved in a community organization with one of Czubinski's brothers, and the officer's wife; and the tax return of a woman Czubinski had dated a few times. Czubinski also accessed the files of various other social acquaintances by performing unauthorized searches.

Nothing in the record indicates that Czubinski did anything more than knowingly disregard IRS rules by observing the confidential information he accessed. No evidence suggests, nor does the government contend, that Czubinski disclosed the confidential information he accessed to any third parties. The government's only evidence demonstrating any intent to use the confidential information for nefarious ends was the trial testimony of William A. Murray, an acquaintance of Czubinski who briefly participated in Czubinski's local Invisible Knights of the Ku Klux Klan ("KKK") chapter and worked with him on the David Duke campaign. Murray testified that Czubinski had once stated at a social gathering in "early 1992" that "he intended to use some of that information to build dossiers on people" involved in "the white supremacist movement." There is, however, no evidence that Czubinski created dossiers, took steps toward making dossiers (such as by printing out or recording the information he browsed), or shared any of the information he accessed in the years following the single comment to Murray. No other witness testified to having any knowledge of Czubinski's alleged intent to create "dossiers" on KKK members.

The record shows that Czubinski did not perform any unauthorized searches after 1992. He continued to be employed as a Contact Representative until June 1995, when a grand jury returned an indictment against him [charging him with] federal wire fraud under 18 U.S.C. §§1343. . . .

The portion of the indictment alleging wire fraud states that Czubinski defrauded the IRS of confidential property . . . by using his valid password to acquire confidential taxpayer information as part of a scheme to: 1) build "dossiers" on associates in the KKK; 2) seek information regarding an assistant district attorney who was then prosecuting Czubinski's father on an unrelated criminal charge; and 3) perform opposition research by inspecting the records of a political opponent in the race for a Boston City Councilor seat. The wire fraud indictment, therefore, articulated particular personal ends to which the unauthorized access to confidential information through interstate wires was allegedly a means. . . .

Discussion

I. The Wire Fraud Counts

We turn first to Czubinski's conviction on the nine wire fraud counts. To support a conviction for wire fraud, the government must prove two elements beyond a reasonable doubt: (1) the defendant's knowing and willing participation in a scheme or artifice to defraud with the specific intent to defraud, and (2) the use of interstate wire communications in furtherance of the scheme. [We hold that] there is insufficient record evidence to permit a rational jury to conclude that the wire transmissions were part of a criminal scheme to defraud under section[] 1343. . . .

A. Scheme to Defraud IRS of Property

The government correctly notes that confidential information may constitute intangible "property" and that its unauthorized dissemination or other use may deprive the owner of its property rights. *See Carpenter*. Where such deprivation is effected through dishonest or deceitful means, a "scheme to defraud," within the meaning of the wire fraud statute, is shown. Thus, a necessary step toward satisfying the "scheme to defraud" element in this context is showing that the defendant intended to "deprive" another of their protected right.

The government, however, provides no case in support of its contention here that merely accessing confidential information, without doing, or clearly intending to do, more, is tantamount to a deprivation of IRS property under the wire fraud statute. . . .

Binding precedents, and good sense, support the conclusion that to "deprive" a person of their intangible property interest in confidential information under section 1343, either some articulable harm must befall the holder of the information as a result of the defendant's activities, or some gainful use must be intended by the person accessing the information, whether or not this use is profitable in the economic sense. Here, neither the taking of the IRS' right to "exclusive use" of the confidential information, nor Czubinski's gain from access to the information, can be shown absent evidence of his "use" of the information. Accordingly, without evidence that Czubinski used or intended to use the taxpayer information (beyond mere browsing), an intent to deprive cannot be proven, and, *a fortiori*, a scheme to defraud is not shown.

All of the cases cited by the government in support of their contention that the confidentiality breached by Czubinski's search in itself constitutes a deprivation of property in fact support our holding today, for they all involve, at a minimum, a finding of a further intended use of the confidential information accessed by the defendants. The government's best support comes from United States v. Seidlitz, 589 F.2d 152, 160 (4th Cir. 1978), in which a former employee of a computer systems firm secretly accessed its files, but never was shown to have sold or used the data he accessed, and was nevertheless convicted of wire fraud. The affirming Fourth Circuit held, however, that a jury could have reasonably found that, at the time the defendant raided a competitor's computer system, he intended to retrieve information that would be helpful for his own start-up, competing computer firm. In the instant case, Czubinski did indeed access confidential information through fraudulent pretenses—he appeared to be performing his duties when in fact he used IRS passwords to perform unauthorized searches. Nevertheless, it was not proven that he intended to deprive the IRS of their property interest through either disclosure or use of that information.

The resolution of the instant case is complex because it is well-established that to be convicted of mail or wire fraud, the defendant need not successfully carry out an intended scheme to defraud. *See, e.g.*, United States v. Serrano, 870 F.2d 1, 6 (1st Cir. 1989) (defendant need only participate in a scheme to defraud with the intent to achieve its illicit objectives); *Seidlitz*, 589 F.2d at 160 (where circumstantial evidence suffices to prove intent to accomplish scheme to defraud, actual use of confidential information need not be shown). The government does not contend either that Czubinski actually created dossiers or that he accomplished some other end through use of the information. It need not do so. All that the government was required to prove was the *intent* to follow through with a deprivation of the IRS's property and the use or foreseeable use of interstate wire transmissions pursuant to the accomplishment of the scheme to defraud. *See, e.g.*, United States v. Silvano, 812 F.2d 754, 760 (1st Cir. 1987). In the case at bar, the government failed to make even this showing.

The fatal flaw in the government's case is that it has not shown beyond a reasonable doubt that Czubinski intended to carry out a scheme to deprive the IRS of its property interest in confidential information. Had there been sufficient proof that Czubinski intended either to create dossiers for the sake of advancing personal causes or to disseminate confidential information to third parties, then his actions in searching files could arguably be said to be a step in furtherance of a scheme to deprive the IRS of its property interest in confidential information. The government's case regarding Czubinski's intent to make any use of the information he browsed rests on the testimony of one witness at trial who stated that Czubinski once remarked at a social gathering that he intended to build dossiers on potential KKK informants. We must assume, on this appeal, that Czubinski did indeed make such a comment. Nevertheless, the fact that during the months following this remark—that is, during the period in which Czubinski made his unauthorized searches—he did not create dossiers (there was no evidence that he created dossiers either during or after the period of his unauthorized searches); given the fact that he did not even take steps toward creating dossiers, such as recording or printing out the information; given the fact that no other person testifying as to Czubinski's involvement in white supremacist organizations had any knowledge of Czubinski's alleged intent to create dossiers or use confidential information; and given the fact that not a single piece of evidence suggests that Czubinski ever shared taxpayer information with others, no rational jury could have found beyond a reasonable doubt that, when Czubinski was browsing taxpayer files, he was doing so in furtherance of a scheme to use the information he browsed for private purposes, be they nefarious or otherwise. In addition, there was no evidence that Czubinski disclosed, or used to his advantage, any information regarding political opponents or regarding the person prosecuting his father.

Mere browsing of the records of people about whom one might have a particular interest, although reprehensible, is not enough to sustain a wire fraud conviction on a "deprivation of intangible property" theory. Curiosity on the part of an IRS officer may lead to dismissal, but curiosity alone will not sustain a finding of participation in a felonious criminal scheme to deprive the IRS of its property.

For the reasons stated in this opinion, we hold the district court's denial of defendant's motion for judgment of acquittal . . . to be in error. The defendant's conviction is thus *reversed* on all counts.

NOTES AND QUESTIONS

1. The *Czubinski* court is correct that a defendant has not committed fraud through the theft of confidential information unless there is proof that he intended to use that information in a manner that would be detrimental to

the interests of the information's "owner." Isn't there sufficient evidence in the case to support the jury's conclusion that Czubinski harbored such an intent? After all, Czubinski *told* Murray about his plans to use some of the information related to the KKK. Could the court of appeals legitimately discount this evidence? Or was it supposed to assume all facts in the light most favorable to the prevailing party, in this case, the prosecution?

2. How is the *Czubinski* case different from *Seidlitz*? There, the defendant never actually used the stolen information, but the conviction was upheld on the ground that, in Judge Torruella's own words, "a jury could reasonably have found that, at the time the defendant raided a competitor's computer system, he intended to retrieve information that would be helpful for his own start-up . . . firm." Couldn't a reasonable juror have inferred from the facts of *Czubinski* that, had he found useful information on the DA who was prosecuting his father, or on his own political opponent, to cite two examples, Czubinski would have used the information? Why else would he look?

CLEVELAND v. UNITED STATES
531 U.S. 12 (2000)

Justice GINSBURG delivered the opinion of the Court.

This case presents the question whether the federal mail fraud statute, 18 U.S.C. §1341, reaches false statements made in an application for a state license. Section 1341 proscribes use of the mails in furtherance of "any scheme or artifice to defraud, or for obtaining money or property by means of false or fraudulent pretenses, representations, or promises." Petitioner Carl W. Cleveland and others were prosecuted under this federal measure for making false statements in applying to the Louisiana State Police for permission to operate video poker machines. We conclude that permits or licenses of this order do not qualify as "property" within §1341's compass. It does not suffice, we clarify, that the object of the fraud may become property in the recipient's hands; for purposes of the mail fraud statute, the thing obtained must be property in the hands of the victim. State and municipal licenses in general, and Louisiana's video poker licenses in particular, we hold, do not rank as "property," for purposes of §1341, in the hands of the official licensor.

I.

Louisiana law allows certain businesses to operate video poker machines. The State itself, however, does not run such machinery. The law requires prospective owners of video poker machines to apply for a license from the State. The licenses are not transferable and must be renewed annually. To qualify for a license, an applicant must meet suitability requirements designed to ensure that licensees have good character and fiscal integrity.

In 1992, Fred Goodson and his family formed a limited partnership, Truck Stop Gaming, Ltd. (TSG), in order to participate in the video poker business at their truck stop in Slidell, Louisiana. Cleveland, a New Orleans lawyer, assisted Goodson in preparing TSG's application for a video poker license. The application required

TSG to identify its partners and to submit personal financial statements for all partners. It also required TSG to affirm that the listed partners were the sole beneficial owners of the business and that no partner held an interest in the partnership merely as an agent or nominee, or intended to transfer the interest in the future.

TSG's application identified Goodson's adult children, Alex and Maria, as the sole beneficial owners of the partnership. It also showed that Goodson and Cleveland's law firm had loaned Alex and Maria all initial capital for the partnership and that Goodson was TSG's general manager. In May 1992, the State approved the application and issued a license. TSG successfully renewed the license in 1993, 1994, and 1995 pursuant to La. Admin. Code, tit. 42, §2405(B)(3) (2000). Each renewal application identified no ownership interests other than those of Alex and Maria.

In 1996, the Federal Bureau of Investigation (FBI) discovered evidence that Cleveland and Goodson had participated in a scheme to bribe state legislators to vote in a manner favorable to the video poker industry. The Government charged Cleveland and Goodson with multiple counts of money laundering under 18 U.S.C. §1957, as well as racketeering and conspiracy under §1962. Among the predicate acts supporting these charges were four counts of mail fraud under §1341. The indictment alleged that Cleveland and Goodson had violated §1341 by fraudulently concealing that they were the true owners of TSG in the initial license application and three renewal applications mailed to the State. They concealed their ownership interests, according to the Government, because they had tax and financial problems that could have undermined their suitability to receive a video poker license.

Before trial, Cleveland moved to dismiss the mail fraud counts on the ground that the alleged fraud did not deprive the State of "property" under §1341. The District Court denied the motion, concluding that "licenses constitute property even before they are issued." A jury found Cleveland guilty on two counts of mail fraud (based on the 1994 and 1995 license renewals) and on money laundering, racketeering, and conspiracy counts predicated on the mail fraud. The District Court sentenced Cleveland to 121 months in prison. . . . The Court of Appeals for the Fifth Circuit . . . affirmed. . . .

We granted certiorari to resolve the conflict among the Courts of Appeals, and now reverse the Fifth Circuit's judgment.

II.

In *McNally v. United States*, this Court held that the federal mail fraud statute is "limited in scope to the protection of property rights." . . . Soon after *McNally*, in *Carpenter v. United States*, we again stated that §1341 protects property rights only. . . . The following year, Congress amended the law specifically to cover one of the "intangible rights" that lower courts had protected under §1341 prior to *McNally:* "the intangible right of honest services." 18 U.S.C. §1346. Significantly, Congress covered only the intangible right of honest services even though federal courts, relying on *McNally*, had dismissed, for want of monetary loss to any victim, prosecutions under §1341 for diverse forms of public corruption, including licensing fraud.

III.

In this case, there is no assertion that Louisiana's video poker licensing scheme implicates the intangible right of honest services. The question presented is whether, for purposes of the federal mail fraud statute, a government regulator parts with "property" when it issues a license. For the reasons we now set out, we hold that §1341 does not reach fraud in obtaining a state or municipal license of the kind here involved, for such a license is not "property" in the government regulator's hands. Again, as we said in *McNally*, "[i]f Congress desires to go further, it must speak more clearly than it has."

To begin with, we think it beyond genuine dispute that whatever interests Louisiana might be said to have in its video poker licenses, the State's core concern is *regulatory*. Louisiana recognizes the importance of "public confidence and trust that gaming activities . . . are conducted honestly and are free from criminal and corruptive elements." The video poker licensing statute accordingly asserts the State's "legitimate interest in providing strict regulation of all persons, practices, associations, and activities related to the operation of . . . establishments licensed to offer video draw poker devices." The statute assigns the Office of State Police, a part of the Department of Public Safety and Corrections, the responsibility to promulgate rules and regulations concerning the licensing process. It also authorizes the State Police to deny, condition, suspend, or revoke licenses, to levy fines of up to $1,000 per violation of any rule, and to inspect all premises where video poker devices are offered for play. In addition, the statute defines criminal penalties for unauthorized use of video poker devices and prescribes detailed suitability requirements for licensees.

In short, the statute establishes a typical regulatory program. It licenses, subject to certain conditions, engagement in pursuits that private actors may not undertake without official authorization. In this regard, it resembles other licensing schemes long characterized by this Court as exercises of state police powers. *E.g.*, Ziffrin, Inc. v. Reeves, 308 U.S. 132 (1939) (license to transport alcoholic beverages); Hall v. Geiger-Jones Co., 242 U.S. 539, 558 (1917) (license to sell corporate stock); Fanning v. Gregoire, 16 How. 524, 534 (1853) (ferry license); *License Cases*, 5 How. 504, 589 (1847) (license to sell liquor) (opinion of McLean, J.), overruled on other grounds, Leisy v. Hardin, 135 U.S. 100 (1890).

Acknowledging Louisiana's regulatory interests, the Government offers two reasons why the State also has a property interest in its video poker licenses. First, the State receives a substantial sum of money in exchange for each license and continues to receive payments from the licensee as long as the license remains in effect. Second, the State has significant control over the issuance, renewal, suspension, and revocation of licenses.

Without doubt, Louisiana has a substantial economic stake in the video poker industry. The State collects an upfront "processing fee" for each new license application, a separate "processing fee" for each renewal application ($1,000 for truck stops), an "annual fee" from each device owner ($2,000), an additional "device operation" fee ($1,000 for truck stops), and, most importantly, a fixed percentage of net revenue from each video poker device (32.5% for truck stops). It is hardly evident, however, why these tolls should make video poker licenses "property" in the hands of the State. The State receives the lion's share of its expected revenue not while the licenses remain in its own hands, but only *after* they have been issued to licensees. Licenses pre-issuance do not generate an ongoing stream of revenue. At most, they entitle the State to collect a processing fee from applicants for new licenses. Were an entitlement of this order sufficient to establish a state property right, one could scarcely avoid the conclusion that States have property rights in any license or permit requiring an upfront fee, including drivers' licenses, medical licenses, and fishing and hunting licenses. Such licenses, as the Government itself concedes, are "purely regulatory."

Tellingly, as to the character of Louisiana's stake in its video poker licenses, the Government nowhere alleges that Cleveland defrauded the State of any money to which the State was entitled by law. Indeed, there is no dispute that TSG paid the State of Louisiana its proper share of revenue, which totaled more than $1.2 million, between 1993 and 1995. If Cleveland defrauded the State of "property," the nature of that property cannot be economic.

Addressing this concern, the Government argues that Cleveland frustrated the State's right to control the issuance, renewal, and revocation of video poker licenses. The Fifth Circuit has characterized the protected interest as "Louisiana's right to choose the persons to whom it issues video poker licenses." But far from composing an interest that "has long been recognized as property," these intangible rights of allocation, exclusion, and control amount to no more and no less than Louisiana's sovereign power to regulate. Notably, the Government overlooks the fact that these rights include the distinctively sovereign authority to impose criminal penalties for violations of the licensing scheme, including making false statements in a license application. Even when tied to an expected stream of revenue, the State's right of control does not create a property interest any more than a law licensing liquor sales in a State that levies a sales tax on liquor. Such regulations are paradigmatic exercises of the States' traditional police powers. . . .

We reject the Government's theories of property rights not simply because they stray from traditional concepts of property. We resist the Government's reading of §1341 as well because it invites us to approve a sweeping expansion of federal criminal jurisdiction in the absence of a clear statement by Congress. Equating issuance of licenses or permits with deprivation of property would subject to federal mail fraud prosecution a wide range of conduct traditionally regulated by state and local authorities. We note in this regard that Louisiana's video poker statute typically and unambiguously imposes criminal penalties for making false statements on license applications. As we reiterated last Term, "'unless Congress conveys its purpose clearly, it will not be deemed to have significantly changed the federal—state balance' in the prosecution of crimes."

Moreover, to the extent that the word "property" is ambiguous as placed in §1341, we have instructed that "ambiguity concerning the ambit of criminal statutes should be resolved in favor of lenity." This interpretive guide is especially appropriate in construing §1341 because, as this case demonstrates, mail fraud is a predicate offense under RICO, 18 U.S.C. §1961(1) and the money laundering statute, §1956(c)(7)(A). In deciding what is "property" under §1341, we think "it is appropriate, before we choose the harsher alternative, to require that Congress should have spoken in language that is clear and definite." . . .

IV.

We conclude that §1341 requires the object of the fraud to be "property" in the victim's hands and that a Louisiana video poker license in the State's hands is not "property" under §1341. Absent clear statement by Congress, we will not read the mail fraud statute to place under federal superintendence a vast array of conduct traditionally policed by the States. Our holding means that Cleveland's §1341 conviction must be vacated. Accordingly, the judgment of the United States Court of Appeals for the Fifth Circuit is reversed, and the case is remanded for further proceedings consistent with this opinion.

It is so ordered.

PASQUANTINO v. UNITED STATES

544 U.S. 349 (2004)

THOMAS, J., delivered the opinion of the Court, in which REHNQUIST, C. J., and STEVENS, O'CONNOR, and KENNEDY, JJ., joined. GINSBURG, J., filed a dissenting opinion, in which BREYER, J., joined, and in which SCALIA and SOUTER, JJ., joined as to Parts II and III.

Justice THOMAS delivered the opinion of the Court.

At common law, the revenue rule generally barred courts from enforcing the tax laws of foreign sovereigns. The question presented in this case is whether a plot to defraud a foreign government of tax revenue violates the federal wire fraud statute, 18 U.S.C. §1343. Because the plain terms of §1343 criminalize such a scheme, and because this construction of the wire fraud statute does not derogate from the common-law revenue rule, we hold that it does.

I.

Petitioners Carl J. Pasquantino, David B. Pasquantino, and Arthur Hilts were indicted for and convicted of federal wire fraud for carrying out a scheme to smuggle large quantities of liquor into Canada from the United States. According to the evidence presented at trial, the Pasquantinos, while in New York, ordered liquor over the telephone from discount package stores in Maryland. They employed Hilts and others to drive the liquor over the Canadian border, without paying the required excise taxes. The drivers avoided paying taxes by hiding the liquor in their vehicles and failing to declare the goods to Canadian customs officials. During the time of petitioners' smuggling operation, between 1996 and 2000, Canada heavily taxed the importation of alcoholic beverages. Uncontested evidence at trial showed that Canadian taxes then due on alcohol purchased in the United States and transported to Canada were approximately double the liquor's purchase price.

Before trial, petitioners moved to dismiss the indictment on the ground that it stated no wire fraud offense. . . . The District Court denied the motion, and the case went to trial. The jury convicted petitioners of wire fraud.

Petitioners appealed their convictions to the United States Court of Appeals for the Fourth Circuit, again urging that the indictment failed to state a wire fraud offense. They argued that their prosecution contravened the common-law revenue rule, because it required the court to take cognizance of the revenue laws of Canada. Over Judge Hamilton's dissent, the panel agreed and reversed the convictions. Petitioners also argued that Canada's right to collect taxes from them was not "money or property" within the meaning of the wire fraud statute, but the panel unanimously rejected that argument.

The Court of Appeals granted rehearing *en banc*, vacated the panel's decision, and affirmed petitioners' convictions. It [rejected the revenue rule argument and] held as well that Canada's right to receive tax revenue was "money or property" within the meaning of the wire fraud statute.

We granted certiorari to resolve a conflict in the Courts of Appeals over whether a scheme to defraud a foreign government of tax revenue violates the wire fraud statute. We agree with the Court of Appeals that it does and therefore affirm the judgment below.

II.

We first consider whether petitioners' conduct falls within the literal terms of the wire fraud statute. The statute prohibits using interstate wires to effect "any scheme or artifice to defraud, or for obtaining money or property by means of false or fraudulent pretenses, representations, or promises." 18 U.S.C. §1343. Two elements of this crime, and the only two that petitioners dispute here, are that the defendant engage in a "scheme or artifice to defraud," and that the "object of the fraud . . . be '[money or] property' in the victim's hands," *Cleveland v. United States*. Petitioners' smuggling operation satisfies both elements.

Taking the latter element first, Canada's right to uncollected excise taxes on the liquor petitioners imported into Canada is "property" in its hands. This right is an entitlement to collect money from petitioners, the possession of which is "something of value" to the Government of Canada. Valuable entitlements like these are "property" as that term ordinarily is employed. Had petitioners complied with this legal obligation, they would have paid money to Canada. Petitioners' tax evasion deprived Canada of that money, inflicting an economic injury no less than had they embezzled funds from the Canadian treasury. The object of petitioners' scheme was to deprive Canada of money legally due, and their scheme thereby had as its object the deprivation of Canada's "property."

The common law of fraud confirms this characterization of Canada's right to excise taxes. . . . The fact that the victim of the fraud happens to be the government, rather than a private party, does not lessen the injury. . . .

Cleveland is different from this case. Unlike a State's interest in allocating a video poker license to particular applicants, Canada's entitlement to tax revenue is a straightforward "economic" interest. There was no suggestion in *Cleveland* that the defendant aimed at depriving the State of any money due under the license; quite the opposite, there was "no dispute that [the defendant's partnership] paid the State of Louisiana its proper share of revenue" due. Here, by contrast, the Government alleged and proved that petitioners' scheme aimed at depriving Canada of money to which it was entitled by law. Canada could hardly have a more "economic" interest than in the receipt of tax revenue. *Cleveland* is therefore consistent with our conclusion that Canada's entitlement is "property" as that word is used in the wire fraud statute.

Turning to the second element at issue here, petitioners' plot was a "scheme or artifice to defraud" Canada of its valuable entitlement to tax revenue. The evidence showed that petitioners routinely concealed imported liquor from Canadian officials and failed to declare those goods on customs forms. By this conduct, they represented to Canadian customs officials that their drivers had no goods to declare. This, then, was a scheme "designed to defraud by representations" and therefore a "scheme or artifice to defraud" Canada of taxes due on the smuggled goods.

[The Court's discussion of the revenue rule, and the dissenting opinion, are omitted.]

NOTES AND QUESTIONS

1. *Cleveland* represents a unanimous opinion of the Supreme Court in a criminal case, a fairly rare event in recent times. Although the outcome is quite defensible on purely formalistic grounds—i.e., that video poker licenses are simply not a form of property when held by the state—it appears that the real motivation underlying the outcome was a much larger policy question. Could it be that the justices were worried about the overfederalization of criminal law? This had become a hotly debated topic in the late 1990s among judges and academics. *See, e.g.*, Steven D. Clymer, *Unequal Justice: The Federalization of Criminal Law*, 70 S. Cal. L. Rev. 643 (1997); Sarah Sun Beale, *Too Many and Yet Too Few: New Principles to Define Proper Limits for Federal Criminal Jurisdiction*, 46 Hastings L.J. 979 (1995); Jamie S. Gorelick & Harry Litman, *Prosecutiorial Discretion and the Federalization Debate*, 46 Hastings L.J. 967 (1995). Note how Justice Ginsburg makes a point of stating that video poker licenses are no different in kind than fishing or drivers licenses. What point is she making through these analogies?
2. Why was *Pasquantino* decided the other way? Consider the very interesting manner in which the justices lined up—conservatives and liberals were on both sides of the case. It seems that, for some of the justices in the *Pasquantino* majority, concluding that tax dollars owed to the Canadian government constituted "money" under §1343 was simply unavoidable. For others, the deciding factor might have been that, because the case did not involve a U.S. state, it did not raise the federalism concerns that had helped to produce the outcome in *Cleveland.*
3. Consider the *Czubinski* case, *supra.* If it were indicted today, how might it be impacted by *Cleveland* and *Pasquantino*?

PROBLEM 4-2

James is a new member of a violent street gang in California that has been targeted for investigation by a joint state-federal task force on gang control. During its investigation, the task force learns that James's main role since being inducted into the gang has been to obtain a dozen or so false drivers licenses for himself and fellow gang-members, in part by using phony credit cards to pay the state for the licenses. As a result of the fraudulent credit card use, California never received drivers' license fees totaling $680. A simultaneous take-down (arrest) of 30 gang members takes place, with James among them. You are the supervising federal prosecutor. The federal agents want you to prosecute James for conspiracy and mail fraud because they believe these charges will get him the longest jail sentence based on the evidence at hand. Should you include James in your indictment or refer him to the state for charging?

B. Honest Services

SKILLING v. UNITED STATES

130 S. Ct. 2896 (2010)

Justice GINSBURG delivered the opinion of the Court.

In 2001, Enron Corporation, then the seventh highest-revenue-grossing company in America, crashed into bankruptcy. We consider in this opinion two questions arising from the prosecution of Jeffrey Skilling, a longtime Enron executive, for crimes committed before the corporation's collapse. First, did pretrial publicity and community prejudice prevent Skilling from obtaining a fair trial? Second, did the jury improperly convict Skilling of conspiracy to commit "honest-services" wire fraud, 18 U.S.C. §§371, 1343, 1346?

[The Court's extensive discussion of the pretrial publicity issue is omitted.]

Enacted in 1872, the original mail-fraud provision, the predecessor of the modern-day mail- and wire-fraud laws, proscribed, without further elaboration, use of the mails to advance "any scheme or artifice to defraud." In 1909, Congress amended the statute to prohibit, as it does today, "any scheme or artifice to defraud, *or for obtaining money or property by means of false or fraudulent pretenses, representations, or promises.*" §1341 (emphasis added). Emphasizing Congress' disjunctive phrasing, the Courts of Appeals, one after the other, interpreted the term "scheme or artifice to defraud" to include deprivations not only of money or property, but also of intangible rights.

In an opinion credited with first presenting the intangible-rights theory, Shushan v. United States, 117 F.2d 110 (1941), the Fifth Circuit reviewed the mail-fraud prosecution of a public official who allegedly accepted bribes from entrepreneurs in exchange for urging city action beneficial to the bribe payers. "It is not true that because the [city] was to make and did make a saving by the operations there could not have been an intent to defraud," the Court of Appeals maintained. "A scheme to get a public contract on more favorable terms than would likely be got otherwise by bribing a public official," the court observed, "would not only be a plan to commit the crime of bribery, but would also be a scheme to defraud the public." *Id.*

The Fifth Circuit's opinion in *Shushan* stimulated the development of an "honest-services" doctrine. Unlike fraud in which the victim's loss of money or property supplied the defendant's gain, with one the mirror image of the other, the honest-services theory targeted corruption that lacked similar symmetry. While the offender profited, the betrayed party suffered no deprivation of money or property; instead, a third party, who had not been deceived, provided the enrichment. For example, if a city mayor (the offender) accepted a bribe from a third party in exchange for awarding that party a city contract, yet the contract terms were the same as any that could have been negotiated at arm's length, the city (the betrayed party) would suffer no tangible loss. Even if the scheme occasioned a money or property *gain* for the betrayed party, courts reasoned, actionable harm lay in the denial of that party's right to the offender's "honest services."

"Most often these cases . . . involved bribery of public officials," but courts also recognized private-sector honest-services fraud. In perhaps the earliest application of the theory to private actors, a District Court, reviewing a bribery scheme, explained:

> "When one tampers with [the employer-employee] relationship for the purpose of causing the employee to breach his duty [to his employer], he in effect is defrauding the employer of a lawful right. The actual deception that is practised is in the continued representation of the employee to the employer that he is honest and loyal to the employer's interests." United States v. Procter & Gamble Co., 47 F. Supp. 676, 678 (D. Mass. 1942).

Over time, "[a]n increasing number of courts" recognized that "a recreant employee"—public or private—"c[ould] be prosecuted under [the mail-fraud statute] if he breache[d] his allegiance to his employer by accepting bribes or kickbacks in the course of his employment"; by 1982, all Courts of Appeals had embraced the honest-services theory of fraud.

2.

In 1987, this Court, in *McNally v. United States*, stopped the development of the intangible-rights doctrine in its tracks. *McNally* involved a state officer who, in selecting Kentucky's insurance agent, arranged to procure a share of the agent's commissions via kickbacks paid to companies the official partially controlled. The prosecutor did not charge that, "in the absence of the alleged scheme[,] the Commonwealth would have paid a lower premium or secured better insurance." Instead, the prosecutor maintained that the kickback scheme "defraud[ed] the citizens and government of Kentucky of their right to have the Commonwealth's affairs conducted honestly."

We held that the scheme did not qualify as mail fraud. . . .

3.

Congress responded swiftly. The following year, it enacted a new statute "specifically to cover one of the 'intangible rights' that lower courts had protected . . . prior to *McNally*: 'the intangible right of honest services.'" . . .

B

Congress, Skilling charges, reacted quickly but not clearly: He asserts that §1346 is unconstitutionally vague. To satisfy due process, "a penal statute [must] define the criminal offense [1] with sufficient definiteness that ordinary people can understand what conduct is prohibited and [2] in a manner that does not encourage arbitrary and discriminatory enforcement." The void-for-vagueness doctrine embraces these requirements.

According to Skilling, §1346 meets neither of the two due process essentials. First, the phrase "the intangible right of honest services," he contends, does not adequately define what behavior it bars. Second, he alleges, §1346's "standardless sweep allows policemen, prosecutors, and juries to pursue their personal predilections," thereby "facilitat[ing] opportunistic and arbitrary prosecutions."

In urging invalidation of §1346, Skilling swims against our case law's current, which requires us, if we can, to construe, not condemn, Congress' enactments. Alert to §1346's potential breadth, the Courts of Appeals have divided on how best to interpret the statute. Uniformly, however, they have declined to throw out the statute as irremediably vague.

We agree that §1346 should be construed rather than invalidated. First, we look to the doctrine developed in pre-*McNally* cases in an endeavor to ascertain the meaning of the phrase "the intangible right of honest services." Second, to preserve what Congress certainly intended the statute to cover, we pare that body of precedent down to its core: In the main, the pre-*McNally* cases involved fraudulent schemes to deprive another of honest services through bribes or kickbacks supplied by a third party who had not been deceived. Confined to these paramount applications, §1346 presents no vagueness problem.

1.

There is no doubt that Congress intended §1346 to refer to and incorporate the honest-services doctrine recognized in Court of Appeals' decisions before *McNally* derailed the intangible-rights theory of fraud. Congress enacted §1346 on the heels of *McNally* and drafted the statute using that decision's terminology. As the Second Circuit observed in its leading analysis of §1346:

> "The definite article 'the' suggests that 'intangible right of honest services' had a specific meaning to Congress when it enacted the statute—Congress was recriminalizing mail- and wire-fraud schemes to deprive others of that 'intangible right of honest services,' which had been protected before McNally, not all intangible rights of honest services whatever they might be thought to be." United States v. Rybicki, 354 F.3d 124, 137-138 (2d Cir. 2003) (en banc).

2.

Satisfied that Congress, by enacting §1346, "meant to reinstate the body of pre-*McNally* honest-services law," we have surveyed that case law. In parsing the Courts of Appeals decisions, we acknowledge that Skilling's vagueness challenge has force, for honest-services decisions preceding *McNally* were not models of clarity or consistency. While the honest-services cases preceding *McNally* dominantly and consistently applied the fraud statute to bribery and kickback schemes—schemes that were the basis of most honest-services prosecutions—there was considerable disarray over the statute's application to conduct outside that core category. In light of this disarray, Skilling urges us, as he urged the Fifth Circuit, to invalidate the statute *in toto*.

It has long been our practice, however, before striking a federal statute as impermissibly vague, to consider whether the prescription is amenable to a limiting construction. We have accordingly instructed "the federal courts . . . to avoid constitutional difficulties by [adopting a limiting interpretation] if such a construction is fairly possible." . . .

Although some applications of the pre-*McNally* honest-services doctrine occasioned disagreement among the Courts of Appeals, these cases do not cloud the doctrine's solid core: The "vast majority" of the honest-services cases involved offenders who, in violation of a fiduciary duty, participated in bribery or kickback schemes. Indeed, the *McNally* case itself, which spurred Congress to enact §1346, presented a paradigmatic kickback fact pattern. Congress' reversal of *McNally* and reinstatement of the honest-services doctrine, we conclude, can and should be salvaged by confining its scope to the core pre-*McNally* applications.

As already noted, the honest-services doctrine had its genesis in prosecutions involving bribery allegations. Both before *McNally* and after §1346's enactment, Courts of Appeals described schemes involving bribes or kickbacks as "core . . . honest services fraud precedents"; "paradigm case[s]"; "[t]he most obvious form of honest services fraud"; "core misconduct covered by the statute"; "most [of the] honest services cases"; "typical"; "clear-cut"; and "uniformly . . . cover[ed]."

In view of this history, there is no doubt that Congress intended §1346 to reach *at least* bribes and kickbacks. Reading the statute to proscribe a wider range of offensive conduct, we acknowledge, would raise the due process concerns underlying the vagueness doctrine. To preserve the statute without transgressing constitutional limitations, we now hold that §1346 criminalizes *only* the bribe-and-kickback core of the pre-*McNally* case law.

3.

The Government urges us to go further by locating within §1346's compass another category of proscribed conduct: "undisclosed self-dealing by a public official or private employee—*i.e.*, the taking of official action by the employee that furthers his own undisclosed financial interests while purporting to act in the interests of those to whom he owes a fiduciary duty." . . .

[The government's] contentions [do not] withstand[] close inspection. *McNally*, as we have already observed, involved a classic kickback scheme [as opposed to mere undisclosed self-dealing]. . . . Nor are we persuaded that the pre-*McNally* conflict-of-interest cases constitute core applications of the honest-services doctrine. Although the Courts of Appeals upheld honest-services convictions for "some schemes of non-disclosure and concealment of material information," they reached no consensus on which schemes qualified. In light of the relative infrequency of conflict-of-interest prosecutions in comparison to bribery and kickback charges, and the intercircuit inconsistencies they produced, we conclude that a reasonable limiting construction of §1346 must exclude this amorphous category of cases.

Further dispelling doubt on this point is the familiar principle that "ambiguity concerning the ambit of criminal statutes should be resolved in favor of lenity." . . .

In sum, our construction of §1346 "establish[es] a uniform national standard, define[s] honest services with clarity, reach[es] only seriously culpable conduct, and accomplish[es] Congress's goal of 'overruling' *McNally*." "If Congress desires to go further," we reiterate, "it must speak more clearly than it has."[44]

4.

Interpreted to encompass only bribery and kickback schemes, §1346 is not unconstitutionally vague. Recall that the void-for-vagueness doctrine addresses concerns about (1) fair notice and (2) arbitrary and discriminatory prosecutions. A prohibition on fraudulently depriving another of one's honest services by accepting bribes or kickbacks does not present a problem on either score.

As to fair notice, "whatever the school of thought concerning the scope and meaning of §1346, it has always been "as plain as a pikestaff that" bribes and kickbacks constitute honest-services fraud." . . .

As to arbitrary prosecutions, we perceive no significant risk that the honest-services statute, as we interpret it today, will be stretched out of shape. Its prohibition on bribes and kickbacks draws content not only from the pre-*McNally* case law, but also from federal statutes proscribing—and defining—similar crimes. *See, e.g.*, 18 U.S.C. §§201(b), 666(a)(2); 41 U.S.C. §52(2) ("The term 'kickback' means any money, fee, commission, credit, gift, gratuity, thing of value, or compensation of any kind which is provided, directly or indirectly, to [enumerated persons] for the purpose of improperly obtaining or rewarding favorable treatment in connection with [enumerated circumstances]."). . . .[45]

It remains to determine whether Skilling's conduct violated §1346. Skilling's honest-services prosecution, the Government concedes, was not "prototypical." The Government charged Skilling with conspiring to defraud Enron's shareholders

44. If Congress were to take up the enterprise of criminalizing "undisclosed self-dealing by a public official or private employee," it would have to employ standards of sufficient definiteness and specificity to overcome due process concerns. The Government proposes a standard that prohibits the "taking of official action by the employee that furthers his own undisclosed financial interests while purporting to act in the interests of those to whom he owes a fiduciary duty," so long as the employee acts with a specific intent to deceive and the undisclosed conduct could influence the victim to change its behavior. That formulation, however, leaves many questions unanswered. How direct or significant does the conflicting financial interest have to be? To what extent does the official action have to further that interest in order to amount to fraud? To whom should the disclosure be made and what information should it convey? These questions and others call for particular care in attempting to formulate an adequate criminal prohibition in this context.

45. Overlap with other federal statutes does not render §1346 superfluous. The principal federal bribery statute, §201, for example, generally applies only to federal public officials, so §1346's application to state and local corruption and to private-sector fraud reaches misconduct that might otherwise go unpunished.

by misrepresenting the company's fiscal health, thereby artificially inflating its stock price. It was the Government's theory at trial that Skilling "profited from the fraudulent scheme . . . through the receipt of salary and bonuses, . . . and through the sale of approximately $200 million in Enron stock, which netted him $89 million." *Id.*, at 51.

The Government did not, at any time, allege that Skilling solicited or accepted side payments from a third party in exchange for making these misrepresentations. It is therefore clear that, as we read §1346, Skilling did not commit honest-services fraud.

Because the indictment alleged three objects of the conspiracy—honest-services wire fraud, money-or-property wire fraud, and securities fraud—Skilling's conviction is flawed. This determination, however, does not necessarily require reversal of the conspiracy conviction; we recently confirmed that errors of th[is] variety are subject to harmless-error analysis. . . . We leave this [matter] for resolution on remand.

Justice Scalia, concurring in part and concurring in the judgment.

I . . . agree that the decision upholding Skilling's conviction for so-called "honest-services fraud" must be reversed, but for a different reason. In my view, the specification in 18 U.S.C. §1346 that "scheme or artifice to defraud" in the mail-fraud and wire-fraud statutes, §§1341 and 1343, includes "a scheme or artifice to deprive another of the intangible right of honest services," is vague, and therefore violates the Due Process Clause of the Fifth Amendment. The Court strikes a pose of judicial humility in proclaiming that our task is "not to destroy the Act . . . but to construe it." But in transforming the prohibition of "honest-services fraud" into a prohibition of "bribery and kick-backs" it is wielding a power we long ago abjured: the power to define new federal crimes. . . .

NOTES AND QUESTIONS

1. *Skilling* is a "private sector" honest services case: The defendant was not a public official, but rather a private CFO accused of defrauding the investors of a publicly traded company. *McNally*, discussed in the *Skilling* case, was a "public sector" honest services fraud case because McNally was a politician and the victims of his fraud were the taxpayers of his jurisdiction. (The victims of public sector honest services fraud can also be "the voters.") By discussing them together, the Supreme Court indicates that the same limitation is placed on both categories of cases: The "honest services" fraud must be the result of receiving or paying bribes or kickbacks.
2. Do you agree that the pre-*Skilling* definition of honest services was unconstitutionally vague? Consider Justice Scalia's discussion of it in his dissent to the denial of *certiorari* in Sorich v. United States, 129 S. Ct. 1308 (2009):

> Though it consists of only 28 words, the statute [18 U.S.C. §1346] has been invoked to impose criminal penalties upon a staggeringly broad swath of

behavior, including misconduct not only by public officials and employees but also by private employees and corporate fiduciaries. Courts have upheld convictions of a local housing official who failed to disclose a conflict of interest; a businessman who attempted to pay a state legislator to exercise "informal and behind-the-scenes influence on legislation"; students who schemed with their professors to turn in plagiarized work; lawyers who made side-payments to insurance adjusters in exchange for the expedited processing of their clients' pending claims; and, in the decision we are asked to review here, city employees who engaged in political-patronage hiring for local civil-service jobs.

If the "honest services" theory—broadly stated, that officeholders and employees owe a duty to act only in the best interests of their constituents and employers—is taken seriously and carried to its logical conclusion, presumably the statute also renders criminal a state legislator's decision to vote for a bill because he expects it will curry favor with a small minority essential to his reelection; a mayor's attempt to use the prestige of his office to obtain a restaurant table without a reservation; a public employee's recommendation of his incompetent friend for a public contract; and any self-dealing by a corporate officer. Indeed, it would seemingly cover a salaried employee's phoning in sick to go to a ball game.

3. Although the Supreme Court's edict in *Skilling* is clear—honest services cases must involve the payment of a bribe or kickback—the Court did not define the meaning of these terms. It did, however, reference the federal bribery statutes, 18 U.S.C. §§201 & 666, and the health care fraud kickback statute, 41 U.S.C. §52(2). As a result, a number of critical questions remain after the *Skilling* decision, such as how much of the interpretation of, say, the concept of bribery found in the jurisprudence surrounding §201 (e.g., that it features a strict *quid pro quo* requirement) will be imported to the honest services area.
4. Almost immediately after *Skilling* came down, the Department of Justice went back to Congress and asked for the decision to be overturned though legislative action. Consider the following:

ROBERT PLOTKIN & NICHOLAS B. LEWIS,
HONEST-SERVICES FRAUD IN THE WAKE OF *SKILLING*
18 No. 4 Bus. Crimes Bull. 1 (2010)

Responding to the Court's call and to these ongoing problems, Sen. Patrick Leahy (D-VT) recently introduced the "Honest Services Restoration Act" to amend §1346 by prohibiting undisclosed self-dealing by public officials and by the officers and directors of public corporations. Assistant Attorney General Breur, urging the Senate Judiciary Committee to fill in what the DOJ sees as a gap left by *Skilling*, has argued that new legislation is necessary because individuals can still improperly steer benefits to entities in which they have an undisclosed interest without engaging in bribery. To preempt potential vagueness challenges, Breur asserted that Congress should require the government to prove both the knowing concealment of an undisclosed interest and a specific intent to defraud, thus minimizing the risk that someone might be convicted for the inadvertent failure to disclose an interest.

> The proposed legislation attempts to avoid vagueness by defining undisclosed self-dealing by a public official to occur when: 1) a public official performs an official act to benefit that official (or someone or some entity closely connected to that official); and 2) the official knowingly conceals or fails to disclose material information that the official had a duty to disclose under an existing law or regulation. Meanwhile, undisclosed self-dealing by a private actor would occur when: 1) officers or directors perform acts which cause or are intended to cause harm to employers and which are undertaken to benefit or further (by $5,000 or more) a financial interest of the officers or directors (or individuals or entities connected to them); and 2) the officer or director knowingly conceals or fails to disclose information required to be disclosed under existing law or regulation.
>
> **Conclusion**
>
> While the proposed legislation contains more detail than the current 1346, it is not clear whether it will address adequately the *Skilling* Court's admonition "to employ standards of sufficient definiteness and specificity to overcome due process concerns." It is also unclear whether there is enough political support to pass legislation that further expands federal authority in a time of anti-federal public sentiment. Honest-services fraud thus remains as murky as it was before *Skilling*. Whether Congress meets the challenge this time around still remains to be seen.

Do you think that Senator Leahy's legislation (drafted by DOJ) appropriately closes the gaps in §1346 created by the *Skilling* decision? If not, how would you redraft §1346 to accomplish this task? Or do you think that the holding in *Skilling* should stand? As you are thinking about these questions, consider the following case.

UNITED STATES v. MILOVANOVIC

627 F.3d 405 (9th Cir. 2010)

KLEINFELD, Circuit Judge:

We address "honest services" mail fraud.

I. Facts

The district court dismissed the indictment before trial, so we describe the facts as though the indictment had been proved, which of course is not the case. The question is whether the charges, if proved, would amount to the crime charged.

According to the indictment, defendants Milovanovic and Lamb corrupted issuance of commercial drivers' licenses in the State of Washington. The other four defendants, Hot, Kovacic, Bilanovic, and Djordjevic, took advantage of the corrupt scheme to defraud the State of Washington into issuing them the undeserved licenses. A person has to be a Washington resident and pass a written test and a driving test to lawfully obtain a Washington commercial drivers' license. Milovanovic and Lamb and their clients allegedly arranged to get commercial drivers' licenses by cheating on the tests and falsifying residency, in exchange for bribes.

Milovanovic worked as a certified Bosnian translator for a firm that the state government used. He contacted Bosnian speakers in other states, and told them that if they came to Spokane and paid him personally $2,500, he could get them Washington commercial drivers' licenses. When the out-of-state Bosnians came, Milovanovic enabled them to cheat on the written test by giving them the answers as they took it. Then Milovanovic bribed Lamb, who worked for a firm the state government hired to administer the driving test, $200 to $500 per person to falsify that test result too. The applicants would bring the falsified forms and the State license fee to the State Department of Licensing for a temporary permit, which would be turned into a permanent permit when Lamb mailed or faxed in his falsified log. The licenses were then mailed by a third contractor to the applicants at the false Washington address Milovanovic had supplied.

Lamb and the firm for which Milovanovic worked both had contracts with the state saying that they were independent contractors, not employees and not agents. The state was not deprived of its fee, and did not lose a nickel on account of the dishonest test and residency certifications. There was no paperwork saying that any fiduciary duty pertained.

The superseding indictment charges mail fraud and conspiracy to commit mail fraud by Milovanovic, Lamb, and four of their customers under 18 U.S.C. §§1341, 1346, and 2. The district court dismissed the indictment on the ground that the mail fraud statute required a fiduciary relationship, and indicated that the jury would be instructed that the crime required economic harm to the victim. The United States appeals.

II. Analysis

. . . Defendants argue that even though we have not said so, we [have] implied that a fiduciary relationship is a sine qua non of "honest services" mail fraud. We have not so held. . . . It remains [an] open question. . . .

Deciding whether Milovanovic and Lamb were fiduciaries would be difficult because they were plainly used as agents to administer the state's commercial drivers' license tests, yet the contracts state that they were not agents. For purposes of this decision, we take the state contracts at their word, and assume without deciding that Milovanovic and Lamb were not agents and were not fiduciaries.

The Supreme Court has not spoken on whether a fiduciary duty is a *sine qua non* of "honest services" mail fraud. Our sister circuits have given varying and conflicting answers, so no decision we make can avoid a circuit split. . . .

As always, we begin our analysis of the mail fraud and "honest service" statutes with the text. The text of the mail fraud statute appears to rule out limiting "honest services" fraud to fiduciaries. Congress provided that "whoever" perpetrates a fraudulent scheme using the mails commits the crime of mail fraud. The perpetrator category "whoever" literally means anyone, whether fiduciary or not.

A purposiveness analysis, considering the social harm the statute addresses, likewise suggests no limitation to fiduciaries. The purpose evident from the face of the statute is prevention and punishment of fraud. Several types of fraud expressly listed, such as selling counterfeit items, do not require a fiduciary relationship. Traditional mail frauds, such as soliciting money for items that are not what they are advertised to be, or collecting remittances by mail and not sending the goods ordered, require no fiduciary relationship. Fraud generally means deception, the use of misrepresentation to obtain something of value or deprive another of something of value. Plenty of traditional fraud is committed in arms-length relationships. If a merchant purports to sell a pound of coffee, but uses false weights to put only fifteen ounces in the bag, he commits fraud despite the arms-length, nonfiduciary relationship. A fiduciary relationship would give him additional duties beyond the honesty required of any seller. He would have to not only provide sixteen ounces in a pound, but also advise if the shop down the street was selling better coffee cheaper (a corporate director renting space to the corporation would have to disclose availability of better, cheaper space to the board because of his fiduciary duty). . . .

Nor do the kinds of honest services fraud to which the statute is limited by Skilling—bribes and kickbacks—imply a fiduciary limitation. One could bribe a blogger to recommend a bistro, or kick back ten percent to a merchant who recommended a particular electrician to customers, without either of them having a fiduciary relationship. One does not have to be a fiduciary to take bribes or kickbacks.

The cases suggest a legitimate and important purpose in trying to find some sort of limitation on federal mail fraud, so that prosecutors cannot convict whoever may be on the wrong end of political shotguns. . . . [O]nce fraud is broadened to deprivation of services, almost anyone can be charged with not doing all that they ought to have done in performing their jobs, and if broadened that far, the notion of bribes may broaden commensurately so that limitations on prosecutors run amuck become illusory. Is "sneak out to the ball game with me, I already have an extra ticket you can use" a bribe by the offeror and a deprivation of honest services by the employee who accepts?

Judge Raggi's concurrence in the Second Circuit *en banc* decision United States v. Rybicki, 354 F.3d 124 (2d Cir. 2003), suggests a sound textual basis for giving some content to the statute so that it distinguishes between corruption and mere nonfeasance. Her limitation makes textual sense, and is not merely picked out of the air, or based on some policy not set out or implied by the statute. We analyze the statute as she does.

The key is, as it should be, reading the words of Section 1346. This post-*McNally* restoration of "honest services" fraud says "scheme or artifice to deprive another of the intangible right of honest services." Both "whoever" and "honest" matter. This language does not limit "whoever" in Section 1341 to fiduciaries or any other subset of "whoever." "While a particular relationship may shed light on whether one person owes another honest services, the language of §1346 indicates that the critical factor is the type of service at issue, not the relationship of the parties."

The words of Section 1346 taken together with Section 1341 imply five limitations. First, there must be a legally enforceable right to have another provide honest services, because without that right, there could be no deprivation of the right. Second, not any deprivation of services provides a predicate for fraud, only deprivation of services the value of which depends on their being performed honestly. The statute says "honest services," not just "services," and every word should be accorded meaning. Dishonest deprivation of services differs from deprivation of honesty in providing services. The statute criminalizes the latter, not the former. Suppose an employee in charge of purchasing office supplies, bribed by a free ticket, sneaks off to the ball game leaving his suit jacket on the chair and having his coworker tell his boss if she inquires that he is in the men's room. He has dishonestly deprived his employer of services in exchange for a bribe, but has not deprived his employer of honesty in the performance of his tasks, as he would if in return for the ticket he steered the employer's business to the provider of the ticket instead of a cheaper, better supplier.

Third, the defendant must intend to defraud, because Section 1341 says "having devised or intending to devise any scheme or artifice to defraud." That the victim may not get all the services it should is insufficient if the specific intent to defraud is absent. Fourth, the scheme must use fraud, that is misrepresentation or concealment of a material fact. And fifth, the mails must be used to further the scheme.

The statute does not say that the fraud must be intended to deprive the victim of money or property. At common law, in the civil context, fraud requires damages, ordinarily a monetary loss, but criminal fraud has always been broader in its reach. Ordinarily, fraud against private victims will have that intent, but fraud against the government often will not. For example, in this case, a commercial drivers' license, though it has considerable economic value to the holder, has no monetary value to the government beyond the fee the government receives when it issues the license, a fee that was paid in this case. What the government seeks, by honest enforcement of the testing requirements, is not money, but safety. The government uses the commercial drivers' license exams to protect its citizens from having to drive their little compact cars alongside big rigs driven by people who have not demonstrated their ability to drive safely. It would make no sense, in terms of the purpose of the fraud statutes or the commercial drivers' license statutes and regulations, to treat as fraud only those schemes that deprived the government of its license issuance fees, yet not of the purpose of the testing, assuring that the drivers honestly passed the tests. All sorts of government services that have to be performed honestly do not involve the financial interest of government—for example, a bribe to a policeman to let a criminal go. The gravamen of the harm prohibited by the statute is dishonesty in providing services where the victim, the government in this case, was entitled to have the services performed honestly.

III. Conclusion

Honest services mail fraud does not require proof of a fiduciary relationship. Nor does it require damages to the money or property of the victim. It is, however, subject to the limitations set out above. The district court thus erred in dismissing the indictment.

REVERSED and REMANDED.

V. USE OF THE MAILS

SCHMUCK v. UNITED STATES

489 U.S. 705 (1989)

Justice BLACKMUN delivered the opinion of the Court.

I.

In August 1983, petitioner Wayne T. Schmuck, a used-car distributor, was indicted in the United States District Court for the Western District of Wisconsin on 12 counts of mail fraud, in violation of 18 U. S. C. §§1341 and 1342.

The alleged fraud was a common and straightforward one. Schmuck purchased used cars, rolled back their odometers, and then sold the automobiles to Wisconsin retail dealers for prices artificially inflated because of the low-mileage readings. These unwitting car dealers, relying on the altered odometer figures, then resold the cars to customers, who in turn paid prices reflecting Schmuck's fraud. To complete the resale of each automobile, the dealer who purchased it from Schmuck would submit a title-application form to the Wisconsin Department of Transportation on behalf of his retail customer. The receipt of a Wisconsin title was a prerequisite for completing the resale; without it, the dealer could not transfer title to the customer and the customer could not obtain Wisconsin tags. The submission of the title-application form supplied the mailing element of each of the alleged mail frauds.

Before trial, Schmuck moved to dismiss the indictment on the ground that the mailings at issue—the submissions of the title-application forms by the automobile dealers—were not in furtherance of the fraudulent scheme and, thus, did not satisfy the mailing element of the crime of mail fraud. . . . The District Court denied [this] motion[]. After trial, the jury returned guilty verdicts on all 12 counts.

The District Court instructed the jury that in order to find Schmuck guilty of mail fraud the jury had to find beyond a reasonable doubt that he knowingly devised a scheme to defraud, and that he caused matter to be sent in the mail for the purpose of executing that scheme. The court also told the jury that it could find Schmuck guilty if the use of the mails was reasonably foreseeable.

A divided panel of the United States Court of Appeals for the Seventh Circuit reversed and remanded the case for a new trial. Although the panel rejected Schmuck's claim that he was entitled to a judgment of acquittal because the mailings were not made in furtherance of his scheme, it ruled that under Rule 31(c) the District Court should have instructed the jury on the lesser offense of odometer tampering. . . .

We granted *certiorari* to define further the scope of the mail fraud statute. . . .

II.

"The federal mail fraud statute does not purport to reach all frauds, but only those limited instances in which the use of the mails is a part of the execution of the fraud, leaving all other cases to be dealt with by appropriate state law."

Kann v. United States, 323 U.S. 88, 95 (1944). To be part of the execution of the fraud, however, the use of the mails need not be an essential element of the scheme. Pereira v. United States, 347 U.S. 1, 8 (1954). It is sufficient for the mailing to be "incident to an essential part of the scheme," *ibid.*, or "a step in [the] plot," Badders v. United States, 240 U.S. 391, 394 (1916).

Schmuck, relying principally on this Court's decisions in *Kann*, Parr v. United States, 363 U.S. 370 (1960), and United States v. Maze, 414 U.S. 395 (1974), argues that mail fraud can be predicated only on a mailing that affirmatively assists the perpetrator in carrying out his fraudulent scheme. The mailing element of the offense, he contends, cannot be satisfied by a mailing, such as those at issue here, that is routine and innocent in and of itself, and that, far from furthering the execution of the fraud, occurs after the fraud has come to fruition, is merely tangentially related to the fraud, and is counterproductive in that it creates a "paper trail" from which the fraud may be discovered. We disagree both with this characterization of the mailings in the present case and with this description of the applicable law.

We begin by considering the scope of Schmuck's fraudulent scheme. Schmuck was charged with devising and executing a scheme to defraud Wisconsin retail automobile customers who based their decisions to purchase certain automobiles at least in part on the low-mileage readings provided by the tampered odometers. This was a fairly large-scale operation. Evidence at trial indicated that Schmuck had employed a man known only as "Fred" to turn back the odometers on about 150 different cars. Schmuck then marketed these cars to a number of dealers, several of whom he dealt with on a consistent basis over a period of about 15 years. Indeed, of the 12 automobiles that are the subject of the counts of the indictment, 5 were sold to "P and A Sales," and 4 to "Southside Auto." Thus, Schmuck's was not a "one-shot" operation in which he sold a single car to an isolated dealer. His was an ongoing fraudulent venture. A rational jury could have concluded that the success of Schmuck's venture depended upon his continued harmonious relations with, and good reputation among, retail dealers, which in turn required the smooth flow of cars from the dealers to their Wisconsin customers.

Under these circumstances, we believe that a rational jury could have found that the title-registration mailings were part of the execution of the fraudulent scheme, a scheme which did not reach fruition until the retail dealers resold the cars and effected transfers of title. Schmuck's scheme would have come to an abrupt halt if the dealers either had lost faith in Schmuck or had not been able to resell the cars obtained from him. These resales and Schmuck's relationships with the retail dealers naturally depended on the successful passage of title among the various parties. Thus, although the registration-form mailings may not have contributed directly to the duping of either the retail dealers or the customers, they were necessary to the passage of title, which in turn was essential to the perpetuation of Schmuck's scheme. As noted earlier, a mailing that is "incident to an essential part of the scheme" satisfies the mailing element of the mail fraud offense. The mailings here fit this description.

Once the full flavor of Schmuck's scheme is appreciated, the critical distinctions between this case and the three cases in which this Court has delimited the reach of the mail fraud statute—*Kann*, *Parr*, and *Maze*—are readily apparent.

The defendants in *Kann* were corporate officers and directors accused of setting up a dummy corporation through which to divert profits into their own pockets. As part of this fraudulent scheme, the defendants caused the corporation to issue two checks payable to them. The defendants cashed these checks at local banks, which then mailed the checks to the drawee banks for collection. This Court held that the mailing of the cashed checks to the drawee banks could not supply the mailing element of the mail fraud charges. The defendants' fraudulent scheme had reached fruition. "It was immaterial to them, or to any consummation of the scheme, how the bank which paid or credited the check would collect from the drawee bank."

In *Parr*, several defendants were charged, *inter alia*, with having fraudulently obtained gasoline and a variety of other products and services through the unauthorized use of a credit card issued to the school district which employed them. The mailing element of the mail fraud charges in *Parr* was purportedly satisfied when the oil company which issued the credit card mailed invoices to the school district for payment, and when the district mailed payment in the form of a check. Relying on *Kann*, this Court held that these mailings were not in execution of the scheme as required by the statute because it was immaterial to the defendants how the oil company went about collecting its payment.[7]

Later, in *Maze*, the defendant allegedly stole his roommate's credit card, headed south on a winter jaunt, and obtained food and lodging at motels along the route by placing the charges on the stolen card. The mailing element of the mail fraud charge was supplied by the fact that the defendant knew that each motel proprietor would mail an invoice to the bank that had issued the credit card, which in turn would mail a bill to the card owner for payment. The Court found that these mailings could not support mail fraud charges because the defendant's scheme had reached fruition when he checked out of each motel. The success of his scheme in no way depended on the mailings; they merely determined which of his victims would ultimately bear the loss.

The title-registration mailings at issue here served a function different from the mailings in *Kann*, *Parr*, and *Maze*. The intrabank mailings in *Kann* and the credit card invoice mailings in *Parr* and *Maze* involved little more than post-fraud accounting among the potential victims of the various schemes, and the long-term success of the fraud did not turn on which of the potential victims bore the ultimate loss. Here, in contrast, a jury rationally could have found that Schmuck by no means was indifferent to the fact of who bore the loss. The mailing of the title-registration

7. *Parr* also involved a second fraudulent scheme through which the defendant school board members misappropriated school district tax revenues. The Government argued that the mailing element of the mail fraud charges was supplied by the mailing of tax statements, checks, and receipts. This Court held, however, that in the absence of any evidence that the tax levy was increased as part of the fraud, the mailing element of the offense could not be supplied by mailings "made or caused to be made under the imperative command of duty imposed by state law." 363 U.S., at 391. No such legal duty is at issue here. Whereas the mailings of the tax documents in Parr were the direct product of the school district's state constitutional duty to levy taxes, *id.*, at 387, and would have been made regardless of the defendants' fraudulent scheme, the mailings in the present case, though in compliance with Wisconsin's car-registration procedure, were derivative of Schmuck's scheme to sell "doctored" cars and would not have occurred but for that scheme.

forms was an essential step in the successful passage of title to the retail purchasers. Moreover, a failure of this passage of title would have jeopardized Schmuck's relationship of trust and goodwill with the retail dealers upon whose unwitting cooperation his scheme depended. Schmuck's reliance on our prior cases limiting the reach of the mail fraud statute is simply misplaced.

To the extent that Schmuck would draw from these previous cases a general rule that routine mailings that are innocent in themselves cannot supply the mailing element of the mail fraud offense, he misapprehends this Court's precedents. In *Parr* the Court specifically acknowledged that "innocent" mailings—ones that contain no false information—may supply the mailing element. In other cases, the Court has found the elements of mail fraud to be satisfied where the mailings have been routine. *See, e.g.*, Carpenter v. United States, 484 U.S. 19, 28 (1987) (mailing newspapers).

We also reject Schmuck's contention that mailings that someday may contribute to the uncovering of a fraudulent scheme cannot supply the mailing element of the mail fraud offense. The relevant question at all times is whether the mailing is part of the execution of the scheme as conceived by the perpetrator at the time, regardless of whether the mailing later, through hindsight, may prove to have been counterproductive and return to haunt the perpetrator of the fraud. The mail fraud statute includes no guarantee that the use of the mails for the purpose of executing a fraudulent scheme will be risk free. Those who use the mails to defraud proceed at their peril.

For these reasons, we agree with the Court of Appeals that the mailings in this case satisfy the mailing element of the mail fraud offenses.

Justice Scalia, with whom Justice Brennan, Justice Marshall, and Justice O'Connor join, dissenting.

. . . The purpose of the mail fraud statute is "to prevent the post office from being used to carry [fraudulent schemes] into effect." The law does not establish a general federal remedy against fraudulent conduct, with use of the mails as the jurisdictional hook, but reaches only "those limited instances in which the use of the mails is *a part of the execution of the fraud*, leaving all other cases to be dealt with by appropriate state law." *Kann*, 323 U.S., at 95 (emphasis added). In other words, it is mail fraud, not mail and fraud, that incurs liability. This federal statute is not violated by a fraudulent scheme in which, at some point, a mailing happens to occur—nor even by one in which a mailing predictably and necessarily occurs. The mailing must be in furtherance of the fraud. . . .

Nor can the force of our cases be avoided by combining all of the individual transactions into a single scheme, and saying, as the Court does, that if the dealers' mailings obtaining title for each retail purchaser had not occurred then the dealers would have stopped trusting petitioner for future transactions. (That conclusion seems to me a *non sequitur*, but I accept it for the sake of argument.) This establishes, at most, that the scheme could not technically have been consummated if the mechanical step of the mailings to obtain conveyance of title had not occurred. But we have held that the indispensability of such mechanical mailings, not strictly in furtherance of the fraud, is not enough to invoke the statute. For example, when officials of a school district embezzled tax funds over the course of several years, we held that no mail fraud had occurred even though the success of the scheme plainly depended on the officials' causing tax bills to be sent by mail (and thus tax payments to be received) every year. *Parr*, 363 U.S., at 388-392. Similarly, when those officials caused the school district to pay by mail credit card bills—a step plainly necessary to enable their continued fraudulent use of the credit card—we concluded that no mail fraud had occurred.

I find it impossible to escape these precedents in the present case. Assuming the Court to be correct in concluding that failure to pass title to the cars would have threatened the success of the scheme, the same could have been said of failure to collect taxes or to pay the credit card bills in *Parr*. And I think it particularly significant that in *Kann* the Government proposed a theory *identical* to that which the Court today uses. Since the scheme was ongoing, the Government urged, the fact that the mailing of the two checks had occurred after the defendants had pocketed the fraudulently obtained cash made no difference. "[T]he defendants expected to receive further bonuses and profits," and therefore "the clearing of these checks in the ordinary course was essential to [the scheme's] further prosecution. . . . The Court rejected this argument, concluding that "the subsequent banking transactions between the banks concerned were merely incidental and collateral to the scheme and not a part of it." I think the mailing of the title application forms equivalently incidental here. . . .

NOTES AND QUESTIONS

1. Though *Schmuck* initially describes the relationship between the mailing and the fraud that is required to satisfy the statute's jurisdictional element, the essential test is set out at the opinion's end: "whether the mailing is part of the execution of the scheme as conceived by the perpetrator at the time [he puts his fraud into motion]." With this in mind, do you think it is a coincidence that Schmuck was charged with defrauding Wisconsin's retail customers—as opposed to the car dealerships with whom he directly conducted business? Was there a risk to the prosecution of charging the case in this manner?
2. Are *Kann, Parr,* and *Maze* truly distinguishable from *Schmuck*? Or is it more accurate to say that, at the very least, *Parr* is no longer good law in light of the *Schmuck* case? Is there really any difference between the credit card statements and corresponding payments mailed in the *Parr* case, for instance, and the title applications and completed titles mailed in the *Schmuck* case? Isn't the dissent correct to say that, in both situations, the continued success of the defendants' fraudulent scheme depended on the recipients of those mailings treating them as routine and non-fraudulent?
3. Reread footnote 7. What, exactly, is the distinction between the tax mailings in *Parr* and the title mailings in *Schmuck*? Is it a distinction that should make a difference? Regardless of the correct answer to these questions, it appears safe to conclude that the holding of *Parr* elucidated in footnote 7

is no longer good law. *See* United States v. Kellogg, 955 F.2d 1244 (9th Cir. 1992) (defendant convicted of mail fraud for sending false tax returns even though the Internal Revenue Service required the mailing); United States v. Helmsley, 941 F.2d 71 (2d Cir. 1991) (rejecting a claim that the mail fraud statute does not apply in circumstances in which the defendant was required to mail the documents).

4. Why would the Supreme Court go to such lengths to distinguish as opposed to overrule earlier precedent?

UNITED STATES v. BRADSHAW

282 Fed. Appx. 264 (4th Cir. 2008)

Per Curiam:

George William Bradshaw, II, former commander of the West Virginia state police detachment at Martinsburg, appeals from his conviction of one count of mail fraud under 18 U.S.C. §1341. At trial the government contended that Bradshaw had devised a fraudulent scheme to steal cash that had been seized as evidence. According to the government, Bradshaw, in furtherance of his scheme, falsely reported to the state treasury department (through the mail) that there was no unclaimed property at the Martinsburg detachment. After the jury returned a guilty verdict, the district court denied Bradshaw's motion for judgment of acquittal and sentenced him to fifteen months' incarceration followed by three years of supervised release. On appeal Bradshaw argues (1) that the evidence was insufficient to support his mail fraud conviction. . . .

To obtain a mail fraud conviction, the prosecution must prove that "the defendant (1) knowingly participated in a scheme to defraud and (2) mailed . . . anything 'for the purpose of executing that scheme.'" A mailing is considered to be "for the purpose of executing" a fraudulent scheme if it is "designed to lull the victims into a false sense of security," even if it is "incident to an essential part of the scheme." Thus, a mailing that is accurate, routine, or sent after the goods have been received can support a mail fraud conviction, so long as the mailing was designed to "make apprehension of the defendant less likely."

Bradshaw advances several arguments in support of his position that his mailing was not in furtherance of the scheme to defraud. First, Bradshaw argues that the mailing and the fraudulent scheme were insufficiently connected because the cash was stolen prior to the mailing. However, "[m]ailings occurring after receipt of the goods obtained by fraud are within the statute if they were designed to lull the victims into a false sense of security, postpone their ultimate complaint to the authorities, and therefore make the apprehension of the defendants less likely than if no mailings had taken place." Here a reasonable jury could have found that Bradshaw sent the mailing, which falsely informed the treasury that there was no unclaimed property, to ensure that the treasury would not come to the detachment to collect the property and discover the missing cash. Because the mailing was designed to "lull the victim"—the state treasury—it is of no moment that the mailing occurred after Bradshaw stole the cash. . . .

Finally, Bradshaw contends that the mailing did not further his fraud because a report of no unclaimed property would be unusual and thus lead to heightened suspicion from the state treasury. But "[t]he relevant question at all times is whether the mailing is part of the execution of the scheme as conceived by the perpetrator at the time, regardless of whether the mailing later, through hindsight, may prove to have been counterproductive." Because a reasonable jury could have concluded that Bradshaw believed at the time that the mailing would conceal his scheme from detection, this argument is foreclosed as well.

Thus, in reviewing the evidence, we find that there was sufficient evidence to support the jury's verdict of guilt. We therefore affirm the district court's denial of the motion for judgment of acquittal. . . .

chapter 5

Bank Fraud

I. INTRODUCTION: COLLAPSE OF THE REAL ESTATE BUBBLE IN 2008 AND NEW EMPHASIS ON BANK AND MORTGAGE FRAUD

In the late 1980s, the Savings and Loan industry in the United States—traditionally a very stable source of homeowner mortgages—came crashing down. Unwise deregulation of the industry coupled with massive amounts of fraud were the culprits. In addition to initiating regulatory remedies, the government, through DOJ, responded to the crisis by setting up criminal task forces and aggressively prosecuted bank and mortgage fraud. This effort lasted about a decade until other problems, particularly the post-9/11 threat of international terrorism, occupied the time and effort of most federal law enforcement officials. A generation after the S&L crisis, however, bank and mortgage fraud returned to the forefront of white collar prosecution as a result of the near collapse of the world's economy in 2008-2009. The "Great Recession," as many called it, had its roots in the bursting of the "real estate bubble." This chapter explains a bit about the economics behind this crisis, and then focuses on the related crime.

CREDIT CRISIS—THE ESSENTIALS

*N.Y. Times, Updated Sept. 22, 2009**

Overview

In the fall of 2008, the credit squeeze, which had emerged a little more than a year before, ballooned into Wall Street's biggest crisis since the Great Depression. As hundreds of billions in mortgage-related investments went bad, mighty investment banks that once ruled high finance have crumbled or reinvented themselves as humdrum commercial banks. The nation's largest insurance company and largest

*http://topics.nytimes.com/top/reference/timestopics/subjects/c/credit_crisis/index.html.

savings and loan both were seized by the government. The channels of credit, the arteries of the global financial system, have been constricted, cutting off crucial funds to consumers and businesses small and large.

In response, the federal government adopted a $700 billion bailout plan in October 2008 meant to reassure the markets and get credit flowing again. But the crisis began to spread to Europe and to emerging markets, with governments scrambling to prop up banks, broaden guarantees for deposits and agree on a coordinated response. In February 2009, a $787 billion economic stimulus measure was also adopted.

Origins

The roots of the credit crisis stretch back to another notable boom-and-bust: the tech bubble of the late 1990s. When the stock market began a steep decline in 2000 and the nation slipped into recession the next year, the Federal Reserve sharply lowered interest rates to limit the economic damage.

Lower interest rates make mortgage payments cheaper, and demand for homes began to rise, sending prices up. In addition, millions of homeowners took advantage of the rate drop to refinance their existing mortgages. As the industry ramped up, the quality of the mortgages went down.

And turn sour they did, when homebuyers had to leverage themselves to the hilt to make a purchase. Default and delinquency rates began to rise in 2006, but the pace of lending did not slow. Banks and other investors had devised a plethora of complex financial instruments to slice up and resell the mortgage-backed securities and to hedge against any risks—or so they thought.

The Crisis Takes Hold

The first shoe to drop was the collapse in June 2007 of two hedge funds owned by Bear Stearns that had invested heavily in the subprime market. As the year went on, more banks found that securities they thought were safe were tainted with what came to be called toxic mortgages. At the same time, the rising number of foreclosures helped speed the fall of housing prices, and the number of prime mortgages in default began to increase.

The Federal Reserve took unprecedented steps to bolster Wall Street. But still the losses mounted, and in March 2008 the Fed staved off a Bear Stearns bankruptcy by assuming $30 billion in liabilities and engineering a sale to JPMorgan Chase for a price that was less than the worth of Bear's Manhattan skyscraper.

Sales, Failures and Seizures

In August, government officials began to become concerned as the stock prices of Fannie Mae and Freddie Mac, government-sponsored entities that were linchpins of the housing market, slid sharply. On Sept. 7, the Treasury Department announced it was taking them over.

Events began to move even faster. On Sept. 12, top government and finance officials gathered for talks to fend off bankruptcy for Lehman Brothers. The talks broke down, and the government refused to step in and salvage Lehman as it had for Bear. Lehman's failure sent shock waves through the global banking system, as became increasingly clear in the following weeks. Merrill Lynch, which had not been previously thought to be in danger, sold itself to the Bank of America to avoid a similar fate.

On Sept. 16, American International Group, an insurance giant on the verge of failure because of its exposure to exotic securities known as credit default swaps, was bailed out by the Fed in an $85 billion deal. Stocks dropped anyway, falling nearly 500 points.

The CIT Group, a lender to hundreds of thousands of small and midsize businesses that received a $2.33 billion bailout from the government in December 2008, announced in July 2009 that it had been unsuccessful in its efforts to receive additional government aid. Federal officials appeared to have concluded that CIT was too troubled to save a second time.

The Government's Bailout Plan

The bleeding in the stock market stopped only after rumors trickled out about a huge bailout plan being readied by the federal government. On Sept. 18, Treasury Secretary Henry M. Paulson Jr. publicly announced a three-page, $700 billion proposal that would allow the government to buy toxic assets from the nation's biggest banks, a move aimed at shoring up balance sheets and restoring confidence within the financial system.

Congress eventually amended the plan to add new structures for oversight, limits on executive pay and the option of the government taking a stake in the companies it bails out. . . .

[The crisis was far from over. . . .]

CONGRESSIONAL TESTIMONY OF ROBERT S. MUELLER, III, DIRECTOR, FEDERAL BUREAU OF INVESTIGATION, BEFORE HOUSE COMMITTEE ON THE JUDICIARY

2009 WLNR 9656026, May 21, 2009

Good morning Chairman Conyers, Ranking Member Smith, and Members of the Committee. I am pleased to be here today. . . .

In the wake of September 11th, we were confronted with radical changes to the FBI—changes that were necessary to address the terrorist threat. Yet at the same time, we faced a rash of corporate wrongdoing, from Enron and WorldCom to Qwest. We needed to prioritize our resources.

Public corruption is our top criminal priority. . . . Apart from public corruption, economic crime remains one of our primary concerns. Our mortgage fraud caseload has more than tripled in the past three years, from over 800 cases to more than 2,400. In addition, the FBI has more than 560 open corporate fraud investigations, including matters directly related to the current financial crisis. To meet this challenge, we have had to re-prioritize our criminal programs to address the current financial crisis. In FY 2007, we had 120 agents investigating mortgage fraud cases. In FY 2008, that number increased to 180 agents, and currently over 260 agents are assigned to mortgage fraud and related cases.

Unfortunately, there is no sign that our mortgage fraud caseload will decrease in the near future. To the contrary, Suspicious Activity Reports (SARs) from financial institutions have indicated a significant increase in mortgage fraud reporting filed with the Financial Crimes Enforcement Network (FinCEN). For example, during FY 2008, mortgage fraud SARs increased more than 36 percent to a total of 63,173. So far in FY 2009, there have been 33,291 mortgage fraud SARs filed. While the total dollar loss attributed to mortgage fraud is unknown, seven percent of SARs filed in FY 2008 indicated a specific dollar loss, which totaled more than $1.5 billion.

To make the best use of our resources, the FBI has found new ways to detect and combat mortgage fraud. One example is the use of a property flipping analytical computer application, first developed by the Washington Field Office, to effectively identify property flipping in the Baltimore and Washington areas. This original concept has evolved into a national FBI initiative that employs statistical correlations and other advanced computer technology to search for companies and persons with patterns of property flipping. As potential targets are analyzed and flagged, information is provided to the respective FBI Field Office for further investigation. In addition, sophisticated investigative techniques, such as undercover operations and wiretaps, not only result in the collection of valuable evidence, they provide an opportunity to apprehend criminals in the commission of their crimes, thus reducing loss to individuals and financial institutions. By pursuing these proactive methods in conjunction with historical investigations, the FBI is able to realize operational efficiencies in large scale investigations.

In December 2008, the FBI dedicated resources to create the National Mortgage Fraud Team at FBI headquarters. The team has specific responsibility for the management of the mortgage fraud program at both the origination and corporate level. They will assist FBI field offices in addressing the mortgage fraud problem at all levels. And they will provide tools to identify the most egregious mortgage fraud perpetrators, prioritize pending investigations, and provide information to evaluate where additional manpower is needed.

One of the best tools the FBI has for combating mortgage fraud is its longstanding partnerships with government and industry partners. Currently, there are 18 mortgage fraud task forces and 50 working groups across the country. These task forces are strategically placed in areas identified as high threat areas for mortgage fraud. Partners are varied, but typically include representatives of Housing and Urban Development, the U.S. Postal Inspection Service, the Internal Revenue Service, Financial Crimes Enforcement Network, the Federal Deposit Insurance Corporation, and State and local law enforcement officers. This multiagency model serves as a force multiplier, providing an array of resources to identify the source of the fraud and finding the most effective way to prosecute each case.

Last June, for example, we worked closely with our partners on "Operation Malicious Mortgage," a multi-agency takedown on mortgage fraud schemes, with more than 400 defendants across the country. Thus far, 164 defendants have been convicted in federal, State, and local courts for crimes that amount to more than $1 billion in losses. Forty six of our 56 field offices took part in the operation, which has also resulted in the forfeiture or seizure of more than $60 million in assets. The FBI is one of the DOJ participants in the national Mortgage Fraud Working Group, which DOJ chairs. Together, we are building on existing FBI intelligence databases to identify large industry insiders and criminal enterprises conducting systemic mortgage fraud.

We also continue to foster relationships with representatives of the mortgage industry to promote mortgage fraud awareness. We are working with industry partners to develop a more efficient mortgage fraud reporting mechanism for those not mandated to report such activity. This Suspicious Mortgage Fraud Activity Report concept is being discussed with FinCEN and is under consideration by the Mortgage Bankers Association. . . .

II. BANK FRAUD: ELEMENTS OF THE CRIME

UNITED STATES v. ROSS

502 F.3d 521 (6th Cir. 2007)

Boyce F. Marting, Jr., Circuit Judge.

Defendant Anthony H. Ross appeals his conviction on two counts of bank fraud in violation of 18 U.S.C. §1344. Defendant challenges . . . the sufficiency of the evidence supporting his conviction. . . . [W]e AFFIRM defendant's conviction. . . .

I.

1. The Nigerian Counterfeit Check Scam

Defendant Anthony Ross [is a real estate agent and commercial real estate broker in Lorain County, Ohio]. In 1997, . . . Ross . . . opened his own business, Northshore Realty. At the time of trial, Northshore Realty had eight full-time employees and seven affiliated independent agents. . . .

Unfortunately, in [2002, Ross suffered significant losses on low-income housing, causing him to owe substantial sums to FirstMerit Bank and some family and friends. In] 2003, Ross filed for personal bankruptcy, though his businesses remained intact. . . .

In 2001, Ross was attending a National Realtors' Association convention in Washington, D.C. where he met an individual by the name of Didi Duke. Duke and Ross agreed to develop commercial real estate in Lorain County. Duke offered to gather approximately $12.5 million in investment capital for the proposed project. Upon his return from the conference, Ross memorialized his agreement with Duke in a contract to represent Duke and a "group of investors in a development or an investment of about $12.5 million." Ross and Duke corresponded several times over the phone before agreeing to enter into this contract, and Ross had his attorney review the contract prior to signing it. . . .

According to Ross's testimony, after the contract was signed, Duke mailed a $90,000 due diligence check to him. Ross received this check via overnight mail on October 25, 2002. The check was drawn on an Associates Credit Card Services Account with the Bank of New York. The check itself appears to be printed on a British Petroleum check. Upon receipt of this $90,000 check, Ross quickly went to a FirstMerit branch in Oakwood (nearest his office) to deposit it and to get $5,000 cash back. The branch informed him a hold would be placed on a check of that size and he would be unable to receive funds from the check until after the check cleared. Ross then decided to take the check to the FirstMerit branch in Sheffield (nearest his home) because "they [knew him] over there." At the Sheffield branch, Ross was able to gain approval from the manager to deposit the check in his E.A.R. Investors account and to receive $5,000 back. Ross needed the $5,000 in order to make payroll at one of his low-income housing construction sites. A few days later, on October 28, 2002, Ross withdrew another $8,000 from the E.A.R. Investors account in order to have cash for a trip he was taking with his girlfriend (now wife) to New Orleans.

While in New Orleans, Ross's bank card and credit card from FirstMerit were frozen and he was unable to withdraw funds. Ross spoke with an official from the bank who informed him that the $90,000 check he had deposited was counterfeit. Upon his return from New Orleans, Ross contacted Duke to inquire about the counterfeit check. Duke informed Ross that his investors were no longer interested in investing in the United States after the events of 9/11 and had backed out of the transaction. Ross's accounts at FirstMerit remained frozen through the time of trial. Ross's financial difficulties subsequently proved too much to bear, and he filed for personal bankruptcy under Chapter 7 of the Bankruptcy Code on April 18, 2003. Ross was discharged from his bankruptcy on July 29, 2003.

During the summer of 2003, several months after the failed transaction with Duke, Ross was contacted by an individual named Didi Hassan. From May 2003 until sometime in the fall of that year, there were several email and telephonic communications between Ross and Hassan discussing the resurrection of the transaction originally arranged with Duke. Hassan led Ross to believe an individual by the name of Bello from Canada was arranging financing for the deal. Ross spoke with Bello on the phone and provided his personal information for purposes of securing financing.

In June 2003, Ross received via overnight mail a check for $346,990.60 drawn on the account of Gregory Dodge Hyundai Car Dealership in Highland Park, Illinois. Ross believed this check was from Mr. Bello and that Gregory Dodge Hyundai was an investor in the proposed real estate deal. Ross called Gregory Dodge Hyundai to confirm they were actually investors in the deal and discovered the check was counterfeit. Ross mailed the counterfeit check to Gregory Dodge Hyundai at their request.

A few days later, Ross received a Bank of America cashier's check for $5,000. Ross deposited this check in his FirstMerit account, believing it to be money sent from Hassan for the purposes of opening up an offshore account to facilitate the proposed deal. After depositing the check, Ross was contacted by the bank and informed the check was counterfeit. Because Ross had not withdrawn any funds from the check, the bank suffered no loss. Ross informed the bank he was dealing with Nigerians who were interested in investing in Lorain County. Ross shared several emails between himself and Hassan with the bank investigator. The bank investigator informed Ross that this was likely a scam and to stop dealing with Hassan or any other Nigerians. Ross promised to cut off his dealings with Hassan. . . .

In the summer of 2004, Hassan contacted Ross again in an attempt to revive the deal with new financing. Hoping to prevent any future counterfeit checks, Ross informed Hassan that he would only accept payment by wire transfer from a United States bank. Hassan agreed to a wire transfer and initiated negotiations with Ace Financial, allegedly based in Chicago, to secure financing in the amount of $700,000. In June of 2004, Ross emailed Hassan stating that he had been contacted by the Chicago financiers about the loan and that the disbursement would occur within seven to ten business days.

On July 15, 2004, National City Bank received an envelope containing a United States Treasury Check for $700,000 payable to A.H. Ross Corp. The account number for A.H. Ross Corp. was typed on the endorsement line on the back of the check. Upon receipt of the check, National City immediately deposited the check in the A.H. Ross Corporation account. No hold was placed on the check as Treasury checks are considered guaranteed funds. . . .

Over the next [few] days, Ross purchased several cashier's checks from the bank in order to pay off debts owed to friends and family. He also moved $505,000 into an investment account at Edward Jones which he had opened approximately a month earlier. Within days, the Treasury check was returned to National City as counterfeit. Thanks to its own quick actions and the cooperation of Ross, National City was able to recover all but $60,824.

Upon learning that the funds were from a check rather than a wire, Ross immediately contacted Hassan and Ace Financial. At some point in the summer of 2004, the phone number for Ace Financial was cut off and Hassan stopped communicating with Ross. At this time, Ross had been in contact with the bank investigator and had attempted to negotiate a payment plan to pay back the money lost by the bank, but the bank turned down his request and referred the case for prosecution.

In November 2004, United States Secret Service agents showed up unannounced at Ross's office. One of the agents told Ross they were investigating a Nigerian counterfeit check scam of which Ross may have been a victim. Believing the agents were there to help him, Ross happily discussed all of his dealings with Duke and Hassan in detail. This meeting lasted several hours in a conference room in Ross's office. At some point during this meeting, Ross deduced that *he* was the actual suspect. The agents informed Ross of his *Miranda* rights and Ross subsequently agreed to offer a written statement. In his testimony and his written statement, Ross revealed that at some point after receiving the first counterfeit check, he researched Nigerian scams on the internet. After that research, Ross insisted that all transactions be done by wire transfer between United States banks and received assurances from Hassan that he and his associates were not part of any scam. Additionally, his written statement said that he was aware through his dealings with Duke and Hassan that they were likely attempting to scam him, but he wanted to "get them before they got me." He also stated that his "business dealing should have been cut off. Greed got the better of me." Finally, he said in his written statement that he had no idea who sent the $700,000 Treasury check.

On December 15, 2004, a federal grand jury in Cleveland, Ohio, returned an indictment charging Ross with two counts of Bank Fraud, in violation of 18 U.S.C. §1344. The first count related to the $90,000 counterfeit check passed at FirstMerit, and the second count related to the $700,000 check deposited at National City. On July 18, 2005, a jury found Ross guilty of both counts of bank fraud. On October 20, 2005, Ross was sentenced to 37 months' incarceration, followed by four years of supervised release. . . .

3. Sufficiency of the Evidence

Ross argues on appeal that the evidence was insufficient to support his convictions for bank fraud. When considering such an argument this Court does not "weigh the evidence presented, consider the credibility of witnesses, or substitute [its] judgment for that of the jury." Our task is to determine "whether, after viewing the evidence in the light most favorable to the prosecution, *and after giving the government the benefit of all inferences that could reasonably be drawn from the testimony,* any rational trier of fact could find the elements of the crime beyond a reasonable doubt." Thus, Ross "bears a very heavy burden" in his sufficiency of the evidence challenge.

In order to prove a violation of 18 U.S.C. §1344, the government must prove three elements: "(1) that the defendant knowingly executed or attempt to execute a scheme to defraud a financial institution; (2) that the defendant did so with the intent to defraud; and (3) that the financial institution was insured by the Federal Deposit Insurance Corporation." At issue is whether the government adequately proved beyond a reasonable doubt that Ross had the requisite knowledge required to be convicted of bank fraud under 18 U.S.C. §1344. In other words, Ross must have "knowingly" participated in a scheme to defraud FirstMerit and National City Bank.

Ross argues that there is no evidence he knew the $90,000 check was counterfeit. He also argues that he believed the $700,000 deposited to his account was via wire transfer and not by check, and thus he had no knowledge a check was even used, let alone a counterfeit check.

As is often the case, direct evidence of knowledge and intent is hard to come by, and thus must be proven by circumstantial evidence. This Circuit has stated that "circumstantial evidence alone is sufficient to sustain a conviction, and such evidence need not remove every reasonable hypothesis except that of guilt."

In the present case, the government offered evidence that over the course of two years Ross passed a counterfeit $90,000 check, received a suspicious and counterfeit $346,000 check in the mail, and deposited a counterfeit $5,000 check. Additionally, during that same period a counterfeit $700,000 Treasury check was mailed to his bank with instructions to be deposited in his account. The jury also considered more than forty emails between Ross and the "Nigerians" and listened to Ross's own testimony from the witness stand. . . .

While this case presents a close evidentiary call, we do not believe Ross has met his very heavy burden of showing the evidence was insufficient. The jury chose not to believe Ross's testimony and found that there was enough circumstantial evidence to prove Ross knowingly intended to defraud a bank. The government offered evidence of Ross's motive to commit bank fraud. Ross was in dire financial straits. Ross had filed for personal bankruptcy. Ross needed money to pay his debts and keep his businesses afloat. . . . He even stated that his greed had got the better of him. And ultimately, Ross did receive four counterfeit checks and deposited three of them. This circumstantial evidence calls into doubt Ross's story that he was simply the victim of an elaborate Nigerian counterfeit check scam. Thus it cannot be said that *no* rational trier of fact could have found beyond a reasonable doubt that Ross knowingly participated in bank fraud. . . .

[Opinion of Alice M. Batchelder, Circuit Judge, concurring in part and dissenting in part, OMITTED].

NOTES AND QUESTIONS

1. What are elements of bank fraud under 18 U.S.C. §1344?
2. The defendant claimed to be a victim of the Nigerians' fraud. The government claimed he was a perpetrator and even went so far as to question whether the first Nigerian even existed. What is the evidence supporting each position? Is the court correct in concluding that there was sufficient evidence to sustain the conviction?
3. The court quotes an earlier case, which stated that "circumstantial evidence alone is sufficient to sustain a conviction, and such evidence need not remove every reasonable hypothesis except that of guilt." How does this statement mesh with the government's burden to prove the defendant's guilt beyond a reasonable doubt? If a "reasonable hypothesis" consistent with innocence exists, could a "reasonable juror" find guilt with no "reasonable doubt"?

III. BANK AS "VICTIM" I: INTENT TO DEFRAUD

UNITED STATES v. CRISCI

273 F.3d 235 (2d Cir. 2001)

PER CURIAM.

George Crisci appeals from the November 2, 2000, judgment of the United States District Court for the Southern District of New York (Barrington D. Parker, Jr., *Judge*) after a trial jury convicted him of seventeen counts of bank fraud in violation of 18 U.S.C. §1344, and one count of making false statements to federal law enforcement agents, in violation of 18 U.S.C. §1001. Although Crisci raised several arguments in his appeal, we write primarily to join our sister circuits in holding that an indictment is not duplicitous or otherwise defective when it charges in a single count bank fraud under both subsections (1) and (2) of Section 1344. Proof of the violation of either subsection, each of which concerns the different means of committing bank fraud, is sufficient to support a conviction.

Background

From November 1998 until April 1999, Crisci worked as the chief engineer at the Wartburg Adult Care Community ("Wartburg"), a residential health care facility for senior citizens located in Mount Vernon, New York. Wartburg officials fired Crisci on April 27, 1999. Between March 11 and April 22, 1999, Crisci carried out a scheme in which he requisitioned and then cashed twenty fraudulently endorsed checks drawn on Wartburg bank accounts and totaling approximately $95,000. Crisci generally created false invoices on the letterhead of contractors doing business for Wartburg and then requisitioned checks from Wartburg's financial officers to satisfy these fictitious accounts payable. Wartburg's accounting department directly gave Crisci checks payable to the various third-party contractors, and the checks were drawn on one of three different Wartburg checking accounts at the Bank of New York and Chase Manhattan Bank. Crisci fraudulently endorsed the checks by forging the signatures of the named payees. Defendant then presented the checks for payment at David's Check Cashing ("David's"), a private company that visited the Wartburg campus weekly in order to cash employees' paychecks. Crisci told David's employees of his position at Wartburg, that he was in charge of security, and that he was going to pay the contractors named on the checks with cash rather than the checks. David's employees gave Crisci the cash and deposited the checks in a separate Wartburg bank account at Chase Manhattan Bank known as the payroll account. The checks cleared against the accounts on which they were drawn, causing funds to move from those three accounts into the payroll account.

After firing Crisci, Wartburg officials discovered and investigated Crisci's activities. On August 19, 1999, agents of the Federal Bureau of Investigation ("FBI") interviewed Crisci about his conduct, and he denied the details of the scheme. Officials arrested Crisci on a criminal complaint in November 1999. A federal grand jury indicted Crisci on March 14, 2000, and charged him with seventeen counts of bank fraud, one for each of seventeen fraudulently endorsed checks totaling $86,311, and one count of making false statements to FBI investigators. A jury trial took place from June 20 to 28, 2000, and the jury convicted defendant on all eighteen counts. Judge Parker denied defendant's post-verdict motions and sentenced Crisci on November 2, 2000, to 33 months imprisonment, three years supervised release, $86,311 restitution, and $1,800 special assessment. Defendant appeals his conviction and sentence.

Discussion

I. Duplicity

Crisci argues that all eighteen of the counts with which the government charged him were improper because they were duplicitous, or charged more than one offense in a single count. With respect to the seventeen bank fraud counts, defendant contends that they defectively charged violations of both Section 1344(1) and

Section 1344(2). Subsection (1) makes it a crime to "defraud a financial institution," while subsection (2) makes it a crime to obtain, among other things, money from a financial institution "by means of false or fraudulent pretenses, representations, or promises." With respect to the false statement count, defendant argues that the indictment's language improperly allowed the jury to convict him on any one of the seven statements that the government alleged were false. We reject both duplicity claims on their merits.

The vice of a duplicitous charge is that it risks to impair "a defendant's rights to notice of the charge against him, to a unanimous verdict, to appropriate sentencing and to protection against double jeopardy in a subsequent prosecution." United States v. Murray, 618 F.2d 892, 896 (2d Cir. 1980). This is so because a general verdict of guilty on a duplicitous count will not reveal whether the jury reached a unanimous verdict on each offense and "whether the jury found defendant guilty of only one crime and not the other, or guilty of both." However, an indictment is not defective if it alleges "in a single count . . . the commission of a crime by several means." We thus distinguish between improperly charging separate offenses in one count and properly charging separate means of committing a single crime in a single count.

Crisci contends that the bank fraud counts are duplicitous because they charge violations of both Section 1344(1), which prohibits a scheme to defraud a financial institution, and Section 1344(2), which prohibits a scheme to obtain a financial institution's money "by means of false or fraudulent pretenses, representations, or promises." According to defendant, it is impossible to know from the general verdict whether the jury convicted him under subsection (1), subsection (2), or both. Crisci's duplicity argument depends on interpreting subsections (1) and (2) to describe distinct crimes rather than two ways of committing the single crime of bank fraud.

We reject defendant's statutory interpretation. Instead, we here join our sister circuits that have considered Section 1344 and held that a single count of an indictment may charge bank fraud under both subsections (1) and (2) and that proof of the violation of either subsection is sufficient to support a conviction. *See* [court cites cases from the First, Third, Fourth, Fifth, Sixth, and Seventh Circuits]. Because the two subsections of Section 1344 are written in the disjunctive, these circuits have interpreted Section 1344 as defining different ways in which a defendant may commit the offense of bank fraud. We agree with this characterization of the statute.

Conclusion

For the foregoing reasons, we affirm the judgment of conviction and sentence.

UNITED STATES v. REAUME

338 F.3d 577 (6th Cir. 2003)

COLE, Circuit Judge. . . .

On August 19, 1999, a federal grand jury returned a one-count indictment charging [defendant Scott A.] Reaume with bank fraud. The indictment alleged that Reaume knowingly executed a scheme to defraud Monroe Bank and Trust ("the Bank").

Reaume's jury trial began on August 14, 2001. At trial, testimony was presented that Reaume opened two checking accounts at the Bank using the aliases Steven D. McIlveen and Robert Sandor. Accounts also were opened at the Bank by Adam Rodriguez and Danny K. Drummond in their own names. Drummond opened an additional account under the alias of John S. Woods.

Reaume, Rodriguez, and Drummond used checks drawn from their accounts to purchase merchandise at various branches of national-chain retailers, and subsequently returned most of the merchandise for cash refunds at other branches of the stores. The Bank flagged the five accounts early on and refused to honor the checks for which there were insufficient funds ("NSF checks"). The losses resulting from the passing of these NSF checks, therefore, fell on either the retailers themselves or the check-guarantee companies that insured the retailers.

On August 16, 2001, the jury returned a guilty verdict. On January 3, 2002, the district court determined that Reaume's guideline range was twenty-seven to thirty-three months, sentenced Reaume to thirty months of imprisonment and four years of supervised release, and ordered him to pay restitution in the amount of $95,649.26.

On appeal, Reaume raises four points of error. First, he argues that the evidence presented at trial was insufficient to maintain a conviction under the federal bank fraud statute because there was no evidence that he intended to defraud the bank itself, as opposed to the individual merchants or their respective insurance companies. . . .

II.

A. Sufficiency of the Evidence and Intent to Defraud

Reaume argues that there was insufficient evidence to find that he specifically intended to defraud the Bank, as opposed to the merchants or their insurers. He contends that an intent to defraud the payee of an NSF check does not provide a basis for a finding that there was an intent to subject the issuing bank to a loss. Accordingly, Reaume argues that the district court erred in denying his motion for a judgment of acquittal. The denial of a motion for a judgment of acquittal is reviewed de novo. United States v. Kone, 307 F.3d 430, 433 (6th Cir. 2002).

Three elements are required for a conviction of bank fraud pursuant to §1344: (1) the defendant must have knowingly executed or attempted to execute a scheme to defraud a financial institution; (2) the defendant must have done so with the intent to defraud; and (3) the financial institution must have been insured by the Federal Deposit Insurance Corporation. United States v. Everett, 270 F.3d 986, 989 (6th Cir. 2001).

This Court previously addressed the intent element of the bank fraud statute in United States v. Hoglund, 178 F.3d 410 (6th Cir. 1999), and *Everett.* While neither of these cases are directly controlling, their explication here is critical because it is from these cases that we distill the principle which we apply to the present case.

In *Hoglund,* an attorney was convicted under §1344 after settling his clients' cases without their permission, forging their signatures on the settlement checks he received, and depositing the money into his own account. . . . [W]e addressed the issue of whether the Government must prove that the defendant exposed a bank to a risk of loss as part of the "scheme to defraud" element. *Hoglund* resolved this question by holding that "risk of loss" is simply "one way of establishing intent to defraud in bank cases." Thus, this Court found that a defendant need not have exposed a bank to a risk of loss as an element of bank fraud. Instead, proof that the defendant "intended to put a bank at a risk of loss" was sufficient to maintain a bank fraud conviction. Thus, *Hoglund* held that the bank fraud statute is violated, even when there is no actual risk of loss on the part of the bank, if the defendant's intent is to expose the bank to such a risk. While informative, *Hoglund* is not controlling in the present case. Here, in contrast to *Hoglund*, the defendant claims that, regardless of whether there was an actual risk of loss, there was no intent to expose the Bank to a risk of loss.

In *Everett*, the defendant, a certified public accountant, was found guilty of bank fraud by a jury. On appeal, the defendant argued that the Government failed to prove the specific intent required by §1344, namely, the intent to defraud a federally insured bank, or at least to put the bank at a risk of loss. The defendant acknowledged that there was evidence that she intended to defraud her client, but argued that the manner in which she defrauded her client did not impose a risk of loss on the bank in question. In affirming the conviction, we held that the specific intent required for bank fraud does not require putting the bank at a risk of a loss or intending to do so "in the usual sense. It is sufficient if the defendant in the course of committing fraud on *someone* causes a federally insured bank to transfer funds under its possession and control." *Everett*, therefore, can be said to stand for the proposition that the bank fraud statute is violated, even if the intended victim of the fraudulent activity is an entity other than a federally insured financial institution, when the fraudulent activity causes the bank to transfer funds. Thus, the holding of *Everett* is also instructive but not squarely on point, as there was no evidence in the present case indicating that the Bank actually did transfer funds in connection with Reaume's fraudulent activities.

Unlike the defendant in *Hoglund*, Reaume contends that he harbored no intent to expose the financial institution to a risk of loss. Moreover, unlike the situation in *Everett*, Reaume contends, and the evidence substantiates, that the Bank never transferred any funds in connection with the fraudulent activity. Thus, it appears that Reaume's particular fact pattern does not fall neatly under the *Hoglund* or *Everett* rubric, which consider both the intended victim and actual loss.

We nevertheless affirm Reaume's conviction. The specific issue that Reaume appeals is the evidence of his intent to defraud the Bank itself. In *Everett*, this Court held that an intent to put the financial institution at a risk of loss is not required, and that the fact that the defendant defrauded someone was sufficient, given that the fraud caused the bank to transfer funds. In the present case, the Bank was clearly at a risk of loss. Evidence was presented at trial to demonstrate that, when the Bank receives an NSF check, it makes a decision to either honor the check anyway or to dishonor the check. If the check is dishonored, the Bank does not lose any money, but if the check is honored, and the account holder fails to pay back that debt to the Bank, the Bank suffers a loss. Therefore, it is clear that Reaume's fraudulent activity, regardless of the intended victim, could have caused the Bank to transfer funds. If in fact the Bank had transferred funds, then this case would clearly be governed by *Everett*, because an intent to defraud someone would have caused the Bank to transfer funds. The issue of Reaume's intent simply cannot logically turn on the course of action chosen by the Bank after receiving the NSF checks. Accordingly, it is a necessary extension of *Everett* to find the intent element of §1344 satisfied in this case.

Everett contains language to support this outcome. In *Everett*, this Court stated that the Government is probably better advised to proceed under the wire or mail fraud statutes where the bank has "minimal involvement, such as where a swindler deceives someone into voluntarily writing checks to the swindler on a good account." Nevertheless, the Court indicated that even such a minimal involvement of the bank is sufficient to find liability under §1344 when the specific intent to defraud someone is present. Therefore, we need not address the question of whether the evidence presented at trial was sufficient for a reasonable jury to find that Reaume intended to defraud the Bank specifically. Applying the reasoning of *Hoglund* and *Everett*, we find that intent to defraud the federally insured institution itself is satisfied where: (1) the intent to defraud some entity was present; and (2) that intended fraud placed a federally insured financial institution at a risk of loss.

. . . [T]herefore, Reaume's argument that the evidence presented at trial was insufficient to demonstrate the intent required by the bank fraud statute fails. . . .

NOTES AND QUESTIONS

1. What, exactly, are the ways that a perpetrator can exhibit an "intent to defraud a federally insured bank" after *Hoglund, Everett,* and *Reaume*?
2. Taking a step back, does it make sense to convict an individual of bank fraud when defrauding a bank was the last thing on his mind? Doesn't the court's interpretation create federal jurisdiction over any fraudulent scheme, no matter how trivial in nature, as long as the perpetrator uses a check or bank account in the course of committing it? Did Congress really intend for bank fraud to be that broadly interpreted?
3. During the Savings and Loan crisis of the late 1980s, Congress amended the mail and wire fraud statutes by increasing the potential penalties and extending the statute of limitations from five to seven years "if the violation affects a financial institution." *See* 18 U.S.C. §§1341, 1343 & 3282(2). In United States v. Pelullo, 964 F.2d 193, 215-16 (3d Cir. 1992), the Third Circuit stated that this phraseology was "clearly" intended to reach a "broader class of crimes" than those in which the financial institution is the "object of fraud." Is this still true after cases like *Reaume*?

IV. BANK AS "VICTIM" II: PARTICIPATION OF BANK EMPLOYEES

UNITED STATES v. DOKE

171 F.3d 240 (5th Cir. 1999)

EDITH H. JONES, Circuit Judge:

Maurice Doke and Larry Bass were convicted of conspiracy, bank fraud, and two counts of making false statements to a bank, all in connection with a $600,000 nominee loan on speculative real estate. On appeal, they raise twelve issues, the most significant of which are the sufficiency of the evidence, potential juror bias, and Doke's competence to stand trial. We affirm the district court's judgment.

I. Facts

Doke was a real estate developer in Houston. Bass was his attorney and had negotiated several of Doke's real estate transactions. In 1984, one of Doke's entities sold a 200-acre tract of undeveloped land in north Houston to General Homes Corporation, retaining two options to buy back small parcels of it. The first option, pertaining to 6.028 acres, was set to expire on August 1, 1985.

On July 11, 1985, Bass notified General Homes that Doke would exercise his option to buy the land. The purchase price would be nearly $788,000. On July 19, Bass requested a $600,000 loan from Champions Point National Bank ("Champions") to pay for the land. Champions approved the loan on July 30, and the next day, in a simultaneous closing, General Homes sold the land to a Doke entity, which sold it to Bass for the same price. This prosecution arose from that loan. The government argues—and the jury must have believed—that Bass told Champions he was borrowing the money to buy the land from Doke, without revealing Doke's continued involvement with the land or the loan.

It is undisputed that Doke gave to Bass the $200,000 Bass used for the down payment. Every six months for the next two years, Doke sent to Bass the money Bass used to make each payment on the loan. By late 1987, however, the Houston real estate market and the stock market had crashed. Doke was no longer able to pay Bass for the loan payments. Just before the February 1988 payment was due, Bass asked Champions to restructure his loan by extending more credit and extending the repayment terms. In the letter making this request, Bass made no mention of Doke. Champions denied Bass's request, and Bass did not make the February 1988 loan payment. Later that year, Champions foreclosed on the property. In 1990, Champions failed and was taken over by the FDIC. Shortly thereafter, the property was sold for a loss.

When regulators took over the bank in 1990, they were unable to find Bass's credit file, in which they were especially interested because the loan was made to an insider and had not been repaid. At the time of the loan, Bass had been on the Champions board of directors. Doke had also been an insider because he was a significant shareholder.

The theory of the government's case is that Doke and Bass failed to disclose Doke's involvement in the loan because Champions could not have loaned the $600,000 directly to Doke without violating civil regulations. Under the limits of the loan-to-one-borrower rule, *see* 12 U.S.C. §84, Champions could loan Doke only about $40,000 more than he had already borrowed. It could, however, lend over $300,000 to Bass. Thus, when Bass borrowed the $600,000, Champions participated out $300,000 of the loan to Park 45 National Bank, a "sister bank" that had several directors in common with Champions.

Doke and Bass were indicted in July 1995. A jury trial was held in February and March 1997. They were found guilty on all four counts: one count of conspiracy under 18 U.S.C. §371, one count of bank fraud under 18 U.S.C. §1344, and two counts of making false statements to a financial institution under 18 U.S.C. §1014.

II. Sufficiency of Evidence

Doke and Bass argue that the evidence was insufficient to support their convictions on any count. The evidence will be sufficient to support the jury's verdict if "a rational jury could have found the essential elements of the crime beyond a reasonable doubt."

As mentioned above, the government argues that Doke and Bass concealed Doke's involvement from Champions, and that the loan exposed Champions to the risk of being in violation of banking regulations. Doke and Bass contend that there was not enough evidence to show that Bass failed to disclose Doke's involvement to the bank. In addition, however, they argue that, even assuming non-disclosure of Doke's involvement, this nominee loan could not have defrauded the bank because the bank received exactly the risk it bargained for: it knew Bass's credit-worthiness, knew what the money would be used for, and knew what collateral would secure the loan.

In order to prove bank fraud under 18 U.S.C. §1344, the government must show that Doke and Bass knowingly executed, or attempted to execute, a scheme to defraud a federally-chartered or -insured financial institution. A scheme to defraud includes any false or fraudulent pretenses or representations intending to deceive others in order to obtain something of value, such as money, from the institution to be deceived. The requisite intent to defraud is established if the defendant acted knowingly and with the specific intent to deceive, ordinarily for the purpose of causing some financial loss to another or bringing about some financial gain to himself.

In this case, the crux is whether Doke and Bass had the intent to deceive and whether the financial gains and losses in the offing demonstrated a scheme to defraud. These are questions of fact, and "[a]ll credibility determinations and reasonable inferences are to be resolved in favor of the verdict."

Doke and Bass argue that Bass disclosed their partnership to the bank when he applied for the loan. They contend that several pieces of evidence, in addition to Bass's own testimony at the trial, show that Bass made this disclosure. The loan file presented at trial was missing the documents that would prove the disclosure. Other documents in the file showed Doke's continued involvement. The files on Bass at other banks show that Bass was not concealing anything. Doke's payments to Bass were routed through Champions. Two bank officers testified they knew of Doke's involvement. Finally, Doke had sufficient credit available at another bank to eliminate any motive to circumvent the lending limits at Champions.

The government, on the other hand, presented testimony from the president of the bank, Ron Karel, who was also Bass's loan officer. Karel strenuously maintained that Bass did not reveal Doke's continued involvement with the loan. Although he knew that Doke was involved in the original sale of the land (selling it to Bass), Karel maintained he did not know Doke would be paying off Bass's loan. The loan application (not filled out by Bass but purportedly reflective of what he had told the bank) stated that Bass would repay the loan out of his "[p]ersonal income and sale of property." Furthermore, Karel testified that at the board of directors meeting where Bass's loan was approved, Bass commented: "This has got to be a good deal because, after all, I'm putting in $200,000 of my own money toward the purchase price of this land." Several other directors testified about the approval of the loan. Bobby Newman testified that he had seen no indication that Doke was involved with the loan. Keith Franze testified that he did not know of Doke's involvement and would not have voted to approve the loan if he had known. Robert Russ testified that he "never heard" that Doke would be the one paying off the loan, but he admitted it had happened so long before trial he could not be sure he would remember if he had.

Aside from the documents in Bass's file at Champions, which were ambiguous because of their incomplete state, this was largely a swearing contest between Bass's and Karel's versions of events. Two bank officers testified that Karel knew of Doke's involvement with the loan. But Karel and the other directors who denied knowledge of Doke's involvement were subject to extensive cross-examination by Bass's able trial counsel. This court is not inclined to interfere with the jury's decision about witnesses' credibility when that issue was so squarely set before it.

In addition, the documents produced by both sides would not necessarily compel a reasonable juror to abandon a determination that Karel's story was more credible. . . .

In sum, taken in the light most favorable to the verdict, there was sufficient evidence for a reasonable juror to have found beyond a reasonable doubt that Doke and Bass intended to deceive Champions about Doke's continued involvement with the loan.

Separate from the issue of how much they concealed from the bank, Doke and Bass argue that the economic validity of the transaction underlying the loan precluded it from being fraudulent. . . .

We agree that the transaction in this case had economic substance and was not a sham. We also agree that a nominee loan is not illegal where there is no evidence that the transaction is concealed from the bank, and where the loan documents "make the relationship between the various transactions very clear." This court has held, however, that fraudulent actions, such as concealing the identity of a silent partner in violation of banking regulations, contravene §1344. . . .

NOTES AND QUESTIONS

1. This is an extremely close case factually. On the one hand, Doke and Bass claimed that the bank knew about Bass's role as a straw man and looked the other way so that it could make a big loan and still be in technical compliance with banking regulations. On the other hand, the government's main witness, bank President Karel, insisted that he knew nothing about this arrangement. Other witnesses split down the middle, and the documentation was inconclusive. How would you have decided this case as a juror? Did Karel have a motive to lie?
2. Two bank officers testified that Karel knew of Doke's involvement with the loan. This must mean that these officers—employees of the bank—knew

of Doke's involvement themselves, undoubtedly within the scope of their employment. Why, then, didn't the court employ the collective knowledge doctrine and instruct the jury that, if these two employees knew, the "bank" as an entity knew, and therefore it was not defrauded? Does the collective knowledge doctrine work both ways—that is, to help defendants in the same way that it helps prosecutors?

3. Though not labeled as such, the last argument made by the defendants seems to be based on a claim that Bass's position as straw man was not a material fact because the bank (1) knew Bass's creditworthiness and (2) knew the purpose of and collateral for the loan. The court rejects this argument, in part because the bank's loan to Doke through Bass caused it to be out of regulatory compliance. But what if this were not the case? What if Bass were a straw man for reasons entirely unrelated to the bank's position (e.g., for tax purposes)? Would the non-disclosure of Doke's involvement still be material?

V. MATERIALITY

UNITED STATES v. RIGAS

490 F.3d 208 (2d Cir. 2007)

WESLEY, Circuit Judge.

Defendants Timothy J. Rigas and John J. Rigas ("Defendants") appeal from a judgment of conviction following a jury trial.... Among other things, [d]efendants were convicted of . . . bank fraud under 18 U.S.C. §1344 (Counts Twenty-Two and Twenty-Three). [Defendants challenge the sufficiency of the evidence with respect to these counts.]

We reverse Defendants' conviction on Count Twenty-Three, and we remand for an entry of a judgment of acquittal on this Count and for resentencing.

Background

Adelphia Communications Company ("Adelphia") announced its 2001 Fourth Quarter and Full-Year results in a March 27, 2002 press release. In a footnote on the final page of that press release, Adelphia, at the recommendation of its accounting firm, Deloitte & Touche, first disclosed publicly that it had approximately $2.2 billion in liabilities not previously reported on its balance sheet. On the day of disclosure, Adelphia's stock price plummeted by about twenty-five percent to $20.39; by the time the stock was delisted in May 2002, the price per share was $1.16. The company filed for bankruptcy in June 2002, wiping out all shareholder value. A month later, John Rigas, his sons Michael and Timothy, and two other Adelphia employees were arrested and charged with looting the company.

The Story of Adelphia

Adelphia, one of the largest cable television providers in the country before its bankruptcy, had modest beginnings. In the early 1950s, John Rigas, the son of Greek immigrants, borrowed money from his family to buy a movie theater in Coudersport, a small town about twenty miles south of the New York-Pennsylvania state line. In 1952, he purchased the rights to wire the town for cable television. By the time John Rigas's sons Michael and Timothy joined Adelphia in the mid-1980s, the privately owned company boasted hundreds of thousands of cable subscribers.

In 1986, John Rigas took Adelphia public. Adelphia issued two classes of common stock: Class A, with one vote per share, and Class B, with 10 votes per share. The Rigas family owned almost all of the Class B shares, and, as a result, was able to maintain control of the company and the Board of Directors. Indeed, Rigas family members filled many of the top positions in Adelphia. John Rigas was Adelphia's President, Chairman of the Board, and Chief Executive Officer until he resigned in May 2002. Timothy Rigas served as Board member, Executive Vice President, and Chief Financial Officer. Michael Rigas was also on Adelphia's Board and was Executive Vice President for Operations. Another son, James, filled out the Rigases' majority control of the seven-member Board of Directors. Peter Venetis, John Rigas's son-in-law, was added to the Board when it expanded to nine members.

Not all of the companies controlled by the Rigas family went public when Adelphia did. Rather, Adelphia managed some of the cable companies—the Rigas Managed Entities ("RMEs")—that the family continued to own privately. Adelphia's management of the RMEs was disclosed in public filings; however, Adelphia did not disclose the amount of the fees charged to, or paid by, the RMEs, or that cash generated from the RMEs was commingled with that generated by Adelphia. Certain transactions between Adelphia and the RMEs were at issue during the trial; the government argued that Defendants utilized the Adelphia-RMEs business arrangement to effect and conceal aspects of their frauds.

Adelphia's business during the time relevant to this case was "cash flow negative." That is, it did not generate enough cash revenue from subscriber fees to pay for its capital expenditures, interest payments, and cost of operations. Adelphia's capital expenditures included $1.5 to $2 billion per year to update its cable systems to higher bandwidth and two-way communication capabilities (the "Rebuild Plan"). Between 1998 and 2002, Adelphia paid approximately $5.2 billion in cash and issued more than 72 million new shares of Class A common stock to acquire other cable entities in an effort to lower costs as a result of operating efficiencies (the "Acquisition Plan"). Banks and holders of Adelphia stocks and bonds watched as Adelphia's leverage ratios climbed. Indeed, as Moody's Investors Service noted in August 2001, Adelphia was "one of the most highly leveraged companies in the cable sector."

Adelphia set about raising sufficient capital to offset its annual operating losses, to fund the Rebuild and Acquisition Plans, and to pay down increasing interest expenses. This new cash mainly came from $4.9 billion in public sales of newly issued common and preferred stock, $4.4 billion in public sales of notes and convertible debentures, and bank loans.

Adelphia's disclosed bank borrowings were $5.4 billion in September 2001, more than a six-fold increase from March 1998. Generally, each separate bank loan was entered into by a group of Adelphia subsidiaries that pledged their assets as collateral; the group was referred to as a "borrowing group." Certain bank loans were set up through a "co-borrowing" arrangement (the "Co-Borrowing Arrangement") between the RMEs and Adelphia subsidiaries. Timothy Rigas proposed the Co-Borrowing Arrangement to the Adelphia Board in 1999, and argued it would lower borrowing costs and prevent competition for bank financing between the RMEs and Adelphia entities. Under this Co-Borrowing Arrangement and at the Rigases' direction, Adelphia entered into three separate "Co-Borrowing Agreements"—loans for which the RMEs and Adelphia subsidiaries were jointly and severally liable. These Co-Borrowing Agreements totaled about $5.5 billion. Adelphia's accounting firm, Deloitte & Touche, reviewed and approved the manner in which Adelphia disclosed and accounted for the co-borrowed debt on its public financial statements. . . .

a. Adelphia's Inflated EBITDA

Several witnesses testified that investors commonly use EBITDA [Earnings Before Interest, Taxes, Depreciation, and Amortization] to assess the earnings from operations of cable companies. [Vice-President of Finance James R.] Brown testified that he told John Rigas Adelphia's real EBITDA and how it compared with its competitors' results. Brown also told John Rigas what would happen if Adelphia reported the actual EBITDA: Adelphia would default on some of its public debt, its stock price could decline, and its interest expenses and the cost of borrowing from banks would increase. While John Rigas told Brown that Adelphia "needed to get away" from using what Brown described as "accounting magic" to manipulate the numbers, he never told Brown to stop manipulating the numbers.

The "accounting magic" used to manipulate EBITDA comprised two schemes: (1) fraudulent allocations of management fees that the RMEs owed to Adelphia and (2) "wash transactions" with Adelphia's suppliers. Brown explained that he would arbitrarily inflate the management fees that an RME owed to Adelphia, and then record a corresponding interest expense that Adelphia "owed" the RME. The interest expense would ensure that there was no real cost to the RME as a result of the scheme but, because it was interest, it would not be included in Adelphia's EBITDA. As a result, then, this scheme—which Timothy Rigas "went along with"—artificially inflated Adelphia's EBITDA.

In his testimony about the wash transactions, Brown indicated that Timothy Rigas discussed, and then implemented, schemes with two separate equipment suppliers, Motorola and Scientific Atlanta. The effect of the wash transaction schemes was to increase Adelphia's EBITDA by $87.1 million. In these schemes, Adelphia increased the price it paid to Motorola and Scientific Atlanta for digital converter boxes, and Motorola and Scientific Atlanta agreed to pay Adelphia the amount of the increase for advertising and market support. Because the payments to the equipment suppliers were booked as capital expenses, and the payments from the suppliers were booked as revenue, this scheme artificially inflated the EBITDA.

According to Brown, Timothy Rigas instructed him to book nearly $20 million in increased advertising revenue even before the two equipment suppliers agreed to the wash transaction scheme; Adelphia never provided any advertising services for these suppliers.

IV. The Scheme to Defraud Adelphia's Bank Lenders

The jury convicted Timothy and John Rigas of conspiracy to commit bank fraud and two substantive counts of bank fraud related to two of the three Co-Borrowing Agreements. The Co-Borrowing Agreements required minimum leverage ratios of debt to EBITDA and tied interest rates to this leverage ratio. The government argued to the jury that the EBITDA manipulations resulted in lower interest payments to the banks than if the EBITDA had been accurately reported. The EBITDA manipulations were carried out at the level of the Adelphia parent company as described above. In addition, when Brown, Timothy Rigas, and Michael Mulcahey (a co-defendant of the Rigases who was Adelphia's Assistant Treasurer) determined that the EBITDA of particular borrowing groups (the Adelphia and RME entities in each Co-Borrowing Agreement) was not high enough, expenses would be moved between the subsidiaries and affiliate or interest income would be transferred from one internal company to another. . . .

[T]he Conviction on Count Twenty-Three Must Be Reversed on Sufficiency Grounds

Defendants challenge their bank fraud convictions [on the ground] that the evidence submitted at trial was insufficient to prove . . . bank fraud. We conclude . . . that the government proffered insufficient evidence to prove that the misrepresentations alleged in Count Twenty-Three were material. We affirm Defendants' convictions on Count Twenty-Two, but reverse their convictions on Count Twenty-Three on sufficiency grounds and instruct the district court to enter a judgment of acquittal on that Count.

II. Sufficiency

. . . "[T]he 'scheme to defraud' clause . . . requires that the defendant engage in . . . a pattern or course of conduct designed to deceive a federally chartered or insured financial institution into releasing property, with the intent to victimize the institution by exposing it to actual or potential loss." First, the government must prove that the defendant engaged in a deceptive course of conduct by making material misrepresentations. "A false statement is material if it has a 'natural tendency to influence, or is capable of influencing, the decision of the decisionmaking body to which it was addressed.'" We have also held that "[t]o be material, the information withheld either must be of some independent value or must bear on the ultimate value of the transaction." Analysis of the misrepresentations must be in the context in which they were made.

Second, the government must prove that the defendant, through the scheme, intended to victimize the bank by exposing it to loss. "[A]ctual or potential loss to the bank is not an element of the crime of bank fraud but merely a description of the required criminal intent." . . .

This is a rather unusual bank fraud case; most bank fraud is committed when a defendant makes a misrepresentation to a bank in an effort to persuade the bank to make a discretionary decision in a way that benefits him. It is clear that any number of misrepresentations made by an applicant for a loan are or can be "material." The bank's subjective decision may be influenced by many variables, including inaccurate leverage ratios. The bank fraud case the government presented to the jury involved misrepresentations intended to yield interest savings—but the Co-Borrowing Agreements constrained the bank's "discretion" to charge different interest rates. The Co-Borrowing Agreements did require that the information submitted be accurate "in all material respects"—but this leaves unanswered the question of what, exactly, was "material." The simple fact that the Co-Borrowing Agreements required information does not make any misstatement of that information *per se* material.

Defendants' misrepresentations certainly concerned a variable that mattered to the banks; the leverage ratio was clearly relevant information. But "relevance" and "materiality" are not synonymous. In Weinstock v. United States, 231 F.2d 699 (D.C. Cir. 1956), the D.C. Circuit explained the distinction between materiality and relevance: "To be 'relevant' means to relate to the issue. To be 'material' means to have probative weight, i.e., reasonably likely to influence the tribunal in making a determination required to be made." We find *Weinstock* persuasive: While the leverage ratio here is certainly relevant, Defendants' misrepresentations were material only if they tended to affect interest rates.

Misrepresentations that are "material" in the context of "an objective decisionmaking process" would tend to be quite different from misrepresentations that are material in subjective decisions such as "the decision to enter a contract or to do some act in detrimental reliance on the assertion of another." In the context of an objective decisionmaking process, whether a misrepresentation is "material" requires examination of the factors the decisionmaker would employ, and the degree to which a misrepresentation would be "capable of influencing[ ] the decision of the decisionmaking body." If a bank's discretion is limited by an agreement, we must look to the agreement to determine what factors are relevant, and when a misstatement becomes material. . . .

With regard to Count Twenty-Two (involving the CCH Co-Borrowing Agreement), the government presented compliance documents and notes regarding manipulations of these documents, and Mulcahey testified that he reduced management fees from the CCH Co-Borrowing Group by $6 million to "put the borrowing group in a better position as far as the [interest] on the agreement." Handwritten notes dated October 1, 2001 state that the leverage ratio was 5.01, and the leverage ratio reported to the banks was 4.98. The term loan component of the CCH Co-Borrowing Agreement provided that a higher interest rate would be charged if the leverage ratio was above 5.0. There was sufficient evidence for the jury to conclude that the misrepresentations were material.

With regard to Count Twenty-Three (involving the OCH Co-Borrowing Agreement), the evidence submitted to the jury cannot support a finding that any misrepresentations regarding the OCH Co-Borrowing Agreement were material. . . . The evidence supporting the leverage ratio/interest rate manipulation scheme appears to boil down to Brown's conclusory opinion that bank debt compliance documents were manipulated in 2000 and 2001 because he had "reviewed documents that make it pretty clear, and had conversations with people while [he] worked there that were consistent with what [he] saw in the documents." This does not suffice to prove that Defendants made material misrepresentations to the banks regarding the OCH Co-Borrowing Agreement.

Conclusion

Defendants' convictions are AFFIRMED, except for their conviction on Count Twenty-Three, which is hereby REVERSED. The case is REMANDED for an entry of ACQUITTAL on Count Twenty-Three and for resentencing.

NOTES AND QUESTIONS

1. The *Adelphia* case is a classic example of what happened to scores of technology companies, which had been soaring in the stock market during the 1990s, when the tech bubble started to show signs of weakness around the turn of the twenty-first century. Hoping against hope that the market's downward spiral would stop, many of these companies used a variety of fraudulent techniques to keep the value of their stock artificially inflated in the meantime. When the bubble burst, their fraud was exposed.
2. Are you convinced by the court's reasoning on Count Twenty-Three? Section 1344 specifically contains an attempt provision; would it be possible to argue that by providing the false leverage ratio information to the bank Adelphia attempted to execute a fraud against it but failed because the number was too low? Why or why not?

PROBLEM 5-1

Assume that Kendra, a recent law school graduate, is applying for a mortgage to purchase her first house. The application asks how long she has been employed. The truth is that she has only been working for a small law firm for eight months. Kendra is worried, however, that if she tells the truth the bank will decline her application. So she lies on the form and claims to have been employed for three years. She tells her firm's HR person about what she's done, and he agrees to substantiate the lie if the bank calls.

Kendra obtains the mortgage but later gets laid off from work and falls behind on her payments. The bank discovers Kendra's lie and refers the case to the FBI for investigation and possible prosecution. The FBI interviews the bank's chief loan officer, who tells him that an applicant's length of steady employment is, in general, a critical predictor of creditworthiness and that three years is an important threshold for most applicants to meet. However, in the case of certain kinds of professionals—such as medical doctors and lawyers—six months of prior employment is usually sufficient to demonstrate the requisite income stability because of their marketable credentials.

Kendra, of course, had no idea about the bank's favorable treatment of professionals. Has Kendra committed bank fraud?

chapter 6

Securities Fraud

I. REGULATORY SETTING: THE SECURITIES ACT OF 1933 AND THE SECURITIES AND EXCHANGE ACT OF 1934 AND BEYOND

The prosecution of securities-related crimes in the United States is cyclical in nature and reflects the business cycle. When the stock market is riding high, crime certainly occurs, but few complain because everyone is making money. When the market comes crashing down, there are suddenly many losers who have an incentive to look for others to blame. This provides prosecutors with complainants and evidence. Politicians are often in the hot seat as well, accused by the public of thoughtless deregulation or of not controlling big business's ability to take advantage of the little guy. They respond not only by enacting new laws, but also by putting pressure on prosecutors to bring more securities-related cases. A crash in the market thus leads to a boom in white collar prosecutions. The worst market crash, of course, was in 1929 and led to the Great Depression. Congress responded by passing two major securities acts: the Securities Act of 1933 ("Securities Act") and the Securities and Exchange Act of 1934 ("Exchange Act") of 1934. These acts remain the centerpiece of federal securities regulation today.

As you read the materials that follow, keep in mind that the vast majority of securities regulation is civil in nature, achieved either through private actions filed by aggrieved plaintiffs (typically shareholders) or civil enforcement actions brought by the Securities and Exchange Commission (SEC), usually pursuant to the 1933 and 1934 Acts. As a general matter, the Securities Act addresses the initial offer and sale of securities to public investors by mandating (absent an applicable exemption) the filing of a registration statement containing specified information with the SEC and the dissemination of a prospectus to investors during the distribution of securities. The Securities Act also imposes a complex liability scheme for misinformation in communications made during the distribution of securities. Finally, it makes unlawful the failure to register nonexempt securities or transactions.

Congress targeted the Exchange Act to deal with matters involving the secondary markets in the trading of securities. The Act created the SEC and provides for the regulation of stock exchanges and securities firms. It requires periodic and event-based disclosure of key information by public companies, and prohibits manipulative stock market practices[1] and misleading statements in mandated reports and other documents.[2] The Exchange Act also regulates margin requirements for stock purchases and has been interpreted to prohibit insider trading in the securities of public companies. Over the years, there have been amendments and supplements to both Acts, for instance, by the Investment Company Act of 1940,[3] and the Investment Advisors Act of 1940.[4]

In what was an essentially unprecedented move at the time, the drafters of the Securities Act and the Exchange Act decided that civil enforcement and private causes of action were not sufficient remedies to punish and deter potential violators. As a result, they grafted a criminal penalty provision onto both statutes. Specifically, §24 of the Securities Act makes it a crime to "willfully" violate any of the Act's provisions or "the rules and regulations promulgated by the Commission under authority thereof."[5] It also establishes as a crime the making "willfully, in a registration statement filed under this title . . . any untrue statement of a material fact or omit[ting] to state any material fact required to be stated therein or necessary to make the statements therein not misleading."[6] Using similar language, §32(a) of the Exchange Act states that "[a]ny person who willfully violates any provision of this chapter . . . or any rule or regulation thereunder the violation of which is made unlawful or the observance of which is required under the terms of this chapter" is guilty of a crime.[7] Additionally, any person who "willfully and knowingly makes, or causes to be made, any statement in any application, report, or document required to be filed under this chapter or any rule or regulation thereunder . . . which statement was false or misleading with respect to any material fact" is also guilty of a crime.[8] Finally, the Exchange Act provides a partial defense for a person who is criminally convicted under a rule or regulation promulgated pursuant to the Act if it can be shown that "he had no knowledge of such rule or regulation."[9]

Thus, the only difference between a civil and criminal violation of the securities laws is whether the defendant acted "willfully." As a result, civil and criminal

1. *See, e.g.*, 15 U.S.C. §§78i-j.

2. *See* 15 U.S.C. §78r. The import of this provision has been significantly reduced given the broad use of §10(b)/Rule 10b-5 to combat fraud and misrepresentation.

3. *See* Investment Company Act of 1940, 15 U.S.C. §§80a (2000)

4. *See* Investment Advisers Act of 1940, 15 U.S.C. §80b (2000).

5. *See* Securities Act of 1933 §24, 15 U.S.C. §77x (2000).

6. *Id.*

7. Securities Exchange Act of 1934 §32, 15 U.S.C. §78ff(a) (2000).

8. *Id.*

9. *Id.*

cases serve as precedent for each other because the courts in these cases are interpreting identical statutory provisions. However, burden of proof and other criminal law doctrines play a role in shaping the application of civil cases to the criminal sphere.

The most recent cycle of boom and bust took place in the years leading up to the beginning of the twenty-first century.[10] Initially, driven by tremendous gains in technology stocks, many listed on the relatively new NASDAQ stock exchange, the markets reached heights never before seen. Some observers theorized that, because of the impact of information technology on the U.S. economy, the market might never decline again.[11] Unfortunately, this prediction turned out to be a pipedream. The soaring equity markets were the result of "irrational exuberance,"[12] and in 2000, the so-called technology bubble burst.[13] It soon became clear that, in the face of declining markets, a great deal of securities crimes had taken place. This led to the initiation of hundreds of major securities fraud prosecutions around the country, as well as to passage of the Sarbanes-Oxley Act of 2002, which—among many other things—created new securities-related offenses and enhanced the penalties for a number of existing ones.

NOTES AND QUESTIONS

1. Why do you think Congress decided to criminalize the securities laws? In answering this question, consider the material you read concerning the debate over the effectiveness of deterrence in the white collar arena in Chapter 1, *supra*.
2. Usually, securities crimes are discovered initially by the SEC in the course of its general monitoring of the markets or its civil enforcement work. If the agency believes that the matter warrants criminal prosecution, it refers it to the local U.S. Attorney's Office for further development.

10. More specifically, this was the last cycle of boom and bust caused by a stock market bubble. The country experienced a near depression after the bust of the real estate bubble in 2008.

11. *See* Jeff Madrick, *Enron, the Media and the New Economy*, The Nation, Apr. 1, 2002, at 17 (commenting on the rhetoric of the "new Economy" of the mid-1990s, which fueled the inflated speculative value of information technology stocks); Steven Weber, *The End of the Business Cycle*, Foreign Aff. (July/Aug. 1997).

12. The term "irrational exuberance" derives from a speech entitled "The Challenge of Central Banking in a Democracy" given by Alan Greenspan, then-chairman of the Federal Reserve Board, before the American Enterprise Institute at the Washington Hilton Hotel on December 5, 1996.

13. *See* Richard W. Stevenson, *Economists Make It Official: U.S. Is in Recession*, N.Y. Times, Nov. 27, 2001, at C1 (noting that the National Bureau of Economic Research concluded that the U.S. economy entered a recession in March 2001); Leslie Eaton & Jayson Blair, *Silicon Valley's Dimming Lights*, N.Y. Times, Oct. 27, 2000, at B1.

II. MENS REA IN SECURITIES OFFENSES

A. Defining "Willfulness"

UNITED STATES v. PELTZ
433 F.2d 48 (2d Cir. 1970)

FRIENDLY, Circuit Judge:

After trial in the District Court for the Southern District of New York, Philip Peltz, an attorney, was convicted on the four counts of an indictment which Judge Weinfeld submitted to the jury. Count One charged that Peltz had conspired with an employee of the Securities and Exchange Commission to defraud the United States and the Commission of their rights to have their business conducted impartially and according to law and to have the securities laws administered impartially and according to their terms, in violation of 18 U.S.C. §371. Counts Three and Four charged willful violations of §10(b) of the Securities Exchange Act of 1934 and the SEC's Rule 10b-5 in that Peltz had told two brokerage houses that sales of the common stock of Georgia Pacific Corporation which he had ordered were long whereas in fact they were short. Count Five charged that Peltz willfully violated §10(a), relating to short sales, and the Commission's Rule 10a-1(a). The court imposed four concurrent one-year sentences, three months of which were to be served in prison; the remainder of the term was suspended as to each count.

The first count charged that from about January 1, 1966, Peltz had conspired with others, including an employee of the SEC, to obtain confidential inside information about matters under consideration by the Commission and use such information for private profit. Specific mention was made of the Georgia Pacific Corporation and Peltz' sales of its stock. The proof identified the employee as Murray B. Weiner, a branch chief of the SEC's corporation finance division. . . .

On April 7, Peltz telephoned a registered representative at Bache & Co., told him he was thinking of selling 1,000 shares of Georgia Pacific which he owned because he had heard there was a lawsuit pending against the company, and directed him to sell the shares at no less than a specific price. In fact, Peltz did not own the shares at that time. On the same day, he instructed a registered representative at Loeb, Rhoades & Co. to sell 2,000 shares allegedly belonging to his mother but, according to the proof, not in fact owned by her. Four days later Weiner asked a former SEC attorney to recommend a broker for Peltz; the attorney suggested a representative at Sterling, Grace & Co., with whom Peltz placed sell orders for 300 shares as long sales. The proof again was that Peltz did not own these shares. All of Peltz' sales instructions were carried out. He made various excuses for not delivering the shares on the settlement dates but, after the SEC suit was announced and the price of Georgia Pacific fell, he borrowed enough money to enable him to cover his short sales and make a tidy profit. . . .

III.

Section 10(a) of the Securities Exchange Act of 1934 makes it unlawful "for any person, directly or indirectly, by the use of any facility of any national securities exchange" to effect a short sale of any security registered on a national securities exchange in contravention of such rules and regulations as the Commission may prescribe as necessary in the public interest or for the protection of investors. . . .

The Government established that Rule 10a-1(a) had been violated in the case of 1700 of the 3000 Georgia Pacific shares Peltz ordered to be sold on April 7, 1966.

Peltz' first contention, that the statute and rule apply only to brokers and dealers, requires little discussion. The statute speaks of "any person" and the intention to go beyond the "person" actually arranging the trade is made manifest by the phrase "directly or indirectly." The rule is even clearer in covering the person for whose account the sale is made as well as the person making it. See United States v. Mandel, 296 F. Supp. 1038, 1040 (S.D.N.Y. 1969). We thus would have no doubt that a customer explicitly instructing a broker to make a short sale in contravention of Rule 10a-1(a) would be as much subject to criminal liability as the broker who carried out the instruction.

However, there was no evidence that Peltz gave any such instruction and we must confront the issue whether a customer "willfully" violates Rule 10a-1(a) when he deliberately makes a false statement to a broker that he owns securities directed to be sold and there is a resulting violation of the rule, because the broker, having no reason to think that the rule was applicable, failed to take the precautions that would prevent such a violation. In considering this question it will be helpful to have the full text of §32(a) of the Securities Exchange Act before us. . . .

[Here the court quotes the full text of §32(a).]

The language makes one point entirely clear. A person can willfully violate an SEC rule even if he does not know of its existence. This conclusion follows from the difference between the standard for violation of the statute or a rule or regulation, to wit, "willfully," and that for false or misleading statements, namely, "willfully and knowingly." It follows also from the proviso whereby lack of knowledge of a rule or regulation prevents imprisonment but not a fine. All this was pointed out in a penetrating article written by the late Judge Herlands many years before his appointment to the federal bench, *Criminal Law Aspects of the Securities Exchange Act of 1934, supra*, 21 Va. L. Rev. at 148-149.

Decision that the Government need not prove knowledge of Rule 10a-1(a) in order to establish criminal liability still leaves the question what mental state it must prove. The Herlands article concluded it was necessary only that "the prosecution establishes a realization on the defendant's part that he was doing a wrongful act," 21 Va. L. Rev. at 149. We accept this with the qualifications, doubtless intended by the author, that the act be wrongful under the securities laws and that the knowingly wrongful act involve a significant risk of effecting the violation that has occurred. *See* A.L.I. Model Penal Code, §2.03 (1962); Study Draft of a New Federal Criminal Code, §305 (1970).

On this analysis the court was clearly justified in submitting the §10(a) counts to the jury under proper instructions. There was ample evidence that Peltz was aware "he was doing a wrongful act," namely, telling the brokers he was long when he knew he was not. His false statements, negating the facts that would have induced the brokers to take the requisite steps to avoid a violation of 10a-1(a), created a serious risk that such a violation would occur, as it did. *Cf.* Pereira v. United States, 347 U.S. 1, 8-9 (1954).

The conviction on all four counts is affirmed.

UNITED STATES v. KAISER

609 F.3d 556 (2010)

The Securities Exchange Act of 1934 criminalizes only "willful" violations of its provisions. 15 U.S.C. §78ff(a). With respect to misstatements in public filings, the defendant must have also acted with knowledge of the falsity of the statement. *See* 15 U.S.C. §78ff(a). But the government is not required to present "[p]roof of a specific intent to violate the law . . . to uphold a conviction under §32(a) of the Act, provided that satisfactory proof is established that the defendant intended to commit the act prohibited." United States v. Schwartz, 464 F.2d 499, 509 (2d Cir. 1972). Instead, a defendant may raise the defense that he did not know the law to avoid imprisonment. *See* 15 U.S.C. §78ff(a) ("[N]o person shall be subject to imprisonment under this section for the violation of any rule or regulation if he proves that he had no knowledge of such rule or regulation.").

In view of this unique statutory language, we have held that, whatever "willful" might mean for purposes of other statutes, for the purposes of Section 32(a), it does not encompass the requirement that a defendant knew he was violating the law. United States v. Dixon, 536 F.2d 1388, 1395 (2d Cir. 1976) ("A person can willfully violate an SEC rule even if he does not know of its existence") (quoting *Peltz)* . . . .

In *Dixon*, the defendant faced charges of failing to disclose in certain SEC statements that his corporation had loaned him money. Dixon had recorded his debts on the corporate books under the names of other individuals, knowing that those debts were in fact his own. At trial, Dixon did "not deny his knowledge that there were SEC rules requiring the reporting of loans to officers." Rather, Dixon contended that he had been incorrectly informed that so long as he had paid back most of the loan by the end of the year, he was exempted from the disclosure rule. We concluded that this was not a "case of a defendant manifesting an honest belief that he was complying with the law." Dixon acted willfully by misstating who had taken out the loans in the corporate books—this was a "wrongful act," in the sense of that term in *Peltz.* Judge Friendly wrote for the Court:

> Dixon may have thought his year-end thimblerig would provide escape from a rule different from the one that existed. But such acts are wrongful "under the Securities Acts" if they lead, as here, to the very violations that would have been prevented if the defendant had acted with the aim of scrupulously obeying the rules (which would have necessarily involved correctly ascertaining them) rather than of avoiding them. Such an intention to deceive is enough to meet the modest requirements of the first clause of section 32(a) when violations occur.

. . . [W]e conclude that *Peltz* and *Dixon* do not require a showing that a defendant had awareness of the general unlawfulness of his conduct, but rather, that he had an awareness of the general wrongfulness of his conduct.

NOTES AND QUESTIONS

1. The *Peltz* and *Kaiser* courts essentially conclude that for §78(ff) purposes, willful means that the defendant must know what he's doing (as opposed to

acting by mistake or accident) plus know that what he's doing is wrong. This latter requirement might be referred to as a "weak" mistake of law defense, because the defendant will prevail only if the government cannot prove that he was aware of the mere "wrongness"—as opposed to the "illegality"—of his conduct. *See* Michael L. Seigel, *Bringing Coherence to Mens Rea Analysis for Securities-Related Offenses*, 2006 Wis. L. Rev. 1563, 1608-1609 (2006). Does the weak mistake of law defense have any real value in the context of fraud prosecutions? Can an individual harbor an intent to defraud and simultaneously be unaware of the wrongfulness of his conduct?

2. If, as suggested in Question 1, an individual who commits securities fraud necessarily acts willfully, is there any doctrinal distinction left between a civil fraud violation and a criminal one? If the answer is "no," can deciding which type of charges to pursue be anything other than arbitrary? Or can an objective set of factors be constructed to guide decision-makers? If so, what would they look like? *See* United States Attorneys' Manual, *Principles of Federal Prosecution*, http://www.usdoj.gov/usao/eousa/foia_reading_room/usam/title9/27mcrm.htm.
3. Was *Dixon* correctly decided? Can you argue it both ways?

B. Willful Blindness

UNITED STATES v. WEINER

578 F.2d 757 (9th Cir.), cert. denied, 439 U.S. 981 (1978)

Per Curiam:

Julian Weiner, Marvin Lichtig, and Solomon Block appeal their respective convictions for securities fraud arising out of their employment as auditors of Equity Funding Corporation of America (Equity Funding) during the time covered by the indictment.

Equity Funding was incorporated in 1960 to sell life insurance, mutual funds, and "equity funding" programs. The company operated legitimately and profitably until 1964, when, the government proved, it began to publish inaccurate and false financial statements. Equity Funding was accused of massive fraud in overstating its income and claiming nonexistent assets in order to increase the market value of its stock.

Wolfson, Weiner, Ratoff, and Lapin were the independent public accountants for Equity Funding from 1961 until 1971. In early 1972, the Los Angeles branch of the Wolfson, Weiner firm joined with the accounting firm of Seidman & Seidman. The combined firm served as Equity Funding's independent public accountant until the exposure of the fraud in 1973.

Julian Weiner was the Wolfson, Weiner partner in charge of the audits of Equity Funding from 1961 to 1973. He was convicted of six counts of securities fraud, 15 U.S.C. §§77x, 77q(a), for accounting practices which fraudulently overstated the income and assets of Equity Funding, and of four counts of willfully making untrue statements to the Securities Exchange Commission (SEC) and the New York or Pacific Coast Stock Exchanges, in violation of 15 U.S.C. §§77x, 77f, 78ff, 78m.

Marvin Lichtig, as an employee and later as a junior partner of Wolfson, Weiner, supervised the audit field work of Equity Funding for the audits between 1963 and 1968. He reported directly to Julian Weiner. From 1968 until 1973, Lichtig served as an officer of Equity Funding and signed registration statements as the principal accounting officer of the company. Lichtig was convicted of the same six counts of securities fraud as Weiner. Lichtig was also convicted of seven counts of filing false statements with the SEC and the New York or Pacific Coast Stock Exchange in violation of 15 U.S.C. §§77x, 77f, 78ff, 78l, 78m.

Solomon Block was employed by Wolfson, Weiner in 1968 and replaced Lichtig as the supervisor of field audits. Block served as supervisor for the 1969 through 1972 audits. Block was charged with the same six counts of securities fraud as Weiner and Lichtig, but Block was convicted of only five of the counts. Block was convicted of two counts of making false statements to the SEC and the New York or Pacific Coast Stock Exchanges in violation of 15 U.S.C. §§77x, 77f, 78ff, 78m. . . .

* * *

P. Jury Instructions Dealing with Intent

We next dispose of defendants' contentions regarding certain jury instructions: those related to the question of the sufficiency of the evidence.

1. Compliance with GAAS and GAAP

Defendants first challenge the court's instruction on the rule of generally accepted auditing standards and generally accepted accounting principles in the jury's deliberations. The instruction is reproduced in the margin.[26]

We have not previously ruled on the propriety of instructions which state that compliance or noncompliance with GAAS or GAAP is relevant to the determination of a defendant's intent. The Second Circuit has dealt with similar instructions in United States v. Simon, 425 F.2d 796 (2d Cir. 1969). . . . In *Simon* three accountants appealed from their convictions on three counts arising out of their drawing up and certifying a misleading and false financial statement. The jury was

26. "One circumstance you are entitled to consider and weigh in determining whether the defendants Weiner, Lichtig, and Block acted willfully and knowingly while in their capacities as independent accountants in relation to Equity Funding is whether they followed or deviated from generally accepted auditing standards or accounting principles in effect at the times here pertinent. . . .

"Generally, when a certified public accountant is engaged to perform an independent audit for a corporation such as Equity Funding, he represents and warrants that he will perform the audit and other accounting work in accordance with generally accepted auditing standards and generally accepted accounting principles and that he will render an opinion as to whether the financial statement of the company fairly represents its financial position and the results of its business operation.

"Proof, if any, that any of these defendants departed from such standards of auditing and accounting as were then applicable or participated in the preparation or approval of an audited financial statement that did not fairly present Equity Funding's financial position is evidence, though not necessarily conclusive evidence, that the individual defendant involved did not act honestly or in good faith, and that the financial statement prepared contrary to such standards may have been materially false or misleading."

instructed that the primary determination was whether the financial statements accurately reflected the company's condition, and, if not, whether the defendants acted in good faith. Proof of compliance with GAAS was deemed "evidence which may be very persuasive but not necessarily conclusive that he acted in good faith."

The prosecution introduced into evidence the Statement on Auditing Standards (1973) issued by the Committee on Auditing Procedure, American Institute of Certified Public Accountants. The Statement outlines the general purpose of the independent audit, and explains the responsibilities of the individual auditor who finds fraud in the entity whose records are being examined:

> "In making the ordinary examination, the independent auditor is aware of the possibility that fraud may exist . . . . However, the ordinary examination directed to the expression of an opinion on financial statements is not primarily or specifically designed and cannot be relied upon, to disclose defalcation and other similar irregularities, although their discovery may result. . . . The responsibility of the independent auditor for failure to detect fraud (which responsibility differs as to clients and others) arises only when such failure clearly results from failure to comply with generally accepted auditing standards."

Under these standards the auditor is not "responsible" for fraud that has gone undetected despite his utilization of generally accepted auditing standards. In our case, failure to apply generally accepted auditing standards is relevant to the issue of knowledge and willfulness.

Sufficient evidence was introduced to raise the issue of conformity with GAAS and GAAP. During the trial several witnesses testified that many of the practices under consideration were not in conformance with GAAS and GAAP. Generally, no audit manual was prepared for each year's audit, no checks on internal controls were made, and basic standards for confirming accounts were not followed. The witnesses included Norman Grosman, a partner in Touche, Ross & Co.; Frank West, who worked on the audits from 1969 through 1972; and William Simpson and Benjamin Karchin, SEC employees who reviewed Equity Funding's books. The jury had evidence from which it could determine whether GAAS and GAAP were properly utilized and whether the failure to utilize them was such as to lead to a reasonable inference of criminal intent.

The judge's instruction, which stated that evidence regarding compliance with GAAS and GAAP was not conclusive but was relevant, was a proper statement. The weight to be given the evidence was for the jury's determination.

2. "Willfulness"

Defendants also assert that the court erred in instructing the jury on the issue of knowledge.[14] The jury was instructed that proof of negligence was insufficient to support a conviction, and that proof of good faith constituted a complete defense

14. [Recall that the *Notes and Questions* section following the *Peltz* case concluded that the "willfulness" standard has two components: first, that the defendant acted knowingly (that is, not recklessly, negligently, or accidentally) and second, that the defendant knew that what he was doing was wrong. The court here is focusing on the former. — Eds.]

to the charges. The court went on to instruct the jury that, in determining intent, the jury could consider whether defendants acted in "reckless, deliberate indifference to or disregard for truth or falsity," and could infer from proof of such acts that defendants acted willfully and knowingly.

. . . The trial court's instruction in the present case followed closely the instruction approved by the Second Circuit in United States v. Natelli, 527 F.2d 311, 322-23. (2d Cir. 1975). There the trial court had instructed the jury that, on proof of "reckless deliberate indifference to or disregard for truth or falsity," the jury could infer the defendants' willful and knowing participation in the filing of false financial information with the SEC. The defendants contended that the instruction erroneously failed to state also that there must be a concurrent, "conscious purpose to avoid learning the truth." The court approved the instruction and stated: The dual instruction is not necessarily required, however, when the defendant is under a specific duty to discover the true facts, the facts tendered are suspect, and he does nothing to correct them." 527 F.2d at 323.

The court properly instructed the jury on the need to find both deliberate avoidance and an awareness of impropriety. Defendants here, as auditors, had a duty carefully to investigate and review the information presented. Because the instruction stated that good faith constituted a complete defense, it was implicit in the instruction that, coupled with a finding of deliberate avoidance of knowledge, the jury also had to find bad faith. . . .

In view of the defendants' duty because of their roles as auditors and financial officer of the company, the jury instruction was proper.

C. Advice of Counsel Defense

UNITED STATES v. WENGER

427 F.3d 840 (10th Cir. 2005)

Tymkovich, Circuit Judge.

Defendant-Appellant Jerome Wenger published a newsletter called *The Next SuperStock* and hosted a syndicated radio program of the same name. After failing to inform his listeners that he had been receiving compensation from certain companies in exchange for touting their stocks on his show, he was indicted and convicted of securities fraud under Section 17(b) of the Securities Act of 1933, 15 U.S.C. §77q(b), which makes it unlawful to publicize a stock for consideration from an issuer, underwriter, or dealer without disclosing the fact and amount of the payment. In addition, for failing to inform readers of *The Next SuperStock* newsletter that he was selling his shares in the companies he had been recommending they buy, he was convicted under Section 10(b) of the Securities Exchange Act of 1934, 15 U.S.C. §78j(b), which makes it unlawful to employ any manipulative or deceptive device in connection with the sale of securities.

On appeal, Wenger challenges his convictions on the ground [that, among other things,] his convictions were against the weight of the evidence presented at trial. . . .

Accepting jurisdiction under 28 U.S.C. §1291, we affirm.

In 1984, Wenger began publishing *Penny Stock News*, a newsletter that gave investment advice concerning "penny stocks," or shares of small companies with large numbers of shares outstanding. After the Securities and Exchange Commission determined that Wenger's *Penny Stock News* had violated the disclosure requirements of Section 17(b) and Section 10(b) because he received money from companies he recommended, Wenger and the SEC entered into a consent decree that stipulated he would disclose the full value of any consideration he was receiving from any issuer about which *Penny Stock News* was giving advice.

Ten years later, Wenger began publishing a similar newsletter called *The Next SuperStock* and also began hosting a radio program based in Salt Lake City. To further these ventures, Wenger approached a company called PanWorld Minerals International, Inc. and told its management that he could help publicize its stock. After PanWorld expressed interest, Wenger offered to provide certain "consulting" services for a standard fee of $15,000. Because PanWorld could not compensate Wenger in cash, Wenger agreed instead to accept 5.5 million shares of PanWorld, of which he had received 2.1 million by April 1994.

In early 1994, Wenger consulted with a law firm to determine how he could comply with Section 17(b)'s disclosure requirements. In a letter dated June 28, 1994, the firm recommended a two-stage disclosure, according to which Wenger would first state on the air that he was a paid consultant to some of the companies mentioned, and second send details regarding his compensation to listeners upon request. Sometime in 1994 Wenger began to tell listeners that they could request a list of his stock holdings. In response to such requests, he would send a form letter, which stated, "I presently charge a company $16,000 for services which may include introducing them to market makers and stock brokers, introduction to newspaper and magazine writers, introduction to newsletter writers and exposure through the radio." The letter then stated that "[a]s far as my portfolio is concerned the following stocks I bought," among which was listed PanWorld.

[Wenger repeatedly touted PanWorld stock on the radio without disclosing the amount of stock Pan World was providing to him in compensation. He continued to urge listeners to buy it long after he sold his own shares for a total of more than $100,000.] Several listeners to Wenger's program testified that they bought PanWorld stock as a result of Wenger's recommendations. They also testified that had Wenger disclosed he was selling his PanWorld stock, they would not have bought any shares in PanWorld. . . .

Wenger was indicted in 1999. . . .

Wenger argues that the jury should have acquitted him because he relied in good faith on the advice of his counsel. Good faith reliance on counsel is a defense to the mens rea element of a criminal prosecution under the Securities Act of 1933. The mens rea element is defined in Section 24 of the Act, 15 U.S.C. §77x, which states that the government must prove that the defendant "willfully violate[d]" the Act's provisions. If the jury finds that the defendant relied in good faith on the advice of counsel, it may acquit him on the grounds that the defendant's conduct was not willful.

Good faith reliance on counsel, however, is not a complete defense, but is merely one factor a jury may consider when determining whether a defendant acted willfully. United States v. Custer Channel Wing Corp., 376 F.2d 675, 683 (4th Cir. 1967). In the Tenth Circuit, to establish a good faith reliance on counsel defense, the defendant must show "(1) a request for advice of counsel on the legality of a proposed action, (2) full disclosure of the relevant facts to counsel, (3) receipt of advice from counsel that the action to be taken will be legal, and (4) reliance in good faith on counsel's advice." C.E. Carlson, Inc. v. SEC, 859 F.2d 1429 (10th Cir. 1988).

We conclude that a reasonable jury could have rejected Wenger's good faith reliance on counsel defense. First, Wenger did not establish that he disclosed all relevant facts to his attorneys. In particular, if Wenger had wanted to avoid future Section 17(b) prosecutions, he would have disclosed to his attorneys that in 1984 he and the SEC had entered into a consent decree governing how he would comply with Section 17(b) in the future. Nonetheless, John Dougherty, one of the lawyers who in 1994 recommended the two-stage disclosure process, testified that he did not know that Wenger had once entered into a consent decree with the SEC that governed Wenger's disclosures. Although Dougherty believed that his partner would have known about the consent decree, Wenger did not present any evidence to substantiate Dougherty's opinion. Wenger therefore did not establish that he had disclosed all relevant facts to his counsel, and thus failed to negate the government's showing of willfulness.

Secondly, the evidence showed that Wenger also failed to accurately disclose to recipients the amount of compensation received. Wenger disclosed (inaccurately) his consulting fee, which far understated the value of the stock given to him for touting PanWorld. Finally, Wenger's prior encounters with the SEC regarding paid promotion for touting belie any lack of knowledge and undercut his claim that he relied on counsel in making the inadequate disclosures at issue here.

On this record, a reasonable jury had sufficient evidence to convict Wenger. . . .

For the foregoing reasons, the decision of the district court is AFFIRMED.

NOTES AND QUESTIONS

1. An ignorance defense ("I did not know what my underlings were up to") is typical when a high-level corporate executive is charged with committing securities fraud. This makes the doctrine of willful blindness especially important in such cases. Moreover, Congress reacted to the ubiquitous use of the defense by corporate CEOs after the collapse of the technology bubble by passing a corporate certification requirement as part of the Sarbanes-Oxley Act, 18 U.S.C. §1350. CEOs now must certify to the accuracy of their company's financial reports subject to personal criminal fines and penalties if it is later discovered that the report was false. How effective do you think §1350 will be in future cases?
2. The advice of counsel defense is a double-edged sword. If the defendant truly acted on counsel's advice, asserting the defense can shortcut charges

in a hurry. On the other hand, if the defendant lied or left out critical facts when seeking counsel's advice, his conduct can come back to haunt him. The prosecutor will seek a waiver of attorney-client privilege based on the crime-fraud exception. Then he will interview counsel. If counsel was unwittingly used to further the perpetration of defendant's crime, she is usually more than willing to tell prosecutors that, had she been given the full picture, she certainly would have advised defendant that his plan was illegal. When counsel testifies to this at trial, it can be a devastating blow to the defense.

3. What are the potential consequences to an attorney who erroneously advises her client that specified transactions are legal? What precautions would you take when providing such advice to protect yourself from future ethical or criminal liability? How would you structure your "opinion letter"?

D. "No Knowledge" Proviso

UNITED STATES v. KNUEPPEL

293 F. Supp. 2d 199 (E.D.N.Y. 2003)

GERSHON, District Judge.

Defendants Jodi L. Knueppel, Mark R. Sonday, Gregory L. Tyrer and Gregory J. Misfeldt have pled guilty to engaging in a criminal conspiracy to violate Securities Exchange Act of 1934 (the "Act") Section 10(b), 15 U.S.C. §§78j(b), and Securities and Exchange Commission ("SEC") Rule 10b-5. Misfeldt and Tyrer each pled guilty pursuant to cooperation agreements, under which they divulged the identity and roles of Knueppel and Sonday. Following the entry of their pleas of guilty, defendants Knueppel, Sonday and Tyrer all moved to avoid the imposition of a prison sentence pursuant to the "no knowledge" provision of 15 U.S.C. §78ff(a). The government opposed the application. . . . I now conclude that the government is correct in that the "no knowledge" provision is inapplicable. . . .

Background

The basic facts underlying the prosecution are not in dispute.

Defendants Misfeldt and Tyrer [were friends who invested in stocks together. Misfeldt was also friendly with Knueppel, who worked with Sonday at a financial magazine called *Business Week*. The four engaged in an insider trading scheme whereby Knueppel or Sonday would provide Misfeldt and Tyrer with information about the magazine's contents prior to its distribution. The latter two would place trades based on their predictions of how the magazine's release would impact the value of certain stocks. Each of the four defendants made money as a result of this activity.]

The government charged all four defendants under the misappropriation theory.

Application of "No Knowledge" Clause of 15 U.S.C. §78ff(a)

Knueppel, Sonday and Tyrer pled guilty to an information which charges that:

> [T]he defendants did knowingly and willfully conspire . . . to use and employ manipulative devices and contrivances in violation of Rule 10b-5 of the Rules and Regulations of the United States Securities and Exchange Commission . . . in that the defendants did knowingly and wilfully conspire . . . to defraud . . . members of the investing public . . . in violation of Title 15, United States Code, Sections 78j and 78ff. . . .

The penalties for violating 15 U.S.C §78j(b) and Rule 10b-5 are codified at 15 U.S.C. §78ff(a), which provides, in relevant part, that:

> Any person who wilfully violates any provision of this chapter (other than section 78dd-1 of this title), or any rule or regulation thereunder the violation of which is made unlawful or the observance of which is required under the terms of this chapter, . . . shall upon conviction be fined not more than $1,000,000, or imprisoned or both, . . . *but no person shall be subject to imprisonment under this section for the violation of any such rule or regulation if he proves that he had no knowledge of such rule or regulation* (emphasis added).

The information to which defendants pled guilty does not, as they suggest, charge just a violation of an SEC Rule but also expressly charges a violation of 18 U.S.C. §371 and Section 10(b) of the Act, 15 U.S.C §78j(b). Criminal penalties attach to violations of Section 78j by virtue of Section 78ff(a), which provides penalties for wilful violations of "any provision of this chapter" as well as for any wilful violation of "any rule or regulation thereunder. . . ."

Section 10(b) is virtually tracked in the language of Rule 10b-5, and the Supreme Court has stated that "the scope of Rule 10b-5 is coextensive with the coverage of §10(b)." . . . Thus, the defendants' pleas of guilty in this case to the charges in the information take them outside the protections of the "no knowledge" provision. Given their allocutions to conspiring to engage in acts which constitute securities fraud prohibited by Section 10(b) and Rule 10b-5, they simply cannot be viewed as intended beneficiaries of the statute.[1] In United States v. Sloan, 399 F. Supp. 982 (S.D.N.Y. 1975), Judge Whitman Knapp found the "no knowledge" provision of Section 78ff(a) inapplicable to a defendant convicted after trial of conspiracy to violate 15 U.S.C. §78q(a) and three SEC regulations promulgated thereunder which required that certain records by accurately made, preserved and filed. In doing so, Judge Knapp analyzed the purposes of the "no knowledge" provision in Section 78ff(a), as follows:

1. Given the unique relationship between Section 10(b) and Rule 10b-5, and the fact that these provisions deal with fraud, with its inherent culpability, it seems difficult to imagine a case in which the "no knowledge" provision could be applicable to a criminal Rule 10b-5 violation, which requires wilfulness.

> This clause is rather unique in that it permits a defendant prior to sentencing to rebut the presumption that he had knowledge of the rule or regulation of which he had been convicted of violating. It was included in the 1934 Act as a compromise measure to allay certain fears in Congress that, by enacting a vast new securities statute giving broad rule-making authority to the SEC, and by making violations of such rules criminal, the legislators were subjecting totally "innocent" people—persons who might act without knowledge that their conduct was now prohibited by a rule—to possible incarceration. The compromise impliedly recognized that under such circumstances, strict adherence to the presumption of knowledge of the law would be unwarranted. *Sloan*, 399 F. Supp. at 984.

Judge Knapp went on to state:

> It is equally clear, however, that Congress did intend to maintain the usual presumption of knowledge with respect to the standards prescribed in the securities acts themselves. The "no knowledge" proviso is explicitly limited to lack of knowledge of a "rule or regulation." Congress did not intend that the protection of the "no knowledge" clause would extend to persons who were charged with knowing their conduct to be in violation of law, but did not happen to know that it was also in violation of a particular SEC rule or regulation. *Id.*

Here, as in *Sloan*, none of these defendants is "a totally innocent person" who committed a mere technical violation of an SEC rule or regulation. As the defense acknowledged at the hearing, the misappropriation theory of securities fraud liability does not involve the technical violation of a rule. They nonetheless argue that the use of that theory of liability relieves them of imprisonment because they had no knowledge of the misappropriation theory. This argument is meritless. . . . Whether or not defendants knew that they faced potential prosecution under a theory labeled by lawyers as the "misappropriation theory," they pled guilty to participating in a conspiracy to use stolen, non-public information to trade in securities to the harm of the investing public, conduct that is inherently culpable both because of the theft and because of the harm to which the information was put. . . .

Even assuming that the "no knowledge" provision were available to the defendants, I find that defendants have failed to carry their burden to prove that they actually had no knowledge within the meaning of Section 78ff(a). Defendants agree that it is their burden to prove by a preponderance of the evidence that they meet the standard for application of the "no knowledge" provision. Defendants also agree that lack of knowledge of the specific rule violated is immaterial and that they must show lack of knowledge of the substance of the rule to which they pled guilty. [The defendants' various statements during their change of plea hearings demonstrated the very opposite.]

Conclusion

For the above stated reasons, defendants' motions are denied, and they will not be allowed to rely on the "no knowledge" provision of 15 U.S.C. §78ff(a) to avoid imprisonment.

NOTES AND QUESTIONS

1. The no knowledge proviso is very unusual. Typically, ignorance or mistake of the criminal law is not a defense of any kind. Why did Congress place it in the Exchange Act? Is the court's interpretation of the proviso consistent with congressional intent?
2. Defendants' invocation of the no knowledge proviso is extremely rare, and their successful use of it is almost nil. This is because, to be liable in the first place, a defendant must have acted "willfully," that is, he must have known that what he was doing was "wrong." For shelter under the proviso, the defendant must demonstrate that he did not know that what he was doing was "illegal." The space between "wrong" and "illegal"—where the defense is operative—is very, very small.
3. Successful use of the no knowledge proviso is much more likely in cases involving a failure to meet a technical regulatory requirement, as opposed to those involving fraud. Why do you think this is the case?

III. MATERIALITY

BASIC v. LEVINSON

485 U.S. 224 (1988)

Justice Blackmun delivered the opinion of the Court.

This case requires us to apply the materiality requirement of §10(b) of the Securities Exchange Act of 1934, (1934 Act), 48 Stat. 881, as amended, 15 U.S.C. §78a *et seq.* and the Securities and Exchange Commission's Rule 10b-5, 17 C.F.R. §240.10b-5 (1987), promulgated thereunder, in the context of preliminary corporate merger discussions. . . .

I.

Prior to December 20, 1978, Basic Incorporated was a publicly traded company primarily engaged in the business of manufacturing chemical refractories for the steel industry. As early as 1965 or 1966, Combustion Engineering, Inc., a company producing mostly alumina-based refractories, expressed some interest in acquiring Basic, but was deterred from pursuing this inclination seriously because of antitrust concerns it then entertained. In 1976, however, regulatory action opened the way to a renewal of Combustion's interest. The "Strategic Plan," dated October 25, 1976, for Combustion's Industrial Products Group included the objective: "Acquire Basic Inc. $30 million."

Beginning in September 1976, Combustion representatives had meetings and telephone conversations with Basic officers and directors, including petitioners here, concerning the possibility of a merger. During 1977 and 1978, Basic made three public statements denying that it was engaged in merger negotiations.

On December 18, 1978, Basic asked the New York Stock Exchange to suspend trading in its shares and issued a release stating that it had been "approached" by another company concerning a merger. On December 19, Basic's board endorsed Combustion's offer of $46 per share for its common stock and on the following day publicly announced its approval of Combustion's tender offer for all outstanding shares.

Respondents are former Basic shareholders who sold their stock after Basic's first public statement of October 21, 1977, and before the suspension of trading in December 1978. Respondents brought a class action against Basic and its directors, asserting that the defendants issued three false or misleading public statements and thereby were in violation of §10(b) of the 1934 Act and of Rule 10b-5. Respondents alleged that they were injured by selling Basic shares at artificially depressed prices in a market affected by petitioners' misleading statements and in reliance thereon.

The District Court . . . granted summary judgment for the defendants. It held that, as a matter of law, any misstatements were immaterial: there were no negotiations ongoing at the time of the first statement, and although negotiations were taking place when the second and third statements were issued, those negotiations were not "destined, with reasonable certainty, to become a merger agreement in principle."

The United States Court of Appeals for the Sixth Circuit . . . reversed the District Court's summary judgment, and remanded the case. The court reasoned that while petitioners were under no general duty to disclose their discussions with Combustion, any statement the company voluntarily released could not be "'so incomplete as to mislead.'" In the Court of Appeals' view, Basic's statements that no negotiations were taking place, and that it knew of no corporate developments to account for the heavy trading activity, were misleading. With respect to materiality, the court rejected the argument that preliminary merger discussions are immaterial as a matter of law, and held that "once a statement is made denying the existence of any discussions, even discussions that might not have been material in absence of the denial are material because they make the statement made untrue." . . .

We granted certiorari to resolve the split . . . among the Courts of Appeals as to the standard of materiality applicable to preliminary merger discussions. . . .

II.

The 1934 Act was designed to protect investors against manipulation of stock prices. Underlying the adoption of extensive disclosure requirements was a legislative philosophy: "There cannot be honest markets without honest publicity. Manipulation and dishonest practices of the market place thrive upon mystery and secrecy." H.R. Rep. No. 1383, 73d Cong., 2d Sess., 11 (1934). This Court "repeatedly has described the 'fundamental purpose' of the Act as implementing a 'philosophy of full disclosure.'"

The Court previously has addressed various positive and common-law requirements for a violation of §10(b) or of Rule 10b-5. . . . The Court also explicitly has defined a standard of materiality under the securities laws, see TSC Industries, Inc. v. Northway, Inc., 426 U.S. 438 (1976), concluding in the proxy-solicitation context that "[a]n omitted fact is material if there is a substantial likelihood that a reasonable shareholder would consider it important in deciding how to vote." Acknowledging that certain information concerning corporate developments could well be of "dubious significance," the Court was careful not to set too low a standard of materiality; it was concerned that a minimal standard might bring an overabundance of information within its reach, and lead management "simply to bury the shareholders in an avalanche of trivial information—a result that is hardly conducive to informed decisionmaking." It further explained that to fulfill the materiality requirement "there must be a substantial likelihood that the disclosure of the omitted fact would have been viewed by the reasonable investor as having significantly altered the 'total mix' of information made available." We now expressly adopt the *TSC Industries* standard of materiality for the §10(b) and Rule 10b-5 context. . . .

As we clarify today, materiality depends on the significance the reasonable investor would place on the withheld or misrepresented information. The fact-specific inquiry we endorse here is consistent with the approach a number of courts have taken in assessing the materiality of merger negotiations. Because the standard of materiality we have adopted differs from that used by both courts below, we remand the case for reconsideration of the question whether a grant of summary judgment is appropriate on this record. . . .

The judgment of the Court of Appeals is vacated, and the case is remanded to that court for further proceedings consistent with this opinion.

It is so ordered.

NOTES AND QUESTIONS

1. Note that *Basic v. Levinson* is a civil case. Should the materiality standard be the same for civil and criminal cases?
2. When testing the safety of new pharmaceutical products, manufacturers study and record each time a recipient of the drug experiences an "adverse event." Can the failure to disclose to investors adverse event reports for a pharmaceutical product be material if the reports have no statistical significance? *See* Matrixx Intiatives Inc. v. Siracusano, 131 S. Ct. 1309 (2011) (reaffirming *Basic* and answering the question "yes," because medical experts rely on other than statistically significant evidence to make causation and other determinations; therefore, such evidence could be material information to investors).

PROBLEM 6-1

About 18 months ago, Garage Doors, Inc., a publicly traded company, introduced a voice-activated garage opener into the market, called "Openme." It operated through a tiny microphone installed in the owner's automobile. Field testing had indicated that the new product, though ground-breaking, still had some serious wrinkles in it. For example, occasionally a loud car radio would cause the opener to operate, either closing the garage door on a car as it was backing out or opening it when an unsuspecting homeowner was driving away. Nevertheless, the company—which had touted the "imminent national launch of a revolutionary new product line" in its previous annual report—pushed forward with the planned release. Unfortunately, due to the frequency and severity of the problems, consumers were uniformly dissatisfied with Openme and the stock price of the company fell dramatically within weeks of its introduction into the market.

Recently, the U.S. Attorney's Office charged Garage Doors with securities fraud pursuant to 17 C.F.R. §240.10b-5 and 15 U.S.C. §78ff. The government's theory of fraud is that the company willfully violated Rule 10b-5 by disseminating an annual report to the investing public that was fraudulent by touting Openme without noting the problems revealed by the testing. The company moves to dismiss this charge. What are the pertinent issues and arguments?

IV. THEORIES OF SECURITIES FRAUD I: MISREPRESENTATION AND CONCEALMENT

Securities fraud violations tend to fall into one of several categories. One ubiquitous kind of fraud occurs when a corporate insider makes material misstatements to the investing public (or fails to correct a material misimpression caused by earlier statements), causing members of the public to engage in market transactions that they otherwise would have forgone. This kind of "fraud on the market" is often termed "Misrepresentation and Concealment." Sometimes the misrepresentations are made directly to investors; on other occasions, they are made to a third-party entity, such as the SEC, with the net result to investors being the same.

A. To Investors

UNITED STATES v. STEWART

305 F. Supp. 2d 368 (S.D.N.Y. 2004)

CEDARBAUM, District Judge.

Defendant Martha Stewart has moved for a judgment of acquittal pursuant to Fed. R. Crim. P. 29. The motion is granted with respect to Count Nine only. . . .

Count Nine of the Indictment charges that defendant Stewart made materially false statements of fact regarding her sale of ImClone securities with the intention of defrauding and deceiving investors by slowing or stopping the erosion of the value of the securities issued by her own company, Martha Stewart Living Omnimedia ("MSLO") [in violation of 15 U.S.C. §§78j & 78ff, and Rule 10(b)-5]. In assessing the sufficiency of the evidence, I have concluded that no reasonable juror can find beyond a reasonable doubt that the defendant lied for the purpose of influencing the market for the securities of her company. Another way of putting it would be that in order to find the essential element of criminal intent beyond a reasonable doubt, a rational juror would have to speculate.

Background

The criminal charges against Stewart and [Peter] Bacanovic arose from Stewart's December 27, 2001 sale of 3,928 shares of stock in ImClone Systems, Inc. ("ImClone"). ImClone is a biotechnology company whose then-chief executive officer, Samuel Waksal, was a friend of Stewart's and a client of Stewart's stockbroker at Merrill Lynch, defendant Bacanovic. On December 28, 2001, the day after Stewart sold her shares, ImClone announced that the Food and Drug Administration had rejected the company's application for approval of Erbitux, a cancer-fighting drug that ImClone had previously described as its lead product.

The Indictment alleges that on the morning of December 27, 2001, defendant Bacanovic learned that Waksal and several of his family members were selling or attempting to sell their ImClone shares. Bacanovic allegedly instructed his assistant, Douglas Faneuil, to inform Stewart of the Waksals' trading activity, and she sold her shares in response to that information.

According to the Indictment, the defendants then lied about the real reason for Stewart's sale in order to cover up what was possibly an illegal trade and to deflect attention from Stewart in the ensuing investigations into suspicious ImClone trading in advance of the Erbitux announcement. The defendants claimed that they had a standing agreement that Stewart would sell her position in ImClone if the stock fell to $60 per share.

The Indictment charges the defendants with conspiracy, obstruction of an agency proceeding, and making false statements to government officials. Bacanovic is also charged with perjury and making and using false documents.

Count Nine of the Indictment charges Stewart, the CEO of MSLO, with fraud in connection with the purchase and sale of MSLO securities in violation of 15 U.S.C. §§78b and 78ff. The count is based on three repetitive public statements she made in June of 2002 after the media began reporting investigations of her ImClone trades by the Securities and Exchange Commission ("SEC"), the United States Attorney's Office, and a congressional subcommittee. In the critical statements, Stewart described the agreement to sell ImClone at a predetermined price, stated that her trade was proper and denied trading on nonpublic information.

Discussion

. . . Taken in the light most favorable to the Government, the evidence presented at trial permits the jury to find the following facts relevant to the securities fraud charge.

Gregory Blatt, MSLO's former general counsel, testified that Stewart held approximately sixty percent of the shares of common stock in MSLO and over ninety percent of the voting shares. The jury could reasonably infer from this evidence that Stewart had a significant financial stake in MSLO. . . .

The Government introduced into evidence MSLO's prospectus, written and disseminated at the time of the IPO in 1999, which detailed the importance of Stewart to the company's revenues and the value of its brands. Under the heading "Risk Factors," the prospectus notes:

> The loss of the services of Martha Stewart or other key employees would materially adversely affect our revenues, results of operations and prospects.
>
> We are highly dependent upon our founder, Chairman and Chief Executive Officer, Martha Stewart. Martha Stewart's talents, efforts, personality and leadership have been, and continue to be, critical to our success.
>
> The diminution or loss of the services of Martha Stewart, and any negative market or industry perception arising from that diminution or loss, would have a material adverse effect on our business.

The prospectus also states that:

> Our success depends on our brands and their value. Our business would be adversely affected if:
>
> Martha Stewart's public image or reputation were to be tarnished.
>
> Martha Stewart as well as her name, her image and the trademarks and other intellectual property rights relating to these, are integral to our marketing efforts and form the core of our brand name. Our continued success and the value of our brand name therefore depends, to a large degree, on the reputation of Martha Stewart.

A reasonable jury could infer from this evidence that Stewart was aware of the importance of her reputation to the continued health of MSLO.

The Government presented evidence, through the testimony of Peter J. Melley, an investigator with the Criminal Prosecution Assistance Group of the National Association of Securities Dealers, that the share price of MSLO stock began to fall on June 7, 2002, the day that the investigations of Stewart's ImClone trade were first reported publicly, and continued falling throughout June of 2002. On June 13 and June 19 the share price experienced brief resurgences, only to continue to fall. The price of MSLO stock, which had closed at \$19.01 on June 6, closed at \$12.55 on June 24. The Government also presented evidence that throughout this period news coverage of Stewart's ImClone trade and the related investigations was widespread and intense. With respect to Stewart's state of mind, a reasonable jury could infer, based on the falling stock price and the ubiquitous news reports, that Stewart believed that the price of MSLO was falling in response to the negative publicity about the investigations. . . .

The Government . . . introduced evidence of the timing, context, and substance of the three allegedly false public statements. The first statement appeared in *The Wall Street Journal* on June 7, 2002. Included in an article entitled "Martha Stewart Sold ImClone Stock," is the following paragraph:

> According to her attorney, John Savarese, Ms. Stewart's sale, involving about 3,000 shares of ImClone, occurred on December 26 or 27. The sale was executed, he said, because Ms. Stewart had a predetermined price at which she planned to sell the stock. That determination, made more than a month before that trade, was to

> sell if the stock ever went below $60, he said. At the time, the stock was trading at about $60.

The second statement appeared in a press release issued after the close of business on June 12, 2002. Attributed to Stewart, the release read as follows:

> In response to media inquiries, I want to reiterate the facts surrounding my sale of ImClone stock. I purchased 5,000 shares of ImClone several years ago in the public market. I tendered all of these shares in the $70 per share tender offer made by Bristol Myers to all public shareholders of ImClone in October 2001. Because the Bristol Myers offer was oversubscribed, I was able to sell only about 20% of my shares.
>
> For the remaining 3,928 shares, I agreed with my broker several weeks after the tender offer, at a time when the ImClone shares were trading at about $70, that, if the ImClone stock price were to fall below $60, we would sell my holdings. On December 27, I returned a call from my broker advising me that ImClone had fallen below $60. I reiterated my instructions to sell the shares. The trade was promptly executed, at $58 per share. I did not speak to Dr. Samuel Waksal regarding my sale, and did not have any nonpublic information regarding ImClone when I sold my ImClone shares. After directing my broker to sell, I placed a call to Dr. Waksal's office to inquire about ImClone. I did not reach Dr. Waksal and he did not return my call.
>
> In placing my trade I had no improper information. My transaction was entirely lawful.

After the close of business on June 18, 2002, Stewart issued a third statement that essentially repeated the June 12 statement, only adding that she was cooperating fully with the investigations. The following day, she read the June 18 statement, with no substantive alterations, at a "Mid-Year Media Review" conference held in midtown Manhattan. Kevin Gruneich, an equities analyst at Bear, Stearns who was present at the conference, testified that it was attended primarily by securities analysts and portfolio managers. Investors were also present. The purpose of the conference was to provide a forum for the executives of media corporations to update the investment community about their companies' outlook and financial health. In addition to MSLO, executives from Gannett, Knight Ridder, and other organizations spoke at the conference. . . .

With respect to inferences that may reasonably be drawn from the evidence, the Second Circuit has emphasized that "where a fact to be proved is also an element of the offense . . . it is not enough that the inferences in the government's favor are permissible. We must also be satisfied that the inferences are sufficiently supported to permit a rational juror to find that the element, like all elements, is established beyond a reasonable doubt. . . .

The Government contends that a reasonable jury could draw inferences from the evidence outlined above that would permit it to find beyond a reasonable doubt that Stewart intended to deceive investors with her statements. Specifically, the Government argues that the evidence supports the inferences that Stewart was aware of the impact of the negative publicity about her ImClone trade on the market value of MSLO securities and on her personal wealth, and that Stewart deliberately directed her statements to investors in MSLO securities.

Second, the Government argues that the effect of the June 12 statement may be considered when contemplating Stewart's intent in issuing the June 18 statement. Her June 12 statement correlated with a temporary rebound of MSLO's share price, and the Government contends that the jury could infer that Stewart was seeking a similar effect on June 19. But the very fact that the rebound was only temporary indicates that this piece of evidence, while possibly relevant to materiality, is not germane to the issue of intent. If anything, the fact that Stewart issued the June 18 statement essentially unrevised, after the failure of the June 12 statement to effect any meaningful improvement in the share price, suggests that she did not intend to affect the market price of the stock.

Mindful of the standards outlined above, and viewing the evidence in its totality and in the light most favorable to the Government's case, I hold that a reasonable juror could not, without resorting to speculation and surmise, find beyond a reasonable doubt that Stewart's purpose was to influence the market in MSLO securities.

As an initial matter, any intent to defraud that could be inferred from the fact that Stewart made the third statement to an audience of analysts and investors cannot retroactively endow her previous statements with a bad purpose. While it is true that for the purposes of a Rule 29 motion, evidence cannot be viewed in isolation, these statements are essentially discrete occurrences, separated from one another by several days' time. They are similar in substance, but that alone does not permit an inference that the defendant's state of mind when making the June 18 statement is sufficient evidence to find beyond a reasonable doubt that she had the same state of mind several days or weeks earlier. Accordingly, the first and second statements must stand or fall without reference to the audience of the third statement. . . .

As for the first statement, the Government contends that an inference of intent can be drawn from the fact that *The Wall Street Journal* is "the most widely read financial publication in the nation." Specifically, by making the statement to that newspaper, Stewart intended to influence investors with her statement. The Government presented no evidence that Stewart or her lawyer reached out to *The Wall Street Journal* as opposed to other publications. Thus, there is no evidence that Stewart chose the forum for the statement. The fact that *The Wall Street Journal*, as a financial publication, had an interest in an investigation into a stock trade by the well-known CEO of a public company does not evidence Stewart's intent.

The Government argues that Stewart's intent with respect to the second statement can be inferred from the fact that she released it knowing that it would be widely disseminated in financial publications. This argument, which can be made with respect to any public statement, adds nothing to the evidence of criminal intent.

With respect to the June 18 statement, the Government contends that Stewart's awareness that she was speaking to analysts and investors, her prefatory statement that she was embarking upon a topic about which her audience was "probably interested," and the timing of the statement, which occurred as the stock continued to fall, are sufficient, in conjunction with the evidence previously outlined, to permit the jury to infer that she intended to deceive investors in MSLO securities when she made the statement.

This statement presents a closer question than the previous two. But just as individual pieces of evidence about intent must be viewed in conjunction when assessing the sufficiency of the whole, the fact that the June 18 statement was read to an audience of analysts and investors on June 19 cannot be viewed in isolation—the entire context of the statement must be considered. Thus, any inference to be drawn from the makeup of the audience must also take into account the fact that Stewart was only one of several representatives of MSLO, and that MSLO was only one of several corporations making presentations at the conference. The evidence does not show that the conference was organized by Stewart or her company. There is no evidence that the negative publicity about ImClone influenced Stewart's decision to attend and take advantage of a platform from which to reach investors directly. To the contrary, her statement — a very brief portion of a much longer presentation—indicates otherwise. The Government argues that her statement indicating an awareness that the audience was "probably interested" in what she had to say about the ImClone trade is meaningful. Yet her remarks at the close of the statement—"I have nothing to add on this matter today. And I'm here to talk about our terrific company, Martha Stewart Living Omnimedia, which I'd like to start doing right now"—support an inference that she wanted to dispose of the issue and begin to address the subjects of the conference.

It is true that the Government "need not refute every possible hypothesis supporting a defendant's innocence." At the same time, however, the Government "must do more than introduce evidence that is 'at least as consistent with innocence as with guilt.'" Insofar as the text of the statement is concerned, the competing intentions appear to be nearly in equipoise. The Government has not offered any evidence that tips the balance in favor of a rational finding of criminal intent beyond a reasonable doubt.

The third statement repeated information that Stewart had already publicized through the previous statements. Because the Government has not presented sufficient evidence of intent for the first two statements, and there is no evidence that Stewart attempted to refine or change this statement in any way that would tailor it to an audience of investors, nothing in the statement itself supports an inference of intent. Moreover, the Government presented no evidence that this statement was developed specifically to be read at the conference. Indeed, it was initially issued as a general press release to the public at large, and only the next day read at the conference.

In sum, when the nature of the audience is viewed within the overall context of the statement, this is too slight an addition to the total mix of evidence of intent to carry the burden of proving criminal intent beyond a reasonable doubt.

The Government also contends that the falsity of the statements supports an inference that Stewart's intention was fraudulent. For the purposes of this motion, it is assumed that the evidence is sufficient for a reasonable jury to find that the statements were materially false. In some securities fraud cases, the falsity of a defendant's statements may lend weight to an inference of intent to deceive. But in this case, the falsehoods lack a direct connection to the supposed purpose of the alleged deception. The falsehoods involve Stewart's personal trade in the securities of ImClone. Evidence of intent to defraud investors of a different company is not readily discernible from the content of the falsehoods. Furthermore, to allow evidence of one essential element of a crime to make up for a dearth of evidence of another element runs dangerously close to ignoring the Second Circuit's injunction that where a fact supporting an essential element is concerned, the court must be assured that inferences in the Government's favor are not only permissible, but supported by sufficient evidence. In the cases that the Government cites, the misrepresentations are directly related to the purpose of the deception. Because the falsehoods about trading in ImClone securities are only circuitously related to the purpose of deceiving investors in MSLO securities, the falsity of Stewart's statements is less significant in assessing the sufficiency of evidence of intent.

Finally, the Government argues that the possibility that Stewart possessed multiple intentions when she made the public statements charged in Count Nine does not negate evidence that she possessed a criminal intent to deceive investors. While it is generally true that the Government is not required to prove that a defendant "have an exclusively illegal intent in order to be subject to the criminal laws," United States v. Woodward, 149 F.3d 46, 70 (1st Cir. 1998), the purpose of a Rule 29 motion is to assess the sufficiency of the evidence actually adduced in a given case. Here, the evidence and inferences the Government presents are simply too weak to support a finding beyond a reasonable doubt of criminal intent. To compound that weak evidence with the reasonable inferences that Stewart possessed many other intents—to protest her innocence or repair her reputation, to reassure her business partners, advertisers, and the consumers of her products—would only invite the jury to speculate. And it would ignore the requirement that the standard of proof be considered in an assessment of the sufficiency of the evidence.

Conclusion

For the foregoing reasons, defendant Stewart's motion for a judgment of acquittal on Count Nine of the Indictment is granted.

NOTES AND QUESTIONS

1. Do you agree with Judge Cedarbaum's conclusion that no reasonable juror could have found that Stewart had the intent to defraud MSLO investors by her (false) protestations of innocence? The test for fraudulent intent, which Judge Cedarbaum conveniently fails to mention, is whether Stewart intended to deceive the investing public for her own gain and to their detriment. (*See Hawkey* case, *supra* Chapter 4.) Does it matter that Stewart owned more than $1 billion in MSLO at the time of her statements and that the value of this investment was slipping because of the ImClone allegations?
2. Do you agree with Judge Cedarbaum that "any intent to defraud that could be inferred from the . . . third statement . . . cannot retroactively endow her previous statements with a bad purpose"? She is right, of course, that fraudulent intent in a later statement is not conclusive proof of the

existence of such intent in an earlier statement, as the speaker may have changed motives over time. Nevertheless, wouldn't the intent surrounding the later statement have *some* evidentiary value when evaluating the intent surrounding the earlier one?

3. The court states that Stewart's "competing intentions [for making the statements] appear to be nearly in equipoise. The government has not offered any evidence that tips the balance in favor of a rational finding of criminal intent beyond a reasonable doubt." Can't one have multiple, yet *complementary*, intentions?
4. Do you think that there might have been an unstated First Amendment issue related to this charge that was bothering Judge Cedarbaum? If so, why do you think the judge decided to dismiss the count on mens rea grounds using a judgment of acquittal instead of deciding the First Amendment issue as a matter of law?
5. Later, you will see that the government decided not to bring criminal charges against Stewart for insider trading, in part because the facts and theory ended up being on somewhat shaky ground. In light of the prosecution's conservative approach on those charges, why do you think it pushed the envelope in charging Stewart with securities fraud for merely asserting her innocence in public?

B. Civil versus Criminal Standard

We know from earlier reading that the standard of criminal versus civil liability in securities fraud cases is very close. It primarily rests on the interpretation of "willfully" in 15 U.S.C. §78ff. However, there are some other critical differences between the two types of cases. Participants in the corporate world—including attorneys and accountants—who are not aware of these distinctions act at their peril. For, as we will see through the cases below, sometimes criminal liability exists despite the absence of civil liability—which is, of course, extremely counterintuitive.

CENTRAL BANK OF DENVER, N.A. v. FIRST INTERSTATE BANK OF DENVER, N.A.

511 U.S. 164 (1994)

Justice KENNEDY delivered the opinion of the Court.

As we have interpreted it, §10(b) of the Securities Exchange Act of 1934 imposes private civil liability on those who commit a manipulative or deceptive act in connection with the purchase or sale of securities. In this case, we must answer a question reserved in two earlier decisions: whether private civil liability under §10(b) extends as well to those who do not engage in the manipulative or deceptive practice, but who aid and abet the violation.

I.

In 1986 and 1988, the Colorado Springs-Stetson Hills Public Building Authority (Authority) issued a total of $26 million in bonds to finance public improvements at Stetson Hills, a planned residential and commercial development in Colorado Springs. Petitioner Central Bank of Denver served as indenture trustee for the bond issues.

The bonds were secured by landowner assessment liens, which covered about 250 acres for the 1986 bond issue and about 272 acres for the 1988 bond issue. The bond covenants required that the land subject to the liens be worth at least 160% of the bonds' outstanding principal and interest. The covenants required AmWest Development, the developer of Stetson Hills, to give Central Bank an annual report containing evidence that the 160% test was met.

In January 1988, AmWest provided Central Bank with an updated appraisal of the land securing the 1986 bonds and of the land proposed to secure the 1988 bonds. The 1988 appraisal showed land values almost unchanged from the 1986 appraisal. Soon afterwards, Central Bank received a letter from the senior underwriter for the 1986 bonds. Noting that property values were declining in Colorado Springs and that Central Bank was operating on an appraisal over 16 months old, the underwriter expressed concern that the 160% test was not being met.

Central Bank asked its in-house appraiser to review the updated 1988 appraisal. . . . After an exchange of letters between Central Bank and AmWest in early 1988, Central Bank agreed to delay independent review of the appraisal until the end of the year, six months after the June 1988 closing on the bond issue. Before the independent review was complete, however, the Authority defaulted on the 1988 bonds.

Respondents First Interstate Bank of Denver and Jack K. Naber had purchased $2.1 million of the 1988 bonds. After the default, respondents sued the Authority, the 1988 underwriter, a junior underwriter, an AmWest director, and Central Bank for violations of §10(b) of the Securities Exchange Act of 1934. The complaint alleged that the Authority, the underwriter defendants, and the AmWest director had violated §10(b). The complaint also alleged that Central Bank was "secondarily liable under §10(b) for its conduct in aiding and abetting the fraud."

The United States District Court for the District of Colorado granted summary judgment to Central Bank. The United States Court of Appeals for the Tenth Circuit reversed.

The Court of Appeals first set forth the elements of the §10(b) aiding and abetting cause of action in the Tenth Circuit: (1) a primary violation of §10(b); (2) recklessness by the aider and abettor as to the existence of the primary violation; and (3) substantial assistance given to the primary violator by the aider and abettor. . . .

We granted certiorari to resolve the continuing confusion over the existence and scope of the §10(b) aiding and abetting action.

In our cases addressing §10(b) and Rule 10b-5, we have confronted two main issues. First, we have determined the scope of conduct prohibited by §10(b). . . .

Second, in cases where the defendant has committed a violation of §10(b), we have decided questions about the elements of the 10b-5 private liability scheme: for example, whether there is a right to contribution, what the statute of limitations is, whether there is a reliance requirement, and whether there is an *in pari delicto* defense. . . .

The latter issue, determining the elements of the 10b-5 private liability scheme, has posed difficulty because Congress did not create a private §10(b) cause of action and had no occasion to provide guidance about the elements of a private liability scheme. We thus have had "to infer how the 1934 Congress would have addressed the issue[s] had the 10b-5 action been included as an express provision in the 1934 Act."

With respect, however, to the first issue, the scope of conduct prohibited by §10(b), the text of the statute controls our decision. In §10(b), Congress prohibited manipulative or deceptive acts in connection with the purchase or sale of securities. It envisioned that the SEC would enforce the statutory prohibition through administrative and injunctive actions. Of course, a private plaintiff now may bring suit against violators of §10(b). But the private plaintiff may not bring a 10b-5 suit against a defendant for acts not prohibited by the text of §10(b). To the contrary, our cases considering the scope of conduct prohibited by §10(b) in private suits have emphasized adherence to the statutory language, "'[t]he starting point in every case involving construction of a statute.'" *Ernst & Ernst*, 425 U.S. 185, 197 (1976). We have refused to allow 10b-5 challenges to conduct not prohibited by the text of the statute. . . .

Our consideration of statutory duties, especially in cases interpreting §10(b), establishes that the statutory text controls the definition of conduct covered by §10(b). That bodes ill for respondents, for "the language of Section 10(b) does not in terms mention aiding and abetting." . . .

Congress knew how to impose aiding and abetting liability when it chose to do so. *See, e.g.*, 18 U.S.C. §2 (general criminal aiding and abetting statute). If, as respondents seem to say, Congress intended to impose aiding and abetting liability, we presume it would have used the words "aid" and "abet" in the statutory text. But it did not.

We reach the uncontroversial conclusion, accepted even by those courts recognizing a §10(b) aiding and abetting cause of action, that the text of the 1934 Act does not itself reach those who aid and abet a §10(b) violation. Unlike those courts, however, we think that conclusion resolves the case. It is inconsistent with settled methodology in §10(b) cases to extend liability beyond the scope of conduct prohibited by the statutory text. To be sure, aiding and abetting a wrongdoer ought to be actionable in certain instances. The issue, however, is not whether imposing private civil liability on aiders and abettors is good policy but whether aiding and abetting is covered by the statute. . . .

Our reasoning is confirmed by the fact that respondents' argument would impose 10b-5 aiding and abetting liability when at least one element critical for recovery under 10b-5 is absent: reliance. A plaintiff must show reliance on the defendant's misstatement or omission to recover under 10b-5. Were we to allow the aiding and abetting action proposed in this case, the defendant could be liable without any showing that the plaintiff relied upon the aider and abettor's statements or actions. Allowing plaintiffs to circumvent the reliance requirement would disregard the careful limits on 10b-5 recovery mandated by our earlier cases. . . .

More to the point, Congress has not enacted a general civil aiding and abetting statute—either for suits by the Government (when the Government sues for civil penalties or injunctive relief) or for suits by private parties. Thus, when Congress enacts a statute under which a person may sue and recover damages from a private defendant for the defendant's violation of some statutory norm, there is no general presumption that the plaintiff may also sue aiders and abettors. . . .

D.

At oral argument, the SEC suggested that 18 U.S.C. §2 is "significant" and "very important" in this case. At the outset, we note that this contention is inconsistent with the SEC's argument that recklessness is a sufficient scienter for aiding and abetting liability. Criminal aiding and abetting liability under §2 requires proof that the defendant "in some sort associate[d] himself with the venture, that he participate[d] in it as in something that he wishe[d] to bring about, that he [sought] by his action to make it succeed." Nye & Nissen v. United States, 336 U.S. 613 (1949) (internal quotation marks omitted). But recklessness, not intentional wrongdoing, is the theory underlying the aiding and abetting allegations in the case before us.

Furthermore, while it is true that an aider and abettor of a criminal violation of any provision of the 1934 Act, including §10(b), violates 18 U.S.C. §2, it does not follow that a private civil aiding and abetting cause of action must also exist. We have been quite reluctant to infer a private right of action from a criminal prohibition alone. . . . There would be no logical stopping point to this line of reasoning: Every criminal statute passed for the benefit of some particular class of persons would carry with it a concomitant civil damages cause of action.

V.

. . . Respondents concede that Central Bank did not commit a manipulative or deceptive act within the meaning of §10(b). Instead, in the words of the complaint, Central Bank was "secondarily liable under §10(b) for its conduct in aiding and abetting the fraud." Because of our conclusion that there is no private aiding and abetting liability under §10(b), Central Bank may not be held liable as an aider and abettor. The District Court's grant of summary judgment to Central Bank was proper, and the judgment of the Court of Appeals is

Reversed.

NOTES AND QUESTIONS

1. Justice Kennedy makes clear that Central Bank could be held criminally liable for securities fraud as an aider and abettor under 18 U.S.C. §2, but that it has no secondary civil liability. This might be an accurate interpretation of the law, but is it good policy? Aren't criminal sanctions supposed to be a last resort?
2. Although the opinion rests heavily on statutory construction, it certainly could have come out the other way. After all, the Supreme Court had

created the private right of action under Rule 10b-5 out of whole cloth; it could easily have added aiding and abetting liability to its own creation. In light of this, the majority's holding must have been motivated by some unarticulated policy concern. What was it? Could it have been the Court's fear that permitting third-party liability in civil cases would open up the floodgates to plaintiffs' pleading aiding and abetting liability in every case to get at "deep pockets" based on conduct only tangentially related to the fraud? Is the same concern applicable in the criminal context?

3. The Court points to the standard of mens rea required for liability in civil cases (recklessness) versus the mens rea it says is required for aiding and abetting in the criminal context ("something that [the defendant] wished to bring about") as a reason why it could not imort 18 U.S.C. §2 into the civil arena. Is there any technical (as opposed to policy) reason why §2 could not have been molded to fit the civil context? If so, how?
4. The Court states that there is no federal common law of crimes. Don't let this statement confuse you. Federal courts no longer create new crimes through the common law, but they constantly interpret criminal statutes legislated by Congress. The body of law resulting from this process is sometimes referred to as "interstitial" federal common law.
5. In Stoneridge Inv. Partners, LLC v. Scientific Atlanta, Inc., 552 U.S. 148 (2008), the Supreme Court affirmed—and perhaps even extended—its holding in *Central Bank of Denver*. In that case, Scientific Atlanta knowingly assisted Charter Communications, Inc. in falsifying Charter's books to meet market expectations. Investors included Scientific Atlanta as a defendant claiming that its participation in the fraud made it liable under Rule 10b-5. The Supreme Court held against the investors, stating, in effect, that their claim against Scientific Atlanta rested solely on an aiding and abetting theory. Writing for the dissent, Justice Ginsburg stated:

> What the Court fails to recognize is that this case is critically different from *Central Bank* because the bank in that case did not engage in any deceptive act and, therefore, did not *itself* violate §10(b). The Court sweeps aside any distinction, remarking that holding respondents liable would "reviv[e] the implied cause of action against all aiders and abettors except those who committed no deceptive act in the process of facilitating the fraud." But the fact that Central Bank engaged in no deceptive conduct whatsoever—in other words, that it was at most an aider and abettor—sharply distinguishes *Central Bank* from cases that do involve allegations of such conduct.

Is this a valid distinction between the cases?

SCHATZ v. ROSENBERG

943 F.2d 485 (4th Cir. 1991)

CHAPMAN, Senior Circuit Judge:

Plaintiffs/appellants Ivan and Joanne Schatz sued defendants Mark E. Rosenberg, MER Enterprises ("MER") and the law firm of Weinberg & Green alleging RICO violations, fraud and securities laws violations. The district judge referred the case to a magistrate judge who recommended that five counts of the seven count complaint be dismissed for failure to state a claim upon which relief can be granted. The district judge agreed and dismissed these five counts under Federal Rule of Civil Procedure 12(b)(6). Three of these counts involved Weinberg & Green. In this appeal, plaintiffs only challenge the dismissal of the three counts against Weinberg & Green.

I.

On December 31, 1986, MER purchased an eighty percent (80%) interest in two companies the plaintiffs owned, Virginia Adjustable Bed Manufacturing Corporation ("VAMCO") and Advanced Bed Concepts ("ABC"). MER is a holding company which Mark Rosenberg created to purchase the VAMCO and ABC stock. As payment for their eighty percent (80%) interests in VAMCO and ABC, Mr. and Mrs. Schatz received $1.5 million in promissory notes issued by MER, which Rosenberg personally guaranteed. The plaintiffs relied on a financial statement dated March 31, 1986 and an update letter delivered at closing on December 31, 1986 which indicated that Rosenberg's net worth exceeded $7 million. These financial documents contained several misrepresentations obscuring the fact that Rosenberg's financial empire had crumbled between April and December of 1986. Rosenberg's largest business, Yale Sportswear Corporation ("Yale"), filed for bankruptcy in September 1987, and Rosenberg filed for personal bankruptcy thereafter. The law firm of Weinberg & Green represented Rosenberg and his entities throughout this period.

The plaintiffs never received payment on their promissory notes and lost an additional $150,000 when they made a "bridge loan" to BBC, the company which was formed when VAMCO and ABC merged with the Back Center, Inc. ("BCI"), another of Rosenberg's companies. To add insult to injury, Rosenberg paid Weinberg & Green's legal fees for the transaction out of VAMCO and ABC's cash reserves. Rosenberg siphoned off operating capital from VAMCO and ABC to prop up Yale. By the time Rosenberg and Yale filed for bankruptcy, VAMCO and ABC were essentially worthless, and plaintiffs had no control over the businesses. Thereafter, plaintiffs filed a seven-count complaint asserting, [among other things]: violations of section 10(b) of the Securities Exchange Act of 1934 against . . . Weinberg and Green (Count III), . . . aiding and abetting liability under the securities laws against Weinberg & Green (Count VI), [and] common law misrepresentation against Weinberg & Green (Count VII). . . .

[The magistrate judge recommended that all of the counts against Weinberg & Green be dismissed.]

On March 8, 1990, the district judge issued an opinion in which he accepted the recommendations to dismiss the counts against Weinberg & Green. . . .

II.

We review *de novo* a district court's decision to dismiss a complaint for failure to state a claim under Federal Rule of Civil Procedure 12(b)(6). In reviewing the legal sufficiency of the complaint, we construe the factual allegations "in the light most favorable to plaintiff." However, we are "not so bound with respect to [the complaint's] legal conclusions. . . . Accordingly, we will affirm a dismissal for failure to state a claim if it appears that the plaintiffs would not be entitled to relief under any facts which could be proved in support of their claim.

III.

Plaintiffs argue that Weinberg & Green committed fraud by remaining silent even though it knew that its client, Rosenberg, was financially insolvent. Plaintiffs allege in their second amended complaint that:

—Weinberg & Green provided legal services to Rosenberg in the past and in connection to the purchase of plaintiffs' business;
—Weinberg & Green had a copy of Rosenberg's financial statement, which it knew to be false as a result of legal services to Rosenberg and his various companies;
—Weinberg & Green prepared draft closing documents for the purchase of plaintiffs' business, which Weinberg & Green then delivered to plaintiffs' lawyers;
—Weinberg & Green gave plaintiffs a letter from Rosenberg at closing in which Rosenberg stated that no material adverse changes had occurred in his financial condition; and
—Weinberg & Green and plaintiffs' lawyers jointly agreed on language in the purchase agreement stating that Rosenberg had delivered his 1986 financial statement and an update letter to the plaintiffs, and that the letters were accurate in all material respects. . . .

A. Section 10(b) and Rule 10b-5

To state a claim for a primary violation of section 10(b) and Rule 10b-5, a plaintiff must allege that the defendant (1) made an untrue statement of material fact or omitted a material fact that rendered the statements misleading, (2) in connection with the purchase or sale of a security, (3) with scienter, and (4) which caused plaintiff's losses. Plaintiffs claim that Weinberg & Green violated section 10(b) and Rule 10b-5 by failing to disclose Rosenberg's misrepresentations and by making affirmative misrepresentations about Rosenberg's financial condition.

1. Weinberg & Green's Nondisclosure of Rosenberg's Misrepresentations

We first address whether Weinberg & Green's failure to disclose Rosenberg's misrepresentations to the Schatzes subjects the law firm to liability under section 10(b) and Rule 10b-5. Silence, absent a duty to disclose, does not violate section 10(b) and Rule 10b-5. Plaintiffs argue that Weinberg & Green had a duty to disclose Rosenberg's misrepresentations on the basis of federal securities cases, Maryland common law, and the Maryland Code of Professional Responsibility. In addition, plaintiffs argue that as a matter of public policy, lawyers should have a duty to disclose a client's fraudulent activity to a third party. We review these claims seriatim.

a. Duty to Disclose Based on Federal Securities Laws

We first address whether the federal securities laws impose upon an attorney a duty of disclosure to third parties who are not the attorney's clients. The Supreme Court has decreed that under the federal securities laws, a duty to disclose "arises from the relationship between parties," Dirks v. SEC, 463 U.S. 646, 658 (1983), and will exist if there is "a fiduciary or other similar relation of trust and confidence between them." Thus, the Supreme Court has established the type of relationship which will create a duty of disclosure. The Court has never determined whether, under circumstances other than fiduciary relationships, the securities laws impose a duty of disclosure to third parties. Plaintiffs urge us to adopt the approach of several federal district courts which have held that a law firm can be liable for misrepresentation under section 10(b) if it disseminates false information "with an intent, knowledge or awareness that the information will be communicated or disseminated to persons . . . in connection with the purchase or sale of a security." We decline this invitation and hold that a lawyer or law firm cannot be held liable for misrepresentation under section 10(b) for failing to disclose information about a client to a third party absent some fiduciary or other confidential relationship with the third party.

[Other federal courts have come to the same conclusion.]

Plaintiffs rely on several federal securities cases which have held attorneys liable under section 10(b) for failing to disclose misrepresentations made by clients to third parties. First, plaintiffs cite cases imposing liability on attorneys for issuing a reckless and misleading bond opinion letter. However, these cases are clearly distinguishable because they involve lawyers who issued misleading legal opinions. In this case, however, plaintiffs do not claim that Weinberg & Green made inaccurate legal representations, only that they failed to tattle on their client for misrepresenting his personal financial condition.

Plaintiffs also cite cases in which courts imposed liability on attorneys who drafted false prospectuses or other securities documents. These cases, however, are also easily distinguished because they involve affirmative misrepresentations made in the solicitation of securities. In our case, Weinberg & Green did not solicit any purchase of securities or prepare any solicitation documents. In fact, Rosenberg and the Schatzes worked out the details of the purchase of the business before involving the attorneys for either side. Accordingly, none of these authorities persuade us to [change our position in this case].

b. Duty of Disclosure Based on Maryland Law

Plaintiffs also claim that the Maryland Rules of Professional Conduct obligated Weinberg & Green to either withdraw from representing Rosenberg or to disclose his financial misrepresentations to the plaintiffs. In support of this claim, plaintiffs' counsel submitted to the Maryland State Bar Committee on Ethics an anonymous request for an ethics ruling on the facts of the present case. The committee concluded that a law firm in Weinberg & Green's position had an ethical duty to either withdraw from representation or disclose the misrepresentations to the third person. This ethical responsibility, plaintiffs argue, establishes a legal duty to disclose and subjects Weinberg & Green to section 10(b) liability.

We reject this argument. An ethical duty of disclosure does not create a corresponding legal duty under the federal securities laws. Courts have consistently refused to use ethical codes to define standards of civil liability for lawyers. More specifically, courts have refused to base a legal duty of disclosure for section 10(b) on a disciplinary rule. . . .

The rationale for these rulings is clear. The ethical rules were intended by their drafters to regulate the conduct of the profession, not to create actionable duties in favor of third parties. The preliminary statement to the Model Code, upon which the Maryland code is patterned, warns that the Code does not "undertake to define standards for civil liability of lawyers for professional conduct." Preliminary Statement, Model Code of Professional Responsibility. We believe this statement accurately reflects the goals and purposes of the Maryland Code of Professional Responsibility. Thus, we hold that the ethical rules do not create a legal duty of disclosure on lawyers and that plaintiffs cannot base a securities fraud or other misrepresentation claim on a violation of an ethical rule. . . .

c. Duty of Disclosure Based on Public Policy

Precedent aside, plaintiffs also argue that, as a matter of public policy, lawyers should not be permitted to perpetrate or assist in a fraud without being held responsible for their wrongdoing. Plaintiffs' counsel urges the court to rule that a lawyer has a duty to disclose misrepresentations to innocent third parties on the basis of public policy. While we sympathize with plaintiff's position and certainly do not condone lawyers making misrepresentations, we find that public policy counsels against imposing such a duty. Attorney liability to third parties should not be expanded beyond liability for conflicts of interest. Any other result may prevent a client from reposing complete trust in his lawyer for fear that he might reveal a fact which would trigger the lawyer's duty to the third party. Similarly, if attorneys had a duty to disclose information to third parties, attorneys would have an incentive not to press clients for information. The net result would not be less securities fraud. Instead, attorneys would more often be unwitting accomplices to the fraud as a result of being kept in the dark by their clients or by their own reluctance to obtain information. The better rule—that attorneys have no duty to "blow the whistle" on their clients—allows clients to repose complete trust in their lawyers. Under those circumstances, the client is more likely to disclose damaging or problematic information, and the lawyer will more likely be able to counsel his client against misconduct. . . .

2. Affirmative Misrepresentations by Weinberg & Green

Plaintiffs also claim that Weinberg & Green violated section 10(b) by making various affirmative misstatements. Plaintiffs complain that Weinberg & Green informed plaintiffs' attorney that it would supply an update letter which would state that Rosenberg's financial position had not materially changed as of December 31, 1986. Weinberg & Green then presented the update letter to plaintiffs' counsel. The letter misrepresented Rosenberg's financial position, and the agreement and closing documents drafted by Weinberg & Green contained representations made by Rosenberg that the financial statement was "true, correct, and complete in all material respects."

Plaintiffs never contend that Weinberg & Green made any representations other than those made by Rosenberg. In fact, plaintiffs only claim that Weinberg & Green stated that Rosenberg would supply an update letter and that Weinberg & Green forwarded the Rosenberg letter to plaintiffs' attorneys. Since Weinberg & Green made no independent affirmative misstatements, Weinberg & Green did not commit a primary violation of section 10(b). . . .

We . . . hold that a lawyer or law firm cannot be liable for the representations of a client, even if the lawyer incorporates the client's misrepresentations into legal documents or agreements necessary for closing the transaction. In this case, Weinberg & Green merely "papered the deal," that is, put into writing the terms on which the Schatzes and Rosenberg agreed and prepared the documents necessary for closing the transactions. Thus, Weinberg & Green performed the role of a scrivener. Under these circumstances, a law firm cannot be held liable for misrepresentations made by a client in a financial disclosure statement.

B. Liability for Aiding and Abetting a Violation of the Securities Laws

Plaintiffs make claims for aider and abettor liability under sections 12(2) and 10(b) of the 1934 Securities Act. Both causes of action require the plaintiff to prove the following three elements to establish an aiding and abetting securities violation: (1) a primary violation by another person; (2) the aider and abettor's "knowledge" of the primary violation; and (3) substantial assistance by the aider and abettor in the achievement or consummation of the primary violation. . . .

In this case, Weinberg & Green did no more than "paper the deal" or act as a scrivener for Rosenberg. These activities cannot form the basis for a securities violation since plaintiffs never allege any facts tending to show an intent on Weinberg & Green's part to violate the securities laws. While it is true that some of Rosenberg's documents prepared by Weinberg & Green (on the basis of information provided by Rosenberg) were misleading, this fact alone does not meet the "substantial assistance" threshold. Otherwise, there would be a *per se* rule holding attorneys liable in every securities fraud case, because in virtually every transaction, attorneys draft the closing documents. Clearly, the fact that an attorney drafts a closing document does not automatically create a warranty that every statement and agreement made by the client is true. Any other result would make attorneys co-guarantors and co-signatories, along with their clients, in every securities transaction. . . .

IV.

The extent of a law firm's liability for knowingly incorporating a client's misrepresentations into closing documents for a financial transaction presents troubling legal issues. However, we do not sit as an ethics or other attorney disciplinary committee, but as a civil court with a duty to interpret the securities laws, and the solution to these legal issues cannot be found in the securities laws. As the Seventh Circuit stated in Barker v. Henderson, Franklin, Starnes & Holt, 797 F.2d 490 (7th Cir. 1986):

> We express no opinion on whether the [law firm] did what [it] should, whether there was malpractice under state law, or whether the rules of ethics . . . ought to require lawyers and accountants to blow the whistle in equivalent circumstances. We are satisfied, however, that an award of damages under the securities laws is not the way to blaze the trail toward improved ethical standards in the legal and accounting professions. Liability depends on an *existing* duty to disclose. The securities laws therefore must lag behind changes in ethical and fiduciary standards.

Id. at 497 (emphasis in original). We agree with this statement of policy and affirm the order of the district court.

NOTES AND QUESTIONS

1. Seriously? An attorney can actively participate in a client's securities fraud by drafting and tendering documents he has written and knows to be false and have no civil liability? Do you find the *Schatz* holding troubling? Or are you convinced by the court's policy arguments in favor of shielding attorneys involved in fraudulent transactions?
2. Could Weinberg & Green be criminally indicted for its role in Rosenberg's fraud?
3. The court cites *Dirks* for the proposition that there must be a fiduciary or other similar relationship between the defendant and plaintiff for there to be liability for securities fraud. Is this a correct reading of *Dirks* and 10b-5?[15] Or does the *Dirks* requirement arise only in cases in which there has been no affirmative misrepresentation and the question is whether there can be liability for an omission? In this case, there was more than a "mere" failure to disclose; the documents tendered to Schatz and his counsel were affirmatively misleading. Doesn't that negate the fiduciary relationship requirement?
4. The court rejects cases that go the other way because those cases "involve[d] affirmative misrepresentations made in the solicitation of securities. In our case, Weinberg & Green did not solicit any purchase of securities or prepare any solicitation documents. In fact, Rosenberg and the Schatzes worked out the details of the purchase of the business before involving the attorneys for either side." Is this a legitimate distinction?
5. The court is correct in stating that an ethical duty of disclosure does not create a corresponding legal duty under the federal securities laws. However, this leads the court to treat the defendant's ethical violation as essentially irrelevant. Is that the case? Shouldn't it have been of importance to the court's determination that the Maryland Bar found that the defendants had acted unethically by passing along Rosenberg's misrepresentations? Doesn't that mean that the Bar likely drew some factual conclusions different from

15. You can find *Dirks* at page 238, *infra*.

those drawn by the court? Also, the court seems to believe that it has a binary choice: determine whether Weinberg & Green had a duty to disclose or not. But, based on the rules of professional conduct, a third choice would have been to hold that Weinberg & Green had a duty to withdraw from the representation rather than participate in the fraud, correct?

6. What about the public policy argument? Note that the court's position is one that is used to defend the attorney-client privilege. Note, too, that the privilege contains an explicit exception for crime and fraud. Is it really better for society to encourage lawyers to remain silent and assist clients in committing fraud?
7. Is the court right to say that knowingly passing along another person's lie is not making an affirmative misrepresentation in its own right? Assume that a classmate told you that he had obtained a fraudulent doctor's note allowing him to postpone a final and asked you to give it to the professor (perhaps because it would strengthen his case that he was ill), and you did so. Do you think that your professor, upon learning of the scheme, would consider your silence when passing the note to be a misrepresentation in and of itself?
8. What do you think about the court's characterization of the role of the lawyers as merely "papering the deal," or as being simple "scriveners"? Is that accurate? Is it an insult to the legal profession?
9. One can read the outcome of *Schatz* as a victory for lawyers because it limits their liability in securities cases. But what are the costs of this victory? Is it helpful to the profession in the long run for the public to learn that lawyers can assist frauds and escape accountability?

PROBLEM 6-2

You are a junior associate working on a disclosure statement for Widget Corp. Your job is to take the information given to you by partners in your firm, Widget employees, and members of Widget's outside accounting firm and draft language for the statement. One day, while at lunch with a friend who works for the accounting firm, you learn that the company has been "cooking its books" and, therefore, that the figures in the disclosure report are way off. If you allow the statement to be released as is, do you have (1) criminal liability; (2) civil liability; (3) ethical liability? What action should you take, if any?

C. To the Security and Exchange Commission

UNITED STATES v. BERGER

473 F.3d 1080 (9th Cir. 2007)

PREGERSON, Circuit Judge.

Defendant Richard I. Berger appeals his conviction of twelve counts of conspiracy, loan fraud, falsifying corporate books, and various securities fraud violations. Berger argues that . . . the district court used the wrong materiality standard for securities fraud violations. . . . For the reasons given below, we affirm the conviction. . . .

I. Offense Conduct

A. Craig Consumer Electronics, Inc. and the Revolving Credit Agreement

Craig Consumer Electronics, Inc. ("Craig Electronics") operated a consumer electronics business that sold products such as car stereos, compact music centers, and small personal stereos to retail stores. Berger was Craig Electronics' President, Chief Executive Officer, and Chairman of the Board. . . .

On August 5, 1994, Craig Electronics entered into a $50 million revolving credit agreement ("Credit Agreement") with a consortium of banks including BT Commercial Corporation ("Bankers Trust"), La Salle National Bank, Nationsbank of Texas, and Sanwa Business Credit Corporation. Bankers Trust acted as the agent for the consortium (collectively "lending banks"). Under the Credit Agreement, Craig Electronics could, subject to certain exclusions, borrow [various sums of money based on its accounts receivable and inventory. Accordingly, the company had to provide Bankers Trust with a report of its financial standing on a daily basis. From 1995 to 1997, Craig Electronic falsified these reports to justify significant over-borrowing. To conceal its bank fraud, the company deceived its own accountants and auditors. This led to false filings with the SEC. Specifically, the false SEC filings were Craig Electronics' Amended S-1 Registration Statement, Amended 1996 10-K Report, and First Quarter 1997 10-Q Report].

Counts 34, 35, and 36 charged that, in three SEC filings, Berger knowingly omitted material facts about Craig Electronics' (1) fraudulent accounting practices, (2) default of the Credit Agreement, and (3) overdrawn status on its line of credit [in violation of §32(a) of the 1934 Act, codified at 15 U.S.C. §78ff]. . . .

Berger contends that when applying section 32(a), courts should assess materiality from the perspective of the SEC. Berger primarily bases his argument on Kungys v. United States, 485 U.S. 759 (1988). In *Kungys*, the Supreme Court interpreted a statute that penalized the "concealment of a material fact" from the Immigration and Naturalization Service. The Supreme Court looked to the federal courts of appeals, which had a "uniform understanding" of "materiality" under a similar statute, 18 U.S.C. §1001. Section 1001 is a general statute that criminalizes acts of material misrepresentation in "any matter within the jurisdiction of the executive, legislative or judicial branch of the Government of the United States." The courts of appeals had, in §1001 cases, assessed materiality from the perspective of the government agency. The Supreme Court agreed with that interpretation and held that a false statement made to a government agency is "material" if it "has a natural tendency to influence, or was capable of influencing, the decision of the decisionmaking body to which it was addressed."

Berger identifies cases that apply the *Kungys* materiality standard to a number of different agencies, including the Environmental Protection Agency and the Food and Drug Administration. Each of those cases dealt with the materiality of false statements made in the context of specific agency decisions. Berger contends that the SEC, as a regulatory body, makes decisions based on the information contained in a company's mandatory filings. Thus, Berger argues that the materiality of false statements made to the SEC under section 32(a) must also be assessed not from the reasonable investor's perspective, but from the SEC's perspective, in the context of its own regulatory decisions.

We disagree with Berger. The purpose of the 1934 Act was to benefit and protect investors, with proper agency decisionmaking as a secondary concern. Furthermore, the Court "repeatedly has described the 'fundamental purpose' of the Act as implementing a 'philosophy of full disclosure.'" Accordingly, the Supreme Court has established a specific materiality standard to be used when assessing fraudulent statements filed with the SEC. In TSC Industries, Inc. v. Northway, Inc., 426 U.S. 438 (1976), the Supreme Court explained in the proxy-solicitation context that "[a]n omitted fact is material if there is a substantial likelihood that a reasonable shareholder would consider it important in deciding how to vote." Thus, the Court held that under section 14(a) and Rule 14a-9, materiality should be assessed, not from the SEC's perspective, but from the investor's perspective. The Court later expanded the reach of the *TSC Industries* materiality standard to section 10(b) and Rule 10b-5, which prohibit fraud in connection with the purchase or sale of securities. *See Basic Inc.*, 485 U.S. at 231-32.

Applying the "reasonable investor" materiality standard to Section 32(a) is consistent with the goals of the SEC. As *amicus curiae*, the SEC noted that the agency itself commences actions on filings it considers materially misleading to *investors*. In addition to being a regulatory body, the SEC acts as a repository of information intended to be disseminated to and used by the public. The mandatory filings at issue in this case, for example, were meant for investors' use. Craig Electronics' Form 10-K and Form 10-Q, which were periodic reports, were filed under Section 13(a) "as necessary or appropriate for the proper protection of investors and to insure fair dealing in the security." 15 U.S.C. §78m(a). . . .

The SEC concedes that the mandatory filings here satisfy a related but separate purpose specific to the agency—the SEC reviews the documents to determine whether to investigate a particular transaction. False filings that relate to specific agency decisions, however, are criminalized by a separate statute, 18 U.S.C. §1001. . . .

Here, the government could have charged Berger with making false statements that related to the SEC's regulatory decisionmaking under §1001 in addition to charging him with filing false statements that were material to investors under Section 32(a). As to the hypothetical §1001 charge, the *Kungys* case's interpretation of materiality—examining the misstatement's ability to influence the SEC's decision-making—would be appropriate. However, under Section 32(a), which was promulgated under an act specifically intended to benefit the investing public, misstated or omitted facts should be evaluated for materiality as to those investors. . . .

For the above reasons, we AFFIRM the conviction. . . .

V. THEORIES OF FRAUD II: INSIDER TRADING

A. Policy

HENRY MANNE, INSIDER TRADING: HAYEK, VIRTUAL MARKETS, AND THE DOG THAT DID NOT BARK

31 J. Corp. L. 167 (2005)

It has been almost forty years since the publication of my book, *Insider Trading and the Stock Market*, and the topic still has the ability to engender heated argument as well as seemingly unending efforts at analytical explication. I apologize at the outset for continuing the debate, especially since I myself thought that it had about run its course. Nonetheless, the topic refuses to die, and it continues to stimulate new hypotheses, one of which is about to be offered.

This taxing of the intellectual tolerance of critics of insider trading may have a redeeming feature for many. In the process of developing this new idea, I have had to reexamine and substantially modify perhaps the most vigorously criticized claim I made for the positive benefits of unregulated insider trading. That claim was the notion that insider trading can be used as an important component of executive compensation. I hope that I am about to offer a much stronger substitute argument.

Fundamentally, my book made only three basic economic arguments. One was that the practice of insider trading did no significant harm to long-term investors. The other two were claims of positive benefits from the practice: one, the compensation argument, and the other, the idea that insider trading contributed importantly to the efficiency of stock market pricing.

By and large the idea that there is no direct harm from the practice has held up very well, especially the point that no real damage is caused to an investor who engages anonymously on an exchange in a trade with an insider on the other side of the transaction. However, one "harm" argument of feasible merit has dominated the academic literature for some time. This is the so-called "adverse selection" argument. Basically the argument is that since specialists on the floor of stock exchanges (or other market makers) systematically lose money when insiders are trading, they will expand their bid-ask spread in order to cover this greater cost of doing business. In this fashion, it is argued, they pass along the cost of insiders' trading to all outside investors with whom they deal, the so-called "insider trading tax."

The first part of this argument is really just a variant of the idea in my book that short-term traders would indeed frequently lose to insiders (a warning against using the stock market as a gambling casino). I suggested that long-term investors had little to worry about quantitatively because of insider trading, and the same thing remains true regardless of the existence of some adverse selection. Furthermore, there is considerable evidence that the harm to market makers exists more in the theoretical world of finance literature than it does in the actual play of the market. Though the argument is theoretically feasible, it seems to be practically irrelevant in the real world.

Of the two arguments that I offered for positive benefits from insider trading, the argument for a strong positive relationship between market efficiency and insider trading has proved to be very robust. I missed the very important and related advantage pointed out by Harold Demsetz that access to valuable trading information may allow controlling shareholders to be compensated for the additional risk they assumed by not being well diversified. This is an especially important factor in corporate governance, since, without a controlling shareholder, agency costs in large corporations, normally dealt with through an exogenous market for corporate control, will be much higher.

There is almost no disagreement that insider trading does always push the price of a stock in the correct direction. This is not to gainsay that there are also other mechanisms that play a significant role in stock pricing, such as the explicit public disclosure of new information, sanctioned transmittal of information to financial analysts, and the so-called "derivative" trading that occurs after some form of market "signaling." A vast literature has developed examining the relative impact of these various mechanisms on stock market pricing, but it is fair to say that none of this has seriously damaged the argument of the stock-pricing benefit of insider trading. This is not the right time or place to review that literature, and for present purposes we merely need to understand that insider trading does have the price vector claimed for it, even though this mechanism alone may play less than an exclusive role in making stock market pricing as efficient as it is. The crucial point for present purposes is that, even if only on a few occasions and either by itself or in tandem with other forces, insider trading may be sufficient to move the price of a company's stock.

My second "positive" argument for insider trading, that it could perform well as a part of an executive compensation package, has been the more forcefully attacked, and it is perhaps less robust than I and other proponents had originally assumed. The insider trading compensation argument has become especially relevant in recent years, as a great debate has swirled through business, regulatory, and legal circles about the proper way to compensate corporate executives. Much of this discussion has focused recently on stock options, since they were so heavily relied upon to compensate employees of the firms that figured heavily in the market collapse of the early 2000s. The focus on stock options in turn logically implicates the insider trading compensation argument, since the two are undoubtedly the closest substitutes in the compensation arena.

A stock option offers the same incentive to employees to work efficiently that would be provided by ownership of an appropriate number of shares, however obtained, but leveraged by non-recourse, interest-free debt. The indirect incentive effects of this leveraging are very difficult to value for corporate accounting purposes or, for that matter, for the purpose of determining the value of the option to an employee. Thus, even though there is a forward look and a leverage feature to options that cannot be obtained, say, with bonuses, there are still real problems with determining the exact incentive effect of stock option grants.

After the option is exercised, and to the extent the employee holds on to the shares, the executive becomes a (larger) shareholder. Stock ownership obviously motivates a manager to maximize share price, especially if the shares represent a substantial part of the employee's portfolio. However, since the shares will represent only a tiny fraction of the company's outstanding shares, free rider reasons dictate that the induced incentive for risky choices may still fall short of what would be dictated by the interest of all shareholders. In other words, as a number of studies suggest, stock options at best offer no greater incentive than would an appropriate, but difficult to determine, number of shares held by the manager, however acquired, and leveraged by debt. At worst, they may provide real adverse incentives.

When stock options are the primary device used to encourage risky decisions by managers, and to the extent that insider trading is effectively, or even substantially, prevented, the financial focus of corporate officials will necessarily be on accounting information, since the real world events underlying those entries cannot be traded on directly as they occur. The legal flow of information to the market will be via formal, SEC-sanctioned disclosures, including press releases, quarterly reports, 10-Ks, and duly publicized conferences with financial analysts. Since future expected profits cannot be shown on the books, and trading on the underlying information is not allowed, the urge to make the accounting picture look better in order to have it conform to management's current view of the company's prospects—biased or not—may become irresistible. It is at least arguable that this constituted part of the underlying pressure for what occurred at Enron and various telecommunications companies.

Insider trading, on the other hand, does not have these disadvantages. It, in effect, allows insiders to meticulously craft their own reward for innovations almost as soon as they occur and to trade without harm to any investors. The incentive is immediate and precise and is never confounded with stock price changes that are not of the managers' making.

If insider trading were legal and used to replace stock options, there would be no "tragedies" of employees being left high and dry with options way out of the money. There would be no loss of reward when an innovation merely resulted in a reduction of an expected loss. There would be no unearned gain because a company's stock appreciates in line with a market or industry rise. There would be no disappointments about the number of shares optioned or granted to particular employees. There would be none of this absurd business of renegotiating the option plan every time the stock takes a nose dive. And there would be no peculiar problems of accounting, since there would be no reason to put the right of employees to trade on undisclosed information on the company's balance sheet at all; such trading would be entirely extraneous to the company's accounts.

The SEC's notoriously ineffective, but highly publicized and politicized, efforts to enforce insider trading laws have merely shifted the identity of the people who may trade first on undisclosed information. In the process, they have perhaps prevented the development of an innovative and useful compensation device and unduly encouraged a problematic second best.

Having said that, however, it must be recognized that insider trading cannot be a perfect form of incentive compensation. While many of the criticisms of the practice are vacuous or even tendentious, there are significant problems with the scheme, which many of my critics hastened to elaborate. Valuable information will undoubtedly get into the hands of individuals inside and outside the company who in no sense should be compensated, usually because they will have done nothing to produce the valuable new information. Another problem is that the value of the information cannot be metered to the value of the contribution of a particular individual. And, as was also pointed out, the value of new information will, in many cases, be a function of the financial ability of someone to trade on the information or of their ability to evaluate new knowledge.

Perhaps the most common objection to insider trading as compensation is that it cannot be metered in advance as part of a compensation plan. It is in its very nature a kind of all-or-nothing proposition, since efforts by a given corporation to police its rules about who can trade, and to what extent, will necessarily involve the company in exactly the kind of post hoc compensation calculations that the practice is argued by its supporters to avoid. It is not too surprising then that even before 1968, in the heyday of insider trading in the United States, no company ever announced that certain executives, but not other employees, would be allowed to engage in the practice. . . .

There is ample evidence that insider trading simply went underground and there is no need for a substitute. SEC rule enforcement is a mess. SEC policies are arbitrary, capricious, political, and extremely inefficient. Nonetheless, illegal insider trading, no matter how robust, is bound to be more expensive and less efficient than the legalized variety. Thus, it is not surprising that other devices might arise for surmounting the SEC's effort to slow insider trading. If the stock market cannot itself be used to gain certain information because of insider trading restrictions, then managers (though, alas, not outside investors) can create a virtual market to provide some of that same information. Virtual markets even have some benefits the actual stock market does not, such as the ability to segregate specific causes of share-price changes. However, virtual markets will never be a complete substitute for the stock market because of the design and motivational problems mentioned earlier. But, these markets can ameliorate some of the costs of the SEC's campaign against insider trading, and we can expect them to flourish.

HAYNE E. LELAND, INSIDER TRADING: SHOULD IT BE PROHIBITED?

100 J. Pol. Econ. 859 (1992)

Is insider trading good for financial markets? In 1934, the U.S. Congress decided "no," and insider trading in the United States has been regulated by the Securities and Exchange Commission since that time.[16] Not all countries have followed the U.S. example, and the debate continues: some countries without regulation are now considering it, whereas in academic circles, the benefits of regulating insider trading are still being contested.

16. [This is an inaccurate statement. The 1934 Exchange Act did not address insider trading directly. It was only later, in the 1960s, that the SEC used the anti-fraud provision of the 1934 Act to attack insider trading—Eds.]

The merits of insider trading have been debated on two levels: (i) Is it "fair" to have trading when individuals are differentially informed? (ii) Is it economically efficient to allow insider trading?

The Securities Exchange Act of 1934 justifies the regulation of insider trading on the presumption that such activity is "unfair" to outside investors. Critics point out that trading is always unfair whenever one investor is better informed than another. Yet no one has advocated that all trading based on private information should (or could) be restricted. The line between what information is fair and what information is unfair has been the subject of considerable legal argument. Recent U.S. cases have emphasized breach of fiduciary duty by employees using privileged information rather than unfairness.

Because there is no commonly accepted definition of "unfair," this aspect of insider trading is not directly addressed. But the second aspect of insider trading, its impact on economic efficiency and welfare, is more susceptible to economic analysis. One can show which parties gain, which lose, and how much is gained or lost. When the sum of monetary gains and losses can be associated with economic welfare, this analysis also provides a measure of the net benefits (or costs) that result from prohibiting insider trading.

To understand the nature of the current debate, it is useful to review the common arguments cited pro and con insider trading.

Pro.—(a) Insider trading will bring new and useful information into asset prices. Decision makers—both portfolio managers and firms making real investment decisions—can reduce risk and improve performance when prices reflect better information. (b) Because of reduced risk, asset prices will be higher and more real investment will occur.

Con.—(a) Outside investors will invest less because the market is "unfair." Asset prices will be lower and less real investment will occur. (b) Market liquidity will be reduced, thereby disadvantaging traders who must trade for life cycle or other reasons not related to information. (c) Insider trading will make current stock prices more volatile, further hurting traders with liquidity needs.

Note that all these points can be true simultaneously—with one exception. The pro-insiders argue that asset prices will rise when insider trading is permitted; the anti-insiders maintain that asset prices will fall.

Elements of a reasonable model to analyze these concerns should include the following: (i) Insiders, who by virtue of their privileged position have more precise information about future stock prices than outside investors. It seems reasonable to presume that insiders will recognize the impact of their purchases on the current stock price. (ii) Outsiders, who have less precise information about future stock prices. Such investors recognize that the current price may reflect (at least partially) the information of insiders. Outsiders are risk averse and, being numerous, behave as perfect competitors. (iii) Liquidity traders who trade for exogenous reasons, such as intertemporal smoothing of income flows. (iv) Real investment, financed by a supply of new shares, which depends on the issuing price per share. A higher current stock price will lead to the issuance of a larger number of shares and to greater real investment.

A model is developed below that contains these elements in as simple a form as possible. The objective is to assess the validity of the arguments pro and con insider trading. Equilibrium prices and welfare are compared in markets in which insider trading is either permitted or restricted. It is assumed that if insider trading is prohibited, the inside information will not be reflected in prices or decisions.

The analysis begins with a model that includes differentially informed investors. In recognition of the monopoly power of the inside trader, the model is similar in spirit to those of [other economists.] However, there are important differences that permit a more appropriate analysis of insider trading.

First, the number of shares issued (and real investment) is endogenously determined. The amount of investment will be affected by prices, which in turn will be affected by information when insiders can trade. Endogenously determined and price-sensitive investment is required of any model that examines the full costs and benefits of insider trading.

Second, the model looks at the impact of insider trading on the welfare of each class of participants rather than simply on the degree to which prices reflect information. Informational efficiency is not an end in itself. It is generally thought to improve welfare, but . . . this will not always be the case . . . .

VIII. Conclusions

The analysis of this paper suggests that insider trading may hurt or help markets, depending on the characteristics of those markets. This should not be surprising: the fact that controversy still exists on the issue suggests that there is no single "best" answer regardless of circumstances.

The analysis does indicate who gains and who loses. It also identifies the characteristics of those markets that are likely to gain from insider trading and those that are likely to lose.

Liquidity traders are major losers when insider trading is permitted. Markets become less liquid when insiders trade: prices move more in response to unobserved random supply shocks because investors believe that price movements might be coming from informed investor activity. If liquidity traders had a way to inform markets that their trades were indeed information-free, they would be less harmed. However, liquidity traders who could not inform markets would suffer more, since market liquidity decreases as Σ_v becomes smaller.

Outside investors also are hurt when insider trading is permitted. Their expected return is reduced. Because they are trading against better-informed investors, they own, on average, more shares when expected returns are low and fewer shares when expected returns are high. But outside investors also have reduced risks: Because some risks are revealed through prices, the remaining risks are less. Both the mean and variance of outsiders' returns are reduced by insider trading. Outsiders' demand for stock may increase, but their welfare always decreases.

Gainers from insider trading of course include the insiders themselves. But owners of firms issuing shares also will, on average, benefit from insider trading. The average issuing price will be higher, and there are additional benefits when the firm's investment level is sensitive to future prospects, as reflected (when insider trading is permitted) in current price.

The net impact of these separate consequences of insider trading can be positive or negative. The results indicate that insider trading is less desirable as (1) investment flexibility decreases, (2) investor risk aversion increases, (3) liquidity trading is more volatile, and (4) future price volatility increases. The single most important factor is the sensitivity of investment to current price. If the sensitivity is great, insider trading is likely to be beneficial. When firms themselves possess inside information, allowing insider trading for personal profit is likely to have negative effects. Firms will pay less attention to current market price if they already possess information superior to that price. Because the sensitivity of investment to current price is lower, the negative aspects of insider trading will tend to dominate the positive aspects. This may well explain why regulation has focused on prohibiting trading based on superior information emanating from *inside* the firm, as contrasted with superior information generated externally.

Typically, insider trading has been *more* tolerated in less developed financial markets. This is somewhat puzzling in light of the results above, if less developed markets are associated with greater future price volatility and, perhaps, greater investor risk aversion as well.

There are a number of possible explanations. First, liquidity trading is likely to be much more important in highly developed capital markets, where investors consider the stock market as a viable alternative for holding assets for retirement and other income-smoothing purposes. Insider trading is particularly harmful to liquidity traders. Second, it is possible (although not obvious) that less developed financial markets have a greater fraction of superior information that is generated outside the firm. Thus the investment level would be more sensitive to stock market price. Third, and most likely, less developed markets may be equally harmed by insider trading, but restrictions are simply impossible to enforce.

The model of this paper captures many of the key ingredients of the insider trading controversy, but it should be extended to multiple time periods. Insider trading "moves up" the resolution of uncertainty. This one-time benefit may be relatively more important in a two-period model than in a multiperiod model. If so, my results may overestimate the benefits of insider trading. But we must await the development of multiperiod rational expectations models to answer this question definitively.

NOTES AND QUESTIONS

1. Professor Manne has made a career out of opposing restrictions on insider trading. Obviously, his arguments have not won the day. What are the arguments in favor of prohibiting insider trading? If you are not prepared to answer this question now, keep it in mind as you read the cases that follow.
2. Manne admits that his argument that insider trading provides incentives for corporate officers to work to improve shareholder value is less robust

than he originally thought. But he fails to address the major criticism of his compensation argument, one so big as to call it into question altogether. This is the fact that insiders can short-sell their company stock and thus make a profit even when the stock's price is declining. Therefore, as insiders, they can be specially rewarded for improving *or* destroying the value of their company.

3. Professor Leland provides a balanced econometric approach to determining the impact of insider trading on various participants in the marketplace. Can you restate his conclusions in laymen's terms?
4. According to Leland, does insider trading have a net positive or net negative impact on the market if the company is in possession of the inside information? As an empirical matter, how often do you think this is the case?
5. Leland says at the beginning of his piece that he draws no "direct" conclusions regarding the fairness of insider trading. But can you draw any conclusions about the fairness of the practice given whom he identifies as the winners and losers?

B. Classic (*Cady, Roberts*) Insider Trading

CHIARELLA v. UNITED STATES

445 U.S. 222 (1980)

Mr. Justice Powell delivered the opinion of the Court.

The question in this case is whether a person who learns from the confidential documents of one corporation that it is planning an attempt to secure control of a second corporation violates §10(b) of the Securities Exchange Act of 1934 if he fails to disclose the impending takeover before trading in the target company's securities.

I.

Petitioner is a printer by trade. In 1975 and 1976, he worked as a "markup man" in the New York composing room of Pandick Press, a financial printer. Among documents that petitioner handled were five announcements of corporate takeover bids. When these documents were delivered to the printer, the identities of the acquiring and target corporations were concealed by blank spaces or false names. The true names were sent to the printer on the night of the final printing.

The petitioner, however, was able to deduce the names of the target companies before the final printing from other information contained in the documents. Without disclosing his knowledge, petitioner purchased stock in the target companies and sold the shares immediately after the takeover attempts were made public. By this method, petitioner realized a gain of slightly more than $30,000 in the course of 14 months. Subsequently, the Securities and Exchange Commission (Commission or SEC) began an investigation of his trading activities. In May 1977, petitioner entered into a consent decree with the Commission in which he agreed to return his profits to the sellers of the shares. On the same day, he was discharged by Pandick Press.

In January 1978, petitioner was indicted on 17 counts of violating §10(b) of the Securities Exchange Act of 1934 (1934 Act) and SEC Rule 10b-5. After petitioner unsuccessfully moved to dismiss the indictment, he was brought to trial and convicted on all counts.

The Court of Appeals for the Second Circuit affirmed petitioner's conviction. We granted certiorari, and we now reverse.

II.

Section 10(b) of the 1934 Act, 48 Stat. 891, 15 U.S.C. §78j, prohibits the use "in connection with the purchase or sale of any security . . . [of] any manipulative or deceptive device or contrivance in contravention of such rules and regulations as the Commission may prescribe." Pursuant to this section, the SEC promulgated Rule 10b-5 which provides in pertinent part:

> "It shall be unlawful for any person, directly or indirectly, by the use of any means or instrumentality of interstate commerce, or of the mails or of any facility of any national securities exchange,
>
> "(a) To employ any device, scheme, or artifice to defraud, [or]
>
> * * *
>
> "(c) To engage in any act, practice, or course of business which operates or would operate as a fraud or deceit upon any person, in connection with the purchase or sale of any security." 17 CFR §240.10b-5 (1979).

This case concerns the legal effect of the petitioner's silence. The District Court's charge permitted the jury to convict the petitioner if it found that he willfully failed to inform sellers of target company securities that he knew of a forthcoming takeover bid that would make their shares more valuable. In order to decide whether silence in such circumstances violates §10(b), it is necessary to review the language and legislative history of that statute as well as its interpretation by the Commission and the federal courts.

Although the starting point of our inquiry is the language of the statute, §10(b) does not state whether silence may constitute a manipulative or deceptive device. Section 10(b) was designed as a catch-all clause to prevent fraudulent practices. But neither the legislative history nor the statute itself affords specific guidance for the resolution of this case. When Rule 10b-5 was promulgated in 1942, the SEC did not discuss the possibility that failure to provide information might run afoul of §10(b).

The SEC took an important step in the development of §10(b) when it held that a broker-dealer and his firm violated that section by selling securities on the basis of undisclosed information obtained from a director of the issuer corporation who was also a registered representative of the brokerage firm. In *Cady, Roberts & Co.*, 40 S.E.C. 907 (1961), the Commission decided that a corporate insider must abstain from trading in the shares of his corporation unless he has first disclosed all material inside information known to him. The obligation to disclose or abstain derives from

> "[a]n affirmative duty to disclose material information[, which] has been traditionally imposed on corporate 'insiders,' particular officers, directors, or controlling stockholders. We, and the courts have consistently held that insiders must disclose material facts which are known to them by virtue of their position but which are not known to persons with whom they deal and which, if known, would affect their investment judgment." *Id.*, at 911.

The Commission emphasized that the duty arose from (i) the existence of a relationship affording access to inside information intended to be available only for a corporate purpose, and (ii) the unfairness of allowing a corporate insider to take advantage of that information by trading without disclosure. *Id.*, at 912, and n.15.[8]

That the relationship between a corporate insider and the stockholders of his corporation gives rise to a disclosure obligation is not a novel twist of the law. At common law, misrepresentation made for the purpose of inducing reliance upon the false statement is fraudulent. But one who fails to disclose material information prior to the consummation of a transaction commits fraud only when he is under a duty to do so. And the duty to disclose arises when one party has information "that the other [party] is entitled to know because of a fiduciary or other similar relation of trust and confidence between them." In its *Cady, Roberts* decision, the Commission recognized a relationship of trust and confidence between the shareholders of a corporation and those insiders who have obtained confidential information by reason of their position with that corporation. This relationship gives rise to a duty to disclose because of the "necessity of preventing a corporate insider from . . . tak[ing] unfair advantage of the uninformed minority stockholders." Speed v. Transamerica Corp., 99 F. Supp. 808, 829 (D. Del. 1951).

The federal courts have found violations of §10(b) where corporate insiders used undisclosed information for their own benefit. The cases also have emphasized, in accordance with the common-law rule, that "[t]he party charged with failing to disclose market information must be under a duty to disclose it." Accordingly, a purchaser of stock who has no duty to a prospective seller because he is neither an insider nor a fiduciary has been held to have no obligation to reveal material facts. . . .

Thus, administrative and judicial interpretations have established that silence in connection with the purchase or sale of securities may operate as a fraud actionable

8. In *Cady, Roberts*, the broker-dealer was liable under §10(b) because it received nonpublic information from a corporate insider of the issuer. Since the insider could not use the information, neither could the partners in the brokerage firm with which he was associated. The transaction in *Cady, Roberts* involved sale of stock to persons who previously may not have been shareholders in the corporation. 40 S.E.C., at 913, and n.21. The Commission embraced the reasoning of Judge Learned Hand that "the director or officer assumed a fiduciary relation to the buyer by the very sale; for it would be a sorry distinction to allow him to use the advantage of his position to induce the buyer into the position of a beneficiary although he was forbidden to do so once the buyer had become one." *Id.*, at 914, n.23 (quoting Gratz v. Claughton, 187 F.2d 46, 49 (2d Cir.), *cert. denied*, 341 U.S. 920 1951).

under §10(b) despite the absence of statutory language or legislative history specifically addressing the legality of nondisclosure. But such liability is premised upon a duty to disclose arising from a relationship of trust and confidence between parties to a transaction. Application of a duty to disclose prior to trading guarantees that corporate insiders, who have an obligation to place the shareholder's welfare before their own, will not benefit personally through fraudulent use of material, nonpublic information.

In this case, the petitioner was convicted of violating §10(b) although he was not a corporate insider and he received no confidential information from the target company. Moreover, the "market information" upon which he relied did not concern the earning power or operations of the target company, but only the plans of the acquiring company. Petitioner's use of that information was not a fraud under §10(b) unless he was subject to an affirmative duty to disclose it before trading. In this case, the jury instructions failed to specify any such duty. In effect, the trial court instructed the jury that petitioner owed a duty to everyone; to all sellers, indeed, to the market as a whole. The jury simply was told to decide whether petitioner used material, nonpublic information at a time when "he knew other people trading in the securities market did not have access to the same information."

The Court of Appeals affirmed the conviction by holding that "*[a]nyone*—corporate insider or not—who regularly receives material nonpublic information may not use that information to trade in securities without incurring an affirmative duty to disclose." Although the court said that its test would include only persons who regularly receive material, nonpublic information, its rationale for that limitation is unrelated to the existence of a duty to disclose. . . .

We see no basis for applying such a new and different theory of liability in this case. As we have emphasized before, the 1934 Act cannot be read "'more broadly than its language and the statutory scheme reasonably permit.'" Section 10(b) is aptly described as a catchall provision, but what it catches must be fraud. When an allegation of fraud is based upon nondisclosure, there can be no fraud absent a duty to speak. We hold that a duty to disclose under §10(b) does not arise from the mere possession of nonpublic market information. The contrary result is without support in the legislative history of §10(b) and would be inconsistent with the careful plan that Congress has enacted for regulation of the securities markets. . . .

IV.

In its brief to this Court, the United States offers an alternative theory to support petitioner's conviction. It argues that petitioner breached a duty to the acquiring corporation when he acted upon information that he obtained by virtue of his position as an employee of a printer employed by the corporation. The breach of this duty is said to support a conviction under §10(b) for fraud perpetrated upon both the acquiring corporation and the sellers.

We need not decide whether this theory has merit for it was not submitted to the jury. . . .

The judgment of the Court of Appeals is
Reversed.

[Concurring opinions of Stevens and Brennan, and dissenting opinion of Blackmun joined by Marshall, omitted.]

Mr. Chief Justice BURGER, dissenting.

I believe that the jury instructions in this case properly charged a violation of §10(b) and Rule 10b-5, and I would affirm the conviction. . . .

I would read §10(b) and Rule 10b-5 to encompass and build on this principle: to mean that a person who has misappropriated nonpublic information has an absolute duty to disclose that information or to refrain from trading. . . .

NOTES AND QUESTIONS

1. What are the elements of "classical" or "*Cady, Roberts*" insider trading? Are they the same or different for criminal versus civil violations? How so?
2. In its discussion of *Cady, Roberts*, what arguments does the Court put forward in support of a prohibition of insider trading?
3. Congress had considered but refused to outlaw insider trading when it passed the 1933 and 1934 Acts. Why do you think this was so? Did the SEC exceed its authority in pursuing the *Cady, Roberts* case?
4. Is it mere coincidence that *Cady, Roberts* was a civil case?

C. Misappropriation Theory

UNITED STATES v. O'HAGAN
521 U.S. 642 (1997)

Justice GINSBURG delivered the opinion of the Court. . . .

I.

Respondent James Herman O'Hagan was a partner in the law firm of Dorsey & Whitney in Minneapolis, Minnesota. In July 1988, Grand Metropolitan PLC (Grand Met), a company based in London, England, retained Dorsey & Whitney as local counsel to represent Grand Met regarding a potential tender offer for the common stock of the Pillsbury Company, headquartered in Minneapolis. Both Grand Met and Dorsey & Whitney took precautions to protect the confidentiality of Grand Met's tender offer plans. O'Hagan did no work on the Grand Met representation. Dorsey & Whitney withdrew from representing Grand Met on September 9, 1988. Less than a month later, on October 4, 1988, Grand Met publicly announced its tender offer for Pillsbury stock.

On August 18, 1988, while Dorsey & Whitney was still representing Grand Met, O'Hagan began purchasing call options for Pillsbury stock. Each option gave him the right to purchase 100 shares of Pillsbury stock by a specified date in September 1988.

Later in August and in September, O'Hagan made additional purchases of Pillsbury call options. By the end of September, he owned 2,500 unexpired Pillsbury options, apparently more than any other individual investor. O'Hagan also purchased, in September 1988, some 5,000 shares of Pillsbury common stock, at a price just under $39 per share. When Grand Met announced its tender offer in October, the price of Pillsbury stock rose to nearly $60 per share. O'Hagan then sold his Pillsbury call options and common stock, making a profit of more than $4.3 million.

The Securities and Exchange Commission (SEC or Commission) initiated an investigation into O'Hagan's transactions, culminating in a 57-count indictment. The indictment alleged that O'Hagan defrauded his law firm and its client, Grand Met, by using for his own trading purposes material, nonpublic information regarding Grand Met's planned tender offer. According to the indictment, O'Hagan used the profits he gained through this trading to conceal his previous embezzlement and conversion of unrelated client trust funds. O'Hagan was charged with, among other things, 20 counts of mail fraud, in violation of 18 U.S.C. §1341 [and] 17 counts of securities fraud, in violation of § 10(b) of the Securities Exchange Act of 1934 (Exchange Act), 15 U.S.C. §78j(b), and SEC Rule 10b-5, 17 CFR §240.10b-5. A divided panel of the Court of Appeals for the Eighth Circuit reversed all of O'Hagan's convictions. Liability under §10(b) and Rule 10b-5, the Eighth Circuit held, may not be grounded on the "misappropriation theory" of securities fraud on which the prosecution relied. . . .

We granted certiorari and now reverse the Eighth Circuit's judgment. . . .

Under the "traditional" or "classical theory" of insider trading liability, §10(b) and Rule 10b-5 are violated when a corporate insider trades in the securities of his corporation on the basis of material, nonpublic information. Trading on such information qualifies as a "deceptive device" under §10(b), we have affirmed, because "a relationship of trust and confidence [exists] between the shareholders of a corporation and those insiders who have obtained confidential information by reason of their position with that corporation." Chiarella v. United States, 445 U.S. 222, 228 (1980). That relationship, we recognized, "gives rise to a duty to disclose [or to abstain from trading] because of the 'necessity of preventing a corporate insider from . . . tak[ing] unfair advantage of . . . uninformed . . . stockholders.'" The classical theory applies not only to officers, directors, and other permanent insiders of a corporation, but also to attorneys, accountants, consultants, and others who temporarily become fiduciaries of a corporation. See Dirks v. SEC, 463 U.S. 646, 655 n.14 (1983).

The "misappropriation theory" holds that a person commits fraud "in connection with" a securities transaction, and thereby violates §10(b) and Rule 10b-5, when he misappropriates confidential information for securities trading purposes, in breach of a duty owed to the source of the information. Under this theory, a fiduciary's undisclosed, self-serving use of a principal's information to purchase or sell securities, in breach of a duty of loyalty and confidentiality, defrauds the principal of the exclusive use of that information. In lieu of premising liability on a fiduciary relationship between company insider and purchaser or seller of the company's stock, the misappropriation theory premises liability on a fiduciary-turned-trader's deception of those who entrusted him with access to confidential information.

The two theories are complementary, each addressing efforts to capitalize on nonpublic information through the purchase or sale of securities. The classical theory targets a corporate insider's breach of duty to shareholders with whom the insider transacts; the misappropriation theory outlaws trading on the basis of nonpublic information by a corporate "outsider" in breach of a duty owed not to a trading party, but to the source of the information. The misappropriation theory is thus designed to "protec[t] the integrity of the securities markets against abuses by 'outsiders' to a corporation who have access to confidential information that will affect th[e] corporation's security price when revealed, but who owe no fiduciary or other duty to that corporation's shareholders."

In this case, the indictment alleged that O'Hagan, in breach of a duty of trust and confidence he owed to his law firm, Dorsey & Whitney, and to its client, Grand Met, traded on the basis of nonpublic information regarding Grand Met's planned tender offer for Pillsbury common stock. This conduct, the Government charged, constituted a fraudulent device in connection with the purchase and sale of securities.

B.

We agree with the Government that misappropriation, as just defined, satisfies §10(b)'s requirement that chargeable conduct involve a "deceptive device or contrivance" used "in connection with" the purchase or sale of securities. We observe, first, that misappropriators, as the Government describes them, deal in deception. A fiduciary who "[pretends] loyalty to the principal while secretly converting the principal's information for personal gain," "dupes" or defrauds the principal.

We addressed fraud of the same species in Carpenter v. United States, 484 U.S. 19 (1987), which involved the mail fraud statute's proscription of "any scheme or artifice to defraud," 18 U.S.C. §1341.[17] Affirming convictions under that statute, we said in *Carpenter* that an employee's undertaking not to reveal his employer's confidential information "became a sham" when the employee provided the information to his co-conspirators in a scheme to obtain trading profits. A company's confidential information, we recognized in *Carpenter*, qualifies as property to which the company has a right of exclusive use. The undisclosed misappropriation of such information, in violation of a fiduciary duty, the Court said in *Carpenter*, constitutes fraud akin to embezzlement—"'the fraudulent appropriation to one's own use of the money or goods entrusted to one's care by another.'" *Carpenter*'s discussion of the fraudulent misuse of confidential information, the Government notes, "is a particularly apt source of guidance here, because [the mail fraud statute] (like Section 10(b)) has long been held to require deception, not merely the breach of a fiduciary duty."

Deception through nondisclosure is central to the theory of liability for which the Government seeks recognition. As counsel for the Government stated in explanation of the theory at oral argument: "To satisfy the common law rule that a trustee may not use the property that [has] been entrusted [to] him, there would

17. [*Carpenter* is set out at pages 126, *supra*—Eds.]

have to be consent. To satisfy the requirement of the Securities Act that there be no deception, there would only have to be disclosure. . . .

We turn next to the §10(b) requirement that the misappropriator's deceptive use of information be "in connection with the purchase or sale of [a] security." This element is satisfied because the fiduciary's fraud is consummated, not when the fiduciary gains the confidential information, but when, without disclosure to his principal, he uses the information to purchase or sell securities. The securities transaction and the breach of duty thus coincide. This is so even though the person or entity defrauded is not the other party to the trade, but is, instead, the source of the nonpublic information. A misappropriator who trades on the basis of material, nonpublic information, in short, gains his advantageous market position through deception; he deceives the source of the information and simultaneously harms members of the investing public.

The misappropriation theory targets information of a sort that misappropriators ordinarily capitalize upon to gain no-risk profits through the purchase or sale of securities. Should a misappropriator put such information to other use, the statute's prohibition would not be implicated. The theory does not catch all conceivable forms of fraud involving confidential information; rather, it catches fraudulent means of capitalizing on such information through securities transactions.

The Government notes another limitation on the forms of fraud §10(b) reaches: "The misappropriation theory would not . . . apply to a case in which a person defrauded a bank into giving him a loan or embezzled cash from another, and then used the proceeds of the misdeed to purchase securities." In such a case, the Government states, "the proceeds would have value to the malefactor apart from their use in a securities transaction, and the fraud would be complete as soon as the money was obtained." In other words, money can buy, if not anything, then at least many things; its misappropriation may thus be viewed as sufficiently detached from a subsequent securities transaction that §10(b)'s "in connection with" requirement would not be met.

Justice Thomas' charge that the misappropriation theory is incoherent because information, like funds, can be put to multiple uses (opinion concurring in judgment in part and dissenting in part), misses the point. The Exchange Act was enacted in part "to insure the maintenance of fair and honest markets," 15 U.S.C. §78b, and there is no question that fraudulent uses of confidential information fall within §10(b)'s prohibition if the fraud is "in connection with" a securities transaction. It is hardly remarkable that a rule suitably applied to the fraudulent uses of certain kinds of information would be stretched beyond reason were it applied to the fraudulent use of money. . . .

The misappropriation theory comports with §10(b)'s language, which requires deception "in connection with the purchase or sale of any security," not deception of an identifiable purchaser or seller. The theory is also well tuned to an animating purpose of the Exchange Act: to insure honest securities markets and thereby promote investor confidence. Although informational disparity is inevitable in the securities markets, investors likely would hesitate to venture their capital in a market where trading based on misappropriated nonpublic information is unchecked by law. An investor's informational disadvantage vis-à-vis a misappropriator with material, nonpublic information stems from contrivance, not luck; it is a disadvantage that cannot be overcome with research or skill.

In sum, considering the inhibiting impact on market participation of trading on misappropriated information, and the congressional purposes underlying §10(b), it makes scant sense to hold a lawyer like O'Hagan a §10(b) violator if he works for a law firm representing the target of a tender offer, but not if he works for a law firm representing the bidder. The text of the statute requires no such result. The misappropriation at issue here was properly made the subject of a §10(b) charge because it meets the statutory requirement that there be "deceptive" conduct "in connection with" securities transactions. . . .

The judgment of the Court of Appeals for the Eighth Circuit is reversed, and the case is remanded for further proceedings consistent with this opinion.

It is so ordered.

[Opinion of Scalia, concurring and dissenting in part, and opinion of Thomas, joined by Rehnquist, concurring and dissenting in part, omitted.]

NOTES AND QUESTIONS

1. Why wasn't O'Hagan a classic insider?
2. How can a misappropriator avoid liability? Is it the same way a classic insider can avoid liability? How realistic is the trading alternative for a misappropriator?
3. What, exactly, is the difference between an individual who misappropriates money (i.e., embezzles) and then uses that money to purchase securities and an individual who misappropriates information and then trades on it? Justice Thomas says there is no difference, and thus claims that misappropriation theory is incoherent. Justice Ginsburg disagrees. Who's right?
4. What arguments does the majority provide in support of outlawing insider trading (including trading based on misappropriated information)? Are they the same arguments set out for the same purpose by the majority in *Chiarella*? If not, what might be an explanation for the difference?
5. Members of Congress and their aides are constantly in a position to learn about nonpublic information that could affect the value of certain companies or sectors of the economy, such as language in a bill that is about to be introduced. If they trade on that information, have they committed insider trading? Believe it or not, the answer is no. They are not corporate insiders, so they are not classic inside traders. And they have not misappropriated the information; they have simply come into possession of it through the normal course of their job. Unlike other government employees, Congress has specifically exempted itself from general ethics obligations, so there is no "owner" of the information to whom they owe a duty. As a result, members of Congress earn 25 percent more on average on their investments than the general public. Is this fair? Many observers don't think so. *See* Peter Cohan, *Former SEC Commissioner: Insider Trading by Congress Is Perfectly Legal*, DailyFinance, available at http://www.dailyfinance.com/story/former-sec-commissioner-insider-trading-by-congress-is-perfectl/19099201/ (last visited July 16, 2009).

D. Tippee Liability

DIRKS v. SEC

463 U.S. 646 (1983)

Justice POWELL delivered the opinion of the Court.

Petitioner Raymond Dirks received material nonpublic information from "insiders" of a corporation with which he had no connection. He disclosed this information to investors who relied on it in trading in the shares of the corporation. The question is whether Dirks violated the antifraud provisions of the federal securities laws by this disclosure.

I.

In 1973, Dirks was an officer of a New York broker-dealer firm who specialized in providing investment analysis of insurance company securities to institutional investors. On March 6, Dirks received information from Ronald Secrist, a former officer of Equity Funding of America. Secrist alleged that the assets of Equity Funding, a diversified corporation primarily engaged in selling life insurance and mutual funds, were vastly overstated as the result of fraudulent corporate practices. Secrist also stated that various regulatory agencies had failed to act on similar charges made by Equity Funding employees. He urged Dirks to verify the fraud and disclose it publicly.

Dirks decided to investigate the allegations. He visited Equity Funding's headquarters in Los Angeles and interviewed several officers and employees of the corporation. The senior management denied any wrongdoing, but certain corporation employees corroborated the charges of fraud. Neither Dirks nor his firm owned or traded any Equity Funding stock, but throughout his investigation he openly discussed the information he had obtained with a number of clients and investors. Some of these persons sold their holdings of Equity Funding securities, including five investment advisers who liquidated holdings of more than $16 million.

While Dirks was in Los Angeles, he was in touch regularly with William Blundell, the *Wall Street Journal*'s Los Angeles bureau chief. Dirks urged Blundell to write a story on the fraud allegations. Blundell did not believe, however, that such a massive fraud could go undetected and declined to write the story. He feared that publishing such damaging hearsay might be libelous.

During the two-week period in which Dirks pursued his investigation and spread word of Secrist's charges, the price of Equity Funding stock fell from $26 per share to less than $15 per share. This led the New York Stock Exchange to halt trading on March 27. Shortly thereafter California insurance authorities impounded Equity Funding's records and uncovered evidence of the fraud. Only then did the Securities and Exchange Commission (SEC) file a complaint against Equity Funding and only then, on April 2, did the *Wall Street Journal* publish a front-page story based largely on information assembled by Dirks. Equity Funding immediately went into receivership.

The SEC began an investigation into Dirks' role in the exposure of the fraud. After a hearing by an administrative law judge, the SEC found that Dirks had aided and abetted violations of §17(a) of the Securities Act of 1933, 15 U.S.C. §77q(a), §10(b) of the Securities Exchange Act of 1934, 15 U.S.C. §78j(b), and SEC Rule 10b-5, 17 CFR §240.10b-5, by repeating the allegations of fraud to members of the investment community who later sold their Equity Funding stock. The SEC concluded: "Where 'tippees'—regardless of their motivation or occupation—come into possession of material 'information that they know is confidential and know or should know came from a corporate insider,' they must either publicly disclose that information or refrain from trading." Recognizing, however, that Dirks "played an important role in bringing [Equity Funding's] massive fraud to light," the SEC only censured him. . . .

In view of the importance to the SEC and to the securities industry of the question presented by this case, we granted a writ of certiorari. We now reverse.

II.

A.

The SEC's position, as stated in its opinion in this case, is that a tippee "inherits" the *Cady, Roberts* obligation to shareholders whenever he receives inside information from an insider:

> "In tipping potential traders, Dirks breached a duty which he had assumed as a result of knowingly receiving confidential information from [Equity Funding] insiders. Tippees such as Dirks who receive non-public material information from insiders become 'subject to the same duty as [the] insiders.' Such a tippee breaches the fiduciary duty which he assumes from the insider when the tippee knowingly transmits the information to someone who will probably trade on the basis thereof. . . . Presumably, Dirks' informants were entitled to disclose the [Equity Funding] fraud in order to bring it to light and its perpetrators to justice. However, Dirks—standing in their shoes—committed a breach of the fiduciary duty which he had assumed in dealing with them, when he passed the information on to traders."

This view differs little from the view that we rejected as inconsistent with congressional intent in *Chiarella*. In that case, the Court of Appeals agreed with the SEC and affirmed Chiarella's conviction, holding that "'[*a*]*nyone*—corporate insider or not—who regularly receives material nonpublic information may not use that information to trade in securities without incurring an affirmative duty to disclose.'" Here, the SEC maintains that anyone who knowingly receives nonpublic material information from an insider has a fiduciary duty to disclose before trading. . . .

Imposing a duty to disclose or abstain solely because a person knowingly receives material nonpublic information from an insider and trades on it could have an inhibiting influence on the role of market analysts, which the SEC itself recognizes is necessary to the preservation of a healthy market. It is commonplace for analysts to "ferret out and analyze information," and this often is done by meeting with and questioning corporate officers and others who are insiders. And information that the analysts obtain normally may be the basis for judgments as to the market worth of a corporation's securities. The analyst's judgment in this respect is made available in market letters or otherwise to clients of the firm. It is the nature of this type of information, and indeed of the markets themselves, that such information cannot be made simultaneously available to all of the corporation's stockholders or the public generally.

B.

The conclusion that recipients of inside information do not invariably acquire a duty to disclose or abstain does not mean that such tippees always are free to trade on the information. The need for a ban on some tippee trading is clear. Not only are insiders forbidden by their fiduciary relationship from personally using undisclosed corporate information to their advantage, but they may not give such information to an outsider for the same improper purpose of exploiting the information for their personal gain. *See* 15 U.S.C. §78t(b) (making it unlawful to do indirectly "by means of any other person" any act made unlawful by the federal securities laws). Similarly, the transactions of those who knowingly participate with the fiduciary in such a breach are "as forbidden" as transactions "on behalf of the trustee himself." As we noted in *Chiarella*," [t]he tippee's obligation has been viewed as arising from his role as a participant after the fact in the insider's breach of a fiduciary duty." Thus, some tippees must assume an insider's duty to the shareholders not because they receive inside information, but rather because it has been made available to them *improperly*. And for Rule 10b-5 purposes, the insider's disclosure is improper only where it would violate his *Cady, Roberts* duty. Thus, a tippee assumes a fiduciary duty to the shareholders of a corporation not to trade on material nonpublic information only when the insider has breached his fiduciary duty to the shareholders by disclosing the information to the tippee and the tippee knows or should know that there has been a breach. . . . Tipping thus properly is viewed only as a means of indirectly violating the *Cady, Roberts* disclose-or-abstain rule.

C.

In determining whether a tippee is under an obligation to disclose or abstain, it thus is necessary to determine whether the insider's "tip" constituted a breach of the insider's fiduciary duty. All disclosures of confidential corporate information are not inconsistent with the duty insiders owe to shareholders. In contrast to the extraordinary facts of this case, the more typical situation in which there will be a question whether disclosure violates the insider's *Cady, Roberts* duty is when insiders disclose information to analysts. In some situations, the insider will act consistently with his fiduciary duty to shareholders, and yet release of the information may affect the market. For example, it may not be clear—either to the corporate insider or to the recipient analyst—whether the information will be viewed as material nonpublic information. Corporate officials may mistakenly think the information already has been disclosed or that it is not material enough to affect the market. Whether disclosure is a breach of duty therefore depends in large part on the purpose of the disclosure. This standard was identified by the SEC itself in *Cady, Roberts*: a purpose of the securities laws was to eliminate "use of inside information for personal advantage." Thus, the test is whether the insider personally will benefit, directly or indirectly, from his disclosure. Absent some personal gain, there has been no breach of duty to stockholders. And absent a breach by the insider, there is no derivative breach. . . .

Determining whether an insider personally benefits from a particular disclosure, a question of fact, will not always be easy for courts. But it is essential, we think, to have a guiding principle for those whose daily activities must be limited and instructed by the SEC's inside-trading rules, and we believe that there must be a breach of the insider's fiduciary duty before the tippee inherits the duty to disclose or abstain. In contrast, the rule adopted by the SEC in this case would have no limiting principle.

IV.

Under the inside-trading and tipping rules set forth above, we find that there was no actionable violation by Dirks. It is undisputed that Dirks himself was a stranger to Equity Funding, with no pre-existing fiduciary duty to its shareholders. He took no action, directly or indirectly, that induced the shareholders or officers of Equity Funding to repose trust or confidence in him. There was no expectation by Dirks' sources that he would keep their information in confidence. Nor did Dirks misappropriate or illegally obtain the information about Equity Funding. Unless the insiders breached their *Cady, Roberts* duty to shareholders in disclosing the nonpublic information to Dirks, he breached no duty when he passed it on to investors as well as to the *Wall Street Journal.*

It is clear that neither Secrist nor the other Equity Funding employees violated their *Cady, Roberts* duty to the corporation's shareholders by providing information to Dirks. The tippers received no monetary or personal benefit for revealing Equity Funding's secrets, nor was their purpose to make a gift of valuable information to Dirks. As the facts of this case clearly indicate, the tippers were motivated by a desire to expose the fraud. In the absence of a breach of duty to shareholders by the insiders, there was no derivative breach by Dirks. . . .

V.

We conclude that Dirks, in the circumstances of this case, had no duty to abstain from use of the inside information that he obtained. The judgment of the Court of Appeals therefore is

Reversed.

[Dissenting opinion of Blackmun, joined by Brennan and Marshall is omitted.]

NOTES AND QUESTIONS

1. The Court holds that "a tippee assumes a fiduciary duty to the shareholders of a corporation not to trade on material nonpublic information only when the insider has breached his fiduciary duty to the shareholders by disclosing the information to the tippee and the tippee knows or should know that there has been a breach." But *Dirks* is a civil case. Is the test for tippee liability different in the criminal context?
2. Where does tippee liability end? Is the tippee of a tippee liable? What about the tippee of a tippee of a tippee? And so on?
3. Is a tipper liable for insider trading when a tippee trades? If so, under what theory?
4. The Court assumes that market analysts, by virtue of their occupation, come into possession of possible inside information on a regular basis. ("In contrast to the extraordinary facts of this case, the more typical situation in which there will be a question whether disclosure [constitutes insider trading] is when insiders disclose information to analysts.") The *Dirks* holding is designed, at least in part, to protect this activity as long as the insider's motives are benign. More recently, however, the SEC and other market participants have begun to view the provision of information to a privileged few as unfair to average investors. Thus, there has been a significant regulatory shift in the direction of encouraging or requiring simultaneous disclosure to all. *See* 17 C.F.R. §§243.100-243.103 (2000) (Regulation "FD," which provides that when an issuer discloses material nonpublic information to securities market professionals and holders of the issuer's securities, it must make public disclosure of that information).

   Do you think that this is a positive or negative trend for the securities markets?

PROBLEM 6-3

The officers of ABC Corporation decide to discuss the pros and cons of a buy-out of XYZ Corporation at a private luncheon. They ask for, and receive, a private dining room. However, the room is located across from the restroom. At one point the discussion becomes heated, and the company CEO says, in a loud voice: "Come on. XYZ is so undervalued that buying it now is a no-brainer. If we wait six months, who knows whether the opportunity will still be there." Fred, a restaurant customer, was coming out of the men's room as this was being said. He recognizes the CEO from having seen his picture in the business pages of the local newspaper a while back. Fred puts two and two together and purchases a large amount of XYZ stock. When ABC announces its buyout, Fred makes a killing. Is Fred liable for insider trading? What if Fred were a waiter serving at the luncheon?

E. Intricacies of the Doctrine

1. Knowing Possession

UNITED STATES v. SMITH
155 F.3d 1051 (9th Cir. 1998)

O'Scannlain, Circuit Judge:

In this appeal from an insider securities trading conviction, we must decide . . . whether conviction requires proof of actual use of that inside information.

PDA Engineering, Inc. ("PDA") was, in 1993, a software design firm with headquarters in Orange County, California. Shares in PDA were publicly traded on the National Association of Securities Dealers Exchange (commonly referred to as "NASDAQ"). Richard Smith served as PDA's Vice President for North American Sales and worked in PDA's Nashville, Tennessee, office. By early 1993, after nearly three years with PDA, Smith had accumulated 51,445 shares of PDA stock.

In a series of transactions between June 10 and June 18, 1993, Smith liquidated his entire position in PDA. In addition to selling his own shares, Smith "sold short"[1] 25,000 shares on July 8, and another 10,000 shares on July 20. Smith's parents also sold and sold short a total of 12,000 shares.

Amidst this flurry of sales activity, on June 19, Smith telephoned Angela Bravo de Rueda ("Bravo"), an employee in the Los Angeles office of PDA, and left her the following voicemail message:

> Hi, Angie, Rich. . . . I talked to Tom last night after I left you some messages and he and Lou discovered that there was about a million and a half dollar mistake in the budget, so now we're back at ground zero and we've got to scramble for the next few days. Anyway, finally I sold all my stock off on Friday and I'm going to short the stock because I know it's going to go down a couple of points here in the next week as soon as Lou releases the information about next year's earnings. I'm more concerned about this year's earnings actually.

Unbeknownst to either Smith or Bravo, another Los Angeles-based PDA employee, Linda Alexander-Gore ("Gore"), guessed correctly Bravo's voicemail password and accessed Bravo's mailbox. When Gore encountered Smith's message, she forwarded it to her own mailbox. In order to retrieve it, she then called her own voicemail from her home telephone, played the message, and recorded it with a handheld audiotape recorder. After recording the message, Gore approached a

1. "Short selling is a device whereby the speculator sells stock which he does not own, anticipating that the price will decline and that he will thereby be enabled to 'cover,' or make delivery of the stock sold, by purchasing it at the lesser price. If the decline materializes, the short seller realizes as a profit the differential between the sales price and the lower purchase or covering price." Louis Loss & Joel Seligman, *Fundamentals of Securities Regulation* 699 (3d ed.1988) (quoting Stock Exchange Practices, Report of Comm. on Banking & Currency, S. Rep. No. 1455, 73d Cong., 2d Sess. 50-51 (1934)) (internal quotation marks omitted).

co-worker, Robert Phillips ("Phillips"). She informed him of the general nature of the communication and provided him with a copy of the recording.

Phillips listened to the message and telephoned the United States Attorney's Office for the Central District of California, where he spoke to Assistant United States Attorney Bart Williams ("Williams"). Phillips told Williams that he believed he had information, in the form of an audiotape, that indicated possible criminal activity. . . .

Smith was indicted on eleven counts of insider trading in violation of §10(b) of the Securities Exchange Act of 1934, 15 U.S.C. §78j(b), and SEC Rule 10b-5, 17 C.F.R. §240.10b-5. . . .

Although the use-possession debate has attracted a good deal of attention from academic commentators, very few courts (and none in this circuit) have addressed the issue head on. In support of their proposed "possession-only" standard, the government and the SEC rely principally upon dictum from a Second Circuit case, United States v. Teicher, 987 F.2d 112, 119 (2d Cir. 1993). The court in *Teicher* suggested, without squarely deciding, that proof of "knowing possession" is sufficient to sustain an insider trading prosecution and that the government need not affirmatively prove that the investor used the information in formulating his trade. For support, the court pointed to "a number of factors." First, it asserted that the SEC has "consistently endorsed" a knowing-possession standard, and that the agency's interpretation of Rule 10b-5 in that respect is "entitled to some consideration." Second, the court found the less exacting knowing-possession standard to be more consistent with the language of §10(b) and Rule 10b-5, both of which require only that a deceptive trade practice be conducted "in connection with" the purchase or sale of a security. Third, the court observed that a knowing-possession standard "comports with the oft-quoted maxim that one with a fiduciary or similar duty to hold material nonpublic information in confidence must either 'disclose or abstain' with regard to trading." Finally, the *Teicher* court pointed to what it believed to be the probable, yet subtle (indeed perhaps unconscious), effect that inside information has on traders:

> Because the advantage [an inside trader has over other traders] is in the form of information, it exists in the mind of the trader. Unlike a loaded weapon which may stand ready but unused, material information can not lay idle in the human brain.

Id. at 120-21.

Despite the Second Circuit's thoughtful analysis, we believe that the weight of authority supports a "use" requirement. Perhaps most significantly, the Supreme Court has consistently suggested, albeit in dictum, that Rule 10b-5 requires that the government prove causation in insider trading prosecutions. Indeed, just last Term, in United States v. O'Hagan, 521 U.S. 642 (1997), the Court indicated that an insider trading suspect must actually use the information to which he is privy, observing that "[u]nder the 'traditional' or 'classical theory' of insider trading liability, §10(b) and Rule 10b-5 are violated when a corporate insider trades in the securities of his corporation *on the basis of* material, nonpublic information." The *O'Hagan* Court was even more explicit in a separate portion of the opinion: "[T]he fiduciary's fraud is consummated, not when the fiduciary gains the confidential information, but when, without disclosure to his principal, he *uses the information* to purchase or sell securities." The Court's earlier decisions sound a similar theme. . . .

In addition to suggestions from the Supreme Court, the only court of appeals squarely to consider the causation issue concluded that Rule 10b-5 does, in fact, entail a "use" requirement. *See* SEC v. Adler, 137 F.3d 1325, 1337-39 (11th Cir. 1998). . . . The *Adler* court also thought a "use" requirement more consistent with the language of §10(b) and Rule 10b-5, which emphasizes "manipulat[ion]," "decept[ion]," and "fraud." We agree. By focusing exclusively upon the phrase "in connection with," the Second Circuit, we think, lost sight of the law's main thrust. After all, §10(b) and Rule 10b-5 do not just prohibit certain unspecified acts "in connection with" the purchase or sale of securities; rather, they prohibit the employment of "manipulative" and "deceptive" trading practices in connection with those transactions. . . .

Moreover, with respect to our colleagues on the Second Circuit, we do not believe that the "oft-quoted maxim" of "disclose or abstain," supports a knowing-possession standard. The trouble with "oft-quoted maxims," of course, is that they rarely, if ever, capture the complexity of the idea that they are supposed to represent. "Disclose or abstain" is no exception. It was absolutely clear both in *Chiarella*, upon which the *Teicher* court relied for its "disclose or abstain" citation, and in *Cady, Roberts*, upon which *Chiarella* relied, that the suspected inside traders had, in fact, *used* inside information in consummating their trades. Indeed, in *Cady, Roberts*, the wellspring of the "disclose or abstain" principle, the SEC premised its decision, at least in part, on the proposition that "[a] significant purpose of the Exchange Act was to eliminate the idea that the *use* of inside information for personal advantage was a normal emolument of corporate office." Consequently, understood in its proper context, we believe that the latter half of the maxim "disclose *or abstain*" enjoins not *all* trading, but trading *on the basis of material nonpublic information.*

We do not take lightly the SEC's argument that a "use" requirement poses difficulties of proof. . . . We nonetheless adhere to our view that Rule 10b-5 entails a "use" requirement. We appreciate that a "use" requirement renders criminal prosecutions marginally more difficult for the government to prove. The difficulties, however, are by no means insuperable. It is certainly not necessary that the government present a smoking gun in every insider trading prosecution. (Not that a smoking gun will always be beyond the government's reach; consider, for instance, that in this case Bravo might herself have gone to the authorities with Smith's statement that "I'm going to short the stock because I know it's going to go down a couple of points here in the next week as soon as Lou releases the information about next year's earnings.") Any number of types of circumstantial evidence might be relevant to the causation issue. Suppose, for instance, that an individual who has never before invested comes into possession of material nonpublic information and the very next day invests a significant sum of money in substantially out-of-the-money call options. We are confident that the government would have little trouble demonstrating "use" in such a situation, or in other situations in which unique trading patterns or unusually large trading quantities suggest that an investor had used inside information.

Consequently, we reject the government's proffered "knowing possession" standard for insider trading violations as contrary the weight of existing authority. Rather, we hold that Rule 10b-5 requires that the government (or the SEC, as the case may be) demonstrate that the suspected inside trader actually used material nonpublic information in consummating his transaction.

Smith contends that the district court's instructions in this case were insufficient as a matter of law. Specifically, he complains that "a jury instruction which allows the government to obtain a conviction *without* proof that the defendant traded in stock '*because of* the material nonpublic information' that he possessed, effectively wipes out the scienter requirement as defined by this Court and the Supreme Court." As a legal matter, he is correct. The trouble for Smith lies not in the law but in the facts, because the district court in this case *did* require proof of causation. It specifically instructed the jury that "the government must prove that the defendant sold or sold short PDA stock *because of* material nonpublic information that he knowingly possessed" and cautioned that "[i]t is *not* sufficient that the government proves that the defendant sold or sold short PDA stock while knowingly in possession of the material nonpublic information." In other words, even under the more rigorous "use" standard that we adopt today, Smith has nothing to complain about. We must therefore reject Smith's challenge to the district court's state-of-mind instruction.

For the foregoing reasons, the district court's decision is affirmed in all respects.

NOTES AND QUESTIONS

1. In 2000, the SEC promulgated Rule 10b5-1, which defines "on the basis of" for purposes of insider trading to mean "knowing possession." It thereby purported to overrule the *Smith* interpretation for future cases. Does the SEC have the authority to manage insider trading through the promulgation of regulations? If so, why did it wait 56 years—and suffer many adverse court opinions—before doing so? Can it reverse a prior court of appeals decision by regulation?
2. In addition to interpreting the phrase "on the basis of," Rule 10b5-1 provides "safe-harbor" provisions through which corporate insiders can trade in the stock of their own company. Without following the strictures of the rule, it is nearly impossible for an insider to trade without running afoul of the insider trading prohibition. Explain the different ways a corporate insider might legally structure her trading under the regulation.
3. Martha Stewart's primary defense against insider trading charges was that she had ordered her stockbroker, Peter Bacanovic, to sell her ImClone holdings when and if the price dropped to $60 per share. The alleged order was made orally during a review of her portfolio and was noted by the number "60" handwritten on a computer printout next to the word "ImClone." If true, was this sufficient evidence to satisfy Rule 10b5-1? Is it relevant that other evidence indicated that, on the day he sold her ImClone shares, Bacanovic tried to call Stewart to let her know he was planning to sell?

2. Closely Held Corporations; Familial Disclosures

UNITED STATES v. CHESTMAN

947 F.2d 551 (1991) (en banc), cert. denied, 503 U.S. 1004 (1992)

MESKILL, Circuit Judge:

The issues [in this case] spring from the alleged insider trading of defendant Robert Chestman. . . . A panel of this Court reversed Chestman's convictions in their entirety. . . .

Background

Robert Chestman is a stockbroker. Keith Loeb first sought Chestman's services in 1982, when Loeb decided to consolidate his and his wife's holdings in Waldbaum, Inc. (Waldbaum), a publicly traded company that owned a large supermarket chain. During their initial meeting, Loeb told Chestman that his wife was a granddaughter of Julia Waldbaum, a member of the board of directors of Waldbaum and the wife of its founder. Julia Waldbaum also was the mother of Ira Waldbaum, the president and controlling shareholder of Waldbaum. From 1982 to 1986, Chestman executed several transactions involving Waldbaum restricted and common stock for Keith Loeb. To facilitate some of these trades, Loeb sent Chestman a copy of his wife's birth certificate, which indicated that his wife's mother was Shirley Waldbaum Witkin.

On November 21, 1986, Ira Waldbaum agreed to sell Waldbaum to the Great Atlantic and Pacific Tea Company (A & P). The resulting stock purchase agreement required Ira to tender a controlling block of Waldbaum shares to A & P at a price of $50 per share. Ira told three of his children, all employees of Waldbaum, about the pending sale two days later, admonishing them to keep the news quiet until a public announcement. He also told his sister, Shirley Witkin, and nephew, Robert Karin, about the sale, and offered to tender their shares along with his controlling block of shares to enable them to avoid the administrative difficulty of tendering after the public announcement. He cautioned them "that [the sale was] not to be discussed," that it was to remain confidential.

In spite of Ira's counsel, Shirley told her daughter, Susan Loeb, on November 24 that Ira was selling the company. Shirley warned Susan not to tell anyone except her husband, Keith Loeb, because disclosure could ruin the sale. The next day, Susan told her husband about the pending tender offer and cautioned him not to tell anyone because "it could possibly ruin the sale."

The following day, November 26, Keith Loeb telephoned Robert Chestman at 8:59 A.M. Unable to reach Chestman, Loeb left a message asking Chestman to call him "ASAP." According to Loeb, he later spoke with Chestman between 9:00 A.M. and 10:30 A.M. that morning and told Chestman that he had "some definite, some accurate information" that Waldbaum was about to be sold at a "substantially higher" price than its market value. Loeb asked Chestman several times what he thought Loeb should do. Chestman responded that he could not advise Loeb what to do "in a situation like this" and that Loeb would have to make up his own mind.

That morning Chestman executed several purchases of Waldbaum stock. At 9:49 A.M., he bought 3,000 shares for his own account at $24.65 per share. Between 11:31 A.M. and 12:35 P.M., he purchased an additional 8,000 shares for his clients' discretionary accounts at prices ranging from $25.75 to $26.00 per share. One of the discretionary accounts was the Loeb account, for which Chestman bought 1,000 shares.

Before the market closed at 4:00 P.M., Loeb claims that he telephoned Chestman a second time. During their conversation Loeb again pressed Chestman for advice. Chestman repeated that he could not advise Loeb "in a situation like this," but then said that, based on his research, Waldbaum was a "buy." Loeb subsequently ordered 1,000 shares of Waldbaum stock.

Chestman presented a different version of the day's events. Before the SEC and at trial, he claimed that he had purchased Waldbaum stock based on his own research. He stated that his purchases were consistent with previous purchases of Waldbaum stock and other retail food stocks and were supported by reports in trade publications as well as the unusually high trading volume of the stock on November 25. He denied having spoken to Loeb about Waldbaum stock on the day of the trades.

At the close of trading on November 26, the tender offer was publicly announced. Waldbaum stock rose to $49 per share the next business day. In December 1986 Loeb learned that the National Association of Securities Dealers had started an investigation concerning transactions in Waldbaum stock. . . . Loeb [eventually] agreed . . . to cooperate with the government. The terms of his cooperation agreement required that he disgorge the $25,000 profit from his purchase and sale of Waldbaum stock and pay a $25,000 fine. . . .

Chestman's Rule 10b-5 convictions were based on the misappropriation theory, which provides that "one who misappropriates nonpublic information in breach of a fiduciary duty and trades on that information to his own advantage violates Section 10(b) and Rule 10b-5. With respect to the shares Chestman purchased on behalf of Keith Loeb, Chestman was convicted of aiding and abetting Loeb's misappropriation of nonpublic information in breach of a duty Loeb owed to the Waldbaum family and to his wife Susan. As to the shares Chestman purchased for himself and his other clients, Chestman was convicted as a "tippee" of that same misappropriated information. Thus, while Chestman is the defendant in this case, the alleged misappropriator was Keith Loeb. The government agrees that Chestman's convictions cannot be sustained unless there was sufficient evidence to show that (1) Keith Loeb breached a duty owed to the Waldbaum family or Susan Loeb based on a fiduciary or similar relationship of trust and confidence, and (2) Chestman knew that Loeb had done so. We have heretofore never applied the misappropriation theory—and its predicate requirement of a fiduciary breach—in the context of family relationships. . . .

3. Fiduciary Duties and Their Functional Equivalent

Against this backdrop, we turn to our central inquiry—what constitutes a fiduciary or similar relationship of trust and confidence in the context of Rule 10b-5 criminal liability? We begin by noting two factors that do not themselves create the necessary relationship.

First, a fiduciary duty cannot be imposed unilaterally by entrusting a person with confidential information. . . .

Second, marriage does not, without more, create a fiduciary relationship. "'[M]ere kinship does not of itself establish a confidential relation.' . . . Rather, the existence of a confidential relationship must be determined independently of a preexisting family relationship." Although spouses certainly may by their conduct become fiduciaries, the marriage relationship alone does not impose fiduciary status. In sum, more than the gratuitous reposal of a secret to another who happens to be a family member is required to establish a fiduciary or similar relationship of trust and confidence.

We take our cues as to what *is* required to create the requisite relationship from the securities fraud precedents and the common law. The common law has recognized that some associations are inherently fiduciary. Counted among these hornbook fiduciary relations are those existing between attorney and client, executor and heir, guardian and ward, principal and agent, trustee and trust beneficiary, and senior corporate official and shareholder. While this list is by no means exhaustive, it is clear that the relationships involved in this case—those between Keith and Susan Loeb and between Keith Loeb and the Waldbaum family—were not traditional fiduciary relationships.

That does not end our inquiry, however. The misappropriation theory requires us to consider not only whether there exists a fiduciary relationship but also whether there exists a "similar relationship of trust and confidence." As the term "similar" implies, a "relationship of trust and confidence" must share the essential characteristics of a fiduciary association. . . .

"[A]t the heart of the fiduciary relationship" lies "reliance, and de facto control and dominance." The relation "exists when confidence is reposed on one side and there is resulting superiority and influence on the other." One acts in a "fiduciary capacity" when

> the business which he transacts, or the money or property which he handles, is not his own or for his own benefit, but for the benefit of another person, as to whom he stands in a relation implying and necessitating great confidence and trust on the one part and a high degree of good faith on the other part.

Black's Law Dictionary 564 (5th ed. 1979).

A fiduciary relationship involves discretionary authority and dependency: One person depends on another—the fiduciary—to serve his interests. In relying on a fiduciary to act for his benefit, the beneficiary of the relation may entrust the fiduciary with custody over property of one sort or another. Because the fiduciary obtains access to this property to serve the ends of the fiduciary relationship, he becomes duty-bound not to appropriate the property for his own use. What has been said of an agent's duty of confidentiality applies with equal force to other fiduciary relations: "an agent is subject to a duty to the principal not to use or to communicate information confidentially given him by the principal or acquired by him during the course of or on account of his agency." Restatement (Second) of Agency §395 (1958). These characteristics represent the measure of the paradigmatic fiduciary relationship. A similar relationship of trust and confidence consequently must share these qualities.

In United States v. Reed, 601 F. Supp. 685 (S.D.N.Y. 1985), the district court confronted the question whether these principal characteristics of a fiduciary relationship—dependency and influence—were necessary factual prerequisites to a similar relationship of trust and confidence. There a member of the board of directors of Amax, Gordon Reed, disclosed to his son on several occasions confidential information concerning a proposed tender offer for Amax. Allegedly relying on this information, the son purchased Amax stock call options. The son was subsequently indicted for violating, among other things, Rule 10b-5 based on breach of a fiduciary duty arising between the father and son. The son then moved to dismiss the indictment, contending that he did not breach a fiduciary duty to his father. The district court sustained the indictment.

Both the government and Chestman rely on *Reed.* The government draws on *Reed*'s application of the misappropriation theory in the family context and its expansive construction of relationships of trust and confidence. Chestman, without challenging the holding in *Reed*, argues that *Reed* cannot sustain his Rule 10b-5 convictions because, unlike Reed senior and junior, Keith and Susan Loeb did not customarily repose confidential business information in one another. Neither party challenges the holding of *Reed.* And we decline to do so *sua sponte.* To remain consistent with our interpretation of a "similar relationship of trust and confidence," however, we limit *Reed* to its essential holding: the repeated disclosure of business secrets between family members may substitute for a factual finding of dependence and influence and thereby sustain a finding of the functional equivalent of a fiduciary relationship. We note, in this regard, that *Reed* repeatedly emphasized that the father and son "frequently discussed business affairs." . . .

4. Application of the Law of Fiduciary Duties

. . . We have little trouble finding the evidence insufficient to establish a fiduciary relationship or its functional equivalent between Keith Loeb and the Waldbaum family. . . .

The government's theory that Keith breached a fiduciary duty of confidentiality to Susan suffers from similar defects. The evidence showed: Keith and Susan were married; Susan admonished Keith not to disclose that Waldbaum was the target of a tender offer; and the two had shared and maintained confidences in the past.

Keith's status as Susan's husband could not itself establish fiduciary status. Nor, absent a pre-existing fiduciary relation or an express agreement of confidentiality, could the coda—"Don't tell." That leaves the unremarkable testimony that Keith and Susan had shared and maintained generic confidences before. The jury was not told the nature of these past disclosures and therefore it could not reasonably find a relationship that inspired fiduciary, rather than normal marital, obligations.

In the absence of evidence of an explicit acceptance by Keith of a duty of confidentiality, the context of the disclosure takes on special import. While acceptance may be implied, it must be implied from a pre-existing fiduciary-like relationship between the parties. . . . The government failed even to establish a pattern of sharing business confidences between the couple. The government, therefore, failed to offer sufficient evidence to establish the functional equivalent of a fiduciary relationship.

In sum, because Keith owed neither Susan nor the Waldbaum family a fiduciary duty or its functional equivalent, he did not defraud them by disclosing news of the pending tender offer to Chestman. Absent a predicate act of fraud by Keith Loeb, the alleged misappropriator, Chestman could not be derivatively liable as Loeb's tippee or as an aider and abettor. Therefore, Chestman's Rule 10b-5 convictions must be reversed. . . .

3. Tippee of Misappropriator?

MICHAEL L. SEIGEL & CHRISTOPHER SLOBOGIN, PROSECUTING MARTHA: FEDERAL PROSECUTORIAL POWER AND THE NEED FOR A LAW OF COUNTS

109 Penn. St. L. Rev. 1107 (2005)

Martha Stewart has just completed her five-month sentence in a West Virginia federal prison, imposed after her conviction on four counts of a five-count indictment. Stewart's case has spawned a cottage industry of commentary. Many have pointed out that the well-known queen of domestic perfection was not prosecuted for insider trading—which was the original focus of the government's investigation and the offense that most casual observers think sent her to jail—but rather for lying about why she traded, charges that have been characterized as both "trivial" and "extraneous." . . .

On December 28, 2001, the value of ImClone stock dropped a precipitous sixteen percent after the announcement that the Food and Drug Administration had declined to review ImClone's key cancer drug, Erbitux. As a matter of routine policy, regulators at the SEC examined the trading of ImClone just prior to its steep decline, looking to see if any insiders or relatives of insiders had traded the stock before the bad news became public. They immediately discovered that both children of ImClone CEO Sam Waksal had, in fact, traded ImClone shares on December 27, one through a Prudential Securities account and one through Merrill Lynch. Inquiries at Merrill Lynch revealed that Sam Waksal had also attempted to sell his own shares of ImClone on the same day, but could not; to its credit, Merrill Lynch blocked the trade. Waksal then transferred these shares to his daughter's account and tried to sell them through her. Once again, Merrill Lynch refused to execute the trade.

It must have been around this time that SEC investigators discovered Martha Stewart's December 27 ImClone trades from her Merrill Lynch account. One can only imagine their reaction at seeing such a famous name appear in the midst of their investigation. They quickly figured out that Waksal and Stewart were close friends. This raised the specter—wrong as it turned out—that Stewart had traded after receiving an inside tip from the company's CEO. The SEC continued its administrative investigation. On January 7, 2002, SEC staff attorneys interviewed Peter Bacanovic, Waksal's former employee as well as his and Stewart's broker at Merrill Lynch. On January 8, the SEC issued a voluntary request for production of documents to ImClone.

It was only at this point, sometime between January 8 and January 25, that the FBI and the U.S. Attorney's Office joined the investigation. Thus, the U.S. Attorney's Office's determination to participate in the Stewart case came only after the SEC's discovery of her potentially illicit trading and its initiation of an official inquiry. From the public record, it is difficult to discern whether the prosecutors were asked aboard by agency investigators or instead read about the case in the media and joined the investigation on their own. Either way, at the time they became involved there was significant circumstantial evidence suggesting that Stewart had committed insider trading as a classic tippee, evidence that could not be ignored.

Of course, the possibility exists that prosecutors decided to pursue Stewart's case for suspect reasons, based on sexism, a political agenda, or a desire to bask in the media limelight. But in a high profile case like Stewart's, the conscientious prosecutor is strongly motivated to take a leading role early in the investigation to ensure that no embarrassing missteps take place. Further, it is perfectly legitimate to target conspicuous violators so that the deterrent effect of criminal law is maximized. Perhaps most important, if a high profile case identified by the SEC were not aggressively investigated under his or her watch, the U.S. Attorney would undoubtedly be accused of favoring the rich and famous. All of these considerations likely influenced the U.S. Attorney's decision to join and pursue the securities investigation.

But what about the prosecutors' ultimate decision to charge Stewart for lying, rather than insider trading? We again can only speculate as to why the latter charge was not brought. Clearly, the original theory of the case—that Stewart had traded on a tip from the company's CEO—did not pan out; instead, the tip had come solely from inside the brokerage house. Although the lower courts have thus far agreed that trading on such a tip constitutes a violation of the insider trading law,[19] the Supreme Court has yet to rule on a case in which a putative inside trader received her tip from a misappropriator. There are several reasons why the U.S. Attorney's Office might not have wanted Stewart's case to be the one to test that proposition in the latter forum (where Stewart surely would have taken it). First, Stewart had the resources to mount the most vigorous, expert defense. Second, the mere fact of Stewart's notoriety might give her a tactical advantage; subconsciously, judges and justices are more likely to have sympathy for someone with fame and fortune. Third, losing to a celebrity at the Supreme Court level would be a conspicuous black eye for the Department of Justice. Better, then, to place this issue on the civil side—which the current SEC case against Stewart does—where the government's burden of proof is lower (critical to success on the mens rea issue) and where a loss would not be so harmful to the government's prestige.

But then why not leave Stewart alone? Others have expressed concern over what have been aptly named "sideshow" charges, especially when those charges are

19. Criminal cases holding that there is liability in this situation include United States v. Mylett, 97 F.3d 663 (2d Cir. 1996), cert. denied 521 U.S. 1119 (1997); United States v. Libera, 989 F.2d 596 (2d Cir.), cert. denied, 510 U.S. 976 (1993); United States v. Falcone, 97 F. Supp. 297 (E.D.N.Y. 2000) (reluctantly following the holding in *Libera*). Regulatory cases imposing such liability, which are precedent for criminal cases, include SEC v. Maio, 51 F.3d 623 (7th Cir. 1995); SEC v. Grossman, 887 F. Supp. 649 (S.D.N.Y. 1995); SEC v. Musella, 748 F. Supp. 1028 (S.D.N.Y. 1989).

primarily based on denials of other, more substantive (alleged) criminal conduct. That concern is appropriate in some cases. But Stewart's cover-up went beyond a simple denial; as we detail in the next section, the prosecution also had solid reason to believe that Stewart had made numerous false statements, altered evidence (if only momentarily), and suborned perjury by her broker.

In short, at the time of charging, the prosecution reasonably could have believed that Stewart had done something plainly wrong, separate and apart from trading on inside information. She not only gave into the understandable but regrettable human instinct to dissemble when confronted with a hand in the cookie jar, but she also tried to muddy the evidentiary trail and lasso a colleague into covering up the swindle. Stewart's conduct may have been near the threshold where prosecutors should avoid filing an indictment. But her conduct was not "trivial." And the charges were not "extraneous" to the criminal justice system's legitimate goals of punishing blameworthy actions and ensuring the efficient prosecution of criminal acts.

NOTES AND QUESTIONS

1. Do you agree with Seigel and Slobogin that "it is perfectly legitimate to target conspicuous violators so that the deterrent effect of criminal law is maximized"? Doesn't that mean that celebrities are treated more harshly than other individuals merely because of their notoriety? On the other hand, as long as they've broken the law, do they really have much standing to complain?
2. Are you bothered by the "sideshow charges" issue? Prosecutors' response to the criticism is that indicting those who try to obstruct criminal and grand jury investigations is essential to vindicate the integrity of the process. Do you agree, or is it a situation in which the tail is wagging the dog?
3. Consider the following excerpt from Stephen Joyce, *Insider Trading Violations Now Evolving Into "Actual Business Model," Official Says*, BNA White Collar Crime Report, 6 WCR 258 (Mar. 25, 2011):

> Insider trading conduct is changing from relatively small, single episodes of illegal behavior to an "actual business model," where rings of sophisticated businesspeople from several distinct industries repeatedly break the law to reap huge illicit gains, [according to] Securities and Exchange Commission Associate Regional Director David Rosenfeld.
>
> In the past, individuals would obtain material nonpublic information about a publicly traded firm—perhaps bad news about the company for which they worked—and trade on that information, Rosenfeld said. Such violations "tended to be one-off, opportunistic trading," he said.
>
> But today, insider trading cases involve sophisticated conspiracies populated by highly paid corporate executives, investors, and financial consultants who engage in frequent and intentional violations of insider trading laws, he said.
>
> "What we're seeing more of recently is not opportunistic, it's not one-off, but rather people who are engaged in multiple instances of insider trading

> and actually going out to try to get material nonpublic information for the sole purpose of trading on it," Rosenfeld said. The SEC official added that it is a "new trend" that the agency is "seeing a lot more."

What do you make of this "new trend?" Is it because technology—e-mail, Facebook, Twitter—make inside communication so much easier than before? Or has there been a diminution of morality among business insiders? Alternatively, is it possible that the conduct has always been there and it's only recently that DOJ has worked aggressively to uncover it?

VI. SARBANES-OXLEY ACT

STUART R. COHN, SECURITIES COUNSELING FOR SMALL AND EMERGING COMPANIES

§1.4 (Sept. 2007)

The Enron and other corporate scandals during 2001-2002 led Congress to enact strong new measures affecting auditing, disclosure, and corporate governance issues. The Sarbanes-Oxley Act of 2002 is a potpourri of measures applicable to public-reporting companies. The legislation does not directly affect smaller, non-public companies, but for those companies that eventually go public they will find reporting and compliance costs to be significant.

Among the principal measures adopted are:

1. *Public Company Accounting Oversight Board:* This newly created board, under the supervision and review of the S.E.C., is charged with establishing auditing, quality control, ethics, and independence standards for public company auditors. The S.E.C. appoints the five members of the Board.
2. *Auditor Independence:* Public accounting firms are prohibited from providing non-audit services contemporaneously with audit services.
3. *Certification of Financial Reports*: The principal executive officer and the principal financial officer are required to [personally] certify annual and quarterly reports to the S.E.C. This provision has caused the greatest consternation and anxiety among corporate management. Each of the officers must attest that, based on their knowledge, their firm's financial results "fairly present" the financial condition of the company. Criminal liability is imposed for false certifications, including fines up to $5 million and 20 years imprisonment for willful violations.
4. *Audit Committees*: The S.E.C. is directed to create rules that call for the de-listing, and prohibition of listing, of securities of any company that does not have an audit committee composed solely of independent directors. The audit committee has authority to engage outside counsel and other advisers as it deems appropriate.
5. *Prohibition of Personal Loans*: No corporate loans may be made to any director or officer, including the arrangement for the extension of credit or the renewal of an extension of credit. Pre-existing loans may continue

as long as they are not materially modified or extended. This provision overrides the authority granted in state corporation laws to provide loans to, or guarantee obligations of, corporate officers.

6. *Prohibition of Certain Bonuses and Compensation*: If a company re-states its financial statements because of prior material non-compliance with financial reporting requirements, the issuer's CEO and CFO must reimburse the company for any bonuses or other incentive-based compensation received, and any profits realized from the sale of issuer's securities, during the 12-month period prior to the restatement.
7. *Accelerated Reporting of Insider Transactions*: Directors, executive officers, and 10% shareholders must report transactions in the issuer's securities within two business days. This materially shortens the reporting time required by Section 16 of the 1934 Exchange Act.
8. *Prohibition of Insider Trading During Pension Fund Blackout Periods*: Directors and executive officers are prohibited from trading in their company's securities during any pension fund blackout period. This provision is a direct response to the sales by certain officers of Enron during a period when the employees' pension fund could not trade because of a blackout period.
9. *Rules of Professional Responsibility for Attorneys*: The S.E.C. is directed to establish rules requiring attorneys that practice securities law to report violations of securities law or breach of fiduciary duty to the CEO or chief legal counsel and, if no action is taken, to the company's audit committee.

The statute contains numerous other provisions affecting securities and corporate law matters. Counsel representing a publicly-held company, or a company about to undertake a public offering, should review all the provisions and advise their clients as to their scope and reach.

NOTES AND QUESTIONS

1. Sarbanes-Oxley also amended the criminal law. It created a new securities fraud crime, 18 U.S.C. §1348, with a maximum penalty of 25 years imprisonment. This provision does away with the requirement under Rule 10b-5 that the fraud must be "in connection with the purchase or sale of any security" and replaces it with the more easily met standard that the fraud be "in connection with any [registered] security." Sarbanes-Oxley also created a new fraud-specific conspiracy crime, 18 U.S.C. §1349, which eliminates the overt act requirement of and has higher penalties than 18 U.S.C. §371. Finally, S-O raised the maximum penalties for a variety of white collar and fraud-related crimes.

2. A Westlaw search conducted on June 1, 2011, indicated that 18 U.S.C. §1348 had been charged in a total of three cases since the statute became effective in 2002. Why do you think that prosecutors are eschewing the use of this powerful tool?

SARITA MOHANTY, SARBANES-OXLEY: CAN ONE MODEL FIT ALL?

12 New Eng. J. Int'l & Comp. L. 231, 246-249 (2006)

The most striking features of the [Sarbanes-Oxley] Act are the creation of the Public Company Accounting Oversight Board, and the increased penalties on public companies and their executives, directors, and auditors. Most of the provisions of the new act apply to public companies (reporting companies) that file a Form 10-K with the SEC.

The Sarbanes-Oxley Act provides for a five-member Public Company Accounting Oversight Board to oversee the audit of public companies, establish audit report standards and rules, and inspect, investigate and enforce compliance by registered public accounting firms. The Act also requires the registration of public accounting firms, domestic and foreign, that audit reports for any issuer. The Board is empowered to set up and amend auditing standards, ethics standards, and quality controls that are used in the preparation of audit reports by the registered public accounting firms. The public accounting firms are required to have a second partner review and approve the audit. They must also evaluate whether the company's internal control system includes records that accurately reflect the nature of transactions and assets, and must report any material weaknesses in the internal controls or any material noncompliance. The Board can bring disciplinary actions against registered firms and their associates for willful or repeated negligent conduct.

To uphold their independence, the act prohibits auditors from performing a number of non-audit services and requires the audit committee to approve the non-audit services that they do perform. It also requires auditors' rotation by prohibiting an audit partner from being the lead or the reviewing auditor for more than five consecutive years. To preserve their independence, the Act prohibits public accounting firms from performing audits of issuers whose senior executives had been employed by the firm and had participated in the audit of the issuer during the one-year period preceding the audit initiation date. The audit committee should be comprised of independent directors of the company and is responsible for the appointment, compensation, and oversight of the registered public accounting firm employed to perform audit services. The audit committee has the authority to hire independent counsel and other advisors.

The act also addresses the issue of corporate responsibility. It instructs the SEC to promulgate rules requiring the CEO and CFO of a company to certify the periodic financial reports. The act also has provisions for enhanced financial disclosures. It mandates that the financial reports filed with the SEC reflect "all material correcting adjustments that have been identified." The Act requires senior management, directors, and principal stockholders to disclose their securities ownership worth ten percent or more within ten days, and any securities based on swap agreements within two business days of acquiring ownership. The annual reports are to include an internal control report, which states that the management is responsible for the internal control structure. They are also to include the procedures for financial reporting and an assessment the effectiveness of the internal controls for the previous fiscal year. The issuer must disclose whether it has adopted a code of ethics and whether its audit committee consists of at least one member who is a financial expert. If not, the issuer must explain why. The act also mandates regular and systematic SEC review of periodic disclosures by issuers, including a review of an issuer's financial statement.

The act has enhanced penalty provisions for both willful and negligent misconduct. It imposes criminal penalties for knowingly destroying or falsifying records with the intent to obstruct a federal investigation or a matter in bankruptcy. The Act also protects whistleblowers by prohibiting a publicly traded company from retaliating against an employee for assisting in an investigation of fraud or other conduct by federal regulators, Congress, or supervisors. . . .

Sarbanes-Oxley also penalizes corporate fraud for tampering with a record or impeding an official proceeding. Additionally, the SEC is authorized to prohibit persons who have violated specified rules from serving as officers or directors of a publicly traded corporation. . . .

LARRY E. RIBSTEIN, MARKET VS. REGULATORY RESPONSES TO CORPORATE FRAUD: A CRITIQUE OF THE SARBANES-OXLEY ACT OF 2002

28 J. Corp. L. 1 (2002)

[B]efore adopting regulatory solutions it is necessary to consider the feasibility of market-based responses. . . . [M]arket-based approaches have high prospects of success now that the risks of defective accounting have become as obvious to market participants as they have become to politicians and regulators. Indeed, it was markets and not regulators that uncovered the problems and adjusted the share prices of offending companies, while years of regulation of securities disclosures and of the membership of boards of directors failed to prevent the frauds. In other words, dishonest insiders were able to outrun the kinds of monitors that regulators favor, but not, ultimately, the markets.

If markets can react, there are significant benefits to allowing them to do so. Market actors are likely to be better informed and motivated than regulators. Markets also lead to a variety of competing solutions. As long as these solutions are evaluated in liquid securities markets, the most efficient solutions are likely to dominate, and firms can pick the approaches that best suit their particular circumstances. A political or regulatory approach will pick a particular approach that may not be the most efficient overall . . . , and may be unsuitable for many firms.

Although market responses are likely to be imperfect, it is necessary to compare market with regulatory imperfections, rather than unrealistically assuming that only markets are flawed. Moreover, it is important to keep in mind that markets have been constrained by past regulation, particularly including of takeovers and of insider trading. Although repeal of this regulation may be politically infeasible amid calls for more regulation of the securities markets, it is worth reflecting on the contribution of past regulation to current problems when considering whether additional regulation is appropriate.

Th[ere are] several potential market-type responses to corporate fraud: relying on newly alerted markets to police corporate frauds (subpart A); signaling by honest firms to differentiate themselves from dishonest competitors for capital (subpart B); [and] more shareholder policing of firms (subpart C)....

A. Market Scrutiny

Most of the corporate frauds that have been exposed so far left tracks in the record that observant market watchers noticed before they caught the public's eye. For example, in February, 2001, long before the disclosures of fall, 2001, a hedge fund manager named Jim Chanos, had figured out that Enron had become a derivatives speculator with unhedged investments. Fundamental risks of Enron's business, particularly including its susceptibility to competition in the various markets it was entering, and the implausibility of the assumptions underlying its market were obvious to astute observers. Moreover, footnotes to financial statements disclosed the basic facts, if not the details, of its potential exposure to debts incurred by special purpose entities.

This discussion indicates that the market can significantly reduce its vulnerability to fraud simply by paying closer attention to warning signs. This might include watching for discrepancies in firms' figures, reading fine print such as financial statement footnotes, and relying on "harder" numbers such as free cash flow that are not affected by firms' decisions on capitalizing and amortizing expenses. Markets also can observe firms' vulnerability to and methods of monitoring fraud, such as relationships with auditors. For example, a recent study showed not only that firms have a greater tendency to "manage" earnings the more non-audit services they bought from their audit firms, but also that investors tended to devalue firms that disclosed unexpected purchases of non-audit services. Market skepticism is more likely now that investor biases have moved from over-optimism to excessive pessimism. In the current environment, firms, analysts, auditors and others have a strong incentive to signal their integrity and independence, as discussed below in subpart B.

Although market scrutiny of corporate conduct can increase without changes in the law, the level of market scrutiny is affected by past regulation. Regulation's perverse effects in this regard counsel caution about the desirability of additional regulation. An example is Regulation FD, which the SEC promulgated in August, 2000. This rule requires firms that disclose material nonpublic information to securities analysts to publicly disclose the same information simultaneously or promptly. The strongest argument for the Regulation is that it reduces the chance of analyst complicity in corporate fraud. The SEC argued in its proposing release that the rule would reduce firms' incentive to "delay general public disclosure so that they can selectively disclose the information to curry favor or bolster credibility with particular analysts or institutional investors," and analysts' incentive "to slant reports in order to maintain access" to disclosing firms' information. Moreover, the Regulation technically leaves corporate insiders free to disclose material information broadly to the market, and to continue private discussions with analysts as long as they do not disclose material non-public information. In any event, the

Regulation might seem to have no effect on disclosure of corporate fraud, which insiders would have no incentive to disclose voluntarily to analysts.

The actual effect of the Regulation, however, may be to reduce analysts' ability to uncover fraud. . . . [S]elective disclosure of material information is an important tool for disclosure of general information about firms that even honest firms would not disclose more broadly. . . .

B. Signaling

Advocates of more regulation would argue that the securities market is now one for "lemons" that investors would tend to avoid because they cannot distinguish the quality products from the defective ones. This is a reference to the theory of George Akerlof, who shared the 2001 Nobel Prize for Economics. Notably, however, the Prize also was awarded to Michael Spence and Joseph Stiglitz for work concerning market responses to this problem, particularly including signaling by potential sellers to avoid being classed with lemons. In securities markets, issuers have strong incentives to demonstrate to investors, consumers, creditors, potential employees and others that they are not like Enron and WorldCom. This is particularly the case for firms using now-suspect devices such as derivatives and special purpose entities. Firms can signal, among other ways, by maintaining a high level of voluntary disclosure, including through meetings with and disclosures to securities analysts and the media, or by voluntarily adopting reforms such as expensing stock options, as several companies have done.

Auditors also can signal the objectivity and care of their services by, for example, clearly separating audit and non-audit services or getting out of the non-audit business. Alternatively, issuers can compete in the way they purchase audit and non-audit services. Issuers can signal the markets about the honesty of their books by, for example, not buying non-audit services from the same firms that audit their books and periodically switching audit firms. Notably, they will do this not just because they are ordered to do so by independent audit committees, but because the securities markets demand it.

Insurance can be an important method of signaling, in which the size of the premium reliably indicates the extent of the insured risk. Insurance is a particularly useful signal because of insurers' strong incentives to be accurate in setting premia, and because firms have non-signaling incentives to buy insurance. There is evidence that the premium a company pays for directors' and officers' liability insurance accurately indicates the quality of a firm's governance arrangements. Premia in the so-called "credit-default-swap" market, in which debt-holders effectively insure against default, recently have appeared reliably to indicate increasing risks associated with debtors. Issuers also might signal honesty by buying "financial statement insurance," where the insurance carrier hires the auditor and provides the signal.

The potential for signaling may not only reduce the benefits of regulation, but also may increase its cost. Mandatory governance rules reduce firms' ability to signal quality by choosing governance forms, auditors, disclosure methods and so forth. If these mechanisms have significant benefits for investors in all companies, *and* if firms have inadequate incentive to signal, then the costs of allowing opting out might exceed the benefits of effectuating signaling. But if firms have incentives to signal quality and regulation is excessively burdensome for some firms, then the availability of signaling is an argument against regulation.

C. Shareholder Monitoring and Takeovers

Firms are subject to scrutiny not only by various capital and other markets, but also by their own shareholders. Shareholders do not need to wait for corporate managers or regulators to decide that firms need protection from fraud. First, institutional shareholders can press for these changes through direct communication with managers, as TIAA-CREF has done regarding expensing of stock options, and through shareholder proposals through which the shareholder can gather support from other shareholders. Even if private institutions do not gain enough from such moves to invest significant resources in them, managers of public funds have political incentives to do so. In light of the political salience of the issue, firms' managers likely would respond positively to high-visibility institutional holders like TIAA-CREF and to shareholder proposals receiving significant, even if minority, votes. The proposals could serve as firm-by-firm referenda testing the level of shareholder acceptance of various alternatives, by contrast with federal laws or SEC rules imposed on all firms. Aggregation of shares in institutional holders may increase because of the declining confidence of amateur investors discussed in subpart A.

Second, and more importantly, there is a theoretical potential for monitoring by outside bidders for control. Bidders have the sort of high-powered, profit-driven incentives that independent directors, auditors and analysts may lack. Even insiders in firms that are never subject to hostile bids may be less likely to take excessive compensation or to engage in fraud if they know potential hostile bidders are watching them. Among other things, bidders for control could buy firms that have hired low-quality auditors, directors or managers, fire the monitors and hire new ones, and pocket the resulting difference in the share price. . . .

NOTES AND QUESTIONS

1. Professor Ribstein takes the position that regulation is counterproductive—that, left alone, the market would regulate itself. Does he make a convincing case? One of the arguments he makes is that historical crashes prove regulation does not work. But can this be said about the stock market crash in 1929? That predates significant government intervention in the marketplace, doesn't it?
2. What does it mean to say that "the market can significantly reduce its vulnerability to fraud simply by paying closer attention to warning signs"? What conditions would make "the market" do that in the future that have not existed in the past?
3. Ribstein contends that "mandatory governance rules reduce firms' ability to signal quality by choosing governance forms, auditors, disclosure methods

and so forth." Implicit in this argument is that, left to their own devices, corporations would do a better job of signaling to the market their financial health. Perhaps. But wouldn't companies also have an incentive to fluff up or even falsify their signals, especially if the firm was not in good health?

4. Does the "Great Recession" of 2008 prove that even the level of Sarbanes-Oxley regulation is insufficient to control market excesses? Or does it help prove Ribstein's contention that regulation is counterproductive?
5. Some observers argued that Sarbanes-Oxley went too far because it made compliance too costly, especially for small publicly traded companies. They claimed that, in response to Sarbanes-Oxley, many of these companies would go private or move to foreign stock exchanges, thereby removing them from U.S. regulatory oversight altogether. Is this a valid argument against S-O? Is there a reason why public corporations merit closer scrutiny compared to private ones? In any event, it turned out that, as an empirical matter, the fear of a mass exodus from U.S. stock exchanges was unfounded. *See* John Gibeaut, *Private Drive: New Twists in Sarbanes-Oxley May Compel More Smaller Companies to Exit the Market*, A.B.A. J. (Jan. 2005) (noting that the "exodus predicted in the law's immediate wake never took off").

chapter 7

False Statements and False Claims

I. INTRODUCTION

The false statements statute, 18 U.S.C. §1001, and the false claims statute, 18 U.S.C. §287, both trace their origins to a Civil War provision passed by Congress to curb the practice of military personnel filing false claims against the Union government.[1] Congress expanded the statute in 1874 to cover the filing of false claims by any person. In 1918, it amended the statute once again to include corporations among its targets. Throughout this period of time, the legislation was limited to instances in which the defendant's intention was to cheat the government out of money or property.

After the rise of the regulatory state that followed the Great Depression, this limitation became a significant weakness. With the federal government now enmeshed in so many aspects of the country's economic life, bureaucrats became increasingly dependent on information supplied to them by people and corporations. This information had to be accurate for the government to succeed in playing its oversight role. As a result, after several attempts at change, in 1948, Congress finally split the old Civil War statute into the two separate provisions we see today: the false claims statute, which retains a pecuniary element at its core, and the false statements statute, which is rooted in simple deception.

This chapter examines the crime of false statements first, and then it takes up the issue of false claims. As you read the cases dealing with the former, you might want to pay attention to how the interpretation of a criminal statute can, over time, increase its scope far beyond the intention of the original drafters.

1. Act of Mar. 2, 1863, ch. 67, 12 Stat. 696, 696-697 (1863).

II. FALSE STATEMENTS TO A DEPARTMENT OR AGENCY OF THE UNITED STATES: 18 U.S.C. §1001

A. Mens Rea

UNITED STATES v. HILDEBRANDT

961 F.2d 116 (8th Cir. 1992)

JOHN R. GIBSON, Circuit Judge.

Norbert L. Hildebrandt appeals both the judgment and his sentence following his conviction of two counts of submitting false statements to a government agency in violation of 18 U.S.C. §1001 (1988). The charges were based on Hildebrandt's sending to the IRS false forms claiming that he had paid various individuals large sums of money. On appeal, Hildebrandt argues that: (1) the district court committed reversible error by failing to instruct the jury that a subjective good faith belief that one is not violating the law negates the willfulness element of section 1001. . . . We affirm the judgment of the district court.

Hildebrandt was a Minnesota farmer who had serious financial troubles during the 1980s. When the bank that had acted as his lender stopped covering checks for which he lacked sufficient funds and also stopped extending him additional credit, Hildebrandt could not keep up the payments on his farm. The State of Minnesota, which held the mortgage, then foreclosed on his property.

Hildebrandt then discovered the teachings of one Roger Elvick, who sold tapes and other materials that informed farmers about their supposed legal rights. Hildebrandt obtained a package of taped and written materials called "Introduction to Redemption."

Following Elvick's teachings, Hildebrandt sent IRS Form 1099 to various individuals whom he believed had conspired to take away his farm and deprive him of his legal rights. Recipients included law enforcement personnel, judges, lenders, attorneys, and creditors who had been involved in some fashion with the foreclosure on Hildebrandt's farm or with other legal proceedings involving Hildebrandt.

IRS Form 1099 is used to report non-wage compensation. Hildebrandt, calculating "all of the damages that had incurred to me and my family through the denial of my rights," treated these losses as the taxable gain of his victims. For instance, law enforcement officers who had enforced court orders against him and judges who had ruled adversely to him received 1099 forms stating that they had received various sums of money from Hildebrandt as non-wage compensation.

Twice in 1989, Hildebrandt filed false 1099 forms with the IRS. With both filings, he included a cover sheet, Form 1096, which summarized the information contained in the attached 1099 forms. On these forms, Hildebrandt claimed to have paid a total of about $68,000,000 in non-wage compensation. He also signed a statement on one of the 1096 forms stating that "under penalties of perjury" he declared that he had "examined this return and accompanying documents" and that to the best of his "knowledge and belief they are true, correct, and complete."

The IRS uses computers to compare the data reported on a particular Form 1099 with the tax return of the individual who purportedly received the income reported on the 1099. Tax examiners investigate any discrepancy between the two forms. Taxpayers bear the burden of explaining any such discrepancy.

Hildebrandt testified at trial that he believed the forms he filed were not false and that he had a legal duty to file them. He further testified that he expected the IRS to collect the taxes due on the income he had reported on the 1099 forms. Based on his sending the false 1096 and 1099 forms to the IRS, a jury convicted Hildebrandt on two counts of knowingly and willfully making false statements to a government agency in violation of 18 U.S.C. §1001. The court sentenced him to one year in prison followed by a two-year period of supervised release.

I.

Hildebrandt asserts that the district court committed reversible error by failing to give a "good faith" defense instruction[3] based on the Supreme Court's recent decision in Cheek v. United States, 498 U.S. 192 (1991).

A jury convicted the defendant in *Cheek* of willfully failing to file federal income tax returns and willfully attempting to evade income taxes. The Supreme Court held that the district court erred by instructing the jury to disregard evidence that Cheek believed that he was not required to file a return or pay income taxes. A defendant's good faith belief that he is not violating the tax laws negates the statutory willfulness requirement, whether or not that good faith belief is objectively reasonable. Although ignorance of the law traditionally is no defense, Congress has carved out an exception to that rule in certain criminal tax statutes by making "specific intent to violate the law" one of the elements. Such special treatment is largely premised on the "complexity of the tax laws," which have so proliferated that the average citizen may have difficulty "comprehend[ing] the extent of [his] duties and obligations."

Although *Cheek* did not address whether its holding extends beyond the criminal tax context, its statement that certain criminal tax offenses are accorded "special treatment" because of the complexity of the tax laws strongly suggests that its holding is limited to the tax area. In United States v. Dashney, 937 F.2d 532 (10th Cir.), *cert. denied*, 502 U.S. 951 (1991), the Tenth Circuit refused to apply *Cheek* to violations of currency reporting statutes, drawing a distinction between the complexity of tax statutes and the "straightforward currency reporting requirements." *Id.* at 540.

We believe a similar distinction exists here. The statutes at issue in *Cheek* required a "willful[ ] attempt[ ] . . . to evade or defeat any tax," 26 U.S.C. §7201 (1988), and a "willful[ ] fail[ure]" to file a required tax return, 26 U.S.C.A. §7203

3. Hildebrandt submitted a proposed instruction that stated:

> Willfulness is defined as a voluntary, intentional violation of a known legal duty.
>
> A good faith misunderstanding of the law or a good faith belief that one is not violating the law negates willfulness, whether or not the claimed belief or misunderstanding is objectively reasonable.

(West Supp. 1991). The Court defined willfulness in this context as the voluntary and intentional violation of a known legal duty. The government must prove that the defendant knew of his duty, and its effort fails "if the jury credits [the defendant's submission] of a good faith misunderstanding and belief."

In contrast, 18 U.S.C. §1001 concerns not a willful failure to act, but the willful doing of a prohibited act. To violate section 1001 in the manner relevant here, the defendant must knowingly and willfully make a material, false statement in any matter within a government agency's jurisdiction. In the context of this statute, the term "willful" simply means that the defendant did the forbidden act "'deliberately and with knowledge.'"

The district court here instructed the jury that to convict the defendant it must find that: (1) he "knowingly made or used a false, fictitious, fraudulent writing or document in submitting 1989 Forms 1096 and 1099 to the IRS"; (2) "[a]t the time [he] did so, he knew that the forms contained a false, fictitious or fraudulent statement"; and (3) "[he] did these acts knowingly, voluntarily and intentionally."

We conclude that these instructions correctly conveyed the substance of the relevant law and that the district court did not err by refusing an instruction based on the Supreme Court's holding in *Cheek.*

Hildebrandt also argues that even if section 1001 does not on its face invite an application of *Cheek*, that a *Cheek* instruction is nonetheless required here because his case arises from a tax matter.

We reject this argument. The *Cheek* holding was premised on the complexity of the tax laws, and Hildebrandt was convicted under a general criminal statute containing a straightforward prohibition against making false, fictitious, or fraudulent statements to the government. If *Cheek* is to be expanded, that expansion must be made by the Supreme Court. . . .

For the foregoing reasons, we affirm the judgment of the district court.

NOTES AND QUESTIONS

1. Given the court's interpretation in *Hildebrandt*, does the term "willfully" add anything to §1001's mens rea requirement? The court says that willfully adds the notion that the defendant's conduct must be deliberate and intentional, not accidental. But isn't that concept already covered by the term "knowingly"? Is it possible to "know" you are providing a false statement to the U.S. government and at the same time do it accidentally? If not, isn't the court violating a fundamental principle of statutory construction: the presumption that legislatures place each word into a statute to serve a useful purpose?
2. We have seen that "willfully" has different meanings in different contexts, including securities fraud, tax fraud, and false statements. Can you articulate and compare the distinct definitions of "willfulness" used for these three purposes?

UNITED STATES v. SHAH

44 F.3d 285 (5th Cir. 1995)

GARWOOD, Circuit Judge. . . .

On June 9, 1992, the General Services Administration (GSA) issued a solicitation for the purchase of irons, ironing boards, and ironing board pads. The solicitation called for a bid from each of a number of prospective suppliers. Because the bid was to be negotiated, not sealed, the offeror was allowed to alter the price after submission but before the award. Among the prospective bidders was Omega Electronics (Omega), a small California company that had held the previous contract for steam irons with GSA. Omega had also previously dealt with GSA and the GSA contract specialist, Linda Brainard (Brainard), on an undisclosed number of small purchase contracts. Brainard testified that these contracts occasioned numerous telephone contacts between her and Shah, Omega's president.

On July 1, 1992, GSA mailed the solicitation for iron products to Omega's address in San Carlos, California. The solicitation contained the following language under section 13, entitled "Certificate of Independent Price Determination":

> "(a) The offeror certifies that—
>
> (1) The prices in this offer have been arrived at independently, without, for the purpose of restricting competition, any consultation, communication, or agreement with any other offeror or competitor relating to (i) those prices, (ii) the intention to submit an offer, or (iii) the methods or factors used to calculate the prices offered;
>
> (2) The prices in this offer have not been and will not be knowingly disclosed by the offeror, directly or indirectly, to any other offeror or competitor before bid opening (in the case of a sealed bid solicitation) or before contract award (in the case of a negotiated solicitation) unless otherwise required by law; and
>
> (3) No attempt has been made or will be made by the offeror to induce any other concern to submit or not to submit an offer for the purpose of restricting competition.
>
> "(b) Each signature on the offer is considered to be a certification . . . that the signatory—
>
> (1) . . . has not participated and will not participate in any action contrary to subparagraphs (a)(1) through (a)(3) above. . . ."

The same solicitation was also sent to Kipper & Company, a New York concern specializing in the supply of hand and power tools to commercial and governmental customers. Jerome Kipper (Kipper), president of Kipper & Company, testified that he and Shah had spoken a "few times" on the telephone. Besides these conversations, which occurred sometime in November or December of 1991, Shah and Kipper communicated only occasionally and very briefly during the early part of 1992.

On July 7, 1992, shortly after Omega received the GSA solicitation but one day before Omega sent it out, Shah telephoned Kipper and suggested that they share their bids. Shah explained that, by fixing and exchanging price information, they could rig the bidding and thus split the award. According to his plan, Shah would acquire the delivery depots west of the Mississippi, while Kipper would take those to the east. In response to this proposal, Kipper told Shah that he "questioned . . . [Shah's] ethic but admired his ambition." Although he clearly did not agree to trade price information, Kipper testified that he was "non-committal" at the close of the conversation. Shah again left his phone number.

The next day, July 8, 1992, Shah signed and mailed the solicitation to GSA, in which he certified that the prices contained in the bid "have not been and will not be disclosed." In the solicitation, he identified himself as the Managing Partner of Omega and listed the San Carlos, California, address as well as the telephone number earlier given to Kipper. Shah also filled in blanks throughout the solicitation, including information above and below section 13, the certification of independent price determination.

Kipper reported his July 7 conversation with Shah to both GSA and his attorney. Under the supervision of a GSA investigator, Kipper made two telephone calls to Shah on July 15, 1992, several days after both Kipper and Shah had submitted their bids to GSA. Both conversations were recorded and transcribed. In the first call, Kipper introduced himself and apologized for not having called him back "the other day." In vague terms, Kipper reminded Shah of their July 7 conversation. After agreeing that they could still withdraw their submitted bids, Shah asserted that the swapping of price information would be to their mutual advantage. When Kipper asked Shah if he had ever swapped prices with other vendors, Shah answered,

> "No. This is the first occasion and I—you sounded that you're a . . . shrewd businessman, and you will understand the logistics and mechanics of it, so that's why I talk to you frankly. I wouldn't be talking . . . like this to anybody else.
>
> "MR. KIPPER: Okay.
>
> "MR. SHAH: I just took a calculated risk, rather. You know, you can only talk . . . to certain people, not all the people would be cooperative and all that. . . . I hope you understand what I'm saying."

Without detailing a plan to swap prices, Kipper ended the conversation and told Shah he would call him back. The jury heard this entire conversation. Although the transcript and audiotape of the second July 15 conversation were not put in evidence, Kipper testified that, during that conversation, they agreed to fax to each other their bids and, further, that Shah requested confidentiality. They then carried out this agreement.

On January 6, 1993, a grand jury returned a one-count indictment against Shah charging him with "knowingly and willfully" having made a "false, fictitious and fraudulent" statement to GSA, a government agency, contrary to 18 U.S.C. §1001, namely "the statement that the prices in this offer have not been and will not be knowingly disclosed by the offeror, directly or indirectly, to any other offeror or competitor before bid opening or contract award." . . . Shah was tried and convicted before a jury in July 1993. . . . [He] filed a timely appeal.

Discussion

On appeal, Shah . . . argues that a promise of future performance cannot, as a matter of law, constitute a violation of 18 U.S.C. §1001. . . .

Section 1001, known as the False [Statements] Act, prohibits the knowing and willful making of "false, fictitious or fraudulent statements or representations" on a matter "within the jurisdiction of any department or agency of the United States." 18 U.S.C. §1001. The purpose of this broadly worded statute is "to protect the authorized functions of governmental departments and agencies from the perversion which might result from . . . deceptive practices." United States v. Gilliand, 312 U.S. 86, 93 (1941). To establish a violation, the government must prove five elements: "(1) a statement, that is (2) false (3) and material, (4) made with the requisite specific intent, [and] (5) within the purview of government agency jurisdiction." United States v. Puente, 982 F.2d 156, 158 (5th Cir.), *cert. denied*, 113 S. Ct. 2934 (1993). With regard to the "requisite specific intent," we have observed, "A false representation is one . . . made with an intent to deceive or mislead." United States v. Guzman, 781 F.2d 428, 431 (5th Cir.), *cert. denied*, 475 U.S. 1143 (1986). In words more relevant to this case, the district court correctly instructed the jury that the government must prove "that the defendant made the false statement for the purposes of misleading the General Services Administration."

The central issue in this case, however, focuses only on the second element, falsity. We are asked to decide whether what Shah stated or represented in the solicitation could violate section 1001, and, if so, whether the government proved that it did. The critical language in the solicitation reads, "The prices in this offer have not been and will not be knowingly disclosed by the offeror . . . to any other offeror or competitor before . . . contract award." The statement was made when Shah submitted the solicitation on July 8, 1992. As of that date, there is no evidence that Shah had disclosed any price information. He had only proposed doing so the day before. It was not until July 15 that Shah actually disclosed the information. Therefore, only the "will not disclose" portion of the statement is at issue.

By disclosing his bid to a competitor, Shah broke a promise made and certified in the solicitation. As the government concedes, however, a broken promise is not alone a basis for criminal liability under section 1001. Otherwise, as Shah correctly points out, every breach of a governmental contract would be converted into a section 1001 false statement, thus exposing the breaching party to criminal prosecution. To establish a violation, then, the government must prove, among other things, that the statement "I will not disclose price information before the contract award" was false *when made*. Shah contends that this statement can be neither true nor false when made because it is simply a *prediction* of future performance. As such, the statement is either true or false only after the promise is carried out or broken. The government, on the other hand, argues that this statement clearly implies and manifests an intent which itself may render a promise true or false when made and which may be proved by circumstantial evidence of Shah's state of mind. According to the government, if Shah all the while intended to disclose price information, but nevertheless promised not to, he made a false and fraudulent statement to GSA in violation of section 1001. . . .

This distinction is critical. In the present context, the statement "I will not disclose prices" is something more than a prediction; it clearly contains a necessary implication, signified by the phrase "I will," that the maker intends to do what he promises. *See Restatement (Second) of Torts* §530(1) cmt. c ("Since a promise *necessarily* carries with it the implied assertion of an intention to perform it follows that a promise made without such an intention is fraudulent. . . .") (emphasis added). The implication is necessary because the statement's meaning depends on it. In the setting of this case, the statement "I will not disclose prices, but I intend to disclose prices" is nonsense because the second clause negates the communicated meaning of the first.

That a promise can inherently be false when made is supported by case law not cited by either party. In Elmore v. United States, 267 F.2d 595 (4th Cir.), *cert. denied*, 361 U.S. 832 (1959), the defendant was convicted of making false statements and representations on an application to the Farmers Home Administration in violation of the Commodity Credit Corporation Act, 15 U.S.C. §714m(a). The defendant purchased surplus wheat from the government on the condition that the wheat be used only to feed livestock or poultry. Although the defendant certified as much, the wheat was later used for other purposes. Following his conviction, the defendant argued that "false statements" should be confined to "false statements of existing fact":

> "Since the statements by the defendant in regard to the 4200 bushels of wheat purchased . . . were not statements of facts but promises as to the future use of the commodity, it is said that he committed no crime. . . . It is said that if Congress had intended to make false promises as to the future a criminal offense . . . , it would have made express provision therefore as it did in 18 U.S.C. §1341 [the mail fraud statute]. . . ." *Id.* at 603.

The court rejected this argument and read the statute to cover "false and fraudulent promises which the maker does not intend to perform." In terms of frustrating the purpose of the act, the court could see no practical difference between false statements and false promises:

> "[I]t cannot be supposed that Congress intended to direct the criminal sanctions of the act only against those who make false statements of existing fact and to exculpate those who should obtain surplus commodities by making false promises which they do not intend to fulfill. In practical effect, *a false promise fraudulently given amounts to a false statement of an existing intent* and it can be as destructive as the false statement of a material fact. We think Congress intended to cover it by the statute." (emphasis added). . . .

Albeit implicit, this Court's assumption in prior cases that a promise can be a false statement is supported by the common law of fraud. Although "[i]t is a general rule that fraud cannot be predicated upon statements which are promissory in their nature at the time they are made and which relate to future action or conduct," 37 *Am. Jur. 2d*, Fraud and Deceit, §60, it is also generally accepted, under common law principles, that

> "fraud may be predicated on promises made with a present intention not to perform them or, as the rule is frequently expressed, on promises made without any intention of performance. . . . The gist of the fraud . . . is not the breach of

> the agreement to perform, but the fraudulent intent of the promisor, the false representation of an existing intention to perform where such intent is in fact nonexistent. . . . The generally accepted modern theory categorizes a promise which the promisor does not intend to carry out, as a misstatement of material and subsisting fact."

Furthermore, "[a] person's statement that he intends to do something when he has no present intention of doing it is a false statement of an existing fact, because it falsely represents the state of his mind, and the state of his mind is a fact." *Id.* §64 (footnote omitted). *See also Restatement (Second) of Torts* §530(1) ("A representation of the maker's own intention to do or not to do a particular thing is fraudulent if he does not have that intention"). This common-law understanding of fraud comports with the words and purpose of section 1001. . . .

For the foregoing reasons, we reject Shah's contention that a "promise to perform" cannot, as a matter of law, ever violate section 1001. We hold that, under section 1001, a promise may amount to a "false, fictitious or fraudulent" statement if it is made without any present intention of performance and under circumstances such that it plainly, albeit implicitly, represents the present existence of an intent to perform.

In the present setting, it is clear that the statement or promise implicitly represents Shah's present intent. We now determine whether the government proved falsity in this case. Shah claims, in his first evidentiary point, that the evidence was inadequate to support the necessary premise that Shah had no intention of carrying out the promise when he made it. We view the evidence in the light most favorable to the jury verdict and will affirm if a rational trier of fact could find that the government proved all essential elements of the crime beyond a reasonable doubt. As mentioned earlier, whether a defendant intended to perform is a question of fact concerning the defendant's state of mind. The mere fact of subsequent nonperformance is not alone sufficient for conviction. Although the call is a close one, we cannot say that the circumstantial evidence in this case was insufficient to justify the verdict. Courts have routinely relied on circumstantial evidence to support such false-promise determinations. . . .

Conclusion

For the foregoing reasons, the judgment of the district court is
AFFIRMED.

NOTES AND QUESTIONS

1. The court in *Shah* does a very nice job of setting out the elements of §1001, including a description of the mens rea requirement. Can you locate this discussion?
2. The mens rea requirement for §1001 is intent to deceive, not intent to defraud. What is the difference between the two? Is it a meaningful distinction? What statutes have we studied that require the latter intent?

3. Do you agree with the court's analysis that a promise can be a false statement if the promissor has no present intention to fulfill it? Could this interpretation lead to a criminal investigation every time a party to a contract with the federal government commited a breach?

UNITED STATES v. YERMIAN

468 U.S. 63 (1984)

Justice POWELL delivered the opinion of the Court.

It is a federal crime under 18 U.S.C. §1001 to make any false or fraudulent statement in any matter within the jurisdiction of a federal agency. To establish a violation of §1001, the Government must prove beyond a reasonable doubt that the statement was made with knowledge of its falsity. This case presents the question whether the Government also must prove that the false statement was made with actual knowledge of federal agency jurisdiction.

I.

Respondent Esmail Yermian was convicted in the District Court of Central California on three counts of making false statements in a matter within the jurisdiction of a federal agency, in violation of §1001. The convictions were based on false statements respondent supplied his employer in connection with a Department of Defense security questionnaire. Respondent was hired in 1979 by Gulton Industries, a defense contractor. Because respondent was to have access to classified material in the course of his employment, he was required to obtain a Department of Defense Security Clearance. To this end, Gulton's security officer asked respondent to fill out a "Worksheet For Preparation of Personnel Security Questionnaire."

In response to a question on the worksheet asking whether he had ever been charged with any violation of law, respondent failed to disclose that in 1978 he had been convicted of mail fraud, in violation of 18 U.S.C. §1341. In describing his employment history, respondent falsely stated that he had been employed by two companies that had in fact never employed him. The Gulton security officer typed these false representations onto a form entitled "Department of Defense Personnel Security Questionnaire." Respondent reviewed the typed document for errors and signed a certification stating that his answers were "true, complete, and correct to the best of [his] knowledge" and that he understood "that any misrepresentation or false statement . . . may subject [him] to prosecution under section 1001 of the United States Criminal Code."

After witnessing respondent's signature, Gulton's security officer mailed the typed form to the Defense Industrial Security Clearance Office for processing. Government investigators subsequently discovered that respondent had submitted false statements on the security questionnaire. Confronted with this discovery, respondent acknowledged that he had responded falsely to questions regarding his criminal record and employment history. On the basis of these false statements, respondent was charged with three counts in violation of §1001.

At trial, respondent admitted to having actual knowledge of the falsity of the statements he had submitted in response to the Department of Defense security questionnaire. He explained that he had made the false statements so that information on the security questionnaire would be consistent with similar fabrications he had submitted to Gulton in his employment application. Respondent's sole defense at trial was that he had no actual knowledge that his false statements would be transmitted to a federal agency.[2]

Consistent with this defense, respondent requested a jury instruction requiring the Government to prove not only that he had actual knowledge that his statements were false at the time they were made, but also that he had actual knowledge that those statements were made in a matter within the jurisdiction of a federal agency. The District Court rejected that request and instead instructed the jury that the Government must prove that respondent "knew or should have known that the information was to be submitted to a government agency." Respondent's objection to this instruction was overruled, and the jury returned convictions on all three counts charged in the indictment. . . .

The Court of Appeals for the Ninth Circuit reversed, holding that the District Court had erred in failing to give respondent's requested instruction. . . . The decision of the Court of Appeals for the Ninth Circuit conflicts with decisions by the three other Courts of Appeals that have considered the issue. We granted certiorari to resolve the conflict and now reverse.

II.

The only issue presented in this case is whether Congress intended the terms "knowingly and willfully" in §1001 to modify the statute's jurisdictional language, thereby requiring the Government to prove that false statements were made with actual knowledge of federal agency jurisdiction.[5] The issue thus presented is one of statutory interpretation. Accordingly, we turn first to the language of the statute.

2. Respondent maintained this defense despite the fact that both the worksheet and the questionnaire made reference to the Department of Defense, and the security questionnaire signed by respondent was captioned "Defense Department." The latter document also contained a reference to the "Defense Industrial Security Clearance Office," stated that respondent's work would require access to "secret" material, and informed respondent that his signature would grant "permission to the Department of Defense to obtain and review copies of [his] medical and institutional records." Nevertheless, respondent testified that he had not read the form carefully before signing it and thus had not noticed either the words "Department of Defense" on the first page or the certification printed above the signature block.

5. The Government never objected to the District Court's instruction requiring proof that respondent reasonably should have known that his false statements were made within the jurisdiction of a federal agency. Thus, in this case the Government was required to prove that federal agency jurisdiction was reasonably foreseeable.

A.

The relevant language of §1001 provides:

> "Whoever, in any matter within the jurisdiction of any department or agency of the United States knowingly and willfully . . . makes any false, fictitious or fraudulent statements or representations, . . . shall be fined. . . ."

The statutory language requiring that knowingly false statements be made "in any matter within the jurisdiction of any department or agency of the United States" is a jurisdictional requirement. Its primary purpose is to identify the factor that makes the false statement an appropriate subject for federal concern. Jurisdictional language need not contain the same culpability requirement as other elements of the offense. Indeed, we have held that "the existence of the fact that confers federal jurisdiction need not be one in the mind of the actor at the time he perpetrates the act made criminal by the federal statute." United States v. Feola, 420 U.S. 671, 676-677, n.9 (1975). Certainly in this case, the statutory language makes clear that Congress did not intend the terms "knowingly and willfully" to establish the standard of culpability for the jurisdictional element of §1001. The jurisdictional language appears in a phrase separate from the prohibited conduct modified by the terms "knowingly and willfully." Any natural reading of §1001, therefore, establishes that the terms "knowingly and willfully" modify only the making of "false, fictitious or fraudulent statements," and not the predicate circumstance that those statements be made in a matter within the jurisdiction of a federal agency. Once this is clear, there is no basis for requiring proof that the defendant had actual knowledge of federal agency jurisdiction. The statute contains no language suggesting any additional element of intent, such as a requirement that false statements be "knowingly made in a matter within federal agency jurisdiction," or "with the intent to deceive the Federal Government." On its face, therefore, §1001 requires that the Government prove that false statements were made knowingly and willfully, and it unambiguously dispenses with any requirement that the Government also prove that those statements were made with actual knowledge of federal agency jurisdiction. Respondent's argument that the legislative history of the statute supports a contrary interpretation is unpersuasive.

B.

The first federal criminal statute prohibiting the making of a false statement in matters within the jurisdiction of any federal agency was the Act of October 23, 1918 (1918 Act).[8] That Act provided in pertinent part:

> "[W]hoever, . . . for the purpose and with the intent of cheating and swindling or defrauding the Government of the United States, or any department thereof, . . .

8. The earliest predecessor of the 1918 Act limited its criminal sanctions to false claims made by military personnel and presented to "any person or officer in the civil or military service of the United States." Act of Mar. 2, 1863, 12 Stat. 696. . . .

> shall knowingly and willfully . . . make . . . any false or fraudulent statements or representations . . . shall be fined. . . ."

Interpreting that provision in United States v. Cohn, 270 U.S. 339 (1926), this Court held that only false statements made with intent to cause "pecuniary or property loss" to the Federal Government were prohibited. The Court rejected the Government's argument that the terms "with the intent of . . . defrauding" the Federal Government "should be construed as being used not merely in its primary sense of cheating the Government out of property or money, but also in the secondary sense of interfering with or obstructing one of its lawful governmental functions by deceitful and fraudulent means." The Court reasoned that if Congress had intended to prohibit all intentional deceit of the Federal Government, it would have used the broad language then employed in §37 of the Penal Code, which "by its specific terms, extends broadly to every conspiracy to defraud the United States 'in any manner and for any purpose,' with no words of limitation whatsoever."

Concerned that the 1918 Act, as thus narrowly construed, was insufficient to protect the authorized functions of federal agencies from a variety of deceptive practices, Congress undertook to amend the federal false-statements statute in 1934. The 1934 provision finally enacted, however, rejected the language suggested in *Cohn*, and evidenced a conscious choice not to limit the prohibition to false statements made with specific intent to deceive the Federal Government.

The first attempt to amend the false-statements statute was unsuccessful. After debates in both Houses, Congress passed H.R. 8046. That bill provided in pertinent part:

> "[E]very person who with the intent to defraud the United States knowingly or willfully makes . . . any false or fraudulent . . . statement, . . . concerning or pertaining to any matter within the jurisdiction of any department, establishment, administration, agency, office, board, or commission of the United States, . . . shall be punished by . . . fine . . . or by imprisonment . . . , or by both. . . ." 78 Cong. Rec. 3724 (1934).

President Roosevelt, however, vetoed the bill because it prohibited only those offenses already covered by the 1918 Act, while reducing the penalties. This was hardly the measure needed to increase the protection of federal agencies from the variety of deceptive practices plaguing the New Deal administration.

To remedy the President's concerns, Congress quickly passed a second bill that broadened the scope of the federal false-statements statute by omitting the specific-intent language of the prior bill. The 1934 provision finally enacted into law provided in pertinent part:

> "[W]hoever shall knowingly and willfully falsify or conceal or cover up by any trick, scheme, or device a material fact, or make . . . any false or fraudulent statements or representations, . . . in any matter within the jurisdiction of any department or agency of the United States . . . shall be fined. . . ." Act of June 18, 1934, ch. 587, 48 Stat. 996.

Noticeably lacking from this enactment is any requirement that the prohibited conduct be undertaken with specific intent to deceive the Federal Government, or with actual knowledge that false statements were made in a matter within federal agency jurisdiction. If Congress had intended to impose either requirement, it would have modified the prior bill by replacing the phrase "with intent to defraud the United States" with the phrase "with intent to deceive the United States," or by inserting the phrase "knowing such statements to be in any matter within the jurisdiction of any federal agency." That Congress did not include such language, either in the 1934 enactment or in the 1948 revision, provides convincing evidence that the statute does not require actual knowledge of federal involvement.

Finally, there is no support in the legislative history for respondent's argument that the terms "knowingly and willfully" modify the phrase "in any matter within the jurisdiction of [a federal agency]." The terms "knowingly and willfully" appeared in the 1918 Act, but the phrase "in any matter within the jurisdiction of [a federal agency]" did not. It is clear, therefore, that in the 1918 Act the terms "knowingly and willfully" did not require proof of actual knowledge of federal involvement. Nor does the legislative history suggest that by adding the jurisdictional prerequisite to the current provision Congress intended to extend the scope of those two terms. The jurisdictional language was added to the current provision solely to limit the reach of the false-statements statute to matters of federal interest.

By requiring proof of specific intent to defraud the United States, Congress limited the 1918 prohibition to matters pertaining to federal concern. There was no reason, therefore, to include the phrase "in any matter within the jurisdiction of [a federal agency]." Once the specific-intent language of the 1918 Act was eliminated, however, the current jurisdictional phrase was necessary to ensure that application of the federal prohibition remained limited to issues of federal concern. There is no indication that the addition of this phrase was intended also to change the meaning of the terms "knowingly and willfully" to require proof of actual knowledge of federal involvement. . . .

III.

Respondent argues that absent proof of actual knowledge of federal agency jurisdiction, §1001 becomes a "trap for the unwary," imposing criminal sanctions on "wholly innocent conduct." Whether or not respondent fairly may characterize the intentional and deliberate lies prohibited by the statute (and manifest in this case) as "wholly innocent conduct," this argument is not sufficient to overcome the express statutory language of §1001. Respondent does not argue that Congress lacks the power to impose criminal sanctions for deliberately false statements submitted to a federal agency, regardless of whether the person who made such statements actually knew that they were being submitted to the Federal Government. That is precisely what Congress has done here. In the unlikely event that §1001 could be the basis for imposing an unduly harsh result on those who intentionally make false statements to the Federal Government, it is for Congress and not this Court to amend the criminal statute.

IV.

Both the plain language and the legislative history establish that proof of actual knowledge of federal agency jurisdiction is not required under §1001. Accordingly, we reverse the decision of the Court of Appeals to the contrary.

It is so ordered.

Justice REHNQUIST, with whom Justice BRENNAN, Justice STEVENS, and Justice O'CONNOR join, dissenting.

It is common ground that in a prosecution for the making of false statements the Government must prove that the defendant actually knew that the statements were false at the time he made them. *See* Bryson v. United States, 396 U.S. 64, 68-70 (1969). The question presented here is whether the Government must also prove that the defendant actually knew that his statements were made in a matter within "the jurisdiction of any department or agency of the United States." The Court concludes that the plain language and the legislative history of 18 U.S.C. §1001 conclusively establish that the statute is intended to reach false statements made without actual knowledge of federal involvement in the subject matter of the false statements. I cannot agree.

The Court nonetheless proceeds on the assumption that some lesser culpability standard is required in §1001 prosecutions, but declines to decide what that lesser standard is. Even if I agreed with the Court that actual knowledge of federal involvement is not required here, I could not agree with the Court's disposition of this case because it reverses the Court of Appeals without determining for itself, or remanding for the lower court to determine, whether the jury instructions in respondent's case were proper. I think that our certiorari jurisdiction is best exercised to resolve conflicts in statutory construction, and not simply to decide whether a jury in a particular case was correctly charged as to the elements of the offense. But here the Court, in a remarkable display of left-footedness, accomplishes neither result: reading its opinion from beginning to end, one neither knows what the congressionally intended element of intent is, nor whether the jury was properly instructed in this case. . . .

NOTES AND QUESTIONS

1. Is the majority's reading of the legislative history correct? True, the original 1918 version of the statute attached the "knowingly and willfully" only to the making of the false statement itself. But that statute required the government to prove that the defendant had the "purpose" of "cheating and swindling or defrauding the government of the United States." Given that language, would it be possible to convict an individual who did not realize his statement was going to be delivered to an agent of the federal government?
2. Although the Supreme Court sidestepped the issue in *Yermian*, later courts of appeals clearly have come down on the side of making defendants strictly liable with respect to the jurisdictional element of §1001. *See, e.g.*, United States v. Dose, 2005 U.S. Dist. LEXIS 526 (N.D. Iowa Jan. 12, 2005); United States v. Green, 745 F.2d 1205 (9th Cir. 1984).

B. Materiality and "Jurisdiction"

UNITED STATES v. RODGERS
466 U.S. 475 (1984)

Justice REHNQUIST delivered the opinion of the Court.

Respondent Larry Rodgers was charged in a two-count indictment with making "false, fictitious or fraudulent statements" to the Federal Bureau of Investigation (FBI) and the United States Secret Service, in violation of 18 U.S.C. §1001. Rodgers allegedly lied in telling the FBI that his wife had been kidnapped and in telling the Secret Service that his wife was involved in a plot to kill the President. Rodgers moved to dismiss the indictment for failure to state an offense on the grounds that the investigation of kidnappings and the protection of the President are not matters "within the jurisdiction" of the respective agencies, as that phrase is used in §1001. The District Court for the Western District of Missouri granted the motion, and the United States Court of Appeals for the Eighth Circuit affirmed. We now reverse. The statutory language clearly encompasses criminal investigations conducted by the FBI and the Secret Service, and nothing in the legislative history indicates that Congress intended a more restricted reach for the statute.

On June 2, 1982, Larry Rodgers telephoned the Kansas City, Missouri, office of the FBI and reported that his wife had been kidnapped. The FBI spent over 100 agent hours investigating the alleged kidnapping only to determine that Rodgers' wife had left him voluntarily. Two weeks later, Rodgers contacted the Kansas City office of the Secret Service and reported that his "estranged girlfriend" (actually his wife) was involved in a plot to assassinate the President. The Secret Service spent over 150 hours of agent and clerical time investigating this threat and eventually located Rodgers' wife in Arizona. She stated that she left Kansas City to get away from her husband. Rodgers later confessed that he made the false reports to induce the federal agencies to locate his wife.

In granting Rodgers' motion to dismiss the indictment, the District Court considered itself bound by a prior decision of the Eighth Circuit in Friedman v. United States, 374 F.2d 363 (1967). *Friedman* also involved false statements made to the FBI to initiate a criminal investigation. In that case, the Court of Appeals reversed the defendant's conviction under §1001, holding that the phrase "within the jurisdiction," as used in that provision, referred only to "the power to make final or binding determinations." . . . The court concluded that false statements made to the FBI were not covered by §1001 because the FBI "had no power to adjudicate rights, establish binding regulations, compel the action or finally dispose of the problem giving rise to the inquiry."

In the present case, the Court of Appeals adhered to its decision in *Friedman* and affirmed the dismissal of the indictment. The court acknowledged that two other Courts of Appeals had expressly rejected the reasoning of *Friedman. See* United States v. Adler, 380 F.2d 917, 922 (CA2), *cert. denied*, 389 U.S. 1006 (1967); United States v. Lambert, 501 F.2d 943, 946 (CA5 1974) (en banc). But the Eighth Circuit found its own analysis more persuasive. We granted certiorari to resolve this conflict.

It seems to us that the interpretation of §1001 adopted by the Court of Appeals for the Eighth Circuit is unduly strained. Section 1001 expressly embraces false statements made "in any matter within the jurisdiction of any department or agency of the United States." A criminal investigation surely falls within the meaning of "any matter," and the FBI and the Secret Service equally surely qualify as "department[s] or agenc[ies] of the United States." The only possible verbal vehicle for narrowing the sweeping language Congress enacted is the word "jurisdiction." But we do not think that that term, as used in this statute, admits of the constricted construction given it by the Court of Appeals.

"Jurisdiction" is not defined in the statute. We therefore "start with the assumption that the legislative purpose is expressed by the ordinary meaning of the words used." The most natural, nontechnical reading of the statutory language is that it covers all matters confided to the authority of an agency or department. Thus, Webster's Third New International Dictionary 1227 (1976) broadly defines "jurisdiction" as, among other things, "the limits or territory within which any particular power may be exercised: sphere of authority." A department or agency has jurisdiction, in this sense, when it has the power to exercise authority in a particular situation. Understood in this way, the phrase "within the jurisdiction" merely differentiates the official, authorized functions of an agency or department from matters peripheral to the business of that body.

There are of course narrower, more technical meanings of the term "jurisdiction." For example, an alternative definition provided by Webster's is the "legal power to interpret and administer the law." *See also* Black's Law Dictionary 766 (5th ed. 1979). But a narrow, technical definition of this sort, limiting the statute's protections to judicial or quasi-judicial activities, clashes strongly with the sweeping, everyday language on either side of the term. It is also far too restricted to embrace some of the myriad governmental activities that we have previously concluded §1001 was designed to protect. . . .

There is no doubt that there exists a "statutory basis" for the authority of the FBI and the Secret Service over the investigations sparked by respondent Rodgers' false reports. The FBI is authorized "to detect and prosecute crimes against the United States," including kidnapping. And the Secret Service is authorized "to protect the person of the President." It is a perversion of these authorized functions to turn either agency into a Missing Person's Bureau for domestic squabbles. The knowing filing of a false crime report, leading to an investigation and possible prosecution, can also have grave consequences for the individuals accused of crime. There is, therefore, a "valid legislative interest in protecting the integrity of [such] official inquiries," an interest clearly embraced in, and furthered by, the broad language of §1001.

Limiting the term "jurisdiction" as used in this statute to "the power to make final or binding determinations," as the Court of Appeals thought it should be limited, would exclude from the coverage of the statute most, if not all, of the authorized activities of many "departments" and "agencies" of the Federal Government, and thereby defeat the purpose of Congress in using the broad inclusive language which it did. If the statute referred only to courts, a narrower construction of the word "jurisdiction" might well be indicated; but referring as it does to "any department or agency" we think that such a narrow construction is simply inconsistent with the rest of the statutory language.

The Court of Appeals supported its failure to give the statute a "literal interpretation" by offering several policy arguments in favor of a more limited construction. For example, the court noted that §1001 carries a penalty exceeding the penalty for perjury and argued that Congress could not have "considered it more serious for one to informally volunteer an untrue statement to an F.B.I. agent than to relate the same story under oath before a court of law." . . . The fact that the maximum possible penalty under §1001 marginally exceeds that for perjury provides no indication of the particular penalties, within the permitted range, that Congress thought appropriate for each of the myriad violations covered by the statute. Section 1001 covers "a variety of offenses and the penalties prescribed were maximum penalties which gave a range for judicial sentences according to the circumstances and gravity of particular violations."

Perhaps most influential in the reasoning of the court below was its perception that "the spectre of criminal prosecution" would make citizens hesitant to report suspected crimes and thereby thwart "the important social policy that is served by an open line of communication between the general public and law enforcement agencies." But the justification for this concern is debatable. Section 1001 only applies to those who "knowingly and willfully" lie to the Government. It seems likely that "individuals acting innocently and in good faith, will not be deterred from voluntarily giving information or making complaints to the F.B.I."

Even if we were more persuaded than we are by these policy arguments, the result in this case would be unchanged. Resolution of the pros and cons of whether a statute should sweep broadly or narrowly is for Congress. Its decision that the perversion of agency resources and the potential harm to those implicated by false reports of crime justifies punishing those who "knowingly and willfully" make such reports is not so "absurd or glaringly unjust," Sorrells v. United States, 287 U.S. 435, 450 (1932), as to lead us to question whether Congress actually intended what the plain language of §1001 so clearly imports.

Finally, respondent urges that the rule of lenity in construing criminal statutes should be applied to §1001, and that because the Friedman case has been on the books in the Eighth Circuit for a number of years a contrary decision by this Court should not be applied retroactively to him. The rule of lenity is of course a well-recognized principle of statutory construction, but the critical statutory language of §1001 is not sufficiently ambiguous, in our view, to permit the rule to be controlling here. . . .

The judgment of the Court of Appeals is reversed, and the case is remanded for further proceedings consistent with this opinion.

It is so ordered.

NOTES AND QUESTIONS

1. *Rodgers* was a seminal case. It took a statute that was rarely used and turned it into a law enforcement staple. Why? Because most suspects at one time or another lie to investigators and *Rodgers* made this ubiquitous act a

federal crime. Suspects are most likely to lie if asked questions in a surprise attack. Thus, it is not uncommon for federal law enforcement officers to appear unannounced at a suspect's home and ask for an informal "chat." After making sure that the suspect understands that he is not under arrest (because they do not want the suspect's *Miranda* rights to kick in), the agents ask away. Almost invariably, the suspect will lie (why is that so?), and a §1001 charge has been created. If the lie is repeated to the agents or to an AUSA, another charge is born. As we will see below, perceived proliferation of this practice led courts to create the "Exculpatory No" doctrine ultimately examined by the Supreme Court in Brogan v. United States, 522 U.S. 398 (1998), *infra* p. 289.

2. Often, §1001 charges for lying to law enforcement are tacked on to the charges that led to the investigation in the first place. On other occasions, however, prosecutors abandon pursuit of the original charges and the entire indictment centers around the allegations of lying. Some commentators have questioned whether prosecutions on such "sideshow charges" should be permitted. *See* Lisa Kern Griffin, *Criminal Lying, Prosecutorial Power, and Social Meaning*, 97 CAL. L. REV. 1515, 1543-1557 (2009) (suggesting that allowing prosecutions in the absence of harm and without accompanying social stigma may produce a variety of counterproductive effects); Erin Murphy, *Manufacturing Crime: Process, Pretext, and Criminal Justice*, 97 GEO. L.J. 1435, 1463-1468 (2009) (noting that the broadening of liability under §1001 results in a statute with a purpose dramatically different from its origins); Dale A. Oesterle, *Early Observations on the Prosecutions of the Business Scandals of 2002: On Sideshow Prosecutions, Spitzer's Clash with Donaldson over Turf, the Choice of Civil or Criminal Actions, and the Tough Tactic of Coerced Cooperation*, 1 OHIO ST. J. CRIM. L. 443, 456-457 (2004) (noting that prosecutions on cover-up charges prevent a public trial on the core charges and that such charges are "an end-run around the more difficult to prove, yet suspected (and hyped), actual offense"). Others, including this author, have defended such prosecutions if the defendant's conduct was serious enough to call into question the integrity of the federal criminal justice system. *See* Michael L. Seigel & Christopher Slobogin, *Prosecuting Martha: Federal Prosecutorial Power and the Need for a Law of Counts*, 109 PENN ST. L. REV. 1107 (2005).

PROBLEM 7-1

Following a lengthy FBI investigation, a grand jury sitting in the Northern District of California indicts Peter Saban for securities fraud in connection with his publicly traded company, SB Investments. The magistrate judge issues an arrest warrant for Saban but places it under seal to prevent Saban from learning about it and fleeing before the FBI can execute the arrest. Two days later, an army of FBI agents surrounds Saban's country estate. The lead agent, Mickey Hawkins, knocks on the front door.

The door is answered by Helen Saban, Peter's wife. When Special Agent Hawkins asks if her husband is home, Mrs. Saban says no. SA Hawkins then tells Mrs. Saban about the indictment and arrest warrant and directs her to tell him where Peter is at that moment.

The day before, Peter told Helen that he was going to New York on business for a few days. He said he would be staying at the Waldorf Astoria Hotel while working at SB Investments' midtown offices. Mrs. Saban repeats all of this information to SA Hawkins.

SA Hawkins contacts the FBI in New York, and agents simultaneously rush to the Waldorf and SB Investments, only to find that Peter Saban is not in either place.

It turns out that Peter had lied to his wife about his whereabouts. Instead of going to New York on business, he had been skiing in Vail, Colorado, with his mistress. After additional investigation, the FBI tracks Saban to Vail and arrests him on the ski slopes.

After Saban's arrest, the AUSA assigned to the case brings a superseding indictment in which she adds a §1001 charge against Saban for the lie to his wife. At a brief press conference after the new charge is brought, the AUSA emphasizes the amount of taxpayer money that was unnecessarily expended trying to find Saban in New York.

Is this a viable charge? Should it be?

UNITED STATES v. TURNER

551 F.3d 657 (7th Cir. 2008)

Sykes, Circuit Judge.

A jury convicted Cecil Turner of two counts of making false statements to the FBI and four counts of wire fraud for his part in a fraudulent scheme by which three janitors employed by the State of Illinois worked only a small fraction of their required 40 hours per week but falsified their attendance logs and collected their full salaries. On appeal, Turner contends that his statements to the FBI were not material because the FBI already knew about his involvement in the scheme and therefore could not have been misled by what he said. . . .

I. Background

Turner was the Director of the Division of Physical Services for the Illinois Secretary of State's office from 1999 to 2005. He supervised over 300 employees who were responsible for cleaning and maintaining various state-owned buildings in Springfield, Illinois. Three of those employees were night janitors Dana Dinora, Steven Boyce, and David Medvesek. Turner promoted Dinora to lead night janitor shortly after being appointed Director in 1999, and the three janitors comprised a cleaning crew responsible for the Herndon Building, the Court of Claims, and the Lincoln Towers. Dinora also worked as an Assistant Superintendent for the City of Springfield Public Works Department where he handled street cleaning and garbage pick-up throughout the city.

Dinora and his crew were required to report to work by 3 P.M. Monday through Friday and stay until 11 P.M. As with any other employee, each was required to submit a leave slip and obtain approval if he was going to be absent during normal work hours. The janitors were supervised by building managers, who in turn reported to the division chief, who was overseen by the deputy director, who reported directly to Turner.

Led by Dinora, the three night janitors devised a scheme to take massive amounts of unauthorized leave without being detected by their supervisors. At its peak the scheme allowed Dinora to collect a full salary while working less than 30 minutes each day and the others to receive full pay while cutting their work hours in half. Sometimes one janitor would remain at work while the other two were absent; the "on duty" janitor would tip off the absent ones if questioned by a supervisor about the whereabouts of the other members of the crew. The absent janitors would then come in to work, call the supervisor who made the inquiry, or submit an appropriate leave slip. Another feature of the scheme involved leaving a note in one building falsely representing that the absent janitor was working in another building. The three janitors also kept two sets of attendance logs. The first accurately recorded occasions when one or more of the janitors did not work a full shift and submitted a proper leave request. If no one checked their work that night, however, the "on duty" janitor would replace the first, accurate attendance log with a second log falsely recording that all three had been working the entire night.

The janitors' scheme could not have succeeded without Turner's help. Prompted by requests from Dinora, Turner repeatedly intervened when the janitors' immediate supervisors began to watch the three more closely. In 1999 Building Manager Randy Lewis forced Dinora to prove that he was actually sick before taking more sick days. Dinora complained to Turner, who reprimanded Lewis and told him to leave Dinora and his crew alone. Two other building managers received similar warnings after attempting to more closely supervise Dinora. Building Manager James Carter was admonished by Turner to "stay the hell away from" Dinora and his crew after Dinora told Turner that Carter was watching the Herndon Building. Turner also instructed Building Manager Harry Fanning to leave Dinora's men alone and to stop checking their work.

Turner's efforts to deflect attention from the night janitors' fraud were successful from 1999 until 2003, when Division Chief Dodie Stannard became involved. After receiving numerous complaints about the unsanitary conditions in the buildings that Dinora's crew was assigned to clean, Stannard began to investigate. . . . [Finally, in mid-2005, Stannard contacted the Inspector General's office. . . . In September [2005], the FBI opened an investigation and Dinora began cooperating. Thereafter Dinora recorded many of his conversations with Turner.]

In mid-October FBI agents questioned Turner about the janitors' scheme. He told them that he never "looked the other way" for Dinora or his crew and that he never reprimanded any of their supervisors for checking on their activities at the Herndon Building. He also claimed that he only learned about the scheme in September 2005 and that he complied with the Inspector General's request to tell no one about the investigation. The FBI interviewed him again in November, and Turner stuck to his story. . . .

Turner was charged with four counts of wire fraud in violation of 18 U.S.C. §§1343 and 1346 and two counts of making false statements in violation of 18 U.S.C. §1001. . . . Turner appeals his conviction on all counts, . . . challeng[ing] the sufficiency of the evidence in a number of respects.

II. Analysis

A. False Statements to the FBI

Turner contends the evidence was insufficient to convict him of making false statements in violation of 18 U.S.C. §1001. On these counts the government was required to prove that Turner's statements were false; material; knowingly and willfully made; and concerned a matter within the jurisdiction of a federal department or agency—here, the FBI. Turner claims there was not enough evidence to prove that . . . his false statements were material. . . .

Turner . . . argues that the statements he made to the special agents were not material because the agents already knew the answers to the questions before they asked him. The FBI was in possession of tape-recorded conversations between Dinora and both Cecil and Doris Turner at the time agents interviewed Turner. During the course of one of the recorded conversations, Doris, on behalf of her husband, warned Dinora about the Inspector General's investigation and told him to be careful about missing work. During a call a few days later, Turner reminded Dinora about the Inspector General's involvement and told him to make sure his crew filled out their leave slips. Turner argues that his statements cannot have been material to the FBI's investigation because the agents had these and other conversations on tape and therefore could not have been misled.

To be material for purposes of §1001, a statement "must have a natural tendency to influence, or be capable of influencing, the decision of the decisionmaking body to which it was addressed." United States v. Gaudin, 515 U.S. 506 (1995). We have held, however, that "[u]nder section 1001 a false statement may be material even though the agency did not rely on it and was not influenced by it." United States v. Dick, 744 F.2d 546, 553 (7th Cir. 1984).

Similarly, we held in *United States v. Ranum*, that "it is not necessary for an allegedly false statement to have any ill effect at all, as long as it is capable of having such an effect." 96 F.3d 1020, 1028 n.12 (7th Cir. 1996). Other circuits are in accord.

In United States v. McBane, 433 F.3d 344 (3d Cir. 2005), the Third Circuit rejected a materiality challenge quite similar to the one Turner advances here. The defendant was a local sheriff who confiscated a rifle from a suspect and later sold it to an FBI informant. When questioned by the FBI about the rifle, the defendant lied and told the agent that it remained in the possession of the sheriff's department at all times. The Third Circuit posed the question presented as follows: "whether the test for 'materiality' necessarily requires that a false statement be capable of influencing an *actual, particular* decision of the agency at issue, or whether the test requires only that a statement be of a type that would naturally tend to influence a *reasonable* decision-making agency in the abstract." Citing the materiality standard we have quoted above, the court concluded that a statement's "natural tendency to influence" suggests not that it must *actually* influence the agency but instead puts the focus more broadly on the "qualities of the statement in question that transcend the immediate circumstances in which it is offered and inhere in the statement itself." The court held that the defendant sheriff's statements to the FBI were material—even though the FBI already had the information from its informant—because the sheriff's "misrepresentations, under normal circumstances, could cause FBI agents to re-direct their investigation to another suspect, question their informant differently or more fully, or perhaps close the investigation altogether."

Here, as in *McBane*, Turner's statements to the FBI probably had very little *actual* influence on the agents because they were already in possession of incriminating recorded conversations between Turner, his wife, and Dinora. The agents were not likely swayed by Turner's false statements because he was on tape saying precisely the opposite to Dinora. But the point of his telling the agents that he did not learn of the trouble in the Herndon Building in September 2005 was to cast suspicion away from him, which in the ordinary course would have an intrinsic capability—a "natural tendency"—to influence an FBI investigation. The same is true of Turner's claim that he had not reprimanded any of his employees for monitoring Dinora's crew, as well as his later denial that he asked his wife to call Dinora on his behalf. Turner's statements were aimed at misdirecting the agents, and this is enough to satisfy the materiality requirement of §1001. . . .

Accordingly, for the foregoing reasons, we AFFIRM Turner's convictions for making false statements in violation of §1001. . . .

UNITED STATES v. HERRING

916 F.2d 1543 (11th Cir. 1990)

HATCHETT, Circuit Judge:

In this case, we affirm the district court's ruling that 18 U.S.C. §1001 is a proper statutory basis for the prosecution of one who receives Georgia Unemployment Insurance benefits as the result of filing false statements in the application for such benefits.

Facts

On January 14, 1987, Dennis D. Herring, the appellant, applied for unemployment insurance benefits from the Georgia Department of Labor. Herring stated on the application that he left his last job in Tucson, Arizona, for lack of work and was unemployed for the week prior to January 14th. Herring, however, began working for an Ohio construction company on January 12, 1987.

Based on his original application, Herring made four subsequent requests for and received unemployment compensation from the Georgia Department of Labor while he was gainfully employed. The Georgia Department of Labor paid Herring a total of $870 in unemployment insurance benefits using Georgia state funds. During a Department of Labor investigation involving State Unemployment Insurance Programs, Herring's false statements were discovered. The United States

Secretary of Labor has approved Georgia's unemployment program, and Georgia receives federal funding for administrative costs from the United States Secretary of Labor. . . .

Contentions

Herring contends that the district court erred in denying his motion to dismiss the indictment. He argues that 18 U.S.C. §1001 does not confer federal jurisdiction to prosecute individuals who make false statements on an application for state unemployment benefits.

The United States contends that the district court correctly denied Herring's motion to dismiss the indictment. The United States argues that federal jurisdiction exists under 18 U.S.C. §1001 because the Georgia Department of Labor receives funding from the United States Department of Labor. . . .

Discussion

. . . A conviction under section 1001 requires proof of five elements: (1) a statement, (2) falsity, (3) materiality, (4) specific intent, and (5) agency jurisdiction. United States v. Lawson, 809 F.2d 1514, 1517 (11th Cir. 1987). Only jurisdiction and materiality are at issue in this case.

A. Jurisdiction

Herring contends that the federal government lacks jurisdiction to prosecute him for false statements made to a state agency. According to Herring, jurisdiction exists under section 1001 only upon a showing of a direct relationship between the false statement and an authorized function of the federal agency or department. United States v. Facchini, 874 F.2d 638 (9th Cir. 1989). Relying extensively on *Facchini*, Herring argues that although the Georgia Department of Labor receives federal funds from the United States Department of Labor for administrative purposes, his false statements did not affect an authorized function of the United States Department of Labor.

In *Facchini*, the Ninth Circuit, sitting en banc, addressed the application of section 1001 to a similar Department of Labor investigation involving State Unemployment Insurance Programs. The court stated that even though jurisdiction may exist under section 1001 when the false statement is not made directly to a federal agency and when the federal agency is not financially affected by the false statement, courts have refused to find jurisdiction unless a direct relationship exists between the false statement and an authorized function of a federal agency or department. The Ninth Circuit reasoned that although the state received funds from the United States Secretary of Labor, the Secretary is authorized to monitor only the administrative structure of the program and is not empowered to act on fraudulent claims for state unemployment benefits. Therefore, false statements to obtain state unemployment funds are not within the proscriptions of section 1001. . . . We reject the Ninth Circuit's narrow and technical definition of section 1001 jurisdiction. . . .

The United States Supreme Court has stated that jurisdiction within the meaning of section 1001 should not be narrowly or technically defined. United States v. Rodgers, 466 U.S. 475, 480 (1984). Moreover, this court has held that false statements need not be presented to an agency of the United States and that federal funds need not actually be used to pay a claimant for federal agency jurisdiction to exist under section 1001. United States v. Suggs, 755 F.2d 1538, 1542 (11th Cir. 1985).

In *Suggs*, the defendant was convicted of falsifying Georgia Department of Labor travel vouchers in violation of 18 U.S.C. §1001. The defendant challenged his conviction on several grounds including lack of jurisdiction. In affirming the conviction, this court found that a state agency's use of federal funds is generally sufficient to establish jurisdiction under section 1001. *Suggs* is controlling. . . .

B. Materiality

Herring next questions the material effects of his statements to the Georgia Department of Labor on the United States government. He argues that his statements did not intrinsically influence the United States Department of Labor's actions because the federal government plays only a limited role in Georgia's unemployment program. Therefore, prosecuting individuals for fraudulent receipt of state funds under section 1001 violates the notice requirement of the due process clause of the United States Constitution.

The test for determining materiality under section 1001 is whether the false statement has the capability of affecting or influencing the exercise of a government function. United States v. Fern, 696 F.2d 1269 (11th Cir. 1983). Materiality is satisfied even if the federal government was not actually influenced by the false statements. The false statements need not be made directly to the federal agency to sustain a section 1001 conviction as long as federal funds are involved. *Suggs*, 755 F.2d at 1542.

In the instant case, Herring received $870 in state unemployment benefits as a result of his false statements. Payment of fraudulent claims frustrates the function of the Georgia unemployment law because such claims are outside the proper and efficient administration of the law. Additionally, the administrative costs involved in processing and paying Herring's unemployment compensation were paid to the Georgia Department of Labor by the Secretary of Labor pursuant to 42 U.S.C. §502(a). The Secretary has an obligation to ensure that the substantial sums the federal government spends to provide an unemployment compensation program are not depleted through false claims which might misdirect or corrupt the functioning of a governmental agency. Consequently, Herring's false statements to the Georgia Department of Labor had the intrinsic capability of influencing the Secretary of Labor in administering the federal unemployment funds.

We further reject Herring's lack of notice argument. As we stated in *Suggs*, notice of the federal agency's involvement in the state unemployment program is not an essential element of a section 1001 conviction.

Conclusion

We hold that the district court properly denied Herring's motion to dismiss the indictment. Section 1001 is the proper vehicle for prosecuting individuals who make false statements on applications for state unemployment benefits. Accordingly, we affirm the district court.

AFFIRMED.

PROBLEM 7-2

(The facts that follow are derived from United States v. Blankenship, 382 F.3d 1110 (11th Cir. 2004)).

The Florida Department of Transportation (the "FDOT") received grants from the United States Department of Transportation (the "USDOT") to subsidize construction of Interstate Highway 4 ("I-4"). As a condition of receiving these grants, the FDOT was contractually obligated to ensure that at least 12% of the USDOT's funds ultimately went to "disadvantaged business enterprises" ("DBEs"). A DBE is a small firm owned and controlled by a woman or minority.

The construction of I-4 was broken down into several smaller segments, including the "3430 project" and the "3431 project." The FDOT contracted with Granite Construction, one of the largest construction companies in the nation, to be its prime contractor on both projects. As part of its agreement with the FDOT, Granite was required to ensure that at least 12% of its subcontracts for both projects were set aside for DBEs. To help fulfill this requirement, Granite hired H.J. Trucking, a licensed DBE owned by Howard Glover (an African-American) to provide hauling services at the 3431 project construction site.

H.J. Trucking, however, never owned more than one dump truck or had any employees, and thus was unable to perform such a large task. Consequently, Glover entered into an oral agreement with Randy and Tammy Blankenship ("the Blankenships"), who owned Tarand Transport, Inc. The Blankenships agreed to use Tarand's equipment and employees to do all the work on the 3431 project, while making Granite believe that it was being done by H.J. Trucking. Tammy Blankenship prepared various documents, including EEO forms, subcontracts, leases, and certified payroll records, to help foster the appearance that H.J. Trucking's employees and owner-operators were performing the hauling at the construction sites, when the people doing the work were really under Tarand's control.

Glover gave Granite the address of Tarand Transport as H.J. Trucking's address, to which Granite sent its payments for the 3431 project. The checks Granite sent to H.J. Trucking's purported address were, appropriately enough, made out to H.J. Trucking. To cash these checks, Randy Blankenship opened an account at his bank in the name of "Randy Blankenship d/b/a H.J. Trucking." He would then deposit the checks into this account, and within a day withdraw most or all of the deposited funds and deposit them into Tarand's account. The Blankenships kept most of this money, giving Glover a payment each month for using his DBE license.

As this plan was being executed, Randy Blankenship (posing as an H.J. Trucking representative) entered into another agreement with Granite to have H.J. Trucking provide hauling services on the 3430 project as well. Blankenship signed Glover's name to the contract and submitted a variety of documents to Granite to make it seem as if H.J. Trucking was actually performing the work on this project, although it was really being done by Tarand. The record does not suggest that Glover knew anything of this second project; Granite sent payment directly to the address it had been given for H.J. Trucking (which, as noted above, was really Tarand's address). Tammy Blankenship prepared several documents in connection with the 3430 project to make it appear as if H.J. Trucking, rather than Tarand, was fulfilling this contract, as well.

During trial, witnesses testified as follows: (1) the Federal Highway Administration and the Florida Department of Transportation agreed that Florida would receive federal funds for the project, provided all federal guidelines were met; (2) Florida was required, prior to receiving funds, to certify all such guidelines would be met; (3) if Florida did not comply with the federal guidelines, it would lose federal funds; and (4) one of the federal guidelines that Florida had to comply with was the DBE requirement.

Howard Glover is convicted of multiple violations of §1001. He appeals on the grounds that his falsehoods, if any, were not made within the jurisdiction of a federal agency and, even if they were, they were not material to the agency's proper functioning. Evaluate his claims, making sure you consider both sides of every argument. *After* you've done so, feel free to look up the case.

C. The Exculpatory No Doctrine

BROGAN v. UNITED STATES

522 U.S. 398 (1998)

Justice Scalia delivered the opinion of the Court.

This case presents the question whether there is an exception to criminal liability under 18 U.S.C. §1001 for a false statement that consists of the mere denial of wrongdoing, the so-called "exculpatory no."

I.

While acting as a union officer during 1987 and 1988, petitioner James Brogan accepted cash payments from JRD Management Corporation, a real estate company whose employees were represented by the union. On October 4, 1993, federal agents from the Department of Labor and the Internal Revenue Service visited petitioner at his home. The agents identified themselves and explained that they were seeking petitioner's cooperation in an investigation of JRD and various individuals. They told petitioner that if he wished to cooperate, he should have an attorney contact the United States Attorney's Office, and that if he could not afford an attorney, one could be appointed for him.

The agents then asked petitioner if he would answer some questions, and he agreed. One question was whether he had received any cash or gifts from JRD when he was a union officer. Petitioner's response was "no." At that point, the agents disclosed that a search of JRD headquarters had produced company records showing the contrary. They also told petitioner that lying to federal agents in the course of an investigation was a crime. Petitioner did not modify his answers, and the interview ended shortly thereafter.

Petitioner was indicted for accepting unlawful cash payments from an employer in violation of 29 U.S.C. §§186(b)(1), (a)(2) and (d)(2), and making a false statement within the jurisdiction of a federal agency in violation of 18 U.S.C. §1001. He was tried, along with several co-defendants, before a jury in the United States District Court for the Southern District of New York, and was found guilty. The United States Court of Appeals for the Second Circuit affirmed the convictions, 96 F.3d 35 (1996). We granted certiorari on the issue of the "exculpatory no."

II.

. . . By its terms, 18 U.S.C. §1001 covers "any" false statement—that is, a false statement "of whatever kind." The word "no" in response to a question assuredly makes a "statement," *see, e.g.*, Webster's New International Dictionary 2461 (2d ed. 1950) (def. 2: "That which is stated; an embodiment in words of facts or opinions"), and petitioner does not contest that his utterance was false or that it was made "knowingly and willfully." In fact, petitioner concedes that under a "literal reading" of the statute he loses.

Petitioner asks us, however, to depart from the literal text that Congress has enacted, and to approve the doctrine adopted by many Circuits which excludes from the scope of §1001 the "exculpatory no." The central feature of this doctrine is that a simple denial of guilt does not come within the statute. There is considerable variation among the Circuits concerning, among other things, what degree of elaborated tale-telling carries a statement beyond simple denial. In the present case, however, the Second Circuit agreed with petitioner that his statement would constitute a "true 'exculpatory n[o]' as recognized in other circuits," but aligned itself with the Fifth Circuit (one of whose panels had been the very first to embrace the "exculpatory no," *see* Paternostro v. United States, 311 F.2d 298 (5th Cir. 1962)) in categorically rejecting the doctrine, *see* United States v. Rodriguez-Rios, 14 F.3d 1040 (5th Cir. 1994) (en banc).

Petitioner's argument in support of the "exculpatory no" doctrine proceeds from the major premise that §1001 criminalizes only those statements to Government investigators that "pervert governmental functions"; to the minor premise that simple denials of guilt to Government investigators do not pervert governmental functions; to the conclusion that §1001 does not criminalize simple denials of guilt to Government investigators. Both premises seem to us mistaken. As to the minor: We cannot imagine how it could be true that falsely denying guilt in a Government investigation does not pervert a governmental function. Certainly the investigation of wrongdoing is a proper governmental function; and since it is the very *purpose* of an investigation to uncover the truth, any falsehood relating to the subject of the investigation perverts that function. It could be argued, perhaps, that a *disbelieved* falsehood does not pervert an investigation. But making the existence of this crime turn upon the credulousness of the federal investigator (or the persuasiveness of the liar) would be exceedingly strange; such a defense to the analogous crime of perjury is certainly unheard of. Moreover, as we shall see, the only support for the "perversion of governmental functions" limitation is a statement of this Court referring to the *possibility* (as opposed to the certainty) of perversion of function — a possibility that exists whenever investigators are told a falsehood relevant to their task. . . .

The second line of defense that petitioner invokes for the "exculpatory no" doctrine is inspired by the Fifth Amendment. He argues that a literal reading of §1001 violates the "spirit" of the Fifth Amendment because it places a "cornered suspect" in the "cruel trilemma" of admitting guilt, remaining silent, or falsely denying guilt. This "trilemma" is wholly of the guilty suspect's own making, of course. An innocent person will not find himself in a similar quandary (as one commentator has put it, the innocent person lacks even a "lemma," Allen, *The Simpson Affair, Reform of the Criminal Justice Process, and Magic Bullets*, 67 U. Colo. L. Rev. 989, 1016 (1996)). And even the honest and contrite guilty person will not regard the third prong of the "trilemma" (the blatant lie) as an available option. The *bon mot* "cruel trilemma" first appeared in Justice Goldberg's opinion for the Court in Murphy v. Waterfront Comm'n of N.Y. Harbor, 378 U.S. 52 (1964), where it was used to explain the importance of a suspect's Fifth Amendment right to remain silent when subpoenaed to testify in an official inquiry. Without that right, the opinion said, he would be exposed "to the cruel trilemma of self-accusation, perjury or contempt." In order to validate the "exculpatory no," the elements of this "cruel trilemma" have now been altered — ratcheted up, as it were, so that the right to remain silent, which was the *liberation* from the original trilemma, is now *itself* a cruelty. We are not disposed to write into our law this species of compassion inflation.

Whether or not the predicament of the wrongdoer run to ground tugs at the heartstrings, neither the text nor the spirit of the Fifth Amendment confers a privilege to lie. "[P]roper invocation of the Fifth Amendment privilege against compulsory self-incrimination allows a witness to remain silent, but not to swear falsely." United States v. Apfelbaum, 445 U.S. 115, 117 (1980). Petitioner contends that silence is an "illusory" option because a suspect may fear that his silence will be used against him later, or may not even know that silence is an available option. As to the former: It is well established that the fact that a person's silence can be used against him — either as substantive evidence of guilt or to impeach him if he takes the stand — does not exert a form of pressure that exonerates an otherwise unlawful lie. And as for the possibility that the person under investigation may be unaware of his right to remain silent: In the modern age of frequently dramatized "Miranda" warnings, that is implausible. Indeed, we found it implausible (or irrelevant) 30 years ago, unless the suspect was "in custody or otherwise deprived of his freedom of action in any significant way," Miranda v. Arizona, 384 U.S. 436, 445 (1966).

Petitioner repeats the argument made by many supporters of the "exculpatory no," that the doctrine is necessary to eliminate the grave risk that §1001 will become an instrument of prosecutorial abuse. The supposed danger is that overzealous prosecutors will use this provision as a means of "piling on" offenses—sometimes punishing the denial of wrongdoing more severely than the wrongdoing itself. The objectors' principal grievance on this score, however, lies not with the hypothetical prosecutors but with Congress itself, which has decreed the obstruction of a legitimate investigation to be a separate offense, and a serious one. It is not for us to revise that judgment. Petitioner has been unable to demonstrate, moreover, any history of prosecutorial excess, either before or after widespread judicial acceptance of the "exculpatory no." And finally, if there is a problem of supposed "overreaching" it is hard to see how the doctrine of the "exculpatory no" could solve it. It is easy enough for an interrogator to press the liar from the initial simple denial to a more detailed fabrication that would not qualify for the exemption. . . .

In sum, we find nothing to support the "exculpatory no" doctrine except the many Court of Appeals decisions that have embraced it. While *communis error facit jus* may be a sadly accurate description of reality, it is not the normative basis of this Court's jurisprudence. Courts may not create their own limitations on legislation, no matter how alluring the policy arguments for doing so, and no matter how widely the blame may be spread. Because the plain language of §1001 admits of no exception for an "exculpatory no," we affirm the judgment of the Court of Appeals.

It is so ordered.

[Concurring opinion by Justice Souter is omitted.]

Justice GINSBURG, with whom Justice SOUTER joins, concurring in the judgment.

Because a false denial fits the unqualified language of 18 U.S.C. §1001, I concur in the affirmance of Brogan's conviction. I write separately, however, to call attention to the extraordinary authority Congress, perhaps unwittingly, has conferred on prosecutors to manufacture crimes. . . .

This case is illustrative. Two federal investigators paid an unannounced visit one evening to James Brogan's home. The investigators already possessed records indicating that Brogan, a union officer, had received cash from a company that employed members of the union Brogan served. (The agents gave no advance warning, one later testified, because they wanted to retain the element of surprise.) When the agents asked Brogan whether he had received any money or gifts from the company, Brogan responded "No." The agents asked no further questions. *After* Brogan just said "No," however, the agents told him: (1) the Government had in hand the records indicating that his answer was false; and (2) lying to federal agents in the course of an investigation is a crime. Had counsel appeared on the spot, Brogan likely would have received and followed advice to amend his answer, to say immediately: "Strike that; I plead not guilty." But no counsel attended the unannounced interview, and Brogan divulged nothing more. Thus, when the interview ended, a federal offense had been completed—even though, for all we can tell, Brogan's unadorned denial misled no one. . . .

At oral argument, the Solicitor General forthrightly observed that §1001 could even be used to "escalate completely innocent conduct into a felony." More likely to occur, "if an investigator finds it difficult to prove some elements of a crime, she can ask questions about other elements to which she already knows the answers. If the suspect lies, she can then use the crime she has prompted as leverage or can seek prosecution for the lie as a substitute for the crime she cannot prove." *Comment, False Statements to Federal Agents: Induced Lies and the Exculpatory No*, 57 U. CHI. L. REV. 1273, 1278 (1990). If the statute of limitations has run on an offense—as it had on four of the five payments Brogan was accused of accepting—the prosecutor can endeavor to revive the case by instructing an investigator to elicit a fresh denial of guilt. Prosecution in these circumstances is not an instance of Government "punishing the denial of wrongdoing more severely than the wrongdoing itself"[;] it is, instead, Government generation of a crime when the underlying suspected wrongdoing is or has become nonpunishable. . . . It is doubtful Congress intended §1001 to cast so large a net. . . .

Although today's decision holds that such prosecutions can be sustained under the broad language of §1001, the Department of Justice's prosecutorial guide continues to caution restraint in each exercise of this large authority. . . .

Justice STEVENS, with whom Justice BREYER joins, dissenting.

Although I agree with nearly all of what Justice Ginsburg has written in her concurrence—a concurrence that raises serious concerns that the Court totally ignores—I dissent for the following reasons.

The mere fact that a false denial fits within the unqualified language of 18 U.S.C. §1001 is not, in my opinion, a sufficient reason for rejecting a well-settled interpretation of that statute. It is not at all unusual for this Court to conclude that the literal text of a criminal statute is broader than the coverage intended by Congress. . . .

NOTES AND QUESTIONS

1. Despite the invitation from the Supreme Court, Congress has never acted to limit the scope or application of §1001. Do you think DOJ's self-imposed "restraint" in this area is part of the reason for congressional apathy?
2. What was the aim of the DOL and IRS agents who confronted Brogan at his house? Was it to make a §1001 case against him? In other words, did they want him to lie? Or did they want him to confess so that they could put him to work in an undercover capacity against other targets before word leaked out on the street that Brogan was cooperating? If the latter was, in fact, their motivation, does it bear on whether concern about the abuse of §1001 is being exaggerated by its critics?
3. Consider this fact as well: A §1001 conviction is considered weak and somewhat trivial for purposes of sentencing. Under the sentencing guidelines, for a defendant with no criminal history, such a conviction is likely to bring no more than 20 months in prison. Indeed, in some circumstances, a conviction on §1001 charges might feel more like a victory for the defense than for the prosecution. Recall, for example, the first trial of ex-Illinois Governor Rod Blagojevich, who was accused of abusing his position to solicit bribes and

extort money, including attempting to sell President Obama's former Senate seat to the highest bidder. The jury hung on all counts other than one for lying to investigators. This was widely reported in the media as a victory for "Blago." *See, e.g., Juror: One Vote Blocked Senate Seat Conviction in Blagojevich Case*, CNN.com, Aug. 18, 2010, available at http://www.cnn.com/2010/CRIME/08/18/illinois.blagojevich.trial/index.html (describing trial's outcome as a "partial victory for the former governor"); Andy Barr, *Rod Blagojevich Jury Convicts on One Count, Hangs on 23*, Politico, Aug. 18, 2010, available at http://www.politico.com/news/stories/0810/41183.html (concluding that verdict "appears to be a big victory for Blagojevich"); Chris Cillizza, *For Rod Blagojevich, Conviction Is Victory*, Wash. Post, Aug. 17, 2010, available at http://voices.washingtonpost.com/thefix/governors/blago-verdict.html (reporting trial outcome as "major victory" for former governor).[2]

D. The Judicial Function Exception

UNITED STATES v. McNEIL

362 F.3d 570 (9th Cir. 2004)

Hug, Circuit Judge:

Christopher McNeil was convicted under 18 U.S.C. §1001 for making false statements on his Criminal Justice Act 23 ("CJA-23") Financial Affidavit. On appeal McNeil argues that his actions should not be subject to punishment under §1001 because §1001(b) specifically excludes "judicial proceeding[s]" from the ambit of the statute. . . .

I. Background

On April 6, 2000, Christopher McNeil was indicted on one count of possessing false documents. He requested that the court appoint counsel to represent him and submitted a CJA-23 Financial Affidavit to support his request. The form requires the defendant to list his assets to determine if he qualifies financially for a court-appointed attorney. McNeil completed the form with the aid of Federal Defender Anthony Gallagher. McNeil admits that he omitted reference to real estate and several financial accounts that he owned at the time. Most of the accounts were in fictitious names, and McNeil argues that he did not list them on Gallagher's advice because of the possibility that such a disclosure would incriminate him. His T. Rowe Price account with a positive balance, however, was in his own name. McNeil admits that he did not tell Gallagher about this account.

2. The prosecution eventually proved its case, convicting Blagojevich on 17 counts of wire fraud, bribery, and extortion for his corruption in office. *See Blagojevich Verdict: The Breakdown*, CBS Chicago.com, June 27, 2001, available at http://chicago.cbslocal.com/2011/06/27/blagojevich-verdict-the-breakdown/.

Gallagher does not remember McNeil's case, but he testified that it was his custom to advise clients not to list assets that could be incriminating. Instead, Gallagher would make a notation on the form and tell the judge when the form was submitted that it was incomplete because of self-incrimination concerns. McNeil's form has no such notations, and Gallagher did not make a declaration to Magistrate Judge Cebull to that effect when the form was submitted.

On June 25, 2001, and on August 17, 2001, two federal grand juries indicted McNeil for making false statements on his CJA-23 Financial Affidavit in violation of 18 U.S.C. §1001. McNeil pleaded not guilty to both counts. . . . The jury convicted McNeil on both counts. . . .

II. Discussion

Questions of statutory interpretation are reviewed de novo. This case presents a question of statutory interpretation of first impression in this circuit. Congress amended 18 U.S.C. §1001 in 1996 to clarify the reach of the statute. This is the first opportunity we have had to address the newly constructed statute. As amended, the first section of the statute imposes criminal liability for, inter alia, knowingly and willfully making false statements "in any matter within the jurisdiction of the executive, legislative, or judicial branch of the Government." Subsection (b) creates an exception for judicial proceedings:

> Subsection (a) does not apply to a party to a judicial proceeding, or that party's counsel, for statements, representations, writings, or documents submitted by such party or counsel to a judge or magistrate in that proceeding.

Thus, to qualify for this exception from liability, McNeil must show that (1) he was a party to a judicial proceeding, (2) his statements were submitted to a judge or magistrate, and (3) his statements were made "in that proceeding."

McNeil was a party to a judicial proceeding when he made the statements because a judicial proceeding had been initiated against him. He had already been indicted on one count of possessing false identification documents when he made his false statements to Magistrate Judge Cebull. *See* Fellers v. United States, 540 U.S. 519 (2004) ("The Sixth Amendment right to counsel is triggered at or after the time that judicial proceedings have been initiated . . . whether by way of formal charge, preliminary hearing, indictment, information, or arraignment.").

Because McNeil's CJA-23 Financial Affidavit was presented to Magistrate Judge Cebull for use in determining whether McNeil qualified for court-appointed counsel, McNeil's statements satisfy the second requirement of submission to a judge or magistrate.

The final requirement to qualify for exemption from liability is that the statement must be made "in [a judicial] proceeding." This brings us to the pivotal issue in this case. We must determine whether the range of judicial activities implied by that phrase includes the inquiry into a defendant's financial status for purposes of appointing counsel. To do so, we start with the language of the statute itself. Because words are to be given their "ordinary, contemporary, common meaning" unless they have been otherwise defined, we turn first to the dictionary. The Oxford

English Dictionary defines "proceeding" as "[t]he fact or manner of taking legal action; a legal action; an act done by authority of the court, assembly or society." (5th ed. 2002). Thus the term "proceeding" refers generally to legal actions and does not distinguish among different phases of an action.

Moreover, the Supreme Court has established the indictment as a definitional starting point for judicial "proceedings" in Sixth Amendment jurisprudence. Logically, every point between the indictment and the disposition would then be considered part of the "judicial proceeding."

Given this background of common understanding, the statute is clear on its face that "in that proceeding" refers to statements that are made as a part of a judicial proceeding, after it has officially begun. Once McNeil was indicted, the criminal proceeding against him had begun. His statement to Magistrate Judge Cebull was made as a part of that proceeding and therefore is exempted from liability under §1001.

Prior to the amendment of §1001 in 1996, this circuit had drawn a distinction between documents submitted for "housekeeping" and "adjudicative" functions, imposing liability for false statements submitted for the former, but making an exception for statements submitted for the latter. *See, e.g.*, United States v. Plascencia-Orozco, 768 F.2d 1074, 1076 (9th Cir. 1985); United States v. Mayer, 775 F.2d 1387, 1391-92 (9th Cir. 1985) (per curiam). We did so because the statute, at that time, did not itself provide an exception for statements made in the context of advocacy in a judicial proceeding. . . .

In crafting the new version of §1001, however, Congress has obviated the concern that led us to create the judicial function exception, and the distinction we drew between "housekeeping" and "adjudicative" functions is no longer necessary. The plain language of §1001(b) carves out an exception to the conduct defined in §1001(a), and that exception applies broadly to all submissions to a judge or magistrate in a proceeding. The statute covers "statements, representations, writings, or documents," without regard to the purpose or nature of the submission. Thus, there is no longer any reason or need to recognize a distinction between "housekeeping" and "adjudicative" functions. In the plain, literal sense, McNeil's submission of the CJA-23 Financial Affidavit was a "document[ ] submitted by[him] to a judge or magistrate in that proceeding." 18 U.S.C. §1001(b). Section 1001(b) therefore exempts McNeil from liability under §1001(a). . . .

UNITED STATES v. MANNING

526 F.3d 611 (10th Cir. 2008)

HENRY, Chief Judge.

. . . This appeal arises from the government's prosecution of Mr. Manning for one count of knowingly and willfully making a materially false, fictitious, or fraudulent statement or representation, in violation of 18 U.S.C. §1001. The government maintains that on August 21, 2003, before he was sentenced for his conviction of misappropriation by a fiduciary under 38 U.S.C. §6101(a), Mr. Manning gave a false statement to United States Probation Officer Tony Budzinsky, who was preparing the PSR [presentencing report]. To determine the appropriate fine and restitution for the misappropriation conviction, Probation Officer Budzinsky inquired as to Mr. Manning's net worth. In response, Mr. Manning failed to disclose his 401(k) retirement plan, which was worth approximately $40,000.

Probation Officer Budzinsky prepared a Net Worth Statement based on Mr. Manning's representations, and subsequently prepared the PSR, relying on the Net Worth Statement. On January 16, 2004, the district court sentenced Mr. Manning to 37 months' imprisonment and 36 months' supervised release. The court did not assess a fine, but it did impose a $100 assessment, and it ordered restitution in the amount of $26,437.34.

The government discovered the omission of the $40,000 401(k) plan a few years after Mr. Manning's sentencing. It then convened a federal grand jury, which indicted Mr. Manning. . . . Before trial, the district court ordered the parties to address "whether the 'judicial proceeding exception' provision in 18 U.S.C. §1001(b) is applicable to this case and whether said provision would invalidate the Indictment issued herein."

At a hearing, the district court concluded that the "judicial proceeding exception" did apply because Mr. Manning made the statement to the probation officer when the probation officer was acting in a "judicial" rather than an "administrative" capacity. . . . Having found that §1001(b) applied, the district court dismissed the indictment.

The government now appeals, arguing that §1001(b) does not exempt false statements such as Mr. Manning's. We agree that the statute does not insulate Mr. Manning's omission, and we therefore reverse and remand.

II. DISCUSSION

The government first argues that §1001(b)'s plain language does not exempt Mr. Manning's wrongful statement to Probation Officer Budzinsky because the judicial function exception is inapplicable in this case. Second, the government argues that, should this court decide to review §1001's legislative history, it is evident that Probation Officer Budzinsky acted in an administrative capacity that did not fall under §1001(b)'s exception. Third and, in conjunction with its second argument, the government asserts that a probation officer's role is an administrative one, and thus §1001(b) cannot apply to Mr. Manning's statements. We agree with the government that the plain language of §1001(b) does not apply to Mr. Manning's false statement and that the legislative history does not support an exemption for his false statement to a probation officer in this context. . . .

Since the [§1001's] amendment in 1996, we have not had occasion to comment upon the breadth of the judicial function exception. Beginning with the plain language of the statute, there is no debate that Mr. Manning was a party to a judicial proceeding and that he made a statement during that proceeding. The question is whether Mr. Manning's failure to mention to Probation Officer Budzinsky the existence of the 401(k) account, which in turn Probation Officer Budzinsky omitted from the PSR submitted to the court, was a false statement "submitted . . . to a judge." 18 U.S.C. §1001(b).

Clearly, if we read §1001(b) strictly and literally ("to a *judge*"), then the false statement, which was contained in the PSR, would not be covered by the judicial function exception. However, the government acknowledges (and we appreciate the government's candor in so doing), that §1001(b)'s exception *must* cover certain *agents* of a judge—such as a judge's secretary or law clerk. Similarly covered might be the judge's courtroom deputy clerk or bailiff, because clerical staff act as conduits to the judge. Because the plain language of §1001(b) leaves some doubt as to the scope of a judicial agency, we look beyond the statute's plain language and consider . . . (2) the statute's legislative history; (3) the role of the probation officer in formulating the PSR; and finally (4) how Mr. Manning's false statement fares against this backdrop. . . .

2. Legislative History Behind the 1996 Amendment

In May, 1995, Congressman Martini introduced H.R. 1678, which applied section 1001 to all three branches of the Federal Government, without exception. At a Crime Subcommittee hearing on June 30, 1995, witnesses expressed concern that the broad application of section 1001 to all three branches would *chill advocacy in judicial proceedings* and also undermine the fact-gathering process that is indispensable to the legislative process. In response to these concerns, Representative Martini introduced H.R. 3166 on March 27, 1996, which included a judicial function exception, exempting from the scope of section 1001 those representations made by a party or party's counsel to a judge during a judicial proceeding. . . .

[In its report on H.R. 3166, the House Committee explained the parameters of the judicial function exception:]

> [S]ubsection (b) provides that section 1001 does not apply to a party to a judicial proceeding, or that party's counsel, for statements, representations, writings or documents submitted by such party or counsel to a judge in that proceeding. As such, section 1001 does not apply to representations made to a court that is acting in its judicial, or adjudicatory capacity; Rather, it applies only to representations made to a court acting in its administrative capacity. . . . Consequently, . . . only those representations made to a court when it is acting in its administrative or "housekeeping" capacity are within the scope of section 1001. Such representations would include any filings not related to a proceeding before the court, *such as submissions related to bar membership, and would also include the submission of information to another entity within the judicial branch, such as the probation service.*

H. Rep. 104-680, 104th Cong., 2nd Sess. 1996, 1996 U.S.C.C.A.N. 3935, 3942-43 (emphasis added). . . . Having concluded the judicial function exception is extant—indeed, codified—and has Congressionally delineated parameters, we consider its application to the case at hand: Was Officer Budzinsky's preparation of the PSR and presentation of the PSR, containing Mr. Manning's statements, equivalent to a party's statement to a judge? To answer this, we consider the role of Probation Officer Budzinsky.

3. Role of the Probation Officer

In fashioning a restitution order, the court is required to "order the probation officer to obtain and include in" the PSR "information sufficient for the court to exercise its discretion in fashioning a restitution order." 18 U.S.C. §3664(a). . . . Pursuant to Rule 32(c)(2), the PSR is to contain (a) information about the history and characteristics of the defendant, including his prior criminal record; (b) the classification of the offense and the defendant under the Sentencing Guidelines, possible sentencing ranges, and any factors that might warrant departure from the Guidelines; (c) any pertinent policy statements issued by the Sentencing Commission; (d) the impact of the defendant's offense upon any victims; (e) information relating to possible sentences not requiring incarceration, unless the court orders otherwise; and (f) any other information requested by the court.

When preparing a PSR under Rule 32, "it is evident . . . that the probation service is an arm of the court. It is not an investigative arm for the prosecution. A presentence report is prepared exclusively at the discretion of and for the benefit of the court." United States v. Dingle, 546 F.2d 1378, 1380-81 (10th Cir. 1976). "The purpose of the presentence report, including associated interviews, is neither prosecutorial nor punitive. It is essentially neutral in those respects. The probation officer acts as an *agent* of the court for the purpose of gathering and classifying information and informing the court in the exercise of its sentencing responsibility." United States v. Rogers, 921 F.2d 975, 979-80 (10th Cir. 1990) (emphasis added). Although the probation officer acts as the court's agent, it seems the role is certainly more substantive than that of a message bearer; indeed, probation officers can exercise some discretion on their own.

There is little doubt that Probation Officer Budzinsky performed his duties as required by the district court pursuant to Rule 32. He filtered all the information he received from his investigation and prepared the Net Worth Statement and finally the PSR, which was subjected to adversarial testing by the parties. *See* Fed. R. Crim. P. 32(i)(1)(c) (mandating that the parties be given an opportunity "to comment on the probation officer's determinations and on other matters relating to an appropriate sentence"). Only after such testing does the court exercise its discretion and fashion a restitution order.

Given this background and the statute's legislative history, we are informed in our analysis by a divided Ninth Circuit decision, [United States v. Horvath, 492 F.3d 1075 (9th Cir. 2007), *reh'g en banc denied*, 522 F.3d 904, 907 (2008),] which recently immunized a similar false statement to a probation officer[, characterizing the officer as a mere "intermediary" between the defendant and judge].

However, we believe that the dissent's logic and reasoning as to the role of the probation officer in this instance appears to be the better approach, and also squares with Congressional intent. The dissent agreed that documents or writing provided to a judge via a courier or a clerk or secretary, are "submitted" to a judge for purposes of §1001(b). However, [the dissenting judge] believed, and we agree, that a probation officer, in preparing the PSR pursuant to Rule 32, acts with greater authority than does a "courier pigeon." "[T]he probation officer's obligation is to submit a report that contains information on the defendant's history and characteristics, not *from* the defendant." Here, as in *Horvath*, the probation officer "picked and chose" what to include and exclude in the PSR, "based on his understanding of what is expected of him and what he believes is important for the court and the parties to know." The process involves the probation officer's exercise of his discretion, and not a mere transmission of information. . . .

This is a close and difficult case. While some aspects of the probation officer's actions seem to be those of an agent, other functions allow discretion. Yet we cannot hold that Congressional intent encompassed allowing a defendant to conceal resources when such evidence is critical to the final judicial decision, at which time the advocates can have their say protected by §1001(b). Thus, although it seems the government could have chosen another route, it was fully empowered to prosecute Mr. Manning under §1001.

III. Conclusion

Mr. Manning's statement to the probation officer that omitted mention of his $40,000 401(k) retirement account is a prosecutable offense under 18 U.S.C. §1001(a) and is not excepted under the judicial function exception of §1001(b). Accordingly, we VACATE and REMAND for trial.

[Concurring and dissenting opinions omitted.]

NOTES AND QUESTIONS

1. According to the *Manning* court's review of the legislative history, Congress created the judicial function exception because giving the prosecution power to wield § 1001 over the defense in criminal cases "would chill advocacy in judicial proceedings." But all agree that prosecutors have other crimes at their disposal with which to combat falsehood during criminal litigation, including perjury, false statements, and obstruction of justice. In light of this latter point, would the application of §1001 to judicial proceedings really alter the balance of power between the adversaries?
2. Can §1001 be used to prosecute a witness who lies during a civil deposition?
3. Federal defendants may be arrested and held in jail or on bond pursuant to a sworn complaint up to 14 days prior to a preliminary hearing or indictment. Fed. R. Crim. P. 5.1(c). Within roughly 24 hours of arrest, arrestees must be brought before a magistrate judge for an initial appearance and bail hearing. *See* Fed. R. Crim. P. 5(a)(1), 5(d)(1)(D) & 5(d)(3). Prior to these proceedings, they are typically interviewed by a Pretrial Services Officer (PSO) who obtains basic information about the defendant for the court's use in fashioning bail. If appropriate, the PSO also has the arrestee fill out an affidavit of indigency so he can qualify for appointed counsel. Usually, the magistrate judge asks the defendant to swear to the accuracy of the

affidavit before making the appointment, resulting in it being subject to the penalties of perjury. On occasion, however, the magistrate judge will accept the affidavit on its face.

Assume that a defendant makes a material misstatement on his indigency affidavit. Is this prosecutable under §1001? How does this situation compare to that of the *McNeil* case? Does the answer depend upon whether the defendant has sworn an oath to tell the truth?

E. The Legislative Branch Provision

UNITED STATES v. PICKETT

353 F.3d 62 (D.C. Cir. 2004)

SENTELLE, Circuit Judge:

. . . On October 15, 2001, an anonymous letter delivered to Senator Thomas Daschle at his Senate office on Capitol Hill contained a white powder that tested positive for Anthrax—a dangerous, often deadly, disease-causing agent. Other similar Anthrax incidents occurred around the same time and geographic area. On November 7, 2001, while the Anthrax investigation was not only ongoing but much on the minds of law enforcement, members of Congress, and the public, Pickett committed what he now admits was a "bad joke." The facts of the incident are not in dispute. Appellant, then a Capitol Police officer, was on duty at a security post at the entrance to the Cannon Office Building tunnel, which connects the House Office Buildings to the Capitol Building. Because of the level of security measures occasioned by the Anthrax incident, which followed close on the heels of the tragic attacks on the United States on September 11, 2001, the tunnel was closed to members of the public, but open to authorized personnel including Members of the House of Representatives. The security post was accessible by members of the public and consisted largely of a podium, a desk, a magnetometer, and an x-ray machine. At approximately 5 P.M. on November 7, Officer Kari Morgansen left her seat at the podium and moved to the desk seat vacated by appellant, who was going on break. At the desk Officer Morgansen discovered a handwritten note and a small pile of white powder. The note read, "PLEASE INHALE YES THIS COULD BE? CALL YOUR DOCTOR FOR FLU—SYMPTOMS. THIS IS A CAPITOL POLICE TRAINING EXERCIZE [sic]! I HOPE YOU PASS!"

Officer Morgansen inquired of Officer John Caldwell, who was also on duty at the post, if he knew anything about the note or the powder. He did not. Neither of the officers believed that the powder was actually Anthrax. Nonetheless, because of the state of alert and the earlier incidents, they called a superior and blocked the powder and note from public view lest anyone become alarmed. The superior, Sergeant Turner, asked who else had been at the desk. Upon learning appellant had been sitting there, he contacted him by phone and asked him what was on the desk. After some delay, appellant advised that "it was a joke" and that the powder "was Equal." Although the powder was never tested, the government has never contended that it was actually Anthrax or anything other than the dietary sugar substitute appellant suggested. Sergeant Turner conducted some further investigation and reported the incident to the Criminal Investigation Division of the Capitol Police.

After some further investigation, the United States Attorney submitted the matter to a grand jury. The grand jury returned an indictment charging Pickett with making false statements in violation of 18 U.S.C. §1001 and obstructing and interfering with the Capitol Police in violation of 40 U.S.C. §212a-2(d). . . . [Pickett was found guilty on the §1001 charge.] The District Court . . . sentenc[ed] appellant to two years probation, 200 hours of community service, and a $100 special assessment. The court suspended execution of the sentence because "significant questions have been raised by [the defense] which deserve attention from the circuit before consequences are visited on [appellant]." Appellant then filed the current appeal. . . .

III. Analysis

The count of conviction in the indictment charged that:

> On or about November 7, 2001, in the District of Columbia, the defendant, JAMES JOSEPH PICKETT, in a matter within the jurisdiction of the legislative branch of the Government of the United States, that is, the United States Capitol Police, did knowingly and willfully make materially false, fictitious, and fraudulent statements and representations; that is, the defendant wrote a note and placed that writing at a United States Capitol Police security station with arrows directed to a nearby quantity of white powder, which writing stated—"PLEASE INHALE YES THIS COULD BE? CALL YOUR DOCTOR FOR FLU—SYMPTOMS. THIS IS A CAPITOL POLICE TRAINING EXERCIZE! [SIC] I HOPE YOU PASS!"—when the defendant knew the powder was not anthrax and his placement of the powder and the writing were not part of a United States Capitol Police training exercise.

Pickett contends that the District Court erred in denying his motion to dismiss this indictment for its failure to allege an essential element of the offense. More specifically, he argues that an indictment charging a violation of §1001 by the making of a false statement "in a matter within the jurisdiction of the *legislative* branch of the Government" must further allege that the charged conduct fell within the specifications of 18 U.S.C. §1001(c)(1) or (2). In this appeal, the Government has at no time claimed that whatever matter may have encompassed Pickett's alleged false statement was an administrative matter covered by subsection (1), and therefore, Pickett argues, the indictment was not valid without allegations that the "statement" was made in an investigation or review. He argues that the allegations of count 1 do not meet the requirements of Fed. R. Crim. P. 7(c)(1) that an "indictment . . . must be a plain, concise, and definite written statement of the essential facts constituting the offense charged." Because §1001 renders unlawful the making of a false statement within the jurisdiction of the legislative branch only with respect to administrative matters, investigations, or reviews, an indictment that charges a false statement made in a matter within the jurisdiction of that branch without alleging that it was within one of the statutory categories has not charged an offense. Otherwise put, it is accepted law that an indictment must "contain[ ] the elements of the offense intended to be charged." Russell v. United States, 369 U.S. 749, 763 (1962).

The Government takes the position that we must hold that the indictment is sufficient and charges all the elements of the offense. The Government contends further that the language of subsection (c) is not elemental and need not be charged in the indictment. . . .

Pickett is correct and the Government incorrect. The Government's argument is built on a foundation of selective quotation. True, the indictment tracks the language of the statute. However, the indictment tracks the language of only a portion of the statute. As Rule 7(c)(1) succinctly requires, the indictment "must be a plain, concise, and definite written statement of the *essential facts constituting the offense charged*." On the plain language of the statute, the conduct charged against Pickett, making false statements and representations in a matter within the jurisdiction of the legislative branch, does not constitute an offense unless it comes within the categories set forth by §1001(c): as applicable here, that it be within an "investigation or review," as delineated by the language of subsection (c)(2). As the Supreme Court taught in *Russell*, it is a fundamental "protection[ ] which an indictment is intended to guarantee," that the indictment "contain[ ] the elements of the offense intended to be charged and sufficiently apprise the defendant of what he must be prepared to meet." 369 U.S. at 763. While the Government is correct that indictments have been upheld where they tracked the language of the statute, this indictment tracks only part of the statutory language. While this is of course the norm, statutes being often lengthy documents and generally only partially applicable to the crime at issue, the indictment against Pickett omits language essential to the definition of the offense which it purports to charge. . . .

This does not, however, end our inquiry. The Government argues that even if the indictment is defective, that defect is harmless "as the evidence of this jurisdictional element was 'overwhelming' and 'essentially uncontroverted.'" . . . This circuit has never considered the question of whether an indictment flawed by omission of an essential element is subject to harmless error review, nor need we today. Contrary to the Government's assertions, the evidence of an "investigation or review" is neither overwhelming nor uncontroverted. Indeed, the evidence is so far from overwhelming that it would have been difficult for Pickett to find it in order to controvert it. Even at the present advanced stage of this litigation, it is not at all clear what the Government's theory is as to the identity of the investigation or review in which the false statement is alleged to have occurred. The Government's primary argument on appeal is that the requirement of §1001 for an investigation is satisfied by the investigation which the false statement occasioned. This theory just does not square with the words of §1001. That section requires first that the false statement be made "in any matter within the jurisdiction of the . . . legislative . . . branch." 18 U.S.C. §1001(a). That it be made *in* a matter within the jurisdiction of the legislative branch would seem to contemplate that the matter existed at the time of the making of the statement. The section further requires that, with specific reference to the legislative branch, it will apply only to an "investigation or review, conducted pursuant to the authority of any committee, subcommittee, commission or office of the Congress, consistent with applicable rules of the House or Senate." 18 U.S.C. §1001(c)(2). Not only was the investigation of the false statement not in existence so that the statement could have been made in it, the Government has pointed us to no evidence supporting the proposition that such investigation was pursuant to the authorities set out in subsection (c)(2). The Government's construction of the statute is not only unnatural and illogical, it would render subsection (2) meaningless. Presumably any false statement made in any matter within the legislative branch which became the subject of a prosecution would have been the subject of an investigation triggered by the statement. Therefore, accepting the Government's interpretation "would require us to eliminate a provision of the statute, a clear violation of a fundamental canon of construction."

To refute the conclusion that the plain language of §1001(c)(2) requires that for prosecution of a statement made in the legislative branch, the statement must occur in a then-pending investigation or review, the Government offers two cases: United States v. Rodgers, 466 U.S. 475 (1984), and United States v. Oakar, 111 F.3d 146 (D.C. Cir. 1997) (Williams, J., concurring in part and dissenting in part). While both those opinions contain language discussing investigations sparked by false statements of a defendant, neither concern a violation of 18 U.S.C. §1001(c). Indeed, at the time of both offenses, Title 18 U.S.C. §1001(c) had not yet been enacted. The Government's reliance on the investigation sparked by the false statement to satisfy the requirements of §1001(c)(2) simply does not work.

This leaves the Government's second theory for satisfaction of the "investigation or review" element. That second theory is that Pickett made a false statement in the concurrent investigation surrounding the Anthrax letters sent to Senator Daschle and others. This theory also fails. Not only has the Government not offered overwhelming and uncontroverted evidence that the statement was made in that investigation, it has offered none at all. The most the evidence shows is that the investigation was ongoing at the time of the alleged making of the statement, and that agents connected to that investigation were sent to all calls involving suspicious packages. The statute does not apply to statements made concurrently with an investigation, even if those statements concerned the same or similar subject matter. The statute requires that the statements be made *in* such a matter. The Government has offered no evidence to meet that requirement. . . .

[Concurring opinion omitted.]

NOTES AND QUESTIONS

1. What is the policy behind the legislative function exception?
2. Do you think the *Pickett* court's attempt to distinguish *Rodgers* is persuasive? If the prank had been more sophisticated—causing the Capitol to be evacuated and streets to be shut down, and leading to a year-long investigation into the perpetrator's identity (on the assumption that the incident was linked to terrorism), would the court have been so quick to conclude that "[t]he Government's reliance on the investigation sparked by the false statement to satisfy the requirements of §1001(c)(2) simply does not work"? Or is this a situation of bad facts making bad law? Do you get the sense that the court is really thinking, "C'mon, this was a practical joke that fooled no one and lasted five minutes. Why are you making a federal (criminal!) case out of it?"

3. On occasion, a congressional investigation into executive decision making leads a Senate or House Committee to subpoena government officials to testify before it because they refuse to appear voluntarily, claiming "executive privilege." A relatively recent example of this occurred when Congress wanted to know why Attorney General Alberto Gonzales had fired seven U.S. Attorneys around the country. *See* Mark J. Rozell & Mitchel A. Sollenberger, *Executive Privilege and the Bush Administration*, 24 J.L. & Pol. 1 (2008). The result is usually a tense showdown between two powerful branches of government. In most instances, a deal is worked out whereby at least some of the officials answer questions while not under oath. *See* Emily Berman, *Lincoln's Legacy: Enduring Lessons of Executive* Power, 3 Alb. Gov't L. Rev. (2010); Stephen C.N. Lilley, *Suboptimal Executive Privilege*, 2009 B.Y.U. L. Rev. (2009). Does §1001 apply to statements made during these informal proceedings? If so, why do both sides view waiver of the oath requirement as a critical part of their compromise?

III. FALSE, FICTITIOUS, OR FRAUDULENT CLAIMS: 18 U.S.C. §287

A. Elements and Mens Rea

UNITED STATES v. BLECKER

657 F.2d 629 (4th Cir. 1981)

James Dickson Phillips, Circuit Judge:

Icarus Corporation (Icarus) and its president, Herbert Blecker, challenge the convictions of each on six counts of presenting false claims to an agency of the United States in violation of 18 U.S.C. §287 and Icarus' conviction on two counts of mail fraud in violation of 18 U.S.C. §1341. Icarus and Blecker contend that venue was improper in the United States District Court for the Eastern District of Virginia. They further argue that there was insufficient evidence to support the convictions for either submitting false claims or mail fraud and that remarks made by the prosecutor in his summation to the jury effectively deprived them of a fair trial. We find all the contentions of the defendants to be without merit and accordingly affirm their convictions.

I.

Briefly stated, the government alleged in its indictment of Icarus and Blecker that the defendants submitted invoices for fees based on false resumes to the Computer Sciences Corporation (CSC) knowing that CSC, in turn, would present the claims to the General Services Administration (GSA) for payment. Icarus was also charged with mail fraud in causing these invoices to be mailed to a CSC office in California.

The evidence presented at trial tended to show that, in March 1972, CSC was awarded a multimillion dollar contract by the GSA to provide federal agencies with computer and data processing services. Under the terms of this National

Teleprocessing System (NTS) contract, CSC provided all the normal supply requirements for computer services for most of the federal government. CSC was authorized to subcontract for consulting services that, under Schedule J of the NTS contract, were to be paid for at rates based upon the consultants' education and experience.

In 1973, CSC subcontracted for consulting services from Icarus. At this time Blecker was told by a CSC official that rates were set according to very specific requirements for education and experience and was given a copy of the NTS contract. Blecker then instructed a number of his employees to embellish their resumes with additional schooling and experience and had the resumes of other employees enhanced without their knowledge. These false resumes were then taken from Icarus' office in Maryland to an official at CSC's Rosslyn, Virginia office for use in computing consultant fees.

In order to receive compensation for services performed under the NTS contract, Icarus was required to prepare and submit invoices to CSC on a monthly basis. At its Rosslyn office, CSC employees checked the rates billed on the Icarus invoices with the resumes of Icarus employees to determine whether Icarus had billed the approved rate for those employees. CSC employees then made the necessary computations and prepared a billing sheet. Information from the billing sheet was transmitted via computer from the CSC office in Rosslyn to the CSC accounting office in El Segundo, California. There, CSC employees prepared a bill for the GSA from the information contained in the Icarus invoices and billing sheets. The bills were then mailed back to the CSC offices in Rosslyn, from which they were hand delivered to the GSA office in Washington, D.C. . . .

Throughout the presentation of their defense to the false claims charges, Icarus and Blecker attempted to introduce evidence that the Government got its money's worth from the services billed by Icarus. The court, however, excluded as irrelevant any testimony about the value of the services performed by Icarus, and it instructed the jury to this effect. The court also refused to give an instruction that the jury should consider whether the "puffing" of resumes engaged in by Icarus was a common business practice for which it should not be held criminally liable. . . .

The defendants . . . argue that the district court misapprehended the elements required for a conviction under 18 U.S.C. §287 and that as a result of this misapprehension the court erroneously excluded certain evidence that the defendants sought to introduce in their defense and improperly instructed the jury. Icarus and Blecker first contend that section 287 prohibits only the submission of false claims directly to the government and that the district court therefore erred in instructing the jury that it could base a conviction on Icarus' submission of false invoices to the GSA through an intermediary such as CSC because Icarus had no direct contractual relationship with the government.

This constitutes an oversimplification of the scope of the false claims statute that has been rejected by every court that has considered the matter. For example, in United States ex rel. Marcus v. Hess, 317 U.S. 537 (1943), the Supreme Court was called upon to construe R.S. §5438, the forerunner of section 287, which in addition to the present statute's prohibition of making or presenting false, fictitious or fraudulent claims to the government also prohibited the causing of another to make or present such claims. The Court in *Hess* held that, when private contractors engaged in collusive bidding practices on contracts made with local governmental units but for which a large portion of the funding was supplied by the federal Public Works Administration, the contractors were "causing to be presented" a fraudulent claim against the United States.

It may be contended that the present version of the false claims statute, from which Congress has deleted the "cause" language, precludes conviction of the defendants in the instant case on the theory of *Hess*. The Reviser's Note to section 287, however, makes it clear that the "cause" language was omitted as unnecessary in view of Congress' enactment of 18 U.S.C. §2(b), which provides that "(w)hoever willfully causes an act to be done which if directly performed by him or another would be an offense against the United States, is punishable as a principal." Therefore, the "intermediary" theory of *Hess* remains good law and has since been applied in a number of cases. . . .

The defendants' next contention with respect to misapprehension of section 287 is that the district court erred in excluding evidence proffered by the defendants that the government got its money's worth for the consultant services performed by Icarus and in refusing to instruct the jury that it must find that the government did not receive adequate value for the money expended on work performed by Icarus in order to convict the defendant of a violation of the false claims statute. This *quantum meruit* argument is simply a restatement of the contention that conviction for violating section 287 requires a showing of specific intent to defraud the government—a contention that we rejected in United States v. Maher, 582 F.2d 842 (4th Cir. 1978). As we stated in *Maher*, section 287 is phrased in the disjunctive, and a conviction under that statute may therefore be based on proof that a claim submitted to the government is either false, fictitious or fraudulent. Thus, the government met its burden of proof in this case by showing that the defendants submitted invoices to CSC with knowledge of their falsity, and evidence that the government got its money's worth was no defense to this proof. . . .

AFFIRMED.

B. Counts

UNITED STATES v. SWEPSTON

289 F.2d 166 (8th Cir. 1961)

VOGEL, Circuit Judge.

This is an appeal from the denial without hearing of a motion for vacation or correction of sentence made under §2255 of Title 28 U.S.C.A.

Owen Walter Swepston, the appellant, after first consulting with his court-appointed counsel, appeared in open court and filed a waiver of indictment. Thereafter upon arraignment and with the assistance of counsel he offered a separate plea of guilty to each count of a five-count information charging five separate offenses, all in violation of §287, Title 18 U.S.C.A. Each count in the information separately charged the appellant with making and presenting a false claim against the government by filing a false, fictitious and fraudulent claim for an income tax refund. After the guilty pleas were offered, the District Court specifically inquired of the appellant: Whether he understood that the penalty for each offense could be five years in the penitentiary or a fine of $10,000 or both, to which appellant answered in the affirmative; if anyone had threatened or intimidated him in any fashion, to which appellant replied in the negative; if he was doing this voluntarily after consulting with his counsel, to which he replied, "Yes"; and if there was anything unusual about his arrest or in regard to the transaction, to which the appellant replied, "No, sir." The court thereupon accepted the pleas of guilty and ordered sentencing suspended pending an investigation by a probation officer.

Subsequent to the pre-sentence investigation and report, which indicated that Swepston had filed many false claims for tax refunds in different districts in the United States, that he had a long history of criminal convictions, including seven previous penitentiary sentences, appellant again appeared in court. After his counsel, who appeared with him, was given an opportunity and did speak in his behalf, he was sentenced to:

> "... imprisonment for a period of three (3) years on each of counts 1, 2, 3, 4 and 5; said sentences of imprisonment to be served consecutively to each other for a total sentence of imprisonment of fifteen (15) years; without costs."

Appellant is presently serving this sentence in the United States Penitentiary at Leavenworth, Kansas.

In his motion to vacate, filed in the District Court on September 22, 1960, appellant set forth the following grounds: (1) illegal arrest; (2) illegal search and seizure; (3) unnecessary delay in being taken before a United States Commissioner; (4) inadmissibility of his confession; (5) failure of the United States Commissioner to inform him of the charges later filed against him in the information; (6) coerced plea of guilty; (7) ineffective assistance of counsel; and (8) failure of the court to clearly and effectively impose consecutive sentences.

Holding that the files and records of the case conclusively show that the appellant was entitled to no relief, the District Court denied the motion without hearing. From such denial Swepston appeals. . . .

[We take up appellant's contention that the sentencing court erred in imposing consecutive sentences. As to this contention,] appellant relies chiefly upon the fact that no statute specifically authorizes a federal court to impose consecutive sentences. None is necessary. The right to impose consecutive sentences is inherent in the courts. Consecutive sentences for separate counts of the same indictment or information have long been sanctioned and cases involving them have been before the Supreme Court of the United States many times.

In a case quite similar to the instant one, Turner v. United States, 271 F.2d 855 (8th Cir. 1959), the appeal was from an order of the District Court denying without a hearing a §2255 motion for vacation or correction of sentence. Appellant there had been convicted and sentenced upon his plea of guilty to an information which in five separate counts charged him with five separate violations of §287, the same statute here involved. Claiming that the consecutive sentences imposed violated his constitutional rights not to be twice put in jeopardy for the same offense, appellant asserted error. In a *per curiam* opinion, this court said at page 856:

> "... He concedes that no authority in support of this contention could be found. It is safe to say that there is no such authority. The information charged five separate offenses and would have sustained an aggregate maximum sentence of twenty-five years."

... While appellant may have had one overall scheme to defraud the government by the filing of many false claims for income tax refunds, he nevertheless committed a separate violation of the statute every time he filed a false claim. Each count of the five-court information charged a separate violation of the statute. Each was a separate crime. Each was punishable separately. They were in no way dependent upon each other. Each false claim for income tax refund was in the name of a different person and was for a separate and different amount. Five crimes were charged and appellant, by his pleas, admitted having committed them. It would seem perfectly clear that the power to impose consecutive sentences under such circumstances rests squarely with the sentencing court. Only [a] Congressional Act could change the inherent power of the court so to do....

The order appealed from is affirmed.

NOTES AND QUESTIONS

1. In line with *Swepston*, courts have consistently held that each presentation of a false claim under §287 constitutes a separate offense. This makes it an especially effective tool to use when the government is the victim of monetary fraud.
2. During the administration of President Bill Clinton, DOJ made the prosecution of health care fraud a priority, in part because of the huge drain caused by such fraud on the federal Medicare system. *See* MALCOLM K. SPARROW, LICENSE TO STEAL: HOW FRAUD BLEEDS AMERICA'S HEALTH CARE SYSTEM 56 (Westview Press 2000) (noting that the Clinton administration recognized the seriousness of health care fraud in the early 1990s and "engaged the problem through a broad array of sustained legislative, administrative, and law enforcement initiatives"). Health care fraud prosecution has been a staple in U.S. Attorneys' offices ever since. One provision that has been regularly employed by health care fraud prosecutors is the anti-kickback statute, 42 U.S.C. §1320a-7b(b), which is designed to prevent health care providers from remunerating others for supplying them with Medicare-eligible patients. *See* MICHAEL K. LOUKS & CAROLO C. LAM, PROSECUTING AND DEFENDING HEALTH CARE FRAUD CASES 143-217 (The Bureau of National Affairs, Inc. 2001). This statute is extremely complex, however, in part because it contains a multitude of safe-harbor provisions. In contrast, the False Claims Act "is popular among health care fraud prosecutors, primarily because of its intuitively simple appeal to juries, combined with case law establishing the broad reaches of the statute." *Id.* at 408.

C. Civil False Claims: Qui Tam Actions

One of the most important features of false claims actions is that 18 U.S.C. §287 has a civil cousin, 31 U.S.C. §3729(a). The civil false claims act makes a person liable if he "(1) knowingly presents, or causes to be presented, to an officer or employee of the United States Government or a member of the Armed Forces of the United States a false or fraudulent claim for payment or approval; [or] (2) knowingly makes, uses, or causes to be made or used, a false record or statement to get a false or fraudulent claim paid or approved by the Government." The remedy under the statute makes it quite powerful: up to $11,000 per claim plus treble damages.

The civil false claims statute also contains a qui tam provision, 31 U.S.C. §3730(b). Under this provision, private third parties who discover fraud against the United States, called relators, can file a qui tam lawsuit against the alleged perpetrator on behalf of the federal government. The lawsuit is initially filed under seal and is reviewed by DOJ to determine if it wants to intervene in the prosecution of the case. Regardless of DOJ's decision, if the suit is successful, the relator is entitled to share in up to 25 percent of any recovered proceeds. Qui tams thus provide private citizens with potent motivation to help the federal government fight fraud and abuse.

Given that billions of dollars of fraud is perpetrated against the United States every year, qui tam lawsuits are common and lucrative. Numerous attorneys specialize in representing relators in qui tam actions as well as in the collateral litigation that is often required to maximize their clients' share of the recovery.

UNITED STATES EX REL. DRC, INC. v. CUSTER BATTLES, LLC

562 F.3d 295 (4th Cir. 2009)

NIEMEYER, Circuit Judge:

In this *qui tam* action, the relators, on behalf of the United States, alleged fraud perpetrated by Custer Battles, LLC, in making fraudulent statements or submitting fraudulent invoices on [a] contract[] entered into in 2003 with the Coalition Provisional Authority in Iraq, in violation of the False Claims Act, 31 U.S.C. §§3729-3732. . . . The district court limited the relators' fraud claim in connection with the . . . contract to a claim for $3 million, which was the amount paid to Custer Battles with a United States Treasury check and, as so limited, submitted the claims to the jury. After the jury found Custer Battles liable for fraud and returned a verdict of $3 million against it, the district court granted Custer Battles' earlier-filed motion for judgment as a matter of law under Federal Rule of Civil Procedure 50(a) on the ground that the evidence was insufficient to demonstrate that Custer Battles "presented" the fraudulent invoices to "an officer or employee of the United States Government or a member of the Armed Forces of the United States," as required by the False Claims Act. . . .

I.

The Coalition Provisional Authority in Iraq ("Coalition Authority") governed Iraq from May 2003 to June 28, 2004, when it turned over governing authority to the Interim Government of Iraq. The Coalition Authority's administrator, L. Paul Bremer, was appointed by the U.S. President and the U.S. Secretary of Defense, and the large majority of the Coalition Authority's personnel were either U.S. civilian contractors and employees or in the U.S. Military. The remainder of the Coalition Authority's personnel were from other countries in the coalition occupying Iraq, including Australia, the Czech Republic, Denmark, Italy, Japan, Poland, Romania, Spain, the United Kingdom, Ukraine, and others.

At the time of the Coalition Authority's formation, the Iraqi currency, the dinar, bore the portrait of Saddam Hussein, the deposed ruler of Iraq. In early July 2003, Administrator Bremer announced an initiative to replace all of these dinars with a new dinar that would not bear Saddam Hussein's portrait. The exchange was a massive undertaking. The new dinars were shipped into Iraq on 28 fully-loaded Boeing 747 cargo planes, and the exchange required the services of multiple contractors, ranging from providers of currency-counting machines to transportation providers.

To build, equip, and service three hubs of the dinar exchange program — to be located in Baghdad, Mosul, and Basra — the Coalition Authority entered into a contract (the "Dinar Exchange Contract") on August 27, 2003, with Custer Battles, LLC. Custer Battles was founded, managed, and owned by two former U.S. Army Rangers, Scott Custer and Michael Battles, and described itself as a "leading international risk management firm with extensive experience assisting large organizations reduce and manage risk in extremely volatile environments." . . .

The Dinar Exchange Contract was a cost-plus contract, meaning that Custer Battles would be reimbursed for its actual expenses, plus 25% of its actual expenses to cover overhead and provide a profit. On the day the contract was signed, the Coalition Authority paid Custer Battles an advance of $3 million. Although the Coalition Authority was funded from multiple sources, it paid Custer Battles the $3 million advance with a U.S. Treasury check funded by its "seized assets" account, consisting of assets seized from Iraqi government sources as part of the war effort. The check was signed by a lieutenant colonel in the U.S. Military. The invoices that Custer Battles thereafter submitted under the contract, however, were paid from the Coalition Authority's "Development Fund for Iraq," which was recognized by United Nations Security Council Resolution 1483 and included funds from various non-U.S. sources but also included $210 million confiscated by the United States from Iraqi bank accounts and transferred to the Development Fund, as well as funds appropriated by Congress. . . . Custer Battles submitted invoices for payment to U.S. personnel who were detailed to work with the Coalition Authority. . . .

Problems developed with the quality of Custer Battles' performance, leading to a meeting on October 18, 2003, between representatives of the Coalition Authority, the U.S. Military, and [Battles and Custer]. After this meeting ended, Battles accidentally left behind an astonishing spreadsheet, which contained rows listing items invoiced under the Dinar Exchange Contract and separate columns listing the "Actual Cost" for the items and the amounts "Invoiced" for the items. This document showed, for example, that for the Baghdad hub of the dinar exchange program, Custer Battles provided two flatbed trucks, for which it paid $18,000 but invoiced the Coalition Authority $80,000. To provide "Life Support, basic level" at the Bagdad hub, it provided generators that cost $74,000 but for which it invoiced the Coalition Authority $400,000. And for the Basra hub, it spent $4,000 to provide laundry facilities but invoiced the Coalition Authority for $12,000. Thus under the Dinar Exchange Contract, Custer Battles improperly received the difference between the actual costs and the inflated invoiced amounts and also 25% of the inflated invoiced amounts. . . .

DRC, Incorporated, a "leading provider of post-conflict management services, with considerable experience and contacts throughout the Middle East," acted as a subcontractor on Custer Battles' contracts in Iraq, and Robert Isakson was DRC's managing director. Based on their belief that Custer Battles defrauded the United States, DRC and Isakson, acting as relators under the False Claims Act, commenced this action against Custer Battles, its subsidiaries, related entities, and employees (collectively hereafter, "Custer Battles"). . . .

The district court . . . proceeded to trial on the Dinar Exchange Contract . . . claim[]. The jury returned a verdict in favor of the relators . . . [and awarded the] maximum amount of damages allowed by the district court—$3 million [paid specifically from the U.S. Treasury]. . . .

Before entering judgment on the verdict, the district court [granted] Custer Battles' motion for judgment as a matter of law under Federal Rule of Civil Procedure 50(a) . . . entering judgment for Custer Battles on Counts I and II. With respect to claims made under §3729(a)(1), the court found that the relators did not prove that the invoices were presented to U.S. government employees or officers, as required by that provision, but rather to the Coalition Authority. For the same reason, the court granted judgment as a matter of law on the claims under §3729(a)(2), which the court concluded had an implied requirement that the false record or statement be *presented* to the U.S. government. . . .

The relators now appeal. . . .

The False Claims Act provides in pertinent part:

> Any person who—
>
> (1) knowingly presents, or causes to be presented, to an officer or employee of the United States Government or a member of the Armed Forces of the United States a false or fraudulent *claim* for payment or approval;
>
> [or]
>
> (2) knowingly makes, uses, or causes to be made or used, a false record or statement to get a false or fraudulent *claim* paid or approved by the Government;
>
> * * *
>
> is liable to the United States Government [for a civil penalty and treble damages].

31 U.S.C. §3729(a) (emphasis added). The Act in turn defines "claim" as follows:

> For purposes of this section, "claim" includes any request or demand . . . for money or property which is made to a . . . grantee, or other recipient if the United States Government provides any portion of the money or property which is requested or demanded, or if the Government will reimburse such . . . grantee, or other recipient for any portion of the money or property which is requested or demanded.

31 U.S.C. §3729(c). The Act thus addresses a false or fraudulent claim even if the claim is "made to a . . . grantee, or other recipient" of U.S. money so long as the claim would draw on money of which the U.S. government provides "any portion."

Textually, therefore, a claim made to a grantee of U.S. money is not defined by the amount of money that the U.S. government paid directly to the claimant. So long as "*any portion*" of the claim is or will be funded by U.S. money *given to the grantee*, the full claim satisfies the definition of claim as used in §3729(a)(1) or (a)(2). The district court thus erred when it concluded that "it is necessary to consider each source of funds separately to determine whether a request for payment therefrom *constitutes a 'claim.'*" And its conclusion that "if the funds used to pay the Custer Battles contracts were 'Iraqi funds,' even if administered or held in the possession of the United States, then the presentment of a fraudulent request for payment from these funds does not constitute a 'claim' within the meaning of the [False Claims Act]" was also erroneous.

The district court also erred in imposing a "control of funds" requirement. The court concluded that when U.S. funds (the $210 million in "vested funds") were transferred to the Development Fund for Iraq, the United States "relinquished control of those funds and they ceased to be United States government property," such that "the United States did not '*provide*' a portion of the money or property requested or demanded from the [Development Fund for Iraq], as §3729(c) requires, even if it, at one time, *provided* a portion of the money now held in the [Development Fund for Iraq].'" This interpretation overlooks the False Claims Act's language that includes claims "*made to a . . . grantee, or other recipient*" of U.S. funds, so long as the United States "provides any portion" of the funds that the grantees or recipients would use to pay the claim. This statutory language precludes an interpretation requiring that the U.S. retain control over funds used to pay claims by extending the reach of the Act to money in the hands of a U.S. government "grantee" or "other recipient." A grantee is one to whom the money is given, and the U.S. need no longer have control over the funds.

In this case, the record demonstrates that over and above the $3 million advance it received, Custer Battles made claims to a grantee of U.S. money, *i.e.*, the Coalition Authority, and that the claims were paid from the grantee's funds, *i.e.*, the Development Fund for Iraq, a portion of which was provided to the grantee by the U.S. government, *i.e.*, $210 million. . . .

Custer Battles also argues that their requests or demands were not "claims" because Custer Battles was not in privity with the United States government. But the statutory language provides no indication that Congress intended to require privity. Indeed, the Supreme Court recently rejected the very notion in Allison Engine Co. v. United States ex rel. Sanders, 553 U.S. 662 (2008). In *Allison Engine*, the Court held that a subcontractor could be liable for submitting a false claim to a prime contractor of the United States. Of course, a subcontractor is by definition not in privity with the U.S. government.

We thus conclude that all false or fraudulent claims made by Custer Battles under the Dinar Exchange Contract were "claims" as defined in 31 U.S.C. §3729(c) and used in §3729(a).

In the end, the district court's source-of-funds analysis might prove harmless because damages sustained by the United States might not have exceeded the $3 million amount found by the jury. . . .

III.

The relators also contend that the district court erred in granting Custer Battles' motion for judgment as a matter of law, filed under Federal Rule of Civil Procedure 50(a). Specifically, relators challenge the court's conclusion that the relators "failed to produce sufficient evidence of presentment," as it construed both §3729(a)(1) and §3729(a)(2) to require. The district court held that because the False Claims Act requires presentment to "an officer or employee of the United States Government," presentment to the Coalition Authority did not satisfy the requirement because the Coalition Authority was not an instrumentality of the United States. . . .

Because the court found the evidence of presentment insufficient, it did not decide three other issues raised in Custer Battles' Rule 50(a) motion, i.e., whether the claims were materially false; whether the United States suffered damage; and whether the individual defendants had sufficient knowledge of the fraudulent conduct to be liable. . . .

Section 3729(a)(1) of the False Claims Act creates liability for any person who "knowingly presents, or causes to be presented, *to an officer or employee of the United States Government or a member of the Armed Forces of the United States* a false or fraudulent claim for payment or approval." 31 U.S.C. §3729(a)(1) (emphasis added). To fulfill this requirement, the relators presented extensive evidence that Custer Battles presented or caused to be presented fraudulently inflated invoices to U.S. government personnel who were detailed to the Coalition Authority. Indeed, the district court observed about the sufficiency of this evidence that "the trial record is replete with evidence that invoices and records were presented to [Coalition Authority] employees, including members of the United States Armed Forces detailed to the [Coalition Authority]."

But the district court found that this evidence did not fulfill the presentment requirement, as "the presentment requirement could not be satisfied by presentment to a United States government employee or officer where the employee or officer is not working in his or her official U.S. capacity." As an example, the district court noted that "if a contractor submitted a false claim to a U.S. government employee for remodeling her kitchen, the presentment requirement would not be satisfied." Because the U.S. government personnel were detailed to the Coalition Authority at the time of presentment, the district court concluded that they could not have been acting in the requisite official capacity as employees of the United States.

While we agree with the district court that §3729(a)(1) requires that presentment be made to U.S. government personnel working in their official capacity, we conclude that the court erred in assuming that U.S. government personnel detailed to the Coalition Authority could not be working in their official capacities as U.S. government employees. This can be demonstrated by reexamining the district court's hypothetical about "a contractor submit[ting] a false claim to a U.S. government employee for remodeling her kitchen." If that employee were a soldier detailed to remodel the kitchen in her government-owned housing, the court would surely have to hesitate in concluding that the soldier was not acting in her official capacity when the soldier's orders required her to remodel the kitchen.

In this case the relators introduced ample evidence to show that the fraudulently inflated invoices were presented to U.S. government employees or officials who were acting in their official capacities. They demonstrated that invoices claiming payment were presented in the first instance to professional U.S. government contracting officers, who were paid and supervised by the U.S. Military. . . .

The district court's interpretation of §3729(a)(1) appears to derive from its assumption that the presentation to a U.S. officer or employee must be for payment or approval "by the U.S. government." But the text of §3729(a)(1) does not contain that language or that requirement. It stands in stark contrast to §3729(a)(2), which *does* contain the requirement of intent to "get" the claim "paid or approved *by the Government*." As the Supreme Court has repeatedly stated, "when Congress includes particular language in one section of a statute but omits it in another section of the same Act, it is generally presumed that Congress acts intentionally and purposely in the disparate inclusion or exclusion." Here, Congress included a requirement of payment or approval "by the Government" in §3729(a)(2), but not in §3729(a)(1). Thus, courts are not free to read "by the Government" into (a)(1) when Congress omitted it.

Moreover, our conclusion comports with the structure created by the juxtaposition of §§3729(a)(1) and 3729(a)(2). Section 3729(a)(1) defines liability in terms of the *person* to whom the claim is presented, whereas §3729(a)(2) defines liability in terms of the intended *source* of the payment or approval. . . .

Because the relators have introduced evidence sufficient for a jury reasonably to conclude that Custer Battles presented or caused to be presented fraudulently inflated invoices to persons acting in their official capacity as U.S. officials or employees, we reverse the district court's order granting Custer Battles' Rule 50(a) motion.

The district court also granted judgment as a matter of law on the relators' claims based on 31 U.S.C. §3729(a)(2), which provides that "[a]ny person who . . . knowingly makes, uses, or causes to be made or used, a false record or statement to get a false or fraudulent claim paid or approved by the Government . . . is liable to the United States Government." The district court concluded that this language implicitly requires *presentment* to a U.S. officer or employee acting in the officer or employee's official capacity. Because the court found the relators' evidence of presentment insufficient, it also granted judgment as a matter of law on their claims made under §3729(a)(2).

The district court's holding that §3729(a)(2) has a "presentment" requirement has subsequently been rejected by the Supreme Court in *Allison Engine*, 128 S. Ct. at 2129-30. The Supreme Court reasoned that because the statutory language in §3729(a)(1) expressly requires presentment, courts should not read such a requirement into § 3729(a)(2) when the statutory language does not expressly contain that requirement. In light of the Supreme Court's holding in *Allison Engine*, we conclude that the district court erred in finding a presentment requirement in §3729(a)(2), recognizing that the district court did not have the benefit of *Allison Engine*.

In short, we hold that the district court erred in basing its order granting Custer Battles' Rule 50(a) motion on an insufficiency of evidence with respect to presentment. This leaves open the other arguments advanced by Custer Battles in its Rule 50(a) motion, which the court did not address. Accordingly, we remand this case to the district court [for further proceedings].

NOTES AND QUESTIONS

1. As one might imagine, litigation over the many issues raised by the civil false claims statute and related qui tam provisions abound. Given that this text focuses on white collar *crime*, the cases presented in this section are intended to do no more than introduce you to the flavor of the proceedings in this arena.
2. Can you delineate the various holdings in *Custer Battles*? Do they make sense? Do they fit together with each other?
3. In May 2009, President Obama signed into law the Fraud Enforcement and Recovery Act of 2009, Pub. L. No. 111-21, 123 Stat. 1620 (FERA), which made significant amendments to the civil False Claims Act (FCA) for the first time in 20 years. The amendments (1) reversed the portion of the *Allison Engine* case in which the Supreme Court had held that, to prevail under the FCA, the government must prove a clear link between the false claim and the government's payment, i.e., that the defendant intended the government itself to pay the claim; (2) imposed and defined a materiality requirement for prosecutions brought pursuant to §3729(a)(2); and (3) expanded the FCA's conspiracy-related offense. In addition, FERA greatly enhanced entities' obligations with regard to overpayments and "reverse false claims."
4. Which do you think provides more deterrence with respect to defrauding the government, 18 U.S.C. §287 or 31 U.S.C. §§3729 *et seq.*? Why?

chapter 8

Perjury and False Declarations

I. INTRODUCTION

The purpose behind the crimes of perjury and false declarations is to protect the integrity of federal judicial proceedings from the taint of lies and false documents. Although perjury and false declarations are usually classified as "white collar crimes," they do not fit the traditional definition because they are not economically motivated and can be committed by individuals of any socioeconomic class. Perhaps they are categorized this way because white collar defendants, usually smart and well-versed in talking themselves out of tight situations, are more prone to committing perjury than their blue collar, street crime, counterparts. Certainly, white collar defendants are more likely to testify at trial because they typically have no prior criminal convictions that can be used to be impeach them on cross-examination, and they probably have an exculpating version of events that is at least plausible. Also, perjury occurs during—indeed, some say pervades—civil litigation, which is typically a white collar "event."

Two distinct statutes address the making of false statements in the federal system. The first, 18 U.S.C. §1621, is derived from the common law crime of perjury and, as such, is subject to a number of defendant-oriented restrictions that judges developed prior to the statutory enactment. The second statute, called "False Declarations," is codified as 18 U.S.C. §1623. It was passed by Congress in 1970 specifically to broaden the net around those whose falsehoods corrupt the judicial system, but its application is limited to certain specific venues. Because of this history, §§1621 and 1623 have an interesting and sometimes confusing relationship. They overlap in many respects, but each applies to circumstances that the other does not.

Specifically:

1. Section 1621 is broader than §1623 in that it applies to individuals who "have taken an oath before [any] competent tribunal, officer, or person, in any case in which a law of the United States authorizes an oath to be administered,"

while §1623 applies only to any "proceeding before or ancillary to any court or grand jury of the United States."

2. Section 1623 is broader than §1621 in that, in addition to covering traditional false declarations (statements), it also applies to the submission of false information in any "book, paper, document, record, recording, or other material."
3. Section 1621 is narrower than §1623 in that its application is limited by the (misleadingly named) "two witness rule" and the requirement that the prosecution prove the actual falsity of any statement, while the statutory language of §1623 exempts it from the former rule and permits the falsity of a declaration to be proven by showing that the defendant made "irreconcilably contradictory declarations" while under oath.
4. Section 1623 is narrower than §1621 in that it is subject to a statutorily created "recantation" defense, while §1621 is not.

These distinctions, and other doctrine applicable to both provisions, are explored in more detail below.

II. THE COMPLEXITIES OF THE DOCTRINE: LITERAL TRUTH, "STARK CONTRAST," MATERIALITY, FUNDAMENTALLY AMBIGUOUS QUESTIONS, AND THE TWO WITNESS RULE (UNDER §1621)

BRONSTON v. UNITED STATES

409 U.S. 352 (1973)

Mr. Chief Justice BURGER delivered the opinion for a unanimous Court.

We granted the writ in this case to consider a narrow but important question in the application of the federal perjury statute, 18 U.S.C. §1621: whether a witness may be convicted of perjury for an answer, under oath, that is literally true but not responsive to the question asked and arguably misleading by negative implication.

Petitioner is the sole owner of Samuel Bronston Productions, Inc., a company that[,] between 1958 and 1964, produced motion pictures in various European locations. For these enterprises, Bronston Productions[] opened bank accounts in a number of foreign countries; in 1962, for example, it had 37 accounts in five countries. As president of Bronston Productions, petitioner supervised transactions involving the foreign bank accounts.

In June 1964, Bronston Productions[] petitioned for an arrangement with creditors under Chapter XI of the Bankruptcy Act. On June 10, 1966, a referee in bankruptcy held a §21(a) hearing to determine, for the benefit of creditors, the extent and location of the company's assets. Petitioner's perjury conviction was founded on the answers given by him as a witness at that bankruptcy hearing, and in particular on the following colloquy with a lawyer for a creditor of Bronston Productions:

"Q. Do you have any bank accounts in Swiss banks, Mr. Bronston?
"A. No, sir.
"Q. Have you ever?
"A. The company had an account there for about six months, in Zurich.
"Q. Have you any nominees who have bank accounts in Swiss banks?
"A. No, sir.
"Q. Have you ever?
"A. No, sir."

It is undisputed that for a period of nearly five years, between October 1959 and June 1964, petitioner had a personal bank account at the International Credit Bank in Geneva, Switzerland, into which he made deposits and upon which he drew checks totaling more than $180,000. It is likewise undisputed that petitioner's answers were literally truthful. (a) Petitioner did not at the time of questioning have a Swiss bank account. (b) Bronston Productions, Inc., did have the account in Zurich described by petitioner. (c) Neither at the time of questioning nor before did petitioner have nominees who had Swiss accounts. The Government's prosecution for perjury went forward on the theory that in order to mislead his questioner, petitioner answered the second question with literal truthfulness but unresponsively addressed his answer to the company's assets and not to his own—thereby implying that he had no personal Swiss bank account at the relevant time.

At petitioner's trial, the District Court instructed the jury that the "basic issue" was whether petitioner "spoke his true belief." Perjury, the court stated, "necessarily involves the state of mind of the accused" and "essentially consists of wilfully testifying to the truth of a fact which the defendant does not believe to be true"; petitioner's testimony could not be found "willfully" false unless at the time his testimony was given petitioner "fully understood the questions put to him but nevertheless gave false answers knowing the same to be false." The court further instructed the jury that if petitioner did not understand the question put to him and for that reason gave an unresponsive answer, he could not be convicted of perjury. Petitioner could, however, be convicted if he gave an answer "not literally false but when considered in the context in which it was given, nevertheless constitute(d) a false statement."[3]

The illustration given by the District Court [see footnote 3] is hardly comparable to petitioner's answer; the answer "five times" is responsive to the hypothetical question and contains nothing to alert the questioner that he may be sidetracked. Moreover, it is very doubtful that an answer which, in response to a specific quantitative inquiry, baldly understates a numerical fact can be described as even "technically true." Whether an answer is true must be determined with reference to the

3. The District Court gave the following example "as an illustration only":

> (I)f it is material to ascertain how many times a person has entered a store on a given day and that person responds to such a question by saying five times when in fact he knows that he entered the store 50 times that day, that person may be guilty of perjury even though it is technically true that he entered the store five times.

question it purports to answer, not in isolation. An unresponsive answer is unique in this respect because its unresponsiveness by definition prevents its truthfulness from being tested in the context of the question—unless there is to be speculation as to what the unresponsive answer "implies."

The jury began its deliberations at 11:30 A.M. Several times it requested exhibits or additional instructions from the court, and at one point, at the request of the jury, the District Court repeated its instructions in full. At 6:10 P.M., the jury returned its verdict, finding petitioner guilty on the count of perjury before us today and not guilty on another charge not here relevant. . . .

There is, at the outset, a serious literal problem in applying §1621 to petitioner's answer. The words of the statute confine the offense to the witness who "willfully . . . states . . . any material matter which he does not believe to be true." Beyond question, petitioner's answer to the crucial question was not responsive if we assume, as we do, that the first question was directed at personal bank accounts. There is, indeed, an implication in the answer to the second question that there was never a personal bank account; in casual conversation this interpretation might reasonably be drawn. But we are not dealing with casual conversation and the statute does not make it a criminal act for a witness to willfully state any material matter that implies any material matter that he does not believe to be true.[4]

The Government urges that the perjury statute be construed broadly to reach petitioner's answer and thereby fulfill its historic purpose of reinforcing our adversary factfinding process. We might go beyond the precise words of the statute if we thought they did not adequately express the intention of Congress, but we perceive no reason why Congress would intend the drastic sanction of a perjury prosecution to cure a testimonial mishap that could readily have been reached with a single additional question by counsel alert—as every examiner ought to be—to the incongruity of petitioner's unresponsive answer. Under the pressures and tensions of interrogation, it is not uncommon for the most earnest witnesses to give answers that are not entirely responsive. Sometimes the witness does not understand the question, or may in an excess of caution or apprehension read too much or too little into it. It should come as no surprise that a participant in a bankruptcy proceeding may have something to conceal and consciously tries to do so, or that a debtor may be embarrassed at his plight and yield information reluctantly. It is the responsibility of the lawyer to probe; testimonial interrogation, and cross-examination in particular, is a probing, prying, pressing form of inquiry. If a witness evades, it is the lawyer's responsibility to recognize the evasion and to bring the witness back to the mark, to flush out the whole truth with the tools of adversary examination.

It is no answer to say that here the jury found that petitioner intended to mislead his examiner. A jury should not be permitted to engage in conjecture whether an

4. Petitioner's answer is not to be measured by the same standards applicable to criminally fraudulent or extortionate statements. In that context, the law goes rather far in punishing intentional creation of false impressions by a selection of literally true representations, because the actor himself generally selects and arranges the representations. In contrast, under our system of adversary questioning and cross-examination the scope of disclosure is largely in the hands of counsel and presiding officer.

unresponsive answer, true and complete on its face, was intended to mislead or divert the examiner; the state of mind of the witness is relevant only to the extent that it bears on whether "he does not believe (his answer) to be true." To hold otherwise would be to inject a new and confusing element into the adversary testimonial system we know. Witnesses would be unsure of the extent of their responsibility for the misunderstandings and inadequacies of examiners, and might well fear having that responsibility tested by a jury under the vague rubric of "intent to mislead" or "perjury by implication." The seminal modern treatment of the history of the offense concludes that one consideration of policy overshadowed all others during the years when perjury first emerged as a common-law offense: "that the measures taken against the offense must not be so severe as to discourage witnesses from appearing or testifying." . . .

[W]e must read §1621 in light of our own and the traditional Anglo-American judgment that a prosecution for perjury is not the sole, or even the primary, safeguard against errant testimony. . . . The cases support petitioner's position that the perjury statute is not to be loosely construed, nor the statute invoked simply because a wily witness succeeds in derailing the questioner—so long as the witness speaks the literal truth. The burden is on the questioner to pin the witness down to the specific object of the questioner's inquiry. . . .

It may well be that petitioner's answers were not guileless but were shrewdly calculated to evade. Nevertheless, we [conclude] that any special problems arising from the literally true but unresponsive answer are to be remedied through the "questioner's acuity" and not by a federal perjury prosecution.

Reversed.

UNITED STATES v. DEZARN

157 F.3d 1042 (6th Cir. 1998)

Rosen, District Judge.

. . . In the spring of 1990, a group of active and retired officers of the Kentucky National Guard, including Defendant Robert DeZarn, Billy Wellman, John Julian, and Ed Gill, met at Billy Wellman's home to discuss raising funds for Brereton Jones' gubernatorial campaign. At that meeting, they selected officers from a list of active officers in the guard from whom funds were to be solicited by designated members of the group. The funds were to be collected at a "Preakness Party" being held at Wellman's home on May 19, 1990.

As indicated, the "Preakness Party" was held in May 1990. Invitations were sent out, inviting guests to "a Preakness Party . . . for an evening of fun on the farm." Sixty guests attended and gubernatorial candidate Jones made a short speech. Contributions to Jones' campaign were collected at that event. DeZarn admitted in his trial testimony that he received contributions to Jones' campaign at that party. Other witnesses testified to giving contributions to DeZarn at that party, to seeing DeZarn, Wellman and others counting checks at the party, and to discussing with DeZarn the sources of cash contributions at the party.

A year later, in June of 1991, Wellman held another party which DeZarn also attended. This was a small dinner party, attended only by six people: Wellman and his wife, DeZarn and his wife, and another couple. They had dinner, watched the Belmont Stakes horse race on television, and then went to a horse show afterwards. No active guardsmen attended, nor were campaign contributions made or collected. Governor Jones neither attended nor was invited to that party.

After Jones was elected governor in November 1991, he appointed DeZarn Adjutant General of the Kentucky National Guard. The Adjutant General is the chief commanding officer of the Kentucky National Guard. In 1992, DeZarn convened a Selective Retention Board. Every few years, a Selective Retention Board, consisting of three officers, is picked by the Adjutant General of the Guard. This board is designed to review the military records of officers eligible for retirement and determine which officers will be retained beyond that point, and which of them have reached their "maximum potential" and should be let go or, in Guard parlance, "non-retained."

Normally, the Board removes only a small number of officers. However, in 1992, an unusually large number of officers were "non-retained," several of whom complained to the Inspector General of the Army, alleging that they were let go because they did not support Jones' gubernatorial campaign. Among other things, these officers alleged that individuals who attended the Preakness Party at Wellman's and made a campaign contribution were not released.

In response to those allegations, the Inspector General sent two army officers, Colonel Thomas Mulrine and Colonel Robert Tripp, to investigate the allegations. The investigators conducted interviews of about 30 witnesses. . . . One of the witnesses interviewed during the investigation was Defendant Robert DeZarn. In pertinent part, the interview, which was conducted by Colonel Tripp under oath pursuant to 10 U.S.C. §936(b), was as follows:

Q: Okay, sir. My question is going to deal with General Wellman, though. Was it traditional for General Wellman to hold parties at his home and invite Guardsman to attend?

A: [by DeZarn]: Well, I suppose you could say that for a number of years that going back to the late 50s he has done this on occasion.

Q: Okay. In 1991, and I recognize this is in the period that you were retired, he held the Preakness Party at his home. Were you aware of that?

A: Yes.

Q: Did you attend?

A: Yes.

* * *

Q: Okay. Sir, was that a political fundraising activity?

A: *Absolutely not.*

Q: Okay. Did then Lieutenant Governor Jones, was he in attendance at the party?

A: I knew he was invited. I don't remember if he made an appearance or not.

Q: All right, sir. You said it was not a political fundraising activity. Were there any contributions to Governor Jones' campaign made at that activity?

A: *I don't know.*

Q: Okay. You did not see any, though?
A: *No.*
Q: And you were not aware of any?
A: *No.*

One witness interviewed by Colonels Mulrine and Tripp indicated that DeZarn received a contribution for Jones at the Preakness Party. The investigators, however, did not credit that witness' testimony because it was not substantiated and because they interpreted one of DeZarn's answers in his interview as denying that he received contributions. Therefore, the investigators' final report indicated that they were unable to sustain the allegations of improper political influence over the Selective Retention Board, although they noted the fact that a retired colonel, Ed Gill, had been brought out of retirement to fill a slot . . . "gave a perception of favoritism."

The report did reveal, however, that there was evidence that one officer, John Julian, had improperly solicited funds from fellow officers, in violation of the Hatch Act, 18 U.S.C. §602. Following that revelation, Julian came forward with additional information about the Preakness Party. He also provided information concerning the planning meeting for that party which had not been disclosed to Colonels Mulrine and Tripp in their witness interviews which formed the basis of their initial report.

In light of the new information provided by Julian, additional investigations were subsequently conducted which revealed DeZarn's involvement in the planning meeting and his collection of contributions at the Preakness Party.

DeZarn was then charged with perjury on the basis of his sworn answers in his interview with the investigators. . . .

On March 11, 1996, DeZarn moved to dismiss the indictment against him arguing that [it] was insufficient to charge him with perjury because when he was questioned by the Inspector General's investigators, he was asked about a Preakness Party at Billy Wellman's house in 1991 as opposed to 1990, and he gave literally truthful answers with respect to Wellman's 1991 dinner party. The District Court denied DeZarn's motion. . . .

At trial, DeZarn testified that Colonel Tripp, by mistakenly setting the questions in his interview about the Preakness Party in 1991, rather than 1990, led him to answer the questions with reference to the 1991 dinner party, which was not a fundraiser and at which he did not collect any contributions.

Evidence was presented at trial, however, to establish that DeZarn was not misled by the 1991 date but had answered the investigators' questions as he had with intent to deceive them. . . .

On September 26, 1996, the jury returned a verdict of guilty. . . . DeZarn now appeals his conviction and sentence. . . .

II. Discussion

B. Sufficiency of the Indictment

In arguing insufficiency of the indictment against him, DeZarn first argues that his conviction must be reversed because the indictment against him did not present a "stark contrast" between the "truth portion" and his allegedly false testimony. Since the indictment alleged that DeZarn accepted contributions at a 1990 Preakness Party and alleged that he testified falsely when he stated that he did not accept contributions at a 1991 Preakness Party, Defendant argues that under the "stark contrast" rule, the indictment was insufficient to charge him with the offense of perjury. As a corollary argument, DeZarn argues that his answers to the investigator's questions dealing with the 1991 Preakness Party were literally true and, therefore, cannot form the basis for a perjury conviction even if there was an intent to mislead or evade.

1. The "Stark Contrast" Rule

The "stark contrast" rule and the "literal truth" defense both had their genesis in Bronston v. United States, 409 U.S. 352 (1973). . . . The *Bronston* Court's decision . . . was premised upon the fact that the defendant had given a nonresponsive answer to the question asked, which the interviewer merely took to imply a negative answer to the question. Specifically, in phrasing the questions, the examiner phrased the initial question in the present tense: "Do you have any bank accounts in Swiss banks?" The response, "No, sir," was literally true, since at the time he was asked the question, Bronston did not have any Swiss bank accounts. The next question asked Bronston, "Have you ever?," to which Bronston gave a partially truthful but incomplete and misleading answer, that his business had had a Swiss bank account for about six months.

Taken in the context of the questioning, this response was really nonresponsive. The Court pointed out that "An unresponsive answer is unique . . . because its unresponsiveness by definition prevents it from being tested in the context of the question—unless there is speculation as to what the unresponsive answer 'implies.'" Thus, because a nonresponsive answer, by its nature, requires speculation by the fact-finder as to what the answer "implies," there cannot be a finding beyond a reasonable doubt that the answer is untruthful.

Where, however, the answer given is responsive to the question asked and "it is entirely reasonable to expect a defendant to have understood the terms used in the question," a charge of perjury may not be dismissed for insufficiency. United States v. Slawik, 548 F.2d 75, 86 (3d Cir. 1977). Thus, the question and answer must be examined in the context of the investigation as a whole and the state of the defendant's knowledge in order to determine whether ambiguity exists.

What is presented in this case is not a nonresponsive, or only partially responsive, answer. Rather, we have a series of categorical answers to questions with a partially mistaken premise or presupposition. In a case very similar to the one now before the court, the Eighth Circuit used factual context to resolve the ambiguity in testimony with a false presupposition, and refused to extend *Bronston* to allow the defendant "to escape a false oath charge by misleading the questioner with false testimony and then supply literally true answers to questions based on his false testimony." United States v. Robbins, 997 F.2d 390, 395 (8th Cir. 1993), *cert. denied*, 510 U.S. 948 (1993). . . .

The question presented here, then, is whether in a perjury case in which a mistaken premise exists in one of the questions asked of the testifier, the Government is entitled to present, and the jury to consider, evidence of the context of the questioning which would establish that the Defendant—despite the false premise of the question—knew exactly what the questions meant and exactly what they were referring to. We hold that the law of perjury not only permits this, but in cases such as this, requires it.

First, perjury must be shown to be willful, and it must be shown that the testifier did not believe his responses to be true. Thus, by its very nature, perjury requires an inquiry into the Defendant's state of mind and his intent to deceive at the time the testimony was given. Indeed, the entire focus of a perjury inquiry centers upon what the testifier knew and when he knew it because in order to make a determination as to whether that person intended to testify falsely, it must be established beyond a reasonable doubt that he knew his testimony to be false when he gave it. In order to prove this, the Government, of necessity, must present evidence of the extent of a Defendant's knowledge of the subject matter of the questioning and the circumstances surrounding how he came to that knowledge. This, of course, requires the Government to show the full context of the Defendant's activities as well as other information of which he may have had knowledge and which may have influenced him. . . .

This is not to say that the question to which the answer is made is not an important part of a perjury inquiry. Of course it is. A question that is truly ambiguous or which affirmatively misleads the testifier can never provide a basis for a finding of perjury, as it could never be said that one intended to answer such a question untruthfully. But, where it can be shown from the context of the question and the state of the testifier's knowledge at the time that the testifier clearly knew what the question meant, the Government must be permitted to present, and the fact-finder to consider, those contextual facts.

The circumstances presented here are just such a case. The context of the investigation in this case establishes that it would be entirely reasonable to expect that DeZarn understood that the questions posed to him concerned the 1990 party. Even if the questioning was not perfectly precise, the context in which the questions were asked made the object of the questioning clear and, more importantly, it is clear that DeZarn knew exactly the party to which Colonel Tripp was referring. The evidence at trial clearly established that Billy Wellman held only one Preakness Party and that was in 1990. No Preakness Party was held in 1991. Furthermore, the characteristics of the 1990 and 1991 parties differed markedly. More than 60 persons were invited to the 1990 Preakness Party, including then Lieutenant Governor Jones who was running for governor. In contrast, only three couples—Billy Wellman and his wife, DeZarn and his wife, and one other couple—attended Wellman's 1991 dinner party. Lieutenant Governor Jones did not attend that gathering, nor was he invited.

With respect to DeZarn's argument that he believed Colonel Tripp's questioning referred to the 1991 party, there was ample evidence to show that it is quite implausible that DeZarn would not remember, as he testified he did not, whether the future governor of the Commonwealth attended or did not attend a dinner party with only six people present.

Perhaps most tellingly, however, the evidence at trial showed that Colonel Tripp's investigation and questioning of DeZarn did not occur in a vacuum of information or news. First, several witnesses testified that the "Preakness Party" was a singular event that was the subject of a great deal of gossip within the Guard because of its ties to the decisions made by the Selective Retention Board. But, the Preakness Party was not only the subject of gossip—it was, two months before DeZarn's testimony, the subject of a series of newspaper articles in the *Louisville Courier Journal*, articles which DeZarn was interviewed for and which he admitted he had read and discussed with others. Indeed, DeZarn was quoted in one of the articles as saying that he attended the 1990 Preakness Party and that, just as he falsely testified to Colonel Tripp, he did not see any fundraising at that party.

Given this factual background, there was certainly abundant evidence from which a jury could find beyond a reasonable doubt that DeZarn knew at the time he answered Tripp's questions exactly which party Tripp was referring to in his questions. . . .

2. The "Literal Truth" Defense

DeZarn also argues that his conviction should be reversed because the testimony upon which his indictment was predicated was literally true with respect to Wellman's 1991 dinner party. We agree with the District Court's determination that the literal truth defense is inapplicable in this case.

As indicated above, the *Bronston* "literal truth" defense applies in cases where a perjury defendant responds to a question with an unresponsive answer. . . . By contrast, in this case, Defendant DeZarn gave unequivocal and directly and fully responsive answers to the questions asked by the Army investigator. Furthermore, as discussed above, there is more than ample context and evidence to test the meaning and falsity of DeZarn's answers.

C. Sufficiency of Evidence at Trial

DeZarn also argues that his conviction should be reversed because the Government did not present sufficient evidence at trial to sustain a finding that his allegedly false statements were material. Defendant contends that materiality requires a showing that the false testimony was the precise factor in the outcome of the proceedings in which the falsity was uttered. The basis for this argument is that although other witnesses had told the investigators that contributions had been made at the Preakness party, the investigators' final report still concluded that the allegations of political influence over the Selective Retention Board were unfounded and no evidence was produced that a different result would have been reached if DeZarn's answers would have been different.

This argument is as misleading as the Defendant's testimony itself. First, the Defendant's legal premise is seriously flawed. Contrary to Defendant's assertions, the test for materiality of a false statement does not require a showing that the outcome of the proceedings in which the statement was uttered would have been different had the defendant answered truthfully. A false statement can be material even if ultimately the conclusion of the tribunal would have been the same. United

States v. Chandler, 752 F.2d 1148 (6th Cir. 1985). To be material, all that must be shown is that the perjurious answer "had the potential or natural *tendency to affect or influence* the [investigator] in, or impede or dissuade [him] from, pursuing [the] investigation." United States v. Gribben, 984 F.2d 47, 51 (2d Cir. 1993) (emphasis added)....

Colonel Tripp testified that truthful statements by General DeZarn would have led to further questions, exposing the pre-Preakness Party planning meeting and the quantity of contributions, which, in turn, would have expanded the focus of the investigation. It could have further led to a finding that the Selective Retention Board was tainted by the appearance of partiality, in violation of army regulations....

In sum, the uncontroverted testimony of Colonel Tripp regarding how different answers by DeZarn would have influenced his investigation provides substantial evidence on which the jury's verdict can be sustained.

D. Two Witness Rule

DeZarn argues that the trial court committed reversible error by refusing to instruct the jury on the "two witness rule." According to the two witness rule, proof of the falsity of the defendant's testimony cannot be established beyond a reasonable doubt by the uncorroborated testimony of a single witness. The two witness rule prevents convictions from resting on "an oath against an oath" for fear that innocent witnesses might be unduly harassed or convicted in perjury prosecutions if a less stringent rule were adopted....

... [T]he Government argues that this case is one in which an instruction on the two witness rule is not required.... [T]his court has previously held that the two witness rule is inapplicable when [the falsity of the accused's statement is uncontested and] the only issue at trial relates to the [accused's] state of mind.

We find that this case falls squarely within th[is] exception since DeZarn admitted in his trial testimony that he took contributions at the 1990 Preakness Party, thereby removing from controversy the question of whether his testimony was false and leaving only the issue of whether his testimony to Colonel Tripp was intentionally false, or only inadvertently false, due to a misunderstanding of the question caused by a false presupposition.... Since there can be no error in refusing to instruct on a rule which has no application, we reject Defendant's argument....

Conclusion

For all of the foregoing reasons, we AFFIRM Defendant DeZarn's conviction and sentence.

NOTES AND QUESTIONS

1. In *Bronston*, the Supreme Court held that a literally truthful answer, though nonresponsive and designed to mislead, does not constitute perjury. Part of the rationale is that the burden of "pinning the witness down" is on the questioner, and ambiguity should be resolved in the witness's favor.

In *DeZarn*, the court holds, in line with most other circuits, that a responsive but willfully misleading answer that is based on a false premise—due to a faulty question—can be the basis of a perjury charge. Why shouldn't the responsibility fall to the questioner to ensure that the premises supporting his question are correct?

2. Both courts stress a difference between literally true responsive answers (which can form the basis of a perjury charge) and literally true nonresponsive answers (which cannot form the basis of a perjury charge). What is the difference between the two? Does the divergent treatment withstand scrutiny?
3. What is the difference between the "stark contrast" defense and the "literal truth" defense?
4. What is the purpose behind the two witness rule? Why doesn't it apply in the *DeZarn* case?
5. Note that, despite its name, the two witness rule does not require two witnesses to testify to the falsity of the accused's statement; as the *DeZarn* court indicates, the testimony of one witness accompanied by corroborating evidence is sufficient. *See also* United States v. Davis, 548 F.2d 840 (1977). Moreover, courts have held that corroboration can come from the defendant's own trial testimony. *See id.* at 843. Would a conviction based on the defendant's testimony constitute *per se* ineffective assistance of counsel? Why or why not?

UNITED STATES v. BONDS

580 F. Supp. 2d. 925 (2008)

SUSAN ILLSTON, District Judge.

[Barry Bonds is a retired Major League Baseball (MLB) player who played for the Pittsburgh Pirates from 1986-1992 and the San Francisco Giants from 1993-2007. Bonds's accomplishments during his baseball career place him among the greatest players of all time. He has a record-setting seven Most Valuable Player awards, including a record-setting four consecutive MVPs. He is a 14-time All-Star and 8-time Gold Glove winner. He holds numerous MLB records, including the all-time MLB home run record with 762. In 2003, Bonds became embroiled in a scandal when his trainer was indicted by a federal grand jury for supplying anabolic steroids to numerous professional athletes. During grand jury testimony on December 4, 2003, Bonds denied receiving steroids from his trainer, claiming instead that the only substances he obtained were the nutritional supplement flax-seed oil and a rubbing balm for arthritis. On November 15, 2007, after the trainer and others began cooperating with prosecutors, a federal grand jury returned an indictment against Bonds, charging him with four counts of perjury and one count of obstruction of justice.]

On November 5, 2008, the Court heard argument on defendant's motion to dismiss Counts One, Two, Five, Seven, Eight, Nine, Eleven, Twelve, Fourteen, and Fifteen of the second superseding indictment. For the reasons set forth below, the motion is GRANTED IN PART. . . .

Defendant argues that Counts Two, Five, Nine, Eleven, Twelve, and Fourteen of the superseding indictment must be dismissed because [the questions] are fundamentally ambiguous.

Generally speaking, the existence of some ambiguity in a falsely answered question will not shield the respondent from a perjury or false statement prosecution. It is for the jury to decide in such cases which construction the defendant placed on a question. If, however, a question is excessively vague, or fundamentally ambiguous, the answer may not, as matter of law, form the basis of a prosecution for perjury or false statement. "A question is fundamentally ambiguous when it 'is not a phrase with a meaning about which men of ordinary intelligence could agree.'" Precise questioning is imperative as a predicate for the offense of perjury.

A. Count Two

Count Two alleges:

> **Q:** Okay. So, I got to ask, Mr. Bonds. There's this number associated on a document with your name, and corresponding to Barry B. on the other document, and it does have these two listed anabolic steroids as testing positive in connection with it. Do you follow my question?
>
> **A:** I follow where you're going, yeah.
>
> **Q:** So, I guess I got to ask the question again, I mean, did you take steroids? And specifically this test the [sic] is in November of 2000. So, I'm going to ask you in the weeks and months leading up to November 2000, were you taking steroids—
>
> **A.** No.
>
> **Q:** —or anything like that?
>
> **A:** No, I wasn't at all. I've never seen these documents. I've never seen these papers.

Defendant maintains that the question was fundamentally ambiguous because the questioner did not identify what substances qualify as "anything like" steroids and because the questioner did not define the starting point of the "weeks and months" time period.

The Court finds that the indefinite time period did not make the question fundamentally ambiguous. If defendant's responses were false as he understood the questions, his conviction is not invalidated by the fact that his answer to the questions might generate a number of different interpretations. The government correctly notes that defendant repeatedly denied that he ever took steroids. Whether he thought the questioner was referring to the time period "weeks" or "months" before November, 2000 is therefore immaterial.

The question regarding "anything like" steroids presents a more serious problem. The government maintains that, in context, this phrase refers to "anything like steroids that could have led to a positive steroid test." This interpretation does not clarify what substances might fall within the category of being "anything like" steroids. The characteristics that make a substance "like" a steroid defy ready definition. The term is therefore not one which could be used with mutual understanding by a questioner and answerer unless it were defined at the time it were sought and offered as testimony. Accordingly, defendant's response to this statement cannot sustain a perjury conviction and the Court GRANTS defendant's motion to dismiss this count. . . .

B. Count Fourteen

Count Fourteen alleges:

> **Q:** And you weren't getting this flax seed oil stuff during that period of time [January 2002]?
>
> **A:** Not that I can recall. Like I say, I could be wrong. But I'm-I'm-going from my recollection it was, like, in the 2002 time and 2003 season.

Defendant raises several arguments in response to this count, all of which arise from the confusing wording of his answer. He argues that if the government proves that defendant received "flax seed oil stuff" in January, 2002, he cannot be convicted on the basis of this statement because at least part of his answer (i.e. that he received the substance "in the 2002 time") was literally true. He also argues that defendant's other qualifiers—"Not that I can recall" and "Like I say, I could be wrong" and "I'm going from my recollection"—render the entire passage fundamentally ambiguous.

The government responds that if such qualifiers could create fatal ambiguity, then every defendant could avoid a perjury charge by qualifying all his answers. The problem here, however, is not that defendant may have attempted to mitigate the effect of his "Not that I recall" response by adding qualifiers. The problem is that defendant's answer is so unclear that it is essentially impossible to parse. When a witness in a grand jury investigation gives answers that are "not entirely responsive," or "evades, it is the lawyer's responsibility to recognize the evasion and to bring the witness back to the mark, to flush out the whole truth with the tools of adversary examination." *Bronston*, 409 U.S. at 358-59. When defendant's interrogator received this meandering, inconclusive and internally inconsistent response, "[t]he burden [was] on the questioner to pin the witness down," *see id.* at 360. The remedy for such evasion, if indeed it was evasion, is "the questioner's acuity, and not[ ] a federal perjury prosecution." *See id.* at 362. Defendant's motion to dismiss this count is GRANTED. . . .

NOTES AND QUESTIONS

1. Judge Illston holds that the vagueness of the time period for the questioning in Count Two is not fatal because Bonds's categorical denial of ever using steroids made the time period "immaterial." Why couldn't the same thing be said with respect to Bonds's denial of ever taking "anything like" steroids? Should it matter that, in the transcript, Bonds appears to interrupt the prosecutor to say "no" even before the prosecutor uses the words "or anything like that?"

2. Some believe that the entire purpose of calling Barry Bonds before the grand jury was not to investigate the use of performance enhancing drugs in baseball, but to "force" the baseball icon into a "perjury trap." As it turns out, perjury defendants often invoke a "perjury trap" defense—usually to no avail. This is because the defense will not be successful if it is based on the claim that the prosecution's underlying motivation was to catch the defendant/witness in a lie. Rather, "[t]he defense requires that the defendant show the false answer was *illegally procured by the government*. Thus, when the grand jury is attempting to obtain useful information in furtherance of its investigation, the perjury trap doctrine does not apply. United States v. Brown, 49 F.3d 1162, 1168 (6th Cir.), *cert. denied*, 516 U.S. 942 (1995); United States v. Chen, 933 F.2d 793, 797 (9th Cir. 1991)." Title 9, United States Attorneys' Manual, Section 1756 (emphasis added).
3. Barry Bonds's case went to trial on March 21, 2011, nearly eight years after the grand jury appearance that led to the filing of the perjury charges against him. By that time, the case had been whittled down to just five counts and, ultimately, only four counts went to the jury. On April 14, the jury convicted Bonds of one count of obstruction of justice; it hung on each of the three perjury charges. At the time of this writing, Bonds's case is on appeal, while the government is still determining whether to retry him on the unresolved counts.
4. The literal truth, materiality, and other doctrines surrounding perjury and false declarations make these crimes difficult to prove. In addition, prosecutors seldom take on cases from the civil realm, not wanting to get caught in the middle of (and potentially manipulated by the parties to) private disputes. (The primary exception to this occurs when a judge contacts the U.S. Attorney and expresses outrage at conduct in his or her courtroom.) As a result, perjury prosecutions are relatively rare. This, of course, undermines the efficacy of the oath requirement in promoting the search for truth in our adversary system—though not as much as one might think. Witnesses seem to overestimate the likelihood of a perjury charge, thereby exercising some degree of self-restraint. Why do you think this is the case? Could it be due to the virility with which prosecutors and other attorneys are typically depicted in television and movies?

III. DOCTRINE SPECIFIC TO FALSE DECLARATIONS UNDER §1623

A. Irreconcilably Inconsistent Declarations

UNITED STATES v. PORTER
994 F.2d 470 (8th Cir. 1993)

KYLE, District Judge.

Introduction

Defendant Quillin Porter appeals his conviction of perjury for making "irreconcilably contradictory declarations material to the point in question" under oath in violation of 18 U.S.C. §1623(c). For the reasons set forth below, we reverse the conviction.

Background

The perjury charge stems from defendant's statements made (a) before a grand jury on May 18, 1989 as part of a plea agreement and (b) during an evidentiary hearing on defendant's own habeas corpus petition. In November, 1988, defendant was indicted on three counts of mail fraud and three counts of securities violations for his role in falsifying newsletters sent out to investors in several investments clubs which he operated. Defendant entered a plea of guilty to two counts of mail fraud and one count of securities law violation pursuant to a plea agreement in which he agreed to testify in grand jury proceedings against two other individuals.

Pursuant to that plea agreement, defendant testified before a grand jury on May 18, 1989. His testimony included the following exchange between himself and the Assistant United States Attorney (AUSA):

Q. How would you keep your individual investors advised on how their investments were doing?
A. I would send out a monthly newsletter that purportedly detailed all the trades and the amount of money that had been made along with a dividend check to each party.
Q. After a period of time, did it become necessary for you to falsify information on those newsletters?
A. Yes, it did.
Q. And is that why you pled guilty to the things you pled guilty to?
A. Yes.
Q. Who was responsible for preparing that newsletter that was sent to the investors?
A. I was.

Following his grand jury testimony and pursuant to his plea of guilty, the district court sentenced defendant to five years in prison on each of the three counts, to be served consecutively. Subsequently, defendant filed a habeas corpus petition to vacate, set aside, or correct his sentence, pursuant to 28 U.S.C. §2255, alleging ineffective assistance of counsel.

On April 14, 1992, an evidentiary hearing on the section 2255 petition was held before the magistrate judge during which the following exchange took place between defendant and the AUSA:

Q. Mr. Porter, you pled guilty because you are guilty, is that not correct?
A. That is not correct.

Q. You mailed newsletters out.
A. I'm not aware of that.
Q. These newsletters that you admitted were misrepresentations of the fact, you mailed these to the various investors?
A. I did not admit that.
Q. You did, though, do it. You mailed it [to] them?
A. I did?
Q. Yes.
A. I did not—
COURT: Sir, the answer is yes or no.
A. No.
Q. Who mailed in on your behalf?
A. I don't know.
Q. Who generated them?
A. I don't know.

During the course of this hearing, defendant, alleging ineffective assistance of counsel, claimed not only that his counsel failed to make certain objections to the pre-sentence investigation report and failed to appeal certain issues, but also failed to inform him of the specific nature of the charges to which he had pleaded guilty. Although the latter basis for a claim of ineffective assistance of counsel was not contained in defendant's habeas corpus petition, the magistrate judge considered the petition to be amended to include such a claim.

The magistrate judge issued a Report and Recommendation on June 8, 1992, finding no evidence of ineffective assistance of counsel and recommending denial of defendant's petition. The district court adopted the Report and Recommendation on July 13, 1992.

Following the habeas petition hearing, defendant was indicted on June 18, 1992 for violating 18 U.S.C. §1623(c), based on the "irreconcilably contradictory" and "material" statements of defendant before the grand jury in 1989 and his testimony before the magistrate judge at the habeas hearing in 1992. The indictment charges that the two statements set out in the preceding paragraphs of this opinion were "inconsistent to the degree that one of them is necessarily false."

At his perjury trial, defendant testified that he had falsified the information in the newsletters and that he was responsible for sending them out, but denied that he had mailed any of them. He also testified that he had pled guilty to the mail fraud charges for reasons other than being guilty of committing acts constituting mail fraud. Such reasons included: he was tired of fighting, his attorney recommended the plea, his life had been threatened, and he did not feel the trial judge could be impartial because he was the same judge who had presided over a civil suit against defendant brought by the investors. Defendant testified that he had given truthful answers to the specific questions asked of him, although he acknowledged that there was some uncertainty in his answers to questions in the habeas petition hearing....

At the close of the government's case and again at the conclusion of the trial, defendant moved for a judgment of acquittal based on the insufficiency of the evidence regarding the alleged irreconcilable inconsistency between his declarations.

The district court denied the motions. On September 10, 1992, the jury returned a verdict of guilty on the single perjury count. Defendant was sentenced to a term of imprisonment of 21 months. This appeal followed.

Defendant appeals his conviction on the grounds that . . . (2) the evidence at trial was insufficient to convict him in that (a) the two statements were not irreconcilably inconsistent. . . .

Discussion

[To sustain a conviction under 18 U.S.C. §1623, the government must prove each of the following elements beyond a reasonable doubt:

1. Defendant, under oath,
2. made two or more declarations,
3. which were irreconcilably inconsistent,
4. each of which was material to the point in question,
and
5. each of which was made within the statute of limitations.]

In reviewing the sufficiency of the evidence to support a conviction, the Court "look[s] at the evidence in the light most favorable to the verdict and accept[s] as established all reasonable inferences supporting the verdict. [The Court] then uphold[s] the conviction only if it is supported by substantial evidence." United States v. Plenty Arrows, 946 F.2d 62, 64 (8th Cir. 1991). An essential element of perjury under 18 U.S.C. §1623(c) is that the statements be "irreconcilably contradictory"—that is, "inconsistent to the degree that one of them is necessarily false." By including this precise and rigorous evidentiary standard in section 1623(c), Congress has enacted a statute under which a conviction requires a variance in testimony that extends beyond mere vagueness, uncertainty, or equivocality. Even though two declarations may differ from one another, the §1623(c) standard is not met unless, taking them in context, they are so different that if one is true there is no way that the other can also be true.[5]

Under this statutory standard, and reviewing the evidence in the light most favorable to the verdict, the Court cannot conclude that there is substantial evidence to support the conviction. At trial, the government introduced the relevant portions of the transcripts of defendant's testimony before the grand jury and at the habeas petition hearing and called two witnesses. The first witness, FBI Agent Richard O'Connell, testified that during his investigation of the mail fraud and

5. In this respect, paragraph (c) of section 1623 differs from the more commonly used paragraph (a) where an offense is committed by any person who "knowingly makes any false material declaration . . ." in a judicial proceeding. Paragraph (a) requires proof of intent and of falsity, whereas paragraph (c) requires proof that the statements are so inconsistent that one is necessarily false without the government having to prove which statement is false. Thus, only in a paragraph (a) prosecution is it necessary that the government submit evidence regarding the defendant's intent to falsify the information or mislead the government. In contrast, section 1623(c) "has eliminated the need for extrinsic evidence of falsity."

securities violations, defendant had made statements to him which were consistent with those defendant made before the grand jury. . . .

The second witness, Scott Sullivan, was a former employee of defendant's company, and testified that defendant provided the information for the newsletters, but that either Mr. Sullivan or the secretary typed up the newsletters, duplicated them, placed them in envelopes and delivered them to the post office. He testified that these activities took place at defendant's request and under his direction. . . .

The jury had the opportunity to compare the transcripts and the portions of those transcripts reproduced in the indictment, but such a comparison could not yield a conclusion that defendant's statements were "irreconcilably inconsistent"—vague, evasive or unresponsive, yes, but not irreconcilably inconsistent. When a defendant's testimony is vague, unresponsive or evasive, there can be no basis for a perjury conviction when the answers given are literally true. *See* Bronston v. United States, 409 U.S. 352 (1973).[7]

In addition, the questions in the two proceedings were not identical, allowing defendant to give answers in the habeas petition hearing which did not directly contradict his previous answers. In order for the government to establish the necessary irreconcilable inconsistency between defendant's statements, the questions asked of him should have focused on the same aspects of defendant's conduct in the mail fraud scheme.

While defendant's statements may appear facially inconsistent with one another, the context of the statements in the two proceedings illustrates that defendant made them in response to different questions emphasizing two different aspects of the charge to which he had pled guilty—the physical generating (including typing, collating, and stuffing envelopes) and mailing of the newsletters and the responsibility for including false information in those letters and directing that they be sent to investors. Defendant did not commit perjury simply by answering the questions in a narrow, arguably evasive fashion, giving a literal meaning to the words "mail" and "generate" and to the reasons and the number of reasons for his pleading guilty. The statements of the defendant must be inconsistent to the degree that "one of them is necessarily false." In our view, the statements in this case do not satisfy such a standard.

On the evidence before it, this Court concludes that a jury could not reasonably conclude that defendant's statements were irreconcilably inconsistent. The statements made during the habeas petition hearing were vague, unresponsive and evasive, and the government did not, or was unable to, elicit testimony from defendant that he was not, in fact, responsible for supplying the false information for the newsletters or for directing that they be sent to investors-testimony which would have been irreconcilably inconsistent with his testimony before the grand jury. The district court should have granted defendant's motion for acquittal made at the close of the government's case.

7. Although Bronston involved a prosecution under 18 U.S.C. §1621, courts have applied its holding to prosecutions under 18 U.S.C. §1623. *See, e.g.*, United States v. Reveron Martinez, 836 F.2d 684, 689 (1st Cir. 1988); United States v. Lighte, 782 F.2d 367, 372 (2d Cir. 1986); United States v. Tonelli, 577 F.2d 194, 198 (3d Cir. 1978).

The government asserts that because defendant, after making a motion for acquittal at the close of the government's case, chose to put on evidence in the form of his own testimony, the sufficiency of the evidence should be judged on the entire record. Having reviewed defendant's testimony at trial, the Court finds nothing which would support a jury's finding that his two previous statements were irreconcilably inconsistent. Defendant admitted that he was responsible for providing the false information for the newsletters and for causing them to be sent to investors. He denied, however, that he typed, copied or collated (what he defined as "generating") the newsletters, or physically mailing them himself. Defendant also testified that he had pled guilty to the mail fraud and securities violation charges not only because he thought he was guilty at the time, but for other reasons as well. Such testimony does not prove that his statements at the habeas petition hearing were irreconcilably inconsistent with his grand jury testimony.

For the reasons discussed above, the judgment of the district court is reversed and the case is remanded for entry of judgment of acquittal.

Floyd R. Gibson, Senior Circuit Judge, concurring specially.

I reluctantly concur with the majority's opinion, and write separately to express my concern that a minute distinction between the word "send" and "mail" has been used to overturn a jury verdict. In everyday life, individuals use the words interchangeably; only under the scrutiny of the judicial microscope could such a distinction be grounds for reversal of a conviction. The New World Dictionary defines "send" as a verb that means "to dispatch, convey, or transmit (a letter, message, etc.) by mail, radio., etc. "Mail" is defined as a verb that means to "send by mail, as by putting into a mailbox; post." Had the government proceeded to question Porter about whether he "sent" the falsified documents, we would not be addressing this issue. Unfortunately, however, the questioning did not go far enough and Porter is able to use an infinitesimal distinction in language to his advantage.

NOTES AND QUESTIONS

1. When he was questioned in front of the grand jury, Porter admitted that he had falsified the information in the newsletters and that he was "responsible for preparing" the newsletters that were "sent out" to investors. During the habeas questioning, Porter claimed that he did "not know" who "generated" the false mailings or "who mailed [them] on [his] behalf." Viewing these two statements as a whole, isn't it a stretch to say that they are not irreconcilably inconsistent?
2. The concurrence states that the case comes down to the distinction between the words "mail" and "send." It claims that there is an infinitesimal distinction between the two. But doesn't the case also involve the distinction between "prepare" and "generate"? In the context of the case, is there even an infinitesimal difference between these two words? How does the majority deal with this issue?

3. As noted above, the cases in this chapter make clear that indicting a defendant for perjury or false declaration can be a dicey proposition because of the unpredictability in how a court will apply the various defendant-friendly limitations to the crime. The same cannot be said for prosecutions under the false statement statute, 18 U.S.C. §1001. (Recall the prosecution-friendly interpretation of the statute in the cases found in Chapter 7.) Why the difference? Is it justified?

B. Requirement of "Proceeding Before or Ancillary to Any Court or Grand Jury"

DUNN v. UNITED STATES
442 U.S. 100 (1979)

Mr. Justice MARSHALL delivered the opinion of the Court.

Title IV of the Organized Crime Control Act of 1970, 18 U.S.C. §1623, prohibits false declarations made under oath "in any proceeding before or ancillary to any court or grand jury of the United States." This case turns on the scope of the term ancillary proceeding in §1623, a phrase not defined in that provision or elsewhere in the Criminal Code. More specifically, we must determine whether an interview in a private attorney's office at which a sworn statement is given constitutes a proceeding ancillary to a court or grand jury within the meaning of the statute.

On June 16, 1976, petitioner Robert Dunn testified before a federal grand jury under a grant of immunity pursuant to 18 U.S.C. §6002. The grand jury was investigating illicit drug activity at the Colorado State Penitentiary where petitioner had been incarcerated. Dunn's testimony implicated a fellow inmate, Phillip Musgrave, in various drug-related offenses. Following petitioner's appearance, the grand jury indicted Musgrave for conspiracy to manufacture and distribute methamphetamine.

Several months later, on September 30, 1976, Dunn arrived without counsel in the office of Musgrave's attorney, Michael Canges. In the presence of Canges and a notary public, petitioner made an oral statement under oath in which he recanted his grand jury testimony implicating Musgrave. Canges subsequently moved to dismiss the indictment against Musgrave, alleging that it was based on perjured testimony. In support of this motion, the attorney submitted a transcript of Dunn's September 30 statement.

The District Court held an evidentiary hearing on Musgrave's motion to dismiss on October 21, 1976. At that hearing, petitioner, who was then represented by counsel, adopted the statement he had given in Canges' office and testified that only a small part of what he had told the grand jury was in fact true. As a result of petitioner's testimony, the Government reduced the charges against Musgrave to misdemeanor possession of methamphetamine.

Petitioner was subsequently indicted on five counts of making false declarations in violation of 18 U.S.C. §1623. The indictment charged that Dunn's testimony before the grand jury was inconsistent with statements made "on September

30, 1976, while under oath as a witness in a proceeding ancillary to *United States v. Musgrave*, . . . to the degree that one of said declarations was false. . . ." In response to petitioner's motion for a bill of particulars, the Government indicated that it would rely on the "inconsistent declarations" method of proof authorized by §1623(c). Under that subsection, the Government must establish the materiality and inconsistency of declarations made in proceedings before or ancillary to a court or grand jury, but need not prove which of the declarations is false.

At trial, the Government introduced over objection pertinent parts of Dunn's grand jury testimony, his testimony at the October 21 evidentiary hearing, and his sworn statement to Musgrave's attorney. After the Government rested its case, petitioner renewed his objections in a motion for acquittal. He contended that the September 30 statement was not made in a proceeding ancillary to a federal court or grand jury as required by §1623(c). . . .

We granted certiorari. Because we disagree with the Court of Appeals' ultimate disposition of the ancillary-proceeding issue . . . , we reverse. . . .

[III.]

Congress enacted §1623 as part of the 1970 Organized Crime Control Act to facilitate perjury prosecutions and thereby enhance the reliability of testimony before federal courts and grand juries. Invoking this broad congressional purpose, the Government argues for an expansive construction of the term ancillary proceeding. Under the Government's analysis, false swearing in an affidavit poses the same threat to the fact-finding process as false testimony in open court. Thus, the Government contends that any statements made under oath for submission to a court, whether given in an attorney's office or in a local bar and grill, fall within the ambit of §1623. In our judgment, the term "proceeding," which carries a somewhat more formal connotation, suggests that Congress had a narrower end in view when enacting §1623. And the legislative history of the Organized Crime Control Act confirms that conclusion.

Section 1623 was a response to perceived evidentiary problems in demonstrating perjury under the existing federal statute, 18 U.S.C. §1621. As Congress noted, the strict common-law requirements for establishing falsity which had been engrafted onto the federal perjury statute often made prosecution for false statements exceptionally difficult. By relieving the Government of the burden of proving which of two or more inconsistent declarations was false, *see* §1623(c), Congress sought to afford "greater assurance that testimony obtained in grand jury and court proceedings will aid the cause of truth." S. Rep. No. 91-617, p. 59 (1969). But nothing in the language or legislative history of the statute suggests that Congress contemplated a relaxation of the Government's burden of proof with respect to all inconsistent statements given under oath. Had Congress intended such a result, it presumably would have drafted §1623 to encompass all sworn declarations irrespective of whether they were made in proceedings before or ancillary to a court or grand jury. Particularly since Congress was aware that statements under oath were embraced by the federal perjury statute without regard to where they were given, the choice of less comprehensive language in §1623 does not appear inadvertent.

That Congress intended §1623 to sweep less broadly than the perjury statute is also apparent from the origin of the term ancillary proceeding. As initially introduced in Congress, the Organized Crime Control Act contained a version of §1623 which encompassed only inconsistent statements made in any "trial, hearing, or proceeding before any court or grand jury." When asked to comment on the proposed statute, the Department of Justice noted that the scope of the inconsistent declarations provision was "not as inclusive" as the perjury statute. Significantly, the Justice Department did not suggest that the provision be made coextensive with the perjury statute. However, in subsequent Senate Subcommittee hearings, Assistant Attorney General Wilson indicated, without elaboration, that the Department advocated "including [under §1623] other testimony, preliminary testimony and other statements, in the perjury field."

In response to that general suggestion, Senator McClellan, on behalf of the Subcommittee, sent a letter to the Assistant Attorney General clarifying its purpose:

> "You also read Title IV not to cover 'pre-trial depositions, affidavits and certifications.' This was not our intent in drafting the bill. We had hoped that it would be applicable, for example, to situations such as [the] kind of pre-trial depositions that the enforcement of S. 1861 would present. If we included in the statute the phrase 'proceedings before or ancillary to any court or grand jury,' do you feel that this intent would be adequately expressed?"

Thus, both the language and history of the Act support the Court of Appeals' conclusion that petitioner's September 30 interview "lack[ed] the degree of formality" required by §1623. For the Government does not and could not seriously maintain that the interview in Canges' office constituted a deposition. Musgrave's counsel made no attempt to comply with the procedural safeguards for depositions set forth in Fed. R. Crim. P. 15 and 18 U.S.C. §3503. A court order authorizing the deposition was never obtained. Nor did petitioner receive formal notice of the proceeding or of his right to have counsel present. Indeed, petitioner did not even certify the transcript of the interview as accurate.

The judgment of the Court of Appeals is

Reversed.

Mr. Justice Powell took no part in the consideration or decision of this case.

NOTES AND QUESTIONS

1. Why wasn't it sufficient to uphold the conviction that Dunn had "adopted the statement he had given in Canges' office" in the hearing before the district court? That was clearly a proceeding, wasn't it?
2. Is Justice Marshall's interpretation of the legislative history persuasive? Can you construct a counterargument?
3. Courts have not been quick to follow the *Dunn* holding. For example, in United States v. Johnson, 325 F.3d 205 (4th Cir. 2003), the defendant was a prisoner who made false statements in sworn notarized documents supporting a petition for habeas corpus. He moved to dismiss §1623 charges

brought against him based on *Dunn*, claiming that the documents, which were created in prison, did not amount to "proceeding[s] before or ancillary to any court or grand jury" under the statute. The Fourth Circuit disposed of Johnson's contention by noting that the documents had been filed with the habeas petition, consequently becoming part of the district court proceeding. *Id.* at 210. Can't the same be said of Dunn's sworn statement, which was attached to Musgrave's motion to dismiss?

IV. THE RECANTATION DEFENSE: DOES "OR" MEAN "AND"?

UNITED STATES v. MOORE

613 F.2d 1029 (D.C. Cir. 1979)

Spottswood W. Robinson, III, Circuit Judge:

. . . This case had its genesis in a grand jury probe into possible corruption and bribery within the Metropolitan Police Department of the District of Columbia. In the early spring of 1977, prior to the grand jury proceeding, the Department's Internal Affairs Division placed Bosco's Carryout, an establishment in Northwest Washington, under observation in an effort to ascertain whether criminal activities were being conducted therein, and, if so, whether any police officers were implicated in them. Physical and photographic surveillance of the carryout was conducted until an officer working undercover in connection with the investigation learned that the vigil had been detected by the carryout's proprietor. Reacting to this discovery, the Internal Affairs Division attempted to mask the real purpose of the operation by circulating selectively a false cover story concerning its objective.

Moore, a police officer, heard the cover story from Walter Whited, a fellow officer. Moore was told that the investigation was aimed at apprehending a suspected narcotics dealer. Moore came under suspicion as a possible conduit of information when shortly thereafter the undercover officer found out that the owner of the carryout had the story as it had been related to Moore by Whited. A month later, at Moore's request, Whited met him at a service station; there, equipped with a concealed recorder, Whited taped their conversation, including Moore's detailed questions concerning the surveillance, the cover story, and the involvement of another police officer in the investigation

After passage of another month, the investigation was terminated, and a grand jury was convened. Early in the proceeding, the grand jury inquired whether Moore and other suspected officers had endeavored to secure information on the carryout surveillance from within the Department, and whether any such information had been passed on to the carryout's proprietor in exchange for remuneration. Moore went before the grand jury and was quizzed on his two conversations with Whited. Moore denied any recollection at all of the first session or the date of the second, though he admittedly did remember a meeting with Whited at a service station. Moore, however, avowed that the latter colloquy was unrelated to police business;

he stated that he had never called anyone, including Whited, to ask about the investigation of the carryout. This testimony formed the basis of the subsequent indictment against Moore for making false statements before the grand jury [pursuant to 18 U.S.C. §1623].

Toward the end of 1977, Moore and his counsel met with representatives of the Internal Affairs Division and an assistant United States attorney in the latter's office. After additional questioning on his rendezvous with Whited at the service station, Moore was informed of the tape recording of their conversation. The tape was played, and counsel informed Moore that by statute he might escape criminal liability for perjurious statements by reappearing before the grand jury and admitting the falsity of his prior testimony. Moore conferred with his attorney and stated that he would do so; he agreed to a tape-recorded rehearsal of the testimony he proposed to give. In that rendition, Moore acknowledged the occurrence of the first conversation with Whited and provided a facially innocent explanation for the second. A few minutes later, however, Government counsel stopped Moore from continuing with his new version, stating that he did not deem it credible. In 1978, Moore was indicted. . . .

[T]he court convened a hearing at which it inquired whether the Government would allow Moore to reappear before the grand jury for the purpose of testifying anew. The Government advised that it was not willing to do so, whereupon the court . . . filed an opinion and an order formally dismissing the indictment. This appeal followed. . . .

III.

The statute under which the Government proceeded offers perjurers a qualified opportunity to recant, . . . Section 1623(d). . . .

In holding that this provision precluded the Government from pressing the charges against Moore, the District Court relied on his representation that he was and had been prepared to reappear before the grand jury and admit the falsity of the statements specified in the indictment. The grand jury was still in session when Moore reached trial, and the court noted that the Government had not undertaken any showing that the impugned statements had affected the proceeding in which Moore had testified. Believing that it was beyond the prosecutor's discretion to deny Moore's request for an opportunity to recant, the court deemed his representation sufficient to bring Section 1623(d) into play. We find it unnecessary to pass on this course of reasoning, for our review of the record before us reveals that in any event there was an insuperable obstacle to Moore's invocation of that section.

By the terms of Section 1623(d), recantation halts a perjury prosecution only "if, at the time the admission (of falsity) is made, the (prior false) declaration has not substantially affected the proceeding, or it has not become manifest that such falsity has been or will be exposed." Assuming without deciding that Moore's original testimony had not disturbed the grand jury's investigation, the tape recording of the Moore-Whited conversation at the service station which at no time has been challenged left undisputed on the record a showing that, before Moore made any effort toward recantation, the Government to Moore's realization knew that he had lied to the grand jury in the several respects charged. We think this circumstance, without more, defeats Moore's claim to the benefit of Section 1623(d).

We are advertent to the consideration that the two events which Section 1623(d) interposes as preconditions to the bar of recantation appear grammatically as alternatives. In the statutory language, falsity of the prior testimony must not have substantially affected the proceeding "or" exposure of the falsity must not have become manifest. Moore obviously assumes, as did the District Court, that he needed to meet only one of these demands. Though the question is difficult, and its solution has taxed our resources severely, we are constrained to hold that satisfaction of both of these requirements was essential.

Normally, of course, "or" is to be accepted for its disjunctive connotation, and not as a word interchangeable with "and." But this canon is not inexorable, for sometimes a strict grammatical construction will frustrate legislative intent. That, we are convinced, is precisely what will occur here unless "or" is read as "and."

Section 1623 was enacted as Title IV of the Organized Crime Control Act of 1970. The legislative history highlights the central purpose of Section 1623 to encourage truthful testimony by witnesses appearing before courts and grand juries. . . .

The congressional effort to improve truthtelling in judicial proceedings was . . . twofold. Congress magnified the deterrent role of the criminal law by easing the Government's path to perjury convictions; and the emphasis here was plainly on pressure calculated to induce the witness to speak the truth at all times. Congress also extended absolution to perjurers who recant under prescribed conditions, admittedly an endeavor to secure truth through correction of previously false testimony. Each of these techniques has its own virtue, and it was, of course, the prerogative of Congress to put them to use; but it is evident that in some degree they unavoidably must work at cross-purposes. Recantation, for all its value in ultimately unveiling the truth, may well prove to be a disincentive to veracity in the first instance; to the extent that a perjurer can sidestep prosecution simply by recanting, he is hardly the more prompted to tell the truth in the beginning. By the same token, the deterrent effect of any statute punishing perjury is weakened in the same measure that recantation holds out the promise of possible escape. And indisputably, maximum deterrence of perjury is necessarily inconsistent with maximum range for recantation.

Mere inspection of the text of Section 1623(d) fails to illuminate satisfactorily just how Congress expected the courts to maintain the delicate balance envisioned for these mutually detracting approaches. Not even the closest examination of the statutory text enables one confidently to locate the point, in terms of breadth of the recantation provision, at which the balance was legislatively struck. Of particular moment for the instant case is the seeming anomaly, on the one hand, of a Congress bent on more truthtelling throughout judicial proceedings and, on the other, the strong temptation to prevaricate initially that an expansive reading of that provision would furnish would-be perjurers. If the two preconditions which Section 1623(d) specifies are alternative in nature, a perjurer can avoid prosecution by the simple expedient of recanting before his perjury adversely affects the proceeding, even after his misdeed has been laid bare; if, however, both preconditions must exist before recantation aborts the prosecution, there is much less tug-of-war within Congress' dual methodology for veracity-promotion. Did Congress contemplate treatment of these statutory demands conjunctively or disjunctively? . . .

With a literal interpretation of Section 1623(d) on this score thus uncomfortably dubious, we turn to the legislative history for assistance. As the committee reports in both Houses disclose, the section was modeled on a New York statute, which has an instructive history of its own. In *People v. Gillette*, the Appellate Division unqualifiedly accepted recantation as a defense, and accordingly quashed a perjury indictment, where the defendant, who had testified falsely before a grand jury, corrected himself before leaving the grand jury room. Subsequently, in *People v. Ezaugi*, the Court of Appeals limited the *Gillette* holding to situations wherein the retraction is made "before the body conducting the inquiry has been deceived or misled to the harm and prejudice of its investigation, and where no reasonable likelihood exists that the witness has learned that his perjury is known or may become known to the authorities." In this form, recantation was incorporated into New York's statutory law as an affirmative defense to a perjury charge, and it summons satisfaction of both of *Ezaugi*'s demands.

Inexplicably, though the New York statute professedly was the paragon of Section 1623(d)'s specification on recantation, the latter as drafted set forth the preconditions in the disjunctive. The fact is, however, that the congressional treatment of the recantation provision never deviated from the understanding that the New York version had been basically incorporated. . . .

Had so drastic a departure from the New York statute as a switch from combinational to alternative satisfaction of its carefully developed preconditions been really intended, we believe Congress would have said so. Had Congress actually intended a nearly complete overruling, in the practical sense, of the Supreme Court's longstanding pronouncement on the serious drawbacks of recantation in the quest for truth, we would expect a much fuller explanation. Had Congress, after making crystal clear its purpose to promote truthtelling to the hilt, intended the almost wide-open door to prevarication that disjunctive construction of the statutory preconditions would furnish, it hardly would have failed to elucidate its logic. . . .

We conclude that Congress did not countenance in Section 1623(d) the flagrant injustice that would result if a witness is permitted to lie to a judicial tribunal and then, upon only learning that he had been discovered, grudgingly to recant in order to bar prosecution. It has been held implicitly that the recantation provision is available to perjurers only if their previous false testimony has not substantially affected the proceeding AND it has not become manifest that the falsity has been or will be exposed. We share that view unreservedly, and hold that the case at bar does not fall within the intendment of Section 1623(d). . . .

The order of dismissal is reversed, and the case is remanded to the District Court for further proceedings consistent with this opinion.

Reversed and remanded.

UNITED STATES v. SMITH

35 F.3d 344 (8th Cir. 1994)

Bowman, Circuit Judge.

Sherry Lynn Smith timely appeals her conviction following her conditional guilty plea to one count of perjury. We vacate and remand for further proceedings.

I.

. . . The perjury charge arose out of Smith's testimony before a grand jury investigating several individuals, including Smith's boyfriend Craig Keltner, and their involvement in a series of crimes including car theft, kidnapping, mail fraud, burglaries, robberies, and money laundering. The grand jury questioned Smith about the source of funds with which Keltner had purchased a Chevrolet Corvette. Keltner first attempted to make the purchase from a dealership with $12,200 in cash. When the dealership informed him that it would have to file a report with the Internal Revenue Service on any cash transaction in excess of $10,000, Keltner arranged to pay with $9,800 in cash and $2,400 in the form of a check from Smith. The dealership held the $12,200 until Keltner returned with Smith's check, then the dealership returned $2,400 in cash to Keltner. Smith deposited $2,400 in cash into her bank account the same day.

Before the grand jury, Smith initially testified that she had invested $3,000 from her savings toward the purchase of the car. She denied that the $2,400 deposited into her bank account after the purchase came from Keltner. After a thirty-eight minute break in the proceeding, during which Smith reviewed her bank records, she resumed her testimony and recanted her previous statements. Smith admitted that the $2,400 belonged to Keltner and was given to her to deposit as part of the transaction to purchase the Corvette.

II.

Prior to her conditional guilty plea to the perjury charge, Smith moved for dismissal of that charge on the ground that 18 U.S.C. §1623(d) (1988) bars prosecution for perjury on the facts of her case. The District Court disagreed with Smith's interpretation of the statute and denied her motion. Her conditional plea preserved the issue for appellate review, and she now asks this court to address it.

We review questions of statutory interpretation de novo. . . . The District Court denied Smith's motion on the ground that §1623(d) "bars prosecution only if the false statement has not substantially affected the proceeding *and* if it has not become manifest that the falsity has been or will be exposed." (Emphasis added.) The District Court construed the two conditions as conjunctive, reading "or" to mean "and," and found that Smith did not satisfy the latter condition. Smith contends that the two conditions are disjunctive and thus satisfaction of either bars her prosecution for perjury.

In interpreting §1623(d), "we adhere to the general principle that when the plain language of a statute is clear in its context, it is controlling." The plain language of the statute indicates that after recantation, a perjury charge is barred if (1) the proceeding has not been substantially affected by the false testimony, or (2) it has not become manifest that the false nature of the testimony has been or will be exposed. Because the wording of §1623(d) "is plain, simple, and straightforward, the words must be accorded their normal meanings." United States v. Jones, 811 F.2d 444, 447 (8th Cir. 1987). The ordinary usage of the word "or" is disjunctive, indicating an alternative. Construing the word "or" to mean "and" is conjunctive, and is clearly in contravention of its ordinary usage. Thus, we find the plain language of §1623(d) controlling and accord the word "or" its ordinary, disjunctive meaning.

According the word "or" its ordinary meaning does not defeat the intent of Congress in enacting the statute and creating the §1623(d) recantation defense. . . . To meet the congressional goal of encouraging truthful testimony, we need only apply the plain language of the statute in its ordinary usage. Reading the two conditions in the alternative, as the word "or" demands, the statute creates an incentive for witnesses to correct false testimony early in the proceeding. Arguably, construing the word "or" to mean "and" creates a statutory scheme providing a stronger incentive for witnesses to testify truthfully at the outset; however, we defer to Congress's chosen scheme as manifested by its language which balances encouragement of truthful testimony and penalties for perjury.

Additionally, because §1623(d) is a penal statute, we must apply the rule of lenity. *See* Dunn v. United States, 442 U.S. 100, 112 (1979). . . .

IV.

On remand, Smith may defeat the perjury charge if she can show that she satisfies either of §1623(d)'s conditions. As to the condition that she recant before her false testimony has substantially affected the proceedings, the District Court did not address the issue at length, but appears to have found that her false statements may not have affected the proceedings. It is not clear to us that the District Court intended to make a definitive finding on this point, and we do not think the court should be precluded from revisiting this issue on remand.

We turn now to the alternative statutory condition, that the declarant recant before it becomes manifest that the falsity of her statement has been or will be exposed, because the District Court relied upon Smith's failure to fulfill this condition in denying her motion to dismiss.

We believe the District Court misapplied the "manifest" test. The court reasoned that because the government had the bank records with which to confront Smith, the falsity of her statements was manifest to the government before she recanted, and the court stopped its analysis at that point. The proper test to apply, however, when determining whether recantation occurred before imminent exposure was manifest, is whether the fact that the statements have been or will be exposed as false is objectively manifest to the declarant. On remand, if the District Court reaches consideration of this condition, it must determine whether it had become objectively manifest to Smith, before she recanted, that the falsity of her statements had been or would be exposed. . . .

NOTES AND QUESTIONS

1. So, should "or" mean "and"? Which court makes the better case? Should a court enforce what Congress says, or what it apparently meant to say? Should it matter that *Smith* was decided 20 years after the first court of appeals, and every other court of appeals to follow, had decided the issue the other way and neither Congress nor the Supreme Court saw fit to intervene? Or is the Eighth Circuit the only court to understand the proper role of a court, which is to interpret law, not legislate?
2. In *Moore*, Judge Robinson eloquently defends the court's interpretation, but was it necessary to reach the question at all? Section 1623 makes clear that, to be effective, recantation must take place "during the same continuous grand jury proceeding." Courts have interpreted this to mean the same meeting of the grand jury, not a different meeting of the same grand jury months later. *See* People v. Ezaugi, 2 N.Y.2d 439, 443 (1957) (holding recantation is only a defense when knowingly false testimony is corrected promptly). Do you think Judge Robinson's unnecessary "tax[ing of the court's] resources" was inadvertent, or did he purposely stretch to address the more important question? A clue to the answer might lie in the fact that the opinion never references the "continuous . . . proceeding" language in the statute.

UNITED STATES ATTORNEYS' MANUAL

Title 9, Section 69.200: Criminal Resource Manual at 1751 (2011)

Recantation was never a defense to perjury in the common law, and is not a complete defense in a Section 1621 prosecution. United States v. Norris, 300 U.S. 564, 573-74 (1937). Recantation in such cases is relevant only as to whether the defendant intended to make a willfully false statement. *Id.*

Section 1623(d), however, makes recantation a bar to a perjury prosecution in certain cases that meet either three or four requirements. . . . Because recantation is a jurisdictional bar to prosecution, Fed. R. Crim. P. 12(b)(2) requires that it be shown before trial.

PRACTICE TIP: The prosecutor has no duty to advise a witness of the possibility of recanting under Section 1623(d), even if the witness is advised of the penalties for perjury. Nor must the government confront a witness with evidence of the untruthfulness of his statements, or, conversely, delay revealing incriminating evidence so that the witness can consider whether to recant. If, however, the prosecutor specifically allows a witness to "straighten out" testimony, the government may be estopped from challenging a witness's eligibility to recant. Normally, no perjury prosecution should be undertaken after a solicited recantation, even if the defendant was technically ineligible under Section 1623(d).

PRACTICE TIP: If a witness who has completed his or her testimony requests the opportunity to appear before the grand jury to recant testimony, the prosecutor should grant the request, provided it is timely and in keeping with the promotion of truthful testimony. A witness's request for reappearance after the falsity of the previous testimony has become manifest does not preclude prosecution of the prior false declaration and may be denied.

NOTES AND QUESTIONS

1. It is the prosecutor's ethical responsibility to see that "justice is done." United States v. Berger, 295 U.S. 78, 88 (1935). Thus, it seems appropriate that DOJ counsels its prosecutors to facilitate recantation when it is done in a timely manner. On the other hand, why "may" a witness's request to recant be denied if it occurs "after the falsity of the previous testimony has become manifest"? True, a late recantation is technically not a defense under the majority reading of §1623, but isn't it in the best interests of all concerned to have the truthful statement on the record anyway? What would motivate a prosecutor to deny such a request? Not wanting his potential perjury case to be weakened by a contrite or sympathetic defendant? Is this fair? Is it in the interests of justice?
2. In United States v. Kahn, 472 F.2d 272 (2d Cir. 1973), the defendant complained that the prosecution had improperly denied him the ability to plead a recantation defense by charging him under §1621 instead of §1623 for conduct covered by both statutes. He supported his position by citing cases for the proposition that, as a matter of statutory construction, the specific controls the general. The government argued that a prosecutor "has the absolute discretion to choose which section a perjurer will be tried under." The court expressed "great skepticism" about the government's claim, but avoided addressing the issue by holding that, in any case, the defendant had not recanted.

Was the court's skepticism warranted? Can a prosecutor pick and choose the charges she will bring against a defendant based in part on strategic considerations such as comparative defenses? Are there any limitations on prosecutorial discretion of this sort?

V. IMMUNIZED TESTIMONY

UNITED STATES v. DESALVO

26 F.3d 1216 (2d Cir. 1994)

McLaughlin, Circuit Judge:

Frank DeSalvo appeals from a judgment entered in the United States District Court for the Eastern District of New York convicting him, after a jury trial, of four counts of perjury, in violation of 18 U.S.C. §1623(a), and four counts of obstructing justice, in violation of 18 U.S.C. §1503. . . . We affirm.

Background

In the early 1980s, Frank DeSalvo was a trial lawyer with the now infamous personal injury firm of Morris J. Eisen, P.C. The Eisen firm dishonored the legal profession by routinely bribing witnesses and manufacturing evidence to win lawsuits or exact favorable settlements. After a federal trial, seven of the firm's lawyers, investigators and administrators were convicted on racketeering charges. *See* United States v. Eisen, 974 F.2d 246 (2d Cir. 1992), *cert. denied*, 507 U.S. 998 (1993).

Although DeSalvo himself was not prosecuted along with his colleagues, his central role as an Eisen insider did not escape the attention of the federal prosecutors. DeSalvo's conviction stems from false testimony he gave under oath during the investigation and prosecution of the Eisen defendants. The facts surrounding DeSalvo's testimony are largely undisputed.

A. DeSalvo's State and Federal Testimony

In September 1987, a New York state grand jury was empanelled to investigate the Eisen firm. It then compelled DeSalvo's testimony under a grant of transactional immunity. DeSalvo appeared and testified about his background and employment with the Eisen firm, and about his participation as a trial lawyer in one Eisen case. DeSalvo was not charged with lying before the state grand jury.

Two years later, a federal grand jury subpoenaed DeSalvo to testify in a federal investigation of the firm. Pursuant to 18 U.S.C. §6002, Judge Eugene Nickerson granted DeSalvo immunity "as to all matters about which he may be interrogated before the [Eisen] Grand Jury." In all, DeSalvo appeared three times before the Eisen federal grand jury in the fall of 1989. On each occasion, he denied complicity in the Eisen firm's crimes.

In his first federal grand jury appearance on September 14, DeSalvo claimed that it was pure coincidence that his cousin testified as an eyewitness on behalf of Eisen clients in two unrelated personal injury cases.

In his second appearance, one week later, in testimony about a different case, DeSalvo denied colluding with two firm investigators who, during a personal injury trial, fabricated an account of a defense witness's whereabouts. This account persuaded the trial judge that the witness was available to be called and thus his deposition testimony should be excluded.

In his third and final appearance before the Eisen grand jury, DeSalvo denied ever knowing that a witness who testified in yet another of his cases was the mother of the Eisen firm's office manager.

In August 1990, the federal grand jury indicted the Eisen defendants, not including DeSalvo. The government, however, called DeSalvo to testify at the Eisen trial. DeSalvo appeared on December 20, 1990, and declined to answer the questions put to him, asserting his Fifth Amendment privilege against self-incrimination. In response, Judge Sifton entered a second federal immunity order pursuant to 18 U.S.C. §6002, covering "all matters about which [DeSalvo] may be interrogated at the [Eisen] trial." DeSalvo's trial testimony essentially tracked his federal grand jury testimony.

B. The Proceedings Below

Following the government's successful prosecution of DeSalvo's colleagues, a federal grand jury indicted DeSalvo for perjury and obstruction of justice in connection with the testimony he gave during his three appearances before the federal grand jury (the "Eisen grand jury") and the trial jury (the "Eisen trial jury"). The government maintained that DeSalvo had repeatedly lied when he denied participating in any wrongdoing at the Eisen firm. . . . The jury convicted DeSalvo on four counts of perjury and four counts of obstruction.

DeSalvo now appeals.

Discussion

I. Use of Immunized Testimony

The Fifth Amendment provides that "[n]o person . . . shall be compelled in any criminal case to be a witness against himself." Consistent with the constitutional guarantee, a court may compel testimony under a grant of immunity so long as the testimony, and any evidence derived therefrom, is not thereafter used against the witness "in any criminal case, *except a prosecution for perjury, giving a false statement, or otherwise failing to comply with the order*." 18 U.S.C. §6002 (emphasis added). *See* Kastigar v. United States, 406 U.S. 441, 453 (1972). Despite the express exception permitting use of immunized testimony in a subsequent perjury prosecution, DeSalvo believes that the government violated 18 U.S.C. §6002 and the Fifth Amendment when it indiscriminately used all of his immunized testimony to indict and convict him on multiple and overlapping perjury charges. To assess DeSalvo's nebulous, not to say inscrutable, grievance, we must plumb the depths of the perjury exception to the immunity statute, and parse DeSalvo's argument into manageable bytes.

Analysis begins with United States v. Apfelbaum, 445 U.S. 115 (1980), where the Supreme Court endeavored to harmonize the varying approaches taken by the lower courts as to the permissible uses of a witness's immunized testimony in a perjury prosecution. The Court rejected the view of the Seventh and Third Circuits, which had held that only the "corpus delicti" or "core" of the false statements charged in the perjury indictment could be used against the witness. The Court also rejected the approach of our Court, which had held that false immunized statements were admissible in a perjury prosecution, but truthful immunized statements were not. In sweeping terms, the Court held that in a perjury prosecution, "neither the [immunity] statute nor the Fifth Amendment requires that the admissibility of immunized testimony be governed by any different rules than other testimony."

A perjury indictment is not carte blanche to admit immunized testimony in all such prosecutions, however. As *Apfelbaum* explained, the perjury exception of 18 U.S.C. §6002 is a "narrow" one precisely because immunized testimony "remains inadmissible in all prosecutions for offenses committed prior to the grant of immunity that would have permitted the witness to invoke his Fifth Amendment privilege absent the grant." *Apfelbaum*, 445 U.S. at 128.

Accordingly, while *Apfelbaum* settled the dispute about how much of a witness's immunized testimony may be used in a prosecution for perjury committed during the course of that testimony (answer: all of it), it did not change the constitutional rules governing when such compelled testimony may be used: The rule remains that none of a witness's immunized testimony may be used in a prosecution for a crime (including perjury) that was "committed prior to the grant of immunity that would have permitted the witness to invoke his Fifth Amendment privilege absent the grant." *Apfelbaum*, 445 U.S. at 128. In other words, nothing in *Apfelbaum* changed the principle that a "witness is entitled to claim the Fifth Amendment privilege if [his testimony] might reveal perjury in a prior proceeding." *In re Corrugated Container Antitrust Litig.*, 644 F.2d 70, 75 n.7 (2d Cir. 1981).

An example may help to illuminate the intersection of these rules and the permissible and impermissible uses of immunized testimony to prove perjury. Assume that a witness makes three sworn statements in a federal proceeding under a grant of use immunity. If one of those three statements is false, and the government then prosecutes for perjury, *Apfelbaum* teaches that neither the Fifth Amendment nor the immunity statute prohibits the admission of the remaining two statements in the perjury prosecution. (The trial judge could, of course, exclude those statements on other evidentiary grounds.)

In addition, it is likely that the government could use all three of the witness's statements in a prosecution for a perjury committed after the proceeding in which the three sworn statements were given. This is so because, at the time the witness was granted immunity in the earlier proceeding, the danger that he might commit perjury in some future proceeding "is not by itself sufficient to create a substantial and real hazard that permits invocation of the Fifth Amendment." *Apfelbaum*, 445 U.S. at 131. Consistent with the Fifth Amendment, however, the government could not use any of the three statements to prove that the witness had committed perjury in some prior proceeding.

In sum, the Fifth Amendment: (1) permits the unrestricted use of a witness's immunized testimony in a prosecution for perjury committed during the course of that immunized testimony; (2) does not permit a witness to invoke the privilege on the ground that he anticipates committing perjury sometime in the future; and (3) prohibits the use of immunized testimony in a prosecution for any offense—including perjury—committed before the grant of immunity if the witness would have had a valid claim of privilege absent the grant.

With these principles as our template, we turn to consider the government's use of DeSalvo's immunized testimony.

A. Use of DeSalvo's Federal Grand Jury Testimony

DeSalvo contends that Judge Sifton should not have allowed the government to present to DeSalvo's grand and petit juries all the testimony DeSalvo earlier gave in his three appearances before the Eisen grand jury. We agree with Judge Sifton that *Apfelbaum* disposes of this argument. Under *Apfelbaum*, such testimony is freely admissible, limited only by the rules of evidence. No evidentiary objection having been raised, all of DeSalvo's immunized testimony given before the Eisen grand jury—both truthful and false, core and peripheral—was properly admitted to prove that DeSalvo committed perjury and obstruction during the course of that testimony. . . .

B. Use of DeSalvo's State Grand Jury Testimony

DeSalvo's argument concerning the government's use of the immunized testimony he gave before the state grand jury in 1987 is more elusive. . . . [We conclude, however, that t]he Fifth Amendment would not have protected DeSalvo against the use of his state grand jury testimony in this future perjury prosecution: The risk that DeSalvo might be prosecuted for lying to a federal jury in 1989 would have been far too speculative to permit him to invoke the privilege in 1987. . . . Accordingly, the Fifth Amendment does not prevent the use of DeSalvo's 1987 state grand jury testimony in this subsequent perjury prosecution "because, at the time he was granted immunity, the privilege would not have protected him against false testimony that he later might decide to give." *Apfelbaum*, 445 U.S. at 130.

C. Use of the Eisen Trial Testimony

Most troublesome is the government's use of the immunized testimony DeSalvo gave before the Eisen trial jury in December, 1990. Without question, all of that testimony was admissible to prove that DeSalvo lied during the course of that trial. However, the instant prosecution was not limited to charges of perjury committed during the course of his Eisen trial testimony; DeSalvo was also charged with committing perjury in a prior proceeding (i.e., the Eisen grand jury proceeding). The question, then, is whether the government was equally free to use the Eisen trial testimony to prove that DeSalvo committed perjury in the prior grand jury proceeding. We believe it was not.

DeSalvo's first federal immunity order, signed by Judge Nickerson, immunized only DeSalvo's grand jury testimony. No doubt, had Judge Sifton not entered the second immunity order on December 20, DeSalvo would have been well within his rights to refuse to testify at the Eisen trial, given the real danger that truthful answers would reveal that he had committed perjury before the Eisen grand jury: "[T]he giving of truthful testimony on the second occasion could surely trigger investigation of whether the original testimony was false. . . . This is a reasonable cause for apprehension, and supports the claim of privilege." United States v. Housand, 550 F.2d 818, 823 (2d Cir.), *cert. denied*, 431 U.S. 970 (1977).

Because the Fifth Amendment thus prohibited the government from compelling DeSalvo's testimony at the Eisen trial, the Eisen trial testimony—given in exchange for a grant of immunity—was inadmissible in a prosecution for perjury committed before the Eisen grand jury. As explained above, the government may not use a witness's immunized testimony in a prosecution for committing perjury in a prior proceeding. Therefore, while the Eisen trial testimony was admissible to prove those counts of the indictment charging perjury and obstruction before the Eisen trial jury, that testimony was not admissible to prove those counts charging perjury and obstruction before the (earlier) Eisen grand jury.

Having identified an error, we turn to the question of remedy. Under the unique facts of this case, we do not believe that the error we have uncovered warrants any relief. When the government violates the Fifth Amendment and 18 U.S.C. §6002 by using immunized testimony, "generally the remedy for the violation is the suppression of the tainted evidence at trial, not a dismissal of the indictment." And, we have held that the improper use of immunized testimony at trial is subject to harmless error analysis.

We are convinced that the error in admitting the Eisen trial testimony at DeSalvo's trial was harmless beyond a reasonable doubt. Notably, this is not a case in which the government proved the falsity of the prior testimony by reference to subsequent, inconsistent testimony. Nor does DeSalvo specifically allege that the government used his Eisen trial testimony to prove the falsity of his Eisen grand jury testimony. To the contrary, DeSalvo testified consistently before the Eisen grand and trial juries; in both appearances, he denied knowing about and participating in the Eisen firm's racketeering.

Accordingly, there is no danger that DeSalvo's jury considered the testimony he gave before the Eisen trial jury to prove that he lied before the Eisen grand jury. Where, as here, the subsequent immunized testimony is the same as the earlier immunized testimony, a *Kastigar* hearing would simply have confirmed what was obvious to Judge Sifton: the government must have had an independent source to discover and prove that the earlier testimony was false. Therefore, we find that the use of DeSalvo's immunized testimony had absolutely no potential to disadvantage him. . . .

AFFIRMED.

NOTES AND QUESTIONS

1. Although confusing, there is logic behind when immunized testimony can be used in a perjury trial. Can you restate the holding in *DeSalvo* in your own words?
2. Why do you think that DeSalvo lied before the Eisen grand and petit juries despite the grants of immunity?

PROBLEM 8-1

(The following facts are derived from United States v. Lee, 359 F.3d 412 (6th Cir. 2004).)

Ryan Lee was arrested on felony charges and brought before a federal magistrate judge for a bail/detention hearing. In an effort to convince the judge that he was a good candidate for pretrial release, Lee testified under oath that, two years ago, he met Jeffrey Bryant and decided to invest money in Bryant's restaurant, Buckeye Fried Chicken ("Buckeye Chicken"). Lee testified that he had a 50 percent interest in the business. Lee stated that he spent most of his weekday mornings at

Buckeye Chicken; when asked who could verify this, he testified that he saw the food vendors making their deliveries nearly every day. When asked what he would do if he got out on bond, Lee stated that he "hoped and expected" that his partner (Bryant) would let him keep a regular working schedule at Buckeye.

During cross-examination, the prosecutor—smelling some kind of rat but not being able to put his finger on it—asked Lee how much money he made on a weekly basis for his work at Buckeye. At that point, much to everyone's surprise, Lee announced that he was refusing to answer any more questions based on his Fifth Amendment privilege. After some private consultation, Lee's attorney withdrew Lee's testimony on direct examination. The magistrate judge stated that he would strike Lee's testimony and not consider it in making his decision regarding Lee's bond.

After the detention hearing, the FBI investigated Lee's statements regarding a connection to Buckeye Chicken. It turned out that (1) Lee did have a 50 percent interest in Buckeye; (2) Lee did spend most weekday mornings at the restaurant and often chatted with the vendors; (3) Lee was at the restaurant to eat breakfast for free; (4) Lee was never employed at the restaurant; (5) Lee had talked to Bryant from the lock-up about working at the restaurant if he got released on bond, but no promises were made.

Lee is charged with one count of perjury in violation of 18 U.S.C. §1621 and one count of false statements under 18 U.S.C. §1623. Evaluate the strength of the case against Lee, along with the defenses that Lee might be able to offer under each statute.

chapter 9

Obstruction of Justice

I. INTRODUCTION

Obstruction of justice is a crime as old as the justice system itself. Upon getting caught up in law enforcement's net, many defendants struggle to escape through illegal means. Their methods of attempted obstruction can take many forms, from the use of intimidation and violence to more peaceful but equally corrosive acts—such as bribing a judge or destroying critically incriminating documents.

Unfortunately, statutes designed to fight obstruction have often been one step behind the imagination of desperate defendants. More often than not, Congress has found itself "closing the barnyard door after the horses have already escaped." As a result, the obstruction statutes, 18 U.S.C. §§1503-1519, are more or less a hodgepodge of overlapping provisions enacted at different times and for different reasons. This unhappy history has created some interpretive problems, including the question—rarely an issue in the criminal law—whether Congress intended one statute to have exclusive application in certain circumstances.

The archetypical obstruction statute is 18 U.S.C. §1503. Although it applies to certain specific conduct (mostly involving threatening letters or communications), it contains a general prohibition stating that whoever "corruptly . . . influences, obstructs, or impedes, or endeavors to influence, obstruct, or impede, the due administration of justice, shall be punished." Because of its applicability across such a wide and unspecified range of corrupt behavior, §1503 has come to be known as the "Omnibus Provision." Of course, as a result of the provision's frequent employment by prosecutors and its sheer expansiveness, it has been the subject of much judicial interpretation over the years.

In 1982, Congress passed the Victim and Witness Protection Act, P.L. 97-291, 96 Stat. 1249. Language relating to interference with or attempts to influence witnesses were deleted from §§1503 and 1505 (which were otherwise left intact) and placed into a new provision, 18 U.S.C. §1512. This newly crafted prohibition deals with tampering with federal witnesses, potential witnesses, or informants, by intimidation, physical force, threats, misleading conduct, or harassment. It also makes it a crime to "mislead" or "corruptly persuade" another person with the intent to

(1) influence, delay, or prevent the testimony of any person in an official proceeding; (2) cause or induce any person to (A) withhold testimony, or withhold a record, document, or other object from an official proceeding; (B) alter, destroy, mutilate, or conceal an object with intent to impair its integrity or use in a judicial proceeding; (C) evade legal process; (D) be absent from a legal proceeding; and (3) hinder the reporting of a possible federal offense to federal authorities.

After the bursting of the technology bubble in 2000 and the resulting criminal investigations and prosecutions, it once again became painfully obvious that the obstruction statutes were lacking in scope. For example, Enron's accounting firm, Arthur Andersen, came under intense scrutiny for shredding millions of documents in the short time between the company's collapse and the SEC's opening of an investigation. Although there seemed little doubt that Andersen acted to prevent the SEC from acquiring these records, it turned out that the closest crime on the books was §1512(b)(1)(C), which makes it a crime to *corruptly persuade another person* to destroy evidence under such circumstances. Concurrently, Congress was extremely frustrated by the parade of CEOs from companies allegedly riddled with fraud who claimed in testimony before congressional committees that they had no idea what had been going on in their own firms.

As a result of these events, Congress devoted portions of the 2002 Sarbanes-Oxley Act to the enhancement of the federal obstruction of justice configuration. It added 18 U.S.C. §1512(c), which, among other things, makes it a crime to corruptly alter, destroy, or conceal a document "with the intent to impair [its] integrity or availability for use in an official proceeding." It also specifically outlawed the destruction of corporate audit records in newly created 18 U.S.C. §1520. Finally, Congress incorporated into the Act 18 U.S.C. §1550, which requires corporate CEOs and CFOs to certify the accuracy of their company's records *personally.*

This chapter begins with a look at some of the critical doctrine surrounding the interpretation of the Omnibus Provision. It then examines the relationship between the Omnibus Provision and other parts of the obstruction-related statutory scheme, particularly 18 U.S.C. §1512. Next, it sets out a few specific applications of §1512. The chapter closes with a sampling of some post–Sarbanes-Oxley cases.

II. THE OMNIBUS CLAUSE, 18 U.S.C. §1503

A. Requirement of Pending Judicial Proceedings

UNITED STATES v. NELSON
852 F.2d 706 (3d Cir. 1988)

GREENBERG, Circuit Judge.

Gilbert Nelson and George Shamy appeal their convictions for conspiracy to obstruct justice (18 U.S.C. §371) and obstruction of justice (18 U.S.C. §1503). . . .

These are the germane facts developed at the trial. After rather complicated negotiations, on March 16, 1983 the City of New Brunswick, New Jersey, entered into an agreement to purchase property from Richard Malouf for use as a central garage for the maintenance and repair of city vehicles. Malouf acquired the property earlier that year and closed on it on March 1, 1983. Malouf's purchase had been partially financed with $20,000 invested by James V. Gassaro, the city's police director who was also an attorney sharing offices with [defendant Gilbert] Nelson, and with $25,000 borrowed from Gassaro's father-in-law, Joseph Perrone. The interests of Gassaro and Perrone were not disclosed to the city council when it authorized the purchase of the property even though Gassaro was to share in the profits.

When Malouf closed on the sale to the city on May 5, 1983 he received a check for $305,000 from the city which he endorsed and gave to Nelson as the New Brunswick city attorney for deposit in Nelson's attorney's trust account. The proceeds of the check were to be disbursed in accordance with a closing statement prepared by Nelson which showed a total of $96,695.56 due Malouf after deductions from Malouf's proceeds for satisfaction of a mortgage and a realty transfer fee, and a credit for outstanding real estate taxes to the city as purchaser. Nelson, however, returned to Malouf a check for only $91,695.56, exactly $5,000 less than due under the statement. Further, Nelson did not pay the $1830.50 which he showed due for the transfer fee or the $1067.50 real estate taxes due. No provision was made at the closing for any distribution to Gassaro or Perrone and their names did not appear on any of the sale documents.

On May 6, 1983 when Malouf went to the Gassaro-Nelson offices to divide the sale proceeds with Perrone and Gassaro, Nelson was there but Gassaro was not. Malouf gave Nelson checks for $20,000 and $25,000 made payable to Gassaro and Perrone, respectively, for their cash contributions and at Nelson's direction he made out a check for $25,000 payable to a defunct paving company to cover Gassaro's share of the profits. In return Nelson gave him a statement showing that this $25,000 was for property improvements but that was a fiction as none were made.

In March 1985, Assistant United States Attorney Thomas L. Weisenbeck, with assistance from the FBI, began an investigation into allegations of corruption in New Brunswick. A grand jury subpoena to Nelson's bank for his records, the first of three grand jury subpoenas secured during the early months of the investigation, was issued on March 7, 1985 from the office of the clerk of the United States District Court pursuant to Weisenbeck's application. In late March an FBI agent visited Malouf and asked to see the closing statement. Although Malouf did not have a copy he obtained one from the attorney who represented him at the closing, an associate of Shamy, and realized for the first time that he had been paid $5,000 less than due.

Nelson soon learned about the investigation from a newspaper reporter and contacted Malouf asking to see his copy of the closing statement. After securing the statement, Nelson added the following language to account for the $5,000 he withheld from Malouf's closing proceeds two years before: "To Seller—$91,695.56. To George Shamy, in payment of outstanding legal fees due him by Richard Malouf—$5,000." At about the same time Nelson also took steps to pay the real estate taxes on the property in an unusual way. Specifically he had the city tax records modified so that a tax payment he made on another property in 1983 was shown as having been partially made on the Malouf property. Naturally this maneuver retroactively created an outstanding balance on the other property which Nelson then paid.

Shamy was served on April 10, 1985 with a grand jury subpoena and on April 16, 1985 he went to the office of the United States Attorney in Newark for an interview. On that occasion he explained that he resigned from the practice of law early in 1983 and entered a hospital in Ohio. He claimed that at the time of his resignation Malouf owed him approximately $5,000 in legal fees and also asserted he borrowed $6,000 from Nelson because of gambling at the racetrack. He said that when he returned from Ohio he arranged for $5,000 to be withheld from Malouf at the closing for payment to Nelson in accordance with a proposal he had made in a letter to Nelson.

Nelson was served with a grand jury subpoena on April 15, 1985, a day before Shamy's interview, and on May 7, 1985 he turned over Shamy's letter, dated April 16, 1983, and a copy of the altered closing statement to the United States Attorney. The letter indicated that Shamy would get Malouf to authorize the withholding of the fees.

During the investigation the government learned that the letter, allegedly dictated by Shamy to his secretary in April 1983, deviated from Shamy's secretary's usual format for correspondence, thus suggesting it was a fabrication. The secretary later testified at the trial that she could not say with certainty that she did not type the letter, though she did not recall doing so, and pointed out how the letter deviated from her usual format.

Weisenbeck left the United States Attorney's office in September 1985 before any evidence was presented to the grand jury on whose authority he had secured the subpoenas. In due course, the investigation went forward and evidence was eventually presented to a new grand jury. On December 30, 1986 Shamy appeared before the grand jury and testified that while he was in the Ohio hospital he called his secretary in New Jersey and dictated a letter to Nelson suggesting that Nelson withhold the fees due from Malouf at the closing and keep the money as payment for the racetrack loan. Shamy claimed he signed the letter when he returned to New Jersey in April 1983.

Ultimately the grand jury returned an indictment charging . . . [among other things] Nelson and Shamy . . . with obstruction of justice and conspiracy to obstruct justice. The conspiracy to obstruct justice count (count 4) alleged that Nelson and Shamy had schemed to cover-up Nelson's wrongful withholding of fees, taxes and proceeds due Malouf and the city at the closing by, among other means, fabricating the April 16, 1983 letter and altering the closing statement, and by Shamy giving false testimony before the grand jury. The first of the two substantive counts charging obstruction of justice (count 5) alleged that Nelson and Shamy had obstructed justice by producing the fabricated letter in response to a grand jury subpoena. The second (count 6) charged Nelson with obstruction of justice by altering the closing statement. [Appellants were convicted on both counts.] . . .

II. Obstruction of Justice

A.

The obstruction of justice statute provides that whoever "corruptly . . . influences, obstructs, or impedes, or endeavors to influence, obstruct, or impede, the due administration of justice, shall be fined . . . or imprisoned . . . or both." 18 U.S.C. §1503. The parties agree that the pendency of some sort of judicial proceeding, which in this case could only be a grand jury investigation, is a necessary prerequisite for a conviction for violation of 18 U.S.C. §1503. *See* United States v. Simmons, 591 F.2d 206, 208 n.2 (3d Cir. 1979). They disagree, however, over whether the three grand jury subpoenas secured by Weisenbeck prior to production of the letter and closing statement on May 7, 1985 are sufficient to establish that there was a pending grand jury investigation which appellants could have obstructed.

When appellants' attorneys attempted to cross-examine Weisenbeck about the pendency of the grand jury investigation, the trial judge barred much of their inquiry as irrelevant as she believed that if a grand jury was sitting at the time the subpoenas were issued, a judicial proceeding was pending as a matter of law. While the appellants do not dispute that a grand jury was sitting at the time Weisenbeck secured the subpoenas, they argue that inquiry into the pendency of the grand jury investigation should not have ended with establishment of that fact. Thus, in their view, the trial court unreasonably limited their cross-examination and infringed their Sixth Amendment right of confrontation. We agree that the cross-examination was unreasonably limited.

B.

The grand jury subpoenas served on Nelson, Shamy and Nelson's bank were issued by the Office of the Clerk for the District of New Jersey on standard forms signed by a deputy clerk. Fed. R. Crim. P. 17(a) provides for issuance of subpoenas "signed and sealed but otherwise blank to a party requesting it, who shall fill in the blanks before it is served." Because these subpoenas are issued without meaningful judicial oversight, the pendency of a grand jury investigation cannot be determined from their face alone. Not every investigation in which grand jury subpoenas are used ripens into a pending grand jury investigation for purposes of 18 U.S.C. §1503. *Simmons*, 591 F.2d at 210.

Although the grand jury's role in the early phase of an investigation can be unclear, we have resisted adoption of rigid standards for determining when a prosecutor's inquiry ripens into a grand jury investigation. In particular, we have rejected suggestions that an investigation be deemed pending only if (1) the grand jury actually hears testimony, (2) the grand jury plays an active role in the decision to issue the subpoena, or (3) the grand jury is aware of the subpoena at the time of the alleged obstruction of justice, for such rules can be easily circumvented by the government and offer the guilty a sanctuary among "empty technicalities." . . . This case by case inquiry is, of course, factual.

C.

In instructing the jury on the obstruction counts, the district judge correctly explained that "a grand jury proceeding is pending for the purposes of this statute if an Assistant U.S. Attorney has issued a subpoena in furtherance of the grand jury investigation." At trial, however, she unreasonably limited inquiry into whether the subpoenas were issued to secure a presently contemplated presentation of evidence before the grand jury.

During cross-examination about his role in the investigation of alleged corruption in New Brunswick, Weisenbeck testified that he scheduled no time for the case before the grand jury prior to leaving the United States Attorney's office in September 1985, he had no recollection of inspecting the records subpoenaed from Nelson's bank, and he could not recall whether those records were delivered to the grand jury before his departure. The judge, however, barred further inquiry into the pendency issue. She explained at sidebar, clearly referring to situations in which a grand jury subpoena has been issued, that if "there is a sitting grand jury . . . there is a judicial proceeding pending. It's not a factual finding. We already have the evidence."

We agree that to establish the pendency of a judicial proceeding for purposes of 18 U.S.C. §1503 a grand jury must be sitting at the time the subpoena issues; otherwise, the United States Attorney cannot be said to be acting as an agent for that body. The sitting panel, however, need not be the one that ultimately receives the evidence. The difficulty with sustaining the trial judge's ruling, however, is that it would unreasonably interfere with the ability of many defendants to challenge an investigative agency's use of grand jury subpoenas for in larger venues there is seldom an occasion when a grand jury is not sitting. Thus, under her ruling the legitimacy of subpoenas issued during a panel's tenure would be inexorably assured. That consequence cannot be reconciled with our precedents and those of other courts of appeal which have rejected mechanical tests for determining whether proceedings are pending in favor of case by case inquiries into the circumstances surrounding the issuance of grand jury subpoenas.

A party on trial for obstruction of a grand jury investigation alleged to have begun upon the issuance of a grand jury subpoena must be afforded an opportunity to question whether the United States Attorney or his or her representative secured the subpoena in furtherance of a then present contemplation that the subpoenaed evidence would be presented to a grand jury. United States v. Walasek, 527 F.2d 676, 678 (3d Cir. 1975). If a decision has been made to present the matter to the grand jury, it makes no difference whether the ultimate presentation includes all, some or none of the materials actually received in response to the subpoena alleged to have commenced the grand jury investigation. Of course, if those materials are not presented to a grand jury, that may be relevant circumstantial evidence as to whether the requisite present intention existed at the time the subpoena was issued.

Because the appellants' inquiry on cross-examination into Weisenbeck's intentions in securing the subpoenas was unreasonably limited, we find that the trial judge's ruling constituted reversible error. The appellants, therefore, must be granted a new trial on counts 5 and 6. . . .

E.

Although we reverse the substantive obstruction convictions on the basis of the district court's improper limitation of Weisenbeck's cross-examination, our ruling is not fatal to the conspiracy convictions. The district court instructed the jury as follows with respect to the count charging a conspiracy to obstruct justice:

> [It is not] necessary that the United States prove that the conspirators used all of the means that are charged in the indictment. It is sufficient if the United States proves, beyond a reasonable doubt, that the conspirators knowingly and intentionally agreed to endeavor to try to obstruct justice by one of the means charged, and that one or more of the conspirators thereafter undertook some specific overt act charged in the indictment with the intent to accomplish this unlawful goal.
>
> With regard to Count 4, it is also not necessary that the United States prove that a grand jury proceeding was pending at all times when defendants conspired to obstruct justice. It is sufficient if the United States proves defendants entered into such a conspiracy expecting that judicial proceedings would be instituted in the future and committed an overt act in furtherance of the conspiracy after grand jury proceedings began.

To the extent this instruction requires that an overt act occur after the grand jury proceedings began, it may have been unduly favorable to the defense. However, it correctly reflects the law of this Circuit that one can conspire to obstruct an anticipated but as yet uncommenced grand jury proceeding. Given the court's instructions, the jury's conclusion of guilt necessarily reflects findings that Nelson or Shamy willfully agreed to obstruct the grand jury investigation referred to in count 4 and that, for the purpose of obstructing that proceeding, one of them committed at least one of the alleged overt acts. No more is required to support their conviction for conspiracy. We further note that count 4 does not charge defendants with conspiring to obstruct a "pending" grand jury investigation. While it does describe the grand jury investigation as having commenced in March 1985, the allegations are sufficiently detailed that there could have been no confusion as to what the government alleged the defendants had done. Accordingly, there was no amendment of or material variance from the indictment. . . .

NOTES AND QUESTIONS

1. In a later case, the Third Circuit put an important gloss on the *Nelson* holding. It stated that a defendant has the right to question *whether* an Assistant U.S. Attorney contemplated presentation of materials obtained from a subpoena to a grand jury, but not the right to *question the AUSA him or herself.* U.S. v. Steele, 241 F.3d 302 (2001). In other words, circumstantial evidence might be (and usually is) sufficient to prove the AUSA's intent.
2. Although most courts of appeals agree with the Third Circuit that a grand jury need not be pending at the time of the defendants' agreement in order to sustain a conviction for conspiracy to obstruct justice, there is not unanimity on this point. *See, e.g.*, United States v. Schwartz, 28 F.3d 76, 105-106 (2d Cir. 2002) (holding that, to convict for conspiracy to obstruct justice under §1503, the government must establish that the defendant *knew about or at least anticipated the existence of a pending judicial proceeding)*; United States v. Cihak, 137 F.3d 252, 263 (5th Cir. 1998).

B. The Distinction Between Perjury and Obstruction

UNITED STATES v. THOMAS

916 F.2d 647 (11th Cir. 1990)

KRAVITCH, Circuit Judge:

Antonio Thomas, an attorney, appeals his conviction on one count of endeavoring to obstruct justice in violation of 18 U.S.C. §1503 by testifying falsely in a federal civil proceeding with knowledge of a pending grand jury investigation. The government concedes that a new trial is warranted because the trial court failed to charge the jury that the alleged false testimony had the effect of obstructing justice. Thomas contends that the government is barred from retrying him on this count because there was insufficient evidence that his allegedly false testimony had such an effect. We hold that the trial court must instruct a jury that the government must prove the alleged statements had the natural and probable effect of obstructing justice. We reverse, however, because we conclude that the evidence was insufficient to support a conviction.

Facts

Thomas was one of the many fish caught in the broad net the government cast over a narcotics trafficking enterprise that was managed and controlled by Rolland Callahan, Jr. The ninety-nine page, thirty-seven count indictment charged Callahan and sixteen other individuals with various offenses relating to the operation of the narcotics conspiracy and the concealment of its activities. Thomas, one of Callahan's attorneys, and Richard Rose, one of Callahan's accountants, were tried together on various counts relating to allegations that they assisted Callahan's narcotics enterprise in concealing, investing, and laundering drug proceeds. Following a jury trial, Rose was acquitted of all twenty of the counts with which he was charged. Thomas was acquitted of seventeen of the eighteen counts with which he was charged, including various counts of racketeering, conspiracy to possess with the intent to distribute drugs, conspiracy to defraud the United States, mail fraud, and money laundering. The sole count on which Thomas was convicted, obstruction of justice in violation of 18 U.S.C. §1503, is the subject of this appeal.

Because we are reviewing Thomas's conviction for sufficiency of the evidence, we present the facts in the light most favorable to the government. The section of the indictment relating to the obstruction of justice count alleged that Thomas

> knowing there was a Federal Grand Jury investigating ROLLAND CALLAHAN, JR., [did] corruptly endeavor to influence, obstruct, and impede the due administration of justice by willfully, knowingly, intentionally, and falsely testify [sic] under oath in the civil trial of the State of Georgia v. Six Hundred Forty Thousand, Seven Hundred and Sixty-Eight Dollars in U.S. Currency, Case No. C85-1700A, then pending in the United States District Court, Northern District of Georgia, before the Honorable Horace T. Ward, United States District Judge.

The alleged false testimony which provided the entire basis for the obstruction of justice count was the following exchange before Judge Ward:

ROBERT WILSON

[Attorney for DeKalb County]: Do you know the intervenor in this case, Mr. Rolland Callahan?

THOMAS: I know Rolland Callahan, yes.

WILSON: Have you ever known him by any other name other [sic] than Rolland Callahan?

THOMAS: No, I have not.

WILSON: Have you ever known him by the name of Robert Johnson?

THOMAS: No, I have not.

WILSON: Have you ever introduced him to anyone as Robert Johnson?

THOMAS: Not that I recall.

In an effort to prove that Thomas's testimony constituted the obstruction of justice, the government introduced evidence attacking the truthfulness and accuracy of Thomas's assertions. The evidence revealed that Callahan had used the name of his wife's ten year old son, Robert Johnson, in negotiating a shopping center construction contract with Weyman Bearden, a builder. Subsequently, Callahan had entered into another contract with Bearden for the construction of a new home. Callahan brought the contract he negotiated with Bearden for the home to Thomas, and informed Thomas that he wanted the home to be in the name of Robert Johnson. In a meeting at Thomas's office where the contract was signed by Thomas as the attorney for Robert Johnson, Bearden referred to Callahan and his wife as Mr. and Mrs. Johnson. Bearden testified that, based upon his prior transaction with Callahan, he believed Callahan to be Robert Johnson. Thomas, although present when Bearden referred to Callahan as Robert Johnson, made no effort to inform Bearden of Callahan's true identity. . . .

The district court charged the jury that they could find Thomas guilty of the obstruction count if the government proved the following facts beyond a reasonable doubt:

> First, that the federal grand jury and the federal district court were conducting proceedings [relating to Callahan]; second, that the defendant endeavored to influence, intimidate or impede such proceedings; and, third, that the defendant's acts were done knowingly and corruptly.

The court followed this instruction by stating that "it is not necessary for the government to prove that any grand juror or trial judge was in fact swayed or changed or prevented in any way from administering justice, only that the defendant corruptly attempted to do so." Thomas's appeal follows from his conviction on this count of obstructing justice.

Discussion

The defendant was prosecuted under the omnibus clause of the obstruction of justice statute. . . .

In order to convict an individual under the omnibus clause, the government must prove that he (1) corruptly or by threats, (2) endeavored, (3) to influence, obstruct, or impede the due administration of justice. "Corruptly" describes the specific intent of the crime and can vary in meaning with the context of the section 1503 prosecution. Generally, the government must show that the defendant knowingly and intentionally undertook an action from which an obstruction of justice was a reasonably foreseeable result. Although the government is not required to prove that the defendant had the specific purpose of obstructing justice, it must establish that the conduct was prompted, at least in part, by a "corrupt motive."

The "endeavor" element of the offense describes any attempt or effort to obstruct justice. It is not necessary that an individual succeed in actually obstructing justice to violate section 1503. Osborn v. United States, 385 U.S. 323, 333 (1966). As the Eleventh Circuit [has] noted . . . , "a section 1503 offense is complete when one corruptly *endeavors* to obstruct or impede the due administration of justice; the prosecution need not prove that the due administration of justice was actually obstructed or impeded."

The final element of a section 1503 violation describes the characteristics of the conduct prohibited by the statute. Under the omnibus clause, an individual is prohibited from engaging in any activity constituting an effort to influence, obstruct, or impede the due administration of justice. The action taken by the defendant does not need to directly and immediately obstruct justice to be prohibited by section 1503. The defendant's conduct must be such, however, that its natural and probable effect would be the interference with the due administration of justice.

The requirement that the government establish that the defendant's conduct has a probable effect of obstructing justice is particularly critical in section 1503 prosecutions premised on false testimony. We have held consistently that false testimony can provide the basis for a conviction under section 1503. In doing so, however, we have heeded the Supreme Court's admonition that not all false or evasive testimony constitutes obstruction of justice. *See* In re Michael, 326 U.S. 224, 227-28 (1945); Ex parte Hudgings, 249 U.S. 378, 383-84 (1919). Proof of perjury alone is, therefore, insufficient to sustain a section 1503 violation.

To show an obstruction of justice based on false testimony, the government must establish a nexus between the false statements and the obstruction of the administration of justice. . . . .

Because proof that the false testimony was of the kind having a probable effect of obstructing justice is critical in distinguishing a section 1503 offense from mere perjury, the trial court must clearly and explicitly instruct the jury of the necessity of finding this relationship between the statements and obstruction. Here, the trial court's instructions were inadequate to convey to the jury the necessity of finding that the alleged false testimony had a natural and probable effect of obstructing justice. We need not decide today whether such an instruction is necessary in all section 1503 prosecutions. In the context of false testimony, however, we hold that the trial court must instruct the jury that false testimony alone will not provide the basis for a section 1503 conviction unless the testimony at issue had the natural and probable effect of impeding the due administration of justice.

Thomas failed to request or object to the absence of this instruction at trial. Therefore, we will not reverse his conviction on this ground unless we find that the failure to provide the jury with this instruction was plain error. We decline to address this issue, however, because we find that the government failed to put forward sufficient evidence that Thomas's alleged false testimony had the natural and probable effect of obstructing justice to sustain his conviction. . . .

After carefully reviewing the record, we are persuaded that the facts as proven by the government are insufficient to support the jury verdict. As a threshold matter, we are not even convinced that the government established that Thomas's testimony was false. . . .

Moreover, even if we believed that a jury could reasonably find that Thomas testified falsely beyond a reasonable doubt, the government's case still fails because no evidence was introduced that the statements had a natural and probable effect of impeding justice. The government's proof at trial of the section 1503 violation was limited to evidence that Thomas knew that Callahan represented himself as Robert Johnson to other individuals. The prosecution did not introduce a shred of evidence from which the jury could infer that the allegedly false testimony before Judge Ward had the potential of obstructing justice. Nor did the government put forward any evidence to show that Thomas's statements had the natural and probable tendency of impeding the grand jury's investigation of Callahan or Judge Ward's civil forfeiture trial relating to Callahan's property.

On appeal, the government now contends that Thomas's allegedly false testimony had the potential of obstructing justice in three ways. First, the "false" testimony hindered the State of Georgia's ability to prove, in the civil forfeiture trial, that Callahan's income was derived from large scale drug dealing. As a result, the government argues, the State of Georgia did not receive a favorable ruling from Judge Ward. Second, "truthful testimony would have led to an expeditious ruling by Judge Ward who otherwise delayed a ruling for a number of months due to the paucity of evidence for the State." Finally, the government argues that Thomas's testimony delayed the grand jury's return of an indictment against Callahan and his associates.

The government's conclusory, highly speculative, and inherently implausible assertions of the statements' tendency to obstruct justice are inadequate to sustain Thomas's conviction. The government does not explain, nor can we conceive a reasonable explanation of, how Thomas's knowledge of Callahan's use of other names had any significant relationship to Georgia's ability to prove the source of Callahan's income. Likewise, we fail to apprehend how Thomas's testimony could have any meaningful impact on the alacrity with which Judge Ward and the grand jury completed their reviews. In any event, because the government presented the jury with no evidence to support any of these assertions, we cannot rely on these claims to support Thomas's conviction.

Conclusion

Because we find insufficient evidence to sustain Thomas's conviction for obstruction of justice, his conviction is REVERSED.

NOTES AND QUESTIONS

1. Do you think that *Thomas* is an unusual case? In other words, wouldn't you expect that in most cases perjury would have the natural and probable effect of obstructing justice? After all, as we have seen, perjury has a materiality requirement. Would it be safe to say that all *material* perjury amounts to obstruction—or is that too simplistic a view?
2. In *United States v. Brown,* the Fifth Circuit held that "false testimony as to one's *knowledge* relating to the subject of a grand jury inquiry does in fact establish obstruction; not because the perjury *ipso facto* establishes obstruction, but because the perjurious testimony has the effect of 'closing off entirely the avenue[] of inquiry being pursued.'" 459 F.3d 509, 530 (5th Cir. 2006), citing United States v. Williams, 874 F.2d 968, 977 (5th Cir. 1989) (emphasis in original). Should certain classes of perjury automatically equate to obstruction, as the Fifth Circuit concluded, or should each case be judged on its own merits?

C. Nexus Requirement

UNITED STATES v. AGUILAR
515 U.S. 593 (1995)

Chief Justice REHNQUIST delivered the opinion of the Court.

A jury convicted United States District Judge Robert Aguilar of one count of illegally disclosing a wiretap in violation of 18 U.S.C. §2232(c), and of one count of endeavoring to obstruct the due administration of justice in violation of §1503. A panel of the Court of Appeals for the Ninth Circuit affirmed the conviction under §2232(c) but reversed the conviction under §1503. After rehearing en banc, the Court of Appeals reversed both convictions. We granted certiorari to resolve a conflict among the Federal Circuits over whether §1503 punishes false statements made to potential grand jury witnesses, and to answer the important question whether disclosure of a wiretap after its authorization expires violates §2232(c).

Many facts remain disputed by the parties. Both parties appear to agree, however, that a motion for postconviction relief filed by one Michael Rudy Tham represents the starting point from which events bearing on this case unfolded. Tham was an officer of the International Brotherhood of Teamsters, and was convicted of embezzling funds from the local affiliate of that organization. In July 1987, he filed a motion under 28 U.S.C. §2255 to have his conviction set aside. The motion was assigned to Judge Stanley Weigel. Tham, seeking to enhance the odds that his petition would be granted, asked Edward Solomon and Abraham Chalupowitz, a.k.a. Abe Chapman, to assist him by capitalizing on their respective acquaintances with another judge in the Northern District of California, respondent Aguilar. Respondent knew Chapman as a distant relation by marriage and knew Solomon from law school. Solomon and Chapman met with respondent to discuss Tham's case, as a result of which respondent spoke with Judge Weigel about the matter.

Independent of the embezzlement conviction, the Federal Bureau of Investigation (FBI) identified Tham as a suspect in an investigation of labor racketeering. On April 20, 1987, the FBI applied for authorization to install a wiretap on Tham's business phones. Chapman appeared on the application as a potential interceptee. Chief District Judge Robert Peckham authorized the wiretap. The 30-day wiretap expired by law on May 20, 1987, but Chief Judge Peckham maintained the secrecy of the wiretap under §2518(8)(d) after a showing of good cause. During the course of the racketeering investigation, the FBI learned of the meetings between Chapman and respondent. The FBI informed Chief Judge Peckham, who, concerned with appearances of impropriety, advised respondent in August 1987 that Chapman might be connected with criminal elements because Chapman's name had appeared on a wiretap authorization.

Five months after respondent learned that Chapman had been named in a wiretap authorization, he noticed a man observing his home during a visit by Chapman. He alerted his nephew to this fact and conveyed the message (with an intent that his nephew relay the information to Chapman) that Chapman's phone was being wiretapped. Respondent apparently believed, in error, both that Chapman's phones were tapped in connection with the initial application and that the initial authorization was still in effect. Chief Judge Peckham had in fact authorized another wiretap on Tham's phones effective from October 1987 through the period in which respondent made the disclosure, but there is no suggestion in the record that the latter had any specific knowledge of this reauthorization.

At this point, respondent's involvement in the two separate Tham matters converged. Two months after the disclosure to his nephew, a grand jury began to investigate an alleged conspiracy to influence the outcome of Tham's habeas case. Two FBI agents questioned respondent. During the interview, respondent lied about his participation in the Tham case and his knowledge of the wiretap. The grand jury returned an indictment; a jury convicted Aguilar of one count of disclosing a wiretap, 18 U.S.C. §2232(c), and one count of endeavoring to obstruct the due administration of justice, §1503. . . .

Section 1503 provides[, in part]:

> "Whoever . . . *corruptly or by threats or force, or by any threatening letter or communication, influences, obstructs, or impedes, or endeavors to influence, obstruct, or impede, the due administration of justice*, shall be fined not more than $5,000 or imprisoned not more than five years, or both." 18 U.S.C. §1503 (emphasis added).

. . . [This so-called] "Omnibus Clause" serves as a catchall, prohibiting persons from endeavoring to influence, obstruct, or impede the due administration of justice. . . . It is far more general in scope than the earlier clauses of the statute. Respondent was charged with a violation of the Omnibus Clause, to wit: with "corruptly endeavor[ing] to influence, obstruct, and impede the . . . grand jury investigation."

The first case from this Court construing the predecessor statute to §1503 was Pettibone v. United States, 148 U.S. 197 (1893). There we held that "a person is not sufficiently charged with obstructing or impeding the due administration of justice in a court unless it appears that he knew or had notice that justice was being administered in such court." The Court reasoned that a person lacking knowledge of a pending proceeding necessarily lacked the evil intent to obstruct. Recent decisions of Courts of Appeals have likewise tended to place metes and bounds on the very broad language of the catchall provision. The action taken by the accused must be with an intent to influence judicial or grand jury proceedings; it is not enough that there be an intent to influence some ancillary proceeding, such as an investigation independent of the court's or grand jury's authority. United States v. Brown, 688 F.2d 596, 598 (CA9 1982) (citing cases). Some courts have phrased this showing as a "nexus" requirement—that the act must have a relationship in time, causation, or logic with the judicial proceedings. . . . This is not to say that the defendant's actions need be successful; an "endeavor" suffices. But as in *Pettibone*, if the defendant lacks knowledge that his actions are likely to affect the judicial proceeding, he lacks the requisite intent to obstruct.

Although respondent urges various broader grounds for affirmance, we find it unnecessary to address them because we think the "nexus" requirement developed in the decisions of the Courts of Appeals is a correct construction of §1503. We have traditionally exercised restraint in assessing the reach of a federal criminal statute, both out of deference to the prerogatives of Congress and out of concern that "a fair warning should be given to the world in language that the common world will understand, of what the law intends to do if a certain line is passed." We do not believe that uttering false statements to an investigating agent—and that seems to be all that was proved here—who might or might not testify before a grand jury is sufficient to make out a violation of the catchall provision of §1503.

The Government did not show here that the agents acted as an arm of the grand jury, or indeed that the grand jury had even summoned the testimony of these particular agents. The Government argues that respondent "understood that his false statements would be provided to the grand jury" and that he made the statements with the intent to thwart the grand jury investigation and not just the FBI investigation. The Government supports its argument with a citation to the transcript of the recorded conversation between Aguilar and the FBI agent at the point where Aguilar asks whether he is a target of a grand jury investigation. The agent responded to the question by stating:

> "[T]here is a Grand Jury meeting. Convening I guess that's the correct word. Um some evidence will be heard I'm . . . I'm sure on this issue." . . .

Because respondent knew of the pending proceeding, the Government therefore contends that Aguilar's statements are analogous to those made directly to the grand jury itself, in the form of false testimony or false documents.

We think the transcript citation relied upon by the Government would not enable a rational trier of fact to conclude that respondent knew that his false statement would be provided to the grand jury, and that the evidence goes no further than showing that respondent testified falsely to an investigating agent. Such conduct, we believe, falls on the other side of the statutory line from that of one who delivers false documents or testimony to the grand jury itself. Conduct of the latter sort all but assures that the grand jury will consider the material in its deliberations. But what use will be made of false testimony given to an investigating agent who has not been subpoenaed or otherwise directed to appear before the grand jury is far more speculative. We think it cannot be said to have the "natural and probable effect" of interfering with the due administration of justice.

Justice Scalia criticizes our treatment of the statutory language for reading the word "endeavor" out of it, inasmuch as it excludes defendants who have an evil purpose but use means that would "only unnaturally and improbably be successful." This criticism is unwarranted. Our reading of the statute gives the term "endeavor" a useful function to fulfill: It makes conduct punishable where the defendant acts with an intent to obstruct justice, and in a manner that is likely to obstruct justice, but is foiled in some way. Were a defendant with the requisite intent to lie to a subpoenaed witness who is ultimately not called to testify, or who testifies but does not transmit the defendant's version of the story, the defendant has endeavored to obstruct, but has not actually obstructed, justice. Under our approach, a jury could find such defendant guilty.

Justice Scalia also apparently believes that *any* act, done with the intent to "obstruct . . . the due administration of justice," is sufficient to impose criminal liability. Under the dissent's theory, a man could be found guilty under §1503 if he knew of a pending investigation and lied to his wife about his whereabouts at the time of the crime, thinking that an FBI agent might decide to interview her and that she might in turn be influenced in her statement to the agent by her husband's false account of his whereabouts. The intent to obstruct justice is indeed present, but the man's culpability is a good deal less clear from the statute than we usually require in order to impose criminal liability.

[Discussion of §2232(c) is omitted.]

We affirm the decision of the Court of Appeals with respect to respondent's conviction under §1503 and reverse with respect to respondent's conviction under §2232(c). We remand for proceedings consistent with this decision.

So ordered.

[The separate opinion of Justice Stevens is omitted.]

Justice Scalia, with whom Justice Kennedy and Justice Thomas join, concurring in part and dissenting in part.

I join all but Part I and the last paragraph of Part II of the Court's opinion. I would reverse the Court of Appeals, and would uphold respondent's conviction, on the count charging violation of 18 U.S.C. §1503. . . .

Today's "nexus" requirement [is unprecedented]. Instead of reaffirming that "natural and probable consequence" is one way of establishing intent, it *substitutes* "'natural and probable effect'" *for* intent, requiring that factor even when intent to obstruct justice is otherwise clear. But while it is quite proper to derive an *intent* requirement from §1503's use of the word "endeavor," it is quite impossible to derive a "*natural and probable consequence*" requirement. One would be "endeavoring" to obstruct justice if he intentionally set out to do it by means that would only unnaturally and improbably be successful. As we said in *Russell*, "any effort or essay" corruptly to influence, obstruct, or impede the due administration of justice constitutes a forbidden endeavor, even, as we held in *Osborn*, an effort that is *incapable* of having that effect.

The Court does not indicate where its "nexus" requirement is to be found in the words of the statute. Instead, it justifies its holding with the assertion that "[w]e have traditionally exercised restraint in assessing the reach of a federal criminal statute, both out of deference to the prerogatives of Congress and out of concern that a fair warning should be given . . . of what the law intends to do if a certain line is passed." But "exercising restraint *in assessing the reach* of a federal criminal statute" (which is what the rule of lenity requires) is quite different from importing extratextual requirements *in order to limit the reach* of a federal criminal statute, which is what the Court has done here. By limiting §1503 to acts having the "natural and probable effect" of interfering with the due administration of justice, the Court effectively reads the word "endeavor," which we said in *Russell* embraced "any effort or essay" to obstruct justice out of the omnibus clause, leaving a prohibition of only actual obstruction and competent attempts.

II.

. . . Recorded conversations established that respondent knew a grand jury had been convened; that he had been told he was a target of its investigation; and that he feared he would be unable to explain his actions if he were subpoenaed to testify. Respondent himself testified that, at least at the conclusion of the interview, it was his "impression" that his statements to the FBI agents would be reported to the grand jury. The evidence further established that respondent made false statements to the FBI agents that minimized his involvement in the matters the grand jury was investigating. Viewing this evidence in the light most favorable to the Government, I am simply unable to conclude that no rational trier of fact could have found beyond a reasonable doubt that respondent lied specifically because he thought the agents *might* convey what he said to the grand jury—which suffices to constitute a corrupt endeavor to impede the due administration of justice. In fact, I think it would be hard for a juror to conclude otherwise. . . .

UNITED STATES v. FASSNACHT

332 F.3d 440 (7th Cir. 2003)

KANNE, Circuit Judge.

[Fassnacht and his co-defendant, Malanga, were charged with tax evasion and obstruction of justice. They were convicted on the latter count. On appeal, they argued that the government's evidence on the obstruction count was insufficient to sustain their convictions in light of *Aguilar*'s nexus requirement.]

. . . The dispute in this case essentially comes down to the question of the intended object of Fassnacht's and Malanga's obstructive efforts. The defendants argue that the government offered evidence which showed that, while they were aware of the grand jury proceeding, they only acted with an intent to mislead the *IRS investigation.* The government contends that there was sufficient evidence from which the jury could have concluded that the *grand jury investigation* was an object of the defendants' efforts. We agree with the government.

This Court has previously held that conviction under §1503's "corruptly endeavors" language requires, as an element of the offense, the specific intent to impede, obstruct, or interfere with a judicial proceeding. In *United States v. Aguilar*, the Supreme Court explained that to prove specific intent, the government must demonstrate some kind of "nexus" between the action taken by the accused and the judicial proceeding: "the act must have a relationship in time, causation, or logic with the judicial proceedings. . . . In other words, the endeavor must have the 'natural and probable effect' of interfering with the due administration of justice." 515 U.S. 593, 599.

On the other hand, "if the defendant lacks knowledge that his actions are likely to affect the judicial proceeding, he lacks the requisite intent to obstruct." *Id.* The Second Circuit phrased the intent element this way: "the conduct offered to evince that intent must be conduct that is directed at the court or grand jury and that, in the defendant's mind, has the 'natural and probable effect' of obstructing or interfering with that entity." United States v. Schwarz, 283 F.3d 76, 109 (2d Cir. 2002) (citing *Aguilar*, 515 U.S. at 599). Mere knowledge of a judicial proceeding is not enough to support a conviction under §1503. . . .

Given this distinction, the Supreme Court warned that it did not believe that "uttering false statements to an investigating agent . . . who might or might not testify before a grand jury is sufficient to make out a violation of the catchall provision of §1503." Under *Aguilar*, therefore, there is a significant difference between an accused who provides a false statement to an investigator with the knowledge that the evidence will be provided to the grand jury (or an accused who provides false evidence directly to the grand jury), and an accused who simply makes false statements to an investigative agent. If an accused makes a false statement to an investigating agent without the knowledge that the agent will forward that information to the grand jury, it is "far more speculative" whether the false statement will have the "natural and probable effect" of obstructing justice. Such speculation is insufficient to support a conviction under §1503.

Further complicating the distinction between judicial proceedings and investigative efforts, we have held that an investigation by a government agency undertaken in direct support of a grand jury investigation constitutes the "due administration of justice." For example, in United States v. Furkin, 119 F.3d 1276, 1278-79 (7th Cir. 1997), the defendant failed to report income from certain gambling machines on his federal tax returns and was convicted of conspiracy to defraud the IRS; he was also convicted of obstruction of justice under §1503 for his efforts to impede the criminal investigation into his tax evasion. In challenging his conviction under §1503, Furkin argued that the evidence against him indicated, at most, an intent to impede the IRS investigation, but not the grand jury investigation. We disagreed, noting that the evidence demonstrated that "Furkin was also aware that the IRS was *integrally involved* in the grand jury investigation. . . . The IRS investigation was not some 'ancillary proceeding' unrelated to the grand jury investigation. Indeed, the IRS investigation and the grand jury investigation were *one and the same*, and the evidence established that Furkin understood this fact." *Id.* at 1282-83 (emphasis added); *see also Aguilar*, 515 U.S. at 600 (noting that obstruction of an investigation by FBI agents may constitute a violation of §1503 if "the agents acted as the arm of the grand jury").

Like the situation in *Furkin*, there was sufficient evidence presented in this case for the jury to have rationally concluded that Fassnacht and Malanga were aware of the grand jury investigation into their tax returns and that they understood that the IRS agents were "integrally involved" in that grand jury investigation or, at the least, that the IRS agents would provide to the grand jury the information they garnered from the defendants.

The government presented evidence that in January 1996, Fassnacht, Malanga, and Newell began to concoct a cover story to obscure any wrongdoing with regard to their handling of the $1.35 million incentive fee, after realizing that terminating [a disgruntled employee] presented the risk that she might go to the authorities with information about LPM's finances. Newell testified that Fassnacht suggested a scenario in which LPM, Inc. would say that it had entered into an agreement with Burke, for the payment to Burke of a finder's fee with respect to the investment work done for ADIA. The three individuals met several times in early 1996 to review false documents prepared by Fassnacht or Newell and to refine the details of their cover story.

There was evidence offered by the government that while the efforts to create a cover story began before the commencement of the grand jury investigation, once Fassnacht and Malanga became aware of the grand jury investigative efforts, they continued to rely on that cover story, making false statements to investigating agents and preparing false documents to back up their story.

First, there was sufficient evidence for the jury to have concluded that Fassnacht and Malanga were aware that a federal grand jury, and not just the IRS, was investigating their tax affairs. Special Agent Lawrence Egan testified that he served Fassnacht with a subpoena from the grand jury on April 1, 1996. On April 2, Fassnacht was recorded in a telephone conversation with Newell discussing the documents requested in "the subpoena I received." Malanga was tape-recorded in an April 3 call with Newell discussing Fassnacht's postponed grand jury testimony. And when Newell was asked on direct examination whether the grand jury was mentioned during his April 23 meeting in Newark with Malanga and Fassnacht, Newell testified: "I believe it was." . . .

NOTES AND QUESTIONS

1. Even under the majority's own interpretation of the nexus requirement, why wasn't the FBI agent's answer to Aguilar's question about whether he was a target of the grand jury's investigation ("[T]here is a Grand Jury meeting. Convening I guess that's the correct word. Um, *some evidence will be heard I'm . . . I'm sure on this issue* (emphasis added).") sufficient to put the judge on notice that his answers were likely going to be transmitted back to the grand jury? Surely a federal judge knows better than anyone that

grand juries listen to hearsay—in the form of agents' summaries of witness interviews—all the time. Is the problem in the case that the agent's answer to the judge was too deferential? Or is it simply that the Supreme Court refused to give the answer its most logical interpretation?

2. If Aguilar had not been a federal judge, would the case have come out the same way? Indeed, might it be fair to say that the majority mangled the interpretation of the omnibus clause to help out a fellow judge? In answering these questions, consider the following additional facts. After the Supreme Court reinstated Aguilar's conviction for disclosing the existence of the wiretap and remanded for "proceedings consistent with this opinion," the *en banc* Ninth Circuit decided to address a second argument that Aguilar had raised on appeal with respect to that count. *See* United States v. Aguilar, 80 F.3d 329 (1996). Aguilar's contention was that the trial judge's instruction on knowledge—specifically regarding his knowledge of the ongoing wiretap—was erroneous because it equated knowledge of a fact with an awareness of a "high probability" of its existence. This instruction (1) was consistent with the Model Penal Code's definition of knowledge, *see* MPC §2.02(7) (1962), and (2) had been upheld by the Ninth Circuit in a very well known (though somewhat confusing) opinion in United States v. Jewell, 532 F.2d 697 (9th Cir.), *cert. denied*, 426 U.S. 951(1976). In addition, the evidence in the case on this point was not ambiguous: The Chief Judge had informed Aguilar of the existence of the wiretap, so he obviously knew of its existence under any interpretation of that word. Any error was clearly harmless. Despite all this, the appeals court, in a 10-1 decision, *again* reversed Aguilar's conviction and sent the case back for retrial.

   By this time, however, retrial was impossible, in part because two of the government's witnesses had died in the intervening years. So, in June 1996, the Department of Justice and Aguilar settled the case. Aguilar—who had continued to sit on the federal bench in California during the litigation of the criminal case—agreed to admit certain facts and step down in return for the government's dismissal of the one remaining charge. *See United States District Judge Robert P. Aguilar Resigns*, June 24, 1996, available at http://www.justice.gov/opa/pr/1996/Jun96/298.crm.htm.

3. Another example of the favorable treatment accorded Aguilar appears in the second paragraph of the opinion. The Court states that "[m]any facts remain disputed by the parties. Both parties appear to agree, however. . . ." But why should this matter? Given Aguilar's conviction, shouldn't the Court have viewed the facts in the light most favorable to the prosecution?

4. If the facts in Questions 2 and 3 convince you that Aguilar got special treatment from his colleagues on the bench, why do you think this is so? Wouldn't you expect judges to be especially offended by someone who has embarrassed their own profession? Should the judges of the Ninth Circuit, who surely knew Aguilar professionally if not personally, have recused themselves and requested that a different circuit hear his appeals?

5. What, if anything, distinguishes *Fassnacht* from *Aguilar*?

D. Distinction Between Vigorous Defense and Obstruction

UNITED STATES v. CINTOLO

818 F.2d 980 (1st Cir. 1987)

SELYA, Circuit Judge.

. . . In December 1984, a grand jury sitting in the District of Massachusetts returned an indictment against William J. Cintolo, a practicing criminal defense attorney, charging him with one count of conspiracy to obstruct justice, 18 U.S.C. §§371, 1503, and two substantive counts of obstruction of justice, 18 U.S.C. §1503. After a lengthy trial, the jury found the defendant guilty on the conspiracy count, but not guilty on the substantive obstruction counts. Cintolo was thereafter sentenced to a prison term, the execution of which was stayed pending appeal. We affirm. . . .

I.

. . . The gravamen of the accusation [against Cintolo] was that [he] did "corruptly endeavor to influence, obstruct and impede the due administration of justice" by befouling the proceedings of a federal grand jury investigating the criminal activities of the Angiulo gang. According to the indictment, Cintolo set out to accomplish this nefarious end through the use of his position as attorney of record for Walter LaFreniere, a witness before the grand jury, to acquire information about the ongoing investigation for Angiulo's benefit. The indictment further charged Cintolo with knowingly assisting Angiulo in his efforts to inhibit LaFreniere, after the latter had been granted immunity, from testifying truthfully before the grand jury, or from cooperating in any way with the investigation.

Tape recordings played for the jury at Cintolo's trial established that LaFreniere and his father-in-law, Louis Venios, possessed damaging information linking various members of Angiulo's organization to illegal gambling and loansharking activities. Among other things, the evidence disclosed that both Venios and LaFreniere had been extended substantial credit to cover unpaid gambling debts, and that each had been subjected to exacting pressure from various of Angiulo's minions to remit the overdue sums. When subpoenas issued to Venios and LaFreniere indicating that the grand jury was investigating possible violations of 18 U.S.C. §§892-94 (making, financing, and collecting extortionate extensions of credit), Angiulo recognized the legal peril which faced him and his confreres. . . .

Following extended discussions among Angiulo and his cohorts, assessing the extent of LaFreniere's knowledge and speculating on the possible foci of the grand jury's investigation, Donato Angiulo sent LaFreniere to meet with the appellant. Shortly thereafter, the lawyer assembled with Gennaro Angiulo and others — not including LaFreniere — to discuss the sweep of the grand jury inquiry and Cintolo's newfound "client." At this session, Angiulo told Cintolo that "about three and a half, four weeks ago, . . . these guys should have gotten you and told you what I wanted." Angiulo explained that LaFreniere had been delivering payments to him on behalf of Venios, and that LaFreniere's name appeared on a "cuff sheet," *i.e.*, a written list kept to show amounts of borrowings and identities of borrowers. . . .

On March 19, 1981, Wendy Collins, a federal prosecutor, notified LaFreniere to report to the grand jury the following Thursday. That evening, Cintolo spoke with Angiulo:

Angiulo: You going to explain to him that you feel that he's gonna get immunity? There's no other way out of it, is there? Huh?

Cintolo: No. I, I'll explain it to him. Figured somebody else might want to talk to him first . . . .

Angiulo: His father-in-law says already that as far as this kid is concerned, one thing you can say he's a . . . man. If he's got time to do, he'll do it. But I don't think they figure on immunity. You understand? They're not that . . . smart. Did we find out anything about this grand jury?

Cintolo: Nothing yet.

Angiulo: I would say you call him in, have a good talk, and give me a reaction.

Cintolo: Yeah.

Angiulo: So that this kid understands that he might just go and do eighteen . . . months.

Later that evening, Angiulo conferred with two of his henchmen, Richard Gambale and Peter "Doc" Limone, soliciting their views as to whether LaFreniere would "stand up." Apparently uneasy at what he heard, Angiulo ordered them to kill LaFreniere. . . .

FBI agents monitoring the electronic surveillance equipment overheard Angiulo hand down this death sentence. They moved immediately to warn the intended victim. . . .

On March 20, Angiulo was told that LaFreniere had been attempting to reach Cintolo. Angiulo advised the lawyer that LaFreniere had been tipped about the "contract" which had been placed on his life:

> [T]he Feds called him and said to him, "we got an informant in the North End. He just informed us that you have been placed on the hit list down there. . . ." Words to that effect.

Cintolo's only response to this grisly piece of news was to mention calmly that he had instructed LaFreniere to talk with no one, and to refer all calls to him. . . .

This particular conversation concluded with Angiulo instructing Cintolo to meet with LaFreniere again and "to evaluate [the situation] very carefully." . . .

Angiulo later told the appellant of Venios's continued assurances that LaFreniere would "stand up." According to Angiulo, Venios had been ordered to remind his son-in-law that this was no avuncular request, but a command from the organization: "You got to tell this kid that we said it, not you. Us. No guy will go to the can here for any reason." So, Angiulo indicated, Cintolo's "client" fully appreciated the personal risk he would run by cooperating with the grand jury. . . .

On April 1, LaFreniere received immunity, thereby stripping him of the fifth amendment's protection against compelled self-incrimination. Not daunted, Cintolo continued to participate in discussions with Angiulo and his subordinates in which the anticipated commission of contempt before the grand jury was frankly acknowledged as an objective. At one point Cintolo remarked, "they've got to figure if they can isolate [LaFreniere] in a sense . . . *if they can pull him away from me,* . . . . Okay. *If they can pull him away from me, then maybe they get something out of him.* Whether he's gonna voluntarily do it, or just by sheer ignorance he's gonna blurt it out. I think that's what they want." (Emphasis supplied). Moments later, Cintolo added:

> I talked to him . . . to evaluate what he's saying to me—in fact, it was like I do with everybody: instill confidence in them, you know. I kept telling him, "I might not be able to help you out, but I can tell ya, I'll fight like a son of a. . . ." *To get him into a confident situation, making him think that we can do what we're saying we can do, and all of a sudden smack, he's a . . . goner.* (Emphasis supplied).

. . . On April 23, LaFreniere appeared before the grand jury and, reading a statement prepared for him by Cintolo, refused to testify. Notwithstanding the immunity which had been conferred, the refusal was predicated on fifth amendment grounds. At a hearing on the government's ensuing motion to compel, the duty judge dismissed Cintolo's argument that the immunity bestowed upon LaFreniere was somehow inadequate as "clearly frivolous." Upon leaving court, the appellant went directly to 98 Prince Street. Angiulo greeted him with the question, "Is he in jail, just say yes or no?" Cintolo responded, "Not yet." The two men then dissected what had transpired at the grand jury in minute detail. . . .

On June 2, 1982, LaFreniere was held in contempt in federal district court and was sentenced to an eighteen month term of incarceration, which he served in full. Cintolo represented him throughout the entire period of his immurement. He was disqualified by court order, however, from continuing to appear for Jason Angiulo.

At his own trial, appellant testified that, although he was aware of Angiulo's involvement in illegal businesses, he had not acted with the intent corruptly to obstruct or impede justice while representing LaFreniere. To the contrary, he claimed to have been cooperating—or pretending to cooperate—with Angiulo solely to enhance his ability to counsel his true client (LaFreniere). The jury obviously disbelieved these assertions and drew a different set of inferences.

II.

From the facts established at trial, a sampling of which we have set out above, we find overwhelming evidence of a conspiracy among Angiulo and his associates to pressure LaFreniere—at all costs and by the nearest means—so as to prevent his testifying before the grand jury; in short, a conspiracy to violate 18 U.S.C. §1503. Drawing reasonable inferences from the evidence in the light most hospitable to the government, we have no difficulty recognizing that the defendant lent his informed assistance to this conspiracy. . . .

Cintolo argues, however, that appearances are deceiving in this case; that his authentic motive in pursuing this perilous course of conduct was to obtain information from Angiulo that would assist him in representing the interests of LaFreniere. He portrays himself as a double agent of sorts, using the ringleader of the mob as the ringleader was attempting to manipulate him. While admitting that his behavior conferred benefits on Angiulo and on the hoped-for conspiracy of silence, the appellant maintains that those rewards were "incidental" to his obligation to represent LaFreniere as he thought best. Inasmuch as he did not intend to obstruct justice, the thesis runs, he cannot be guilty of conspiring to commit the substantive offense.

The short answer to this plaint is that the jurors, armed with considerable circumstantial evidence to support their assessment of the situation, deemed these protestations to be apocryphal. . . .

This notwithstanding, appellant and the amici beseech us to announce an unprecedented rule of law designed, they contend, to insulate lawyers from encroachments on the "zealous representation" of clients accused of crime. So long as an attorney tenders a facially legitimate explanation for conduct performed in the course of his defense of a client, they urge, a factfinder must evaluate the behavior *on that basis.* In constructing this sort of paradigm, the lawyer's word alone creates what amounts to an irrebuttable presumption which debars the jury—despite the existence of mounds of circumstantial evidence—from drawing contradictory inferences as to the attorney's motives or intent. Put another way, if defense counsel's actions of and by themselves do not amount to a crime, then a factfinder may not criminalize the conduct on the basis of conclusions reached, no matter how reasonably, about *why* the actions were performed. Hidden motivations, howsoever corrupt, remain forever hidden in a world where veniremen are not allowed to peer beneath the surface of things.

We find no support in precedent, principle, or policy for such an anti-lapsarian rule, and decline to cleave so deep a chasm in the criminal law for the exclusive benefit of attorneys who knowingly involve themselves in the corruption of their clients. As important a role as defense counsel serve . . . the acceptance of a retainer by a lawyer in a criminal case cannot become functionally equivalent to the lawyer's acceptance of a roving commission to flout the criminal law with impunity. A criminal lawyer has no license to act as a lawyer-criminal. . . .

We have held before, and reaffirm now, that "[i]f reasonable jurors could conclude, from the circumstances of the conversation[s], that the defendant had sought, however cleverly and with whatever cloaking of purpose, to influence improperly a [witness], the offense was complete." Correct application of §1503 thus requires, in a very real sense, that the factfinder discern—by direct evidence or from inference—the motive which led an individual to perform particular actions. As Justice Holmes once aptly observed, "[i]ntent may make an otherwise innocent act criminal, if it is a step in a plot." Badders v. United States, 240 U.S. 391, 394, (1916). The appellant's suggestion that the jury be precluded, as a matter of law, from drawing its own (reasonable) conclusions as to why any defendant—or, more narrowly put, a lawyer-defendant—committed acts not unlawful in and of themselves would do enormous violence to the statute and play unwarranted havoc with its enforcement. . . .

Once it is conceded that the existence *vel non* of intent under §1503 is a question of fact for the jury, it remains to define the parameters of behavior that can fairly be labeled as "corrupt," ergo, criminal under the statute. . . . Courts have tended to interpret the requirement broadly, holding that it applies to the ends of an actor's conduct rather than merely the means. . . . Thus, any act by any party—whether lawful or unlawful on its face—may abridge §1503 if performed with a corrupt motive. . . .

The appellant and the amici pay lip service to this principle, but maintain that different considerations come into play where criminal defense lawyers are concerned. In those purlieus, they assert, a corrupt motive may not be found in conduct which is, itself, not independently illegal. We regard this argument as being in conflict with persuasive caselaw, and as wrongheaded from the standpoint of sound public policy.

In Cole v. United States, 329 F.2d 437 (9th Cir.), *cert. denied*, 377 U.S. 954 (1964), the court affirmed the §1503 conviction of an individual who had pressed a grand jury witness to stand mute by invocation of his fifth amendment prerogative. The defendant's motive, the prosecution contended, was to protect both himself and a close friend from the slings and arrows of a pending grand jury investigation. The Ninth Circuit noted that: "the constitutional privilege against self-incrimination is an integral part of the due administration of justice, designed to do and further justice, and to the exercise of which there is an absolute right in every witness." Nevertheless, while "[a] witness violates no duty to claim it, . . . one who bribes, coerces, forces or threatens a witness to claim it, or advises with corrupt motive the witness to take it, can and does himself obstruct or influence the due administration of justice." *Id.* . . .

On this unhappy record, a factfinder could well have believed beyond a reasonable doubt that Cintolo acted as part of a high pressure, no-holds-barred campaign to induce his nominal client, LaFreniere, to commit a criminal contempt. Though Cintolo's acts in fostering the intimidation of LaFreniere were not in themselves *overtly* unlawful, they seem to us, in this context, to have been fully actionable under 18 U.S.C. §1503.

A few simple illustrations may be useful. Purchasing a chisel at a hardware store is, usually, a lawful act, commonplace in the extreme. Yet, if an individual were to purchase the same chisel at the same hardware store with the avowed (evil) purpose that it be used as part of a planned break-in by persons in league with him, the iniquitous motive alone would transmogrify the innocent transaction into an overt act carrying undeniable criminal consequences. . . .

Whatever the contours of the line between traditional lawyering and corrupt intent may be, they must inevitably be drawn case-by-case. The question of whether an attorney who does no more than file motions, make court appearances, and the like—however dilatory they may seem, however much they may slow the progress of a grand jury probe—can ever be subject to §1503 liability for such conduct alone, is not before us. We recognize the dangers that are present if prosecutors can be allowed to inquire into motive in such confined circumstances, and we respect the importance of allowing defense counsel to perform legitimate activities without let or hindrance. We do not see this case, however, edging into that forbidden terrain. Where, as here, it is proven beyond any reasonable doubt that a lawyer has purposefully acted as an advisor to third-party criminals and as a participant in the illegal plot which they have hatched, that he has served knowingly and willingly as a go-between linking the conspirators to his nominal client, that he has performed functions apart from (and alien to) the traditional chores of a lawyer, and that he has done all of this with the corrupt aim of frustrating a federal grand jury on its appointed rounds, then he cannot hide behind his law degree when the presence or absence of the essential elements of an obstruction of justice charge are considered. Having called the tune, Cintolo cannot be excused from paying the piper on the basis of his vocation. . . .

In sum, the government presented plethoric evidence from which the jury could reasonably have found the appellant guilty of conspiring to obstruct the due administration of justice. His role as a defense attorney did not insulate him from the criminal consequences of his corruptly-motivated actions. Accordingly, the district court did not err in denying the defendant's motion for judgment of acquittal. . . .

NOTES AND QUESTIONS

1. Cases in which a criminal defense attorney is prosecuted for litigation-related conduct are extremely rare. Why do you think this is so?
2. The Seventh Circuit reached a conclusion similar to *Cintolo* in United States v. Cueto, 151 F.3d 620 (7th Cir. 1998). In the latter case, defense attorney Cueto cleverly used an emergency injunction proceeding in state court to force an undercover witness to reveal a covert FBI (and shortly thereafter, grand jury) probe into his client's (and business partner's) illegal gambling and loan-sharking operation. (The witness had 15 minutes to respond to a subpoena to testify, was denied counsel, and was thus forced to reveal the truth about the investigation under oath.) Even after the injunction proceeding was removed to federal court and the involvement of the U.S. Attorney's Office and the FBI were known to Cueto, he pressed the State Attorney (and even wrote a congressman) to charge the witness with corruption based on his *undercover* conduct. The §1503 charge was based, in part, on Cueto's appeal of the district court's ruling in the injunction case and his petition for certiorari. The Seventh Circuit stated:

> Whatever the contours of the line between traditional lawyering and criminal conduct, they must inevitably be drawn case-by-case. We refuse to accept the notion that lawyers may do anything, including violating the law, to zealously advocate their clients' interests and then avoid criminal prosecution by claiming that they were "just doing their job." . . . We respect the importance of allowing defense counsel to perform legitimate activities without hindrance and recognize the potential dangers that could arise if prosecutors were permitted to inquire into the motives of criminal defense attorneys ad hoc. This case, however, does not create that avenue of inquiry; our conclusion is limited to the specific facts of this case. . . . [T]here was ample basis for the jury to find that Cueto corruptly endeavored to obstruct the due administration of justice. The jury was justified in concluding that Cueto had the requisite knowledge of the FBI's investigation of [his client], the grand jury's inquiry, and

> the district court's proceedings and then acted in a manner that had the natural and probable effect of interfering with the lawful function of those governmental entities and the due administration of justice. His role as a defense attorney did not insulate him from the criminal consequences of his corruptly-motivated actions. Accordingly, we affirm Cueto's convictions on Counts 2, 6, and 7.

Id. at 634-635. Although this outcome feels right, isn't the court suggesting that Cueto had an obligation to accept as true the facts claimed by the government and found by the federal district court? At what point must a criminal defense attorney accept "reality," as it were? Is the case distinguished by the fact that the "dispute" centered around the existence of the federal investigation itself, which was impossible to deny?

3. The court in *Cueto* seemed heavily influenced by the fact that Cueto and his client were also business partners in numerous ventures. The government's theory was that Cueto's corrupt motive arose mainly because he needed to protect his own economic interests. How important should that factor be? Is a generous fee sufficient to create a corrupt motive under §1503? Or is the decisive feature of *Cueto* the fact that attorney and client were mutually engaged in *criminal* economic activity?
4. Where should we draw the line between vigorous defense and obstruction with respect to lawful litigative maneuvers? Isn't a zealous defense attorney's motivation *always* to obstruct the course of the investigation and prosecution? When does that motive turn corrupt? *Cintolo* and *Cueto* both seem to suggest that the determination must be made on a case-by-case basis—in other words, a "we'll know it when we see it" approach. Is that the best we can do?

III. WITNESS TAMPERING

A. Relationship Between §§1503 and 1512

UNITED STATES v. MASTERPOL
940 F.2d 760 (2d Cir. 1991)

MESKILL, Circuit Judge:

. . . In 1988, Nicholas Masterpol was indicted on charges of racketeering, bribery, mail fraud, conspiracy, false statements, perjury and tax fraud. The charges arose in part from Masterpol's attempt to defraud Oliver Schools, Inc. by overcharging it for renovation work that Masterpol's construction company had performed. During the ensuing trial on several of these charges two former employees of Masterpol, Daniel Tagliamonte and Royal Cooper, testified against Masterpol. Both witnesses testified that they had been paid less for their work on the renovation project than

Masterpol reported to Oliver Schools. On November 2, 1989, a jury convicted Masterpol on several of the charges in the indictment. Masterpol subsequently pleaded *nolo contendere* to other charges in the indictment. Sentencing was scheduled for January 19, 1990 before Judge Munson.

Shortly before sentencing, Masterpol met individually with Tagliamonte and Cooper. Masterpol urged them to write letters to Judge Munson recanting portions of their trial testimony. At Masterpol's behest, Tagliamonte and Cooper wrote the letters, indicating that they had received either a combination of cash and gifts, or cash alone, from Masterpol equaling the amount that Masterpol claimed to have paid them—in other words, that Masterpol had in fact paid both employees what he had reported to Oliver Schools. According to the government, Masterpol made a copy of the Tagliamonte letter and submitted it to Judge Munson as an attachment to Masterpol's sentencing memorandum. During the sentencing proceedings, Masterpol's attorney presented a copy of the Cooper letter to Judge Munson for consideration in imposing Masterpol's sentence. Judge Munson sentenced Masterpol to three years' imprisonment.

On February 21, 1990, a federal grand jury returned a second indictment against Masterpol. This indictment was directed at Masterpol's conduct in seeking to influence Tagliamonte and Cooper. Count one alleged that Masterpol attempted to obstruct justice in violation of 18 U.S.C. §1503 when he urged Cooper and Tagliamonte to recant their trial testimony. . . . After a four day trial, the jury returned a guilty verdict. . . .

Discussion

A. Obstruction of Justice—18 U.S.C. §1503

Masterpol was prosecuted under the residual ["Omnibus"] clause of 18 U.S.C. §1503. . . . Masterpol contends that he was improperly convicted of violating section 1503. He claims that section 1503, after its amendment in 1982, no longer covers witness tampering. In his view, if he was to be charged under the "Obstruction of Justice" chapter of Title 18, section 1501 through section 1517, he should have been charged under section 1512 or not at all. We agree.

We confronted a similar issue in United States v. Hernandez, 730 F.2d 895 (2d Cir. 1984). There the defendant was convicted of violating 18 U.S.C. §1503 . . . for threatening a witness in order to obtain documentary evidence. The defendant in *Hernandez* . . . argued . . . that the enactment in 1982 of the Victim and Witness Protection Act removed from section 1503's purview witness tampering. In support of this argument, he noted that Congress in 1982 deleted all references to witnesses from section 1503, entitled "Influencing or injuring officer or juror generally," and enacted a new provision, section 1512, which was entitled "Tampering with a witness, victim, or an informant" and which was addressed specifically to contacts with witnesses. The government sought to counter this argument by contending "that although §1512 absorbs some of the jurisdiction previously given to §1503, Congress intended, in effect, to create two crimes, making witness intimidation and harassment punishable not only under §1512, but also under the residual clause of

§1503." After examining what Congress did in simultaneously enacting section 1512 and deleting all references to witnesses in section 1503, as well as what Congress said it did in the relevant legislative history, we rejected the government's argument. We noted that congressional intent was "graphically demonstrated by examining those portions of §1503 that congress expressly deleted" and "conclude[d] that congress affirmatively intended to remove witnesses entirely from the scope of §1503."

The government now seeks to limit *Hernandez.* It notes that *Hernandez* involved a coercive attempt to influence a witness, whereas in this case Masterpol urged witnesses to make false statements without resort to intimidation or harassment. Such noncoercive witness contacts, says the government, are still covered by the residual clause of section 1503 because, otherwise, "noncoercive witness tampering, including corrupt efforts to urge witnesses to make false statements, would not be proscribed by either Section 1512 or Section 1503." This limiting construction of *Hernandez* has been accepted by other circuits and by district courts in this Circuit. The force of these precedents, however, was diminished significantly in 1988 when Congress amended section 1512.

Section 1512(b), as amended, reads in pertinent part:

> Whoever knowingly uses intimidation or physical force, threatens, *or corruptly persuades* another person, or attempts to do so . . . with intent to—
>
> (1) influence, delay, or prevent the testimony of any person in an official proceeding . . . [violates the laws of the United States].

(emphasis added). The "corruptly persuades" language was added to the statute in 1988—well before Masterpol's obstructive conduct in January 1990. Notably, this language reaches noncoercive witness contacts. In fact the conduct described in Masterpol's indictment is nearly identical to that which may be charged under section 1512. The indictment charges that Masterpol "*corruptly* . . . attempted to *persuade*" witnesses Cooper and Tagliamonte. The government, moreover, candidly admits in its sur-reply brief that if it "had been aware of the 1988 amendment of Section 1512, the Assistant United States Attorney responsible for the case might have sought to charge Masterpol . . . under both 18 U.S.C. §1503 and §1512." Thus, what justification there once was for giving *Hernandez* a narrow construction now lacks merit, at least where, as in this instance, there appears to be no statutory vacuum. In any event, to the extent a gap remains in the legislative scheme covering noncoercive witness contacts, "the proper remedy is not for the courts to distort the plain language of [the statute] but for Congress to enact legislation to close the gap." Furthermore, the government points to no cases decided after the 1988 amendment to section 1512 that have given *Hernandez* a narrow reading. In view of these developments and the plain import of Congress' actions in both adopting section 1512 and deleting from section 1503 all references to witnesses, we see no reason at this juncture to retreat from the position we took in *Hernandez,* that "congress affirmatively intended to remove witnesses entirely from the scope of §1503."

Masterpol's obstruction of justice conviction under section 1503 therefore must be reversed. . . .

B. Corrupt Persuasion, 18 U.S.C. §1512

ARTHUR ANDERSEN LLP v. UNITED STATES
544 U.S. 696 (2005)

Chief Justice REHNQUIST delivered the opinion of the Court.

As Enron Corporation's financial difficulties became public in 2001, petitioner Arthur Andersen LLP, Enron's auditor, instructed its employees to destroy documents pursuant to its document retention policy. A jury found that this action made petitioner guilty of violating 18 U.S.C. §§1512(b)(2)(A) and (B). These sections make it a crime to "knowingly us[e] intimidation or physical force, threate[n], or corruptly persuad[e] another person . . . with intent to . . . cause" that person to "withhold" documents from, or "alter" documents for use in, an "official proceeding."[1] The Court of Appeals for the Fifth Circuit affirmed. We hold that the jury instructions failed to convey properly the elements of a "corrup[t] persua[sion]" conviction under §1512(b), and therefore reverse.

Enron Corporation, during the 1990's, switched its business from operation of natural gas pipelines to an energy conglomerate, a move that was accompanied by aggressive accounting practices and rapid growth. Petitioner audited Enron's publicly filed financial statements and provided internal audit and consulting services to it. Petitioner's "engagement team" for Enron was headed by David Duncan. Beginning in 2000, Enron's financial performance began to suffer, and, as 2001 wore on, worsened.[2] On August 14, 2001, Jeffrey Skilling, Enron's Chief Executive Officer (CEO), unexpectedly resigned. Within days, Sherron Watkins, a senior accountant at Enron, warned Kenneth Lay, Enron's newly reappointed CEO, that Enron could "implode in a wave of accounting scandals." She likewise informed Duncan and Michael Odom, one of petitioner's partners who had supervisory responsibility over Duncan, of the looming problems.

On August 28, an article in the Wall Street Journal suggested improprieties at Enron, and the SEC opened an informal investigation. By early September, petitioner had formed an Enron "crisis-response" team, which included Nancy Temple, an in-house counsel.[3] On October 8, petitioner retained outside counsel to represent it in any litigation that might arise from the Enron matter. The next day,

1. We refer to the 2000 version of the statute, which has since been amended by Congress.

2. During this time, petitioner faced problems of its own. In June 2001, petitioner entered into a settlement agreement with the Securities and Exchange Commission (SEC) related to its audit work of Waste Management, Inc. As part of the settlement, petitioner paid a massive fine. It also was censured and enjoined from committing further violations of the securities laws. In July 2001, the SEC filed an amended complaint alleging improprieties by Sunbeam Corporation, and petitioner's lead partner on the Sunbeam audit was named.

3. A key accounting problem involved Enron's use of "Raptors," which were special purpose entities used to engage in "off-balance-sheet" activities. Petitioner's engagement team had allowed Enron to "aggregate" the Raptors for accounting purposes so that they reflected a positive return. This was, in the words of petitioner's experts, a "black-and-white" violation of Generally Accepted Accounting Principles.

Temple discussed Enron with other in-house counsel. Her notes from that meeting reflect that "some SEC investigation" is "highly probable."

On October 10, Odom spoke at a general training meeting attended by 89 employees, including 10 from the Enron engagement team. Odom urged everyone to comply with the firm's document retention policy. He added: "'[I]f it's destroyed in the course of [the] normal policy and litigation is filed the next day, that's great. . . . [W]e've followed our own policy, and whatever there was that might have been of interest to somebody is gone and irretrievable.'" On October 12, Temple entered the Enron matter into her computer, designating the "Type of Potential Claim" as "Professional Practice—Government/Regulatory Inv[estigation]." Temple also e-mailed Odom, suggesting that he "'remin[d] the engagement team of our documentation and retention policy.'"

On October 16, Enron announced its third quarter results. That release disclosed a $1.01 billion charge to earnings. The following day, the SEC notified Enron by letter that it had opened an investigation in August and requested certain information and documents. On October 19, Enron forwarded a copy of that letter to petitioner.

On the same day, Temple also sent an e-mail to a member of petitioner's internal team of accounting experts and attached a copy of the document policy. On October 20, the Enron crisis-response team held a conference call, during which Temple instructed everyone to "[m]ake sure to follow the [document] policy." On October 23, Enron CEO Lay declined to answer questions during a call with analysts because of "potential lawsuits, as well as the SEC inquiry." After the call, Duncan met with other Andersen partners on the Enron engagement team and told them that they should ensure team members were complying with the document policy. Another meeting for all team members followed, during which Duncan distributed the policy and told everyone to comply. These, and other smaller meetings, were followed by substantial destruction of paper and electronic documents.

On October 26, one of petitioner's senior partners circulated a New York Times article discussing the SEC's response to Enron. His e-mail commented that "the problems are just beginning and we will be in the cross hairs. The marketplace is going to keep the pressure on this and is going to force the SEC to be tough." On October 30, the SEC opened a formal investigation and sent Enron a letter that requested accounting documents.

Throughout this time period, the document destruction continued, despite reservations by some of petitioner's managers.[6] On November 8, Enron announced that it would issue a comprehensive restatement of its earnings and assets. Also on November 8, the SEC served Enron and petitioner with subpoenas for records. On

6. For example, on October 26, John Riley, another partner with petitioner, saw Duncan shredding documents and told him "this wouldn't be the best time in the world for you guys to be shredding a bunch of stuff." On October 31, David Stulb, a forensics investigator for petitioner, met with Duncan. During the meeting, Duncan picked up a document with the words "smoking gun" written on it and began to destroy it, adding "we don't need this." Stulb cautioned Duncan on the need to maintain documents and later informed Temple that Duncan needed advice on the document retention policy.

November 9, Duncan's secretary sent an e-mail that stated: "Per Dave-No more shredding. . . . We have been officially served for our documents." Enron filed for bankruptcy less than a month later. Duncan was fired and later pleaded guilty to witness tampering.

In March 2002, petitioner was indicted in the Southern District of Texas on one count of violating §§1512(b)(2)(A) and (B). The indictment alleged that, between October 10 and November 9, 2001, petitioner "did knowingly, intentionally and corruptly persuade . . . other persons, to wit: [petitioner's] employees, with intent to cause" them to withhold documents from, and alter documents for use in, "official proceedings, namely: regulatory and criminal proceedings and investigations." A jury trial followed. When the case went to the jury, that body deliberated for seven days and then declared that it was deadlocked. The District Court delivered an "*Allen* charge," and, after three more days of deliberation, the jury returned a guilty verdict. The District Court denied petitioner's motion for a judgment of acquittal.

The Court of Appeals for the Fifth Circuit affirmed. It held that the jury instructions properly conveyed the meaning of "corruptly persuades" and "official proceeding"; that the jury need not find any consciousness of wrongdoing; and that there was no reversible error. Because of a split of authority regarding the meaning of §1512(b), we granted certiorari. . . .

In this case, our attention is focused on what it means to "knowingly . . . corruptly persuad[e]" another person "with intent to . . . cause" that person to "withhold" documents from, or "alter" documents for use in, an "official proceeding."

"We have traditionally exercised restraint in assessing the reach of a federal criminal statute, both out of deference to the prerogatives of Congress and out of concern that 'a fair warning should be given to the world in language that the common world will understand, of what the law intends to do if a certain line is passed.'" *Aguilar*, 515 U.S. at 600.

Such restraint is particularly appropriate here, where the act underlying the conviction—"persua[sion]"—is by itself innocuous. Indeed, "persuad[ing]" a person "with intent to . . . cause" that person to "withhold" testimony or documents from a Government proceeding or Government official is not inherently malign. Consider, for instance, a mother who suggests to her son that he invoke his right against compelled self-incrimination or a wife who persuades her husband not to disclose marital confidences.

Nor is it necessarily corrupt for an attorney to "persuad[e]" a client "with intent to . . . cause" that client to "withhold" documents from the Government. In Upjohn Co. v. United States, 449 U.S. 383 (1981), for example, we held that Upjohn was justified in withholding documents that were covered by the attorney-client privilege from the Internal Revenue Service (IRS). No one would suggest that an attorney who "persuade[d]" Upjohn to take that step acted wrongfully, even though he surely intended that his client keep those documents out of the IRS' hands.

"Document retention policies," which are created in part to keep certain information from getting into the hands of others, including the Government, are common in business. It is, of course, not wrongful for a manager to instruct his employees to comply with a valid document retention policy under ordinary circumstances.

Acknowledging this point, the parties have largely focused their attention on the word "corruptly" as the key to what may or may not lawfully be done in the situation presented here. Section 1512(b) punishes not just "corruptly persuad[ing]" another, but "*knowingly* . . . corruptly persuad[ing]" another. (Emphasis added.) The Government suggests that "knowingly" does not modify "corruptly persuades," but that is not how the statute most naturally reads. It provides the *mens rea*—"knowingly"—and then a list of acts—"uses intimidation or physical force, threatens, or corruptly persuades." We have recognized with regard to similar statutory language that the *mens rea* at least applies to the acts that immediately follow, if not to other elements down the statutory chain. The Government suggests that it is "questionable whether Congress would employ such an inelegant formulation as 'knowingly . . . corruptly persuades.'" Long experience has not taught us to share the Government's doubts on this score, and we must simply interpret the statute as written.

The parties have not pointed us to another interpretation of "knowingly . . . corruptly" to guide us here.[9] In any event, the natural meaning of these terms provides a clear answer. "[K]nowledge" and "knowingly" are normally associated with awareness, understanding, or consciousness. "Corrupt" and "corruptly" are normally associated with wrongful, immoral, depraved, or evil. Joining these meanings together here makes sense both linguistically and in the statutory scheme. Only persons conscious of wrongdoing can be said to "knowingly . . . corruptly persuad[e]." And limiting criminality to persuaders conscious of their wrongdoing sensibly allows §1512(b) to reach only those with the level of "culpability . . . we usually require in order to impose criminal liability." *Aguilar*, 515 U.S. at 602.

The outer limits of this element need not be explored here because the jury instructions at issue simply failed to convey the requisite consciousness of wrongdoing. Indeed, it is striking how little culpability the instructions required. For example, the jury was told that, "even if [petitioner] honestly and sincerely believed that its conduct was lawful, you may find [petitioner] guilty." The instructions also diluted the meaning of "corruptly" so that it covered innocent conduct.

The parties vigorously disputed how the jury would be instructed on "corruptly." The District Court based its instruction on the definition of that term found in the Fifth Circuit Pattern Jury Instruction for §1503. This pattern instruction defined "corruptly" as "'knowingly and dishonestly, with the specific intent to subvert or undermine the integrity'" of a proceeding. The Government, however, insisted on excluding "dishonestly" and adding the term "impede" to the phrase "subvert or undermine." The District Court agreed over petitioner's objections, and the jury was told to convict if it found petitioner intended to "subvert, undermine, or impede" governmental factfinding by suggesting to its employees that they enforce the document retention policy.

These changes were significant. No longer was any type of "dishonest[y]" necessary to a finding of guilt, and it was enough for petitioner to have simply "impede[d]" the Government's factfinding ability. As the Government conceded

9. The parties have pointed us to two other obstruction provisions, 18 U.S.C. §§1503 and 1505, which contain the word "corruptly." But these provisions lack the modifier "knowingly," making any analogy inexact.

at oral argument, "'[i]mpede'" has broader connotations than "'subvert'" or even "'[u]ndermine,'" and many of these connotations do not incorporate any "corrupt[ness]" at all. The dictionary defines "impede" as "to interfere with or get in the way of the progress of" or "hold up" or "detract from." By definition, anyone who innocently persuades another to withhold information from the Government "get[s] in the way of the progress of" the Government. With regard to such innocent conduct, the "corruptly" instructions did no limiting work whatsoever.

The instructions also were infirm for another reason. They led the jury to believe that it did not have to find *any* nexus between the "persua[sion]" to destroy documents and any particular proceeding. In resisting any type of nexus element, the Government relies heavily on §1512(e)(1), which states that an official proceeding "need not be pending or about to be instituted at the time of the offense." It is, however, one thing to say that a proceeding "need not be pending or about to be instituted at the time of the offense," and quite another to say a proceeding need not even be foreseen. A "knowingly . . . corrup[t] persuade[r]" cannot be someone who persuades others to shred documents under a document retention policy when he does not have in contemplation any particular official proceeding in which those documents might be material.

We faced a similar situation in *Aguilar*. Respondent Aguilar lied to a Federal Bureau of Investigation agent in the course of an investigation and was convicted of "'corruptly endeavor[ing] to influence, obstruct, and impede [a] . . . grand jury investigation'" under §1503. All the Government had shown was that Aguilar had uttered false statements to an investigating agent "who might or might not testify before a grand jury." We held that §1503 required something more—specifically, a "nexus" between the obstructive act and the proceeding. "[I]f the defendant lacks knowledge that his actions are likely to affect the judicial proceeding," we explained, "he lacks the requisite intent to obstruct."

For these reasons, the jury instructions here were flawed in important respects. The judgment of the Court of Appeals is reversed, and the case is remanded for further proceedings consistent with this opinion.

It is so ordered.

NOTES AND QUESTIONS

1. The *Andersen* case received considerable attention, and caused the Department of Justice to receive a great deal of criticism, as the mere indictment of the public accounting firm effectively led to its demise. (As of November 2005, the firm employed approximately 200 administrators solely for the purpose of dealing with outstanding lawsuits. *See U.S. Ends Prosecution of Arthur Andersen*, Nov. 28, 2005, available at http://arthur-andersen-news.newslib.com/story/4381-3071314/.) This outcome of Andersen was not unforeseen. Public accounting firms certify audits of publicly traded companies, and the value of their certifications rests, in large part, on their reputation. Once indicted, Andersen's reputation was destroyed, and its clients jumped ship en masse. The result was the loss of 28,000 jobs in the United States. *See*

id. On the other hand, downplayed by the Court was the huge number of documents shredded by Andersen in light of Enron's collapse—literally truckloads—and the fact that that the accounting firm had been in serious trouble with the SEC before (*see* footnote 2 of the Court's opinion). Should DOJ have charged Arthur Andersen in light of the significant "collateral damage" the prosecution caused? Why or why not? Do the DOJ guidelines on the prosecution of corporate entities (found in Chapter 2, *supra*) assist in making this judgment?

2. The Court goes to great lengths to demonstrate that Congress placed the term "knowingly" in §1512(b)(2) as a modifier of "corruptly" for the purpose of adding consciousness of wrongdoing as an essential element of the crime. Was this (arguably strained) interpretation really necessary? Isn't the notion of wrongdoing imbedded in the word "corruptly" standing alone? Indeed, the Fifth Circuit Pattern Jury Instruction defined "corruptly" as "knowingly and dishonestly." Can someone act dishonestly without knowing they are doing something wrong?
3. The prosecutors apparently fought hard for the jury instruction that eliminated the word "dishonestly" from the definition of corruptly, which eliminated any sense of wrongdoing from the crime and invited the jury to convict based on completely innocent conduct. This requested instruction begged for reversal. Can you think of a reason, other than ignorance, why the prosecutors would act in this way?
4. The Court makes clear that there is a "nexus" requirement imbedded in §1512(b)(2) (overruling without mentioning several circuits that had concluded otherwise, *see, e.g.*, United States v. Gabriel, 125 F.3d 89, 103-105 (2d Cir. 1997)). What, exactly, is this requirement, and how did the case fail to meet it? (Hint: Re-read the wording of the allegation in the indictment.) Is this nexus requirement the same as the one in *Aguilar*?
5. Many observers claimed that the Supreme Court's reversal of Andersen's conviction was a vindication of the company's behavior. Do you agree? Consider that the government claimed that its decision not to retry the case was because, at the time of remand, the company was essentially no longer in existence. *See U.S. Ends Prosecution of Arthur Andersen*, Nov. 28, 2005, available at http://arthur-andersen-news.newslib.com/story/4381-3071314/.) Moreover, as noted in the introduction to this chapter, the case had led Congress, as part of the Sarbanes-Oxley Act in 2002, to amend the obstruction of justice scheme to account for conduct similar to Andersen's in the future.
6. David Duncan was both the main player in the destruction of the documents at Andersen and the main witness for the government in its case against his former employer. After the Supreme Court's reversal, Duncan successfully withdrew his guilty plea to one count of obstruction of justice under 18 U.S.C. §1512(b). In the end, Duncan settled his (remaining administrative) case with the government by agreeing never to appear before the SEC again as an accountant. He paid no fine. *See Accountant and S.E.C. Reach Deal in Enron Case*, N.Y. TIMES, Jan. 29, 2008, available at http://www.nytimes.com/2008/01/29/business/29enron.html?_r=1. The successful withdrawal of a guilty plea is a very rare event. Was it justified in Duncan's case?

C. Post–Sarbanes-Oxley Cases

UNITED STATES v. TAMPAS

493 F.3d 1291 (11th Cir. 2007)

GIBSON, Circuit Judge:

Nicky J. Tampas . . . was president and executive director of the YMCA of Valdosta-Lowndes County, Georgia, where he had a 26-year career. As president, he ran the day to day operations of the YMCA, managed its finances, and reported to the board of directors. Tampas worked closely with finance director Toni Fillyaw, who was responsible for the YMCA's payroll and accounts payable. In addition, Tampas was the YMCA's listed representative on several of its American Express cards.

Tampas hired W. Lee Patrick and his landscaping company to perform maintenance, repair, and some construction projects at the YMCA, and to perform landscaping work and home improvement projects at Tampas's own house. Tampas arranged for Patrick's employees to be paid directly by the YMCA as contractors, an arrangement the YMCA board never authorized. Tampas and Fillyaw issued YMCA checks to Patrick and his employees based on handwritten slips of paper Patrick submitted listing his employees' names and dollar amounts to be paid, rather than the descriptive invoices the YMCA typically used. Unlike other bills, Patrick's were handled solely by Fillyaw and not by the other bookkeeper responsible for entering expenses into the YMCA's computer system. Fillyaw also handled bills for the YMCA American Express account Tampas used.

In December 2002, it was discovered that Fillyaw had failed to remit payroll taxes that had been withheld from YMCA employees' checks to the federal and state taxing authorities; instead, the funds were kept in the YMCA's general operating account. This resulted in an unpaid principal tax liability of $1.4 million, plus penalties. Fillyaw was terminated and eventually was convicted of theft of government property and mail fraud. After the unpaid taxes were discovered, the FBI began an investigation into the YMCA's books. As YMCA officials also began to examine and organize the books, they noticed other financial irregularities. Don Pope, treasurer of the board of directors, took over signing YMCA checks in Fillyaw's stead and became suspicious of large payments the YMCA had issued to Patrick without documentation of what work he had done, and large charges on the YMCA American Express card used by Tampas, where Pope was able to find only three months' worth of statements for the account. The YMCA's outside auditor also was troubled by the size of YMCA payments to Patrick and his discovery that Tampas had endorsed one of his YMCA paychecks over to Patrick. Tampas became angry when questioned about the payments. In the spring of 2003, Tampas asked one of his subordinates, Paul Arambula, to prepare a spreadsheet attributing two years' worth of Patrick's job receipts to various YMCA projects. Seeing that the value of the receipts far exceeded the value of the work Patrick and his employees had done at the YMCA, Arambula reported the matter to the YMCA board and its attorney and resigned from his position. The board voted to request that Tampas resign, and he acceded to that request.

In February 2005, a grand jury indicted Tampas . . . on one count of conspiracy to commit embezzlement . . . [and two counts of] embezzlement from an organization receiving federal funds, in violation of 18 U.S.C. §666. . . . A superseding indictment was filed in July 2005 . . . adding a count against each defendant for misleading conduct in violation of 18 U.S.C. §1512(b)(3). The case proceeded to separate trials for Patrick and Tampas. . . .

The government's evidence on the misleading conduct count consisted primarily of the testimony of former YMCA employee Paul Arambula. Arambula testified that Tampas asked him to create a spreadsheet reconciling two years' worth of Patrick's "hand receipts" with various YMCA projects. Tampas's request came at a time when suspicion was mounting about the YMCA's sizable payments to Patrick and his employees. Arambula testified that he refused to make the spreadsheet because he was disturbed by the large disparity between the value of the work done and Patrick's receipts, which did not contain detailed information to explain the charges.

The jury convicted Tampas [on all counts]. This appeal followed. . . . .

D. Misleading Conduct Count

Tampas . . . challenges the sufficiency of the evidence on his conviction for misleading conduct. To prove that Tampas engaged in misleading conduct, the government had to show: 1) Tampas knowingly and willfully engaged in misleading conduct toward another person, 2) with the intent to hinder, delay, or prevent the communication of information to a federal law enforcement officer, 3) about the commission or the possible commission of a federal crime. 18 U.S.C. §1512(b); United States v. Veal, 153 F.3d 1233, 1253 (11th Cir. 1998), *cert. denied*, 526 U.S. 1147 (1999). This charge was based on Tampas's actions in asking Arambula to make a spreadsheet attributing two years' worth of Patrick's hand receipts to jobs Patrick's company performed at the YMCA. *See Veal*, 153 F.3d at 1247 (misleading conduct statute encompasses "a wide range of conduct that thwarts justice," including "us[ing] unwitting third parties" to conceal the truth). Tampas contends that the evidence shows only that he asked for a spreadsheet organizing legitimate financial documents, and no reasonable juror could conclude his conduct was misleading because Fillyaw had left the YMCA's books in disarray and everyone, including Tampas, was sorting through various receipts in an organization-wide effort to straighten out the financial records. The government produced sufficient evidence, however, from which a reasonable juror could conclude that Tampas's superficially benign request was really an effort to mislead Arambula into creating a record that would hide the scheme Tampas had undertaken with Patrick. A reasonable juror could conclude that the receipts Tampas tendered to Arambula were not legitimate business records, but fraudulent, padded bills, in light of the government's evidence that Patrick's employees frequently received paychecks issued by the YMCA for time they spent at other clients' sites. It is also reasonable to infer that Tampas's goal was to create a record justifying the YMCA's inflated payments to Patrick, which the YMCA treasurer and auditor both had begun to question. In light of this evidence and Arambula's testimony on the "great disparity" between the vague receipts and the value of the jobs Tampas asked him to reconcile, the jury was free to reject Tampas's innocent explanation for his conduct. . . .

Thus, we conclude that the evidence is sufficient to support Tampas's convictions on all counts. . . .

UNITED STATES v. HO

2009 WL 2591345 (D. Haw. Aug 20, 2009)

J. Michael Seabright, District Judge.

I. Introduction

The Second Superseding Indictment ("SSI"), filed March 11, 2009, charges Defendant Robert Tam Ho ("Defendant") with three counts of unlawful use of force under color of law in violation of 18 U.S.C. §242 (Counts 1-3), and four counts of witness tampering in violation of 18 U.S.C. §§1512(b)(1) and 1512(b)(3) (Counts 4-7). Currently before the court is Defendant's Motion for *In Camera* Review of Grand Jury Transcripts, in which Defendant requests the court to review the grand jury transcripts *in camera* and disclose to him any portion of the transcripts supporting his belief that the witness tampering counts should be dismissed. Defendant makes this request because he believes—based on his interpretations of 18 U.S.C. §§1512(b)(1) and 1512(b)(3)—that the government misunderstands the required elements of each offense. Based on the following, the court finds that Defendant has carried his burden regarding only his argument that the government may have misled the grand jury regarding the "nexus" requirement of 18 U.S.C. §1512(b)(1), and therefore GRANTS in part and DENIES in part Defendant's Motion for *In Camera* Review of Grand Jury Transcripts. Further, upon an *in camera* review of the government's instructions to the grand jury, the court finds nothing that would support a motion to dismiss based on any misstatement of law regarding 18 U.S.C. §1512(b)(1).

II. Background

. . . Defendant was the Security Manager for Wackenhut Security Corporation at the Kahului Airport in Maui, which provides on-site security for the airport through a contract with the State of Hawaii Department of Transportation. Defendant was the direct supervisor of the "Law Enforcement Officers," ("LEOs"), who have full "peace officer" authority pursuant to Hawaii state law, including the authority to arrest and detain individuals suspected of criminal activity.

On October 20, 2005, during a meeting with Pacific Wings Airline employees G.K., W.G., and others, Defendant got into a verbal confrontation with G.K. and left the meeting. Defendant returned with two LEOs, advised G.K. that he was placing him under "citizen's arrest" for "harassment," and directed the LEOs to effectuate the arrest. Defendant also ordered the other individuals to leave the conference room, and then repeatedly struck W.G. after he refused to leave. When Maui Police Department ("MPD") officers arrived, Defendant requested them to place both G.K. and W.G. in custody, where they were held until bail was posted for their release.

. . . [O]n that same day, Defendant approached J.W. to discuss the witness statement she intended to give to MPD and told her that she should state that she was heading home for the day at the time of the incident and did not see what happened because her view was blocked by other people. J.W. knew this version was untrue, but repeated this version to MPD anyway. Count 4 therefore alleges that Defendant "did knowingly and corruptly persuade J.W. to give false information with respect to the physical assault perpetuated by [Defendant] upon W.G., with the intent to influence, delay or prevent the testimony of J.W. in an official proceeding." Count V similarly alleges that Defendant "did knowingly and corruptly persuade J.W. to give false information with respect to the physical assault perpetuated by [Defendant] upon W.G., with the intent to hinder, delay and prevent the communication to a law enforcement officer of the United States of information relating to the commission and possible commission of a Federal offense, namely the deprivation of rights under color of law. . . ."

Finally, the SSI alleges that on the next day, October 21, 2005, Defendant directed J.W. to prepare a written witness statement summarizing a false version of events of October 20, 2005. As in Count 4, Count 6 alleges that Defendant "did knowingly and corruptly persuade J.W. to give false information with respect to the physical assault perpetuated by [Defendant] upon W.G., with the intent to influence, delay or prevent the testimony of J.W. in an official proceeding." Similar to Count 5, Count 7 alleges that Defendant "did knowingly and corruptly persuade J.W. to give false information with respect to the physical assault perpetuated by [Defendant] upon W.G., with the intent to hinder, delay and prevent the communication to a law enforcement officer of the United States of information relating to the commission or possible commission of a Federal offense, namely the deprivation of rights under color of law. . . ."

* * *

IV. Discussion

Defendant requests that the court review the grand jury transcripts *in camera* and disclose to him any portion that supports a claim that the witness tampering counts pursuant to 18 U.S.C. §§1512(b)(1) and 1512(b)(3) should be dismissed because the government misinstructed the grand jury about the applicable law and failed to adduce evidence sufficient to establish probable cause for the elements of these offenses. Defendant argues that he has reason to believe there were errors before the grand jury due to the government's on-the-record comments about the elements of these offenses. As explained below, the court finds that Defendant has carried his burden in showing a particularized need that the government may have misinstructed the grand jury regarding only the nexus requirement for §1512(b)(1), and rejects Defendant's other arguments. The court's *in camera* review, however, reveals nothing in the government's instructions to the grand jury that would support a motion to dismiss and therefore the court does not order disclosure of the grand jury instructions to Defendant.

A. 18 U.S.C. §1512(b)(1)

[Under 18 U.S.C. §1512(b)(1)(A), an] "official proceeding" includes, among other things, "a proceeding before a judge or court of the United States, a United States magistrate judge, a bankruptcy judge, a judge of the United States Tax Court, a special trial judge of the Tax Court, a judge of the United States Court of Federal Claims, or a Federal grand jury." Defendant argues that the government misunderstands the statutory elements such that the government may have misled the grand jury. The court addresses Defendant's arguments in turn.

1. The Nexus Requirement

Defendant argues that the government misunderstands that to prove a violation of §1512(b)(1), Defendant must have foreseen that the natural and probable effect of his conduct would be to interfere with a person's testimony in a future official proceeding. Because the conduct the government has identified involves only alleged interference with an MPD and employer's investigations, Defendant suggests that the government believes it can prove an offense without showing any foreseeability of a federal official proceeding.

Defendant's argument stems from Arthur Andersen LLP v. United States, 544 U.S. 696 (2005), which interpreted §1512(b)(2), §1512(b)(1)'s companion statute, and found that §1512(b)(2) requires a "nexus" between the obstructive act and a particular official proceeding. The government had argued against a "nexus" requirement because §1512(f)(1) explicitly provides that "an official proceeding 'need not be pending or about to be instituted at the time of the offense.'"

[The Supreme Court] rejected the government's argument, explaining:

> It is . . . one thing to say that a proceeding "need not be pending or about to be instituted at the time of the offense," and quite another to say a proceeding need not even be foreseen. A "knowingly . . . corrupt persuader" cannot be someone who persuades others to shred documents under a document retention policy when he does not have in contemplation any particular official proceeding in which those documents might be material.

Id. at 707-08. . . .

. . . [Based on the AUSA's statements during a hearing, t]he court cannot rule out that the government did not properly instruct the grand jury regarding the nexus requirement. If the government did in fact instruct the grand jury that Defendant need not foresee that his actions may affect a future official proceeding, such misstatement would mislead the grand jury into believing that there need be no nexus between the conduct at issue and the official proceeding. . . .

The court therefore GRANTS Defendant's Motion with respect to this limited issue. Consistent with the principles of secrecy of the grand jury and tailoring disclosure to only those relevant portions of the transcript, the court has reviewed *in camera* the government's instructions to the grand jury. Because the court's review reveals no misstatements regarding the nexus requirement that would support a motion to dismiss, the court concludes that Defendant is not entitled to disclosure of the grand jury transcripts.

2. Conduct Prior to the Beginning of Any "Investigation"

Defendant also argues that the government may have misinstructed the grand jury because it "has insisted that interfering with a county law enforcement investigation and, even more removed, with an employer's internal investigation of its own employees, constitutes a violation of subsection (b)(1) just as much as it constitutes a violation of subsection (b)(3)." Defendant reasons that this conduct—to the extent it can support a violation of any witness tampering statute—is directed to a violation of §1512(b)(3), which criminalizes tampering with witness statements to a law enforcement officer, and therefore cannot also support a violation of §1512(b)(1). In other words, Defendant seeks the court to draw a line between conduct that violates §1512(b)(1) versus §1512(b)(3) by finding that tampering with a witness in a law enforcement investigation that precedes an official proceeding is not a violation of §1512(b)(1). . . . [T]he court rejects Defendant's line-drawing.

As an initial matter, the plain language of §1512(b)(1) does not appear to be limited to any particular scenario or timing. That §1512(b)(1) includes no timing limitation is confirmed by §1512(f)(1), which eschews any timing requirement for the "official proceeding" by providing that an "official proceeding need not be pending or about to be instituted at the time of the offense. . . ." Indeed, Congress adopted this language so that §1512(b)(1) would encompass a defendant's actions even before an investigation has begun. Specifically, the 1982 Senate Report explains that §1512(f)(1) expands the scope of §1512(b)(1) to encompass acts that occur even before a crime is reported, much less investigated. . . .

Nor does §1512(b)(3) appear to limit the scope of §1512(b)(1). Section 1512(b)(3) states a violation for knowingly corruptly persuading another person with intent to hinder, delay, or prevent the communication to a federal law enforcement officer of information relating to the commission or possible commission of a federal offense. It is axiomatic that a single act or course of conduct—in this case, convincing J.W. to give a false statement to MPD and in a witness statement—may violate more than one criminal statute, and nothing in the statutory framework suggests that the same conduct cannot be the basis for violations of different sections of the statute. So long as the government can prove the elements of these separate violations, it does not matter that the violations stem from the same conduct.

The court further rejects Defendant's argument that an interpretation of "official proceeding" allowing the government to assert a violation under these circumstances makes §1512(b)(3) superfluous because every statement to any kind of law enforcement officer would also count as a statement in a future official proceeding. Defendant's concern is illusory—Defendant ignores that the government must still prove the nexus between the obstructive act and the official proceeding. A defendant may violate §1512(b)(3) by believing that he is preventing a witness from communicating with a law enforcement officer, but at the same time not violate §1512(b)(1) by not foreseeing an official proceeding. Accordingly, every statement to a law enforcement officer is not a statement in a future official proceeding, and every violation of §1512(b)(3) is not a violation of §1512(b)(1). Rather, each provision has its own clear boundaries based on Defendant's intentions in "knowingly corruptly persuading" the witness.

In sum, the court rejects Defendant's argument that the government may have misled the grand jury simply because the allegations that Defendant violated §1512(b)(1) are based on interfering with a county law enforcement investigation and an employer's internal investigation. Accordingly, the court DENIES Defendant's request for disclosure of the grand jury proceedings that may address this issue.

B. 18 U.S.C. §1512(b)(3)

. . . Section 1515(a)(4) defines a "law enforcement officer" as "an officer or employee of the Federal Government, or a person authorized to act for or on behalf of the Federal Government. . . ." Section 1512(g)(2) provides that "no state of mind need be proved with respect to the circumstance . . . that the judge is a judge of the United States or that the law enforcement officer is an officer or employee of the Federal Government or a person authorized to act for or on behalf of the Federal Government or serving the Federal Government as an adviser or consultant."

Defendant argues that the government misunderstands that it must prove that J.W. made these false statements *directly* to a federal law enforcement officer. Defendant interprets this limitation based on a statutory reading of §1512(b)(3) with §1512(g), as well as applying *Arthur Andersen*'s holding and its predecessor *United States v. Aguilar*, that certain witness tampering violations require a "nexus." . . .

According to the plain language of §1512(b)(3), the government must prove that Defendant (1) knowingly used intimidation, threatened, or corruptly persuaded another person, (2) with the intent to hinder, delay, or prevent the communication of information to a federal official, (3) relating to the commission or the possible commission of a federal crime. The statutory language does not limit the meaning of "the communication" and no other provision evinces any requirement that Defendant tamper with a communication that was made directly to a federal law enforcement official.

Further, courts interpreting §1512(b)(3) have found that it is not limited as Defendant suggests. Rather, §1512(b)(3) "criminalizes the *transfer* of misleading information which actually relates to a *potential* federal offense." United States v. Veal, 153 F.3d 1233, 1252 (11th Cir. 1998). Accordingly, the government need only show that "the misleading information" was "*likely* to be transferred to a federal agent." *Veal*, 153 F.3d at 1251.

Finally, the court rejects that *Arthur Andersen* or *Aguilar* require that the government prove a "nexus" as shown through a direct communication between J.W. and a federal law enforcement officer. While the Ninth Circuit has not addressed this issue, other courts have expressly rejected that the nexus requirement developed in *Aguilar* and *Arthur Andersen* applies to §1512(b)(3) offenses. For example, the Eleventh Circuit has explained that unlike §1512(b)(1), "federal jurisdiction under §1512(b)(3) is based on the federal interest of protecting the integrity of *potential* federal investigations by ensuring that transfers of information to federal law enforcement officers and judges relating to the *possible* commission of federal offenses be truthful and unimpeded." Accordingly, "§1512(b)(3) does not depend on the existence or immanency of a federal case or investigation but rather on the *possible* existence of a federal crime and a defendant's intention to thwart an inquiry into that crime."

Courts have relied on these statutory and jurisdictional differences between §1512(b)(1) and §1512(b)(3) to find that *Arthur Andersen*'s reasoning does not apply to §1512(b)(3) offenses . . . .

The court finds the reasoning of these cases persuasive and agrees that §1512(b)(3) does not require the nexus described in *Arthur Andersen* to prove a violation. Accordingly, Defendant has not carried his burden to show that he is entitled to the grand jury transcripts on the basis that the government improperly based these offenses on the fact that J.W. made these false statements to MPD and in a witness statement. . . .

IT IS SO ORDERED.

NOTES AND QUESTIONS

1. Are you comfortable with the number of inferences the *Tampas* court draws from the evidence to sustain the conviction? Based on the court's recitation of the evidence, isn't it equally likely that Tampas was trying to get a handle on the magnitude of his problem, rather than trying to cover it up? Can a verdict be sustained if there are two equally plausible interpretations of it—one indicating guilt and the other indicating innocence?
2. Assume you are a new Assistant U.S. Attorney assigned the prosecution of a case involving the destruction of documents with facts identical to those found in *Andersen*. Is your case more winnable than *Andersen* as a result of the Sarbanes-Oxley amendments to the obstruction statutes? Why or why not?
3. What is the *Ho* court's rationale for applying the *Andersen* §1512(b)(2)'s nexus requirement to §1512(b)(1) prosecutions but not to §1512(b)(3) prosecutions? Is it convincing?

PROBLEM 9-1

The following facts are derived from United States v. Stevens, 2011 WL 1033707 (D. Md. Mar. 23, 2011):

> On October 9, 2002,* the Food and Drug Administration (FDA) sent a letter to pharmaceutical manufacturer GlaxoSmithKline (GSK) stating that the FDA had recently received information indicating that GSK had possibly promoted antidepressant drug Wellbutrin for weight loss, a use not approved by the FDA. The FDA asked GSK to provide it with materials related to Wellbutrin promotional programs sponsored by GSK, including copies of all slides, videos, handouts, and other materials presented or distributed at any GSK program or activity related to Wellbutrin. Lauren Stevens, former Vice President and Associate General Counsel of GSK, was in charge of" GSK's response to the FDA's inquiry and investigation and led a team of lawyers and paralegals who gathered documents and information.

*[The Sarbanes-Oxley Act was passed in July 2002—Eds.]

> The United States alleges that Stevens withheld and concealed documents and other information about GSK's promotional activities for Wellbutrin, including for unapproved uses, while representing to the FDA that she had completed her response to its inquiry, and that Stevens falsified and altered documents in order to impede the FDA's investigation of GSK. In particular, the Government alleges Stevens withheld slide sets used by speakers at GSK promotional events that promoted off-label use of Wellbutrin and withheld information regarding compensation received by attendees at promotional events. The Government alleges that Stevens signed and sent to the FDA six letters containing materially false statements regarding GSK's promotion of Wellbutrin for off-label uses.
>
> In responding to the FDA's inquiry, Stevens was assisted by GSK in-house counsel and outside counsel from the law firm of King & Spalding. Stevens' primary defense to the charges in the indictment is that she relied in good faith on the advice of counsel in responding to the FDA's inquiry, and that such reliance negated the requisite intent to obstruct the FDA's investigation.

You are defense counsel representing Lauren Stevens. What obstruction crimes do you anticipate she might be charged with? How effective will her advice of counsel defense be? What other defenses—legal or factual—might you argue on her behalf?

chapter 10

Public Corruption

I. INTRODUCTION

When measured by direct dollar losses, public corruption is not the most serious form of white collar crime, but when measured by its overall negative impact on society, it very well may be. Corruption is uniquely harmful because it involves the distortion and betrayal of the political system. Historically, countries that have been unable to control official corruption have suffered severe consequences in terms of economic development and national morale.[1] Therefore, it is critical to the health of the republic that law enforcement stays one step ahead of corrupt officials, thereby preventing the corrosion of politics and the obstruction of governmental functions.

Corruption occurs at both the state and federal levels. Federal prosecutors and investigators have traditionally been the main players on both stages: at the state level, because local law enforcement is typically not good at self-policing; and at the federal level, because there is no one else to do the job. Historically, the "feds" have been relatively successful in their anti-corruption work. This can probably be attributed to two factors. First, federal investigators and career federal prosecutors are generally well insulated against political influence.[2] Second, their professional careers are advanced by successfully bringing down "big fish"—the bigger, the better—rather than by looking the other way.

Four statutes are most commonly employed to combat corruption. The first is honest services mail and wire fraud, which we have already studied in Chapter 4.

1. *See generally* Ted Constantini, *International Security in a New Millennium*, 12 INT'L HUM. RESOURCES J. 2 (Winter 2003) (discussing the limiting effects of widespread corruption on doing business in Russia).

2. This explains why, when Attorney General Alberto Gonzales fired seven U.S. Attorneys in 2006, at least some for apparent political reasons, the reaction was quite negative and intense. The firings themselves led to a corruption investigation, but no charges were ever filed. *See* Mark J. Rozeel & Mitchel A. Sollenberger, *Executive Privilege and the Bush Administration*, 24 J.L. & POL. 1 (2008); *see also* Amy Goldstein, *Report Suggests Laws Broken in Attorney Firing*, WASH. POST, July 25, 2007, available at http://www.washingtonpost.com/wp-dyn/content/article/2007/07/24/AR2007072402311.html.

The other three are examined here. They are Bribery of Public Officials, 18 U.S.C. §201; Theft or Bribery Concerning Programs Receiving Federal Funds, 18 U.S.C. §666; and the "Hobbs Act," 18 U.S.C. §1951, which—among other things—prohibits extortion under color of official right.

Section 201 covers not only bribery (which requires a very specific quid pro quo) but also the promising of gratuities to public officials "for or because of any official act performed or to be performed by such public official." This latter restriction is called the "nexus requirement," and delineating its parameters has caused courts significant consternation in recent years. Other interpretive challenges under the statute include identifying who is a "public official" and what constitutes an "official act."

Compared to §201, §666 is a relatively straightforward provision criminalizing the theft of more than $5,000 from any organization or state, local, or tribal government that receives more than $10,000 in federal funds in any one-year period. It also outlaws bribery of non-federal officials involving $5,000 or more, with the same $10,000 jurisdictional element. Section 666 has sparked considerable litigation testing the limits of the relationship between the federal funding and the criminal activity.

The Hobbs Act comes into play when a public official obtains property from another person in return for an official act. It is jurisdictionally based on interference with interstate commerce, though this requirement has been minimized over many years of judicial interpretation. A critical question under the Hobbs Act is whether the public official must demand (or even request) payment to come within its reach, or whether mere acceptance of property is good enough.

All of these issues, and a few more, are examined below.

II. BRIBERY AND GRATUITIES, 18 U.S.C. §201

A. The Nexus Requirement

UNITED STATES v. SUN-DIAMOND GROWERS OF CALIFORNIA
526 U.S. 398 (1999)

Justice Scalia delivered the opinion of the Court.

Talmudic sages believed that judges who accepted bribes would be punished by eventually losing all knowledge of the divine law. The Federal Government, dealing with many public officials who are not judges, and with at least some judges for whom this sanction holds no terror, has constructed a framework of human laws and regulations defining various sorts of impermissible gifts, and punishing those who give or receive them with administrative sanctions, fines, and incarceration. One element of that framework is 18 U.S.C. §201(c)(1)(A), the "illegal gratuity statute," which prohibits giving "anything of value" to a present, past, or future public official "for or because of any official act performed or to be performed by such public official." In this case, we consider whether conviction under the illegal gratuity statute requires any showing beyond the fact that a gratuity was given because of the recipient's official position.

I.

Respondent is a trade association that engaged in marketing and lobbying activities on behalf of its member cooperatives, which were owned by approximately 5,000 individual growers of raisins, figs, walnuts, prunes, and hazelnuts. Petitioner United States is represented by Independent Counsel Donald Smaltz, who, as a consequence of his investigation of former Secretary of Agriculture Michael Espy, charged respondent with, *inter alia*, making illegal gifts to Espy in violation of §201(c)(1)(A). . . .

Count One of the indictment charged Sun-Diamond with giving Espy approximately $5,900 in illegal gratuities: tickets to the 1993 U.S. Open Tennis Tournament (worth $2,295), luggage ($2,427), meals ($665), and a framed print and crystal bowl ($524). The indictment alluded to two matters in which respondent had an interest in favorable treatment from the Secretary at the time it bestowed the gratuities. First, respondent's member cooperatives participated in the Market Promotion Plan (MPP), a grant program administered by the Department of Agriculture to promote the sale of U.S. farm commodities in foreign countries. [Respondent was concerned about a possible change in the program that could negatively impact its members.] . . .

Second, respondent had an interest in the Federal Government's regulation of methyl bromide, a low-cost pesticide used by many individual growers in respondent's member cooperatives. . . .

Although describing these two matters before the Secretary in which respondent had an interest, the indictment did not allege a specific connection between either of them—or between any other action of the Secretary—and the gratuities conferred. . . . At trial, the District Court instructed the jury along these same lines. . . . It . . . [stated] that "[i]t is sufficient if Sun-Diamond provided Espy with unauthorized compensation simply because he held public office," and that "[t]he government need not prove that the alleged gratuity was linked to a specific or identifiable official act or any act at all." The jury convicted respondent on, *inter alia*, Count One (the only subject of this appeal), and the District Court sentenced respondent on this count to pay a fine of $400,000. The Court of Appeals reversed. . . . We granted certiorari.

II.

Initially, it will be helpful to place §201(c)(1)(A) within the context of the statutory scheme. Subsection (a) of §201 sets forth definitions applicable to the section. . . . [Subsection (b) defines the crime of bribery and subsection (c) defines the crime of giving or receiving an illegal gratuity.] . . .

The distinguishing feature of each crime is its intent element. Bribery requires intent "to influence" an official act or "to be influenced" in an official act, while illegal gratuity requires only that the gratuity be given or accepted "for or because of" an official act. In other words, for bribery there must be a *quid pro quo*—a specific intent to give or receive something of value *in exchange* for an official act. An illegal gratuity, on the other hand, may constitute merely a reward for some future act that the public official will take (and may already have determined to take), or for a past act that he has already taken. The punishments prescribed for the two offenses reflect their relative seriousness: Bribery may be punished by up to 15 years' imprisonment, a fine of $250,000 ($500,000 for organizations) or triple the value of the bribe, whichever is greater, and disqualification from holding government office. Violation of the illegal gratuity statute, on the other hand, may be punished by up to two years' imprisonment and a fine of $250,000 ($500,000 for organizations).

The District Court's instructions in this case, in differentiating between a bribe and an illegal gratuity, correctly noted that only a bribe requires proof of a *quid pro quo*. The point in controversy here is that the instructions went on to suggest that §201(c)(1)(A), unlike the bribery statute, did not require any connection between respondent's intent and a specific official act. It would be satisfied, according to the instructions, merely by a showing that respondent gave Secretary Espy a gratuity because of his official position—perhaps, for example, to build a reservoir of goodwill that might ultimately affect one or more of a multitude of unspecified acts, now and in the future. . . .

In our view, this interpretation does not fit comfortably with the statutory text, which prohibits only gratuities given or received "for or because of *any official act* performed or to be performed" (emphasis added). It seems to us that this means "for or because of some particular official act of whatever identity"—just as the question "Do you like any composer?" normally means "Do you like some particular composer?" . . . Why go through the trouble of requiring that the gift be made "for or because of any official act performed or to be performed by such public official," . . . when, if the Government's interpretation were correct, it would have sufficed to say "for or because of such official's ability to favor the donor in executing the functions of his office"? The insistence upon an "official act," carefully defined, seems pregnant with the requirement that some particular official act be identified and proved.

Besides thinking that this is the more natural meaning of §201(c)(1)(A), we are inclined to believe it correct because of the peculiar results that the Government's alternative reading would produce. It would criminalize, for example, token gifts to the President based on his official position and not linked to any identifiable act—such as the replica jerseys given by championship sports teams each year during ceremonial White House visits. Similarly, it would criminalize a high school principal's gift of a school baseball cap to the Secretary of Education, by reason of his office, on the occasion of the latter's visit to the school. That these examples are not fanciful is demonstrated by the fact that counsel for the United States maintained at oral argument that a group of farmers would violate §201(c)(1)(A) by providing a complimentary lunch for the Secretary of Agriculture in conjunction with his speech to the farmers concerning various matters of USDA policy—so long as the Secretary had before him, or had in prospect, matters affecting the farmers. Of course the Secretary of Agriculture *always* has before him or in prospect matters that affect farmers, just as the President always has before him or in prospect matters that affect college and professional sports, and the Secretary of Education matters that affect high schools.

It might be said in reply to this that the more narrow interpretation of the statute can also produce some peculiar results. In fact, in the above-given examples, the gifts could easily be regarded as having been conferred, not only because of the official's position as President or Secretary, but also (and perhaps principally) "for or because of" the official acts of receiving the sports teams at the White House, visiting the high school, and speaking to the farmers about USDA policy, respectively. The answer to this objection is that those actions—while they are assuredly "official acts" in some sense—are not "official acts" within the meaning of the statute, which, as we have noted, defines "official act" to mean "any decision or action on any question, matter, cause, suit, proceeding or controversy, which may at any time be pending, or which may by law be brought before any public official, in such official's official capacity, or in such official's place of trust or profit." 18 U.S.C. §201(a)(3). Thus, when the violation is linked to a particular "official act," it is possible to eliminate the absurdities *through the definition of that term.* When, however, no particular "official act" need be identified, and the giving of gifts by reason of the recipient's mere tenure in office constitutes a violation, nothing but the Government's discretion prevents the foregoing examples from being prosecuted. . . .

Our refusal to read §201(c)(1)(A) as a prohibition of gifts given by reason of the donee's office is supported by the fact that when Congress has wanted to adopt such a broadly prophylactic criminal prohibition upon gift giving, it has done so in a more precise and more administrable fashion. . . .

Finally, a narrow, rather than a sweeping, prohibition is more compatible with the fact that §201(c)(1)(A) is merely one strand of an intricate web of regulations, both administrative and criminal, governing the acceptance of gifts and other self-enriching actions by public officials. . . .

More important for present purposes, however, this regulation, and the numerous other regulations and statutes littering this field, demonstrate that this is an area where precisely targeted prohibitions are commonplace, and where more general prohibitions have been qualified by numerous exceptions. Given that reality, a statute in this field that can linguistically be interpreted to be either a meat axe or a scalpel should reasonably be taken to be the latter. Absent a text that clearly requires it, we ought not expand this one piece of the regulatory puzzle so dramatically as to make many other pieces misfits. As discussed earlier, not only does the text here not require that result; its more natural reading forbids it.

* * *

We hold that, in order to establish a violation of 18 U.S.C. §201(c)(1)(A), the Government must prove a link between a thing of value conferred upon a public official and a specific "official act" for or because of which it was given. We affirm the judgment of the Court of Appeals, which remanded the case to the District

Court for a new trial on Count One. Our decision today casts doubt upon the lower courts' resolution of respondent's challenge to the sufficiency of the indictment on Count One—an issue on which certiorari was neither sought nor granted. We leave it to the District Court to determine whether that issue should be reopened on remand.

NOTES AND QUESTIONS

1. No one disputes that Secretary of Agriculture Espy was offered and accepted gifts from members of the very industry he was supposed to be regulating. Many would say that this kind of behavior is one of the most corrupting influences on good government. *See generally* James M. Lager, *Overcoming Cultures of Compliance to Reduce Corruption and Ethics in Government*, 41 McGeorge L. Rev. 63 (2009) (identifying the practice of government employees accepting gifts from the industries they regulate as "flourishing" corruption). Why, then, should legislation designed to prevent such behavior be treated like a "scalpel" rather than a "meat axe"? Wouldn't the latter approach be much more effective in minimizing the influence of money on the political system? Couldn't the Court just as easily have stated that the intent of the statute was to root out corruption, which only a broad interpretation would accomplish, and that Congress could modify the law if the Court has misunderstood congressional intention?
2. How convincing is the Court's argument that the alternative interpretation of the statute would produce perverse results? Isn't there a qualitative difference between the President accepting a baseball cap or championship sports jersey and the Secretary of Agriculture accepting a free lunch from industry representatives? Moreover, what would be wrong with requiring that the President give such "token" gifts to the "Office of the Presidency" rather than keep them for his personal use?
3. Note that *Sun-Diamond* grew out of the work of an Office of Independent Counsel. These were statutorily created entities designed to eliminate potential conflicts of interest with respect to investigations and prosecutions involving individuals close to the President and other high government officials. At first, ICs seemed like a great idea. After a while, however, it became evident to most observers that they could too easily run amok. IC's had unlimited budgets, and unlike any other prosecutor's office, they essentially focused on one case. In the eyes of many, this led to a lack of perspective, and to the pursuit of very questionable prosecutions, such as the Monica Lewinsky case. Indeed, in the main case prosecuted by IC Smaltz, Mike Espy was acquitted of all charges. *See* Donald C. Smaltz, Final Report of the Independent Counsel In Re: Alphonso Michael (Mike) Espy, Oct. 25, 2001, available at http://www.gpo.gov/fdsys/pkg/GPO-ICREPORT-ESPY/html/GPO-ICREPORT-ESPY-1.html. The unaccountability of IC offices also led to the handing down of some very anti-law enforcement decisions on appeal because, unlike DOJ, IC's did not have to worry about

the larger ramifications of a possible loss on future cases. For these reasons and others, the IC statute was permitted to sunset in 1999. *See* 28 U.S.C. §599 (1994).

PROBLEM 10-1

AUTO, a lobbying group formed on behalf of the three major German automobile manufacturers—Mercedes-Benz, BMW, and Volkswagen—is concerned about three pieces of legislation that may be considered during the next session of Congress. The first is environmental legislation that would drive up all automakers' costs. The second is a tightening of antitrust laws that could cause an investigation into how the German car companies are interrelated. The third involves automobile tariffs that would make imported cars more expensive compared to their American rivals.

Hermann Ward, the Executive Director of AUTO, meets with the presidents and other top officials of its member companies during Congress's summer recess to discuss strategy for the upcoming session. All concur that their lobbying efforts should be more aggressive than ever before, and they increase AUTO's funding by 50 percent to hire more staff to coordinate events and "meet and greets." In addition, they decide to specially target Mitchell MacDonald, the Senate Majority Leader. They do not discuss why they are singling out MacDonald, but of course every lobbyist knows that the majority leader controls whether and when legislation comes to the Senate floor for consideration and a vote.

The group fashions a plan to give MacDonald the free, unlimited use of three automobiles: the first, a $75,000 Mercedes-Benz for MacDonald himself; the second, a $55,000 BMW for his wife; and the third, a $22,000 Volkswagen for the Senator's 21-year-old daughter. They discuss the fact that it is only "fair" that each member of AUTO supply one car. They do not discuss the fact that "three" is an important number for another reason.

Ward follows through on the plan. He tells Senator MacDonald in a privately mailed letter that the automobiles are for "your extraordinary service to the United States and international automobile industries, both of which are of critical importance to the health of the US and world economies." They have no other discussion about it.

The three bills arrive on MacDonald's desk at different times throughout the session. Coincidentally, MacDonald gets a notice (from the various dealerships) that he is due a free service on his cars within two weeks prior to each bill's arrival. In any event, the environmental legislation passes over MacDonald's "no" vote. The antitrust legislation never gets off MacDonald's desk. And finally, through MacDonald's efforts, the tariff bill—which is very popular—ends up being attached to another, very unpopular, piece of legislation, and it goes down to defeat.

Evaluate the potential for a bribery and/or gratuity case against Ward, AUTO, and MacDonald. How about an honest services mail fraud case under 18 U.S.C. §§1341 and 1346?

B. Defining "Official Act"

UNITED STATES v. JEFFERSON

634 F. Supp. 2d 595 (E.D. Va. 2009)

T.S. Ellis, III, District Judge.

. . . On June 4, 2007, a federal grand jury sitting in the Eastern District of Virginia returned a sixteen-count indictment (the "Indictment") charging defendant, then a sitting congressman, with a variety of crimes including conspiracy, bribery, wire fraud, foreign corrupt practices, money laundering, obstruction of justice, and racketeering. The Indictment is lengthy and detailed; it spans some ninety-four pages. Pertinent here are the bribery allegations. . . .

The Indictment's bribery-related counts set forth several broad descriptions of acts defendant allegedly undertook, or agreed to undertake, in exchange for things of value from individuals seeking to advance various business ventures in Africa and elsewhere. Those acts generally involved defendant's efforts to obtain financial and other business development assistance for those business ventures by exerting his influence as a Member of Congress on various U.S. and African government officials and agencies, including, *inter alia*, the Nigerian government, the Export-Import Bank of the United States, and the United States Trade Development Agency. More specifically, defendant, acting either directly or through his congressional staff, allegedly exerted his influence by engaging in a pattern of meetings and correspondence that included, *inter alia*, (i) "official travel" overseas to meet with foreign government officials; (ii) meetings with U.S. and foreign government officials in the United States; and (iii) correspondence, in some instances on congressional letterhead, with U.S. and foreign government officials and agencies. In connection with the overseas travel, defendant, again acting either directly or through his congressional staff, also allegedly lobbied various U.S. and foreign embassies to expedite visa requests and otherwise assist with travel arrangements.

The Indictment alleges that during the course of the alleged bribery schemes, defendant's conduct suggested that he considered himself to be acting—and indeed, hoped those he dealt with would consider him to be acting—in his official capacity as a congressman. For example, the Indictment alleges that when defendant solicited the alleged bribes from the individuals seeking his assistance, he did so as both a congressman and as a member of certain congressional committees and caucuses relating to international—and more specifically, African-trade matters. Defendant's positions in that regard allegedly included (i) membership on the Subcommittee on Trade of the House Committee on Ways and Means, (ii) membership on the House Committee on the Budget, (iii) co-chairmanship of the Africa Trade and Investment Caucus, and (iv) co-chairmanship of the Congressional Caucus on Nigeria. Further, defendant allegedly used official congressional letterhead and represented himself as a congressman when he wrote to U.S. and foreign government officials seeking to gain financial and other business development assistance on behalf of those who had made or promised payments to him. Moreover, defendant allegedly filed several travel forms with the Clerk of the U.S. House of

Representatives on which he stated that his travel to Africa was "in connection with [his] duties as a Member or Officer of the U.S. House of Representatives."

B. The Prior Opinion and the Parties' Motions

In [a] May 2008 Opinion [of this Court], the sufficiency of the Indictment's "official act" allegations was squarely addressed. . . . In denying defendant's motion, the May 2008 Opinion essentially relied upon a two-pronged analysis of the statutory definition of "official act":

> First, the act must be among the official duties or among the settled customary duties or practices of the official charged with bribery. And second, performance of the act must involve or affect a government decision or action.

Applying that two-pronged test, the May 2008 Opinion held that the Indictment's "official act" allegations were legally sufficient. Yet, the May 2008 Opinion also cautioned that "[w]hether . . . the government is able to prove each of the[ ] [required] elements with regard to each of the alleged acts . . . is a question properly addressed at trial, not on a motion to dismiss the Indictment."

Nearly ten months later, . . . the government filed a motion to clarify the May 2008 Opinion . . . , while defendant filed a motion for reconsideration of the denial of his motion to dismiss or, in the alternative, to exclude evidence of conduct that defendant argues does not fall within the statutory definition of "official act." The parties' positions with respect to those motions merit brief discussion here. . . .

II.

As the parties' motions reflect, clarification of the May 2008 Opinion is warranted. . . . First, analysis of what constitutes an "official act" must begin with — and indeed, must be anchored in — the plain language of the statute defining that term. . . . [T]he plain language of §201(b)(2)(A) and §201(a)(3), taken together and applied to a specific case like this one, requires the government to adduce proof with respect to the "official act" element that defendant solicited a thing of value in exchange for being influenced in his performance of (i) a decision or action (ii) on a question, matter, cause, suit, proceeding or controversy (iii) which could at any time have been pending, or which could by law have been brought before him, in his official capacity, or in his place of trust or profit.

The parties' briefs demonstrate that two points of clarification are warranted. First, the second prong of the May 2008 Opinion's test — that the "official act" must "involve or affect a government decision or action" — could be misinterpreted as suggesting that the "decision or action" required by the statute may be, or is required to be, a decision or action by someone *other* than the charged public official. This is neither correct, nor what was intended by the May 2008 Opinion. Rather, the statute clearly requires that in exchange for the alleged bribe, *defendant* — and not some third party, government or otherwise — be *influenced* in the *performance* of a decision or action.

Second, it is important to clarify the meaning of the phrase "any public official" in §201(a)(3). Specifically, the May 2008 Opinion cited that phrase in a manner that may have led the parties to believe that the "question, matter," *etc.*, at issue could be one that may at any time be pending, or could by law be brought before "*any* public official," even if that public official is not the charged public official. This is incorrect; in context, the reference to "any public official" means the charged official. Any contrary implication is inconsistent with the plain language, context, and legislative history of the bribery statute. . . .

. . . Next, it is important to address what constitutes a "question, matter, cause, suit, proceeding or controversy," and what must be shown for that "question, matter," etc., to be one "which may at any time be pending, or which may by law be brought before . . . the charged official . . . in such official's official capacity, or in such official's place of trust or profit." §201(a)(3). In this respect, it has long been settled that these phrases do not require proof that the alleged "official act" was taken pursuant to responsibilities explicitly assigned by law; rather, as the Supreme Court held long ago, these phrases are intended to describe those activities that have been "clearly established by settled practice" as part of a public official's position. United States v. Birdsall, 233 U.S. 223, 231 (1914). Courts since *Birdsall* have consistently applied this principle. *See, e.g.*, United States v. Carson, 464 F.2d 424, 431-34 (2d Cir. 1972); United States v. Biaggi, 853 F.2d 89, 96-99 (2d Cir. 1988). Thus, where, as here, the charged public official is a congressman, the universe of "official acts" described by §201(a)(3) is not limited to so-called "legislative acts" such as voting on or introducing a piece of legislation; rather, §201(a)(3) has been read "sufficiently broadly to encompass all of the acts normally thought to constitute a congressman's legitimate use of his office." Moreover, it is also settled that the charged public official need not have authority to make a final decision or take binding action on the "question, matter," *etc.*, at issue. Rather, §201(a)(3) "cover[s] any situation in which the advice or recommendation of a [public official] would be influential, irrespective of the [official]'s specific authority (or lack of same) to make a binding decision."

These principles, applied here, compel the conclusion that the Indictment's "official act" allegations in this case are sufficient to withstand defendant's attempts to dismiss the bribery-related charges at this stage of the prosecution. Yet, the Indictment's legal sufficiency on the "official act" element does not relieve the government of its burden to prove at trial that the alleged "official acts" meet the statutory definition of that term. . . . [I]t is sufficient for the government to adduce proof, including expert testimony or evidence of defendant's admissions and conduct, that it was customary, as a matter of clearly established settled practice, for members of Congress in defendant's position to exert influence—by advice, recommendation, or otherwise—on the issues in question.

Instructive in demonstrating how the government might meet this burden are *Carson* and *Biaggi*, two Second Circuit cases addressing exertion of influence by a congressman or his staff on resolution of questions, matters, causes, suits, proceedings or controversies not by law within a congressman's purview to resolve. First, in *Carson*, the Second Circuit rejected a senatorial administrative assistant's argument on appeal that his attempts to persuade a deputy attorney general to quash a federal criminal prosecution could not support a jury verdict for solicitation of bribes in exchange for "official acts." . . . Similarly, in *Biaggi* the Second Circuit rejected a congressman's arguments that his actions in lobbying various municipal and federal entities on behalf of individuals who made payments "were not 'official act[s]' within the meaning of §201 because they were not legislative acts and because they were directed principally toward municipal, not federal, agencies." 853 F.2d at 97 (alteration in original). Rather, the Second Circuit held that "[a] congressman's own invocation of his position and of congressional interest in his intercession with others on behalf of a constituent" constituted an official act. . . .

Thus, the government might meet its burden on the "official act" element in this case by showing that defendant's action (of exerting his influence in person or by written correspondence) was on a question, matter, cause, suit, proceeding or controversy (such as the question of how various federal agencies allocate funds, the question of how embassies handle visa requests, or the matter of how the Nigerian government pursues business development in Nigeria) that may at any time be pending before a member of Congress for advice or recommendation as a matter of custom and settled practice. . . .

In sum, although the result reached by the May 2008 Opinion is reaffirmed for the reasons stated, the May 2008 Opinion's explanation of the "official act" element is superseded by the analysis contained herein. . . .

An appropriate Order has issued.

UNITED STATES v. PARKER

133 F.3d 322 (5th Cir. 1998)

Emilio M. Garza, Circuit Judge:

Joann A. Parker ("Mrs. Parker") appeals her conviction and sentence for conspiracy to commit public bribery and five counts of public bribery in violation of 18 U.S.C. §§201(b)(2)(C) and 371. Ralph Parker ("Mr. Parker") appeals his conviction for conspiracy to commit public bribery and three counts of public bribery under the same statutes. We affirm.

I.

The Social Security Administration ("SSA") Office of Hearings and Appeals employed Mrs. Parker as a clerk to Administrative Law Judge ("ALJ") John Aronson. She led a group that helped certain individuals to fraudulently obtain Supplemental Security Income ("SSI") benefits in return for money. The scheme began when Mrs. Parker met Niknitta Simmons ("Simmons") at a hearing where Simmons was appealing the denial of SSI benefits for her son, Kevin Simmons. ALJ Aronson advised Simmons that additional documentation would be necessary for a favorable ruling on Kevin's claim. Mrs. Parker approached Simmons after the hearing and offered to help. A few days later, Mrs. Parker gave Simmons a letter approving Kevin's benefits. Mrs. Parker thereafter called Simmons and demanded money for her help. Simmons refused to pay, and Kevin's benefits were terminated. Mrs. Parker advised Simmons that Kevin's benefits would be reinstated if Simmons paid her.

Simmons went to several SSA offices and reported Mrs. Parker's demands. Investigators from the SSA and FBI contacted Simmons, and she agreed to assist them by permitting FBI Agent Karen Jenkins to record her telephone conversations with Mrs. Parker. In multiple recorded conversations, Mrs. Parker demanded payment for having Kevin's benefits approved initially and for having those benefits reinstated. At a meeting at Simmons' home, Mrs. and Mr. Parker took $500, as captured on videotape by the FBI. Mrs. Parker thereafter demanded more money, which Simmons paid, and Mrs. Parker gave Simmons a letter purportedly bearing ALJ Aronson's signature reinstating Kevin's benefits. . . .

II.

A.

Mrs. Parker first argues that the indictment charging her with conspiracy to commit public bribery and public bribery under 18 U.S.C. §201(b)(2)(C) was deficient because she lacked the authority to grant or deny benefits. Mrs. Parker's duties included assisting ALJ Aronson before and during the hearings, recording and taking notes at those hearings, and typing and mailing ALJ Aronson's decisions. Mrs. Parker had access to the office's computer system, but was not authorized to approve benefits or sign ALJ Aronson's name. Thus, Mrs. Parker essentially argues that the only acts which we should examine in determining whether she violated section 201(b)(2)(C) are those within the scope of her authority, such as typing and mailing opinions.

Section 201(b)(2)(C) prohibits public officials from being induced to do or omit any act in violation of their official duty. Acts that violate an official's duty are extremely broad in scope. Section 201(a) broadly defines an "official act" as "any decision or action on any question, matter, cause, suit, proceeding or controversy, which may at any time be pending, or which may by law be brought before any public official, in such official's official capacity, or in such official's place of trust or profit." 18 U.S.C. §201(a)(3). This broad definition of "official act" reflects Congress' intent to "include any decision or action taken by a public official in his capacity as such." S. Rep. No. 87-2213 (1962). Official acts that violate an official's official duty are not limited to those proscribed by statutes and written rules and regulations, but may also be found in "established usage," because duties not completely defined by written rules are established by settled practice, and action taken in the course of their performance must be regarded as within the provisions of the above-mentioned statutes against bribery. Official acts that violate an official's official duty are also not limited to those within the official's specific authority. *See, e.g.*, United States v. Gjieli, 717 F.2d 968, 972 (6th Cir. 1983).

Mrs. Parker does not dispute that the individuals for whom she fraudulently approved benefits had appeals pending in her office. Because the appeals were pending in her "place of trust or profit," her actions fall within the statutory definition of "official act." Her abuse of the SSA facilities and equipment and the responsibility that ALJ Aronson gave her enabled her to alter and forge the decisions. Mrs. Parker could create fictitious letters approving benefits because she had access to the official networked computer system. She was able to "cut and paste" segments of one document onto another and make them appear real. As access to government computer systems becomes more prevalent, opportunities for this kind of nefarious behavior will become more common. We therefore hold that the term "official act" encompasses use of governmental computer systems to fraudulently create documents for the benefit of the employee or a third party for compensation, even when the employee's scope of authority does not formally encompass the act. Mrs. Parker's actions were thus covered by section 201(b)(2)(C) and the indictment was not deficient. . . .

The convictions of Joann Parker and Ralph Parker are AFFIRMED and the sentence of Joann Parker is AFFIRMED.

NOTES AND QUESTIONS

1. The case against Congressman Jefferson received significant notoriety not only because he was a sitting congressman when arrested, but also because a simultaneous search of his congressional office turned up $90,000 cash in a freezer. Despite some excellent defense lawyering and a partially successful challenge to the search based on the "Speech and Debate Clause" of the U.S. Constitution, Jefferson was ultimately convicted on multiple counts of bribery and sentenced to 13 years' incarceration. *See* U.S. v. Rayburn House Office Building, Room 2113, 497 F.3d 654 (D.C. Cir. 2007); *see also* Associated Press, *Former La. Congressman Sentenced to 13 Years*, CRIMES & COURTS ON MSNBC.COM, Nov. 13, 2009, available at http://www.msnbc.msn.com/id/33915800/ns/us_news-crime_and_courts/t/former-la-congressman-sentenced-years/.
2. Consider the following facts:

> A guy walks into a bar. He meets a police detective, asks him to search a law enforcement database for the names and home addresses of individuals holding certain Virginia automobile license plates, and then hands the detective some cash. He gives the detective more cash after the detective provides the information, and still more as an "incentive" to determine whether a "friend" of his has an outstanding arrest warrant in New York. The guy—who wears a gold Rolex, drives a leased Mercedes-Benz, will meet only at night at a local gas station, and advises the detective to "read between the lines"—tells the detective that he is a "federal judge." He says that he wants the information because "these f***ing people owe me a lot of money."
>
> The detective cannot know who the "judge" really is, or why he wants the information. He cannot know whether the "judge" is a loan shark seeking to find and punish his debtors, or whether he wants the information because the individuals are his associates in a criminal enterprise, police officers who are surveilling him, witnesses against him, or targets of identity theft. The detective is wary: he uses another officer's code to access the restricted database and then runs the license number of the "judge's" own Mercedes, learning only that the Mercedes is leased. Nonetheless, in the end he takes the cash—repeatedly—and gives the "judge" the information he seeks.

Valdes v. United States, 475 F.3d 1319, 1333 (D.C. Cir. 2007) (Henderson, J., dissenting). Is the police officer guilty of accepting a gratuity under §201? Much to the dismay of the dissenting judges, the en banc D.C. Circuit said no, holding that looking up information in a police data bank is not an "official act," that is, it is not a "decision or action on any question, matter, cause, suit, proceeding or controversy, which may at any time be pending, or which may by law be brought before any public official, in such official's official capacity." 18 U.S.C. §201(a)(3). Do you agree? The Jefferson court distinguished and rejected Valdes, stating, "Insofar as language in Valdes addressing those vastly different circumstances is inconsistent with the result reached here, Valdes is unpersuasive."

3. The *Valdes* court relied in part on the fact that, in addition to containing an "official act" clause, the bribery provisions in §201 also prohibit being induced to do or omit to do any act in violation of an "official duty." The gratuity provisions, on the other hand, lack a reference to duty. Thus, according to the court, Valdes could have been convicted of bribery but not gratuity. (Valdes had in fact been charged in the alternative under both provisions, but the jury apparently reached a compromise verdict by convicting him on the lesser included offense.) Does interpreting the more serious crime as prohibiting a wider swath of behavior than the less serious crime make sense? The court says yes, arguing that the broader coverage of the bribery statute is counterbalanced by the requirement of a specific quid pro quo.

C. Mens Rea

UNITED STATES v. ALFISI

308 F.3d 144 (2d Cir. 2002)

WINTER, Circuit Judge.

Mark Alfisi appeals from a conviction by a jury . . . on counts of: (i) bribery of a public official in violation of 18 U.S.C. §201(b)(1)(A); (ii) paying an unlawful gratuity to a public official in violation of 18 U.S.C. §201(c)(1)(A); and (iii) engaging in a conspiracy to commit bribery in violation of 18 U.S.C. §371.

The charges against Alfisi arose out of payments he made to a United States Department of Agriculture ("USDA") produce inspector at the Hunts Point Terminal Market. On appeal, Alfisi contends principally that the district court's jury instructions failed to delineate accurately the difference between the crime of bribery, which includes a *quid pro quo* element, and that of paying unlawful gratuities, which does not. He also claims that the instructions erroneously allowed the jury to convict him of bribery even though his payments were intended only to procure lawful action from a government official. Alfisi further argues that the jury should not have been allowed to consider the payment of an unlawful gratuity as a lesser-included offense of bribery. . . .

We reject these arguments and affirm.

Background

. . . This appeal involves purchases and sales of fresh produce at the Hunts Point Terminal Market, the world's largest wholesale produce market. Growers ship their produce to the Hunts Point Market where it is sold to wholesalers. The sales are consummated through purchase contracts negotiated between wholesalers and commercial brokers who act as agents for the growers. Generally, purchase contracts set a price and stipulate a particular required quality of the produce, stated by grade levels, to be met at the time of delivery. . . . [I]f a load of produce does not meet the contractually stipulated grade level upon delivery, the price of the produce must be renegotiated downward by the parties to reflect this change. . . .

If commercial brokers and wholesalers disagree as to the grade level of a load of produce, they have the option of requesting an inspection by the USDA's Agricultural Marketing Service for a nominal fee. When they opt for such an inspection, a USDA produce inspector will examine random samples from the disputed load of produce to determine the frequency of "quality" and "condition" defects among the produce. The inspector will then record the percentage of defects on an official USDA inspection certificate. . . .

At some point, federal officials undertook an investigation of corruption among USDA inspectors at the Hunt's Point Terminal Market. One such inspector, William Cashin, was arrested and thereafter cooperated in the investigation. Cashin and other USDA officials had routinely accepted money from wholesalers at the Hunts Point Market since about 1980. In the course of the scheme, an inspector would receive $50 in cash per inspection from wholesalers. That inspector would kick back a portion of this payoff to his or her supervisor as payment for receiving profitable assignments, i.e., assignments to bribing wholesalers. According to Cashin, the payoffs from the wholesalers were in exchange for downgrading the grade level of a load of produce by recording a higher percentage of defects than were actually observed. When applied to the unofficial "good delivery" standards, a false downgrade allowed the wholesalers to renegotiate downward the price of a load of produce.

As part of Cashin's cooperation with the government, he continued his work as a USDA inspector while also serving as an undercover agent. Cashin was assigned by his supervisor to the produce wholesaler Post & Taback. Alfisi was employed by Post & Taback, and Cashin's supervisor informed Cashin that Alfisi was prepared to make payoffs. After Cashin contacted Alfisi, Alfisi agreed to pay Cashin $50 in cash per inspection performed for the firm. Cashin and Alfisi also devised code phrases by which Alfisi was able to alert Cashin when Alfisi needed "help" with a load of produce. Cashin testified that in exchange for the $50 payments, he would falsely downgrade loads of produce except where they were already "legitimately bad." Many of Cashin's discussions with Alfisi were videotaped and audiotaped. On these recordings, Alfisi gave Cashin money and discussed Cashin's inspection of produce. . . .

After six days of trial and four days of deliberation, the jury convicted Alfisi of seven counts of bribery, six counts of paying unlawful gratuities as a lesser-included offense to bribery, and one count of conspiracy to commit bribery. The district court sentenced Alfisi to a prison term of a year and a day, two years of supervised release, and a fine of $6,000.

Discussion

a) The Instructions on Bribery and Payment of Unlawful Gratuities

. . . Alfisi's principal argument on appeal is that the jury was erroneously instructed on the elements of bribery and paying unlawful gratuities.

As we understand Alfisi's argument, he claims first that the instruction given by the district court failed to explain sufficiently the difference between bribery, which requires a *quid pro quo* element, and paying unlawful gratuities, which does not. Second, he argues that the instruction erroneously allowed the jury to convict him for bribery even if the jury found that the payments were a *quid pro quo* exchange for Cashin to perform his job faithfully. . . . We are satisfied that the district court's jury instructions, viewed in their entirety, were correct.

We begin by examining the pertinent elements of bribery and paying unlawful gratuities. The bribery provision, 18 U.S.C. §201(b)(1)(A), renders it unlawful for any person to "directly or indirectly, corruptly give[ ], offer[ ] or promise[ ] anything of value to any public official . . . with intent . . . to influence any official act." The payment of an unlawful gratuity involves an act where a person "directly or indirectly gives, offers, or promises anything of value to any public official . . . for or because of any official act performed or to be performed." 18 U.S.C. §201(c)(1)(A). Bribery therefore requires that the payor intend "to influence" an official act "corruptly" while the payment of an unlawful gratuity requires only that the payment be "for or because of" an official act. *See* United States v. Sun-Diamond Growers of California, 526 U.S. 398, 404 (1999).

The "corrupt" intent necessary to a bribery conviction is in the nature of a *quid pro quo* requirement; that is, there must be "a specific intent to give . . . something of value *in exchange* for an official act." Putting it only slightly differently, bribery involves the giving of value to procure a specific official action from a public official. The element of a *quid pro quo* or a direct exchange is absent from the offense of paying an unlawful gratuity. To commit that offense, it is enough that the payment be a reward for a past official act or made in the hope of obtaining general good will in the payee's performance of official acts off in the future.

Turning to the instructions in the present case, the district court initially informed the jury that Alfisi could be convicted of bribery if the government proved beyond a reasonable doubt that he paid money "wilfully, corruptly and with intent to influence an official act to be performed by Inspector Cashin." In defining "corruptly," the district court stated that the term entailed a "specific intent to influence Inspector Cashin's official acts of performing inspections and certifying the condition and grade of fruits and vegetables." The payment of an unlawful gratuity was described as the giving of money "for or because of official acts performed or to be performed by William Cashin." More specifically, the district court told the jury that to prove the payment of an unlawful gratuity, the government must show a link between the payment and some official act, but not corrupt intent as earlier defined.

As we understand the first aspect of Alfisi's argument, he believes that these instructions were not sufficiently specific as to the *quid pro quo* element of bribery to spell out adequately the difference between that crime and paying unlawful gratuities. In that regard, it is significant that the district court's explanation of bribery and paying unlawful gratuities virtually mirrors the statutory language contained in 18 U.S.C. §§201(b)(1)(A), 201(c)(1)(A) and used by many courts to distinguish the two crimes. Where a district court's jury instructions accurately track the language and meaning of the relevant statute, we generally will not find error. However, we need not affirm here on the court's initial instructions, because the court later erased all doubt as to the need for proof of a *quid pro quo* arrangement to convict Alfisi of bribery.

The jury evidently found the instructions somewhat ambiguous with regard to the difference between bribery and paying unlawful gratuities and asked the court for clarification. In response, the court described bribery as the giving of money to a public official "for or because of an official act [and] with a corrupt intention specifically to influence the outcome of the official act." This instruction clearly set out the *quid pro quo* requirement, and, accordingly, any ambiguity in the original jury instructions was cured. The events here suggest that it might be well to add similar language in the future for such jury instructions.

Alfisi also argues that he should not be found guilty of bribery if he paid money to Cashin solely to induce him to perform his job faithfully. Put another way, Alfisi contends that the term "corruptly" requires evidence of an intent to procure a violation of the public official's duty. For this reason, he contends, it was not "corrupt" for him to give Cashin money to ensure that Cashin inspect and report accurately on the produce because that was Cashin's legal duty. We are not persuaded.

First, Alfisi's suggested reading of the bribery statute does not rest comfortably within the statutory language. Subsection (b)(1)(A), the basis for Alfisi's bribery convictions, outlaws payments made with a corrupt intent—to procure a *quid pro quo* agreement—"to influence any official act." It cannot be seriously argued that Alfisi's payments did not fall within that broad language, even if he was paying Cashin solely to make accurate inspections. . . .

[Second, a broad reading of the bribery provision makes good policy sense. Otherwise,] many highly culpable payments would go underpunished as unlawful gratuities, or unpunished altogether.

For example, if a party to litigation were to pay a judge money in exchange for a favorable decision, that conduct would-and should-constitute bribery, even if a trier of fact might conclude *ex post* that the judgment was on the merits legally proper. This principle was at stake and upheld in a decision arising from the most lamentable episode in this court's history. *See* United States v. Manton, 107 F.2d 834, 845-46 (2d Cir. 1939) (rejecting Chief Circuit Judge's defense that payments in exchange for particular decisions were not obstruction of justice where decisions rendered were legally correct). In such a case, the key element of the offense is the intent of the payor to purchase a particular decision without regard to the merits, as opposed to an impartial judgment. The legal merits, or lack thereof, of the judgment rendered is not an element of the offense. . . .

For the reasons indicated above, we affirm.

NOTES AND QUESTIONS

1. Think back to the definition of "corruptly" used in connection with obstruction of justice cases. There it had a very stringent meaning. Here, in the context of bribery, the word is treated almost as duplicative of the requirement that bribery must involve a specific quid pro quo. In other words, it has almost no independent meaning. Can taking two approaches to the interpretation of the same word in two different contexts be justified? How?
2. Relying on *Sun-Diamond*, the court states that, to be guilty of making an illegal gratuity, "it is enough that the payment be a reward for a past official act or made in the hope of obtaining general good will in the payee's performance of official acts off in the future." Is this a correct statement of the law?
3. Is a public official guilty of accepting a bribe even if he never intended to be influenced by it? The courts have answered this question in the affirmative. *See, e.g.*, United States v. Peleti, 576 F.3d 377 (7th Cir. 2009) (army food service officer's claim that he took $50,000 from a potential supplier without an intent to be influenced is not relevant to his guilt); United States v. Valle, 538 F.3d 341 (5th Cir. 2008) (ICE agent guilty of accepting a bribe despite claim that he had no intention to fulfill his end of the bargain). Is there a persuasive policy reason for interpreting the statute in this fashion?

D. Definition of "Public Official"

DIXSON v. UNITED STATES
465 U.S. 482 (1984)

Justice MARSHALL delivered the opinion of the Court.

These consolidated cases present the question whether officers of a private, nonprofit corporation administering and expending federal community development block grants are "public officials" for purposes of the federal bribery statute. 18 U.S.C. §201(a).

I.

In 1979, the City of Peoria received two federal block grants from the Department of Housing and Urban Development (HUD). The first was a $400,000 Community Development Block Grant; the second a $636,000 Metro Reallocation Grant. Both grants were funded through the Housing and Community Development Act of 1974, 42 U.S.C. §§5301-5320. Under that Act, the Secretary of HUD is authorized to dispense federal block grants to state and local governments and nonprofit community organizations for urban renewal programs such as the rehabilitation of residential structures, code enforcement in deteriorating areas, and the construction of public works projects.

The City of Peoria subsequently designated United Neighborhoods, Inc. (UNI), a community-based, social-service organization, to be the City's subgrantee in charge of the administration of the federal block grant funds. UNI in turn hired petitioner Dixson to serve as the corporation's Executive Director and petitioner Hinton as its Housing Rehabilitation Coordinator. Petitioner Dixson was responsible for the general supervision of UNI's programs, including fiscal control and execution of contracts. Petitioner Hinton's duties included contracting with persons applying for housing rehabilitation assistance, and contracting with demolition firms.

A federal grand jury named petitioners in an 12-count indictment filed on March 12, 1981. The indictment charged that petitioners, as "public officials" under 18 U.S.C. §201(a), had sought a series of bribes in return for "being influenced in their performance of an official act in respect to the awarding of housing rehabilitation contracts" in violation of 18 U.S.C. §201(c)(1), (2).

According to the Government's evidence at trial, petitioners used their positions to extract $42,604 in kick-backs from contractors seeking to work on UNI's housing rehabilitation projects. One contractor testified how he was approached by petitioner Hinton and persuaded to pay petitioners 10 percent of each housing rehabilitation contract that petitioners awarded him. The contractor explained that on ten occasions, he received first draw checks from UNI for 20 percent of the contract price, deposited the check at his bank, and paid half the amount of the check in cash to petitioners. A second contractor testified as to substantially the same arrangement.

Before trial, petitioners moved to dismiss the indictment on the grounds that they were not "public officials" within the meaning of the federal statute. Their motions were denied, and following a jury trial in the United States District Court for the Central District of Illinois, petitioners were convicted as charged. The District Court sentenced each to 7½ years imprisonment, to be followed by 3 years' probation. Petitioners appealed to the United States Court of Appeals for the Seventh Circuit, which affirmed. We now affirm.

II.

. . . The HCDA creates a "consistent system of Federal aid," §5301(d), by distributing funds committed by Congress through organizations outside the federal government, while retaining federal control to assure compliance with statutory federal objectives and implementing regulations. Congress itself specified the 17 categories of community projects upon which HCDA grants can be spent. Within the federal constraints, grant recipients design programs addressing local needs. To obtain federal funds, local communities must submit to the Secretary a plan made in accordance with national urban growth policies, and supplement the plan with annual performance reports. The federal government retains the right to audit the records of HCDA programs, and to recover improperly expended funds.

HCDA grantees give assurances to HUD that they, and their subgrantees, will abide by specific financial accountability, equal opportunity, fair labor, environmental, and other requirements. . . .

III.

. . . Petitioners argue that they cannot be considered to have acted "for or on behalf of the United States" because neither they nor their employer UNI ever entered into any agreement with the United States or any subdivision of the federal government. . . . The Government, in response, argues that the term "public official" has a broader sweep, covering not only parties in privity with the United States, but also any private individuals responsible for administering federally-funded and federally-supervised programs. The Government defends the decision of the Seventh Circuit in the instant case, which held that the "substantial federal supervision over the cities and all sub-grantees responsible for local distribution of grant funds" made petitioners' public officials for purposes of section 201. The court reasoned that petitioners "were acting as federal agents in the sense of having discretion in ad-ministering the expenditure of federal funds."

As is often the case in matters of statutory interpretation, the language of section 201(a) does not decide the dispute. The words can be interpreted to support either petitioners' or the Government's reading. We must turn, therefore, to the legislative history of the federal bribery statute to determine whether these materials clarify which of the proposed readings is consistent with Congress's intent. If the legislative history fails to clarify the statutory language, our rule of lenity would compel us to construe the statute in favor of petitioners, as criminal defendants in this case.

A.

Congress passed the current federal bribery provision, including section 201(a), in 1962, as part of an effort to re-formulate and rationalize all federal criminal statutes dealing with the integrity of government. At the time of the 1962 revisions, general federal bribery statutes had been in existence for more than a century. From the start, Congress drafted its bribery statutes with broad jurisdictional language, and periodically amended the provisions to ensure that the scope of federal criminal liability kept pace with the growth and diversification of the federal government. Prior to 1962, in recognition of Congress's apparent desire for the federal bribery statutes to have wide application, the federal judiciary interpreted the statutes and, indeed, the phrase "person acting for or on behalf of the United States" to have a broad jurisdictional reach.

When drafting section 201(a), Congress was aware of previous federal bribery statutes, as well as the judicial interpretation given those statutes. The phrase at issue here—"person acting for or on behalf of the United States"—was taken directly from predecessor bribery statutes. Moreover, the reenactment of this language was no happenstance. Earlier versions of the 1962 statute omitted the phrase, but Department of Justice testimony that "its removal would be undesirable" convinced Congress to retain the language.

Standing alone, Congress' purposeful retention of the "acting for or on behalf of the Government" phrase does not advance our inquiry into the scope and meaning of those words. When, however, we compare the phrase as enacted with the proposed definition of "public official" in earlier draft bills that were not enacted, we conclude that Congress could not have meant to restrict the definition, as petitioners argue, to those persons in an employment or agency relationship with the federal government. Such persons were clearly covered by successive, rejected versions of the reform bill, which defined "public official" in pertinent part as "an officer, agent, or employee of the United States in the executive, legislative, or judicial branch of the Government, or of any agency." If Congress intended courts to restrict their reading of the jurisdictional definition to persons in a formal employment or agency relationship with the Government, it would have had no reason to accede to the Department of Justice's urging to retain the "acting for or on behalf of" language.

Moreover, we find the legislative history of section 201(a) inconsistent with the view that the words "person acting for or on behalf of the United States" were added simply to bring within the jurisdiction of the federal bribery laws those individuals tied to the federal government by direct contractual obligations. Committee reports from both Houses of Congress emphasized that the new bribery laws made "no significant changes of substance" and "would not restrict the broad scope of the present bribery statutes as construed by the courts." S. Rep. No. 2213, 87th Cong., 2d Sess. 4 (1962); H.R. Rep. No. 748, 87th Cong., 1st Sess. 17 (1961). Federal courts interpreting the federal bribery laws prior to 1962 had generally avoided formal distinctions, such as the requirement of a direct contractual bond, that would artificially narrow the scope of federal criminal jurisdiction.

Of particular relevance to the instant case is the House Judiciary Committee's citation of the Second Circuit's decision in United States v. Levine, 129 F.2d 745 (2d Cir. 1942), as an example of how the judiciary had in the past properly construed the federal bribery laws. The *Levine* decision involved the application of the 1909 bribery statute to a low-level official in a decentralized federal assistance program. The defendant in *Levine* worked for a locally-administered price stabilization program, the Market Administrator of the New York Metropolitan Milk Marketing Area, and was responsible for receiving milk handlers' market surplus claims, and checking them for accuracy. Levine solicited a bribe from one of the handlers within his jurisdiction in return for his promise to prevent investigations of the claims.

Although hired by a Market Administrator who, in turn, had been appointed by the Secretary of Agriculture, Levine himself was neither employed by the United States nor paid with federal funds. Nevertheless, Levine's duties were critical to the proper administration of the federally assisted New York Milk Marketing Area. Because claims for payment were not rechecked by anyone else, his duties resulted in expenditures from the federal treasury. After reviewing these facts, the Second Circuit concluded that, notwithstanding the absence of a direct contractual bond between the defendant and the United States, Levine's responsible position made him a "public official" for purposes of the federal bribery laws. By explicitly endorsing the Second Circuit's analysis in *Levine*, the House Judiciary Committee strongly intimated that the phrase "acting for or on behalf of the United States" covers something more than a direct contractual bond. . . .

B.

By finding petitioners to be public officials within the meaning of section 201(a), we do not mean to suggest that the mere presence of some federal assistance brings a local organization and its employees within the jurisdiction of the federal bribery statute or even that all employees of local organizations responsible for administering federal grant programs are public officials within the meaning of section 201(a). To be a public official under section 201(a), an individual must possess some degree of official responsibility for carrying out a federal program or policy. . . .

We recognize that the manner in which the HCDA block grant program combines local administration with federal funding initially creates some confusion as to whether local authorities administering HCDA grants should be considered public officials under the federal bribery statute. However, when one examines the structure of the program and sees that the HCDA vests in local administrators like petitioners Hinton and Dixson the power to allocate federal fiscal resources for the purpose of achieving congressionally-established goals, the confusion evaporates and it becomes clear that these local officials hold precisely the sort of positions of national public trust that Congress intended to cover with the "acting for or on behalf of" language in the bribery statute. The federal government has a strong and legitimate interest in prosecuting petitioners for their misuse of government funds. . . .

It is so ordered.

[The dissenting opinion of Justice O'Connor is omitted.]

UNITED STATES v. EVANS

344 F.3d 1131 (11th Cir. 2003)

EDMONDSON, Chief Judge:

. . . Following a jury trial, [Audley] Evans was convicted of one count of conspiracy (count 8), two counts of bribery (counts 14 and 15), six counts of gratuity (counts 34, 35, and 45-48), and six counts of false statements (counts 120-125). . . . We vacate . . . Evans's gratuity convictions on counts 45-48 and Evans's false statement convictions on counts 120 and 121. Discovering no other reversible error, we affirm without discussing the remainder of Evans's convictions.

Background

From 1988 through August 1996, Audley Evans was the Executive Director of the Tampa Housing Authority (The Authority). After resigning as Executive Director, Evans was an unpaid consultant at the Authority until December 1996. While an unpaid consultant for the Authority, Evans became the Executive Director of the Meridian River Development Corp. (MRDC).

The City of Tampa created the Authority to develop and operate public housing units for eligible families. The Authority received millions of dollars annually from the United States Department of Housing and Urban Development (HUD) to assist it in providing housing. Among the HUD funds received by the Authority were "Section 8" funds which were used by the Authority to pay the rent of qualified families who lived outside of Authority-owned public housing. The Authority made rent payments for low income families who became clients of the Authority and resided in private housing.

MRDC is a non-profit corporation created at the direction of the Authority to provide and develop affordable housing opportunities for low income persons. MRDC was created as an instrumentality of the Authority for the purpose of implementing the housing plans and programs of the Authority. As a private non-profit corporation, MRDC could perform public housing functions that the Authority, as a state agency, could not. The Authority was the sole member of MRDC.

MRDC owned and operated several residential properties. MRDC received Section 8 funds from the Authority for eligible families who resided in MRDC properties. In 1996 and 1997, MRDC received more than $350,000.00 in HUD funds. All of these funds were paid by the Authority to MRDC to offset the rent payments of eligible low income residents in MRDC properties. MRDC's excess funds were to be returned to the Authority, or used as the Authority directed.

In July 1996, Evans resigned his Director's position at the Authority. Immediately thereafter, Evans became the director of MRDC. Beginning in September 1996, Evans awarded several MRDC contracts to Concorde, Inc. Concorde was formed by C. Hayward Chapman and Terri Keirn (Chapman's daughter). Concorde was controlled by Chapman. In December 1996, Chapman had Concorde post a $25,000 letter of credit as collateral to allow Evans to take out a loan. In May 1997, Chapman had Concorde pay $125,000.00 to three of Evans's creditors. Although Evans claims that Chapman paid these sums to purchase an interest in Caribbean Properties (a company owned by Evans), Evans, after the time of Chapman's payments, executed a financial affidavit stating that he and his wife owned 100% of Caribbean Properties....

Discussion

... Counts 45-48 and 69-72 charged that Chapman, through Concorde, had given and Evans had received gratuities because of official acts to be performed by Evans. Evans ... challenge[s] the convictions claiming [he] was no public official, no link existed between the gratuities and an official act, and nothing evidenced the intent to give or accept an unlawful gratuity. Because Evans was not a public official (at MRDC), we vacate these convictions.

... "To determine whether any particular individual [is a public official], the proper inquiry is ... whether the person occupies a position of public trust with official federal responsibilities." Dixson v. United States, 465 U.S. 482 (1984).

"To be a public official under section 201(a), an individual must possess some degree of official responsibility for carrying out a federal program or policy." *Id.* at 1181. The person need not be an employee of the federal government: the definition of "public official" is broad enough to cover persons working for private organizations. *See* United States v. Kenney, 185 F.3d 1217, 1222 (11th Cir. 1999) (saying that employee of government contractor who provided information and made recommendations that were relied on by government's decision makers was public official). But the Supreme Court has cautioned that the "mere presence of some federal assistance" is not enough to "bring[ ] a local organization and its employees within the jurisdiction of the federal bribery statute. . . ." *Dixson.*

The Government claims that Evans was a public official because he was a "person acting for or on behalf of the United States." They point out that MRDC was closely related to the Authority. MRDC was the only nonprofit entity associated with the Authority. The Authority set MRDC up for the Authority's benefit. MRDC's excess funds were to be returned to the Authority or spent as the Authority directed. Two Authority board members sat on the board of MRDC. MRDC received a substantial amount of HUD Section 8 funds from the Authority for Authority clients residing in MRDC properties. The Government argues that these facts show that Evans was "acting on behalf of a federal agency, by the authority of a federal agency, and was responsible for carrying out a federal program or policy."

The only federal program identified by the Government is the "Section 8" program. Under that program, HUD makes annual contribution contracts with local public housing agencies, in this case the Authority, which the agencies can use to make rental payments to the owners of dwelling units. 42 U.S.C. 1437f(b)(1). The record shows that MRDC participated in this program as the owner of dwelling units. In this way, MRDC is no different from any other landlord renting to eligible low income tenants. MRDC was a final recipient of federal funds.

The final recipients of federal funds are usually not public officials under section 201(a)(1). The Government argues that MRDC differs from other landlords because of its relationship with the Authority and that this relationship makes Evans a public official. In the light of the record in this case, we disagree.

The relationship between MRDC and the Authority cannot by itself make an MRDC employee a public official. In fact, not every employee of the Authority is a public official. "To be a public official . . . an individual must possess some degree of official responsibility for carrying out a federal program or policy." *Dixson* at 1181. The evidence does not show and the Government does not really argue that Evans possessed this kind of official responsibility. Because Evans while at MRDC did not have authority for carrying out a federal program or policy, he was not a public official as defined by section 201(a)(1). Evans's convictions on Counts 45-48 and Chapman's convictions on counts 69-72 are vacated. . . .

NOTES AND QUESTIONS

1. Compare the introductory language of *Dixson* to that of *Sun-Diamond.* In *Dixson*, the Court observes, "From the start, Congress drafted its bribery statutes with broad jurisdictional language, and periodically amended the provisions to ensure that the scope of federal criminal liability kept pace with the growth and diversification of the federal government." The Court uses this rationale to support its interpretation that the bribery statute covers private citizens employed by local agencies funded by the federal government. In *Sun-Diamond*, on the other hand, the Court limited the scope of the gratuity provision, claiming, "[A] narrow, rather than a

sweeping, prohibition is more compatible with the fact that §201(c)(1)(A) is merely one strand of an intricate web of regulations, both administrative and criminal, governing the acceptance of gifts and other self-enriching actions by public officials. . . . [T]his regulation, and the numerous other regulations and statutes littering this field, demonstrate that this is an area where precisely targeted prohibitions are commonplace, and where more general prohibitions have been qualified by numerous exceptions. Given that reality, a statute in this field that can linguistically be interpreted to be either a meat axe or a scalpel should reasonably be taken to be the latter." So which is it? Did Congress intend a sweeping ("meat axe") or hypertechnical ("scalpel") reading of §201?

2. Consider the following. Dixson and his co-defendant used HUD funds to compensate program beneficiaries and to enter into contracts with demolitions companies. The Supreme Court holds that the discretion they derived as a result of the latter activity qualified them as federal officials under the bribery statute.

   Evans, on the other hand, received Section 8 funds as reimbursement for rents owed him by that program's beneficiaries. The Eleventh Circuit says that this makes him the "final recipient" of these funds and, as such, not a public official. However, the court mentioned earlier in the opinion that Evans also had the discretion to use Section 8 funds to "award[] several . . . contract[s] to Concord, Inc." (The court neglects to tell us what the contracts were for.) It was in connection with this activity that the receipt of gratuities took place.

   Is *Evans* truly distinguishable from *Dixson*?

II. FEDERAL PROGRAM BRIBERY, THEFT, AND FRAUD, 18 U.S.C. §666

A. General Requirements

SABRI v. UNITED STATES
541 U.S. 600 (2004)

Justice Souter delivered the opinion of the Court.

The question is whether 18 U.S.C. §666(a)(2), proscribing bribery of state, local, and tribal officials of entities that receive at least $10,000 in federal funds, is a valid exercise of congressional authority under Article I of the Constitution. We hold that it is.

I.

Petitioner Basim Omar Sabri is a real estate developer who proposed to build a hotel and retail structure in the city of Minneapolis. Sabri lacked confidence, however, in his ability to adapt to the lawful administration of licensing and zoning laws, and offered three separate bribes to a city councilman, Brian Herron, according to the grand jury indictment that gave rise to this case. At the time the bribes were allegedly offered (between July 2 and July 17, 2001), Herron served as a member of the Board of Commissioners of the Minneapolis Community Development Agency (MCDA), a public body created by the city council to fund housing and economic development within the city.

Count 1 of the indictment charged Sabri with offering a $5,000 kickback for obtaining various regulatory approvals and according to Count 2, Sabri offered Herron a $10,000 bribe to set up and attend a meeting with owners of land near the site Sabri had in mind, at which Herron would threaten to use the city's eminent domain authority to seize their property if they were troublesome to Sabri. Count 3 alleged that Sabri offered Herron a commission of 10% on some $800,000 in community economic development grants that Sabri sought from the city, the MCDA, and other sources. . . .

For criminal liability to lie under 18 U.S.C. §666(a)(2), the statute requires that

> "the organization, government, or agency receiv[e], in any one year period, benefits in excess of $10,000 under a Federal program involving a grant, contract, subsidy, loan, guarantee, insurance, or other form of Federal assistance."

§666(b).

In 2001, the City Council of Minneapolis administered about $29 million in federal funds paid to the city, and in the same period, the MCDA received some $23 million of federal money.

Before trial, Sabri moved to dismiss the indictment on the ground that §666(a)(2) is unconstitutional on its face for failure to require proof of a connection between the federal funds and the alleged bribe, as an element of liability. The Government responded that "even if an additional nexus between the bribery conduct and the federal funds is required, the evidence in this case will easily meet such a standard" because Sabri's alleged actions related to federal dollars. Although Sabri did not contradict this factual claim, the District Court agreed with him that the law was facially invalid. A divided panel of the Eighth Circuit reversed, holding that there was nothing fatal in the absence of an express requirement to prove some connection between a given bribe and federally pedigreed dollars, and that the statute was constitutional under the Necessary and Proper Clause in serving the objects of the congressional spending power. . . .

We granted certiorari to resolve a split among the Courts of Appeals over the need to require connection between forbidden conduct and federal funds. We now affirm.

II.

Sabri raises what he calls a facial challenge to §666(a)(2): the law can never be applied constitutionally because it fails to require proof of any connection between a bribe or kickback and some federal money. It is fatal, as he sees it, that the statute does not make the link [to] an element of the crime, to be charged in the indictment and demonstrated beyond a reasonable doubt. Thus, Sabri claims his attack meets the demanding standard set out in United States v. Salerno, 481 U.S. 739, 745 (1987), since he says no prosecution can satisfy the Constitution under this statute, owing to its failure to require proof that its particular application falls within Congress's jurisdiction to legislate.

We can readily dispose of this position that, to qualify as a valid exercise of Article I power, the statute must require proof of connection with federal money as an element of the offense. We simply do not presume the unconstitutionality of federal criminal statutes lacking explicit provision of a jurisdictional hook, and there is no occasion even to consider the need for such a requirement where there is no reason to suspect that enforcement of a criminal statute would extend beyond a legitimate interest cognizable under Article I, §8.

Congress has authority under the Spending Clause to appropriate federal moneys to promote the general welfare, Art. I, §8, cl. 1, and it has corresponding authority under the Necessary and Proper Clause, Art. I, §8, cl. 18, to see to it that taxpayer dollars appropriated under that power are in fact spent for the general welfare, and not frittered away in graft or on projects undermined when funds are siphoned off or corrupt public officers are derelict about demanding value for dollars. *See generally* McCulloch v. Maryland, 4 Wheat. 316 (1819) (establishing review for means-ends rationality under the Necessary and Proper Clause). Congress does not have to sit by and accept the risk of operations thwarted by local and state improbity. Section 666(a)(2) addresses the problem at the sources of bribes, by rational means, to safeguard the integrity of the state, local, and tribal recipients of federal dollars.

It is true, just as Sabri says, that not every bribe or kickback offered or paid to agents of governments covered by §666(b) will be traceably skimmed from specific federal payments, or show up in the guise of a *quid pro quo* for some dereliction in spending a federal grant. But this possibility portends no enforcement beyond the scope of federal interest, for the reason that corruption does not have to be that limited to affect the federal interest. Money is fungible, bribed officials are untrustworthy stewards of federal funds, and corrupt contractors do not deliver dollar-for-dollar value. Liquidity is not a financial term for nothing; money can be drained off here because a federal grant is pouring in there. And officials are not any the less threatening to the objects behind federal spending just because they may accept general retainers. It is certainly enough that the statutes condition the offense on a threshold amount of federal dollars defining the federal interest, such as that provided here.

For those of us who accept help from legislative history, it is worth noting that the legislative record confirms that §666(a)(2) is an instance of necessary and proper legislation. The design was generally to "protect the integrity of the vast sums of money distributed through Federal programs from theft, fraud, and undue influence by bribery," *see* S. Rep. No. 98-225, p. 370 (1983), in contrast to prior federal law affording only two limited opportunities to prosecute such threats to the federal interest: 18 U.S.C. §641, the federal theft statute, and §201, the federal bribery law. Those laws had proven inadequate to the task. The former went only to outright theft of unadulterated federal funds, and prior to this Court's opinion in Dixson v. United States, 465 U.S. 482 (1984), which came after passage of §666, the bribery statute had been interpreted by lower courts to bar prosecution of bribes directed at state and local officials. Thus we said that §666 "was designed to extend federal bribery prohibitions to bribes offered to state and local officials employed by agencies receiving federal funds," thereby filling the regulatory gaps. Congress's decision to enact §666 only after other legislation had failed to protect federal interests is further indication that it was acting within the ambit of the Necessary and Proper Clause. . . .

No piling is needed here to show that Congress was within its prerogative to protect spending objects from the menace of local administrators on the take. The power to keep a watchful eye on expenditures and on the reliability of those who use public money is bound up with congressional authority to spend in the first place. . . .

IV.

We remand for proceedings consistent with this opinion. The judgment of the Court of Appeals for the Eighth Circuit is

Affirmed.

[The concurring opinions of Justice Kennedy and Justice Thomas are omitted.]

FISCHER v. UNITED STATES

529 U.S. 667 (2000)

Justice KENNEDY delivered the opinion of the Court.

The federal bribery statute prohibits defrauding organizations which "receiv[e], in any one year period, benefits in excess of $10,000 under a Federal program." 18 U.S.C. §666(b). We granted certiorari to determine whether the statute covers fraud perpetrated on organizations participating in the Medicare program. Upon consideration of the role and regulated status of hospitals as health care providers under the Medicare program, we hold they receive "benefits" within the meaning of the statute. We affirm petitioner's convictions.

I.

Petitioner Jeffrey Allan Fischer was president and partial owner of Quality Medical Consultants, Inc. (QMC), a corporation which performed billing audits for health care organizations. In 1993 petitioner, on QMC's behalf, negotiated a $1.2 million loan from West Volusia Hospital Authority (WVHA), a municipal agency responsible for operating two hospitals located in West Volusia County, Florida. Both hospitals participate in the Medicare program, and in 1993 WVHA received between $10 and $15 million in Medicare funds.

A February 1994 audit of WVHA's financial affairs raised questions about the QMC loan. An investigation revealed QMC used the loan proceeds to repay creditors and to raise the salaries of its five owner-employees, including petitioner. It was determined that petitioner had arranged for QMC to advance at least $100,000 to a private company owned by an individual who had assisted QMC in securing a letter of credit in connection with the WVHA loan. QMC, at petitioner's directive, also committed portions of the loan proceeds to speculative securities. These investments yielded losses of almost $400,000. The investigation further uncovered use of the loan proceeds to pay, through an intermediate transfer, a $10,000 kickback to WVHA's chief financial officer, the individual with whom petitioner had negotiated the loan in the first instance. QMC defaulted on its obligation to WVHA and filed for bankruptcy.

In 1996 petitioner was indicted by a federal grand jury on 13 counts, including charges of defrauding an organization which receives benefits under a federal assistance program, 18 U.S.C. §666(a)(1)(A), and of paying a kickback to one of its agents, §666(a)(2). A jury convicted petitioner on all counts charged. . . .

II.

A.

The nature and purposes of the Medicare program give us essential instruction in resolving the present controversy. Established in 1965 as part of the Social Security Act, 42 U.S.C. §1395 *et seq.* (1994 ed. and Supp. III), Medicare is a federally funded medical insurance program for the elderly and disabled. In fiscal 1997 some 38.8 million individuals were enrolled in the program, and over 6,100 hospitals were authorized to provide services to them. Medicare expenditures for hospital services exceeded $123 billion in 1998, making the Federal Government the single largest source of funds for participating hospitals. This amount constituted 32% of the hospitals' total receipts.

Providers of health care services, such as the two hospitals operated by WVHA, qualify to participate in the program upon satisfying a comprehensive series of statutory and regulatory requirements, including particular accreditation standards. Hospitals, for instance, must satisfy licensing standards, 42 CFR §482.11 (1999); possess a governing body to "ensure that there is an effective, hospital-wide quality assurance program to evaluate the provision of patient care," §482.21; and employ a "well organized" medical staff accountable on matters relating to "the quality of the medical care provided to patients," §482.22(b). . . . The regulations go further, requiring hospital facilities to "be constructed, arranged, and maintained to ensure the safety of the patient, and to provide facilities for diagnosis and treatment and for special hospital services appropriate to the needs of the community." §482.41. Compliance with these standards provides the Government with assurance that participating providers possess the capacity to fulfill their statutory obligation of providing "medically necessary" services "of a quality which meets professionally recognized standards of health care." 42 U.S.C. §1320c-5(a). . . .

Medicare attains its objectives through an elaborate funding structure. Participating health care organizations, in exchange for rendering services, receive federal funds on a periodic basis. The amounts received reflect the "reasonable cost" of services rendered, defined as "the costs necessary in the efficient delivery of needed health services to individuals covered [by the program]." §1395x(v)(1)(A). Necessary costs are not limited to the immediate costs of an individual treatment procedure. Instead they are defined in broader terms: "Necessary and proper costs are costs that are appropriate and helpful in developing and maintaining the operation of patient care facilities and activities." 42 CFR §413.9(b)(2) (1999). Allowable costs include amounts which enhance the organization's capacity to provide ongoing, quality services not only to eligible patients but also to the community at large. By way of example, amounts incurred for "certain educational programs for interns and residents, known as [graduate medical education] programs, are 'allowable cost[s]' for which a hospital (a provider) may receive reimbursement." . . .

B.

. . . Liability for the acts prohibited by subsection (a) is predicated upon a showing that the defrauded organization "receive[d], in any one period, benefits in excess of $10,000 under a Federal program." §666(b). Those benefits can be in the form of "a grant, contract, subsidy, loan, guarantee, insurance, or other form of Federal assistance." All agree Medicare is a federal assistance program, *see* 42 CFR §400.200 (1999), and that WVHA, as the organization defrauded by petitioner's actions, received in excess of $10,000 in payments under the program. The sole point in contention is whether those payments constituted "benefits" within the meaning of subsection (b).

Petitioner argues that the Medicare program provides benefits to the elderly and disabled but not to the health care organizations. Provider organizations, in petitioner's view, do no more than render services in exchange for compensation. Under petitioner's submission the Medicare program envisions a single beneficiary, the qualifying patient. The Government, in opposition, urges that a determination whether an organization receives "benefits" within the meaning of §666(b) turns on whether the Federal Government was the source of the payment. Funds received under a federal assistance program, the Government asserts, can be traced from federal coffers, often through an intermediary or carrier, to the health care provider. Under its view, the "federal-program source of the funds" satisfies the benefits definition.

We reject petitioner's reading of the statute but without endorsing the Government's broader position. We conclude Medicare payments are "benefits," as the term is used in its ordinary sense and as it is intended in the statute. The noun "benefit" means "something that guards, aids, or promotes well-being: advantage, good"; "useful aid"; "payment, gift [such as] financial help in time of sickness, old age, or unemployment"; or "a cash payment or service provided for under an annuity, pension plan, or insurance policy." Webster's Third New International Dictionary 204 (1971). These definitions support petitioner's assertion that qualifying patients receive benefits [and are indeed the primary beneficiaries] under the Medicare program.

That one beneficiary of an assistance program can be identified does not foreclose the existence of others, however. . . . For present purposes it cannot be disputed the providers themselves derive significant advantage by satisfying the participation standards imposed by the Government. These advantages constitute benefits within the meaning of the federal bribery statute, a statute we have described as "expansive," "both as to the [conduct] forbidden and the entities covered."

Subsection (b) identifies several sources as providing benefits under a federal program—"a grant, contract, subsidy, loan, guarantee, insurance, or other form of Federal assistance." This language indicates that Congress viewed many federal assistance programs as providing benefits to participating organizations. Coupled with the broad substantive prohibitions of subsection (a), the language of subsection (b) reveals Congress' expansive, unambiguous intent to ensure the integrity of organizations participating in federal assistance programs.

Subsection (c) of the statute bears on the analysis. The provision removes from the statute's coverage any "bona fide salary, wages, fees, or other compensation paid, or expenses paid or reimbursed, in the usual course of business." §666(c). . . .

We do not accept the view [put forward by petitioner] that the Medicare payments here in question are for the limited purposes of compensating providers or reimbursing them for ordinary course expenditures. The payments are made for significant and substantial reasons in addition to compensation or reimbursement, so that neither these terms nor the usual course of business conditions set forth in subsection (c) are met here. The payments in question have attributes and purposes well beyond those described in subsection (c). These attributes and purposes are consistent with the definition of "benefit." While the payments might have similarities to payments an insurer would remit to a hospital quite without regard to the Medicare program, the Government does not make the payment unless the hospital complies with its intricate regulatory scheme. The payments are made not simply to reimburse for treatment of qualifying patients but to assist the hospital in making available and maintaining a certain level and quality of medical care, all in the interest of both the hospital and the greater community. . . .

Our discussion should not be taken to suggest that federal funds disbursed under an assistance program will result in coverage of all recipient fraud under §666(b). Any receipt of federal funds can, at some level of generality, be characterized as a benefit. The statute does not employ this broad, almost limitless use of the term. Doing so would turn almost every act of fraud or bribery into a federal offense, upsetting the proper federal balance. To determine whether an organization participating in a federal assistance program receives "benefits," an examination must be undertaken of the program's structure, operation, and purpose. The inquiry should examine the conditions under which the organization receives the federal payments. The answer could depend, as it does here, on whether the recipient's own operations are one of the reasons for maintaining the program. Health care organizations participating in the Medicare program satisfy this standard. . . .

Other cases may present questions requiring further examination and elaboration of the term "benefits." Here it suffices to hold that health care providers such as the one defrauded by petitioner receive benefits within the meaning of the statute. The judgment of the Court of Appeals is affirmed.

It is so ordered.

[The dissenting opinion of Justice Thomas is omitted.]

NOTES AND QUESTIONS

1. In *Sabri*, the Court makes a convincing case that not requiring a specific connection between the federal funds and the impact of the bribery does not undermine §666's underlying goal of protecting the federal fisc:

   > *Money is fungible, bribed officials are untrustworthy stewards of federal funds,* and corrupt contractors do not deliver dollar-for-dollar value. Liquidity is not a financial term for nothing; money can be drained off here because a federal grant is pouring in there. *And officials are not any the less threatening to the objects behind federal spending just because they may accept general retainers.* It is certainly enough that the statutes condition the offense on a threshold amount of federal dollars defining the federal interest, such as that provided here.

   Couldn't the same thing be said (in a very different context) about the federal officials in the *Sun-Diamond* case? If the Supreme Court viewed the two cases congruently, would the outcome of *Sun-Diamond* be different? How?
2. After *Sabri*, can a mayor who accepts bribes be convicted under §666 if his city receives federal funding, even if the bribes are totally unrelated to the federal dollars? *See* United States v. Caro-Muñiz, 406 F.3d 22 (1st Cir. 2005) (answering in the affirmative).
3. Is an employee of a defense contractor who accepts bribes covered under §666? *See* United States v. Copeland, 143 F.3d 1439 (11th Cir. 1998) (no, because federal dollars received by contractors, though obtained by way of a "contract," are not "federal assistance").

B. Does §666 Cover Gratuities?

UNITED STATES v. BONITO
57 F.3d 167 (2d Cir. 1995)

COFFIN, Senior Circuit Judge.

. . . Benjamin Bonito was a landlord and real estate developer in the New Haven area. He was charged in the indictment with giving a car bribe to his co-defendant at trial, Joseph DeMatteo, who was the Director of Real Estate Services for the City of New Haven and also a member of a joint New Haven-New Haven Housing Authority committee established to select sites for low income housing. The New Haven Housing Authority is an organization created by Connecticut statute, which administers projects funded by the federal Department of Housing and Urban Development (HUD), and operates under close HUD supervision. It exists independently of the City of New Haven, which is a municipality of the state of Connecticut.

Bonito purchased a 1991 Mercury Tracer at a fundraising auction in October 1990 for $9,500. He paid for the car, but never picked it up from the lot. Instead, three months later, DeMatteo, who had originally obtained the car from a local

Budget Rent-a-Car for the auction organizing committee, paid the tax and registration fee on the vehicle and took possession of it. Budget transferred the title directly to DeMatteo, though no Budget employee could remember receiving authorization from Bonito to do so. Bonito later told the police that he had bought the car at DeMatteo's request.

On January 25, 1991, DeMatteo executed a document captioned "Promissory Note." According to Bonito's statement to the police, the Note guaranteed repayment for the car. On its face, the Note described a repayment schedule for an interest free loan from Bonito in the amount of $8,200, with no mention of the car or description of the consideration given. DeMatteo was to pay monthly installments of $300 for one year starting on February 15, 1991, with the balance due in February 1992. Any default made the entire balance payable immediately and triggered a 10% interest rate. DeMatteo never made any payments on the Note. Nonetheless, Bonito did not bring suit to collect until June 30, 1992, when a corruption investigation was well under way.

The car allegedly was given primarily in connection with Bonito's attempted sale of Bonito Village to the Housing Authority. The government introduced evidence showing that Bonito had tried unsuccessfully to sell the property on the open market, and had tried but failed to sell the property to the Housing Authority in 1989. In 1990, DeMatteo was appointed to represent New Haven on a joint New Haven-Housing Authority committee established by the mayor to identify and approve sites for a few hundred units of low income housing to be purchased by the Housing Authority. The relationship between the two entities was one of cooperation; while final legal authority to choose sites may have remained with the Housing Authority, the mayor had issued a directive saying that his approval was required. During the months following the car transfer, DeMatteo allegedly used his position on the committee to advance the Housing Authority's purchase of Bonito Village in a number of ways: he set up meetings between Bonito and an aide to the Mayor concerning the deal; he became involved in the negotiations over price; and he contacted both New Haven and Housing Authority officials involved in the decision making process to try to push the deal through. Government evidence showed that DeMatteo frequently met with Bonito throughout this period of advocacy, during which DeMatteo's installment payments on the Note were falling due, and going unpaid. On April 4, 1991, the Housing Authority submitted a proposal to HUD to purchase Bonito Village for over $1.1 million. HUD rejected the deal, citing excessive price, the presence of hazardous conditions on the property, and problems with maintaining the property's one accessible road. . . .

II. Discussion

Bonito challenges his conviction and sentence on several grounds. We address them seriatim.

A. The Jury Charge

Bonito argues that the instructions were faulty in three basic respects. We note that he failed to lodge any objection to the instructions below, so we review for plain error only. A defendant satisfies this standard by showing that there was error, that it was clear or obvious, and that it affected a substantial right. None of his assigned errors meets this stringent test.

1. The Gratuity Claim

Bonito's first claim is that §666 applies only to bribery, and not gratuities. He argues that the court's instructions erroneously told the jury to convict if he corruptly gave DeMatteo a thing of value in connection with any business "past, present or future," and incorrectly defined the word "corrupt." These errors, he maintains, allowed conviction without requiring the jury to find the requisite mens rea for bribery.

In United States v. Crozier, 987 F.2d 893, 898-99 (2d Cir. 1993), we held that the former version of §666 applied to both illegal gratuities and bribes. Bonito argues that the new version does not because it no longer contains the language upon which the *Crozier* court relied for its holding. Fatal to his argument, however, is the fact that the deleted language has been replaced with language that is to the same effect. *Compare id.* at 899 (under the former version of §666, the payment must be "for or because of" the official conduct) *with* §666(a)(1)(B) (under the current version, the payment must be "to influence or reward" the official conduct). Thus, the current statute continues to cover payments made with intent to reward past official conduct, so long as the intent to reward is corrupt.

Bonito also argues that the term "corrupt" was inadequately explained to the jury. We disagree. The court specifically instructed that the government had to prove that Bonito acted with corrupt intent, which it defined as acting

> voluntarily and intentionally and with the purpose, at least in part, of accomplishing either an unlawful end result or a lawful end result by some unlawful method or means. A person acts corruptly, for example, when he gives or offers to give something of value intending to influence or reward a government agent in connection with his official duties.

Because it told the jury that the bribe had to be made "with the purpose . . . of accomplishing . . . an . . . end," this instruction made clear that the corrupt agreement, offer or payment must precede the official act to be influenced or rewarded. It then accurately tracked the statutory language as an example. No more was required. *Cf.* United States v. Medley, 913 F.2d 1248, 1261 (7th Cir. 1990) (failure to use the word "corrupt" not plain error where jury was told that defendant must have accepted or agreed to accept payment intending to be influenced or rewarded in his official conduct). . . .

The judgment of conviction and the sentence are affirmed.

NOTES AND QUESTIONS

1. Did the *Bonito* court read its own opinion? Doesn't its holding on the gratuity issue flatly contradict its holding with respect to the proper definition of corruption? With respect to the former, the court states that

§666 covers gratuities because the statute prohibits the rewarding of "past official conduct." It then upheld the jury instruction because the court made clear "that the bribe [sic?] must precede the official act to be influenced or rewarded." How can a reward for *past* conduct *precede* it?

2. Doesn't the *Medley* holding simply read the word "corruptly" out of the statute? Is that what Congress intended? If not, what should the definition of "corruptly" be?

PROBLEM 10-2

The following facts are derived from United States v. Thompson, 848 F.3d 877 (7th Cir. 2007):

Georgia Thompson is a procurement officer for the State of Wisconsin. She is overseeing the awarding of a state-wide contract for travel agency services. Under state law, the process is supposed to be purely merit-based, with interested companies making proposals that are scored by procurement officials. Included in the score are points for price, service, and quality of presentation.

At the end of the process, Omega World Travel receives the highest overall score; Adelman Travel comes in second. Thompson tells her colleagues that awarding east-coast based Omega would not go over well with her boss. She says that, for political reasons, Adelman had to get the contract. Accordingly, Thompson orders that the contract be rebid on a "best and final" basis, which Wisconsin law allows. This results in Adelman winning the contract. Three months later, Thompson receives a $1,000 raise.

The government charges Thompson with a violation of §666. On what theory could such charges rest? What elements would the government need to prove to convict? What are Thompson's best arguments for why the statute does not apply to her conduct? How would you decide the case?

III. EXTORTION UNDER COLOR OF OFFICIAL RIGHT, 18 U.S.C. §1951(a)(2)

A. Inducement and Quid Pro Quo Requirements

EVANS v. UNITED STATES

504 U.S. 255 (1992)

Justice STEVENS delivered the opinion of the Court.

We granted certiorari to resolve a conflict in the Circuits over the question whether an affirmative act of inducement by a public official, such as a demand, is an element of the offense of extortion "under color of official right" prohibited by the Hobbs Act, 18 U.S.C. §1951. We agree with the Court of Appeals for the Eleventh Circuit that it is not, and therefore affirm the judgment of the court below.

Petitioner was an elected member of the Board of Commissioners of DeKalb County, Georgia. During the period between March 1985 and October 1986, as part of an effort by the Federal Bureau of Investigation (FBI) to investigate allegations of public corruption in the Atlanta area, particularly in the area of rezonings of property, an FBI agent posing as a real estate developer talked on the telephone and met with petitioner on a number of occasions. Virtually all, if not all, of those conversations were initiated by the agent and most were recorded on tape or video. In those conversations, the agent sought petitioner's assistance in an effort to rezone a 25-acre tract of land for high-density residential use. On July 25, 1986, the agent handed petitioner cash totaling \$7,000 and a check, payable to petitioner's campaign, for \$1,000. Petitioner reported the check, but not the cash, on his state campaign-financing disclosure form; he also did not report the \$7,000 on his 1986 federal income tax return. Viewing the evidence in the light most favorable to the Government, as we must in light of the verdict, we assume that the jury found that petitioner accepted the cash knowing that it was intended to ensure that he would vote in favor of the rezoning application and that he would try to persuade his fellow commissioners to do likewise. Thus, although petitioner did not initiate the transaction, his acceptance of the bribe constituted an implicit promise to use his official position to serve the interests of the bribegiver.

In a two-count indictment, petitioner was charged with extortion in violation of 18 U.S.C. §1951 and with failure to report income in violation of 26 U.S.C. §7206(1). He was convicted by a jury on both counts. With respect to the extortion count, the trial judge gave the following instruction:

> "The defendant contends that the \$8,000 he received from agent Cormany was a campaign contribution. The solicitation of campaign contributions from any person is a necessary and permissible form of political activity on the part of persons who seek political office and persons who have been elected to political office. Thus, the acceptance by an elected official of a campaign contribution does not, in itself, constitute a violation of the Hobbs Act even though the donor has business pending before the official.
>
> "However, if a public official demands or accepts money in exchange for [a] specific requested exercise of his or her official power, such a demand or acceptance does constitute a violation of the Hobbs Act regardless of whether the payment is made in the form of a campaign contribution."

In affirming petitioner's conviction, the Court of Appeals noted that the instruction did not require the jury to find that petitioner had demanded or requested the money, or that he had conditioned the performance of any official act upon its receipt. The Court of Appeals held, however, that "passive acceptance of a benefit by a public official *is* sufficient to form the basis of a Hobbs Act violation if the official knows that he is being offered the payment in exchange for a specific requested exercise of his official power. The official need not take any specific action to induce the offering of the benefit." *Id.* (emphasis in original). . . .

II.

It is a familiar "maxim that a statutory term is generally presumed to have its common-law meaning." As we have explained: "[W]here Congress borrows terms of art in which are accumulated the legal tradition and meaning of centuries of practice, it presumably knows and adopts the cluster of ideas that were attached to each borrowed word in the body of learning from which it was taken and the meaning its use will convey to the judicial mind unless otherwise instructed. In such case, absence of contrary direction may be taken as satisfaction with widely accepted definitions, not as a departure from them." Morissette v. United States, 342 U.S. 246, 263 (1952).

At common law, extortion was an offense committed by a public official who took "by colour of his office" money that was not due to him for the performance of his official duties. A demand, or request, by the public official was not an element of the offense. Extortion by the public official was the rough equivalent of what we would now describe as "taking a bribe." It is clear that petitioner committed that offense. The question is whether the federal statute, insofar as it applies to official extortion, has narrowed the common-law definition. . . .

There is nothing in either the statutory text or the legislative history that could fairly be described as a "contrary direction," Morissette v. United States, 342 U.S., at 263, from Congress to narrow the scope of the offense. . . .

The two courts that have disagreed with the decision to apply the common-law definition have interpreted the word "induced" as requiring a wrongful use of official power that "begins with the public official, not with the gratuitous actions of another." If we had no common-law history to guide our interpretation of the statutory text, that reading would be plausible. For two reasons, however, we are convinced that it is incorrect.

First, we think the word "induced" is a part of the definition of the offense by the private individual, but not the offense by the public official. In the case of the private individual, the victim's consent must be "induced by wrongful use of actual or threatened force, violence or fear." In the case of the public official, however, there is no such requirement. The statute merely requires of the public official that he obtain "property from another, with his consent, . . . under color of official right." The use of the word "or" before "under color of official right" supports this reading.

Second, even if the statute were parsed so that the word "induced" applied to the public officeholder, we do not believe the word "induced" necessarily indicates that the transaction must be *initiated* by the recipient of the bribe. Many of the cases applying the majority rule have concluded that the wrongful acceptance of a bribe establishes all the inducement that the statute requires. They conclude that the coercive element is provided by the public office itself. And even the two courts that have adopted an inducement requirement for extortion under color of official right do not require proof that the inducement took the form of a threat or demand.

Petitioner argues that the jury charge with respect to extortion allowed the jury to convict him on the basis of the "passive acceptance of a contribution." He contends that the instruction . . . did not properly describe the *quid pro quo* requirement for conviction if the jury found that the payment was a campaign contribution.

We reject petitioner's criticism of the instruction, and conclude that it satisfies the *quid pro quo* requirement of McCormick v. United States, 500 U.S. 257 (1991), because the offense is completed at the time when the public official receives a payment in return for his agreement to perform specific official acts; fulfillment of the *quid pro quo* is not an element of the offense. We also reject petitioner's contention that an affirmative step is an element of the offense of extortion "under color of official right" and need be included in the instruction. As we explained above, our construction of the statute is informed by the common-law tradition from which the term of art was drawn and understood. We hold today that the Government need only show that a public official has obtained a payment to which he was not entitled, knowing that the payment was made in return for official acts.

Our conclusion is buttressed by the fact that so many other courts that have considered the issue over the last 20 years have interpreted the statute in the same way. Moreover, given the number of appellate court decisions, together with the fact that many of them have involved prosecutions of important officials well known in the political community, it is obvious that Congress is aware of the prevailing view that common-law extortion is proscribed by the Hobbs Act. The silence of the body that is empowered to give us a "contrary direction" if it does not want the common-law rule to survive is consistent with an application of the normal presumption identified in *Taylor* and *Morissette*. . . .

The judgment is affirmed.

[The concurring opinions of Justices O'Connor and Kennedy, and the dissenting opinion of Justice Thomas, are omitted.]

NOTES AND QUESTIONS

1. The Supreme Court's resolution of the inducement issue relies exclusively on methods of statutory interpretation. Is there also a policy argument behind criminalizing public officials' acceptance of money in return for official acts, even in the absence of an inducement?
2. This case could be framed as one in which two interpretations of a criminal statute are equally plausible, depending upon whether the word "induced" means "demanded" and whether, in any event, it applies to the phrase "color of official right." The Court clears up the ambiguity by interpreting the statute *against* the criminal defendant. What happened to the Rule of Lenity?
3. The *Evans* Court cites McCormick v. United States, 500 U.S. 257 (1991), for the proposition that, in campaign contribution cases, there must be a *quid pro quo* between the public official and the extortion "victim." As the Supreme Court explained in *McCormick*:

   > Serving constituents and supporting legislation that will benefit the district and individuals and groups therein is the everyday business of a legislator. It is also true that campaigns must be run and financed. Money is constantly being solicited on behalf of candidates, who run on platforms and who claim support on the basis of their views and what they intend to do or have done. Whatever ethical considerations and appearances may indicate, to hold that legislators commit the federal crime of extortion when they act for the benefit of constituents or support legislation furthering the interests of some of their constituents, shortly

> before or after campaign contributions are solicited and received from those beneficiaries, is an unrealistic assessment of what Congress could have meant by making it a crime to obtain property from another, with his consent, "under color of official right." To hold otherwise would open to prosecution not only conduct that has long been thought to be well within the law but also conduct that in a very real sense is unavoidable so long as election campaigns are financed by private contributions or expenditures, as they have been from the beginning of the Nation. It would require statutory language more explicit than the Hobbs Act contains to justify a contrary conclusion. *Cf.* United States v. Enmons, 410 U.S. 396 (1973).
>
> This is not to say that it is impossible for an elected official to commit extortion in the course of financing an election campaign. Political contributions are of course vulnerable if induced by the use of force, violence, or fear. The receipt of such contributions is also vulnerable under the Act as having been taken under color of official right, but only if the payments are made in return for an explicit promise or undertaking by the official to perform or not to perform an official act. In such situations the official asserts that his official conduct will be controlled by the terms of the promise or undertaking. This is the receipt of money by an elected official under color of official right within the meaning of the Hobbs Act.

Does it make sense to have a political system in which public officials can be captured by money interests as long as no specific quid pro quo is mentioned? Or is half a cure (this interpretation of the Hobbs Act) better than no cure at all?

4. Does a *mere candidate* for public office qualify as a "public official" who violates §1951(a) by accepting bribes in return for a promise of future action? *See* United States v. Manzo, __ F.3d ___, 2011 WL 538746 (3d. Cir. Feb 17, 2011) (not unless the candidate wins the election).

B. Interstate Commerce Requirement

UNITED STATES v. CARTER

530 F.3d 565 (7th Cir. 2008)

FLAUM, Circuit Judge.

Defendant Morris Carter, who served as the elected Recorder for Lake County, Indiana, was convicted for . . . extortion in violation of the Hobbs Act, 18 U.S.C. §1951(a). . . . Carter challenges the sufficiency of the evidence for his conviction[], claiming that the government failed to prove that his actions affected interstate commerce. . . .

I. Background

A. Defendant's Criminal Conduct

Carter was elected to two consecutive terms as the Lake County Recorder, with his second term concluding in December 2004. The acts of extortion for which Carter was convicted all occurred during the summer of his last year in this office. Central to the Government's case was the assistance it received from Peter Livas, an FBI informant. Livas owned three Indiana-based Subchapter S corporations—GIN Development, B & L Construction, and API Construction, Inc.—all of which were real estate rehab and development companies. Livas first came into contact with Carter through a mutual acquaintance, Javier Miranda, a subcontractor. . . .

The first audio recorded meeting between Carter, Livas, and Miranda occurred on June 2, 2004 in Gary, Indiana. . . . During this meeting, the three discussed two things Livas sought: a contractor's license for building in unincorporated areas of Lake County, and lists of homes in foreclosure that would be placed on sheriff's tax and commissioner's sales. With respect to the lists of homes, Carter maintained that he could get "the first look at the list" since he was "taking care of" a woman working in the department that had access to the lists. Livas was later told that these lists would cost $1,000.

Carter, Livas, and Miranda next met on June 11, 2004. This conversation was videotaped by the Government. At this meeting, Livas paid Carter $1,000, which Livas testified at trial was for the property lists, although Carter maintained that this money was for work he had already done as part of their consulting relationship. Carter then supplied Livas with the tax and commissioner's lists. . . .

The other matter discussed at the June 11 meeting was the county contractor's license Livas sought, the receipt of which partially depended upon passing a written test. Carter instructed Livas to report to Carter's office on June 16, 2004, where Carter would "hook up" Livas with a "guy," who Livas later found out was Jan Donald Allison, the person who administered the test and served as the Assistant Lake County Building Administrator. Carter instructed Livas not to discuss money with the "guy," but instructed Livas to bring $500 to Carter's office at the June 16 meeting.

The June 16 meeting at Carter's office was also videotaped. Once both Miranda and Livas had arrived, Carter started the meeting by warning them not to use his name when calling him, and pointed out a recent newspaper article discussing criminal charges related to tax sales in Lake County. Carter made clear that "things have to be done a certain way" because he "don't want nobody to get the wrong impression" and "ain't trying to go to jail." The three then turned to discussing [Livas's] contractor's license. With respect to the $500 Carter was charging Livas for the license (the license itself only cost $150), Livas explained that he would have the money after he got paid for one of his rehabbing projects. In response, Carter instructed Livas to pay him by giving the money to Miranda, who would then pass it along to Carter. Carter then called Allison and sent Livas and Miranda upstairs to meet with him, instructing Livas not to mention money with Allison. Carter had told Allison that Livas was a "friend" and asked if Allison could "help" Livas get a contractor's license. During the meeting with Allison, Livas received a license application, which he later completed on behalf of B & L Construction and submitted along with a $50 application fee drawn from B & L's bank account.

On June 24, a hidden camera captured Livas paying Miranda the $500 for the contractor's license, which Miranda then passed along in full to Carter. Approximately one month later, on July 23, Livas took the contractor's license exam. Livas intentionally failed the exam and Allison, when grading it, filled out a new examination with a passing score. Later that day, Allison went to Carter's office to tell Carter that Livas had passed the test. Carter later sent Allison a thank you card which included $100 in cash. . . .

II. Analysis

A. Sufficiency of the Evidence

. . . The Hobbs Act makes it a criminal offense to obstruct, delay, or affect interstate commerce by actual or attempted extortion. 18 U.S.C. §1951(a). "Extortion" under this Act is defined in part as "the obtaining of property from another, with his consent, . . . under color of official right." 18 U.S.C. §1951(b)(2). Carter contends that the Government failed to provide sufficient evidence to show that interstate commerce was affected. . . .

While the Hobbs Act requires that the extortion must have an effect on interstate commerce, this Court has repeatedly held that only a *de minimis* effect must be shown. United States v. Peterson, 236 F.3d 848, 851-52 (7th Cir. 2001). Furthermore, because the Hobbs Act also criminalizes attempted crimes, it is not required that there be an actual effect on interstate commerce; a showing that the conduct "had the potential to impact commerce" is sufficient. United States v. Re, 401 F.3d 828, 835 (7th Cir. 2005).

The Government in this case sought to satisfy the interstate commerce requirement through the "depletion of assets" theory. Under this method, it is sufficient for the Government to show that a business that customarily purchases items through interstate commerce had its assets depleted through the acts of extortion, thus limiting its ability to purchase goods in interstate commerce. There is no requirement that the business directly purchase its items through interstate commerce, rather, it is enough if the business purchases such items through a wholesaler or other intermediary. Moreover, it is of no consequence if the money used was the FBI's, rather than that of the business itself.

The applicability of the depletion of assets theory in this case largely turns on whether the Government provided sufficient evidence showing that [Livas's] three Indiana-based corporations purchased items through interstate commerce. To establish this link, the Government called Donald Cook as a witness, Store Manager of ICI Paints in Hammond, Indiana. Cook testified that ICI Paints purchases its paints from Huron, Ohio, and that Livas was a "contractor customer" at ICI Paints, having held an account at the store for more than three years. Additionally, Livas himself testified that as part of his work rehabbing homes, he purchased paint from ICI Paints. Nonetheless, Carter argues on appeal that there was no evidence presented to specifically show that Livas's *businesses* purchased the paint from ICI Paints, rather than Livas purchasing the supplies in his individual capacity. While this distinction was not specifically addressed in the trial testimony, given the standard of review for sufficiency of the evidence, this is certainly a reasonable inference for the jury to have drawn. Livas testified that he purchased paint from ICI Paints for his rehabbing projects, and Cook testified that he knew Livas as a "*contractor* customer." Given that Livas's corporations were all engaged in developing and rehabbing homes, a jury could reasonably conclude that the paint purchases were made for these businesses.

Carter additionally argues, however, that even if the paint purchases were made by Livas's corporations, there was insufficient evidence for a jury to conclude that the payments made to Carter would have depleted Livas's corporate assets, rather than his own personal accounts. This argument also fails. Again, to the extent this money was provided by the FBI, this is of no consequence to the depletion of assets theory's applicability. Turning specifically to the $1,000 Livas paid for the property lists, given that it is reasonable to infer that any property purchased through these lists would then be developed by Livas's companies, it is also reasonable to infer that the $1,000, if not provided by the FBI, would have come from Livas's corporate funds. Similarly, the contractor's license Livas received was for B & L Construction, one of Livas's companies, and the $500 Livas paid to Carter for this license came from his receipt of funds from a "side job." Here too, there was sufficient evidence for the jury to link the payment to a depletion of Livas's corporate assets. . . .

NOTES AND QUESTIONS

1. The court's not kidding when it states that a mere de minimis effect on interstate commerce satisfies the jurisdiction element of §1951(a), is it? Is this interpretation an abuse of federal power, allowing federal law enforcement to act in areas of exclusive state interest? Or, even if it is a stretch definitionally, does the interpretation at least serve legitimate federal policy goals?
2. Does a scheme whereby a local police commissioner embezzles the proceeds from travelers caught speeding on an interstate highway satisfy the Hobbs Act's interstate commerce requirement? *See* United States v. Mann, 493 F.3d 484 (5th Cir. 2007) (yes, but only if the traveler has an out-of-state destination).
3. The defendant's impact on interstate commerce is an element of Hobbs Act extortion; therefore, it must be specifically alleged in the indictment. Stirone v. United States, 361 U.S. 212 (1960).

PROBLEM 10-3

The facts that follow are largely derived from United States v. Abbey, 560 F.3d 513 (6th Cir. 2009). Some additional facts have been added for context and clarification. Analyze whether the defendant is liable under 18 U.S.C. §§201, 666, and 1951.

> Albert Louis-Blake Rizzo, a local land developer, implicated defendant Charles Abbey, Burton, Michigan, City Administrator, in statements he made to county prosecutors following the filing of perjury and fraud charges against him. Rizzo stated that he had given numerous bribes to various Burton public officials, including . . . Abbey. He further claimed that he gave Abbey a free subdivision lot in return for unspecified future official favors. These statements formed the basis of Abbey's federal indictment.

Trial testimony indicated that Abbey had been looking for a lot on which to build a new home. Rizzo had one, and, after some machinations (the lot was deeded to Rizzo's secretary and possible mistress, who then deeded it to Abbey) Abbey received it without any cash exchanging hands. Rizzo testified that, in giving Abbey the lot "for free," he had hoped that he would be considered favorably for future Burton real-estate developments. Abbey argued that the lot was not free because he paid various encumbrances to clear title after receiving it and that this equaled what he believed the land was worth. The value of the lot was $35,000; the encumbrances totaled $22,000.

The government did not introduce any evidence establishing that, when the lot was transferred, Rizzo and Abbey had an express agreement for specific official acts to be done in return for Rizzo's gift. The government did prove, however, that—after the transfer—Abbey used his influence and position to assist Rizzo with one particular land development called Pebble Creek. Roughly a year after the free lot transfer, Abbey proposed that the City of Burton issue municipal bonds to finance Pebble Creek's development. At that time, though Rizzo had already contracted to purchase Pebble Creek, the title change had not yet become public. Also, despite the fact that the sale was already final, it was the seller—and not Rizzo—who had publicly petitioned for a municipal bond issue. (The result was that no one in city government other than Abbey knew of Rizzo's ownership of Pebble Creek.) After bond financing was agreed upon, but without a formal bidding process, Rizzo was named general contractor to develop Pebble Creek (even though he owned it). The government characterized this arrangement as the City of Burton paying Rizzo with municipal bond financing to develop his own property.

An initial contracting fee was agreed upon but Rizzo protested. In response, officials substantially increased Rizzo's fee after he met with city officials, including Abbey. Thus, in 2003, Rizzo received an initial payment of $199,222.14 and, six months later, another payment of $124,166.93. The City of Burton characterized this latter fee as "Overhead and Profit" on the Pebble Creek project. Rizzo was allowed to handle the improvements and contracting as he wished and to submit his invoice at the end, rather than up front.

Both before and after the time period in question, Rizzo's land development company purchased materials from numerous manufacturers located in states other than Michigan.

chapter 11

Investigating White Collar Crime

I. INTRODUCTION: THE UNIQUE NATURE OF WHITE COLLAR CASES

White collar prosecutions are typically different in kind from their street crime counterparts. The investigation of street crime is usually reactive: An injurious event occurs, the police investigate and, if warranted, arrest one or more suspects, and the case is either pleaded out or goes to trial. As a general rule, there is no method of dealing with street criminals other than prosecution. They either face criminal charges or go free. As a result, district or state attorneys' offices do not have the luxury of "passing" on even insignificant cases brought to their attention. Everything that has a reasonable chance of being proven must be charged.

By way of contrast,

> [f]ar more white collar crime takes place in the United States than federal prosecutors have the resources to pursue. As a result, only a small percentage of this alleged criminal conduct is targeted for federal prosecution. A close look at the winnowing process reveals that prosecutors—and even criminal investigators—play a smaller role in selecting cases for criminal treatment than is commonly believed. Most of the time, white collar investigations are initiated, not by members of the Department of Justice, but by employees of regulatory agencies such as the SEC, IRS, or EPA. Often, the administrative investigation is triggered by a flag raised during a routine screening process. In other cases, the conduct would have escaped official notice (as most white collar crime probably does) but for a citizen's tip—for example, from an estranged spouse, nosy neighbor, or a disgruntled shareholder or employee.[1]
>
> Most white collar crime detected by the government is fully disposed of at the regulatory level. On occasion, however, agency personnel decide, for one reason or another, that the behavior of the putative defendant warrants a criminal

1. [If the tipster is working within the company he reports, he is often called a "whistle-blower."—Eds.]

> investigation. When lower level bureaucrats make such a determination, some form of supervisory review takes place to confirm that a referral for criminal treatment is appropriate. Thus, only a small percentage of white collar cases ever make it to the U.S. Attorney's doorstep.
>
> Even fewer cases get in the door. Due to their relative lack of resources, U.S. Attorney's Offices usually employ a set of intake guidelines to screen out potential cases that are too insignificant to warrant a federal prosecutor's attention. These guidelines vary from office to office, administration to administration, and crime to crime. They depend to some degree on priorities set by the Department of Justice as well as on local conditions. If an agency refers a matter that does not meet the guidelines, it is promptly declined. If the matter meets the guidelines, it is assigned to an Assistant United States Attorney for evaluation and further development.

Michael L. Seigel & Christopher Slobogin, *Prosecuting Martha: Federal Prosecutorial Power and the Need for a Law of Counts*, 109 Penn. St. L. Rev. 1107, 1109 (2005).

Once the U.S. Attorney's Office comes into a case, there is a subtle shift of power from the investigators to the prosecutors. Technically, the investigators are "in charge" of a case until the grand jury returns an indictment, with the prosecutor merely providing "legal support" to the investigation. After indictment, the roles reverse, and the investigators are tasked with assisting the AUSA in bringing the case to a successful conclusion. The reality, however, is usually different. Even during the investigative stage, the AUSA is quite powerful; after all, she is going to have the ultimate call on whether sufficient evidence has been obtained to bring charges. So, if she says the case cannot be won without a wiretap, a wiretap is typically sought. In the best-case scenario, and probably accounting for the majority of cases, the investigation and prosecution of a federal case features teamwork and trust among the investigators and prosecutors as it runs its course.

Once a white collar case lands in the lap of an AUSA, she and the agents must decide how best to structure the investigation. First thought is almost always given to secret, undercover operations. If the putative defendant is not yet aware of the investigation (or at least of its criminal nature), the investigative team will consider the feasibility of placing a body recorder on an undercover witness (or an undercover agent introduced into the situation) to capture the suspects committing criminal acts or to get them to incriminate themselves on tape. Especially in what would otherwise be a labor-intensive, document-laden fraud case, a successful undercover operation can help pare down considerably the quantity and complexity of proof needed for conviction. In all cases, having incriminating words coming from the defendant's own mouth is powerful evidence.

Sometimes an undercover case is not possible because the defendant is already aware of the investigation. (In such cases, trying to record the defendant "secretly" is likely to produce only self-serving exculpatory comments.) If so, the prosecutor will typically initiate a grand jury investigation. Technically an arm of the court, the federal grand jury is an extremely potent tool for prosecutors to employ. This is because it has the power to issue subpoenas for both witness testimony ("*ad testificandum*") and documents ("*duces tecum*"). If a witness fails or refuses to comply with a subpoena, the prosecutor can move the court to hold the witness in civil contempt. Also, the grand jury operates in secret,[2] for two reasons: first, to protect the integrity of an ongoing investigation and, second, to protect the reputation of individuals who are investigated by the grand jury but never charged.

Subpoenas can be directed both to a suspect (particularly a corporate suspect, for documents) or to third-party witnesses. Using a subpoena to obtain evidence from a suspect has its pros and cons. On the one hand, subpoenas (in contrast to search warrants) do not require a showing of probable cause, and a carefully crafted document subpoena can force the defendant to search for and identify the incriminating evidence among lots of irrelevant material, saving investigators countless hours of work. On the other hand, supplying the suspect with a subpoena can sometimes also provide him with a blueprint of the government's theory of the case. At the very least, it will tell him which documents to destroy behind the scenes if he is so inclined. For this reason, prosecutors try to size up the integrity of the suspect as well as opposing counsel—who can and often does step in to ensure that there is no spoliation of potential evidence—when determining if a subpoena is the best way to proceed.

The alternative to a subpoena, of course, is a search warrant. In addition to being an effective vehicle for the gathering of evidence, search warrants often constitute a "wake-up call" to a putative defendant, particularly a corporation. Unlike a subpoena, a search tends to create a huge stir both within company ranks (as employees witness "the feds" cart off truckloads of company documents and computers) and among the public (who will read about the search online or in the next day's newspapers). Thus, a search warrant can bring "heat" on a company and its employees to start contemplating a plea. The downsides to document searches from the prosecutor's perspective, however, are that (1) they raise some tricky Fourth Amendment issues; and (2) they may result in investigators needing to sort through company records for months—if not years.

This chapter focuses on legal issues surrounding the various tools federal agents and prosecutors use to investigate white collar crime. Given the diverse nature of white collar criminal investigations, the chapter should be considered introductory rather than comprehensive. Readers who desire more detail are advised to undertake an in-depth study of federal criminal procedure.

II. TOOLS AVAILABLE TO INVESTIGATE AND PROSECUTE WHITE COLLAR CASES

A. Whistleblowers

1. Sarbanes-Oxley Act

We have already seen one category of whistleblowers in Chapter 7: qui tam relators in false claims cases. After the technology bubble burst at the turn of the century, Congress passed the Sarbanes-Oxley Act, which empowered the SEC to set up a similar whistleblower framework to encourage knowledgeable corporate insiders

2. *See* Fed. R. Crim. P. 6(e).

to report suspected securities fraud.[3] Sarbanes-Oxley also fashioned a new role for corporate auditors and lawyers: It made them responsible for reporting criminal behavior up the chain of authority within the corporation and, if necessary, to the SEC.[4] Not surprisingly, neither profession welcomed its new role. In addition, as we will see, federal courts also have, to some degree, undermined it.

RICHARD E. MOBERLY, SARBANES-OXLEY'S STRUCTURAL MODEL TO ENCOURAGE CORPORATE WHISTLEBLOWERS

2006 B.Y.U. L. Rev. 1107 (2006)

Effective corporate monitoring benefits corporate shareholders and employees, as well as the general public. Traditional monitoring occurs through a variety of overlapping means. A board of directors monitors a corporation's professional management on behalf of the shareholders, who are too dispersed and diverse to monitor management themselves. Professional corporate "gatekeepers," such as auditors and attorneys, provide outside monitoring of corporations that protects shareholders as well as the investing public. Further, the government monitors companies through government inspectors and by requiring various corporate reports to be filed.

A primary advantage of each of these traditional corporate monitors is that they are external to the company. Independent directors purportedly provide dispassionate oversight of management. Gatekeepers have reputational concerns outside of their contractual relationship with corporations to inspire them to provide effective monitoring. When the government enforces laws and regulations, accountability to the public at large keeps regulators from being influenced by the corporation's own goals.

Despite the advantage of external monitors, however, their external position presents a significant challenge: monitoring the inner workings of a company from the outside. External monitors must rely upon information they receive from corporate executives to fulfill their monitoring function. Even under the best circumstances, this information is certain to be incomplete and self-serving due to information blocking and filtering by executives and subordinate managers. Under the worst circumstances, corporate executives may affirmatively hide or misrepresent information in order to evade a monitor's oversight. Thus, flow-of-information problems can arise because these traditional corporate monitors do not have enough information, and the information that they do have is often distorted and filtered. . . .

Corporate employees could be instrumental in solving the inherent information problems of traditional external corporate monitors. Employees have an information advantage over traditional corporate monitors because they have more complete knowledge regarding the inner workings of a large corporation. Financial misconduct on the scale that occurred during the recent corporate scandals necessarily requires the assistance of low- and mid-level employees because

3. *See* 18 U.S.C. §1514A (2002).
4. *See* 15 U.S.C. §7245 (2002).

of its scope and complexity. Additionally, even if an employee does not participate in the wrongdoing, corporate accounting and finance employees, who are trained in the proper methods of conducting business, should recognize when corporate actions fall outside legal boundaries. In fact, even with few corporate or legal incentives provided to whistleblowing employees, roughly one-third of fraud and other economic crimes against businesses are reported by whistleblowers. Given their central role in corporate activity, information from rank-and-file employees is essential to uncovering wrongdoing in a timely manner. Accordingly, effectively encouraging employees to disclose their knowledge of wrongdoing is a critical step in discovering fraud and other corporate misconduct.

1. The Few Who Succeeded

Unlike the traditional corporate monitors during the recent scandals, some corporate employees successfully identified and reported the corporate fraud, particularly at WorldCom, Kmart, and several mutual fund companies. These whistleblowing employees succeeded for two reasons. First and foremost, they simply spoke out and disclosed their inside knowledge regarding the corporate misconduct. Second, the successful whistleblowers spoke out effectively by disclosing their information directly to traditional corporate monitors rather than to corporate executives.

The most famous example of a successful individual employee whistleblower may be Cynthia Cooper, the former head of internal auditing at WorldCom. Cooper uncovered a wide variety of illegal accounting practices at WorldCom in 2002 and reported the illegalities directly to WorldCom's Board of Directors. The Board publicly admitted the financial manipulations and fired WorldCom's CFO Scott Sullivan, who allegedly orchestrated the fraud and tried to stop Cooper's investigation. By reporting Sullivan's misconduct directly to the Board, Cooper successfully avoided Sullivan's attempt to block disclosure of the fraud.

Other whistleblowers were similarly effective because they disclosed information directly to the government, another traditional corporate monitor. For example, separate, anonymous whistleblowers brought to light fraud at Symbol Technologies and Kmart when they sent letters to government regulators. More recently, the mutual fund industry paid hundreds of millions of dollars to settle charges arising out of allegations made by employee whistleblowers to government investigators regarding improper practices in the industry.

Alone, these whistleblowing employees could not stop corporate misconduct; but by providing information directly to traditional monitors, the employees circumvented the barriers corporate executives erected to shield external monitors from uncovering wrongdoing.

2. The Many Who Failed

The success of these few individual whistleblowers does not indicate that employee whistleblowing worked effectively. Rather, the small number of successful whistleblowers highlights the overall failure of corporate employees to promptly identify and report the wrongdoing occurring in these companies and others, such as Enron. Employees failed in two respects. First, employees failed to speak out;

and second, when they did, they failed to effectively report the misconduct they witnessed.

a. Failing to speak out. Unlike the few successful individual whistleblowers, the vast majority of knowledgeable employees failed to reveal wrongdoing because they were unable or unwilling to speak out. The misconduct at many of the corporations affected by recent scandals occurred over a period of several years. During this time, rank-and-file employees certainly participated, at some level, in the improper practices that led to the fraud. For example, when corporate executives at Enron made outlandish profit predictions, employees knew they must "gin . . . up" earnings and revenues to match the predictions. Thus, executives may have hatched accounting scams, but often their underlings were sent to do the dirty work of executing the plan despite the underlings' knowledge that such accounting was illegal. . . . Importantly, this failure to report is not unique to Enron. In fact, studies reveal that the majority of corporate employees who witnessed wrongdoing did not report it. Successful whistleblowers, by definition, overcame this inherent hesitation to speak out.

b. Executive blocking and filtering. A second flow-of-information failure occurred because of executive blocking and filtering of whistleblower reports, so that even if employees spoke out, their disclosures of wrongdoing were ineffective. Many whistleblowers reported information to corporate executives rather than to traditional corporate monitors, such as the board of directors. Executives subsequently prevented such information from reaching corporate monitors in order to protect the company from penalties and scandal. Such problems were apparent in many recent cases of corporate fraud. . . .

Even when employees avoided management's information blocking, corporate executives often filtered or slanted employee reports before the information reached the monitors. For example, Sherron Watkins, the famed Enron whistleblower, was unsuccessful in stopping Enron's fraud because the information she disclosed about misconduct at Enron was sanitized before it reached the Board of Directors. Watkins's error was that she complained to Enron's CEO, Kenneth Lay, rather than to the full Board of Directors. Lay subsequently hired the law firm of Vinson & Elkins to investigate the allegations—the very same law firm that approved many of the transactions about which Watkins complained. When the Board ultimately learned of Watkins's allegations, the report was whitewashed by Vinson & Elkins's conclusion that the transactions Watkins reported were proper. . . .

[The Sarbanes-Oxley Act] sought to improve corporate whistleblowing by making changes on two fronts. First, it provided for additional protection for whistleblowers against company retaliation. Second, it created new, specific channels (structures) through which whistleblowing would take place: from the employee to members of the corporation's board of directors. Although improvements over existing law, neither change is sufficient to encourage an optimal level of whistleblowing in securities fraud cases.

[First,] Sarbanes-Oxley's anti-retaliation provision suffers from significant limitations. The Act only protects employees of public corporations and only if such employees report violations of federal securities laws. Its statute of limitations period of ninety days is unreasonably short because it does not give employees enough time to deal with the after-effects of retaliation, consider their options, hire an attorney, and have the attorney investigate the merits of the case before filing a complaint. The remedies do not include any sort of punitive or liquidated damages to provide extra encouragement for whistleblowers. Finally, requiring employees to jump through OSHA's administrative hoops before bringing a claim in federal district court can be "cumbersome rather than expeditious, biased rather than expert, [and] ineffective rather than efficient."

These statutory restrictions likely contribute to the low success rates of employees who bring claims under Sarbanes-Oxley. According to OSHA, of the 784 cases resolved at the initial investigative level prior to September 30, 2006, OSHA investigators found only 17 to have merit, while another 106 cases settled. The percentage of meritorious and settled cases for Sarbanes-Oxley is slightly lower than the percentage of successful claimants for other whistleblower statutes administered by OSHA, perhaps suggesting that the "stronger" whistleblower protections of Sarbanes-Oxley do not result in more protections for whistleblowers. Moreover, of the 119 OSHA-level decisions that were appealed by April 28, 2005, the Department of Labor's Administrative Law Judges (ALJs) decided in favor of employees only 4 times, while another 19 settled.

The decisions issued by the ALJs further exacerbate Sarbanes-Oxley's statutory shortcomings. Procedural issues eviscerate claimants' cases. Several decisions dismissed complaints because the wrong corporate entity was named or because a corporation filed a registration statement with the SEC but withdrew it before it became effective, thus denying coverage under the Act. Claims have also been dismissed for missing the ninety-day statute of limitations window, including claims that missed the deadline by less than two weeks. ALJs routinely reject equitable tolling of the statute of limitations. ALJs dismissed other claims because employees made whistleblower disclosures about topics not strictly addressed by Sarbanes-Oxley, such as underpayment of employees, racial discrimination, or environmental violations, rather than securities fraud.

These problems with Sarbanes-Oxley's anti-retaliation provision reflect larger problems with the Anti-retaliation Model. First, anti-retaliation provisions in general do not provide realistic encouragement for employees to become corporate monitors because they focus on protection only after a disclosure is made. Surveys demonstrate that most employees are unaware of the protections they may (or may not) receive should they report wrongdoing. Moreover, even if an employee is aware that a disclosure might be protected, it is exceedingly difficult to determine the extent of any protection because there is little consistency among whistleblower statutes. Whether a whistleblower is protected depends upon the employee's state of residence, the industry in which the employee works, the type of misconduct reported, the type of retaliation endured, and, under some statutes, the willingness of administrative agencies to enforce the law. Sarbanes-Oxley only adds to this confusion because of its applicability to specific types of employees making specific kinds of disclosures.

The second failure of the Anti-retaliation Model is that it does not address the flow-of-information problems revealed by recent scandals. Even if whistleblowing occurs and is protected, the Model does not produce effective whistleblowing because anti-retaliation laws rarely indicate to whom an employee should make a disclosure. Therefore, although an employee may be protected from retaliation if she reports corporate misconduct to a supervisor or corporate executive, such information may never reach traditional corporate monitors because of executive blocking and filtering. As discussed above, in order for whistleblowers to act effectively as part of the corporate monitoring system, employees must be able to report misconduct to those with the authority and responsibility to end it rather than to a supervisor who has less incentive to relay potentially damaging information. The Anti-retaliation Model simply does not address this issue. . . .

C. Sarbanes-Oxley's Structural Model

Sarbanes-Oxley implements a new and improved version of the Structural Model. Under Section 301 of Sarbanes-Oxley, the audit committee of the board of directors of public companies must establish procedures for receiving complaints regarding accounting, internal accounting controls, or auditing matters. Additionally, the audit committee must be able to receive anonymous disclosures by employees regarding accounting or auditing matters. These requirements significantly alter the pre-scandal Structural Model in two ways.

First, Sarbanes-Oxley improves the legitimacy of the disclosure channel. It requires that independent directors on the board's audit committee receive whistleblower disclosures. This direct line to a traditional corporate monitor with the authority and responsibility to address whistleblower concerns enables whistleblowers to avoid the blocking and filtering from corporate executives. As recognized by the SEC when it amended its general rules and regulations by implementing Section 301, directors typically rely upon company managers to provide information, but managers "may not have the appropriate incentives to self-report all questionable practices." Accordingly, the SEC rightfully asserted that "[t]he establishment of formal procedures for receiving and handling complaints should serve to facilitate disclosures, encourage proper individual conduct and alert the audit committee to potential problems before they have serious consequences." Moreover, Sarbanes-Oxley provides for anonymous disclosures, which should improve the willingness of employees to come forward with information. Requiring a legitimate disclosure channel will unleash the true potential of the Structural Model and reveal its power to overcome the information problems that undermined employee effectiveness as corporate monitors during the corporate scandals. . . .

Second, for the first time in the private sector, the Structural Model is broadly imposed rather than merely encouraged. The Act instructs the Securities and Exchange Commission to direct the national securities exchanges and national securities associations (e.g., the New York Stock Exchange and the National Association of Securities Dealers) to prohibit the listing of any security of a company that is not in compliance with this requirement. The penalty for noncompliance with Section 301 and the corresponding listing rules is delisting, which can harm corporations and their shareholders significantly. . . .

GUYDEN v. AETNA, INC.
544 F.3d 376 (2d Cir. 2008)

Hall, Circuit Judge:

Plaintiff-Appellant Linda Guyden sued Defendant-Appellee Aetna, Inc. for terminating her employment in violation of the whistleblower protection provision of the Sarbanes-Oxley Act. Based on an arbitration clause in an agreement between Guyden and Aetna, the district court dismissed the complaint in favor of arbitration. On appeal, Guyden argues that her whistleblower claim under the Sarbanes-Oxley Act is nonarbitrable because arbitration is inconsistent with the purpose and structure of the Act. . . .

Background

I. Guyden's Relationship with Aetna

In January 2004, Guyden joined Aetna as its Director of Internal Audit. Soon after starting, Guyden alleges that she discovered that Aetna's Internal Audit Department was "ineffective, demoralized, and without independence or objectivity." According to Guyden's complaint, these problems were so serious that she believed that Aetna was in danger of violating the Sarbanes-Oxley Act of 2002 ("SOX"). SOX, and regulations promulgated thereunder, require corporate officers to report on the effectiveness of internal controls over financial reporting, and they prohibit those officers from characterizing the controls as "effective" if "there are one or more material weaknesses. . . ." 17 C.F.R. §229.308(a)(3). Guyden claims that she reasonably believed that Aetna was at risk of violating this regulation because (1) the Internal Audit Department was ineffective, and (2) that ineffectiveness, if left unaddressed, would become a material weakness in the company's internal controls.

Guyden responded by attempting to rehabilitate the Internal Audit Department. In need of more resources and greater authority to make changes within the Department, she also brought her concerns to the attention of senior management. During the course of her discussions with senior management about those concerns, Guyden and management clashed over a number of issues, including the possibility of an outside audit and Guyden's efforts to restructure her Department. Over the spring of 2004, Guyden sought assistance from Aetna's Chief Financial Officer, Alan Bennett. Guyden found Bennett's response wanting, and on August 16, 2004, she raised her concerns to Chairman and Chief Executive Officer John ("Jack") Rowe, President Ron Williams, and General Counsel Lou Briskman. About one week after this meeting, Bennett gave Guyden a "withering" performance review, despite having given her a positive review one month earlier.

Guyden eventually prevailed in hiring an outside auditor to review Aetna's internal controls. According to the complaint, senior management prevented the distribution of the outside auditor's report until September 30, 2004, one week after the Audit Committee had held its scheduled meeting. That Committee's next scheduled meeting was to take place on December 2, 2004. Guyden planned to discuss her concerns with the Committee at that meeting, where she also hoped to present the outside auditor's report.

Ten days before the meeting, however, Aetna terminated Guyden's employment. After being terminated, Guyden requested to speak at the Audit Committee meeting about her concerns. Senior management denied that request. Guyden believes that Aetna fired her to prevent her from bringing attention to deficiencies in Aetna's internal controls, and she points to management's refusal to allow her to speak at the Committee meeting as evidence of its desire to prevent further discussion of her concerns.

II. Guyden's Lawsuit Against Aetna

A. Guyden's Complaint

Within ninety days of Aetna's termination of her employment, Guyden filed an administrative complaint with the Secretary of Labor alleging that Aetna's action had violated the SOX whistleblower protection provision, 18 U.S.C. §1514A. Section 1514A prohibits public companies from "discharg[ing] . . . an employee . . . because of any lawful act done by the employee . . . to provide information . . . regarding any conduct which the employee reasonably believes constitutes a violation of [federal securities law], when the information or assistance is provided to . . . a person with supervisory authority over the employee. . . ." 18 U.S.C. §1514A(a)(1)(C). An aggrieved employee may file an administrative complaint with the Secretary of Labor, and if the Secretary takes no action on the complaint within 180 days, the employee may bring an action in federal district court. Id. §1514A(b)(1). When the Secretary did not act on Guyden's administrative complaint within 180 days, she filed this action in the district court[, which] dismissed the complaint in favor of arbitration.

Guyden appeals.

Discussion

. . . A court determining whether to stay proceedings pending arbitration must resolve four issues:

> first, it must determine whether the parties agreed to arbitrate; second, it must determine the scope of that agreement; third, if federal statutory claims are asserted, it must consider whether Congress intended those claims to be nonarbitrable; and fourth, if the court concludes that some, but not all, of the claims in the case are arbitrable, it must then decide whether to stay the balance of the proceedings pending arbitration.

Guyden does not challenge the existence of the arbitration agreement or that it covers most employment-related disputes. Her appeal concerns the third prong: "whether Congress intended [SOX whistleblower] claims to be nonarbitrable." She asserts that Congress did so intend. . . .

Guyden urges this Court to find an "inherent conflict" between SOX's underlying purposes and arbitration as a mechanism for resolving related disputes. The premise of Guyden's inherent conflict argument is that the SOX whistleblower provision has a public purpose in addition to its private compensatory function. In Guyden's view, an individual who brings a SOX whistleblower claim is acting as a private attorney general, and the resulting litigation serves as a vehicle for transmitting to the public information about the corporation's fraudulent activity. Her argument thus connects the SOX whistleblower provision with the policies of SOX more generally, the purpose of which is to enforce the accountability and transparency needed for well-functioning capital markets. In other words, Guyden sees her lawsuit against Aetna as having twin objectives: first, to compensate Guyden for her own injuries; and second, "to bring serious auditing and accounting issues to the attention of Defendant's Board of Directors, shareholders, and . . . the investing public." . . .

Our review of the legislative history of the SOX whistleblower provision confirms that the . . . primary purpose of the statute is to provide a private remedy for the aggrieved employee, not to publicize alleged corporate misconduct. Although Guyden correctly points out that the broad purpose of the Sarbanes-Oxley Act is to strengthen the integrity of capital markets, the whistleblower provision in particular fills a far narrower gap in the law – it protects "employees when they take lawful acts to disclose information or otherwise assist . . . in detecting and stopping actions which they reasonably believe to be fraudulent." S. Rep. No. 107-146, at pt. III. That protection, designed to "make [the] victim whole," takes the form of remedies that include "both reinstatement of the whistleblower, backpay, and compensatory damages. . . ." *Id.* Remedies that "make [the] victim whole" protect and compensate whistleblowers, but they do little to publicize the conduct of the corporate defendant. Tellingly, and further undermining Guyden's argument that the public purpose of SOX should preclude arbitration, both Houses of Congress, acting separately, rejected versions of SOX that would have prohibited mandatory arbitration of whistleblower claims. . . .

We recognize that arbitration is more private than litigation and that Guyden will not have the same opportunity to expose publicly Aetna's alleged wrongdoing. . . . [H]owever, the loss of a public forum in which to air allegations of fraud does not undermine the statutory purpose of a whistleblower protection provision.

Because we find no inherent conflict between the purpose of the SOX whistleblower protection provision and mandatory arbitration, we hold that such claims are arbitrable. . . .

NOTES AND QUESTIONS

1. According to Moberly, what are the anti-retaliatory measures put into place by the Sarbanes-Oxley Act? What are the structural measures? What improvements over prior law does he see from each set of measures? What are the deficiencies?
2. Think back to the civil qui tam provisions of the False Claims Act. They provide a whistleblower with up to 25 percent of any recovery of money paid by the government due to fraud, which has led to a huge number of qui tam lawsuits. Why did Sarbanes-Oxley fail to do the same? Is it surprising that, without such a carrot, most potential whistleblowers look the other way?

3. Do you think the *Guyden* court is correct in its conclusion that the Sarbanes-Oxley whistleblower remedy is primarily a private one for compensation, or is it equally designed to further the public policy of exposing corporate fraud to the SEC and to the investing public (by encouraging whistleblowers)? Does the fact that the Sarbanes-Oxley Act also features a provision making it a felony to retaliate against whistleblowers, 18 U.S.C. §1513(e), bear on this issue? If so, how?
4. Is the prospect of exposing her company's fraud the only reason why someone like Guyden would want to have her case heard in federal court? Could it be that she also perceives that her claim of retaliation based on SOX would receive more careful attention by a federal judge as opposed to an industry arbitrator? If this is so, why did Guyden fail to raise this issue in her appeal?

2. Dodd-Frank Act

Following the near-collapse of the international banking system in 2008, Congress passed a new round of regulations related to banking and investing in the landmark legislation called the Dodd-Frank Act.[5] This legislation, without question the most comprehensive attempt to regulate the financial system since the Depression-era 1933 and 1934 Acts, sought—among many other things—to enhance the whistleblowing scheme devised by Sarbanes-Oxley. As the Dodd-Frank Act goes into effect, it remains to be seen whether the incentives provided for whistleblowing hit the mark or, as some are predicting, cause corporate chaos.

ROBERT B. FITZPATRICK, PLLC, ABA SECTION OF LABOR AND EMPLOYMENT LAW FEDERAL LABOR STANDARDS LEGISLATION COMMITTEE 2011 MIDWINTER MEETING REPORT: SUBCOMMITTEE ON THE SARBANES-OXLEY ACT OF 2002

Mar. 31 – Apr. 2, 2011

I. Introduction

On July 21, 2010, President Obama signed into law the Dodd-Frank Wall Street Reform and Consumer Protection Act ("Dodd-Frank"), Pub. L. 111-203. Dodd-Frank, *inter alia*, significantly expands SOX's civil whistleblower protections and creates additional anti-retaliation requirements for employers. The Dodd-Frank amendments . . . reflect Congress's response to criticism that [SOX] has been interpreted in an unduly restrictive, pro-employer manner which has limited whistleblowers' ability to have their claims heard on the merits. . . .

Section 922 of the Dodd-Frank Act established new whistleblower protections, including a bounty system which allows the SEC . . . to compensate whistleblowers. . . . Furthermore, Title X of Dodd-Frank creates the Bureau of Consumer

5. Dodd-Frank Wall Street Reform and Consumer Protection Act, Pub. L. No. 111-203, §§929P(b), 929Y, 124 Stat. 1376 (July 21, 2010).

Financial Protection, which is empowered to regulate the offering and provision of consumer financial products and services. The Bureau is granted certain enforcement powers, including the authority to investigate and commence civil actions. Section 1057 prohibits retaliation against financial services employees who engage in protected conduct, which includes: (1) providing an employer, the Bureau, or any state, local of federal agency any information the employee reasonably believes to be a violation of Title X; (2) participating in Bureau proceedings; (3) filing any proceeding "under any federal consumer financial law"; and (4) objecting to, or refusing to participate in, any activity, policy, practice, or assigned task that the employee reasonably believes to be in violation of any law, rule, order, standard or prohibition subject to the Bureau's jurisdiction. Complaints must be filed with the [Department of Labor (DOL)] within 180 days of the alleged violation. The SEC is in the process of promulgating regulations interpreting the Dodd-Frank whistleblower provisions.

II. Overview of Sox's [and Dodd-Frank's] Civil Whistleblower Provision[s]

Under Section 806 [of SOX], publicly traded companies may not "discharge, demote, suspend, threaten, harass or in any other manner discriminate against an employee in the terms and conditions of employment" because of any protected whistle blowing activity. 18 U.S.C. §1514A(a). This Section applies to companies with a class of securities registered under Section 12 of the Securities Exchange Act of 1934 . . . or that are required to file reports under Section 15(d) of the Securities Exchange Act of 1934 . . . , or to any officer, employee, contractor, subcontractor, or agent of such companies. In 2010, Dodd-Frank amended SOX to cover "any subsidiary or affiliate whose financial information is included in the consolidated financial statements of such company." . . .

A broad range of activities relating to corporate fraud is protected under [SOX], including providing information to federal agencies, Congress or internally within the company, and filing, causing to be filed, testifying, participating in, or assisting in proceedings. Protected activity involves providing information that the employee "reasonably believes" constitutes a violation of federal mail, wire, bank or securities fraud . . . , or a violation of any SEC rule or other provision of federal law relating to fraud against shareholders. . . .

Dodd-Frank added [special] protections for whistleblowers who complain to the SEC. Specifically, [the new Act] allows an employee who complains to the SEC to file a claim directly in federal court, bypassing the current DOL administrative process. Unlike [its SOX counterpart], this provision does not contain a reasonable belief standard. Dodd-Frank also provides for double back-pay damages to prevailing whistleblowers in such cases, with a statute of limitations period of six years from the date of the violation or three years from the date the employee discovers the violation (but no more than ten years from the date of violation). Moreover, Section 922 allows the SEC, in any action involving sanctions in excess of $1 million, to compensate whistleblowers with up to 30% but not less than 10% of the amount of the sanctions. The amounts paid are within the sole discretion of the SEC, subject to judicial review.

Employees of covered companies who believe they have been subjected to adverse action for having engaged in protected activity may file a complaint with the Secretary of Labor within 180 days of the alleged retaliatory act. Prior to Dodd-Frank, this time period was limited to 90 days.... [In addition, under Dodd-Frank,] a claimant proceeding in district court will be ... entitled to a jury trial....

NOTES AND QUESTIONS

1. It took only eight years—from the enactment of SOX to the enactment of Dodd-Frank—before Congress added a carrot (and a whopping one at that!) to encourage whistleblowing in the financial industry. It took only two *days* after the new statute's enactment for the first Dodd-Frank whistleblower claim to be filed. *See* Yin Wilczek, *SEC Already Receiving Whistleblower Claims; More Coming in Near Future, Law Firms Say*, BNA Securities Regulation & Law Report, 42 SRLR 1662 (Sept. 6, 2010). Though it is too soon to tell what the long-term impact of the Dodd-Frank provisions will be, if experience with qui tams is any guide, there will soon be an entire legal field dedicated to D-F whistleblower actions.
2. Naysayers point out that Dodd-Frank has with one stroke wiped out the benefit of Sarbanes-Oxley's structural reform. Under the latter scheme, whistleblowers are directed to report company fraud ultimately to the board of directors or the audit committee, thereby enabling the company to investigate and remedy the fraud on its own. Now, under Dodd-Frank, the whistleblower will have a very strong incentive to go directly to the SEC, cutting the company out of the equation. Critics argue that this is inefficient because (1) companies are in a much better position than outside government regulators to ferret out internal crime and fix the underlying problems; and (2) Dodd-Frank claims will soon overwhelm an already very busy SEC. What do you think?
3. The SEC is in the process of receiving public comment on proposed rules designed to implement the new whistleblower provisions. In the introductory comments to the rules, it notes the structural discordance between Sarbanes-Oxley and Dodd-Frank and claims the regulations have taken this into account:

> In fashioning these proposed rules, the Commission has considered and weighed a number of potentially competing interests that are presented in implementing the statute. Among them was the potential for the monetary incentives provided to whistleblowers by Section 21F of the Exchange Act to reduce the effectiveness of a company's existing compliance, legal, audit and similar internal processes for investigating and responding to potential violations of the federal securities laws. With this possible tension in mind, we have included provisions in the proposed rules intended not to discourage whistleblowers who work for companies that have robust compliance programs to first report the violation to appropriate company personnel, while at the same time preserving the whistleblower's status

as an original source of the information and eligibility for an award. At the same time, the proposed rules would not prohibit a whistleblower in a compliance function from reporting information to the Commission where the company did not provide the information to the Commission within a reasonable time or acted in bad faith.[6]

4. Other critics of the Dodd-Frank whistleblower provisions claim that they will lead to innumerable allegations against companies that are later deemed to be false. The U.S. Attorney for the Southern District of New York tried to counter this fear by promising that whistleblowers who provide false information will be prosecuted. *See* Dena Aubin, *Prosecutor Warns of Whistleblowers "Run Amok,"* REUTERS, available at http://www.reuters.com/article/2010/11/12/us-whistleblowers-idUSTRE6AB4U720101112 (last visited Nov. 12, 2010). Do you think this promise is likely to be fulfilled? Why or why not?

B. Gatekeepers

SUNG HUI KIM, NAKED SELF-INTEREST? WHY THE LEGAL PROFESSION RESISTS GATEKEEPING

63 Fla. L. Rev. 129 (2011)

The last major scandal plagued with allegations of lawyer misconduct is now known by the single word "Enron." When that disaster was brought to light, Congress responded swiftly by enacting §307 of the Sarbanes-Oxley Act of 2002 ("Sarbanes-Oxley §307" or just "§307"),[7] the "first federal statute in American history to regulate lawyers directly and broadly." The statute gave to the Securities and Exchange Commission (SEC) an explicit, sweeping mandate to establish "minimum standards of professional conduct" for lawyers "appearing and practicing before the Commission in any way in the representation of [public] issuers." By enacting Sarbanes-Oxley §307, Congress formally recognized lawyers' role as gatekeepers"—"private intermediaries who can prevent harm to the securities markets by disrupting the misconduct of their client representatives."

But, as any lawyer then practicing recalls, the legal profession was horrified by this pro-regulatory turn of events. Just as it had done in previous battles with the SEC over lawyers' gatekeeping obligations, the organized bar aggressively lobbied against the passage of §307. When those efforts failed, lawyers circled the wagons and fought against the SEC's rulemaking to implement §307. The bar took special aim at the SEC's two "noisy withdrawal" proposals. These proposals (1) required lawyers to resign if intra-corporate remedies to rectify material law violations proved to be futile and (2) required lawyers (or, alternatively, companies) to report lawyers' withdrawal "based on professional considerations" to the SEC. (Auditors

6. Proposed Rules for Implementing the Whistleblower Provisions of Section 21F of the Securities Exchange Act of 1934, Securities and Exchange Commission, available at http://www.sec.gov/rules/proposed/2010/34-63237.pdf.

7. [15 U.S.C. §7245—EDS.]

have been subject to a similar reporting obligation since 1995.) Just as predictably, the SEC backed down from its noisy withdrawal proposals, making both the notice to the SEC and the lawyer's withdrawal entirely discretionary.

At the core of the bar's opposition was hostility to the general notion of "lawyer as gatekeeper"—that lawyers should have any obligations to the public or the capital markets that could put them at odds with their client representatives. Although the bar might tolerate lawyers as attack dogs (at least unofficially in advertisements and beauty contests), it rejects both officially and unofficially the idea of lawyers as watchdogs. Official comments in the SEC administrative rulemaking process complained that the proposed rules could "eviscerate the attorney's traditional role as advocate, confidant and advisor" and "risk destroying the trust and confidence many issuers have up to now placed in their legal counsel." They worried that the proposals would "drive a wedge between client and the counsel who advised it on a matter" and decried that "the Commission would be using the attorney as the Commission's eyes and ears to build a case against the client." Lawyers maintained that by "requiring attorneys to police and pass judgment on their clients," lawyers for corporations would slide down the slippery slope from trusted counselor to policeman.

Since the SEC's retraction of its noisy withdrawal proposals, much of the furor over gatekeeping has waned. But the battles are far from over. After the regulations promulgated under Sarbanes-Oxley §307 were enacted, the American Bar Association (ABA) published a carefully crafted statement asserting that "lawyers for the corporation . . . are not 'gatekeepers' of corporate responsibility in the same fashion as public accounting firms." Also, the Washington and California state bar associations openly flouted the SEC's authority to adopt its regulations (notwithstanding §307). Still today, the bar continues to denounce the SEC for targeting lawyers who are merely "engaged in what lawyers do," as if to suggest that lawyers should be immune from liability so long as their complicity is mediated through "legal services."

And Sarbanes-Oxley §307 may turn out to be just a prelude of things to come. As recently as July 30, 2009, Senator Arlen Specter of Pennsylvania introduced a bill that would effectively reverse a 1994 U.S. Supreme Court decision that shielded law firms, accounting firms, and investment banks from investor lawsuits alleging aiding and abetting violations of §10(b) and Rule 10b-5, the principal anti-fraud provisions of the Securities Exchange Act of 1934.[35] And in a brief filed on August 6, 2009, the SEC argued that law firms should be held primarily liable for knowingly providing false and misleading statements in companies' public disclosures. . . . [L]awyers' complicity in corporate securities fraud remains a timely, if understudied, issue.

[Here's] a fundamental question: *why* does the legal profession so stridently resist gatekeeping? After all, aren't lawyers supposed to be "officers of the legal system," as touted by the ABA Model Rules of Professional Conduct? Or, even if you reject that characterization, *why* do lawyers resist duties that only require them to avert gross harm to their corporate clients? We are now too familiar with the chaos unleashed by the massive frauds at Enron, WorldCom, Refco, Bernard L. Madoff Investment Securities, and Bear Stearns Asset Management Fund. So, why does the legal profession resist measures designed to avert potential financial calamity?

35. Cent. Bank of Denver, N.A. v. First Interstate Bank of Denver, N.A., 511 U.S. 164, 191 (1994).

For many readers, the answer will be obvious: "It's the money, stupid!" Or in more scholar-speak, "It's about economic self-interest." Indeed, no lawyer wants to expand her financial liability with duties backed by civil or administrative sanction, and no profession wants to be shackled with additional rules that raise the costs of legal practice. On the one hand, economic self-interest is an undeniable force fueling the bar's opposition to gatekeeping. On the other hand, the characterization of naked rent-seeking behavior misses crucial subtleties and portrays a degree of "naïve cynicism"—the inclination to think that others are more prone to bias than oneself could ever be. While economic self-interest plays an important role here, it exerts a more complex influence than conventionally understood. Moreover, there are motivations other than self-interest that loom large in the bar's resistance to gatekeeping. And these complexities should inform our legal and social responses.

[There are] two other psychological forces that influence the bar's motivations in subtle ways. First, lawyers overwhelmingly tend to internalize the antiregulatory attitudes held by those senior corporate managers who typically serve as lawyers' de facto clients. Although lawyers' self-interest is a factor here as well, cognitive dissonance mechanisms more robustly explain this internalization phenomenon. Second, lawyers are inclined to be indifferent to (if not downright dismissive about) the interests of their clients' shareholders who stand to be the greatest beneficiaries of lawyer gatekeeping. Again, I do not deny the likely contributions of lawyers' self-interest here. But . . . the abstractness of shareholders greatly hinders lawyers' ability to empathize with these particular victims of corporate malfeasance. . . .

NOTES AND QUESTIONS

1. Kim's article provides only a taste of the firestorm that broke out when Congress and the SEC took the position that lawyers should report ongoing fraud publicly if they failed to stop it internally. The ABA fiercely opposed the idea, claiming that it struck at the heart of the attorney-client privilege. Does the privilege cover ongoing criminal behavior of a client who is using his lawyer's advice to further his illegal activity?
2. One of the arguments that the ABA made, noted in Kim's piece, is that if attorneys "rat" on their clients, they will be cut out of important transactions engaged in by the company, making criminal activity even more rampant. Does this claim hold up under close scrutiny? Can a corporation accomplish complex transactions without its attorneys' assistance? In any event, is it really good for the profession to have its members constantly in the center of major fraud cases?
3. Kim notes that corporate lawyers often forget that they are representing the shareholders, not the individual officers with whom they work. The argument can be taken a step further: Corporate lawyers often become social equals and friends with the officers, sharing family events, golf outings, and so on. Could this be another reason why corporate lawyers find the idea of being gatekeepers against corporate crime so horrifying?

C. Undercover Operations

As noted in the introduction, prosecutors and investigative agents will almost always consider whether they can gather evidence in a surreptitious manner if the targets of the investigation are not aware of its existence. The theory behind this approach is that the most convincing proof of a defendant's guilt is a video- or audio-recording of him in the act of committing the crime. Undercover operations, however, carry with them concomitant risks, including the possibility of being discovered by the defendant (and thus "blowing" the investigation) or failing to limit the governmental intrusion into the defendant's sphere of privacy in accordance with the strictures of the U.S. Constitution and relevant statutory provisions.

The cases below are designed to give the reader some basic insight into three undercover techniques used in white collar cases: (1) the use of informant/witnesses who are willing to wear a body recorder and "consensually monitor" conversations with the defendant; (2) the use of video surveillance of suspects; and (3) the use of wiretaps, i.e., recording devices placed in a suspect's home, place of business, or on his telephone lines without the knowledge or consent of any party to the intercepted conversations.

1. Consensual Monitoring

UNITED STATES v. CACERES
440 U.S. 741 (1979)

Mr. Justice STEVENS delivered the opinion of the Court.

The question we granted certiorari to decide is whether evidence obtained in violation of Internal Revenue Service (IRS) regulations may be admitted at the criminal trial of a taxpayer accused of bribing an IRS agent.

Unbeknown to respondent, three of his face-to-face conversations with IRS Agent Yee were monitored by means of a radio transmitter concealed on Yee's person. Respondent moved to suppress tape recordings of the three conversations on the ground that the authorizations required by IRS regulations had not been secured. The District Court granted the motion. The Court of Appeals for the Ninth Circuit reversed as to the third tape; it concluded that adequate authorization had been obtained. As to the first two tapes, however, the Court of Appeals agreed with the District Court both that the IRS regulations had not been followed and that exclusion of the recordings was therefore required. It is the latter conclusion that is at issue here.

The Government argues that exclusion of probative evidence in a criminal trial is an inappropriate sanction for violation of an executive department's regulations. In this case, moreover, it argues that suppression is especially inappropriate because the violation of the regulation was neither deliberate nor prejudicial, and did not affect any constitutional or statutory rights. We agree that suppression should not have been ordered in this case, and therefore reverse the judgment of the Court of Appeals. . . .

On March 14, 1974, Agent Yee met with respondent and his wife in connection with an audit of their 1971 income tax returns. After Mrs. Caceres left the meeting, respondent offered Yee a "personal settlement" of $500 in exchange for a favorable resolution of the audit. When he returned to the IRS office, Yee reported the offer to his superiors and prepared an affidavit describing it.

On January 27, 1975, Yee had a meeting with respondent that was not recorded. [T]he meeting proceeded in two stages. First, he discussed his calculations with respondent, Mrs. Caceres, and their accountant. When respondent and his wife asked for an additional week to check their records, Yee told them it would be necessary to sign an extension because the statute of limitations would otherwise expire soon. Respondent stated that he would have to consult his attorney before signing any extension, and would call Yee with his decision later that day.

Yee then left the office to return to his car. He was followed by respondent, who revived the subject of a "personal settlement." This time, respondent indicated that he had $500 that he would give Yee immediately, with an additional $500 to be paid when the matter was finally settled. Yee refused the offer, but at respondent's insistence, eventually stated that he might consider it.

In subsequent conversations initiated by Agent Yee, all of which were monitored, respondent indicated that he was not prepared for another meeting with Yee. Finally, in a conversation on January 30 at 5:15 P.M., respondent agreed to a meeting the following day at 2 P.M. At 8:15 A.M. on the 31st, the Regional Inspector in San Francisco telephoned the Director of Internal Security in Washington and obtained emergency approval for the use of electronic equipment to monitor the meeting that afternoon. On the same day, a written request for authority to monitor face-to-face conversations for a period of 30 days was initiated and, in due course, forwarded to Washington for submission to the Department of Justice.

At the meeting on the 31st, respondent gave Yee $500 and promised to give him an additional $500 when he received a notice from IRS showing his deficiency at an amount upon which he and Yee had agreed. As in all his future meetings with respondent, Yee wore a concealed radio transmitter which allowed other agents to monitor and record their conversation.

Yee next called respondent on February 5 and arranged a meeting for the next day to review the audit agreement. Because the Department of Justice had not yet acted on, or perhaps even received, the request for a 30-day authorization, the Regional Inspector again requested and obtained emergency approval to monitor the meeting with respondent. At the February 6 meeting, respondent renewed his promise to pay an additional $500 in connection with the 1971 return, and also offered Yee another $2,000 for help in settling his 1973 and 1974 returns.

On February 11, a Deputy Assistant Attorney General approved the request for authority to monitor Yee's conversations with respondent for 30 days. The approval was received in time to cover a meeting held that day at which Yee was paid the additional $500. Because the 30-day period did not commence until February 11, however, no approval from the Department of Justice was ever obtained for the earlier monitorings of January 31 and February 6. . . .

III.

A court's duty to enforce an agency regulation is most evident when compliance with the regulation is mandated by the Constitution or federal law. . . .

In this case, however . . . , the agency was not required by the Constitution or by statute to adopt any particular procedures or rules before engaging in consensual monitoring and recording. While Title III of the Omnibus Crime Control and Safe Streets Act of 1968, 18 U.S.C. §2510 *et seq.*, regulates electronic surveillance conducted without the consent of either party to a conversation, federal statutes impose no restrictions on recording a conversation with the consent of one of the conversants.

Nor does the Constitution protect the privacy of individuals in respondent's position. In Lopez v. United States, 373 U.S. 427, 439 (1963), we held that the Fourth Amendment provided no protection to an individual against the recording of his statements by the IRS agent to whom he was speaking. In doing so, we repudiated any suggestion that the defendant had a "constitutional right to rely on possible flaws in the agent's memory, or to challenge the agent's credibility without being beset by corroborating evidence that is not susceptible of impeachment," concluding instead that "the risk that petitioner took in offering a bribe to [the IRS agent] fairly included the risk that the offer would be accurately reproduced in court, whether by faultless memory or mechanical recording." The same analysis was applied in United States v. White, 401 U.S. 745 (1971), to consensual monitoring and recording by means of a transmitter concealed on an informant's person, even though the defendant did not know that he was speaking with a Government agent:

> "Concededly a police agent who conceals his police connections may write down for official use his conversations with a defendant and testify concerning them, without a warrant authorizing his encounters with the defendant and without otherwise violating the latter's Fourth Amendment rights. For constitutional purposes, no different result is required if the agent instead of immediately reporting and transcribing his conversations with defendant, either (1) simultaneously records them with electronic equipment which he is carrying on his person; or (2) carries radio equipment which simultaneously transmits the conversations either to recording equipment located elsewhere or to other agents monitoring the transmitting frequency. If the conduct and revelations of an agent operating without electronic equipment do not invade the defendant's constitutionally justifiable expectations of privacy, neither does a simultaneous recording of the same conversations made by the agent or by others from transmissions received from the agent to whom the defendant is talking and whose trustworthiness the defendant necessarily risks."

Our decisions in *Lopez* and *White* demonstrate that the IRS was not required by the Constitution to adopt these regulations. It is equally clear that the violations of agency regulations disclosed by this record do not raise any constitutional questions. . . .

IV.

Respondent argues that the regulations concerning electronic eavesdropping, even though not required by the Constitution or by statute, are of such importance in safeguarding the privacy of the citizenry that a rigid exclusionary rule should be applied to all evidence obtained in violation of any of their provisions. We do not doubt the importance of these rules. Nevertheless, without pausing to evaluate the Government's challenge to our power to do so, we decline to adopt any rigid rule requiring federal courts to exclude any evidence obtained as a result of a violation of these rules.

Regulations governing the conduct of criminal investigations are generally considered desirable, and may well provide more valuable protection to the public at large than the deterrence flowing from the occasional exclusion of items of evidence in criminal trials. Although we do not suggest that a suppression order in this case would cause the IRS to abandon or modify its electronic surveillance regulations, we cannot ignore the possibility that a rigid application of an exclusionary rule to every regulatory violation could have a serious deterrent impact on the formulation of additional standards to govern prosecutorial and police procedures. Here, the Executive itself has provided for internal sanctions in cases of knowing violations of the electronic-surveillance regulations. To go beyond that, and require exclusion in every case, would take away from the Executive Department the primary responsibility for fashioning the appropriate remedy for the violation of its regulations. But since the content, and indeed the existence, of the regulations would remain within the Executive's sole authority, the result might well be fewer and less protective regulations. In the long run, it is far better to have rules like those contained in the IRS Manual, and to tolerate occasional erroneous administration of the kind displayed by this record, than either to have no rules except those mandated by statute, or to have them framed in a mere precatory form. . . .

The judgment of the Court of Appeals is *Reversed*.

UNITED STATES v. NERBER

222 F.3d 597 (9th Cir. 2000)

James R. Browning, Circuit Judge:

The government appeals an order of the district court suppressing evidence derived from video surveillance of a hotel room. For the reasons stated below, we affirm.

I.

On December 24, 1998, defendants Nerber and Betancourt-Rodriguez went to La Quinta Inn in Seattle to conduct a narcotics transaction with confidential informants. The informants brought defendants to Room 303. The FBI and the King County Police had rented the room for the operation and installed a hidden video camera without first obtaining a warrant. The parties entered the room at 9:54 A.M., the informants gave defendants one kilogram of sample cocaine, and the defendants briefly "flashed" money in a briefcase. The informants left the room at 10:00 A.M., telling defendants they would return to deliver 24 more kilograms of cocaine. They did not return, however, because they believed defendants intended to rob them. For three hours thereafter, law enforcement agents used the surveillance equipment to monitor defendants' activities in the hotel room. They observed the other two defendants—Betancourt and Alvarez—enter the room, and watched as the defendants brandished weapons and sampled cocaine. All four defendants left the hotel at approximately 1:00 P.M. and were arrested shortly thereafter.

A grand jury returned an indictment charging all four defendants with narcotics offenses and two with possessing a firearm during the commission of a narcotics offense. Defendants moved to suppress the evidence derived from the video surveillance. . . .

III.

In finding for defendants, the district court distinguished Minnesota v. Carter, 525 U.S. 83 (1998), in which the Supreme Court held that the defendants had no legitimate expectation of privacy in another person's apartment which they entered for a brief period to conduct a narcotics transaction. The district court held that *Carter* was not controlling because the governmental intrusion in this case (the use of a hidden surveillance camera) was far more egregious than the intrusion in *Carter* (visual observation through a ground-floor apartment window).

The government responds that the severity of the intrusion is irrelevant to whether a defendant has a legitimate expectation of privacy in a particular place. Once the severity of the intrusion is removed from the equation, the government argues, this case is indistinguishable from *Carter*, which compels a ruling that the defendants may not invoke the protection of the Fourth Amendment. [We disagree. . . .]

[N]umerous Supreme Court and appellate decisions—handed down before and after *Carter*—suggest a contrary principle: the legitimacy of a citizen's expectation of privacy in a particular place may be affected by the nature of the intrusion that occurs. . . .

B.

The district court did not err in finding that defendants had a subjective expectation not to be videotaped in the hotel room. In addition to closing the door, drawing the blinds, and exercising dominion over the room after the informants left at 10:00 A.M., defendants ingested cocaine and brandished weapons in a way they clearly would not have done had they thought outsiders might see them.

The objective reasonableness of defendants' privacy expectation presents a closer question. The governmental intrusion was severe. Hidden video surveillance is one of the most intrusive investigative mechanisms available to law enforcement. The sweeping, indiscriminate manner in which video surveillance can intrude upon us, regardless of where we are, dictates that its use be approved only in limited circumstances. As we pointed out in *Taketa*, the defendant had a reasonable expectation to be free from hidden video surveillance because "the video search was directed straight at him, rather than being a search of property he did not own or control . . . [and] the silent, unblinking lens of the camera was intrusive in a way that no temporary search of the office could have been." As Judge Kozinski has stated, "every court considering the issue has noted [that] video surveillance can result in extraordinarily serious intrusions into personal privacy. . . . If such intrusions are ever permissible, they must be justified by an extraordinary showing of need." United States v. Koyomejian, 970 F.2d 536, 551 (9th Cir. 1992) (Kozinski, J., concurring). And, as the Fifth Circuit said, hidden video surveillance invokes images of the "Orwellian state" and is regarded by society as more egregious than other kinds of intrusions.

Despite the pause the government's use of video surveillance gives us, we agree with the district court that defendants had no reasonable expectation that they would be free from hidden video surveillance while the informants were in the room. Defendants' privacy expectation was substantially diminished because of where they were. They were not "residents" of the hotel, they were not overnight guests of the occupants, and they were there solely to conduct a business transaction at the invitation of the occupants, with whom they were only minimally acquainted. Moreover, as the parties agree, when the informants were in the room the video surveillance was conducted with their consent, and defendants bore the risk that their activities with the informants were being surveilled. *Cf.* Hoffa v. United States, 385 U.S. 293, 302 (1966). These factors coalesce to support the district court's finding that the defendants may not invoke the Fourth Amendment to suppress the evidence gathered during this period.[5]

We also agree with the district court, however, that once the informants left the room, defendants' expectation to be free from hidden video surveillance was objectively reasonable. When defendants were left alone, their expectation of privacy increased to the point that the intrusion of a hidden video camera became unacceptable. People feel comfortable saying and doing things alone that they would not say or do in the presence of others. This is clearly true when people are alone in their own home or hotel room, but it is also true to a significant extent when they are in someone else's home or hotel room. Even if one cannot expect total privacy while alone in another person's hotel room (i.e., a maid might enter, someone might peek through a window, or the host might reenter unannounced), this diminished privacy interest does not eliminate society's expectation to be protected from the severe intrusion of having the government monitor private activities through hidden video cameras.

The fact that society is prepared to accept as reasonable defendants' expectation to be free from video surveillance while alone in the hotel room is confirmed by the way the law treats audio surveillance in identical circumstances. The government conceded that audio surveillance conducted after the informants departed was inadmissible, because the federal wiretap statute permits warrantless audio surveillance only if one of the participants in the monitored conversation consents. Absent such consent, the government must obtain a warrant and satisfy the statute's stringent particularity requirements. The limitations in the wiretap statute reflect a societal determination that the threat to liberty inherent in audio surveillance requires that this intrusive investigative technique be permitted only in

5. We do not intend to imply that video surveillance is justifiable whenever an informant is present. For example, we suspect an informant's presence and consent is insufficient to justify the warrantless installation of a hidden video camera in a suspect's home. We hold only that when defendants' privacy expectations were already substantially diminished by their presence in another person's room to conduct a brief business transaction, the presence and consent of the informants was sufficient to justify the surveillance.

limited circumstances. . . . Defendants' expectation to be free from hidden video surveillance when alone in the hotel room was, therefore, objectively reasonable.

In sum, although the video surveillance conducted while the informants were present is admissible, defendants had a legitimate expectation to be free from such surveillance after they were left alone in the hotel room. Because the government infringed upon defendants' expectation of privacy without first obtaining a warrant, the Fourth Amendment requires that the fruits of the surveillance be suppressed. . . .

NOTES AND QUESTIONS

1. The lesson taught by *Caceres* and a plethora of cases like it is that, according to the federal government, you have no right to trust those whom you believe are your friends. Anything you say to another person can be recorded by that person and used against you in a later criminal proceeding. *Nerber* comes to the same conclusion for video surveillance. Not all states agree, however, and a state may be more protective of an individual's rights than what is required by the U.S. Constitution. So, for example, in Florida, state investigators must obtain a warrant before they can make consensual recordings. *See* Fla. Stats. 934.03-.09. Note, however, that federal agents operating in a state such as Florida do not have to follow the state's procedures because of the Supremacy Clause, U.S. Const. Art. VI, cl. 2.
2. What is the two-part test for determining when the Fourth Amendment provides an individual with privacy protection? How does the level of government intrusion get factored into the equation? Note that, under this test, individuals generally have no legitimate expectation of privacy with respect to video surveillance on public streets or other places traversed by the public.
3. Does the line drawn in *Nerber* feel right to you? Ask yourself this: Are there things you might do in a hotel room alone (or with an intimate partner) that you would not do if other people—just friends or acquaintances—were also present? If so, then you have a higher subjective expectation of privacy when alone.

2. Wiretaps

ANNUAL REVIEW OF CRIMINAL PROCEDURE, THIRTY-SEVENTH EDITION

37 Geo. L.J. Ann. Rev. Crim. Proc. 133 (2008)

I. Investigations and Police Practices

Recognizing the threat to privacy rights that would result from unrestricted use of electronic monitoring devices, Congress passed Title III of the Omnibus Crime Control and Safe Streets Act of 1968 to regulate the interception and recording of wire, oral, and electronic communications. . . .[8]

8. [Codified in 18 U.S.C. §§2510-22.—Eds.]

Orders for Electronic Surveillance. Both the Fourth Amendment and Title III require that certain procedures be followed when law enforcement officials conduct electronic surveillance. Law enforcement officials must first receive authorization to apply for a court order permitting the interception of wire, oral, or electronic communications in connection with the investigation of certain enumerated crimes. Only the United States Attorney General or certain deputies of the Attorney General may authorize an application for wire or oral interceptions. However, any government attorney may authorize an application for an electronic communication interception. The application must identify the applicant and the person authorizing it and, once authorized, it must be submitted to a court to secure the requisite court order.

In considering an application, a court may rely on factual statements contained in the application and supporting affidavits. An application for a surveillance order must include: (1) a full and complete statement of the alleged offense; (2) the facilities from which the communications are to be intercepted; (3) a particular description of the communications sought to be intercepted; (4) the identity of the persons committing the offense, if known, and of the persons whose communications are to be intercepted; (5) a full and complete statement of whether other investigative procedures have been tried, have failed, or why they appear unlikely to succeed or are too dangerous; and (6) a full and complete statement of the period of time for which the interception is to be maintained. The application must also include information concerning previous applications involving any of the same persons, facilities, or places. A defendant may challenge the validity of the government's affidavit by making a substantial preliminary showing that a false statement was included in the warrant affidavit knowingly and intentionally or with reckless disregard for the truth. Although the Supreme Court has not ruled on this issue, a number of circuit courts have held that reckless omissions are also challengeable. If a challenged statement was necessary to support probable cause for the search, the court must hold an evidentiary hearing on the matter. If the defendant proves at the evidentiary hearing by a preponderance of the evidence that a false statement was knowingly or recklessly included in the warrant affidavit, any evidence seized pursuant to that warrant must be suppressed.

A court may issue a surveillance order for the interception of wire or oral communications only if it finds probable cause to believe that: (1) a person is committing one of the crimes enumerated in Title III; (2) communications concerning the offense will be obtained through interception; and (3) the facilities from which the communications are to be intercepted are being used in connection with the commission of the offense The court must also find that normal investigative techniques have failed, appear unlikely to succeed, or would be too dangerous.

Upon finding that probable cause exists and that normal investigative techniques are inadequate, the court will issue an [appropriate] order. . . .

[The] order . . . must be executed "as soon as practicable." Title III requires that surveillance "terminate upon attainment of the authorized objective." Without an extension, surveillance cannot last more than thirty days. The thirty-day period begins on the first day of interception or ten days after the order is entered, whichever comes first. A court may grant extensions of an order for additional thirty-day periods. The court may also require the government to submit reports on the progress of the surveillance and on the need for continued interception.

Although a state may not apply less stringent requirements than those imposed by Title III, it may place greater restrictions on electronic surveillance. In general, federal courts will admit evidence obtained by federal officials in violation of a more restrictive state law, provided the evidence was obtained in accordance with Title III. The circuits, however, are split over whether to apply more restrictive state surveillance statutes in federal proceedings when state law enforcement officials conducted the surveillance. . . .

Statutory Post-Authorization Duties. Title III imposes at least four post-authorization duties upon those acting under an electronic surveillance order. Failure to comply with any of these duties may result in suppression of evidence obtained pursuant to the order.

First, the police must minimize the interception of communications outside the scope of the authorization and order. The effort to minimize must be objectively reasonable in light of the circumstances confronting the interceptor. If the intercepted communications concern crimes not listed in the interception order, the government can use the contents of the communication as evidence only upon applying to the court "as soon as practicable" for a determination that the interception complied with Title III requirements. The trial court has discretion to determine the necessity of holding an evidentiary hearing on the adequacy of the minimization effort.

Second, to protect confidentiality and to prevent tampering, the court must seal the application for a Title III order and the order itself, as well as all recordings made pursuant to it, immediately after the specified surveillance period or any relevant extensions have expired. Intercepted communications are admissible in a criminal proceeding only if the communications were properly sealed or if the government satisfactorily explains the delay or absence of a seal.

Third, after the interception is completed, an "inventory" must be issued to those persons named in the surveillance order and, if the judge requires, to other persons whose conversations have been intercepted. The inventory must include notice of the authorization order or application, the surveillance dates, and whether any interception occurred. Failure to give inventory notice is not grounds for suppression unless the failure has caused incurable prejudice.

Fourth, if the government wishes to disclose the contents at a trial, hearing, or other proceeding, it must provide each party with a copy of the application and court order at least ten days before the proceeding.

Intercepted communications obtained in an authorized fashion and in compliance with these duties may be lawfully used in the following situations: (1) a law enforcement officer may disclose the contents of an intercepted communication to another law enforcement officer "to the extent that such disclosure is appropriate"; (2) a law enforcement officer may use the contents of an intercepted communication in the performance of his or her official duties; (3) any person may disclose the contents of an intercepted communication while giving testimony "in any proceeding held under the authority of the United States or of any State . . ."; (4) a law enforcement officer or government attorney may disclose the contents of an intercepted communication to certain enumerated federal officials "to the extent that such contents include foreign intelligence or counterintelligence"; (5) a law enforcement officer or federal official may disclose the contents of an intercepted communication to foreign law enforcement officers for the necessary performance of his or her official duties; and (6) a law enforcement officer or federal official may disclose the contents of an intercepted communication to any appropriate government official, domestic or foreign, for the purpose of responding to a threat of hostile acts by a terrorist or foreign power.

Suppression. Title III allows any aggrieved person to move to suppress the contents of intercepted oral and wire communications, or evidence derived therefrom, obtained in violation of the statute. The statutory exclusionary rule applies to all federal and state proceedings, but does not cover illegally intercepted electronic communications. Standing to challenge evidence obtained under Title III is limited to persons whose Fourth Amendment rights were violated by the surveillance. Thus, to bring such a challenge, one must have been a party to the illegally intercepted conversation or the owner of the premises where the illegal interception occurred.

Aggrieved persons may move to suppress unlawfully-intercepted oral or wire communications if the order authorizing the surveillance was insufficient on its face or the interception violated the requirements of the order. Improper sealing of interception evidence may also constitute grounds for suppression. A violation of Title III does not require suppression, however, if the provision violated is not central to the legislative purpose of the statute.

NOTES AND QUESTIONS

1. In recent years, white collar prosecutors and investigators have grown increasingly enamored with the use of undercover agents, consensual monitoring, and wiretaps in their cases. For example, a recent prosecution involving a $25 million insider trading ring was based in large part on taps on the defendants' phones. *See* Susan Pulliam & Chad Bray, *Jury Hears Galleon Wiretaps*, WALL ST. J., Mar. 11, 2011, available at http://online.wsj.com/article/SB10001424052748704823004576192530075087702.html. As noted in the introduction to this chapter, one reason for this trend is the devastating impact this type of evidence has on the defense. Another critical reason is that such evidence can usually simplify the path to proving guilt. A statement that "we've got to shred these documents or we're toast" can take the place of reconstructing exactly what crime the documents (hundreds of thousands or millions of them, perhaps) actually reveal.
2. The requirements of Title III make obtaining a wiretap considerably more time-consuming and difficult than obtaining a search warrant. Is the additional burden justified?

D. The Grand Jury

If an undercover investigation is not possible or has run its course, the next step in virtually every federal white collar criminal matter will be a grand jury investigation. Although proceedings before a grand jury are secret, *the fact that the grand jury is meeting and taking testimony from witnesses is not.* Consequently, reporters and other interested parties often "camp out" in front of the courthouse or the grand jury room to determine the identity of the witnesses. As a result, it is typically at the opening of the grand jury probe that a defendant becomes aware of the possibility that federal criminal charges may be brought against him. No matter how well represented he or she is regarding civil matters, the smart defendant wastes no time in hiring a criminal defense attorney (or a team of them) at this point in time.

The Supreme Court has described the grand jury in the following way (citations omitted):

> The grand jury has always occupied a high place as an instrument of justice in our system of criminal law—so much so that it is enshrined in the Constitution. It serves the dual function of determining if there is probable cause to believe that a crime has been committed and of protecting citizens against unfounded criminal prosecutions. It has always been extended extraordinary powers of investigation and great responsibility for directing its own efforts. Traditionally the grand jury has been accorded wide latitude to inquire into violations of criminal law. No judge presides to monitor its proceedings. It deliberates in secret and may determine alone the course of its inquiry. The grand jury may compel the production of evidence or the testimony of witnesses as it considers appropriate, and its operation generally is unrestrained by the technical procedural and evidentiary rules governing the conduct of criminal trials. It is a grand inquest, a body with powers of investigation and inquisition, the scope of whose inquiries is not to be limited narrowly by questions of propriety or forecasts of the probable result of the investigation, or by doubts whether any particular individual will be found properly subject to an accusation of crime.
>
> These broad powers are necessary to permit the grand jury to carry out both parts of its dual function. Without thorough and effective investigation, the grand jury would be unable either to ferret out crimes deserving of prosecution, or to screen out charges not warranting prosecution.

United States v. Sells Engineering, 463 U.S. 418, 423-424 (1983).

1. Overview of the Grand Jury's Functions and Powers

JUDGE JAMES F. HOLDERMAN & CHARLES B. REDFERN, PREINDICTMENT PROSECUTORIAL CONDUCT IN THE FEDERAL SYSTEM REVISITED

96 J. Crim. L. & Criminology 527

The decision to investigate and prosecute a suspected crime is inherently the province of the executive branch. Although the Attorney General of the United States is the head of the Department of Justice of the United States, the United States Attorneys of the federal judicial districts throughout the country are the chief federal law enforcement officers of the United States within their particular jurisdiction, and serve as the nation's principal federal litigators under the direction of the Attorney General. Congress has statutorily directed the United States Attorneys to prosecute all offenses against the United States that occur in their districts. . . .

[T]he district court of the judicial district in which the grand jury sits will summon grand juries when required by the public's interest.[9] A grand jury must have at least sixteen jurors for a quorum and the number cannot exceed twenty-three.[10] A grand jury can be summoned to sit as members of either a "regular" or "special" grand jury.

The Fifth Amendment establishes the need and existence of the grand jury in the federal system.[11] Although the grand jury interacts with both the prosecutor and the courts, federal courts have recognized that the grand jury is not assigned to any of the three branches of government but is instead a constitutional fixture in its own right. The grand jury in a particular federal district is responsible for investigating possible criminal violations of federal laws and returning indictments after finding probable cause to believe that a crime has been committed. The grand jury's investigatory power is tremendously broad. Grand juries have jurisdiction to investigate conduct merely because that conduct might have been a federal crime within the jurisdiction of the federal court convening the grand jury.

Both the prosecutor and the grand jury serve dual roles in the process. Grand juries, while responsible for determining if probable cause exists that a crime has been committed and returning indictments in accordance with those findings, must also act to protect against unfounded criminal prosecutions. The prosecutor must seek indictments when warranted and must also be an advisor to the grand jury. A prosecutor's use of the grand jury's power is limited only by the grand jury's obligation to evaluate evidence to determine whether to return an indictment. It is not an abuse of the grand jury process if, in addition to conducting investigation, a prosecutor seeks to obtain evidence of additional criminal conduct or seeks to "lock in" witnesses' testimony under oath for further investigation of wrongdoing. [A] federal prosecutor cannot use the grand jury for the sole or dominant purpose of: (1) obtaining additional evidence on charges already made against an indicted defendant, or (2) eliciting evidence for a civil case. A prosecutor also cannot use the grand jury solely as an investigative aid in the search for a fugitive in whose testimony the grand jury has no interest.

IV. The Use of Grand Jury Subpoena Power

The rules governing the use of the federal court's criminal subpoena power, including grand jury subpoena power, are set forth in Rule 17 of the Federal Rules of Criminal Procedure. Rule 17 authorizes nationwide service of subpoenas but a grand jury's subpoena authority is contingent on issuance by the federal district

9. [Typically, the court will summon a grand jury at the request of the U.S. Attorney's Office. — Eds.]

10. [Grand jurors are adult citizens who reside in the jurisdiction of the federal court for whom they serve. They are subpoenaed for jury service and chosen by the court in a manner similar to the selection of a petite (trial) jury, except that only the prosecution participates in the process. As a general rule, grand jurors come to the courthouse to hear evidence for multiple cases once a week. They consider indictments when presented to them by the prosecutors. A federal grand jury's term is 12 months but can be extended to 18 months. *See* Fed. R. Crim. P. 6(g). — Eds.]

11. [U.S. Const. Art. V. "No person shall be held to answer for a capital, or otherwise infamous crime, unless on a presentment or indictment of a Grand Jury. . . ." — Eds.]

court that summoned the grand jury. The clerk of a federal district court issues blank grand jury subpoenas which are ready for federal prosecutors to fill-in and serve. The subpoena can order a witness to appear and give testimony or produce non-testimonial physical evidence....

A. Preappearance Interview or Review and the "Office" Subpoena

[T]he issuance of a grand jury subpoena does not necessarily require prior grand jury authorization or awareness. A prosecutor's collection of information using a grand jury subpoena without the intended participation of the grand jury, however, is an improper use of the grand jury....

B. Requiring Production of Documents and Other Materials

[Issuing a subpoena for n]on-testimonial evidence[,] such as a DNA sample, fingerprints, handwriting exemplars, or financial records[,] typically requires [the evidence] to be useful to the grand jury. Courts have held that a prosecutor may first have the subpoenaed materials analyzed, and can even issue the initial subpoena when the grand jury is not in session, as long as the return date on the subpoena is for a date that the grand jury is in session. Furthermore, the material [need] not ultimately be presented to the grand jury if the witness can voluntarily provide the sample to the prosecutor or government agents outside of the grand jury's presence. In order to avoid an abuse of the grand jury, however, the prosecutor must have intended to obtain useable evidence for the grand jury when the subpoenas were initially issued....

V. Inside the Grand Jury

A. The Prosecutor's Role and Function

When appearing before the grand jury, a federal prosecutor has the dual roles of both pressing for an indictment and being a legal advisor to the grand jury. Additionally, "[t]he ex parte character of grand jury proceedings makes it peculiarly important for a federal prosecutor to remember that, in the familiar phrase, the interest of the United States in a criminal prosecution is not that it shall win a case, but that justice shall be done...."

B. Who May Attend Sessions

Rule 6(d) expressly identifies who may be present while the grand jury is in session and while the grand jury is deliberating and voting. Excluded from Rule 6(d)'s listing of persons allowed to attend grand jury sessions are the putative defendant, an attorney for the witness testifying before the grand jury, and the district court judge responsible for supervising the grand jury. Only one witness may appear at a time before the grand jury and a witness must leave the grand jury once he or she has completed testifying....

The prosecutor has the responsibility to safeguard the propriety of the grand jury's proceedings by leaving the grand jury room during the grand jury's deliberations and voting. Nor should the prosecutor partake in the presentation of the government's case to the grand jury if that prosecutor will testify as a witness before the grand jury. Additionally, a prosecutor who has had some previous involvement with the persons under investigation should not participate in the grand jury investigation and should be screened from it.

C. The Presentation of Evidence and Prosecutors' Comments to the Grand Jury

Although the grand jury can consider matters brought to its attention from sources other than the prosecutor, such as the court that impaneled it or from the personal knowledge of a grand jury member, the grand jury's efforts are usually focused on receiving evidence presented by an attorney for the government. The Federal Rules of Evidence do not apply in a grand jury proceeding except for the privilege provisions. The prosecutor can present hearsay to the grand jury and the grand jury can use the hearsay as the basis of its indictment. The prosecutor's presentation is ex parte and he or she can provide legal advice to the grand jury, discuss the prosecution's strategy with grand jury and can respond to grand juror questions.

D. Recording of Proceedings

. . . Rule 6(e)(1) . . . require[s] that all grand jury proceedings, other than grand jury deliberation and voting, be recorded by a court reporter or a suitable recording device. The attorney for the government is ordered under Rule 6(e)(1) to retain control of the grand jury recording, reporters' notes and any transcripts of grand jury proceedings. However, the grand jury's records, although in the government's possession, are the court's records. . . .

F. Right of Putative Defendant to Testify or Present Evidence

Although a putative defendant has no right to testify in front of the grand jury, the [U.S. Attorney's] Manual encourages the prosecutor to allow voluntary appearances by subjects and targets before the grand jury because a prosecutor's refusal of a request to appear before the grand jury may appear unfair. As one commentator has suggested, a "savvy [defense] counsel will not allow his 'target' clients to testify before the grand jury . . . because it is the rare target who can talk his way out of an indictment." Therefore, a prosecutor should allow the putative defendant to testify as long as (1) there is no burden on the grand jury or delay of its proceedings, (2) the witness explicitly waives his privilege against self-incrimination on the record before the grand jury, (3) the witness is represented by counsel or voluntarily or knowingly appears without counsel, and (4) the witness consents to a full examination under oath.

It is up to the sound discretion of the grand jury to determine whether to allow a putative defendant to supplement his or her testimony with testimony from third parties. It is also up to the grand jury as to whether the putative defendant can read a prepared statement although there is Department of Justice policy that opposes such a reading. . . .

H. The Duty to Present Favorable Evidence to the Grand Jury

... [S]ince a putative defendant has no right to present any evidence to the grand jury, it is up to the prosecutor to decide whether to present evidence favorable to the putative defendant to the grand jury. The Department of Justice's policy is that a prosecutor must disclose to the grand jury, before seeking an indictment, "substantial evidence that directly negates the guilt of the subject of the investigation" when the prosecutor is "personally aware" of that evidence. The ABA Prosecution Standards go further by prohibiting the prosecutor from knowingly not disclosing favorable evidence to the grand jury.

Despite Department of Justice policy, the law is settled that a prosecutor is not constitutionally required to include exculpatory evidence in the presentation to the grand jury. Once the grand jury indictment is returned and the case proceeds through the pretrial discovery stage, the prosecutor faces the due process requirement of having to disclose this same material pursuant to the Federal Rules of Criminal Procedure and to the Supreme Court's decision in Brady v. Maryland, 373 U.S. 83 (1963).... Thus, a prosecutor who fails to disclose exculpatory evidence to the grand jury not only violates Department of Justice policy but also will not gain any advantage in the trial of the case.

NOTES AND QUESTIONS

1. Federal grand jury practice has been the subject of much criticism over the years, as many observers wonder whether—given prosecutors' considerable influence over the process—it provides any real protection for citizens against unwarranted intrusion and indictment. *See, e.g., The Hyde Amendment and Prosecutorial Investigation: the Promise of Protection for Criminal Defendants*, 28 FORDHAM URB. L.J. 1967 (2001); Roger Roots, *If It's Not a Runaway, It's Not a Real Grand Jury*, 33 CREIGHTON L. REV. 821 (2000); Lynn R. Singband & Andrew D. Leipold, *Why Grand Juries Do Not (and Cannot) Protect the Accused*, 80 CORNELL L. REV. 260 (1995). In your casebook author's ten years' experience as a federal prosecutor, he is aware of only one occasion on which a grand jury refused to return a True Bill to *any prosecutor* in his two offices. (The next grand jury was more compliant.) More interesting, perhaps, is that grand jurors generally got most upset when they learned that a suspect whom they believed to be guilty was *not* going to be indicted, in effect cheering on rather than reigning in prosecutors.
2. Despite how rare it is that grand juries exercise their protective function, is it possible that they serve a significant prophylactic role? In other words, is it possible that prosecutors are deterred from blatantly abusing their immense power because they know that, if they did, the grand jury would balk?
3. The primary downside to providing more rights to a suspect during the grand jury phase of a case is the potential interference it would have with the progress of the investigation, costing time and money and risking the success of the ultimate prosecution. Indeed, the more protections added

(such as permitting the defendant to be present, offering exculpatory evidence, etc.), the more the grand jury proceeding starts to look like a trial before the trial. *See generally* Michael L. Seigel, *The Moment of Truth: The Decision to Institute Charges in a Rape Case,* in Race to Injustice: Lessons Learned from the Duke Lacrosse Rape Case (Carolina Academic Press) (M. Seigel ed., 2009).

Do you think the federal grand jury strikes the right balance between protecting suspects' interests and promoting the investigation and prosecution of crime?

2. Grand Jury Secrecy

IN RE SEALED CASE NO. 99-3091 (OFFICE OF INDEPENDENT COUNSEL CONTEMPT PROCEEDING)

192 F.3d 995 (D.C. Cir. 1999)

Before: Wald, Silberman, and Henderson, Circuit Judges.

Opinion for the court filed Per Curiam.

The Office of Independent Counsel (OIC) seeks summary reversal of the district court's order to show cause why OIC should not be held in contempt for violating the grand jury secrecy rule, and its order appointing the United States Department of Justice as prosecutor of OIC in a criminal contempt proceeding. In the alternative, OIC seeks a stay of those orders pending appeal. We conclude we have jurisdiction to consider the interlocutory appeal and grant the motion for summary reversal.

I.

On January 31, 1999, while the Senate was trying President William J. Clinton on articles of impeachment, the New York Times published a front page article captioned "Starr is Weighing Whether to Indict Sitting President." As is relevant here, the article reported:

> Inside the Independent Counsel's Office, a group of prosecutors believes that not long after the Senate trial concludes, Mr. Starr should ask the grand jury of 23 men and women hearing the case against Mr. Clinton to indict him on charges of perjury and obstruction of justice, the associates said. The group wants to charge Mr. Clinton with lying under oath in his Jones deposition in January 1998 and in his grand jury testimony in August, the associates added.

The next day, the Office of the President (the White House) and Mr. Clinton jointly filed in district court a motion for an order to show cause why OIC, or the individuals therein, should not be held in contempt for disclosing grand jury material in violation of Federal Rule of Criminal Procedure 6(e). . . .

[W]e conclude that the disclosures made in the *New York Times* article do not constitute a prima facie violation of Rule 6(e). A prima facie violation based on a news report is established by showing that the report discloses "matters occurring before the grand jury" and indicates that sources of the information include government attorneys. Because OIC [concedes that] its attorneys w[ere] the source of the disclosures in the *New York Times* article at issue here, the only remaining issue is whether those disclosures qualify as "matters occurring before the grand jury." Fed. R. Crim. P. 6(e)(2).

The district court concluded that only one excerpt from the *New York Times* article constituted a prima facie violation of Rule 6(e). That excerpt . . . disclosed the desire of some OIC prosecutors to seek, not long after the conclusion of the Senate trial, an indictment of Mr. Clinton on perjury and obstruction of justice charges, including lying under oath in his deposition in the Paula Jones matter and in his grand jury testimony. These statements, according to the district court, reveal a specific time frame for seeking an indictment, the details of a likely indictment, and the direction a group of prosecutors within OIC believes the grand jury investigation should take. Not surprisingly, Mr. Clinton and the White House agree with the district court's expansive reading of Rule 6(e). OIC takes a narrow view of the Rule's coverage, arguing that matters occurring outside the physical presence of the grand jury are covered only if they reveal grand jury matters. DOJ generally supports OIC with respect to the Rule's coverage, but emphasizes the importance of the context and concreteness of disclosures.

The key to the district court's reasoning is its reliance on this court's definition of "matters occurring before the grand jury." In In re Motions of Dow Jones & Co., 142 F.3d 496, 500 (D.C. Cir.), *cert. denied*, 525 U.S. 820 (1998), we noted that this phrase encompasses "not only what has occurred and what is occurring, but also what is likely to occur," including "the identities of witnesses or jurors, the substance of testimony as well as actual transcripts, the strategy or direction of the investigation, the deliberations or questions of jurors, and the like." In the earlier contempt proceeding against Independent Counsel Starr, however, we cautioned the district court about "the problematic nature of applying so broad a definition, especially as it relates to the 'strategy or direction of the investigation,' to the inquiry as to whether a government attorney has made unauthorized disclosures." Despite the seemingly broad nature of the statements in *Dow Jones*, we have never read Rule 6(e) to require that a "veil of secrecy be drawn over all matters occurring in the world that happen to be investigated by a grand jury." Indeed, we have said that "[t]he disclosure of information 'coincidentally before the grand jury [which can] be revealed in such a manner that its revelation would not elucidate the inner workings of the grand jury" is not prohibited. Thus, the phrases "likely to occur" and "strategy and direction" must be read in light of the text of Rule 6(e)—which limits the Rule's coverage to "matters occurring before the grand jury"—as well as the purposes of the Rule.

As we have recited on many occasions,

> Rule 6(e) . . . protects several interests of the criminal justice system: First, if preindictment proceedings were made public, many prospective witnesses would be hesitant to come forward voluntarily, knowing that those against whom they testify would be aware of that testimony. Moreover, witnesses who appeared before the grand jury would be less likely to testify fully and frankly, as they would be open

> to retribution as well as to inducements. There also would be the risk that those about to be indicted would flee, or would try to influence individual grand jurors to vote against indictment. Finally, by preserving the secrecy of the proceedings, we assure that persons who are accused but exonerated by the grand jury will not be held up to public ridicule.

In re Sealed Case No. 98-3077, 151 F.3d 1059, 1070 (D.C. Cir. 1998). These purposes, as well as the text of the Rule itself, reflect the need to preserve the secrecy of the grand jury proceedings themselves. It is therefore necessary to differentiate between statements by a prosecutor's office with respect to its own investigation, and statements by a prosecutor's office with respect to a grand jury's investigation, a distinction of the utmost significance upon which several circuits have already remarked.

Information actually presented to the grand jury is core Rule 6(e) material that is afforded the broadest protection from disclosure. Prosecutors' statements about their investigations, however, implicate the Rule only when they directly reveal grand jury matters. To be sure, we have recognized that Rule 6(e) would be easily evaded if a prosecutor could with impunity discuss with the press testimony about to be presented to a grand jury, so long as it had not yet occurred. Accordingly, we have read Rule 6(e) to cover matters "likely to occur." And even a discussion of "strategy and direction of the investigation" could include references to not yet delivered but clearly anticipated testimony. But that does not mean that any discussion of an investigation is violative of Rule 6(e). Indeed, the district court's Local Rule 308(b)(2), which governs attorney conduct in grand jury matters, recognizes that prosecutors often have a legitimate interest in revealing aspects of their investigations "to inform the public that the investigation is underway, to describe the general scope of the investigation, to obtain assistance in the apprehension of a suspect, to warn the public of any dangers, or otherwise aid in the investigation." . . .

Thus, internal deliberations of prosecutors that do not directly reveal grand jury proceedings are not Rule 6(e) material. . . . It may be thought that when such deliberations include a discussion of whether an indictment should be sought, or whether a particular individual is potentially criminally liable, the deliberations have crossed into the realm of Rule 6(e) material. This ignores, however, the requirement that the matter occur before the grand jury. Where the reported deliberations do not reveal that an indictment has been sought or will be sought, ordinarily they will not reveal anything definite enough to come within the scope of Rule 6(e).

For these reasons, the disclosure that a group of OIC prosecutors "believe" that an indictment should be brought at the end of the impeachment proceedings does not, on its face, or in the context of the article as a whole, violate Rule 6(e). We acknowledge, as did OIC, that such statements are troubling, for they have the potential to damage the reputation of innocent suspects. But bare statements that some assistant prosecutors in OIC wish to seek an indictment do not implicate the grand jury; the prosecutors may not even be basing their opinion on information presented to a grand jury.

The fact that the disclosure also reveals a time period for seeking the indictment of "not long after the Senate trial concludes" does not in any way indicate what is "likely to occur" before the grand jury within the meaning of Rule 6(e). That disclosure reflects nothing more than a desire on the part of some OIC prosecutors to seek an indictment at that time, not a decision to do so. The general uncertainty as to whether an indictment would in fact be sought (according to the article, only some prosecutors in OIC thought one should be) leads us to conclude that this portion of the article did not reveal anything that was "occurring before the grand jury."

. . . In ordinary circumstances, Rule 6(e) covers the disclosure of the names of grand jury witnesses. Therefore, the statement that members of OIC wished to seek an indictment based on Mr. Clinton's alleged perjury before a grand jury would ordinarily be Rule 6(e) material. In this case, however, we take judicial notice that the President's status as a witness before the grand jury was a matter of widespread public knowledge well before the *New York Times* article at issue in this case was written; the President himself went on national television the day of his testimony to reveal this fact. Where the general public is already aware of the information contained in the prosecutor's statement, there is no additional harm in the prosecutor referring to such information. . . .

Similarly, it would ordinarily be a violation of Rule 6(e) to disclose that a grand jury is investigating a particular person. Thus, the statement that a grand jury is "hearing the case against Mr. Clinton" would be covered by Rule 6(e) if it were not for the fact that the *New York Times* article did not reveal any secret, for it was already common knowledge well before January 31, 1999, that a grand jury was investigating alleged perjury and obstruction of justice by the President. Once again, the President's appearance on national television confirmed as much.

V.

In light of our conclusion that the excerpt from the *New York Times* article does not constitute a prima facie violation of Rule 6(e), we reverse and remand with instructions to dismiss the Rule 6(e) contempt proceedings against OIC. Because we have granted OIC's request for summary reversal, we dismiss as moot the alternative request for a stay, as well as the consolidated petition for mandamus. The administrative stay is lifted.

NOTES AND QUESTIONS

1. The court admits that one of the purposes of grand jury secrecy it articulated in its 1998 case—to "assure that persons who are accused but exonerated by the grand jury will not be held up to public ridicule"—was implicated here. Indeed, President Clinton was never charged with perjury. Certainly he was harmed by the leak that some prosecutors believed the evidence before the grand jury had been strong enough to do so. How does the court reconcile this policy with the outcome of the case?
2. Isn't this case particularly egregious because the motive of the leakers appears to have been to raise the public's expectations and thereby to put pressure on their boss, IC Starr, to bring an indictment against the President? Weren't

they abusing their knowledge of the status of the grand jury proceeding as a tactic to prejudice the outcome?

3. The court indicates that disclosure of facts that are already public does not violate Rule 6(e) because such facts are not secret. Should that matter? Isn't most of the information provided to a grand jury already known by some segment of the population? Isn't the protection of Rule 6(e) really designed to protect against public knowledge of the *grand jury's* interest in that information? Moreover, who is to say that the same culprits did not leak the information earlier, making it public now?
4. The Starr investigation of President Bill Clinton was, of course, a highly charged case politically. Do you think that politics influenced this opinion? Can you otherwise explain how the court takes its circuitous and sometimes contradictory route to its conclusion? Is this another example of bad (here, notorious) facts making bad law?

3. Subpoenas Ad Testificandum (for Testimony)

a. Threshold Showing

IN RE GRAND JURY PROCEEDINGS (SCHOFIELD II)

507 F.2d 963 (3d Cir. 1975)

JAMES HUNTER, III, Circuit Judge:

This case raises questions concerning the district court's application of our holding in In re Grand Jury Proceedings, 486 F.2d 85 (3d Cir. 1973) (*Schofield I*). Because we conclude that the requirements of *Schofield I* have been met, the district court order is affirmed.

I.

In *Schofield I* this court soundly rejected any contention that the district court should "rubber stamp" petitions for the enforcement of grand jury subpoenas. Instead we held that the trial court would first be required to satisfy itself of the propriety of the subpoena. Under our supervisory powers we required the party seeking enforcement of a grand jury subpoena to make some minimal showing by affidavit of the existence of a proper purpose.We suggested three tests for determining whether the required showing had been made.

> . . . (W)e think it reasonable that the Government be required to make some preliminary showing by affidavit that each item is at least relevant to an investigation being conducted by the grand jury and properly within its jurisdiction, and is not sought primarily for another purpose.

2. Our supervisory power over grand juries is derived from several sources. Under 18 U.S.C. §3331 and F. R. Cr. P. 6(a) a district court is given power to call a grand jury into existence; under F. R. Cr. P. 17(a), and 28 U.S.C. §1826(a) respectively, the district court is given the power to issue and the duty to enforce grand jury subpoenas.

Despite the fact that the burden is generally on the witness to show abuse of the grand jury process, *Schofield I* requires the government to present affidavits in every case irrespective of whether the witness has challenged the propriety of the subpoena. This broad rule is designed to prevent abuse of the grand jury process by requiring a minimum disclosure of the grand jury's purpose in every case.

Schofield I emphasizes that where the district court is not satisfied with the affidavits presented by the government, whether because the matters set forth challenge the [government's] credibility or because the witness has made some colorable challenge to the affidavits, the court can require something more.

The district judge is vested with considerable discretion in determining whether additional proceedings are warranted. Various avenues of inquiry are open to a court which questions the sufficiency of the affidavits, among them discovery, in camera inspection, additional affidavits and a hearing. If it was not made clear in *Schofield I*, we emphasize now that the decision to require additional investigation is committed to the sound discretion of the district court. In *Schofield I* we stated:

> . . . the court must in deciding that request (for additional proceedings,) weigh the quite limited scope of an inquiry into abuse of the subpoena process, and the potential for delay, against any need for additional information which might cast doubt upon the accuracy of the Government's representations.

We will not disturb a decision to deny additional review unless we find that the district court's "weighing" was an abuse of discretion. . . .

Our holding in *Schofield I* did not require a showing of reasonableness, it did not require any determination of probable cause and it clearly did not require a hearing in every case.

What *Schofield I* did require, however, was a minimum showing by affidavit in every case that each item sought was (1) relevant to an investigation, (2) properly within the grand jury's jurisdiction, and (3) not sought primarily for another purpose.

None of the Supreme Court cases deal with the precise issue raised in *Schofield I*. Nevertheless, we feel that the three-pronged showing requirement of that case is perfectly compatible with Supreme Court decisions. . . .

II.

In January of 1974, Mrs. Schofield was subpoenaed to testify before the grand jury. After being granted immunity, she did in fact testify for seven hours.

The present appeal deals with a subpoena issued in July of 1974 which . . . directed the witness to permit photographs, fingerprints and handwriting exemplars to be taken. When Mrs. Schofield refused to comply, the United States Attorney's office moved to enforce the subpoena in the district court. Appellant filed an answer to the enforcement motion averring, among other things, that the affidavit was insufficiently detailed to determine relevancy and that the government already had in its possession a photograph and a handwritten letter. The court nevertheless denied further discovery and ordered enforcement of the subpoena. Mrs. Schofield refused to comply and was ultimately adjudged in civil contempt.

In a detailed opinion the district court concluded that the government affidavit in support of the enforcement motion had in fact complied with the *Schofield I* three-pronged affidavit requirement. We agree. The affidavit states:

> Walter S. Batty, Jr., Assistant United States Attorney in and for the Eastern District of Pennsylvania, states as follows:
>
> 1. The January 25, 1974 Grand Jury for the Eastern District of Pennsylvania is now conducting investigations of various alleged illegal activities in the said District; said investigations involve possible violations of federal criminal statutes, including 18 U.S.C. §§1621 (perjury), 1623 (giving false declarations). Jacqueline Schofield has been subpoenaed by the said Grand Jury and has been fully advised that she is a potential defendant in its investigation.
> 2. It is essential and necessary to the said Grand Jury investigation that Jacqueline Schofield furnish before and to the Grand Jury, or to any duly appointed agent of the said Grand Jury, exemplars of her handwriting and/or handprinting, and to permit that her photograph and fingerprints be taken. Such items will be used solely as a standard of comparison to determine whether or not the witness uttered any forged, falsely made, altered or counterfeited checks.

While the information supplied was scant, it was not insufficient as a matter of law. The affidavit gave the trial judge some basis for determining that the three-pronged test of *Schofield I* had been met. Considering the slender information supplied and Mrs. Schofield's allegation that the government already had the information it sought in the affidavit, the district court could have required something more of the government. We state again, however, that we will not review the trial court's refusal to grant additional inquiry except where we find the refusal to be abuse of discretion.

The government affidavits state that the grand jury was investigating violations of criminal statutes and that the witness was a potential defendant, thus clearly satisfying the requirement that the items be relevant[4] to the grand jury investigation and properly within the grand jury's jurisdiction. The last requirement of *Schofield I*, that the item not be sought for another purpose, is less clearly laid out in the affidavit but sufficiently met in the district judge's and our view. Paragraph two of the affidavit states that the material will be used solely as a standard of comparison to determine whether the witness had committed forgery. The district judge knew that the grand jury was investigating perjury and that the witness had been granted immunity from prosecution for forgery during her seven hours of grand jury testimony. A viable conclusion is that the exemplars were relevant to determine whether Mrs. Schofield perjured herself during her earlier testimony before the grand jury.

4. We cite an appropriate definition of relevancy: Relevancy, in the context of a Grand Jury proceeding is not a probative relevancy, for it cannot be known in advance whether the document produced will actually advance the investigation. It is rather a relevancy to the subject matter of the investigation.

Having satisfied the minimum showing requirements of *Schofield I*, we can only disturb the failure to require more if an abuse of discretion is shown. Although Mrs. Schofield contested the need for the exemplars, alleging that the government already had copies of her photograph and handwriting, the district judge satisfactorily explained his refusal to require more. Because of the limited scope of inquiry into abuse of the grand jury process, the court concluded that there had been no charge of harassment or unreasonableness and that additional review was, therefore, unnecessary. The slight burden of compliance did not warrant further inquiry into the grand jury's reasons for requesting the information. We find no abuse of discretion and consequently hold meritless appellant's contention that additional proceedings are required in this case. . . .

NOTES AND QUESTIONS

1. Two key words appear at the end of *Schofield I*: "harassment" and "unreasonableness." Essentially, these harms are what the prosecutor's affidavit is supposed to prevent.
2. The Third Circuit's *Schofield* approach is fairly unique among the courts of appeals; most presume a subpoena to be regular unless the opposing party can produce evidence to the contrary. Which is the better rule?

b. Fifth Amendment, Immunity, and Contempt

KASTIGAR v. UNITED STATES

406 U.S. 441 (1972)

Mr. Justice POWELL delivered the opinion of the Court.

This case presents the question whether the United States Government may compel testimony from an unwilling witness, who invokes the Fifth Amendment privilege against compulsory self-incrimination, by conferring on the witness immunity from use of the compelled testimony in subsequent criminal proceedings, as well as immunity from use of evidence derived from the testimony.

Petitioners were subpoenaed to appear before a United States grand jury in the Central District of California on February 4, 1971. The Government believed that petitioners were likely to assert their Fifth Amendment privilege. Prior to the scheduled appearances, the Government applied to the District Court for an order directing petitioners to answer questions and produce evidence before the grand jury under a grant of immunity conferred pursuant to 18 U.S.C. §§6002, 6003. Petitioners opposed issuance of the order, contending primarily that the scope of the immunity provided by the statute was not coextensive with the scope of the privilege against self-incrimination, and therefore was not sufficient to supplant the privilege and compel their testimony. The District Court rejected this contention, and ordered petitioners to appear before the grand jury and answer its questions under the grant of immunity.

Petitioners appeared but refused to answer questions, asserting their privilege against compulsory self-incrimination. They were brought before the District Court, and each persisted in his refusal to answer the grand jury's questions, notwithstanding the grant of immunity. The court found both in contempt, and committed them to the custody of the Attorney General until either they answered the grand jury's questions or the term of the grand jury expired. The Court of Appeals for the Ninth Circuit affirmed. This Court granted *certiorari* to resolve the important question whether testimony may be compelled by granting immunity from the use of compelled testimony and evidence derived therefrom ("use and derivative use" immunity), or whether it is necessary to grant immunity from prosecution for offenses to which compelled testimony relates ("transactional" immunity).

I.

The power of government to compel persons to testify in court or before grand juries and other governmental agencies is firmly established in Anglo-American jurisprudence. The power with respect to courts was established by statute in England as early as 1562, and Lord Bacon observed in 1612 that all subjects owed the King their "knowledge and discovery." . . . The first Congress recognized the testimonial duty in the Judiciary Act of 1789, which provided for compulsory attendance of witnesses in the federal courts. . . .

But the power to compel testimony is not absolute. There are a number of exemptions from the testimonial duty, the most important of which is the Fifth Amendment privilege against compulsory self-incrimination. The privilege reflects a complex of our fundamental values and aspirations, and marks an important advance in the development of our liberty. It can be asserted in any proceeding, civil or criminal, administrative or judicial, investigatory or adjudicatory; and it protects against any disclosures which the witness reasonably believes could be used in a criminal prosecution or could lead to other evidence that might be so used. This Court has been zealous to safeguard the values which underlie the privilege.

Immunity statutes, which have historical roots deep in Anglo-American jurisprudence, are not incompatible with these values. Rather, they seek a rational accommodation between the imperatives of the privilege and the legitimate demands of government to compel citizens to testify. The existence of these statutes reflects the importance of testimony, and the fact that many offenses are of such a character that the only persons capable of giving useful testimony are those implicated in the crime. Indeed, their origins were in the context of such offenses, and their primary use has been to investigate such offenses. . . .

III.

Petitioners' . . . contention is that the scope of immunity provided by the federal witness immunity statute, 18 U.S.C. §6002, is not coextensive with the scope of the Fifth Amendment privilege against compulsory self-incrimination, and therefore is not sufficient to supplant the privilege and compel testimony over a claim of the privilege. The statute provides that when a witness is compelled by district court order to testify over a claim of the privilege:

> "the witness may not refuse to comply with the order on the basis of his privilege against self-incrimination; but no testimony or other information compelled under the order (or any information directly or indirectly derived from such testimony or other information) may be used against the witness in any criminal case, except a prosecution for perjury, giving a false statement, or otherwise failing to comply with the order."

18 U.S.C. §6002.

The constitutional inquiry, rooted in logic and history, as well as in the decisions of this Court, is whether the immunity granted under this statute is coextensive with the scope of the privilege. If so, petitioners' refusals to answer based on the privilege were unjustified, and the judgments of contempt were proper, for the grant of immunity has removed the dangers against which the privilege protects. If, on the other hand, the immunity granted is not as comprehensive as the protection afforded by the privilege, petitioners were justified in refusing to answer, and the judgments of contempt must be vacated.

Petitioners draw a distinction between statutes that provide transactional immunity and those that provide, as does the statute before us, immunity from use and derivative use. They contend that a statute must at a minimum grant full transactional immunity in order to be coextensive with the scope of the privilege. . . .

The statute's explicit proscription of the use in any criminal case of "testimony or other information compelled under the order (or any information directly or indirectly derived from such testimony or other information)" is consonant with Fifth Amendment standards. We hold that such immunity from use and derivative use is coextensive with the scope of the privilege against self-incrimination, and therefore is sufficient to compel testimony over a claim of the privilege. While a grant of immunity must afford protection commensurate with that afforded by the privilege, it need not be broader. Transactional immunity, which accords full immunity from prosecution for the offense to which the compelled testimony relates, affords the witness considerably broader protection than does the Fifth Amendment privilege. The privilege has never been construed to mean that one who invokes it cannot subsequently be prosecuted. Its sole concern is to afford protection against being "forced to give testimony leading to the infliction of 'penalties affixed to . . . criminal acts.'" Immunity from the use of compelled testimony, as well as evidence derived directly and indirectly therefrom, affords this protection. It prohibits the prosecutorial authorities from using the compelled testimony in any respect, and it therefore insures that the testimony cannot lead to the infliction of criminal penalties on the witness. . . .

We conclude that the immunity provided by 18 U.S.C. §6002 leaves the witness and the prosecutorial authorities in substantially the same position as if the witness had claimed the Fifth Amendment privilege. The immunity therefore is coextensive with the privilege and suffices to supplant it. The judgment of the Court of Appeals for the Ninth Circuit accordingly is

Affirmed.

Mr. Justice Brennan and Mr. Justice Rehnquist took no part in the consideration or decision of this case.

[Dissenting opinions of Douglas and Marshall, JJ., omitted.]

NOTES AND QUESTIONS

1. Generally speaking, courts enforce *Kastigar* by holding a "*Kastigar* hearing" anytime the government indicts an individual who previously received use and derivative use immunity in the same or related matter. At these hearings, the government carries the burden of showing that its case was not tainted in any way by the earlier testimony. *See* United States v. Slough, 677 F. Supp. 2d 112 (2009). As one might imagine, proving this negative after the fact is nearly impossible. Accordingly, prosecutors generally seek immunity for witnesses only if (1) they are satisfied that the witness does not merit prosecution; (2) they have already convicted the witness on charges pertinent to the matters about which he will be questioned; or (3) the prosecutors have prepared a case against the witness that they have sealed up and stored away prior to the immunity grant.
2. Congress, which has the authority to investigate matters related to its legislative functions, has independent power to grant immunity to witnesses who testify before its committees. *See* 18 U.S.C. §§6002, 6005. The Department of Justice often tries to convince Congress to forgo exercising this power to prevent a *Kastigar* problem from arising in a future criminal prosecution, and Congress usually complies. Sometimes, however, the political forces are just too strong, and the country obtains information at the expense of justice. One example of this was the criminal conviction of Oliver North in connection with the Iran-Contra affair, a major scandal that occurred during the administration of President Ronald Reagan. North's conviction was later overturned on *Kastigar* grounds due to an earlier congressional inquiry. *See* United States v. North, 910 F.2d 843 (1990), *opinion withdrawn*, 920 F.2d 940 (1990). Should there be some mechanism to prevent this kind of outcome, or is it simply a cost we must bear to maintain the separation of powers in our government?

PROBLEM 11-1

On January 10, 2005, in connection with an investigation of corruption in the New Jersey Department of Labor (DOL), Thomas Byrd testified before a federal grand jury under a grant of use and derivative use immunity. The case was led by AUSA John Stubbs and FBI Special Agent Tom Coleman. Byrd testified that he was a former employee of DOL and that he had witnessed and participated in numerous acts of bribery with other DOL employees, including the commissioner, over a period of about five years. A dozen or more other current and former employees of DOL testified similarly. In addition, Agent Coleman showed the grand jury records of bank deposits into various targets' accounts on days and in amounts corresponding to some of the alleged bribes.

On February 10, the grand jury returned indictments against Byrd, the DOL commissioner, and other officials of the Department. On March 20, AUSA Stubbs shredded and destroyed all copies of Byrd's immunized testimony, except the original, which was sealed and preserved for later court review, if needed.

In May 2005, the district court dismissed the indictment against Byrd because it had been returned by the same grand jury that had heard his immunized testimony, a clear violation of *Kastigar*. The order of dismissal was unopposed by the government.

On July 10, 2006, a different grand jury returned a new indictment against Byrd. The case was now being handled by AUSA Beatrice Chance. Byrd promptly filed a motion to dismiss this second indictment, also on *Kastigar* grounds. The court held a hearing on July 22.

At the hearing, FBI Agent Coleman testified that the only evidence presented to the second grand jury was his own testimony, which included (1) oral summaries of the testimony of various witnesses who had appeared before the first grand jury (except Byrd's, of course); (2) testimony concerning the contents of reports of witness interviews by FBI agents and other investigators which had been conducted prior to January 10, 2005; and (3) his bank records analysis. Coleman further testified that, although he had read a transcript of Byrd's immunized testimony prior to its destruction, he had not had access to any transcripts since then. He testified that he did not present any evidence to the second grand jury that was derived from his reading of Byrd's immunized testimony, nor did he in any way refer to such testimony. Finally, Coleman testified that he did not present any evidence to the second grand jury that had been obtained after Byrd's immunized testimony of June 16, 1983.

To corroborate Coleman's testimony, the government submitted the following evidence for *in camera* review: (1) the evidence against Byrd obtained by the government prior to the grant of immunity, which the government intended to use at trial; (2) Byrd's immunized testimony before the first grand jury; and (3) the transcript of Coleman's testimony before the second grand jury. In addition, AUSA Morehead testified that he had neither seen a transcript of the immunized testimony nor discussed any aspect of it with anyone who had.

Has the government overcome its *Kastigar* burden? Counsel for Byrd argues in the negative, claiming that, even if he testified in good faith, Agent Coleman could not help but use the immunized testimony in his decision making. AUSA Chance's position is that (1) the mere "possibility" that the immunized testimony influenced Agent Coleman in some unspecified way is not sufficient to rebut the government's evidence; and (2) a ruling for Byrd would mean that in all situations of this kind the government would be required to switch case agents, which would be a waste of valuable time and resources.

Who has the better position? What are the arguments on either side of the issue? What evidentiary burden should be used to weigh the adequacy of the government's position?

Cf. United States v. Byrd, 765 F.2d 1524 (11th Cir. 1985).

c. Targets and Warnings

Not every witness who appears before the grand jury is "equal." Many witnesses are solely that—innocent individuals who have information pertinent to the grand jury's investigation. Some witnesses, however, may be a target or subject of the grand jury's probe. The United States Attorneys' Manual describes a "target" as "a person as to whom the prosecutor or the grand jury has substantial evidence linking him or her to the commission of a crime and who, in the judgment of the prosecutor, is a putative defendant." A "subject" is an individual whose conduct has come within the scope of the grand jury's investigation. *See* USAM §9-11.151.

A grand jury may properly issue a subpoena *ad testificandum* to a subject or target of an investigation and question him about his involvement in the alleged crime. *See* United States v. Washington, 431 U.S. 181, 190 n.6 (1977); United States v. Wong, 431 U.S. 174, 179 n.8 (1977); United States v. Mandujano, 425 U.S. U.S. 564, 573-575 and 584 n.9 (1976). However, because subpoenaing a target can seem unfair, the Department of Justice requires that the line prosecutor first try to obtain the target's testimony voluntarily; if that fails, the prosecutor must get personal permission from the U. S. Attorney or (if she works in Main Justice) the responsible Assistant Attorney General before proceeding. *See* USAM §9-11.150.

In *Washington*, *supra* at 1820, the Supreme Court specifically held that targets of grand jury proceedings are not entitled to be warned of their status prior to testifying for their grand jury statements to be admissible against them later at trial. Moreover, in *Washington* and the other cited cases, the Court consistently declined to decide whether a target is entitled to be warned of his Fifth Amendment right against compulsory self-incrimination prior to giving grand jury testimony. This is one area, however, in which DOJ has decided to play it safe. The USAM requires that a target must be notified of his status prior to testifying, typically by means of a "target letter," *see* USAM §9-11.151. It also requires that an "Advice of Rights" form be attached to any subpoena issued to a target, and that the target be advised of—and acknowledge that he understands—his status and rights orally on the record in the grand jury room. The Advice of Rights form reads as follows:

- The grand jury is conducting an investigation of possible violations of Federal criminal laws involving: (State here the general subject matter of inquiry, e.g., conducting an illegal gambling business in violation of 18 U.S.C. §1955).
- You may refuse to answer any question if a truthful answer to the question would tend to incriminate you.
- Anything that you do say may be used against you by the grand jury or in a subsequent legal proceeding.
- If you have retained counsel, the grand jury will permit you a reasonable opportunity to step outside the grand jury room to consult with counsel if you so desire.

Occasionally, a target will request the opportunity to testify before the grand jury to tell his side of the story. Although a prosecutor has no obligation to grant such a request, *see, e.g.*, United States v. Leverage Funding System, Inc., 637 F.2d 645

(9th Cir. 1980), *cert. denied*, 452 U.S. 961 (1981); United States v. Gardner, 516 F.2d 334 (7th Cir. 1975), *cert. denied*, 423 U.S. 861 (1976), failing to do so might lend the proceeding a sense of unfairness. As a result, the USAM encourages prosecutors to grant such requests in the normal course. *See* USAM §9-11.152.

4. Subpoenas Duces Tecum (for Documents and Records)

Federal Rule of Criminal Procedure 17(c) addresses the requirements for the issuance and enforcement of subpoenas *duces tecum*. The critical language states that "the court may quash or modify the subpoena if compliance would be unreasonable or oppressive." Fed. R. Crim. P. 17(c)(2). Similarly, the Supreme Court held in Hale v. Henkel, 201 U.S. 43 (1906), that an overbroad subpoena for books and records "may constitute an unreasonable search and seizure within the Fourth Amendment." *See also* United States v. Dionisio, 410 U.S. 1, 11 (1973) (the "Fourth Amendment provides protection against a grand jury subpoena *duces tecum* too sweeping in its terms to be regarded as reasonable.") Although the Supreme Court has never directly addressed the specifications of reasonableness for Fourth Amendment purposes, one court set out the requirements as follows:

> [T]hree interrelated requirements appear critical: (1) that the subpoena command only the production of materials relevant to the investigation; (2) that the subpoena specify the materials to be produced with reasonable particularity; and (3) that the subpoena command production of materials covering only a reasonable period of time.

In re Corrado Brothers, 367 F. Supp. 1126 (D. Del. 1973).

In the following case, the Court was faced with the task of defining what reasonable means in the context of Rule 17(c).

UNITED STATES v. R. ENTERPRISES, INC.
498 U.S. 292 (1991)

Justice O'CONNOR delivered the opinion of the Court.

This case requires the Court to decide what standards apply when a party seeks to avoid compliance with a subpoena *duces tecum* issued in connection with a grand jury investigation.

I.

Since 1986, a federal grand jury sitting in the Eastern District of Virginia has been investigating allegations of interstate transportation of obscene materials. In early 1988, the grand jury issued a series of subpoenas to three companies—Model Magazine Distributors, Inc. (Model), R. Enterprises, Inc., and MFR Court Street Books, Inc. (MFR). Model is a New York distributor of sexually oriented paperback books, magazines, and videotapes. R. Enterprises, which distributes adult materials, and MFR, which sells books, magazines, and videotapes, are also based in New York. All three companies are wholly owned by Martin Rothstein. The grand jury subpoenas sought a variety of corporate books and records and, in Model's case, copies of 193 videotapes that Model had shipped to retailers in the Eastern District of Virginia. All three companies moved to quash the subpoenas, arguing that the subpoenas called for production of materials irrelevant to the grand jury's investigation and that the enforcement of the subpoenas would likely infringe their First Amendment rights.

The District Court, after extensive hearings, denied the motions to quash. As to Model, the court found that the subpoenas for business records were sufficiently specific and that production of the videotapes would not constitute a prior restraint. As to R. Enterprises, the court found a "sufficient connection with Virginia for further investigation by the grand jury." The court relied in large part on the statement attributed to Rothstein that the three companies were "all the same thing, I'm president of all three." Additionally, the court explained in denying MFR's motion to quash that it was "inclined to agree" with "the majority of the jurisdictions," which do not require the Government to make a "threshold showing" before a grand jury subpoena will be enforced. . . .

The Court of Appeals for the Fourth Circuit upheld the business records subpoenas issued to Model, but remanded the motion to quash the subpoena for Model's videotapes. Of particular relevance here, the Court of Appeals quashed the business records subpoenas issued to R. Enterprises and MFR. In doing so, it applied the standards set out by this Court in United States v. Nixon, 418 U.S. 683, 699-700 (1974). The court recognized that *Nixon* dealt with a trial subpoena, not a grand jury subpoena, but determined that the rule was "equally applicable" in the grand jury context. Accordingly, it required the Government to clear the three hurdles that Nixon established in the trial context—relevancy, admissibility, and specificity—in order to enforce the grand jury subpoenas. The court concluded that the challenged subpoenas did not satisfy the *Nixon* standards, finding no evidence in the record that either company had ever shipped materials into, or otherwise conducted business in, the Eastern District of Virginia. . . .

We granted certiorari to determine whether the Court of Appeals applied the proper standard in evaluating the grand jury subpoenas issued to respondents. We now reverse.

II.

The grand jury occupies a unique role in our criminal justice system. It is an investigatory body charged with the responsibility of determining whether or not a crime has been committed. Unlike this Court, whose jurisdiction is predicated on a specific case or controversy, the grand jury "can investigate merely on suspicion that the law is being violated, or even just because it wants assurance that it is not." The function of the grand jury is to inquire into all information that might possibly bear on its investigation until it has identified an offense or has satisfied itself that none has occurred. As a necessary consequence of its investigatory function, the grand jury paints with a broad brush. "A grand jury investigation 'is not fully carried out until every available clue has been run down and all witnesses examined in every proper way to find if a crime has been committed.'" A grand jury subpoena is thus much different from a subpoena issued in the context of a prospective criminal trial, where a specific offense has been identified and a particular defendant charged. "[T]he identity of the offender, and the precise nature of the offense, if there be one, normally are developed at the conclusion of the grand jury's labors, not at the beginning." In short, the Government cannot be required to justify the issuance of a grand jury subpoena by presenting evidence sufficient to establish probable cause because the very purpose of requesting the information is to ascertain whether probable cause exists. . . .

III.

A.

The investigatory powers of the grand jury are nevertheless not unlimited. Grand juries are not licensed to engage in arbitrary fishing expeditions, nor may they select targets of investigation out of malice or an intent to harass. In this case, the focus of our inquiry is the limit imposed on a grand jury by Federal Rule of Criminal Procedure 17(c), which governs the issuance of subpoenas *duces tecum* in federal criminal proceedings. The Rule provides that "[t]he court on motion made promptly may quash or modify the subpoena if compliance would be unreasonable or oppressive."

This standard is not self-explanatory. As we have observed, "what is reasonable depends on the context." . . .

To the extent that Rule 17(c) imposes some reasonableness limitation on grand jury subpoenas, however, our task is to define it. In doing so, we recognize that a party to whom a grand jury subpoena is issued faces a difficult situation. As a rule, grand juries do not announce publicly the subjects of their investigations. A party who desires to challenge a grand jury subpoena thus may have no conception of the Government's purpose in seeking production of the requested information. Indeed, the party will often not know whether he or she is a primary target of the investigation or merely a peripheral witness. Absent even minimal information, the subpoena recipient is likely to find it exceedingly difficult to persuade a court that "compliance would be unreasonable." As one pair of commentators has summarized it, the challenging party's "unenviable task is to seek to persuade the court that the subpoena that has been served on [him or her] could not possibly serve any investigative purpose that the grand jury could legitimately be pursuing." 1 S. Beale & W. Bryson, Grand Jury Law and Practice §6:28 (1986).

Our task is to fashion an appropriate standard of reasonableness, one that gives due weight to the difficult position of subpoena recipients but does not impair the strong governmental interests in affording grand juries wide latitude, avoiding minitrials on peripheral matters, and preserving a necessary level of secrecy. We begin by reiterating that the law presumes, absent a strong showing to the contrary, that a grand jury acts within the legitimate scope of its authority. Consequently, a grand jury subpoena issued through normal channels is presumed to be reasonable, and the burden of showing unreasonableness must be on the recipient who seeks to avoid compliance. Indeed, this result is indicated by the language of Rule

17(c), which permits a subpoena to be quashed only "on motion" and "if compliance would be unreasonable" (emphasis added). To the extent that the Court of Appeals placed an initial burden on the Government, it committed error. Drawing on the principles articulated above, we conclude that where, as here, a subpoena is challenged on relevancy grounds, the motion to quash must be denied unless the district court determines that there is no reasonable possibility that the category of materials the Government seeks will produce information relevant to the general subject of the grand jury's investigation.

B.

It seems unlikely, of course, that a challenging party who does not know the general subject matter of the grand jury's investigation, no matter how valid that party's claim, will be able to make the necessary showing that compliance would be unreasonable. After all, a subpoena recipient "cannot put his whole life before the court in order to show that there is no crime to be investigated." Consequently, a court may be justified in a case where unreasonableness is alleged in requiring the Government to reveal the general subject of the grand jury's investigation before requiring the challenging party to carry its burden of persuasion. We need not resolve this question in the present case, however, as there is no doubt that respondents knew the subject of the grand jury investigation pursuant to which the business records subpoenas were issued. In cases where the recipient of the subpoena does not know the nature of the investigation, we are confident that district courts will be able to craft appropriate procedures that balance the interests of the subpoena recipient against the strong governmental interests in maintaining secrecy, preserving investigatory flexibility, and avoiding procedural delays. For example, to ensure that subpoenas are not routinely challenged as a form of discovery, a district court may require that the Government reveal the subject of the investigation to the trial court *in camera*, so that the court may determine whether the motion to quash has a reasonable prospect for success before it discloses the subject matter to the challenging party.

Applying these principles in this case demonstrates that the District Court correctly denied respondents' motions to quash. It is undisputed that all three companies—Model, R. Enterprises, and MFR—are owned by the same person, that all do business in the same area, and that one of the three, Model, has shipped sexually explicit materials into the Eastern District of Virginia. The District Court could have concluded from these facts that there was a reasonable possibility that the business records of R. Enterprises and MFR would produce information relevant to the grand jury's investigation into the interstate transportation of obscene materials. . . .

The judgment is reversed insofar as the Court of Appeals quashed the subpoenas issued to R. Enterprises and MFR, and the case is remanded for further proceedings consistent with this opinion.

It is so ordered.

[Opinion of Stevens, J., concurring in part and concurring in the judgment, omitted.]

IN RE GRAND JURY SUBPOENAS, SERVED ON WHITE & CASE LLP, LIEFF, CABRASER, HEINEMANN, BERNSTEIN LLP, K&L GATES LLP, AND NOSSAMAN LLP

627 F.3d 1143 (9th Cir. 2010)

NOONAN, Circuit Judge:

The United States appeals an order of the district court quashing certain subpoenas directed to the respondent law firms named in the caption of the case (the Law Firms). The subpoenas sought nonprivileged material in aid of a grand jury investigating the clients of the Law Firms. The material had been obtained by the firms as a result of civil discovery in an antitrust suit. Holding that the district court abused its discretion, we reverse its order.

Background

In 2006, the United States was conducting an antitrust investigation into alleged criminal conduct. Soon after this investigation became public, a number of civil suits were filed by private plaintiffs against the companies under investigation. These suits were consolidated in the Northern District of California before District Judge Illston. The litigation resulted in the production by the civil defendants of documents originating outside the United States. The documents at issue here came into the possession of the Law Firms in the United States.

In this case the United States subpoenaed these documents. Invoking Federal Rule of Criminal Procedure 17, the Law Firms moved to quash. The district court stated that it found no authority governing the case. It concluded: "However, because the motions to quash raise novel issues with potentially far-reaching implications about the power of the grand jury and the relationship between grand jury proceedings and civil discovery of unindicted foreign defendants, the Court finds it is more prudent to quash the subpoenas and allow the DOJ to raise these issues on appeal to the Ninth Circuit."

This appeal followed.

Analysis

On appeal, the Law Firms argue that the district court exercised its discretion under Fed. R. Crim. Proc. 17 to quash the subpoenas and that the court of appeals should respect its reasonable exercise of discretion. We do not read the district court's decision as an exercise of discretion but as a passing of the decision to this court. We are not reviewing an exercise of discretion but a request for guidance.

No collusion between the civil suitors and the government has been established or even suggested by the Law Firms. Indeed, the district court determined that the government had not engaged in any bad faith tactics. Moreover, the Law Firms do not claim that the documents are privileged. Accordingly, we apply our per se rule that a grand jury subpoena takes precedence over a civil protective order. In re Grand Jury Subpoena Served on Meserve, Mumper & Hughes, 62 F.3d 1222, 1226-27 (9th Cir. 1995). By a chance of litigation, the documents have been moved from outside the grasp of the grand jury to within its grasp. No authority forbids the government from closing its grip on what lies within the jurisdiction of the grand jury. *See* 18 U.S.C. §3332.

For this reason, the order of the district court is REVERSED. The subpoenas may be enforced.

NOTES AND QUESTIONS

1. What exactly is the standard of reasonableness set out in *R. Enterprises*? Does it appropriately balance the interests of the government in being unfettered in the investigative stage of a case against the right of citizens not to be subjected to harassment or fishing expeditions?
2. Does the definition of reasonableness set out in *R. Enterprises* comport with the Fourth Amendment's reasonableness requirement as interpreted by the court in *In re Corrado Brothers*?
3. In 1997, the Third Circuit extended its *Schofield II* procedure (see *supra* p. 479) to subpoenas duces tecum, *see* In re Grand Jury, 103 F.3d 1140 (3d Cir. 1997). It continues to enforce *Schofield II* even after *R. Enterprises*. But is *Schofield* still good law? Note that the Court in *R. Enterprises* specifically states, "We begin by reiterating that the law presumes, absent a strong showing to the contrary, that a grand jury acts within the legitimate scope of its authority. Consequently, a grand jury subpoena issued through normal channels is presumed to be reasonable, and the burden of showing unreasonableness must be on the recipient who seeks to avoid compliance."

   On the other hand, the Court also says that "a court may be justified in a case where unreasonableness is alleged in requiring the Government to reveal the general subject of the grand jury's investigation before requiring the challenging party to carry its burden of persuasion." Moreover, it specifically emphasizes the discretion lower courts have in fashioning a remedy to handle claims of unreasonableness. Could it be argued that the Third Circuit is merely exercising its discretion by requiring an affidavit from prosecutors up front, perhaps for the sake of efficiency?
4. Was the district court's refusal to decide the legal issue in the "*Law Firms*" case—thereby passing it along to the Ninth Circuit—appropriate? How does Judge Noonan appear to feel about it? One hint is Judge Noonan's decision to name the district court judge in the opinion reversing the lower court's order, which is usually considered a form of censure for a judge who has acted out of line.

In addition to the Fourth Amendment, the Fifth Amendment's right against compelled self-incrimination also impacts the enforcement of subpoenas *duces tecum*. For more than a century, the Supreme Court struggled with trying to define the exact relationship between the two. In recent years, it appears to have settled on the view that the contents of subpoenaed documents are not protected by the Fifth Amendment because their author was not compelled by the government to create them in the first place. This interpretation clearly applies to business records and likely applies to personal papers, such as diaries and journals, as well. On the other hand, compliance with a subpoena—that is, the act of producing the documents—*is* compelled by the court through its contempt power, and the act of production can have testimonial aspects. For example, the act of production might later be used at trial by the government as proof that the documents are authentic, which is a prerequisite for their admission into evidence under Federal Rule of Evidence 901.[12]

DOE v. UNITED STATES

487 U.S. 201 (1988)

Justice BLACKMUN delivered the opinion of the Court.

This case presents the question whether a court order compelling a target of a grand jury investigation to authorize foreign banks to disclose records of his accounts, without identifying those documents or acknowledging their existence, violates the target's Fifth Amendment privilege against self-incrimination.

I.

Petitioner, named here as John Doe, is the target of a federal grand jury investigation into possible federal offenses arising from suspected fraudulent manipulation of oil cargoes and receipt of unreported income. Doe appeared before the grand jury pursuant to a subpoena that directed him to produce records of transactions in accounts at three named banks in the Cayman Islands and Bermuda. Doe produced some bank records and testified that no additional records responsive to the subpoena were in his possession or control. When questioned about the existence or location of additional records, Doe invoked the Fifth Amendment privilege against self-incrimination.

The United States branches of the three foreign banks also were served with subpoenas commanding them to produce records of accounts over which Doe had signatory authority. Citing their governments' bank-secrecy laws, which prohibit the disclosure of account records without the customer's consent, the banks refused to comply. The Government then filed a motion with the United States District Court for the Southern District of Texas that the court order Doe to sign 12 forms consenting to disclosure of any bank records respectively relating to 12 foreign bank accounts over which the Government knew or suspected that Doe had control. . . .

12. A common method of authenticating subpoenaed records at trial is to call a government agent to testify that the records were produced by the party responding to the subpoena, asking the jury, in effect, to infer the records' legitimacy from the fact that they originated from a place where one would expect to find them in the normal course. This would constitute reliance on the implicit out-of-court testimonial statement of the subpoenaed party to the effect of, "Here are real and unadulterated documents that match the description specified in the subpoena." Unless the authenticity of the records were raised as a serious issue in the case, such testimony would meet the government's burden under Fed. R. Evid. 104(b) and 901.

The District Court denied the motion, reasoning that by signing the consent forms, Doe would necessarily be admitting the existence of the accounts. The District Court believed, moreover, that if the banks delivered records pursuant to the consent forms, those forms would constitute "an admission that [Doe] exercised signatory authority over such accounts." The court speculated that the Government in a subsequent proceeding then could argue that Doe must have guilty knowledge of the contents of the accounts. Thus, in the court's view, compelling Doe to sign the forms was compelling him "to perform a testimonial act that would entail admission of knowledge of the contents of potentially incriminating documents," and such compulsion was prohibited by the Fifth Amendment. . . .

The Court of Appeals for the Fifth Circuit reversed in an unpublished per curiam opinion judgment order. . . .

On remand, the District Court ordered petitioner to execute the consent directive. He refused. The District Court accordingly found petitioner in civil contempt and ordered that he be confined until he complied with the order. The court stayed imposition of sanction pending appeal and application for writ of certiorari.

The Fifth Circuit affirmed the contempt order. . . . We conclude that a court order compelling the execution of such a directive as is at issue here does not implicate the [Fifth] Amendment.

II.

It is undisputed that the contents of the foreign bank records sought by the Government are not privileged under the Fifth Amendment. *See* Braswell v. United States, 487 U.S. 99, 108-110 (1988); United States v. Doe, 465 U.S. 605 (1984); Fisher v. United States, 425 U.S. 391 (1976). There also is no question that the foreign banks cannot invoke the Fifth Amendment in declining to produce the documents; the privilege does not extend to such artificial entities. *See* Braswell v. United States, 487 U.S., at 102-103; Bellis v. United States, 417 U.S. 85, 89-90 (1974). Similarly, petitioner asserts no Fifth Amendment right to prevent the banks from disclosing the account records, for the Constitution "necessarily does not proscribe incriminating statements elicited from another." Couch v. United States, 409 U.S. 322 (1973). Petitioner's sole claim is that his execution of the consent forms directing the banks to release records as to which the banks believe he has the right of withdrawal has independent testimonial significance that will incriminate him, and that the Fifth Amendment prohibits governmental compulsion of that act. . . .

A.

Petitioner contends that a compelled statement is testimonial if the Government could use the content of the speech or writing, as opposed to its physical characteristics, to further a criminal investigation of the witness. The second half of petitioner's "testimonial" test is that the statement must be incriminating, which is, of course, already a separate requirement for invoking the privilege. Thus, Doe contends, in essence, that every written and oral statement significant for its content is necessarily testimonial for purposes of the Fifth Amendment. Under this view, the consent directive is testimonial because it is a declarative statement of consent made by Doe to the foreign banks, a statement that the Government will use to persuade the banks to produce potentially incriminating account records that would otherwise be unavailable to the grand jury. . . .

The Government's view of the privilege, apparently accepted by the Courts of Appeals that have considered compelled consent forms, is derived largely from this Court's decisions in *Fisher* and *Doe*. The issue presented in those cases was whether the act of producing subpoenaed documents, not itself the making of a statement, might nonetheless have some protected testimonial aspects. The Court concluded that the act of production could constitute protected testimonial communication because it might entail implicit statements of fact: by producing documents in compliance with a subpoena, the witness would admit that the papers existed, were in his possession or control, and were authentic. Thus, the Court made clear that the Fifth Amendment privilege against self-incrimination applies to acts that imply assertions of fact. . . .

This understanding is perhaps most clearly revealed in those cases in which the Court has held that certain acts, though incriminating, are not within the privilege. Thus, a suspect may be compelled to furnish a blood sample; to provide a handwriting exemplar or a voice exemplar; to stand in a lineup; and to wear particular clothing. These decisions are grounded on the proposition that "the privilege protects an accused only from being compelled to testify against himself, or otherwise provide the State with evidence of a testimonial or communicative nature." The Court accordingly held that the privilege was not implicated in each of those cases, because the suspect was not required "to disclose any knowledge he might have," or "to speak his guilt." It is the "extortion of information from the accused," the attempt to force him "to disclose the contents of his own mind," that implicates the Self-Incrimination Clause. . . .

B.

The difficult question whether a compelled communication is testimonial for purposes of applying the Fifth Amendment often depends on the facts and circumstances of the particular case. This case is no exception. We turn, then, to consider whether Doe's execution of the consent directive at issue here would have testimonial significance. We agree with the Court of Appeals that it would not, because neither the form, nor its execution, communicates any factual assertions, implicit or explicit, or conveys any information to the Government.

The consent directive itself is not "testimonial." It is carefully drafted not to make reference to a specific account, but only to speak in the hypothetical. Thus, the form does not acknowledge that an account in a foreign financial institution is in existence or that it is controlled by petitioner. Nor does the form indicate whether documents or any other information relating to petitioner are present at the foreign bank, assuming that such an account does exist. The form does not even identify the relevant bank. Although the executed form allows the Government access to a potential source of evidence, the directive itself does not point the Government toward hidden accounts or otherwise provide information that will assist the prosecution in uncovering evidence. The Government must locate that evidence "'by the independent labor of its officers,'" As in *Fisher*, the Government is not relying upon the "'truthtelling'" of Doe's directive to show the existence of, or his control over, foreign bank account records.

Given the consent directive's phraseology, petitioner's compelled act of executing the form has no testimonial significance either. By signing the form, Doe makes no statement, explicit or implicit, regarding the existence of a foreign bank account or his control over any such account. Nor would his execution of the form admit the authenticity of any records produced by the bank. Not only does the directive express no view on the issue, but because petitioner did not prepare the document, any statement by Doe to the effect that it is authentic would not establish that the records are genuine. Authentication evidence would have to be provided by bank officials.

Finally, we cannot agree with petitioner's contention that his execution of the directive admits or asserts Doe's consent. The form does not state that Doe "consents" to the release of bank records. Instead, it states that the directive "shall be construed as consent" with respect to Cayman Islands and Bermuda bank-secrecy laws. Because the directive explicitly indicates that it was signed pursuant to a court order, Doe's compelled execution of the form sheds no light on his actual intent or state of mind. The form does "direct" the bank to disclose account information and release any records that "may" exist and for which Doe "may" be a relevant principal. But directing the recipient of a communication to do something is not an assertion of fact or, at least in this context, a disclosure of information. In its testimonial significance, the execution of such a directive is analogous to the production of a handwriting sample or voice exemplar: it is a nontestimonial act. In neither case is the suspect's action compelled to obtain "any knowledge he might have." . . .

We read the directive as equivalent to a statement by Doe that, although he expresses no opinion about the existence of, or his control over, any such account, he is authorizing the bank to disclose information relating to accounts over which, in the bank's opinion, Doe can exercise the right of withdrawal. When forwarded to the bank along with a subpoena, the executed directive, if effective under local law, will simply make it possible for the recipient bank to comply with the Government's request to produce such records. As a result, if the Government obtains bank records after Doe signs the directive, the only factual statement made by anyone will be the bank's implicit declaration, by its act of production in response to the subpoena, that it believes the accounts to be petitioner's. The fact that the bank's customer has directed the disclosure of his records "would say nothing about the correctness of the bank's representations." Indeed, the Second and Eleventh Circuits have concluded that consent directives virtually identical to the one here are inadmissible as an admission by the signator of either control or existence.

III.

Because the consent directive is not testimonial in nature, we conclude that the District Court's order compelling petitioner to sign the directive does not violate his Fifth Amendment privilege against self-incrimination. Accordingly, the judgment of the Court of Appeals is affirmed.

It is so ordered.

[Dissenting opinion of Stevens, J., omitted.]

UNITED STATES v. HUBBELL

530 U.S. 27 (2000)

Justice STEVENS delivered the opinion of the Court.

The two questions presented concern the scope of a witness' protection against compelled self-incrimination: (1) whether the Fifth Amendment privilege protects a witness from being compelled to disclose the existence of incriminating documents that the Government is unable to describe with reasonable particularity; and (2) if the witness produces such documents pursuant to a grant of immunity, whether 18 U.S.C. §6002 prevents the Government from using them to prepare criminal charges against him.

I.

This proceeding arises out of the second prosecution of respondent, Webster Hubbell, commenced by the Independent Counsel appointed in August 1994 to investigate possible violations of federal law relating to the Whitewater Development Corporation. The first prosecution was terminated pursuant to a plea bargain. In December 1994, respondent pleaded guilty to charges of mail fraud and tax evasion arising out of his billing practices as a member of an Arkansas law firm from 1989 to 1992, and was sentenced to 21 months in prison. In the plea agreement, respondent promised to provide the Independent Counsel with "full, complete, accurate, and truthful information" about matters relating to the Whitewater investigation.

The second prosecution resulted from the Independent Counsel's attempt to determine whether respondent had violated that promise. In October 1996, while respondent was incarcerated, the Independent Counsel served him with a subpoena *duces tecum* calling for the production of 11 categories of documents before a grand jury sitting in Little Rock, Arkansas. On November 19, he appeared before the grand jury and invoked his Fifth Amendment privilege against self-incrimination. In response to questioning by the prosecutor, respondent initially refused "to state whether there are documents within my possession, custody, or control responsive to the Subpoena." Thereafter, the prosecutor produced an order, which had previously been obtained from the District Court pursuant to 18 U.S.C. §6003(a), directing him to respond to the subpoena and granting him immunity "to the extent allowed by law." Respondent then produced 13,120 pages of documents and records and responded to a series of questions that established that those were all of the documents in his custody or control that were responsive to the commands in the subpoena, with the exception of a few documents he claimed were shielded by the attorney-client and attorney work-product privileges.

The contents of the documents produced by respondent provided the Independent Counsel with the information that led to this second prosecution. On April 30, 1998, a grand jury in the District of Columbia returned a 10-count indictment charging respondent with various tax-related crimes and mail and wire fraud. The District Court dismissed the indictment relying, in part, on the ground that the Independent Counsel's use of the subpoenaed documents violated §6002 because all of the evidence he would offer against respondent at trial derived either directly or indirectly from the testimonial aspects of respondent's immunized act of producing those documents. Noting that the Independent Counsel had admitted that he was not investigating tax-related issues when he issued the subpoena, and that he had "'learned about the unreported income and other crimes from studying the records' contents,'" the District Court characterized the subpoena as "the quintessential fishing expedition."

The Court of Appeals vacated the judgment and remanded for further proceedings. The majority concluded that the District Court had incorrectly relied on the fact that the Independent Counsel did not have prior knowledge of the contents of the subpoenaed documents. The question the District Court should have addressed was the extent of the Government's independent knowledge of the documents' existence and authenticity, and of respondent's possession or control of them. It explained:

> "On remand, the district court should hold a hearing in which it seeks to establish the extent and detail of the [G]overnment's knowledge of Hubbell's financial affairs (or of the paperwork documenting it) on the day the subpoena issued. It is only then that the court will be in a position to assess the testimonial value of Hubbell's response to the subpoena. Should the Independent Counsel prove capable of demonstrating with reasonable particularity a prior awareness that the exhaustive litany of documents sought in the subpoena existed and were in Hubbell's possession, then the wide distance evidently traveled from the subpoena to the substantive allegations contained in the indictment would be based upon legitimate intermediate steps. To the extent that the information conveyed through Hubbell's compelled act of production provides the necessary linkage, however, the indictment deriving therefrom is tainted."

... On remand, the Independent Counsel acknowledged that he could not satisfy the "reasonable particularity" standard prescribed by the Court of Appeals and entered into a conditional plea agreement with respondent. In essence, the agreement provides for the dismissal of the charges unless this Court's disposition of the case makes it reasonably likely that respondent's "act [of] production immunity" would not pose a significant bar to his prosecution. The case is not moot, however, because the agreement also provides for the entry of a guilty plea and a sentence that will not include incarceration if we should reverse and issue an opinion that is sufficiently favorable to the Government to satisfy that condition. Despite that agreement, we granted the Independent Counsel's petition for a writ of certiorari in order to determine the precise scope of a grant of immunity with respect to the production of documents in response to a subpoena. We now affirm....

IV.

The Government correctly emphasizes that the testimonial aspect of a response to a subpoena *duces tecum* does nothing more than establish the existence, authenticity, and custody of items that are produced. We assume that the Government is also entirely correct in its submission that it would not have to advert to respondent's act of production in order to prove the existence, authenticity, or custody of any documents that it might offer in evidence at a criminal trial; indeed, the Government disclaims any need to introduce any of the documents produced by respondent into evidence in order to prove the charges against him. It follows, according to the Government, that it has no intention of making improper "use" of respondent's compelled testimony.

The question, however, is not whether the response to the subpoena may be introduced into evidence at his criminal trial. That would surely be a prohibited "use" of the immunized act of production. But the fact that the Government intends no such use of the act of production leaves open the separate question whether it has already made "derivative use" of the testimonial aspect of that act in obtaining the indictment against respondent and in preparing its case for trial. It clearly has.

It is apparent from the text of the subpoena itself that the prosecutor needed respondent's assistance both to identify potential sources of information and to produce those sources. Given the breadth of the description of the 11 categories of documents called for by the subpoena, the collection and production of the materials demanded was tantamount to answering a series of interrogatories asking a witness to disclose the existence and location of particular documents fitting certain broad descriptions. The assembly of literally hundreds of pages of material in response to a request for "any and all documents reflecting, referring, or relating to any direct or indirect sources of money or other things of value received by or provided to" an individual or members of his family during a 3-year period is the functional equivalent of the preparation of an answer to either a detailed written interrogatory or a series of oral questions at a discovery deposition. Entirely apart from the contents of the 13,120 pages of materials that respondent produced in this case, it is undeniable that providing a catalog of existing documents fitting within any of the 11 broadly worded subpoena categories could provide a prosecutor with a "lead to incriminating evidence," or "a link in the chain of evidence needed to prosecute."

Indeed, the record makes it clear that that is what happened in this case. The documents were produced before a grand jury sitting in the Eastern District of Arkansas in aid of the Independent Counsel's attempt to determine whether respondent had violated a commitment in his first plea agreement. The use of those sources of information eventually led to the return of an indictment by a grand jury sitting in the District of Columbia for offenses that apparently are unrelated to that plea agreement. What the District Court characterized as a "fishing expedition" did produce a fish, but not the one that the Independent Counsel expected to hook. It is abundantly clear that the testimonial aspect of respondent's act of producing subpoenaed documents was the first step in a chain of evidence that led to this prosecution. The documents did not magically appear in the prosecutor's office like "manna from heaven." They arrived there only after respondent asserted his constitutional privilege, received a grant of immunity, and—under the compulsion of the District Court's order—took the mental and physical steps necessary to provide the prosecutor with an accurate inventory of the many sources of potentially incriminating evidence sought by the subpoena. It was only through respondent's truthful reply to the subpoena that the Government received the incriminating documents of which it made "substantial use . . . in the investigation that led to the indictment."

For these reasons, we cannot accept the Government's submission that respondent's immunity did not preclude its derivative use of the produced documents because its "possession of the documents [was] the fruit only of a simple physical act—the act of producing the documents." It was unquestionably necessary for respondent to make extensive use of "the contents of his own mind" in identifying the hundreds of documents responsive to the requests in the subpoena. The assembly of those documents was like telling an inquisitor the combination to a wall safe, not like being forced to surrender the key to a strongbox. The Government's anemic view of respondent's act of production as a mere physical act that is principally nontestimonial in character and can be entirely divorced from its "implicit" testimonial aspect so as to constitute a "legitimate, wholly independent source" (as required by *Kastigar*) for the documents produced simply fails to account for these realities.

In sum, we have no doubt that the constitutional privilege against self-incrimination protects the target of a grand jury investigation from being compelled to answer questions designed to elicit information about the existence of sources of potentially incriminating evidence. That constitutional privilege has the same application to the testimonial aspect of a response to a subpoena seeking discovery of those sources. . . .

Given our conclusion that respondent's act of production had a testimonial aspect, at least with respect to the existence and location of the documents sought by the Government's subpoena, respondent could not be compelled to produce those documents without first receiving a grant of immunity under §6003. As we construed §6002 in *Kastigar*, such immunity is coextensive with the constitutional privilege. *Kastigar* requires that respondent's motion to dismiss the indictment on immunity grounds be granted unless the Government proves that the evidence it used in obtaining the indictment and proposed to use at trial was derived from legitimate sources "wholly independent" of the testimonial aspect of respondent's immunized conduct in assembling and producing the documents described in the subpoena. The Government, however, does not claim that it could make such a showing. . . .

Accordingly, the indictment against respondent must be dismissed. The judgment of the Court of Appeals is affirmed.

It is so ordered.

Justice THOMAS, with whom Justice SCALIA joins, concurring.

Our decision today involves the application of the act-of-production doctrine, which provides that persons compelled to turn over incriminating papers or other physical evidence pursuant to a subpoena *duces tecum* or a summons may invoke the Fifth Amendment privilege against self-incrimination as a bar to production only where the act of producing the evidence would contain "testimonial" features. I join the opinion of the Court because it properly applies this doctrine, but I write separately to note that this doctrine may be inconsistent with the original meaning of the Fifth Amendment's Self-Incrimination Clause. A substantial body of evidence suggests that the Fifth Amendment privilege protects against the compelled production not just of incriminating testimony, but of any incriminating evidence. In a future case, I would be willing to reconsider the scope and meaning of the Self-Incrimination Clause. . . .

[Dissenting opinion of Rehnquist, CJ., omitted.]

NOTES AND QUESTIONS

1. Has the exception swallowed the rule? *Fisher* and *Doe* winnowed down Fifth Amendment protection for subpoenas to the act of production (which is compelled) rather than the contents of the documents (which is not). This led to the notion of "act of production immunity": the government could satisfy *Fisher* and *Doe* simply by obtaining §6002 immunity for the custodian of the records for the act of producing the records (as was done in the *Hubbell* case), and could then use the records at trial as long as it could authenticate them from another source. After *Hubbell*, can this technique be used successfully if the government does not have prior knowledge, with "reasonable particularity," of the existence and location of the documents it seeks? How often does the government know in advance exactly what documents a records custodian has in his possession? If the answer is rarely, isn't the result the functional equivalent of protecting the contents of documents themselves?
2. Should we start over as Justice Thomas suggests and interpret the Fifth Amendment as protecting against the giving of *any* evidence against oneself?
3. Does *Hubbell* apply to records custodians who are not targets of the grand jury's investigation? How?
4. Could the additional Fifth Amendment protection provided by *Hubbell* actually backfire on targeted records custodians? Arguably, yes. Once a custodian invoked privilege, the prosecutor might "back away" from using a subpoena for fear that *Hubbell* would taint any evidence gathered through a grant of act of production immunity. However, the custodian's invocation of privilege will have telegraphed to the prosecutor that the sought-after documents contain incriminating evidence, which is likely to encourage the prosecutor to focus her efforts on obtaining probable cause for a search warrant. The execution of the warrant would be far more intrusive than compliance with the subpoena, wouldn't it? Is there anything wrong with the prosecutor's use of this strategy?

BRASWELL v. UNITED STATES
487 U.S. 99 (1988)

Chief Justice REHNQUIST delivered the opinion of the Court.

This case presents the question whether the custodian of corporate records may resist a subpoena for such records on the ground that the act of production would incriminate him in violation of the Fifth Amendment. We conclude that he may not.

From 1965 to 1980, petitioner Randy Braswell operated his business—which comprises the sale and purchase of equipment, land, timber, and oil and gas interests—as a sole proprietorship. In 1980, he incorporated Worldwide Machinery Sales, Inc., a Mississippi corporation, and began conducting the business through that entity. In 1981, he formed a second Mississippi corporation, Worldwide Purchasing, Inc., and funded that corporation with the 100 percent interest he held in Worldwide Machinery. Petitioner was and is the sole shareholder of Worldwide Purchasing, Inc.

Both companies are active corporations, maintaining their current status with the State of Mississippi, filing corporate tax returns, and keeping current corporate books and records. In compliance with Mississippi law, both corporations have three directors, petitioner, his wife, and his mother. Although his wife and mother are secretary-treasurer and vice-president of the corporations, respectively, neither has any authority over the business affairs of either corporation.

In August 1986, a federal grand jury issued a subpoena to "Randy Braswell, President Worldwide Machinery Sales Inc. [and] Worldwide Purchasing, Inc.," requiring petitioner to produce the books and records of the two corporations. The subpoena provided that petitioner could deliver the records to the agent serving the subpoena, and did not require petitioner to testify. Petitioner moved to quash the subpoena, arguing that the act of producing the records would incriminate him in violation of his Fifth Amendment privilege against self-incrimination. The District Court denied the motion to quash, ruling that the "collective entity doctrine" prevented petitioner from asserting that his act of producing the corporations' records was protected by the Fifth Amendment. The court rejected petitioner's argument that the collective entity doctrine does not apply when a corporation is so small that it constitutes nothing more than the individual's alter ego.

The United States Court of Appeals for the Fifth Circuit affirmed. . . . We granted certiorari to resolve a conflict among the Courts of Appeals. . . . We now affirm.

There is no question but that the contents of the subpoenaed business records are not privileged. Similarly, petitioner asserts no self-incrimination claim on behalf of the corporations; it is well established that such artificial entities are not protected by the Fifth Amendment. Petitioner instead relies solely upon the argument that his act of producing the documents has independent testimonial significance, which would incriminate him individually, and that the Fifth Amendment prohibits Government compulsion of that act.

Had petitioner conducted his business as a sole proprietorship, [precedent] would require that he be provided the opportunity to show that his act of production would entail testimonial self-incrimination. But petitioner has operated his business through the corporate form, and we have long recognized that, for purposes of the Fifth Amendment, corporations and other collective entities are treated differently from individuals. This doctrine—known as the collective entity rule—has a lengthy and distinguished pedigree.

[Here the Court reviews the early history of the collective entity rule.]

The next significant step in the development of the collective entity rule occurred in United States v. White, 322 U.S. 694 (1944), in which the Court held that a labor union is a collective entity unprotected by the Fifth Amendment. . . .

The frontiers of the collective entity rule were expanded even further in Bellis v. United States, 417 U.S. 85 (1974), in which the Court ruled that a partner in a small partnership could not properly refuse to produce partnership records. . . .

The plain mandate of these decisions is that without regard to whether the subpoena is addressed to the corporation, or as here, to the individual in his capacity as a custodian, a corporate custodian such as petitioner may not resist a subpoena for corporate records on Fifth Amendment grounds. . . .

[T]he Court has consistently recognized that the custodian of corporate or entity records holds those documents in a representative rather than a personal capacity. Artificial entities such as corporations may act only through their agents and a custodian's assumption of his representative capacity leads to certain obligations, including the duty to produce corporate records on proper demand by the Government. Under those circumstances, the custodian's act of production is not deemed a personal act, but rather an act of the corporation. Any claim of Fifth Amendment privilege asserted by the agent would be tantamount to a claim of privilege by the corporation—which of course possesses no such privilege. . . .

We note further that recognizing a Fifth Amendment privilege on behalf of the records custodians of collective entities would have a detrimental impact on the Government's efforts to prosecute "white-collar crime," one of the most serious problems confronting law enforcement authorities. "The greater portion of evidence of wrongdoing by an organization or its representatives is usually found in the official records and documents of that organization. Were the cloak of the privilege to be thrown around these impersonal records and documents, effective enforcement of many federal and state laws would be impossible." . . .

Petitioner suggests, however, that these concerns can be minimized by the simple expedient of either granting the custodian statutory immunity as to the act of production, 18 U.S.C. §§6002, 6003, or addressing the subpoena to the corporation and allowing it to choose an agent to produce the records who can do so without incriminating himself. We think neither proposal satisfactorily addresses these concerns. Taking the last first, it is no doubt true that if a subpoena is addressed to a corporation, the corporation "must find some means by which to comply because no Fifth Amendment defense is available to it." The means most commonly used to comply is the appointment of an alternate custodian. But petitioner insists he cannot be required to aid the appointed custodian in his search for the demanded records, for any statement to the surrogate would itself be testimonial and incriminating. If this is correct, then petitioner's "solution" is a chimera. In situations such as this—where the corporate custodian is likely the only person with knowledge about the demanded documents—the appointment of a surrogate will simply not ensure that the documents sought will ever reach the grand jury room; the appointed custodian will essentially be sent on an unguided search.

This problem is eliminated if the Government grants the subpoenaed custodian statutory immunity for the testimonial aspects of his act of production. But that "solution" also entails a significant drawback. All of the evidence obtained under a grant of immunity to the custodian may of course be used freely against the corporation, but if the Government has any thought of prosecuting the custodian, a grant of act of production immunity can have serious consequences. Testimony obtained pursuant to a grant of statutory use immunity may be used neither directly nor derivatively. And "[o]ne raising a claim under [the federal immunity] statute need only show that he testified under a grant of immunity in order to shift to the government the heavy burden of proving that all of the evidence it proposes to use was derived from legitimate independent sources." Even in cases where the Government does not employ the immunized testimony for any purpose—direct or derivative—against the witness, the Government's inability to meet the "heavy burden" it bears may result in the preclusion of crucial evidence that was obtained legitimately.

Although a corporate custodian is not entitled to resist a subpoena on the ground that his act of production will be personally incriminating, we do think certain consequences flow from the fact that the custodian's act of production is one in his representative rather than personal capacity. Because the custodian acts as a representative, the act is deemed one of the corporation and not the individual. Therefore, the Government concedes, as it must, that it may make no evidentiary use of the "individual act" against the individual. For example, in a criminal prosecution against the custodian, the Government may not introduce into evidence before the jury the fact that the subpoena was served upon and the corporation's documents were delivered by one particular individual, the custodian. The Government has the right, however, to use the corporation's act of production against the custodian. The Government may offer testimony—for example, from the process server who delivered the subpoena and from the individual who received the records—establishing that the corporation produced the records subpoenaed. The jury may draw from the corporation's act of production the conclusion that the records in question are authentic corporate records, which the corporation possessed, and which it produced in response to the subpoena. And if the defendant held a prominent position within the corporation that produced the records, the jury may, just as it would had someone else produced the documents, reasonably infer that he had possession of the documents or knowledge of their contents. Because the jury is not told that the defendant produced the records, any nexus between the defendant and the documents results solely from the corporation's act of production and other evidence in the case.

The judgment is therefore

Affirmed.

NOTES AND QUESTIONS

1. In *Braswell*, the Court decides that a corporate records custodian acts solely in a representative capacity when delivering subpoenaed records. Think back to *United States v. Wise*, *supra* p. 59 (Chapter 2). In that case, the Court held that an individual cannot avoid criminal liability by claiming that actions he took on behalf of his corporation were in a representative capacity only. Can the two cases be reconciled?
2. The *Braswell* Court holds that a corporate records custodian is not entitled to act of production immunity because this could lead to an inability to prosecute the custodian altogether. But it also holds that the custodian is protected by the fact that the jury may not be told that the custodian personally delivered the subpoenaed records. Isn't this act of production immunity? If not, how do the two differ?

3. The Court puts forward a number of utilitarian/policy-based arguments in support of the *Braswell* outcome. What are they? Do they convince you that the collective entity doctrine is justified?

PROBLEM 11-2

Natural Products, Inc. (NP) is a publicly traded company that manufactures supplements sold to health food stores. Its President is Vincent Kruger. Until 2009, NP's best seller was "Muscle-Up," a dietary supplement with a "secret ingredient" that helped young athletes build bigger muscles in the course of several months. Muscle-Up brought measurable results.

In March 2009, rumors began to circulate that Muscle-Up's secret ingredient was, in fact, a steroid banned by the Food and Drug Administration (FDA). Sure enough, the FDA opened an investigation of Muscle-Up in May 2009. A grand jury investigation followed soon after, assigned to AUSA Wanda Geiger.

Geiger's first act was to issue a subpoena to NP for "all corporate documents, correspondence (including e-mails and other electronic communications), and other written or electronically stored materials related in any manner whatsoever to the chemical composition of Muscle-Up." The subpoena was addressed to "Pres. & CEO Vincent Kruger, Custodian of Records."

Kruger refused to comply with the subpoena, claiming that it would violate his Fifth Amendment right against self-incrimination. AUSA Geiger moved in the district court to compel Kruger's compliance. The court held that, as a custodian of corporate records, Kruger was not entitled to claim the privilege due to the "collective entity doctrine." She therefore ordered Kruger to comply with the subpoena or be held in contempt. Kruger complied by turning over thousands of corporate records, including an e-mail from Kruger to NP's Vice President for Public Relations early in the corporation's history in which Kruger stated, "Vickie—whatever you do, make sure that the public does not find out about the steroids in Muscle-Up. They are very controversial. If asked, be mysterious—say that Muscle-Up has a 'secret ingredient' or something like that." The government was not aware of the existence of this e-mail until the grand jury received it in response to the subpoena.

NP and Kruger are eventually indicted for violations of the Food and Drug Act. Kruger moves to dismiss the indictment against him as being brought in violation of *Hubbell*.

How should the trial judge rule, and why?

Cf. Armstrong v. Guccione, 470 F.3d 89 (2d Cir. 2006).

E. Search Warrants

The procedure for obtaining a federal warrant to conduct a search of a private place is contained in Federal Rule of Criminal Procedure 41. Under Rule 41, any federal law enforcement officer or attorney for the government may apply to a federal magistrate judge for a warrant. The warrant must specify the person or property to be searched and seized and the magistrate judge to whom the warrant must be returned. Attached to the warrant is an affidavit sworn to under oath by the law enforcement officer (often ghost written by the prosecutor) setting out all of the facts and circumstances demonstrating that probable cause exists to conduct the search. The warrant is good for a maximum of 14 days (after which it goes "stale"), and must be executed during the daytime, unless special permission is requested and granted to conduct the search at night. Constitutionally, search and seizures are regulated by the Fourth Amendment.

The Supreme Court has consistently shied away from articulating a clear measurement of probable cause. The closest it came to defining the term was in Illinois v. Gates, 462 U.S. 213 (1983):

> Perhaps the central teaching of our decisions bearing on the probable cause standard is that it is a "practical, nontechnical conception." "In dealing with probable cause, . . . as the very name implies, we deal with probabilities. These are not technical; they are the factual and practical considerations of everyday life on which reasonable and prudent men, not legal technicians, act."
>
> Our observation in United States v. Cortez, 449 U.S. 411, 418 (1981), regarding "particularized suspicion," is also applicable to the probable cause standard:
>
>> The process does not deal with hard certainties, but with probabilities. Long before the law of probabilities was articulated as such, practical people formulated certain common-sense conclusions about human behavior; jurors as factfinders are permitted to do the same—and so are law enforcement officers. Finally, the evidence thus collected must be seen and weighed not in terms of library analysis by scholars, but as understood by those versed in the field of law enforcement.
>
> As these comments illustrate, probable cause is a fluid concept—turning on the assessment of probabilities in particular factual contexts—not readily, or even usefully, reduced to a neat set of legal rules. Informants' tips doubtless come in many shapes and sizes from many different types of persons. As we said in Adams v. Williams, 407 U.S. 143 (1972), "Informants' tips, like all other clues and evidence coming to a policeman on the scene, may vary greatly in their value and reliability." Rigid legal rules are ill-suited to an area of such diversity "One simple rule will not cover every situation." . . .
>
> As early as Locke v. United States, 7 Cranch 339 (1813), Chief Justice Marshall observed, in a closely related context, that "the term 'probable cause,' according to its usual acceptation, means less than evidence which would justify condemnation. . . . It imports a seizure made under circumstances which warrant suspicion." More recently, we said that "the quanta . . . of proof" appropriate in ordinary judicial proceedings are inapplicable to the decision to issue a warrant. Finely-tuned standards such as proof beyond a reasonable doubt or by a preponderance of the evidence, useful in formal trials, have no place in the magistrate's decision. While an effort to fix some general, numerically precise degree of certainty corresponding to "probable cause" may not be helpful, it is clear that "only the probability, and not a prima facie showing, of criminal activity is the standard of probable cause." . . .
>
> Similarly, we have repeatedly said that after-the-fact scrutiny by courts of the sufficiency of an affidavit should not take the form of de novo review. A magistrate's "determination of probable cause should be paid great deference by reviewing

courts." "A grudging or negative attitude by reviewing courts toward warrants" is inconsistent with the Fourth Amendment's strong preference for searches conducted pursuant to a warrant "courts should not invalidate . . . warrant[s] by interpreting affidavit[s] in a hypertechnical, rather than a commonsense, manner."

UNITED STATES v. FORD

184 F.3d 566 (6th Cir. 1999)

John R. Gibson, Circuit Judge.

Don Ford and his wife, Sandra Hutchins Ford appeal their convictions for operation of an illegal gambling business, 18 U.S.C. §1955 (1994), and money laundering, 18 U.S.C. §§1957 (1994) (both defendants) and 1956(a)(1)(B)(1994) (Ford only). Ford also appeals his conviction under 26 U.S.C. §7206(1) (1994) for filing a false income tax return. Both raise numerous claims of error in denying various motions and in sentencing. Ford and Hutchins raise Fourth Amendment issues concerning the search of Ford's bingo hall and another building. . . . We reverse Ford's tax conviction because it is based on evidence that was seized in violation of his Fourth Amendment rights. We affirm Ford's and Hutchins's gambling and money laundering convictions, but remand Ford's case for resentencing in light of the reversal of his tax conviction.

Don Ford owned and operated the Arcade Bingo Plaza, which was in the business of conducting bingo games for the benefit of charities. Under Kentucky law, it is illegal to promote gambling (which includes bingo) other than "charitable gaming" subject to complex rules that were amended twice during the time periods relevant to this case. Throughout the time in question, gambling could only be legal "charitable gaming" if it was operated by a tax exempt organization; if that organization had maintained tax exempt status for five years before the gaming; if the gaming was conducted exclusively by unpaid volunteers for the charity; and if the proceeds were used solely for the charitable purposes of the organization. . . .

Ford first operated the Arcade Bingo Plaza in Louisville, Kentucky in 1990, conducting bingo games for various charities, such as the Knights of Columbus. Ford would charge the charities rental and overhead for use of the hall. Hutchins was Ford's second in command at the Arcade Plaza, and when he was not there she conducted the business. Instead of using volunteers from the sponsoring charities to run the bingo games in accordance with Kentucky law, Ford hired workers. The workers were paid from money "cut" or "skimmed" from the bingo proceeds. The skim was made by the controller for the session, then given to Hutchins. The workers were paid in cash, often surreptitiously handed to them in a handshake. The amount of money skimmed varied with the size of the crowd, because the more players there were, the larger the amount that could be skimmed without the players detecting the diminution of the prize money. Sometimes there was cash left over from the skim after the workers were paid; this money would be put in the safe in "Mr. Ford's compartment."

. . . Ford reactivated a lapsed post of the Regular Veterans Association on December 16, 1991. Later, he registered several other RVA Posts and suborganizations. Because of the statutory limitations on the number of sessions one organization could sponsor and the amount of prize money an organization could award in one day, once the limits had been reached for one RVA sponsor, Ford would substitute another RVA sponsor. . . .

After police executed a search warrant on the Arcade Bingo Plaza and the RVA Hall across the street, Ford and Hutchins were indicted. . . . Ford was also indicted in a separate case of eleven counts of tax offenses completely unrelated to the bingo operation. During the search of the RVA Hall at 2902 South Seventh Street Road, across from the Arcade Plaza, police seized documents that had no relation to the bingo operation, including files from 1984 to 1988 relating to a real estate transaction known as the "Huber's deal." In the Huber's deal, Ford [earned more than $330,000 on which he paid no federal income tax].

I.

Ford contends that the search of his buildings violated his Fourth Amendment rights because the warrant was not sufficiently particular. . . .

Louisville Police Department officers conducted the search under a state warrant based on an affidavit. Three IRS agents also assisted in executing the warrants. The affidavit supporting the warrant described the Louisville Police Department's investigation of Donald Ford's bingo operations. Police had visited the Arcade Bingo Plaza building, where Donald Ford and his subordinates Sandra Hutchins and Clay Ballinger conducted bingo games, which they claimed were for the benefit of charities. The affidavit described numerous violations of the statutory requirements for charitable gaming, such as payment of the "volunteer" workers, payment of prizes exceeding $5,000 per day, and operation of bingo games supposedly sponsored by charities that had no representatives present during the game. The affidavit also stated facts indicating that the RVA sponsors were actually shells having no charitable or fraternal function, but existing only as alter egos of Donald Ford. The affiant recited facts that would support an inference that Hutchins and Ballinger had taken home the proceeds from the bingo games, and that Ford kept numerous lock boxes at various banks containing cash.

The warrant contained ten clauses listing items to be seized. Some of the clauses were expressly limited by reference to illegal gambling or bingo. However, some clauses had no such limitation, in particular the category authorizing seizure of: "Books, records, receipts, bank statements and records, money drafts, letters of credit, money orders and cash checks, money wrappers, passbooks, bank checks, automatic teller machine receipts, Western Union receipts, safety deposit box keys, and other items evidencing the obtaining, secreting, transfer, and/or concealment of assets and the obtaining, secreting, transfer, concealment and or expenditure of money."

The police executing the warrant seized several file cabinets and eleven boxes of documents. The officer in charge testified at the suppression hearing that they seized "basically most of the documents" at 2902 South Seventh. Another officer agreed that they "pretty much took everything." Many of the documents related to Ford Industries and Durrett Investigations, auto-financing and private investigation businesses, respectively, also owned by Ford. Among the documents seized were promissory notes, deeds, and related papers, all dated between 1984 and 1988, concerning the Huber's deal, which was completely unrelated to the gambling operation.

The search took place in the late night and early morning of August 28 and 29, 1992. The documents seized were kept at the Louisville Police headquarters until September 23, when they were transferred to the IRS offices. In November 1992, the IRS officially obtained custody of the documents by grand jury subpoena.

A.

The tax prosecution was based on documents seized in the August 28-29 search. Ford moved to suppress the documents on the grounds that if the documents were within the scope of the search warrant, the search warrant was overbroad, and if the search warrant was read narrowly enough to be valid, the documents were not within its scope. The government did not contend that the warrant should be narrowed by construction, *see* Andresen v. Maryland, 427 U.S. 463 (1976), and therefore limited to documents related to bingo. Instead, the government contended that it needed all of Ford's financial documents in order to determine his "overall financial picture" and thus establish what money he had available, where the money came from, and what happened to it. This could require law enforcement officials to go back "ten years or more." Therefore, according to the government, the warrant properly permitted seizure of all financial documents in the buildings, whether or not related to the bingo operations in time or subject matter. . . .

The Fourth Amendment guarantees that "no Warrants shall issue, but upon probable cause, supported by Oath or affirmation, and *particularly* describing the place to be searched, and the persons or things to be seized." (Emphasis added.) The particularity requirement prohibits the issuance of warrants that would let officers seize "one thing under a warrant describing another." "A general order to explore and rummage through a person's belongings is not permitted." . . .

[I]n this case, the quoted language authorized a broader search than was reasonable given the facts in the affidavit supporting the warrant. The affidavit stated that the first of Ford's RVA posts was incorporated in December 1991, and there was no indication in the affidavit of criminal activity before that date. The affidavit described an investigation beginning on April 24, 1992. It also reported an interview with Clay Ballinger, who said he had operated the bingo himself but had "sold the Arcade Plaza Bingo back to Mr. Ford in 1991." However, the police seized promissory notes, deeds, and related papers dated between 1984 and 1988, which had no relation to the bingo operation. . . . Failure to limit broad descriptive terms by relevant dates, when such dates are available to the police, will render a warrant overbroad.

The government argues that it was necessary to seize documents antedating the bingo operation to establish what money Ford had before the bingo business started. This would help the government to identify which of his present assets could be bingo proceeds. This argument would allow virtually unlimited seizure of a lifetime's worth of documentation, which is extremely intrusive. Moreover, the impracticability of tracing the origin of every dollar Ford owned to show whether it came from some enterprise other than bingo, casts doubt on whether the government really means to take on such a herculean task. At any rate, this rationale was not articulated in the affidavit, and therefore we need not decide whether it would have provided a justification for the warrant if it had been presented to the magistrate.

Similarly, we reject the government's argument that it seized the Huber's, Inc. documents because the storage of Ford's personal documents at the RVA Hall showed Ford and the RVA were alter egos. Again, this argument would allow an extreme intrusion for evidence of very little probative value. The government at trial used the documents for an entirely different purpose than simply to prove that they were stored at the RVA Hall.

The government further argues that there was probable cause to seize all the documents at the RVA Hall because the business carried on there was "permeated with fraud." Other circuits have upheld extremely broad warrants on such a theory. The affidavit definitely contained evidence that Ford was abusing the form of charitable organizations in order to run bingo games for personal profit. However, the affidavit did not disclose any reason to believe that the scheme began before December 1991, the date given in the affidavit as the date when Ford reactivated his first RVA post. Even if one business carried on at a site is permeated with fraud, if other businesses run at the same site are separable and are not shown to be related to the suspected crime, a warrant permitting seizure of all documents at the site is not justified. [T]he overbreadth of the warrant in this case is illustrated by the items actually seized under it—here, documents dating from years before the bingo operation began and which pertain to an entirely unrelated crime.

The government argues that even if the warrant was overbroad, the documents relating to the Huber's, Inc. deal would inevitably have been discovered in the course of the IRS's pending civil investigation of Ford's 1988 tax return. Under the inevitable discovery doctrine, illegally seized evidence may be admitted despite the exclusionary rule if the government can prove that it would have obtained the evidence from lawful sources even if the illegal seizure never happened. . . .

In this case, before the illegal search took place, the IRS had issued a notice of deficiency to Ford for the 1988 tax year, based on his claimed net operating loss carryforward from 1986. Ford petitioned the United States Tax Court for relief on November 2, 1992, contending that the IRS had incorrectly disallowed the net operating loss carryforward. On December 28, 1992, the IRS filed an answer conceding the case: "[R]eview of taxpayer's records, not available to respondent's agent at the time notice was issued, has persuaded respondent that petitioners' 1988 return was substantially correct as filed." [Thus, the government's claim of "inevitable discovery" contradicts actual reality and, accordingly, fails.]

We therefore hold that the documents seized from 2902 South Seventh Street Road pertaining to the Huber's deal, the sale of the Huber's note to the accountant and the accountant's reassignment of the note to Ford must be suppressed because they were seized in violation of Ford's Fourth Amendment rights. Ford's tax conviction must be reversed.

B.

Ford and Hutchins contend that the district court should have suppressed the evidence seized in the August 28-29 search in the gambling case as well as the tax case. They argue that since the warrant was overbroad, all the evidence seized under it should be suppressed. To the contrary, the remedy for an overbroad warrant is to sever the overbroad portions of the warrant from those portions that are sufficiently particular. The portions of the warrant limited to fruits and evidence of gambling are sufficiently particular; even though those portions do not contain a time limitation, their subject-matter limitation (fruits and evidence of gambling) fulfills the same function as a time limitation would have done, by limiting the warrant to evidence of the crimes described in the affidavit. The portions of the warrant limited to fruits and evidence of bingo can be severed from the part of the warrant which is not so limited. Therefore, seizure of the documents pertaining to the gambling and the closely related money laundering charges was permissible.

NOTES AND QUESTIONS

1. The specific challenge to the warrant in this case is lack of particularity, which allegedly transformed the government's exploits into an illegal "general search." Note, however, the variety of Fourth Amendment doctrine touched on by the court: (1) a search warrant can be narrowed in scope by construing it in the context of the accompanying affidavit; (2) broad, general categories of documents listed in a warrant can be narrowed by tying them to a specific subject matter (e.g., "related to gambling activity") or date (e.g., "on or after 1991"); (3) in the right case (not this one) the argument that an entity is "permeated by fraud" may be sufficient to save an otherwise overbroad warrant; (4) the "inevitable discovery" doctrine can prevent the suppression of illegally seized evidence; and (5) the remedy for an overbroad warrant is the suppression only of the materials seized pursuant to the overbreadth, not of all materials seized under the warrant.
2. All the government needs to do to "narrow a warrant by construction" is to state in the warrant that the affidavit supporting the warrant is "hereby incorporated into the warrant itself." Why did the government fail to incorporate the affidavit in this case? Is there ever a good reason to forgo incorporation?
3. As this case demonstrates, drafting a search warrant in a white collar case is difficult because the warrant must be specific—but the government is often not in a position to know what specific records the target of the subpoena has in his possession. If the warrant is too broad, the government risks suppression of evidence; if it is too narrow, the government will not be able to collect the evidence it needs in the first place.

IN RE SEARCH OF 3817 W. WEST END, FIRST FLOOR, CHICAGO, ILLINOIS 60621

321 F. Supp. 2d 953 (N.D. Ill. 2004)

SCHENKIER, United States Magistrate Judge.

We begin by recounting the relevant background events. Late in the afternoon of April 30, 2004, the government applied for the issuance of a search warrant for a residence at 3817 W. West End in Chicago, Illinois. The affidavit in support of the application set forth information offered by the government to establish probable cause to believe that Jacqueline Williams (also known by other names) was the occupant of that residence, and that she was engaged in acts of federal income tax fraud, in violation of 26 U.S.C. §7206(2), in connection with her preparation and filing of federal income tax returns for various individuals during 2002 and 2003.

The government sought authority to search for and to seize certain enumerated items that it claimed would show the alleged tax fraud. However, with respect to any computers or related media (generally referred to hereafter collectively as "computers"), the government sought a warrant authorizing it to seize those items before conducting any search of their contents for evidence of tax fraud. The government explained that . . . a search of the computers would be better conducted in a laboratory setting. . . .

[T]he Court expressed concern over the request as it pertained to any computers the government might find at the residence. The Court was satisfied by the government's explanation of why a search of the contents of any computers while at the residence might not be practicable, and thus authorized the government to seize any computer without an on-site search of its contents. But, the Court explained to the government that a computer found during the search of a home likely would contain a wide variety of documents having nothing to do with the alleged criminal activity intermingled with documents that might fall within the scope of the alleged criminal activity. The affidavit provided no information that would suggest otherwise. Neither the application nor the affidavit set forth the types of documents relating to the alleged criminal activity that the government expected to find on the computers. Nor did the government's submission describe the means by which the government planned to search the computer, to avoid a general rummaging through all information on the computer, much of which would be irrelevant to the alleged criminal activity. To the contrary, the government represented that its search of the computer might involve "an examin[ation of] all the stored data to determine which particular files are evidence or instrumentalities of a crime."

The Court told the government that in order to address these concerns, prior to allowing any search of the contents of the computers, the Court would require the government to provide a protocol outlining the methods it would use to ensure that its search was reasonably designed to focus on documents related to the alleged criminal activity. The purpose of this protocol was to provide the Court with assurance that the search of the computer after its seizure would not consist merely of a random or general examination of other documents — which, on a home computer, might contain sensitive information regarding health or other personal and private matters completely unrelated to the alleged criminal activity. . . .

On May 4, 2004, the government met with the Court to discuss the [search]. . . . The government attorney informed the Court that the search had been conducted, and that a computer had been seized. At that time, the government attorney argued that the government should be permitted to search the contents of the computer without providing the Court with any search protocol. . . . There was nothing in the responses by the government representatives that indicated that there was some technical or practical reason that a protocol could not be provided.

What emerged clearly during the discussion was the government position that the Court lacked the authority to require a protocol. . . .

II.

The government's motion raises a serious question, one which we believe to be of first impression in this district: whether, when deciding to issue a warrant that would involve the seizure and subsequent search of a home computer, a magistrate judge has the authority to require the government to set forth a search protocol that attempts to ensure that the search will not exceed constitutional bounds. For the reasons set forth below, we believe that the answer to that question is yes.

A.

. . . The degree of particularity that is required in any given situation may not be determined by resorting to some simple formulaic approach, but instead "varies depending on the circumstances of the case and the types of items involved." A number of courts addressing the issue have found that the search and seizure of a computer requires careful scrutiny of the particularity requirement. . . . [For several reasons, we agree.]

First, it is frequently the case with computers that the normal sequence of "search" and then selective "seizure" is turned on its head. Because of the difficulties of conducting an on-site search of computers, the government frequently seeks (and, as here, obtains), authority to seize computers without any prior review of their contents.

Second, that is significant in this case because of the substantial likelihood that the computer contains an "intermingling" of documents evidencing the alleged tax fraud, with documents that the government has no probable cause to seize. . . . Third, we consider the extraordinary volume of information that may be stored even on a home computer. . . . The capacity of the computer to store these large quantities of information increases the risk that many of the intermingled documents will have nothing to do with the alleged criminal activity that creates the probable cause for a search and seizure.

Fourth, while computers present the possibility of confronting far greater volumes of documents than are typically presented in a paper document search, computers also present the tools to refine searches in ways that cannot be done with hard copy files. When confronting a file cabinet full of papers, there may be no way to determine what to seize without doing some level of review of everything in the cabinet, as "few people keep documents of their criminal transactions in a folder marked '[crime] records.'" Thus, in that setting, it may be inevitable that innocuous records must be examined to determine whether they fall into the category of those papers covered by the search warrant. Andresen v. Maryland, 427 U.S. 463, 482 n.11 (1976).

By contrast, computer technology affords a variety of methods by which the government may tailor a search to target on the documents which evidence the alleged criminal activity. These methods include limiting the search by date range; doing key word searches; limiting the search to text files or graphics files; and focusing on certain software programs. Of course, these are not the exclusive means of focusing a computer search, and they are not the means that might be appropriate in every case. But, the existence of these tools demonstrates the ability of the government to be more targeted in its review of computer information than it can be when reviewing hard copy documents in a file cabinet. . . .

D.

The government urges that any questions about the manner in which a search is executed may not be addressed by a judge when approving the warrant, but only when a judge later is confronted with a motion to suppress. If adopted, such an approach would unnecessarily run the risk of [having] evidence seized in a search of a computer . . . suppressed because of a failure to provide the magistrate judge with search protocols.

An approach that leads to such results is neither desirable nor legally required. We do not believe that is the approach that the Supreme Court had in mind when it stated that "responsible officials, including judicial officials," must take care to assure that searches are conducted so as to "minimize[ ] unwarranted intrusions upon privacy." *Andresen.* The purpose of review of warrant applications by "neutral, disinterested magistrates" is to ensure that the requirements of probable cause and particularity are met. When there are concerns about the particularity of a given search, as is the case here, it is both sensible and constitutionally required to address those concerns at the front end of the process, and to resolve them in a way that avoids the later suppression of evidence. . . .

. . . Accordingly, the Court denies the government's motion to reconsider. In light of this ruling, the Court orders that within 21 days the government inform the Court in writing of the following: (a) whether there is good cause that this Opinion, which does not disclose sensitive material from the application, should remain under seal; and (b) whether the government still wishes to search the computer. If so, within that 21 day period the government shall submit for review a proposed protocol for searching the contents of the computer. If the government informs the Court that it no longer wishes to search the computer, then the Court will direct that the computer be returned.

UNITED STATES v. STABILE

2011 WL 294036 (3d Cir. Feb. 1, 2011)

VAN ANTWERPEN, Circuit Judge.

[Defendant] Stabile resided in Mahwah, New Jersey, with Debbie Deetz. . . . The house shared by Stabile and Deetz was secured by a mortgage and home equity credit line in the name of Stabile's brother. Stabile defaulted on these loans and tried to mask his default by passing more than $156,000 in counterfeit checks. These counterfeit checks initially formed the basis for investigating Stabile [for financial fraud]. . . .

At 1:00 P.M. on July 24, 2006, Secret Service Special Agents Christopher Albanese and John Croes, and Detective Joseph Nieciecki of the Bergen County Sheriff's Department, arrived at Stabile's house to question Stabile about counterfeiting checks. Stabile was not at home, but Deetz answered the door, invited the agents inside, asked the officers to sit at a table near the living room, and offered them something to drink. . . . Albanese . . . asked Deetz for consent to search the house. Albanese provided Deetz with a consent form and informed Deetz that she could refuse consent. Deetz reviewed the consent form for approximately thirty minutes and then signed it. . . .

[Pursuant to Deetz's consent, law enforcement on the scene searched a personal computer on the premises. Defendant objected to the validity of her consent. The issue is whether the party consenting had authority over the computer.] Here, the facts weigh in favor of a determination that Deetz had the authority to consent to a search and seizure of the shared hard drives. First, the computer was not password-protected. The failure to use password protection indicates that Stabile relinquished his privacy in the contents of the computer. . . . Moreover, all of the computers and seized hard drives were located in common areas of the home, such as on the main floor and in the basement, rather than in a private bedroom. These factors indicate that, under the totality of the circumstances, Deetz had unfettered access to the hard drives and had authority to consent to the seizure of all of them. . . .

Stabile argues that even assuming Deetz validly consented to this search and seizure, the seizure of six entire hard drives was unreasonable because it was unconstitutionally overbroad. Stabile notes that by seizing six entire hard drives, the Government also seized personal emails and other information not related to financial crimes. Therefore, according to Stabile, the Government's failure to "segregate" data on-site (at Stabile's house) renders this seizure unconstitutionally overbroad. The Government defends the seizure on the grounds that Deetz did not limit the scope of her consent, that evidence of financial crimes could be found anywhere on any computer hard drive, and that the practical considerations of investigating and seizing electronic evidence counsel against on-site data collection. We agree with the Government and reject Stabile's argument.

The seizure of the six entire hard drives was reasonable. First, except for the restriction as to financial crimes, Deetz did not limit the scope of her consent in any way. Second, a broad seizure was required because evidence of financial crimes could have been found in any location on any of the six hard drives, and this evidence very likely would have been disguised or concealed somewhere on the hard drive. Third, as a practical matter, "[w]hen a search requires review of a large collection of items, such as papers, 'it is certain that some innocuous documents will be examined, at least cursorily, in order to determine whether they are, in fact, among those papers authorized to be seized.'" Finally, Stabile argues for an "on-site" search requirement, but the practical realities of computer investigations preclude on-site searches. For example, a hard drive search requires a "controlled environment." Computer searches are also time consuming and require trained forensic investigators. In short, such on-site searches would be "fraught with difficulty and risk," and cannot be rushed by a cursory on-site search. All these reasons suggest that the seizure of the six entire hard drives was reasonable. . . .

Agent Albanese obtained [a] state search warrant on October 19, 2006[, to search the computer hard drives that had been taken from the premises]. In mid-November, Detective Vanadia commenced a warranted search of the 120 GB hard drive solely for evidence of financial crimes. During this search, Vanadia noticed a folder named "Kazvid." The folder contained files bearing names indicative of child pornography. Vanadia then opened these files and "confirmed" that they did contain child pornography. Stabile argued that this search violated the Fourth Amendment and that the fruits of the search had to be suppressed. . . .

On appeal, Stabile challenges each step of this search. . . .

The first issue is whether, pursuant to the state search warrant to search for evidence of financial crimes, Detective Vanadia properly viewed the files in the Kazvid folder. . . .

Resolution of this issue forces us to reconcile two competing principles. On one hand, it is clear that because criminals can—and often do—hide, mislabel, or manipulate files to conceal criminal activity, a broad, expansive search of the hard drive may be required. *See* United States v. Burgess, 576 F.3d 1078, 1092-94 (10th Cir. 2009) ("[T]here may be no practical substitute for actually looking in many (perhaps all) folders and sometimes at the documents contained within those folders, and that is true whether the search is of computer files or physical files."). On the other hand, as Stabile argues, granting the Government a carte blanche to search every file on the hard drive impermissibly transforms a "limited search into a general one." Marron v. United States, 275 U.S. 192, 196 (1927) ("The requirement that warrants shall particularly describe things to be seized makes general searches under them impossible and prevents the seizure of one thing under a warrant describing another."); *see* United States v. Tracey, 597 F.3d 140, 146 (3d Cir. 2010). To reconcile these competing aims, many courts have suggested various strategies and search methodologies to limit the scope of the search. . . .

In United States v. Carey, 172 F.3d 1268, 1276 (10th Cir. 1999), the Tenth Circuit suggested methods to avoid searching files of the type not identified in the warrant, such as "observing files types and titles listed on the directory, doing a key word search for relevant terms, or reading portions of each file stored in the memory." The Tenth Circuit has refined its approach since *Carey*. In *Burgess*, the Tenth Circuit considered the appropriate standards for searching a hard drive, offering the following guidance: "while officers must be clear as what it is they are seeking on the computer and conduct the search in a way that avoids searching files of types not identified in the warrant, a computer search may be as extensive as reasonably required to locate the items described in the warrant" based on probable cause. But the search warrant itself need not "contain a particularized computer search strategy." Given that it would be "folly for a search warrant to structure the mechanics of the search" because "imposing such limits would unduly restrict legitimate search objectives," the scope of the search must be "constrained by content." . . . To avoid transforming a limited search into a general one, the court cautioned that "[a]s the description of such places and things becomes more general, the method by which the search is executed become[s] more important—the search method must be tailored to meet allowed ends." . . . [We agree with *Carey* and *Burgess.*]

Turning to the instant case, the scope of the consent and state search warrant were limited to evidence of financial crimes. For a number of reasons, we believe that Detective Vanadia's decision to highlight and view the contents of the Kazvid folder was reasonable and permissible under the Fourth Amendment.

First, Detective Vanadia's decision to highlight and view the contents of the Kazvid folder was objectively reasonable because criminals can easily alter file names and file extensions to conceal contraband. Second, Detective Vanadia's search procedures complied with the search procedures outlined in *Carey*. . . . For example, *Carey* suggested search methods such as focusing on the file type identified in the warrant, file names, key word search, and directory structure. . . . Here, Vanadia took steps to ensure that his investigation complied with the state search warrant. Vanadia began by physically inspecting the hard drive and creating a copy of the drive to ensure that the original drive was not damaged or corrupted during the search. Next, Vanadia examined the file signatures to see if any files had been corrupted. He then conducted a "hash value analysis" to see if any files had been copied. Finally, he examined suspicious and out-of-place folders, such as the Kazvid folder. These procedures demonstrate that Vanadia engaged in a focused search of the hard drives rather than a general search. . . .

For the foregoing reasons, we conclude that highlighting the Kazvid folder was reasonable and did not exceed the scope of the state search warrant.

After highlighting the Kazvid folder, Detective Vanadia observed in the folder a list of files with lurid names. The Government argues that these file names may be examined pursuant to the plain view doctrine. Stabile disagrees. This brings us to the question of whether evidence of other crimes in a computer can be examined under the plain view doctrine. We hold that the plain view doctrine applies to seizures of evidence during searches of computer files, but the exact confines of the doctrine will vary from case to case in a common-sense, fact-intensive manner. What is permissible in one situation may not always be permissible in another.

There are three requirements for valid seizures of evidence in plain view. "First, the officer must not have violated the Fourth Amendment in 'arriving at the place from which the evidence could be plainly viewed.' Second, the incriminating character of the evidence must be 'immediately apparent.' Third, the officer must have 'a lawful right of access to the object itself.'" Detective Vanadia's examination of the file names in the Kazvid folder, to the extent that he may arguably be said to have "seized" the names by, for example, making a screen print, satisfies all three plain view requirements.

First, Detective Vanadia did not violate the Fourth Amendment in arriving at the place from which the evidence could be viewed. Deetz consented to the seizure of all six hard drives and a magistrate issued a state search warrant to search all six hard drives for evidence of financial crimes. Vanadia began executing the state search warrant by searching the 120 GB hard drive. Within the 120 GB hard drive, Vanadia noticed the Kazvid folder. He lawfully highlighted the Kazvid folder to view its contents because a thorough computer search requires a broad examination of files on the computer to ensure that file names have not been manipulated to conceal their contents. Nor did Vanadia unreasonably expand the scope of his search by highlighting the Kazvid folder and viewing its contents. Therefore, the first plain view requirement is satisfied because Vanadia "lawfully arrived at the point from which the evidence could be viewed."

Second, there is no doubt that the incriminating character of the evidence—in this instance the names themselves—was "immediately apparent." The Kazvid folder contained files with lurid names. These file names suggested that Stabile illegally possessed contraband (child pornography).

Third, Detective Vanadia had a "lawful right of access" to the object of the search because he was authorized by a state search warrant to search the 120 GB hard drive for evidence of Stabile's financial crimes.

Therefore, we conclude that the Government properly examined the file names listed in the Kazvid folder pursuant to the plain view doctrine.

After highlighting the Kazvid folder, Detective Vanadia viewed a list of file names with file extensions suggesting child pornography videos. Vanadia testified that he opened these video files to "confirm" they contained child pornography. The Government claims in their brief that under the plain view doctrine, once Detective Vanadia saw the lurid file names he was then empowered to seize and examine the contents of those files. Stabile argues, and the District Court concluded, that opening the video files to view their contents exceeded the scope of the state search warrant and that plain view did not apply, resulting in an illegal search. The state search warrant issued on October 19, 2006 authorized Vanadia to search all six hard drives only for evidence of financial crimes.

We need not resolve whether the plain view doctrine applies to examination of contents of the video files because the independent source and inevitable discovery doctrines apply to the contents of all the video files. Therefore, we ultimately conclude that suppression is not required. . . .

NOTES AND QUESTIONS

1. Who's right here, Magistrate Judge Schenkier in *3817 W. West End*, or Judge Van Antwerpen in *Stabile*? Should the government be required to outline in the search warrant a protocol designed to avoid general searches of computer files? Is that even possible if the government does not know exactly what it is going to find? On the other hand, in the absence of a protocol, is there any real protection against an unreasonable "general search"?
2. The reader should note that search warrants often describe a protocol that will be used to minimize the government's intrusion into attorney-client or other privileged material. *See, e.g.*, United States v. Hunter, 13 F. Supp. 2d 574 (D. Vt. 1998). Is there a good reason to treat computer information differently?
3. Magistrate Judge Schenkier rejects the comparison between a file cabinet and a computer hard drive, contending that available search tools obviate the need to peruse the totality of the latter. But how true is that? Just as a

criminal using a file cabinet is not likely to store the evidence against him in a neat file labeled "Crime," neither is one employing a computer likely to use searchable words like "fraud" in the documents that prove his crime.

4. Why was the government so resistant to providing a protocol in *3818 W. West End*? After all, if it submitted a plan to the magistrate judge and he approved it, a later attack on the warrant would likely fail under the "good faith" exception to the exclusionary clause set out by the Supreme Court in United States v. Leon, 468 U.S. 897 (1984) (if law enforcement applies and obtains a warrant in good faith, exclusion is not an appropriate remedy if it turns out that the warrant was technically flawed). One reason, alluded to in Note 3, might be a concern that protocols, by definition, screen certain files from law enforcement's view and are certainly not perfect, meaning that lots of pertinent evidence might never be discovered. Another reason might be that investigators actually *want* the ability to "stumble upon" evidence in "plain view," because such evidence can be quite valuable.
5. If you were a prosecutor, would you include a protocol in a case similar to *3818 W. West End*? If so, what would it look like?

chapter 12

Defending *Alleged* White Collar Criminals

I. INTRODUCTION

One of the distinguishing characteristics of this casebook is the fact that the materials are presented, to some degree, from the prosecution's point of view. This chapter is the primary counterweight. It sets out the defense perspective in white collar cases, including the defendant's goals and strategies. It also focuses on the numerous pitfalls that defense counsel must avoid to bring a white collar case to a successful conclusion.

Unlike their street crime counterparts, white collar criminals usually hold a position of respect and even admiration in their community. Socioeconomically, they are upper-middle to upper class, which means that not only do they live well, but quite often they are noted philanthropists and supporters of the arts. They may also be esteemed professionals, such as doctors, lawyers, bankers, and accountants. Their personal networks run long and deep.

As a result of all this, it is not good enough for a white collar defense attorney to think about a case in terms of obtaining a not guilty verdict after trial. Such would be a pyrrhic victory: By that time, her client's reputation and livelihood would likely be destroyed. Instead, the white collar attorney's primary objective is to prevent her client from being indicted in the first place. Ideally, the prosecution's decision not to bring charges will come in a manner that either keeps the underlying investigation secret or, in the worst case, preserves the client's ability to claim innocence. That way, the client's professional position and standing in the community, though tarnished, will be salvageable. Accordingly, a civil settlement in which the client pays damages but admits no liability is better than a grant of immunity in exchange for the client's testimony against others.

Of course, if efforts to avoid charges fail, the attorney's fallback position is to obtain her client's post-indictment exoneration. In addition to the employment of a wide variety of traditional defenses, experience has taught white collar defense attorneys that sometimes the best defense is a good offense. Thus, there has been an ever increasing rise in the number of claims of prosecutorial misconduct leveled against government attorneys in recent years.[1] More often than one would hope, such charges have stuck, sometimes taking down entire prosecutions in their wake.[2]

Short of outright victory, of course, a plea to minimal charges is defense counsel's goal. Finally, in cases where proof of the defendant's guilt is a foregone conclusion, defense counsel's most important role is arguing for a favorable calculation of the victims' losses and/or for a downward departure at the time of sentence.

KENNETH MANN, DEFENDING WHITE COLLAR CRIME: A PORTRAIT OF ATTORNEYS AT WORK

6-7 (Yale University Press 1985)

If an attorney does in the white-collar case what is done in the street-crime case, he takes the evidence presented against his client, and other evidence known to him that is exculpatory of the client, and makes the appropriate legal argument. This evidence, so the attorney argues, fails to show adequately, that is, beyond a reasonable doubt, that the client committed a crime. The defense attorney's task is to draw on conventional sources of law—statutory and case law—to show his adversary that the client's behavior falls on the "not guilty" side of the line created by the substantive standard of criminal responsibility. This task is conventional legal argument and takes place at all stages of the criminal process. [This defense strategy is called a] substantive defense. . . .

The substantive defense is not, however, the initial defense strategy for a competent [white collar] attorney. The defense attorney's first objective is to prevent the government from obtaining evidence that could be inculpatory of his client and used by the investigator or prosecutor to justify issuance of a formal criminal charge. Instead of preparing legal argument, the defense attorney first devotes himself to keeping evidence out of any prospective adversary forum in which legal argument about the client's criminal responsibility might take place. This action is crucial to prevent issuance of a criminal charge. . . . [T]his task is called information control and the defense strategy built on these actions [is] an information control defense. . . .

Attorneys act in two ways to control information. First, they oppose their adversaries in quasi-judicial and court settings [such as motions to quash an overly

1. *See* Andrea Elliot & Benjamin Weiser, *When Prosecutors Err, Others Pay the Price*, N.Y. Times, June 24, 2007, available at http://www.nytimes.com/2004/03/21/nyregion/21prosecute.html ("misconduct by prosecutors has become a national concern in recent years . . .").

2. *See, e.g.*, James Oliphant, *Ted Stevens' charges dismissed as judge excoriates prosecutors*, L.A. Times, Apr. 8, 2009, available at http://articles.latimes.com/2009/apr/08/nation/na-stevens8 (prosecution of former Senator Ted Stevens dismissed because of prosecutors' *Brady* violation); Adam Liptak, *Prosecutor Becomes Prosecuted*, N.Y. Times, June 24, 2007, available at http://query.nytimes.com/gst/fullpage.html?res=9B05E1D6113FF937A15755C0A9619C8B63 (charges dropped against Duke lacrosse players when district attorney Mike Nifong admitted to prosecutorial misconduct; Nifong was disbarred).

burdensome subpoena]. . . . Second, the defense attorney uses an information control strategy that focuses on the potential source of the inculpatory information. . . . The defense attorney's aim is to instruct the client or third party holding inculpatory information how to refrain from disclosing it to the government and, if necessary, to persuade or force him to refrain.

II. THE INVERSE OF WHAT WE HAVE STUDIED ELSEWHERE IN THIS VOLUME (AND MORE)

Although this is the first time we are directly addressing defenses, the doctrine set out in virtually every other chapter in this book provides ample opportunities for a defendant to thwart the prosecution's attempts to prove him guilty beyond a reasonable doubt. Obviously, this doctrine will not be repeated here; it is up to the reader to consider how a defendant could exploit any number of deficiencies in a case brought against him under the statutes, regulations, and procedural requirements covered in this volume. Here, however, is a non-exhaustive and general list of defense possibilities, along with some other defenses not explored elsewhere in the book:[3]

A. Actus Reus

1. Defendant did not participate in the criminal activity.
2. Defendant did not aid or abet the criminal activity.
3. Defendant did not supervise the individuals who carried out the criminal activity.
4. Defendant relied on his underlings to perform this function without his supervision.
5. Defendant's actions were authorized by the company's board of directors.

B. Mens Rea

1. Defendant did not possess the requisite mens rea required by the statute.
2. Defendant was not aware of the criminal activity in his company.
3. Defendant was merely reckless or negligent, and criminal liability for the crime in question requires knowledge (or more).
4. Defendant made an honest and reasonable mistake of fact.
5. Defendant did not know what he was doing was against the law.
6. Defendant did not know that what he was doing was wrong.
7. Defendant acted in good faith.

3. *See generally* Joel M. Androphy, White Collar Crime (Shepard's McGraw-Hill, Inc. 1992); F. Lee Bailey & Henry B. Rothblatt, Defending Business and White Collar Crimes, Federal and State (2d ed., The Lawyers Co-operative Publishing Co. 1984 & Supp. 1990).

8. Defendant acted on advice of counsel.
9. Defendant is not an expert in accounting, and acted on good-faith reliance on his accountants.

C. Other Defenses

1. The statute of limitations has run on the charges.
2. The court does not have jurisdiction, or the case was brought in an improper venue.
3. Defendant acted out of duress.
4. Defendant's criminal conduct constituted the lesser of evils.
5. Defendant was entrapped by government overreaching.
6. Double jeopardy precludes this prosecution.

Additional defenses are explored in more detail below.

III. HOLDING FIRM: FIGHTING THE ALLEGATIONS

A. Prosecutorial Misconduct

1. Grand Jury Abuse

As noted above, defense attacks alleging prosecutorial misconduct have increased in recent years. Such allegations serve a number of useful purposes. First, if they are meritorious, the appropriate remedy might be dismissal of the case with prejudice. Second, meritorious or not, they divert the attention of the prosecution away from building its case against one's client to defending against a personal attack, possibly resulting in a less effective government presentation. In addition, even unsubstantiated misconduct allegations have a potential chilling effect on prosecutors, causing them to be more cautious than the substantive law might otherwise allow. There is nothing more frightening to a litigator than facing the possibility of professional discipline, including the "death penalty" of disbarment.[4]

Because prosecutors work out of the public's eye during the grand jury phase of a case, this is a time when they are particularly prone to cutting ethical corners. Of course, claims of prosecutorial misconduct in front of the grand jury usually do not arise until sometime later, after the grand jury has found probable cause and the defendant has been indicted. The cases that follow address the issues surrounding allegations of prosecutorial abuse of grand jury proceedings.

4. Of course, if defense counsel knowingly files a false claim of prosecutorial misconduct, she has acted unethically herself and could face a counterattack.

BANK OF NOVA SCOTIA v. UNITED STATES
487 U.S. 250 (1988)

Justice KENNEDY delivered the opinion of the Court.

The issue presented is whether a district court may invoke its supervisory power to dismiss an indictment for prosecutorial misconduct in a grand jury investigation, where the misconduct does not prejudice the defendants.

I.

In 1982, after a 20-month investigation conducted before two successive grand juries, eight defendants, including petitioners William A. Kilpatrick, Declan J. O'Donnell, Sheila C. Lerner, and The Bank of Nova Scotia, were indicted on 27 counts. The first 26 counts charged all defendants with conspiracy and some of them with mail and tax fraud. Count 27 charged Kilpatrick with obstruction of justice. The United States District Court for the District of Colorado initially dismissed the first 26 counts for failure to charge a crime, improper pleading, and, as to charges against the bank, for failure to allege that the bank or its agents had the requisite knowledge and criminal intent. Kilpatrick was tried and convicted on the obstruction of justice count.

The Government appealed the dismissal of the first 26 counts. Before oral argument, however, the Court of Appeals granted a defense motion to remand the case to the District Court for a hearing on whether prosecutorial misconduct and irregularities in the grand jury proceedings were additional grounds for dismissal. United States District Judge Fred M. Winner first presided over the post-trial motions and granted a new trial to Kilpatrick on the obstruction of justice count. The cases were later reassigned to United States District Judge John L. Kane, Jr., to complete the post-trial proceedings. After 10 days of hearings, Judge Kane dismissed all 27 counts of the indictment. The District Court held that dismissal was required for various violations of Federal Rule of Criminal Procedure 6. Further, it ruled dismissal was proper under the "totality of the circumstances," including the "numerous violations of Rule 6(d) and (e), Fed. R. Crim. P., violations of 18 U.S.C. §§6002 and 6003, violations of the Fifth and Sixth Amendments to the United States Constitution, knowing presentation of misinformation to the grand jury and mistreatment of witnesses." We shall discuss these findings in more detail below.

The District Court determined that "[a]s a result of the conduct of the prosecutors and their entourage of agents, the indicting grand jury was not able to undertake its essential mission" to act independently of the prosecution. In an apparent alternative holding, the District Court also ruled that

> "[t]he supervisory authority of the court must be used in circumstances such as those presented in this case to declare with unmistakable intention that such conduct is neither 'silly' nor 'frivolous' and that it will not be tolerated."

The Government appealed once again, and a divided panel of the Court of Appeals reversed the order of dismissal. . . .

We hold that, as a general matter, a district court may not dismiss an indictment for errors in grand jury proceedings unless such errors prejudiced the defendants.

II.

In the exercise of its supervisory authority, a federal court "may, within limits, formulate procedural rules not specifically required by the Constitution or the Congress." Nevertheless, it is well established that "[e]ven a sensible and efficient use of the supervisory power . . . is invalid if it conflicts with constitutional or statutory provisions. . . . Our previous cases have not addressed explicitly whether this rationale bars exercise of a supervisory authority where, as here, dismissal of the indictment would conflict with the harmless-error inquiry mandated by the Federal Rules of Criminal Procedure.

We now hold that a federal court may not invoke supervisory power to circumvent the harmless-error inquiry prescribed by Federal Rule of Criminal Procedure 52(a). Rule 52(a) provides that "[a]ny error, defect, irregularity or variance which does not affect substantial rights shall be disregarded." The Rule was promulgated pursuant to 18 U.S.C. §687 (currently codified, as amended, at 18 U.S.C. §3771), which invested us with authority "to prescribe, from time to time, rules of pleading, practice, and procedure with respect to any or all proceedings prior to and including verdict. . . ." Like its present-day successor, §687 provided that after a Rule became effective "all laws in conflict therewith shall be of no further force and effect." It follows that Rule 52 is, in every pertinent respect, as binding as any statute duly enacted by Congress, and federal courts have no more discretion to disregard the Rule's mandate than they do to disregard constitutional or statutory provisions. The balance struck by the Rule between societal costs and the rights of the accused may not casually be overlooked "because a court has elected to analyze the question under the supervisory power." . . .

Having concluded that our customary harmless-error inquiry is applicable where, as in the cases before us, a court is asked to dismiss an indictment prior to the conclusion of the trial, we turn to the standard of prejudice that courts should apply in assessing such claims. We adopt for this purpose, at least where dismissal is sought for nonconstitutional error, the standard articulated by Justice O'Connor in her concurring opinion in *United States v. Mechanik*. Under this standard, dismissal of the indictment is appropriate only "if it is established that the violation substantially influenced the grand jury's decision to indict," or if there is "grave doubt" that the decision to indict was free from the substantial influence of such violations. . . .

To be distinguished from the cases before us are a class of cases in which indictments are dismissed, without a particular assessment of the prejudicial impact of the errors in each case, because the errors are deemed fundamental. These cases may be explained as isolated exceptions to the harmless-error rule. We think, however, that an alternative and more clear explanation is that these cases are ones in which the structural protections of the grand jury have been so compromised as to render the proceedings fundamentally unfair, allowing the presumption of prejudice. These cases are exemplified by Vasquez v. Hillery, 474 U.S. 254 (1986), where we held that racial discrimination in selection of grand jurors compelled dismissal of the indictment. In addition to involving an error of constitutional magnitude, other remedies were impractical and it could be presumed that a discriminatorily selected grand jury would treat defendants unfairly. We reached a like conclusion in Ballard v. United States, 329 U.S. 187 (1946), where women had been excluded from the grand jury. The nature of the violation allowed a presumption that the defendant was prejudiced, and any inquiry into harmless error would have required unguided speculation. Such considerations are not presented here, and we review the alleged errors to assess their influence, if any, on the grand jury's decision to indict in the factual context of the cases before us.

III.

Though the standard we have articulated differs from that used by the Court of Appeals, we reach the same conclusion and affirm its decision reversing the order of dismissal. We review the record to set forth the basis of our agreement with the Court of Appeals that prejudice has not been established.

The District Court found that the Government had violated Federal Rule of Criminal Procedure 6(e) by: (1) disclosing grand jury materials to Internal Revenue Service employees having civil tax enforcement responsibilities; (2) failing to give the court prompt notice of such disclosures; (3) disclosing to potential witnesses the names of targets of the investigation; and (4) instructing two grand jury witnesses, who had represented some of the defendants in a separate investigation of the same tax shelters, that they were not to reveal the substance of their testimony or that they had testified before the grand jury. The court also found that the Government had violated Federal Rule of Criminal Procedure 6(d) in allowing joint appearances by IRS agents before the grand jury for the purpose of reading transcripts to the jurors.

The District Court further concluded that one of the prosecutors improperly argued with an expert witness during a recess of the grand jury after the witness gave testimony adverse to the Government. It also held that the Government had violated the witness immunity statute, 18 U.S.C. §§6002, 6003, by the use of "pocket immunity" (immunity granted on representation of the prosecutor rather than by order of a judge), and that the Government caused IRS agents to mischaracterize testimony given in prior proceedings. Furthermore, the District Court found that the Government violated the Fifth Amendment by calling a number of witnesses for the sole purpose of having them assert their privilege against self-incrimination and that it had violated the Sixth Amendment by conducting postindictment interviews of several high-level employees of The Bank of Nova Scotia. Finally, the court concluded that the Government had caused IRS agents to be sworn as agents of the grand jury, thereby elevating their credibility.

As we have noted, no constitutional error occurred during the grand jury proceedings. . . . The Court of Appeals . . . found that no Fifth Amendment violation occurred as a result of the Government's calling seven witnesses to testify despite an avowed intention to invoke their Fifth Amendment privilege. We agree that, in the circumstances of these cases, calling the witnesses was not error. The Government was not required to take at face value the unsworn assertions made by these witnesses outside the grand jury room. Once a witness invoked the privilege on the record, the prosecutors immediately ceased all questioning. Throughout the proceedings, moreover, the prosecution repeated the caution to the grand jury that it was not to draw any adverse inference from a witness' invocation of the Fifth Amendment. . . .

We must address, however, whether, despite the grand jury's independence, there was any misconduct by the prosecution that otherwise may have influenced substantially the grand jury's decision to indict, or whether there is grave doubt as to whether the decision to indict was so influenced. Several instances of misconduct found by the District Court . . . might be relevant to an allegation of a purpose or intent to abuse the grand jury process. Here, however, it is plain that these alleged breaches could not have affected the charging decision. We have no occasion to consider them further.

We are left to consider only the District Court's findings that the prosecutors: (1) fashioned and administered unauthorized "oaths" to IRS agents in violation of Rule 6(c); (2) caused the same IRS agents to "summarize" evidence falsely and to assert incorrectly that all the evidence summarized by them had been presented previously to the grand jury; (3) deliberately berated and mistreated an expert witness for the defense in the presence of some grand jurors; (4) abused its authority by providing "pocket immunity" to 23 grand jury witnesses; and (5) permitted IRS agents to appear in tandem to present evidence to the grand jury in violation of Rule 6(d). . . .

In considering the prejudicial effect of the foregoing instances of alleged misconduct, we note that these incidents occurred as isolated episodes in the course of a 20-month investigation, an investigation involving dozens of witnesses and thousands of documents. In view of this context, those violations that did occur do not, even when considered cumulatively, raise a substantial question, much less a grave doubt, as to whether they had a substantial effect on the grand jury's decision to charge.

Errors of the kind alleged in these cases can be remedied adequately by means other than dismissal. For example, a knowing violation of Rule 6 may be punished as a contempt of court. *See* Fed. Rule Crim. Proc. 6(e)(2). In addition, the court may direct a prosecutor to show cause why he should not be disciplined and request the bar or the Department of Justice to initiate disciplinary proceedings against him. The court may also chastise the prosecutor in a published opinion. Such remedies allow the court to focus on the culpable individual rather than granting a windfall to the unprejudiced defendant.

IV.

We conclude that the District Court had no authority to dismiss the indictment on the basis of prosecutorial misconduct absent a finding that petitioners were prejudiced by such misconduct. The prejudicial inquiry must focus on whether any violations had an effect on the grand jury's decision to indict. If violations did substantially influence this decision, or if there is grave doubt that the decision to indict was free from such substantial influence, the violations cannot be deemed harmless. The record will not support the conclusion that petitioners can meet this standard. The judgment of the Court of Appeals is affirmed.

It is so ordered.

UNITED STATES v. WILLIAMS

504 U.S. 36 (1992)

Justice Scalia delivered the opinion of the Court.

The question presented in this case is whether a district court may dismiss an otherwise valid indictment because the Government failed to disclose to the grand jury "substantial exculpatory evidence" in its possession.

I.

On May 4, 1988, respondent John H. Williams, Jr., a Tulsa, Oklahoma, investor, was indicted by a federal grand jury on seven counts of "knowingly mak[ing] [a] false statement or report . . . for the purpose of influencing . . . the action [of a federally insured financial institution]," in violation of 18 U.S.C. §1014. According to the indictment, between September 1984 and November 1985 Williams supplied four Oklahoma banks with "materially false" statements that variously overstated the value of his current assets and interest income in order to influence the banks' actions on his loan requests.

Williams' misrepresentation was allegedly effected through two financial statements provided to the banks, a "Market Value Balance Sheet" and a "Statement of Projected Income and Expense." The former included as "current assets" approximately $6 million in notes receivable from three venture capital companies. Though it contained a disclaimer that these assets were carried at cost rather than at market value, the Government asserted that listing them as "current assets"—i.e., assets quickly reducible to cash—was misleading, since Williams knew that none of the venture capital companies could afford to satisfy the notes in the short term. The second document—the Statement of Projected Income and Expense—allegedly misrepresented Williams' interest income, since it failed to reflect that the interest payments received on the notes of the venture capital companies were funded entirely by Williams' own loans to those companies. The Statement thus falsely implied, according to the Government, that Williams was deriving interest income from "an independent outside source."

Shortly after arraignment, the District Court granted Williams' motion for disclosure of all exculpatory portions of the grand jury transcripts. *See* Brady v. Maryland, 373 U.S. 83 (1963). Upon reviewing this material, Williams demanded that the District Court dismiss the indictment, alleging that the Government had failed to . . . present "substantial exculpatory evidence" to the grand jury. His contention was that evidence which the Government had chosen not to present to the grand jury—in particular, Williams' general ledgers and tax returns, and Williams' testimony in his contemporaneous Chapter 11 bankruptcy proceeding—disclosed that, for tax purposes and otherwise, he had regularly accounted for the "notes receivable" (and the interest on them) in a manner consistent with the Balance Sheet and the Income Statement. This, he contended, belied an intent to mislead the banks, and thus directly negated an essential element of the charged offense.

The District Court initially denied Williams' motion, but upon reconsideration ordered the indictment dismissed without prejudice. It found, after a hearing, that the withheld evidence was "relevant to an essential element of the crime charged," created "'a reasonable doubt about [respondent's] guilt'" and thus "render[ed] the grand jury's decision to indict gravely suspect." *See Bank of Nova Scotia.* Upon the Government's appeal, the Court of Appeals affirmed the District Court's order. . . . We granted certiorari. . . .

III.

Respondent does not contend that the Fifth Amendment itself obliges the prosecutor to disclose substantial exculpatory evidence in his possession to the grand jury. Instead, building on our statement that the federal courts "may, within limits, formulate procedural rules not specifically required by the Constitution or the Congress," United States v. Hasting, 461 U.S. 499 (1983), he argues that imposition of the Tenth Circuit's disclosure rule is supported by the courts' "supervisory power." We think not. *Hasting*, and the cases that rely upon the principle it expresses, deal strictly with the courts' power to control their own procedures. That power has been applied not only to improve the truth-finding process of the trial, but also to prevent parties from reaping benefit or incurring harm from violations of substantive or procedural rules (imposed by the Constitution or laws) governing matters apart from the trial itself). Thus, Bank of Nova Scotia v. United States, 487 U.S. 250 (1988), makes clear that the supervisory power can be used to dismiss an indictment because of misconduct before the grand jury, at least where that misconduct amounts to a violation of one of those "few, clear rules which were carefully drafted and approved by this Court and by Congress to ensure the integrity of the grand jury's functions."[6]

We did not hold in *Bank of Nova Scotia*, however, that the courts' supervisory power could be used, not merely as a means of enforcing or vindicating legally compelled standards of prosecutorial conduct before the grand jury, but as a means of prescribing those standards of prosecutorial conduct in the first instance. . . . It is this latter exercise that respondent demands. Because the grand jury is an institution separate from the courts, over whose functioning the courts do not preside, we think it clear that, as a general matter at least, no such "supervisory" judicial authority exists, and that the disclosure rule applied here exceeded the Tenth Circuit's authority. . . .

6. Rule 6 of the Federal Rules of Criminal Procedure contains a number of such rules, providing, for example, that "no person other than the jurors may be present while the grand jury is deliberating or voting," Rule 6(d), and placing strict controls on disclosure of "matters occurring before the grand jury," Rule 6(e). Additional standards of behavior for prosecutors (and others) are set forth in the United States Code. See 18 U.S.C. §§6002, 6003 (setting forth procedures for granting a witness immunity from prosecution); §1623 (criminalizing false declarations before grand jury); §2515 (prohibiting grand jury use of unlawfully intercepted wire or oral communications); §1622 (criminalizing subornation of perjury). That some of the misconduct alleged in Bank of Nova Scotia was not specifically proscribed by Rule, statute, or the Constitution does not make the case stand for a judicially prescribable grand jury code, as the dissent suggests. All of the allegations of violation were dismissed by the Court—without considering their validity in law—for failure to meet Nova Scotia's dismissal standard. See *Bank of Nova Scotia*, supra, at 261.

. . . The judgment of the Court of Appeals is accordingly reversed, and the cause is remanded for further proceedings consistent with this opinion.

So ordered.

[Dissenting opinion of Stevens, J., omitted.]

UNITED STATES v. MECHANIK

457 U.S. 66 (1986)

Justice Rehnquist delivered the opinion of the Court.

Federal Rule of Criminal Procedure 6(d) states that only specified persons including "the witness under examination" may be present at a grand jury proceeding. In these cases, two Government witnesses testified in tandem before the grand jury, which indicted respondents and cross-petitioners (hereafter defendants) Mechanik and Lill for various drug-related offenses and conspiracy to commit such offenses. The Court of Appeals for the Fourth Circuit held that the simultaneous presence of these two witnesses violated Rule 6(d), and that even though the petit jury subsequently returned a verdict of guilty against defendants, the verdict must be set aside on any count that corresponds to a "tainted" portion of the indictment. We believe that the petit jury's verdict of guilty beyond a reasonable doubt demonstrates *a fortiori* that there was probable cause to charge the defendants with the offenses for which they were convicted. Therefore, the convictions must stand despite the rule violation.

A fairly detailed summary of the District Court proceedings will help to illustrate the nature and extent of our holding. A grand jury returned an indictment charging defendants with drug-related offenses and conspiracy. This indictment was concededly free from any claim of error. The grand jury then returned a superseding indictment in which the conspiracy charge was expanded. In support of this superseding indictment, the United States Attorney presented the testimony of two law enforcement agents who were sworn together and questioned in tandem before the grand jury.

The defendants did not learn about this joint testimony until after trial began. Before trial, they filed an omnibus motion requesting, *inter alia*, the names of all the people who appeared before the grand jury. The Government responded that there were no unauthorized persons appearing before the grand jury, and the District Court denied the motion. Trial began in February 1980, and concluded in early July of the same year. During the second week of trial, one Jerry Rinehart, an agent of the Drug Enforcement Administration, testified as a Government witness. At the time of his testimony, the Government furnished the defendants with a portion of the transcript of his grand jury testimony as required by the Jencks Act, 18 U.S.C. §3500. The transcript disclosed that Rinehart and his fellow agent, Randolph James, had testified in tandem before the grand jury.

The defendants moved for dismissal of the indictment on the ground that the simultaneous presence of the two agents had violated Federal Rule of Criminal Procedure 6(d). Chief Judge Knapp, presiding over the trial, concluded that the presence and testimony of the two agents had not violated Rule 6(d), and he denied the motion. In May 1980, however, Chief Judge Knapp was unexpectedly hospitalized, and Judge Copenhaver took over as the trial judge. The defendants then moved for a rehearing of their motion to dismiss the indictment. Judge Copenhaver took the motion under advisement until the conclusion of trial.

In August 1980, after the jury had returned its guilty verdict, Judge Copenhaver ruled upon and denied the defendants' motion for dismissal of the indictment. He first decided, contrary to Chief Judge Knapp's earlier ruling, that the joint testimony of Agents Rinehart and James did constitute a violation of Rule 6(d). But he declined to set aside the defendants' indictment and convictions because, on the basis of a comparison between the two indictments and the evidence on which the indictments rested, the violation of Rule 6(d) had not harmed the defendants. . . .

A divided Court of Appeals reversed the conspiracy convictions, affirmed the others, and dismissed the conspiracy portion of the indictment. It reasoned that the language of Rule 6(d) is so "plain and unequivocal in limiting who may appear before a grand jury," that its transgression requires automatic reversal of any subsequent conviction regardless of the lack of prejudice. But the court reversed only the conspiracy convictions because it found that the violation of Rule 6(d) tainted only the portion of the superseding indictment that related to them. A divided en banc decision agreed.

We assume for the sake of argument that the simultaneous presence and testimony of the two Government witnesses before the grand jury violated Rule 6(d), and that the District Court would have been justified in dismissing portions of the indictment on that basis had there been actual prejudice and had the matter been called to its attention before the commencement of the trial. But although the defendants appear to have been reasonably diligent in attempting to discover any error at the grand jury proceeding, they did not acquire the transcript showing that the two agents had appeared jointly in the grand jury proceeding until the second week of trial. Nor is there any suggestion that the Government designedly withheld the information. When the defendants made their motion to dismiss the indictment based on the joint testimony, Chief Judge Knapp denied the motion because of his view that there had been no violation of Rule 6(d). Judge Copenhaver eventually issued a contrary ruling on the resubmitted motion, but not until after the long and costly trial had been brought to its conclusion. Although we do not believe that the defendants can be faulted for any lack of diligence, we nonetheless hold that the supervening jury verdict made reversal of the conviction and dismissal of the indictment inappropriate.

. . . Rule [6(d)] protects against the danger that a defendant will be required to defend against a charge for which there is no probable cause to believe him guilty. The error involving Rule 6(d) in these cases had the theoretical potential to affect the grand jury's determination whether to indict these particular defendants for the offenses with which they were charged. But the petit jury's subsequent guilty verdict means not only that there was probable cause to believe that the defendants were guilty as charged, but also that they are in fact guilty as charged beyond a reasonable doubt. Measured by the petit jury's verdict, then, any error in the grand jury proceeding connected with the charging decision was harmless beyond a reasonable doubt.

It might be argued in some literal sense that because the Rule was designed to protect against an erroneous charging decision by the grand jury, the indictment should not be compared to the evidence produced by the Government at trial, but to the evidence produced before the grand jury. But even if this argument were accepted, there is no simple way after the verdict to restore the defendant to the position in which he would have been had the indictment been dismissed before trial. He will already have suffered whatever inconvenience, expense, and opprobrium that a proper indictment may have spared him. In courtroom proceedings as elsewhere, "the moving finger writes; and, having writ, moves on." Thus reversal of a conviction after a trial free from reversible error cannot restore to the defendant whatever benefit might have accrued to him from a trial on an indictment returned in conformity with Rule 6(d). . . .

The reversal of a conviction entails substantial social costs: it forces jurors, witnesses, courts, the prosecution, and the defendants to expend further time, energy, and other resources to repeat a trial that has already once taken place; victims may be asked to relive their disturbing experiences. The "[p]assage of time, erosion of memory, and dispersion of witnesses may render retrial difficult, even impossible." Thus, while reversal "may, in theory, entitle the defendant only to retrial, in practice it may reward the accused with complete freedom from prosecution," and thereby "cost society the right to punish admitted offenders." Even if a defendant is convicted in a second trial, the intervening delay may compromise society's "interest in the prompt administration of justice" and impede accomplishment of the objectives of deterrence and rehabilitation. These societal costs of reversal and retrial are an acceptable and often necessary consequence when an error in the first proceeding has deprived a defendant of a fair determination of the issue of guilt or innocence. But the balance of interest tips decidedly the other way when an error has had no effect on the outcome of the trial.

We express no opinion as to what remedy may be appropriate for a violation of Rule 6(d) that has affected the grand jury's charging decision and is brought to the attention of the trial court before the commencement of trial. We hold only that however diligent the defendants may have been in seeking to discover the basis for the claimed violation of Rule 6(d), the petit jury's verdict rendered harmless any conceivable error in the charging decision that might have flowed from the violation. In such a case, the societal costs of retrial after a jury verdict of guilty are far too substantial to justify setting aside the verdict simply because of an error in the earlier grand jury proceedings. The judgment of the Court of Appeals is therefore reversed to the extent it set aside the conspiracy convictions and dismissed the indictment, but is otherwise affirmed.

It is so ordered.

NOTES AND QUESTIONS

1. What is the combined effect of the *Bank of Nova Scotia* and *Williams* holdings? What kinds of prosecutorial misconduct in connection with the grand jury are cognizable, and what impact must they have on the grand jury's decision to indict before they are actionable?
2. In addition to promulgating model Rules of Professional Conduct, the American Bar Association has also promulgated model Standards for the

Criminal Justice System, including Standards for the Prosecution Function. According to Standard 3-3.6(b),

> No prosecutor should knowingly fail to disclose to the grand jury evidence which tends to negate guilt or mitigate the offense.

How does this standard interact with the *Williams* holding? Should a State Bar be able to enforce a rule of conduct that has a substantive impact on the operation of federal law?

3. After *Mechanik*, are there *any* circumstances under which a defendant can obtain, post-verdict, a new trial for an irregularity that took place before the grand jury? Although the *Mechanik* rule might be efficient in the short term, does it encourage grand jury abuse by taking off the table the one remedy that might get prosecutors' attention?
4. How can a diligent defense attorney maximize her opportunities to review (or at least convince the court to conduct an ex parte review of) grand jury transcripts to discover prosecutorial abuse? Or does she face a classic Catch-22: She needs to make a credible allegation of abuse to gain access to the transcripts, but she needs to see the transcripts to make a credible allegation of abuse?
5. Is the game worth the candle? What is the typical remedy for a finding of prejudicial grand jury abuse?

PROBLEM 12-1

A federal grand jury is investigating an alleged multi-million dollar fraud by Acme International Bank's (AIB) Chairman and CEO, Henry Hudson. In 2009, Hudson received $52 million in compensation on which he paid no federal taxes. Documents located in the bank's accounting department specify that the $52 million was a "no interest loan" payable only "upon demand by the bank with 180-days prior notice." Federal investigators suspect that the loan papers are a fictitious cover for regular income, and even have some reason to believe that they were created after the federal inquiry began. Minutes from a Board of Directors meeting show approval of a very vague item, buried in lots of other financial minutia, permitting loans to officers "as long as the terms are not contrary to AIB's interest."

It is obvious that someone had to have assisted Hudson in his scheme. Suspicion falls on Arnold Schwisser, AIB's Vice President for Finance and Accounting. AUSA Gregory Waurton obtains immunity for Schwisser and questions him before the grand jury in part as follows:

AUSA WAURTON: You directed your underlings to "cover your behind" by drawing up false loan papers, didn't you?

SCHWISSER: No, Sir, that's just not true.

WAURTON: Come on, why are you lying to me? Is it because you are afraid of Hudson?

SCHWISSER: I don't know what you are talking about.

WAURTON: Get real. You heard the rumors that Hudson is tied to organized crime. You knew that he was seen with mob bosses at the exclusive clubs in town every night. You figured that if you did not cover-up and lie for him, he might have you killed. Isn't that so?

SCHWISSER: Honestly, this is all news to me.

WAURTON: All right, let's move on.

AUSA Waurton makes similar references to Hudson's alleged connection to organized crime with other witnesses as well. All deny knowing about it. Despite being a close case, tthe grand jury indicts Hudson for conspiracy, 18 U.S.C. §371, tax evasion, 26 U.S.C. §7501, and wire fraud, 18 U.S.C. §1343.

It turns out that Hudson's connection to organized crime was a figment of AUSA Waurton's imagination. Hudson had once been seen sitting next to an alleged "mob boss" at a gala charity event, but the seats had been pre-assigned.

Defense counsel hears about this line of questioning from Schwisser. The court grants her pretrial motion to obtain nearly all of the grand jury transcripts to document AUSA Waurton's numerous references to organized crime and fear throughout the proceedings. Counsel has now moved, again pretrial, for dismissal of the indictment *with prejudice.*

You are the judge. How would you rule, and why?

2. Discovery Violations

In addition to statutory and rule-based discovery, prosecutors—alone among litigators—have a constitutional duty to turn exculpatory evidence over to the defense. As one might imagine, failure to obey this requirement often gets prosecutors in trouble; in any adversarial situation, helping one's opponent runs counter to human nature. Thus, it is an area ripe for claims of misconduct by the defense.

This section starts with an overview of prosecutors' responsibilities, and then provides a recent and notorious example of a case destroyed by the government's failure to live up to its discovery obligations.

GEORGETOWN LAW JOURNAL ANNUAL REVIEW OF CRIMINAL PROCEDURE, DISCOVERY AND ACCESS TO EVIDENCE

37 Geo. L.J. Ann. Rev. Crim. Proc. 334 (2008)

The Fifth and Fourteenth Amendments require the government to disclose certain specific types of evidence to defendants. For example, in Brady v. Maryland, 373 U.S. 83 (1963), the Supreme Court held that due process requires the prosecution to disclose evidence favorable to an accused upon request when such evidence is material to guilt or punishment. In United States v. Bagley, 473 U.S. 667 (1985), the Court held that evidence is material under *Brady* if there is a reasonable probability that disclosure of the evidence would have changed the outcome of the proceeding. A "reasonable probability" under Bagley is "a probability sufficient to undermine confidence in the outcome." When assessing evidence's materiality, the court must take into account the cumulative effect of the suppressed evidence in light of other evidence, not merely the probative value of the suppressed evidence standing alone.

The government's obligation to disclose favorable evidence under *Brady* covers exculpatory evidence and information that could be used to impeach government witnesses. Giglio v. United States, 405 U.S. 150 (1972). In particular, an agreement with a government witness for testimony in exchange for monetary compensation or favorable treatment in the criminal justice system should be disclosed as impeachment evidence, especially where the witness's testimony is an important part of the government's case. The government's duty under *Brady* arises regardless of whether the defendant specifically requests the favorable evidence. The *Brady* doctrine does not require the prosecution to disclose material impeachment information prior to the entry of a guilty plea. However, it is unclear whether the prosecution must disclose [other] material exculpatory evidence under *Brady* before a guilty plea is entered.

The government's duty to disclose favorable evidence does not compel the government to draw and disclose inferences from the evidence; nor does the *Brady* doctrine mandate open file discovery. The government need not disclose: (1) neutral, irrelevant, speculative, or inculpatory evidence; (2) evidence available to the defense from other sources; (3) evidence the defense already possesses; or (4) evidence the prosecutor could not reasonably be imputed to have knowledge of or control over. Nevertheless, even when the prosecutor does not possess *Brady* material, he or she has a duty to learn of any favorable evidence known to other government agents, including the police, who are involved in the investigation. Although the government's constitutional duty to disclose continues throughout the proceedings, tardy disclosure of *Brady* material does not itself constitute a *Brady* violation and will not result in sanctions unless the defendant can show a reasonable probability that the delay changed the outcome.

UNITED STATES v. STEVENS

No. 08-231 (EGS) (D.D.C.) (Dec. 5, 2008)

Memorandum in Support of Senator [Ted] Stevens's Motion for a New Trial

* * *

VII. The Government's Multiple Instances of Misconduct Warranted a New Trial.

[Alaska Senator Ted Stevens was charged and convicted of making false statements on his financial disclosure forms because he accepted unreported gifts of various kinds including, according to the government, $188,000 worth of renovations on what was known as his "Girdwood" residence. The company that carried out the renovations was known as VECO, owned by Bill Allen; one of Allen's employees, supposedly supervising the job on-site, was Rocky Williams.]

As the Court recognized during the trial, the government engaged in severe and intentional misconduct, including: (i) knowingly presenting false evidence to the jury in the form of VECO's accounting records; [and] (ii) intentionally concealing critical exculpatory statements by the government's star witness, Bill Allen. . . . In addition, the conclusion is now unmistakable that the government (iv) elicited fabricated testimony by Mr. Allen about his alleged "CYA" conversation with Mr. Persons, which the government must have known to be false.

The Court endeavored to assure a fair and speedy trial, but defense counsel were forced nonetheless to spend hundreds of hours attempting to deal with government misconduct. As each instance of misconduct came to light, the Court attempted to deal fairly and promptly with the issues without unduly delaying the trial. It is apparent, however, that the government's repeated and intentional misconduct violated the Senator's constitutional rights and severely prejudiced him at trial. There can be no confidence in the verdict, and a new trial is warranted.

The government's misconduct violated at least two separate constitutional rules, either of which requires a new trial. First, the Due Process Clause forbids the government from introducing or failing to correct testimony that it knows or reasonably should know to be false. . . . Second, under *Brady v. Maryland*, "suppression of material evidence justifies a new trial irrespective of the good faith or bad faith of the prosecution." . . .

A. Knowing Presentation of False Evidence.

In an attempt to prove that Senator Stevens knew the Girdwood renovations were worth more than the $160,000 that the Stevens family paid, the government presented evidence at trial, in the form of VECO's internal accounting records, that VECO had incurred over $188,000 in unreimbursed labor and material costs. A substantial portion of these costs, if the records were to be believed, was composed of hours worked by two VECO employees, Robert "Rocky" Williams and David Anderson, whom the VECO accounting records portray as working virtually full time on the renovation project throughout its duration.

What the defense did not know—but the government did—at the time the government introduced the VECO accounting records at trial was that Mr. Williams and Mr. Anderson had not worked anywhere near the amount of time on the project that the VECO accounting records reflect. Mr. Williams had told the government, and testified to an Anchorage grand jury that he worked approximately 24 hours per week on the Girdwood project, while the VECO accounting records show him working an average of 60-70 hours per week. Even more remarkably, Mr. Anderson had testified to the Anchorage grand jury that he was in Portland, Oregon during a 2 to 3 month period when the VECO accounting records show him working nearly full time on the project in Girdwood, Alaska. Three members of the prosecution team were in attendance when Mr. Williams and Mr. Anderson testified before the Anchorage grand jury, and they clearly knew that the VECO accounting records were false. Yet these same prosecutors presented the false records to the jury at trial as supposedly "reliable" business records under the business records exception to the hearsay rule.

In a clear violation of the Due Process Clause, the prosecution team never informed counsel for Senator Stevens of the fundamental unreliability of the government's evidence. On the contrary, the government took affirmative steps to conceal this information by denying the defense access to Mr. Williams and Mr. Anderson. Mr. Williams, while under a defense subpoena, was in Washington, D.C. for the two weeks prior to trial, but the government sent him back to Alaska on the day of opening statements — the same day the lead prosecutor emphasized to the jury the importance of the VECO accounting records and the $188,000 figure. While government counsel claim they sent Mr. Williams 3,300 miles home to receive medical attention (which apparently was unavailable in our Nation's Capital), the prosecutors instructed Mr. Williams to call defense counsel to discuss his obligations under the defense subpoena only *after* he got back to Alaska. Similarly, Mr. Anderson was in D.C. in preparation for his testimony, but the government affirmatively refused to disclose his whereabouts or make him available for a defense subpoena until after the Court criticized its conduct with regard to Mr. Williams.

Based on the above information, the Court specifically concluded that the prosecution team had knowingly presented false evidence of VECO's costs relating to the renovations. . . .

B. Concealing and Manufacturing Information.

The prosecution team also concealed highly material, exculpatory information from the defense regarding prior statements by the government's star witness, Bill J. Allen. The most critical issue in the trial was Senator Stevens's knowledge and intent regarding the allegedly unpaid home renovations. Unbeknownst to the defense, Bill Allen had for nearly two years told prosecutors that he believed Senator Stevens *would have paid bills* relating to the renovations if they had been sent to him. Two interview memoranda contain such statements from Allen:

> — "If Rocky Williams or Dave Anderson had invoiced Ted or Catherine Stevens for VECO's work, BILL ALLEN believes *they would have paid the bill.*" Memorandum of Interview (Dec. 11-12, 2006), at 9 (emphasis added); Tr. (Oct. 2, A.M.), at 4.
>
> — "The source [Allen] did not invoice STEVENS for the work that [VECO engineer John] Hess performed; however, *the source believes that STEVENS would have paid an invoice if he had received one.*" Form 302 Interview Memorandum (Mar. 1, 2007), at 2 (emphasis added); Tr. (Oct. 2, A.M.), at 4.

Despite multiple *Brady* requests, this information was not provided to the defense. Instead, on September 9, 2008, one day before the Court was to hear argument on Senator Stevens's *Brady* motion, the government re-interviewed Allen by telephone and procured a contrary statement that Senator Stevens would *not* have paid a VECO bill because it would have been too high. The government that same day sent the defense a purported *Brady* letter revealing only the new, inculpatory statement and *not* the prior exculpatory ones.

[In a subsequent response to an order by the Court to disclose all *Brady* material, the prosecution once again provided the revised 302 but not the original contradictory statements. In fact, prosecutors affirmatively *redacted* the contradiction out of an earlier 302.]

The conclusion is unmistakable. The government intentionally chose to suppress the critical exculpatory information that Bill Allen believed Senator Stevens would have paid VECO bills if they had been sent. The government did so by procuring a new and inconsistent statement from Mr. Allen on the eve of producing *Brady* material, and then turning over to the defense only the newly created, inculpatory statement while affirmatively redacting and withholding the earlier, exculpatory statements. The government concealed material information, apparently manufactured new information that better suited its theory of the case, and then sought to cover up what it had done.

D. Presenting Mr. Allen's False, Recently Fabricated Testimony.

The prosecution team's misconduct runs much deeper than what it has admitted and what the Court previously found. Bill Allen's most critical testimony, which the prosecutors intentionally elicited, was demonstrably false, and the prosecution team must have known that. The following facts prove the point and warrant a new trial.

The government's theory at trial—that Senator Stevens had no intention of paying for work performed—was directly at odds with (a) the over $160,000 his family paid for the renovations, and (b) the Senator's repeated written and oral requests to Bill Allen, in which Senator Stevens demanded bills for the work performed and, in one instance, reminded Allen of the Senate Ethics Rules. The heart of the defense was Government Exhibit 495, a handwritten note from Senator Stevens to Mr. Allen:

> 10/6/02
>
> Dear Bill—
>
> When I think of the many ways in which you make my life easier and more enjoyable, I lose count!
>
> Thanks for all the work on the chalet. You owe me a bill—remember Torricelli, my friend. Friendship is one thing—compliance with these ethics rules entirely different. I asked Bob P[ersons] to talk to you about this so don't get P.O.'d at him—it just has to be done right.
>
> Hope to see you soon.
>
> My best,
> Ted

To overcome this exculpatory evidence, the government dramatically elicited the following testimony from Mr. Allen:

Q: . . . Did you send Senator Stevens a bill or an invoice after you received this note from him?

A: No.

* * *

Q: Mr. Allen, do you remember having a conversation with Mr. Persons after you got the note from Senator Stevens?

A: Yes.

Q: What did Mr. Persons tell you?

A: He said oh, [B]ill, don't worry about getting a bill. He said, Ted is just covering his ass. . . .

With this bombshell, the government sought not only to erase Senator Stevens's repeated requests for bills, but also to transform these exculpatory requests, particularly Government Exhibit 495, into further evidence of a scheme to deceive the Senate Ethics Committee.

It is readily apparent that Bill Allen's testimony was false—and that the government must have known that it was false. First, Mr. Allen was interviewed by government agents on more than 20 separate occasions, from the date of his initial contact and agreement to cooperate, August 30, 2006, through at least September 9, 2008—two weeks before trial. More than 50 government memoranda (including FBI Form 302s and IRS Memoranda of Interview) relating to Mr. Allen were eventually provided to the defense during the trial pursuant to court order. Not one of these memoranda references this purported comment from Bob Persons, or even hints at the existence of such a conversation. On the contrary, as detailed in section B, above, the memoranda provide that Mr. Allen stated that Senator Stevens would have paid the bills.

Second, even as late as September 9, 2008—a mere two weeks before trial—Mr. Allen provided the FBI with three reasons why he did not send the requested bills to Senator Stevens. None of these reasons had anything to do with the purported comment from Bob Persons or Mr. Allen's supposed belief that Senator Stevens was "just covering his ass." Instead, Mr. Allen explained that he did not send Senator Stevens the requested invoices because: (1) he "wasn't sure how to produce an invoice"; (2) he "felt that VECO's costs were higher than they needed to be"; and (3) he "simply wanted to do the work for Stevens." FBI Form FD-1023 (memorializing 9/9/08 telephonic interview).

Third, the government actually had to prod Mr. Allen to remember this fabrication during his trial testimony. On direct examination, the government showed Mr. Allen yet another letter from Senator Stevens to Mr. Allen requesting a bill for work done on his home. When asked why he did not send Senator Stevens a bill after receiving this follow-up letter, Mr. Allen responded "I don't know why." Only after being reminded by the government of his alleged "CYA" conversation with Mr. Persons did Mr. Allen alter his recollection to state that he had not sent a bill "[b]ecause I had talked to Bob Person[s] before this but I thought, well, it's the same thing, you know." . . .

Fourth, although the government relied heavily on this hearsay statement of Bob Persons, it never once asked Mr. Persons whether he made that statement to Mr. Allen. The government had ample opportunity to ask Mr. Persons about this, having questioned him on five separate occasions between August 31, 2006 and June 1, 2007, including two days worth of grand jury testimony and three interviews. When questioned at trial, Mr. Persons adamantly denied ever having made the "CYA" statement, and reasserted that the government never asked him whether he had made it. . . .

UNITED STATES v. STEVENS

No. 08-cr-231 (EGS) (D.C.C.) (Apr. 7, 2009)

EMMET G. SULLIVAN, District Judge.

At the direction of the Attorney General, on April 1, 2009, a newly-appointed team of prosecutors filed a Motion to Set Aside the Verdict and Dismiss the Indictment, citing the failure to produce notes taken by prosecutors in an April 15, 2008 interview of Bill Allen. At a hearing on April 7, 2009, the government conceded that these notes contained information that the government was constitutionally required to provide to the defense for use at trial. Despite repeated defense requests and the Court's repeated admonitions to provide exculpatory information, the notes were not produced to the defense until March 25-26, 2009, nearly five months after trial. The Court will grant the Motion.

There was never a judgment of conviction in this case. The jury's verdict is being set aside and has no legal effect.

The government's Motion is GRANTED. The verdict is hereby set aside and the indictment is hereby dismissed with prejudice. *See* Fed. R. Crim. P. 48(a).

IT IS SO ORDERED.

RYAN J. REILLY, TED STEVENS PROSECUTOR FELT "SCAPEGOATED" DURING MISCONDUCT INVESTIGATION

*tpmmuckraker.talkingpointsmemo.com, Sept. 28, 2010**

Nicholas A. Marsh, the federal prosecutor who had been involved in the botched prosecution of the late Sen. Ted Stevens and took his own life over the weekend, felt abandoned by some at the Justice Department because of its handling of a probe into allegations of misconduct, friends tell TPMMuckraker.

Marsh felt that he had been sidelined during the course of an investigation into allegations of prosecutorial misconduct while other colleagues also under investigation were able to continue prosecuting cases, according to friends familiar with Marsh's views. They say waiting for the investigation to play out its course was difficult for him to handle.

"Particularly when you're dealing with someone like Nick, who is someone with the utmost character and integrity . . . for him to sort of have to sit by and wait for this investigation to run its course while he is waiting to have his name cleared is very hard for him," Josh Waxman, a longtime friend who was a summer law associate with Marsh, told TPMMuckraker.

"I think he felt scapegoated," one friend speaking on the condition of anonymity told TPMMuckraker.

Stevens, the longtime Republican Senator from Alaska, was convicted in October 2008 of lying on Senate financial disclosure forms about gifts he received, including a massage chair and a stained glass window. But prosecutorial misconduct in the

*http://tpmmuckraker.talkingpointsmemo.com/2010/09/stevens_prosecutor_felt_hung_out_to_dry_during_misconduct_investigation.php.

case—including the prosecution's admission that it withheld from the defense team notes from an interview with a witness that contradicted what he eventually said on the stand—convinced Attorney General Eric Holder to request that the charges be dropped in the spring of 2009. At the trial, Marsh had defended the prosecution, arguing the testimony wouldn't have changed the basic issues in the case.

The prosecutors were taken off the case, and the judge appointed a special prosecutor to look into whether the team was guilty of misconduct for failing to hand over evidence. A separate probe was opened by DOJ's Office of Professional Responsibility.

The circumstances of Marsh's suicide on Sunday were not made public, but Beverley Fields of the Office of the Chief Medical Examiner told TPMMuckraker on Monday that the case and manner of the death would be available shortly.

While the ongoing investigation was expected to wrap up soon and reportedly focused on misconduct by prosecutors besides Marsh, friends said he took the situation pretty hard.

Waxman said he thought Marsh was doing well in his most recent job in the DOJ's Office of International Affairs, which sent Marsh traveling around the world. Two weeks ago, Marsh was in Moldova, and a previous DOJ trip had brought him to Budapest, said Waxman. He also wanted to emphasize that Marsh had worked on several important public corruption cases well before the Stevens trial.

"He was not just the Stevens case. He had a long career of working on public corruption cases and great success in prosecuting," Waxman said. "I just want to make sure that people understand that his career was much more than just the Stevens case and that he had a long record of success."

But Marsh was bothered by the fact that William Welch III and Brenda Morris, two other prosecutors who were also under investigation, were allowed to continue prosecuting cases. Morris popped up in a corruption case in Alabama, while Welch is stationed in the U.S. Attorney's office for the District of Massachusetts and has a role in the prosecution of some high-profile leak cases.

"When the shit hit the fan—regardless of what happened or who was at fault—in a high profile case like this, the mistakes go higher up the chain," the friend told TPMMuckraker.

"It seems odd that if four people are under investigation for possible criminal wrongdoing, two would be taken out of litigation, and two would continue on working on high profile matters," the friend said. "That raised questions with Nick."

Another close friend of Marsh's, former prosecutor Joshua Berman, told The Wall Street Journal that Marsh was anxious that the probe had dragged on. "He became so concerned that the inaction of these bureaucrats would lead to something bad. Their inaction absolutely caused distress for Nick," Berman said. . . .

Marsh's lawyer Robert Luskin said that the special prosecutor looking into allegations had been "thorough, but also fair and utterly professional" in the probe.

"This is an awful tragedy, but I don't know anyone who is inclined to assign personal blame," Luskin told TPMMuckraker in an e-mail. "To the contrary, one of the lessons here is that being the subject of accusations is a very cruel process even when conducted fairly." . . .

NOTES AND QUESTIONS

1. The *Stevens* case was surrounded by misfortune and tragedy all the way around. The indictment likely caused Stevens to lose the Senate seat he had held for 40 years. (Regardless of how one feels about Stevens's performance as a senator, he should not have lost his seat based on a tainted ethics prosecution.) Then, in August 2010, Stevens was killed in a private plane crash at the age of 86. *See* Alex Johnson et al., *Former Sen. Ted Stevens Dies in Alaska Plane Crash*, LIFE ON MSNBC.COM, Aug. 10, 2010, http://www.msnbc.msn.com/id/38637072/ns/us_news-life/t/former-sen-ted-stevens-dies-alaska-plane-crash/.
2. The prosecutorial misconduct in this case, as in most others, was eventually uncovered only because extremely competent defense counsel was relentless in demanding discovery and complaining to the court when it was not received in a timely fashion. Some observers argue that, because only defendants with a lot of money can afford counsel of such high quality, we have a "two-tiered" system of justice. *See, e.g.*, Rodney Uphoff, *The Duke Defendants Reaped the Benefits of a Zealous Defense—But Do Only the Rich Get Real Lawyers? in* RACE TO INJUSTICE, LESSONS LEARNED FROM THE DUKE LACROSSE RAPE CASE (M. Seigel ed., 2009). Do you think that the type of *Brady* violations in this case would have come to light in a run-of-the-mill prosecution?
3. We know that the prosecutors' misconduct in the *Stevens* case was particularly egregious because it provoked an insider (FBI Special Agent Joy) to file a complaint and caused the Attorney General to dismiss the case outright rather than press for a new trial. These are extremely rare events. What motivated the prosecutors' misconduct? Is it especially disturbing that they were members of the *Public Integrity* Section at DOJ, supposedly comprised of the cream of the prosecutorial crop?
4. Beyond reversal of the conviction, what should the penalty be for outrageous prosecutorial misconduct of the type found in *Stevens*? Should the offending prosecutors be fired? Disbarred? Prosecuted? Regarding the last question, what would the possible offenses be?
5. Initial investigations of alleged misconduct by DOJ lawyers are conducted by DOJ's Office of Professional Responsibility (OPR). Defense attorneys have long criticized OPR for routinely failing to find fault with federal prosecutors' conduct. Until 1998, DOJ also faced scathing criticism from the private bar for taking the position that, in line with the Supremacy Clause of the U.S. Constitution, its prosecutors were not subject to state ethics codes. This changed in 1998 when Congress enacted the "McDade Amendment," which declares that "an attorney for the Government shall be subject to State laws and rules . . . governing attorneys in each State where such attorney engages in that attorney's duties, to the extent and in the same manner as other attorneys in that State." 28 U.S.C. §530B(a). Interestingly, Congressman McDade authored his amendment upon returning to Congress after being acquitted on charges of bribery, racketeering, and conspiracy for allegedly accepting gifts and trips in exchange for diverting government contracts to specific groups. *See Lawmaker Acquitted in Bribery Case*, L.A. TIMES,

Aug. 2, 1996, available at http://articles.latimes.com/1996-08-02/news/mn-30554_1. Accordingly, many prosecutors consider this statute "The Revenge of McDade."

6. Many argue that *Stevens* and cases like it demonstrate the need for "open discovery"—that is, allowing defense counsel access to essentially everything in the prosecution's files. *See, e.g.*, John H. Beisner, *Discovering a Better Way: The Need for Effective Civil Litigation Reform*, 60 DUKE L.J., 547 (2010). They say that it is impossible to expect a prosecutor to know in advance of trial what evidence might be material to the defense's case. Is open discovery a good idea?

B. Other Useful Strategic Tools

1. Attorney-Client Privilege (and Work Product Protection) as a Shield

The purpose behind the attorney-client privilege, as it is traditionally formulated, is to encourage individuals seeking legal advice to provide counsel with complete and accurate information to maximize counsel's ability to provide effective representation. Few doubt the value of the privilege in this regard. A necessary consequence of the privilege, however, is that it shields pertinent information from those seeking the underlying "truth," such as government investigators in white collar cases. It should thus come as no surprise that, as part of a strategy to limit investigators' access to incriminating information, savvy defense attorneys use the privilege to their client's advantage.

In United States v. United Shoe Machinery Corp., 89 F. Supp. 357 (D. Mass. 1950), Judge Wyzanski set out the seminal definition of the attorney-client privilege, which is still intact today:

> The privilege applies only if (1) the asserted holder of the privilege is or sought to become a client; (2) the person to whom the communication was made (a) is a member of the bar of a court, or his subordinate and (b) in connection with this communication is acting as a lawyer; (3) the communication relates to a fact of which the attorney was informed (a) by his client (b) without the presence of strangers (c) for the purpose of securing primarily either (i) an opinion on law or (ii) legal services or (iii) assistance in some legal proceeding, and not (d) for the purpose of committing a crime or tort; and (4) the privilege has been (a) claimed and (b) not waived by the client.

Id. at 358-359. The "communication" referenced in Judge Wyzanski's definition includes documents prepared by the client for the purpose of obtaining legal advice. If, in anticipation of litigation, counsel also participates in the creation of documents, or if counsel organizes documents into a form that would reveal his thought processes, "work product" protection combines with the attorney-client privilege to keep the documents out of the hands of opposing counsel.[5]

5. *See* Upjohn v. United States, 449 U.S. 383 (1981); Hickman v. Taylor, 392 U.S. 495 (1947).

Although attorney-client privilege and work product protection are important factors in every case, they are of the utmost importance in cases involving a corporation or other collective entity.

MICHAEL L. SEIGEL, CORPORATE AMERICA FIGHTS BACK: THE BATTLE OVER WAIVER OF THE ATTORNEY-CLIENT PRIVILEGE

49 B.C. L. Rev. 1 (2008)

[U]pon learning about potential criminal conduct by corporate employees, corporations typically launch an internal investigation. This is the only way the "corporation" can figure out "what happened." The corporation needs to know this for a variety of reasons: to avoid or reduce liability to the victims of the alleged illegality, be they creditors, consumers, or shareholders; to avoid or reduce liability in the administrative context, such as an enforcement proceeding by the SEC; to avoid or reduce corporate criminal liability; and, hopefully, because halting any criminal activity is the right thing to do. If the corporate officer initiating the investigation were exclusively to use non-lawyers — forensic accountants, for instance — as investigators, the results of the investigation — witness statements, notes of the investigators, the final report — would not be attorney-client protected. Nor would they be protected by any other privilege. If the government later undertook an investigation, these materials would have to be turned over pursuant to subpoena or other appropriate process.

Of course, corporations typically choose to employ counsel, either in-house, outside, or both to conduct their internal investigations. This practice is eminently rational. As experts in the legal and regulatory landscape, lawyers are in the best position to advise the corporation whether a crime has been committed and, if so, what course of action it should take. Moreover, by using lawyers to conduct the investigation, the materials generated thereby gain protection under the attorney-client privilege. This gives the corporation the ability to control whether it will reveal such materials to outsiders at a later time through privilege waiver.

Corporations generate other attorney-client protected material as well. This occurs when ideas or proposals are "run by" counsel to determine whether (or how) they can be done legally. It also occurs when counsel functions in a general compliance capacity, either through structured compliance programs or on a more informal, ad hoc basis. The privilege does not apply, however, when counsel renders business, as opposed to legal, advice.

UPJOHN CO. v. UNITED STATES

449 U.S. 383 (1981)

Justice REHNQUIST delivered the opinion of the Court.

We granted certiorari in this case to address important questions concerning the scope of the attorney-client privilege in the corporate context. . . .

I.

Petitioner Upjohn Co. manufactures and sells pharmaceuticals here and abroad. In January 1976 independent accountants conducting an audit of one of Upjohn's foreign subsidiaries discovered that the subsidiary made payments to or for the benefit of foreign government officials in order to secure government business. The accountants, so informed petitioner, Mr. Gerard Thomas, Upjohn's Vice President, Secretary, and General Counsel. Thomas is a member of the Michigan and New York Bars, and has been Upjohn's General Counsel for 20 years. He consulted with outside counsel and R.T. Parfet, Jr., Upjohn's Chairman of the Board. It was decided that the company would conduct an internal investigation of what were termed "questionable payments." As part of this investigation the attorneys prepared a letter containing a questionnaire which was sent to "All Foreign General and Area Managers" over the Chairman's signature. . . . The letter indicated that the Chairman had asked Thomas, identified as "the company's General Counsel," "to conduct an investigation for the purpose of determining the nature and magnitude of any payments made by the Upjohn Company or any of its subsidiaries to any employee or official of a foreign government." The questionnaire sought detailed information concerning such payments. Managers were instructed to treat the investigation as "highly confidential" and not to discuss it with anyone other than Upjohn employees who might be helpful in providing the requested information. . . .

On March 26, 1976, the company voluntarily submitted a preliminary report to the Securities and Exchange Commission on Form 8-K disclosing certain questionable payments. A copy of the report was simultaneously submitted to the Internal Revenue Service, which immediately began an investigation to determine the tax consequences of the payments. Special agents conducting the investigation were given lists by Upjohn of all those interviewed and all who had responded to the questionnaire. On November 23, 1976, the Service issued a summons pursuant to 26 U.S.C. §7602 demanding production of:

> "All files relative to the investigation conducted under the supervision of Gerard Thomas to identify payments to employees of foreign governments and any political contributions made by the Upjohn Company or any of its affiliates since January 1, 1971 and to determine whether any funds of the Upjohn Company had been improperly accounted for on the corporate books during the same period.
>
> "The records should include but not be limited to written questionnaires sent to managers of the Upjohn Company's foreign affiliates, and memorandums or notes of the interviews conducted in the United States and abroad with officers and employees of the Upjohn Company and its subsidiaries."

The company declined to produce the documents specified in the second paragraph on the grounds that they were protected from disclosure by the attorney-client privilege and constituted the work product of attorneys prepared in anticipation of litigation. . . .

II.

Federal Rule of Evidence 501 provides that "the privilege of a witness . . . shall be governed by the principles of the common law as they may be interpreted by the courts of the United States in light of reason and experience." The attorney-client privilege is the oldest of the privileges for confidential communications known to the common law. Its purpose is to encourage full and frank communication between attorneys and their clients and thereby promote broader public interests in the observance of law and administration of justice. The privilege recognizes that sound legal advice or advocacy serves public ends and that such advice or advocacy depends upon the lawyer's being fully informed by the client. . . . Admittedly complications in the application of the privilege arise when the client is a corporation, which in theory is an artificial creature of the law, and not an individual; but this Court has assumed that the privilege applies when the client is a corporation, and the Government does not contest the general proposition.

The Court of Appeals, however, considered the application of the privilege in the corporate context to present a "different problem," since the client was an inanimate entity and "only the senior management, guiding and integrating the several operations, . . . can be said to possess an identity analogous to the corporation as a whole." The first case to articulate the so-called "control group test" adopted by the court below, Philadelphia v. Westinghouse Electric Corp., 210 F. Supp. 483, 485 (E.D. Pa.), reflected a similar conceptual approach:

> "Keeping in mind that the question is, Is it the corporation which is seeking the lawyer's advice when the asserted privileged communication is made?, the most satisfactory solution, I think, is that if the employee making the communication, of whatever rank he may be, is in a position to control or even to take a substantial part in a decision about any action which the corporation may take upon the advice of the attorney, . . . then, in effect, *he is (or personifies) the corporation* when he makes his disclosure to the lawyer and the privilege would apply." (Emphasis supplied.)

Such a view, we think, overlooks the fact that the privilege exists to protect not only the giving of professional advice to those who can act on it but also the giving of information to the lawyer to enable him to give sound and informed advice. The first step in the resolution of any legal problem is ascertaining the factual background and sifting through the facts with an eye to the legally relevant. . . .

In the case of the individual client the provider of information and the person who acts on the lawyer's advice are one and the same. In the corporate context, however, it will frequently be employees beyond the control group as defined by the court below—"officers and agents . . . responsible for directing [the company's] actions in response to legal advice"—who will possess the information needed by the corporation's lawyers. Middle-level—and indeed lower-level—employees can, by actions within the scope of their employment, embroil the corporation in serious legal difficulties, and it is only natural that these employees would have the relevant information needed by corporate counsel if he is adequately to advise the client with respect to such actual or potential difficulties. . . .

The communications at issue were made by Upjohn employees to counsel for Upjohn acting as such, at the direction of corporate superiors in order to secure legal advice from counsel. . . . Information, not available from upper-echelon management, was needed to supply a basis for legal advice concerning compliance with securities and tax laws, foreign laws, currency regulations, duties to shareholders, and potential litigation in each of these areas. The communications concerned matters within the scope of the employees' corporate duties, and the employees themselves were sufficiently aware that they were being questioned in order that the corporation could obtain legal advice. . . . Consistent with the underlying purposes of the attorney-client privilege, these communications must be protected against compelled disclosure.

The Court of Appeals declined to extend the attorney-client privilege beyond the limits of the control group test for fear that doing so would entail severe burdens on discovery and create a broad "zone of silence" over corporate affairs. Application of the attorney-client privilege to communications such as those involved here, however, puts the adversary in no worse position than if the communications had never taken place. The privilege only protects disclosure of communications; it does not protect disclosure of the underlying facts by those who communicated with the attorney. . . . Here the Government was free to question the employees who communicated with Thomas and outside counsel. Upjohn has provided the IRS with a list of such employees, and the IRS has already interviewed some 25 of them. While it would probably be more convenient for the Government to secure the results of petitioner's internal investigation by simply subpoenaing the questionnaires and notes taken by petitioner's attorneys, such considerations of convenience do not overcome the policies served by the attorney-client privilege. As Justice Jackson noted in his concurring opinion in Hickman v. Taylor, 329 U.S., at 516: "Discovery was hardly intended to enable a learned profession to perform its functions . . . on wits borrowed from the adversary."

Needless to say, we decide only the case before us, and do not undertake to draft a set of rules which should govern challenges to investigatory subpoenas. . . . At the same time we conclude that the narrow "control group test" sanctioned by the Court of Appeals, in this case cannot, consistent with "the principles of the common law as . . . interpreted . . . in the light of reason and experience," Fed. Rule Evid. 501, govern the development of the law in this area. . . .

Accordingly, the judgment of the Court of Appeals is reversed, and the case remanded for further proceedings.

It is so ordered.

[Opinion of Burger, C.J., concurring in part and concurring in the judgment, omitted.]

NOTES AND QUESTIONS

1. The most significant exception to the attorney-client privilege, at least in the criminal context, is the crime-fraud exception. Communications made to further a crime or fraud are not privileged. The controlling point of view is that of the client: The exception applies if the client was intending to seek information from an attorney to aid a future criminal act. The attorney's state of awareness versus the client's intention is immaterial. To take advantage of the exception, the government must

convince the court that there is a reasonable basis to believe that it applies. The court will then conduct an *in camera* review of the contested materials to decide the issue.

2. The upshot of *Upjohn* is that, in the corporate context, a robust version of the attorney-client privilege applies, but it is the *corporation*, not the individual employees, who holds it. *See, e.g.*, United States v. International Brotherhood of Teamsters, 119 F.3d 210 (2d Cir. 1997). Thus, if an employee incriminates herself in an statement made as part of the corporation's internal investigation, she is protected against the government obtaining that statement and using it against her—as long as the corporation continues to assert its privilege. As we will see below, however, the situation quickly changes if the corporation decides to waive its privilege in connection with a pledge of cooperation with law enforcement.
3. In In re Bevill, Bresler & Schulman Asset Mgmt. Corp., 805 F.2d 120, 124-125 (3d Cir. 1986), the Third Circuit set out five factors that must be met before a conversation between corporate counsel and a corporate officer will be entitled to *personal* attorney-client privilege. They are:

   - the officer approached corporate counsel for the purpose of seeking legal advice;
   - he made it clear that he was seeking legal advice in his individual capacity rather than in his representative capacity;
   - counsel saw fit to communicate with the officer in his individual capacity, knowing that a possible conflict could arise;
   - the conversations with counsel were confidential; and
   - the substance of the communications with counsel did not concern matters within the company or the general affairs of the company.

4. Are conversations between an outside (non-employee) consultant to a corporation and the corporation's general counsel concerning corporate matters subject to the *Upjohn* privilege? The Ninth Circuit Court of Appeals has answered this question in the affirmative. *See* United States v. Graf, 610 F.3d 1148 (2010) (corporate counsel permitted to testify that he advised the "functional employee" that contemplated action would constitute health care fraud).
5. Counsel representing a corporation often faces delicate conflict issues when dealing with insiders who might have committed a crime. On the one hand, counsel wants—and may use considerable pressure to obtain[6]—information from the employee, even if it is self-incriminating. On the other hand, counsel must be very careful to abide by Model R. Prof. Conduct 4.3, which states that "[t]he lawyer shall not give legal advice to an unrepresented person, other than the advice to secure counsel, if the lawyer knows or reasonably should know that the interests of such a person are or have a reasonable possibility of being in conflict with the interests of the client." An employee

6. For example, the corporation can instruct that employees who do not cooperate with counsel be fined, suspended, or even terminated.

who has committed an offense and an employer who wants to root it out (perhaps to turn it over to law enforcement as part of its cooperation) have a definite conflict of interest. Thus, attorneys who practice in this area have developed "*Upjohn* Warnings," which are protective of the employee's rights. *See* GARY H. COLLINS & DAVID Z. SEIDE, WARNING THE WITNESS: A GUIDE TO INTERNAL INVESTIGATIONS AND THE ATTORNEY-CLIENT PRIVILEGE (American Bar Association 2010).

6. Collins and Seide suggest that *Upjohn* Warnings be delivered orally rather than in writing, so as not to unduly intimidate the employee/witness. They suggest the warnings be as follows:

> I am a lawyer for . . . Corporation A. I represent only Corporation A, and I do not represent you personally.
>
> I am conducting this interview to gather facts in order to provide legal advice for Corporation A. This interview is part of an investigation to determine the facts and circumstances of X in order to advise Corporation A how best to proceed.
>
> Your communications with me are protected by the attorney-client privilege. But the attorney-client privilege belongs solely to Corporation A, not you. That means that Corporation A alone may elect to waive the attorney-client privilege and reveal our discussion to third parties. Corporation A alone may decide to waive the privilege and disclose this discussion to such third parties as federal or state agencies, at its sole discretion, and without notifying you.
>
> In order for this discussion to be subject to the privilege, it must be kept in confidence. In other words, with the exception of your own attorney, you may not disclose the substance of this interview to any third party, including other employees or anyone outside of the company. You may discuss the facts of what happened but you may not discuss this discussion.
>
> Do you have any questions?
>
> Are you willing to proceed?

Id. at 31-32. Although these warnings undoubtedly satisfy Rule 4.3, are they truly adequate to inform the employee of the potential consequences of answering questions? Note, in particular, that the warning is careful not to mention self-incrimination or even the potential for future criminal cases. Likewise, it references "your own attorney" in passing, but never reveals that the employee has a right to obtain counsel prior to deciding whether to cooperate.

7. For a fascinating, spy novel-type account of an internal corporate investigation, *see* JOE ANASTASI, THE NEW FORENSICS: INVESTIGATING CORPORATE FRAUD AND THE THEFT OF INTELLECTUAL PROPERTY (2003).

2. Joint Defense Agreements

One way a defendant can expand the scope of the attorney-client privilege is to enter into a "joint defense agreement" with parties who share a "common interest."

This option can bestow significant benefits on the participants, but it also brings with it certain risks, as specified in the materials below.

THOMSON/REUTERS WESTLAW, CRIMINAL PRACTICE MANUAL DATABASE PART II. INVESTIGATION, CHAPTER 11. JOINT DEFENSE AGREEMENTS

Updated Mar. 2011

Joint defense agreements are assuming increasing importance—and attracting increasing controversy—as a means of protecting confidential information shared among counsel for codefendants, among counsel for subjects and targets in criminal investigations, and among counsel in various civil and administrative proceedings. While lawyers for codefendants in "street crime" cases have long participated in informal pooling agreements, use of joint defense agreements is becoming more and more important in white collar criminal defense practice. . . . The undergirding for joint defense agreements is partly contractual and partly related to the joint defense privilege, which protects confidential communications intended to facilitate potential representation among those who share common interests. Most of the federal appeals courts have recognized the joint defense privilege, also called the "common interest rule," as necessary for effective assistance of counsel and a full opportunity to defend. As with the attorney-client privilege, the party who furnishes information must reasonably believe that he is making the statements in confidence. Despite its name, the joint defense privilege is not limited to codefendants; for example, it can apply as well to confidential communications between counsel for subjects and targets in the pre-indictment, investigative stages of a criminal case or to two corporations with a common interest in an administrative claim against the government. The protection of the privilege has been explicitly recognized for communications with attorneys, with their agents, and at [attorney-client] conferences, but not yet for communications solely between the clients or codefendants themselves.

Although it is not an absolute requirement that joint defense agreements be in writing, a well-drafted written agreement is preferable to an oral understanding. The written agreement not only furnishes a clear basis for invoking the privilege, but also provides heightened protections for shared information. . . .

While the U.S. Department of Justice does not deem joint defense agreements illegal per se, and many prosecutors accept them as a fact of life, concern has been stirred within the white collar criminal defense bar by events in several cases, including a motion for an inquiry into conflicts of interest in one case, an outright motion to disqualify in another case, subpoenas to signatories of a joint defense agreement, and an attempt to condition an immunity grant on withdrawal from a joint defense agreement. These developments have intensified the debate over joint defense agreements and heightened the defense bar's awareness of potential problem areas. At present, however, widespread judicial acceptance of joint defense agreements supports their continued use and usefulness.

* * *

Joint defense agreements offer several important benefits to participants: they increase access to information, especially in the case of employees and companies sharing information; they present the potential to conserve resources by dividing witness interview and legal research tasks, and they diminish the government's ability to "divide and conquer" by reducing the possibility of cooperation with the government.

There is another perspective on the "divide and conquer" issue, however, i.e., that once a participant learns what the others say he may decide to cooperate in order to reap the substantial benefit under the Federal Sentencing Guidelines. Thus, safeguards must be built into the agreement anticipating the possibility of a participant who "flips."

Joint defense agreements are "of great value in preparing for criminal or civil cases," according to attorney Gerald Lefcourt, New York City, who has used such agreements in his practice for years. "Courts shouldn't be led to believe this is some way to obfuscate." These agreements "make cases that are large and unwieldy more manageable," he said, adding that he prefers to call these arrangements "pooling agreements" rather than joint defense agreements.

Lefcourt said that in many cases "where what used to be civil is now criminal," such as antitrust, RICO, mail fraud, and "Wall Street" cases, "there is no reasonable way you can gather information and get access to documents without a joint defense agreement. People who have the documents are not going to give them to you without some protection." In these cases, he pointed out, investigations may go back five or six years, and "people's memories are jello. You can't reconstruct what happened so long ago without pooling."

In an article on joint defense planning, Lefcourt listed several advantages of a joint defense. First, a joint defense promotes harmony among defendants and helps avoid "ugly finger-pointing." Information sharing can provide each defendant with the factual and/or legal basis for pretrial motions and help a defendant discover what evidence possessed by codefendants is helpful or harmful to him. Second, a joint defense offers protection against informants, in that defectors and cooperators can be identified more easily in joint defense situations, and pooling information about informants can lead to more effective cross-examination. Third, a joint defense can help achieve a coordinated trial strategy, minimizing repetitious arguments and questioning, avoiding conflicts among defendants' interests and lawyers' egos, and achieving more informed cross-examination. "A coordinated, common defense provides the jury with a consistent, comprehensible, and cogent presentation that is far more effective than conflicting and confusing versions proffered by different defense factions."

Pooling agreements benefit the government and the courts as well as the members of the agreement, Lefcourt emphasized. For example, a client might decide to plead guilty because of knowledge learned from another attorney through the agreement. In fact, Lefcourt said, pooling agreements sometimes lead to "widespread settlements of entire cases" instead of a piecemeal disposition. Additionally, the government may benefit because a witness's recollection has been refreshed by the information shared among agreement participants. Finally, these agreements can reduce the paperwork burden on the prosecution. "Instead of having to respond to five or 10 sets of motions, the government typically gets one set of motions, more intelligently framed," Lefcourt observed.

* * *

. . . No magic formula need be followed to draft a joint defense agreement; instead, counsel should be sure to include a basis for invoking the joint defense privilege and then think creatively about what additional protections to include. These components [are] suggested as a minimum . . . :

- mutuality of interest;
- that materials previously confidential will remain confidential when communicated to counsel for codefendants;
- that the parties believe their disclosures are covered by the joint defense doctrine;
- that codefendants may not disclose information obtained from other parties;
- that parties may withdraw from the agreement, but that information obtained under the agreement will remain privileged;
- that counsel intend to pursue the separate but common interests of their clients.

* * *

Even the most carefully crafted joint defense agreement cannot eliminate the risk that information will later be disclosed, but some circumstances heighten this risk. Joint conferences with clients pose special dangers, both in terms of the technical coverage of the privilege and the practical risk of later disclosure. A client may, for example, make an extraneous statement about his own personal situation or motivations that is arguably outside the common interest and thus outside the joint defense privilege. Moreover, a prosecutor may later try to paint such meetings as "a chance for the defendants to get together and make up their story."

Most problematic is the possibility that a codefendant who is subpoenaed or compelled to testify or who later starts cooperating with the government may in fact reveal information learned at the meeting, either because he does not remember the confidential source of this information or simply because he decides not to honor the agreement. This risk can be minimized to some extent . . . by limiting the number of defendants present at the conference and thus reducing the defendants' exposure to disclosures of the individual clients. . . .

Risks are present even when individual defendants do not attend meetings among defense counsel if the attorneys then share the information learned at the meeting with their clients. . . . Although it would technically be hearsay for an individual not present at the meeting to testify about statements made there, that evidentiary problem would not diminish the information's value to the government as a lead in the case, he pointed out.

Clearly, inter-attorney communications are the least risky and thus most desirable. On the other hand, the value of discussing with clients information learned from participants in a joint defense effort may outweigh the risk of its later inadvertent or even intentional disclosure. "The ability to share information with the client is beneficial in that it allows the participants in the relevant transaction to discuss it, through counsel, and thereby sharpen their recall and gain insight concerning the underlying facts. . . . A strong argument can be made that the agreement is not as useful if the information cannot be shared among the parties to the litigation." . . .

UNITED STATES v. SCHWIMMER

924 F.2d 443 (2d Cir. 1991)

Miner, Circuit Judge:

Defendant-appellant Martin Schwimmer appeals from a judgment of conviction entered after a jury trial in the United States District Court for the Eastern District of New York (McLaughlin, J.). Schwimmer was convicted of[, among other things,] receipt of illegal payments to influence the operations of employee benefit plans, 18 U.S.C. §1954 (1988), conspiracy to defraud the United States, 18 U.S.C. §371 (1988), and income tax evasion, 26 U.S.C. §7201 (1988). The offenses all relate to the receipt of commissions [he received] from a number of financial institutions for investing the funds of employee benefit plans in Certificates of Deposit issued by the institutions.

Schwimmer argues that his sixth amendment right to counsel was violated when the government intentionally obtained from his accountant information protected by the attorney-client privilege. . . .[7]

* * *

7. [The privilege arose out of a joint defense agreement, described as follows:

> When the government began its investigation into their employee benefit plan investment activities, Schwimmer and Renda each retained counsel. Schwimmer retained the law firm of Kostelanetz Ritholz Tigue & Fink, and was represented principally by Robert S. Fink of that firm. Renda retained the law firm of Russo, Silverman and Vitaliano and was represented principally by Ronald Russo and Larry Silverman of that firm, which also represented the interests of First United. Schwimmer, Renda and their attorneys agreed to cooperate in all matters of mutual concern related to the investigation and to the defense of any charges that might be made against them. The attorneys decided that it was necessary to hire an accountant to analyze the financial transactions in which their clients had engaged as well as the tax consequences of those transactions. Ralph Glickman, a certified public accountant, was hired by attorney Silverman in June of 1984 to serve the joint interests.
>
> Although Silverman, attorney for Renda and First United, worked most closely with Glickman, Schwimmer's attorney, Fink, also met with the accountant from time to time. Fink told his client to speak freely with Glickman and that any conversations with the accountant would be protected by the attorney-client privilege. Schwimmer spoke to Glickman at some length on the occasion of their first meeting, which took place at the offices of First United in June of 1984. Present for all or part of that meeting, besides Glickman and Schwimmer, were Renda, Silverman, Ronald Russo of Silverman's law firm, Stewart Steinberg, another attorney for Renda, Kenneth Gould, a partner of Glickman, and Joseph DeCarlo. Schwimmer spoke to Glickman on several occasions thereafter. He also furnished information to the accountant through Fink and Silverman.

United States v. Schwimmer, 892 F.2d 237, 241 (2d Cir. 1989).—Eds.]

In United States v. Schwimmer, 892 F.2d 237 (2d Cir. 1989) (*Schwimmer I*), we remanded Schwimmer's case to the district court for an evidentiary hearing because there was insufficient evidence in the record to determine whether the government had obtained information by invading the attorney-client privilege, and whether any information that might have been obtained was used to prepare the prosecution's case. We directed the court to determine whether the government's case was in any respect derived from a violation of the attorney-client privilege and, if so, to determine what use was made of the derivative information and whether that use affected a substantial right of the appellant.

On March 2 and 12, 1990, Judge McLaughlin conducted evidentiary hearings on the attorney-client privilege issue and found that no direct or indirect use of privileged information by the government had occurred.

Judge McLaughlin focused on meetings between Schwimmer's accountant and government representatives occurring on April 26, May 6, and August 18, 1988, and on copies of the accountant's workpapers that the government had obtained. The accountant, Ralph Glickman, had been hired by Schwimmer and his co-defendant, Mario Renda, to assist in the preparation of their defense, and the workpapers described the allocation between the two men of the commissions they received for investing the funds of employee benefit plans.

Based on the testimony of government agents Frank Devine and Eugene Brozen, the district court found that the information derived from the meetings of April 26 and May 6 was not used to prepare for the prosecution of Schwimmer. Rather, the meetings were conducted to determine a reasonable forfeiture amount for co-defendant Renda, who had pleaded guilty, and there was little, if any, reference to Schwimmer. Regarding the August 18 meeting, the district court heard uncontroverted testimony from Assistant United States Attorney ("AUSA") Bruce Maffeo that he had cautioned Glickman at the outset of the meeting not to disclose any information regarding conversations with Schwimmer, and that no inquiries into such confidential communications between Glickman and Schwimmer were made.

The court determined that there had been no derivative use of the information contained in the workpapers examined and copied at Glickman's office. Agent Brozen, who had retrieved the papers, testified that he had told AUSA Maffeo that the workpapers contained "nothing new" and that they never had discussed the matter again. Agent Devine, who along with Brozen was responsible for investigating the financial aspects of the case, testified that he never was in possession of the workpapers and never had discussed them with Brozen. AUSA Maffeo testified that the first time he had looked at the workpapers was the day of the hearing on remand, and that, while preparing to prosecute Schwimmer, he had considered their acquisition a "non-event."

The district court also found that the workpapers had not been used by the prosecution either to prepare for cross-examination of witnesses or to gain an understanding of the strengths and weaknesses of its case so that evidence could be presented in the light most favorable to the government. The cross-examination of defense witnesses in the case was conducted entirely by AUSA Alan Friedman. Both Maffeo and Brozen testified that Friedman had neither seen the workpapers nor discussed the workpapers with them. Similarly, the record contained no evidence that the government used the papers to structure its presentation of evidence. Rather, AUSA Maffeo testified that the government was ready for trial in March of 1988, well before the workpapers were obtained. Finally, Judge McLaughlin rejected Schwimmer's contention that the workpapers had provided new information used by the government to alter the figures on its spreadsheets. Judge McLaughlin found that, although several figures were different, the substance of the workpapers and of the government's original spreadsheets was the same. Alterations that had been made to the government's spreadsheets were predicated not upon Glickman's workpapers, but upon Glickman's negotiations with the government regarding the amount of Renda's forfeiture and upon the independent cooperation of a business associate of Renda.

We think the district court's rulings regarding the attorney-client privilege . . . were correct.

Discussion

A district court's determination of whether the government improperly has used privileged information in a criminal prosecution is an issue of fact that will not be reversed unless the district court's finding is clearly erroneous. The government must demonstrate that the evidence it uses to prosecute an individual was derived from legitimate, independent sources. Kastigar v. United States, 406 U.S. 441 (1972). We believe that the district court's finding that no privileged information was used by the government in its prosecution of Schwimmer was not clearly erroneous because it is amply supported by the evidence produced at the hearing.

. . . Schwimmer argues that even the indirect use of privileged information by the prosecution is prohibited. However, we have expressly rejected [this view] as being too restrictive. . . . [W]e have held that the mere "tangential[ ] influence[ ] [that privileged information may have on] the prosecutor's thought processes in . . . preparing for trial" was not an unconstitutional use. Schwimmer contends that possession of the information contained in the workpapers allowed the government to confirm the information it had already acquired on its own; however, this use would not require reversal because confirmatory use is not prohibited under the circumstances of this case. Here, the findings of the district court indicate that, at most, any influence on the government's case by information obtained at the interviews or from the workpapers was "wholly conjectural and insubstantial." This does not constitute an improper use.

Schwimmer also contends that the intentional intrusion into the attorney-client domain that occurred when the government agents obtained the workpapers requires an automatic reversal of his conviction. Although such an intentional intrusion warrants careful scrutiny, this Circuit never has gone so far as to adopt the per se rule for which Schwimmer argues. Rather, we have held that, unless "the conduct of the Government has . . . been . . . manifestly and avowedly corrupt," a defendant must show prejudice to his case resulting from the intentional invasion of the attorney-client privilege.

Here, we find that the prosecution's conduct was not manifestly corrupt. Glickman was cautioned not to reveal confidential communications during the course of the interviews with government attorneys and investigators. Moreover, although the agents obviously obtained the workpapers intentionally, Schwimmer suffered no prejudice as a result. The hearing evidence demonstrated that no preview of defense strategy was derived from the workpapers and that no other violative use of privileged information had occurred. . . .

NOTES AND QUESTIONS

1. *Schwimmer* represents an "easy" case because it was fairly clear that the government obtained no additional evidence from the jointly hired accountant. But what about the case of co-defendants who begin cooperating with the government? Even if counsel has followed the advice of the Criminal Practice Manual and has limited his client's exposure to the other members of the joint defense team, and even assuming that the government warns the witness to avoid revealing attorney-client information, isn't there a colorable risk that such information will be conveyed to prosecutors nonetheless? Realistically, will the witness be able to compartmentalize his knowledge based upon its source? If not, is this simply a risk that must be considered and potentially tolerated by the defense? Would a clause in the joint defense agreement prohibiting the signatories from cooperating with the government be enforceable? Would it be ethical?
2. Another risk associated with joint defense agreements is the possibility that, if a member of the defense group cooperates with the government and testifies, counsel for the other group members might be saddled with serious conflicts of interest because they would not be permitted to cross-examine the cooperator based on privileged information—that is, information provided to counsel while the agreement was in effect. The fear—unfounded so far—is that a court will deem the conflict unwaivable and disqualify counsel from the case (presumably because counsel could not realistically quarantine the privileged information during cross). The last thing counsel wants is to be disqualified—it would mean a significant personal monetary loss and potentially severe prejudice to the client, who must wait for new counsel to get up to speed in the case. Should the potential for this conflict be a basis for disqualification?
3. In United States v. Almeida, 341 F.3d 318 (11th Cir. 2003), the court answered the question raised in Note 2 with a resounding "no." It held that, at least where the alleged confidential information was communicated by the now-cooperating witness directly to another party's lawyer, the decision to cooperate amounts to a waiver of the privilege. Further, the court noted that, despite the existence of a joint defense agreement, one party's lawyer does not owe a duty of loyalty to a former member of the group who abandoned it in favor of cooperation. Therefore, when cross-examining the cooperating witness, the lawyer has just one objective, which is vindication of his current client.

   At first glance, the Eleventh Circuit's solution to the conflict issue seems elegant: By not recognizing the existence a conflict, the problem (of potential attorney disqualification) disappears. But does this solution throw the baby out with the bath water? Will defendants enter into joint defense agreements knowing that, if they ever decide to cooperate, whatever they said pursuant to the agreement will be used against them during cross?

III. COOPERATING WITH THE GOVERNMENT

A. Pleading Guilty

In the end, federal prosecutors do not lose many of their cases. This is as it should be: Unlike nearly every other litigator—criminal or civil—federal prosecutors have complete discretion in determining which matters they pursue. Given that there is far more federal crime than they can ever hope to attack, it makes no sense for them to spend time on marginal cases. (There are a few exceptions to this rule: For example, organized crime prosecutors might indict a very close case on a known mafia figure because it is worth risking defeat in an attempt to get a very bad person off the street.) The flip side of this, of course, is that defense attorneys who handle federal cases are most often representing a guilty party. In some instances, the government might not be able to withstand being put to the test, and in other cases, there might be a procedural or constitutional error on which defense counsel can hang her hat. But in many situations, the best alternative for a criminal defendant might be to enter into a plea agreement with the government.

A plea agreement is a contract between the prosecution and defense in a criminal case in which each side makes certain promises (and the defendant makes certain admissions of guilt) in exchange for the case to be settled. Usually, the defendant is willing to plead guilty because he knows that, if he proceeds to trial, he will ultimately be convicted—and he will have paid a very high price in terms of much higher attorneys fees and a significantly longer jail sentence. The prosecutor, on the other hand, is willing to enter into a plea deal to obtain an assured conviction while avoiding the tremendous time and energy necessary to put a case together for trial. In addition, the plea frees him up to address other important cases on his docket.

The customary plea agreement is drafted by the prosecutor and is designed to make sure that, once the defendant signs on the dotted line, he cannot turn back. The agreement will state that, if the defendant violates any part of it, anything he has said pursuant to it can be used against him in a future prosecution. The Supreme Court has held that trying a defendant who has breached his plea agreement for the same crimes to which he had earlier pled guilty does not violate his right against double jeopardy. Ricketts v. Adamson, 483 U.S. 1 (1987). Since 1995, federal plea agreements have also included a waiver of appeal, which courts have found to be enforceable. *See* United States v. Teeter, 257 F.3 14 (1st Cir. 2001).

Due process requires that the terms of a plea agreement be enforced against the government as well. Remedies for a government breach might include specific performance or providing the defendant with the opportunity to withdraw his plea. Good faith on the part of prosecutors, or the lack thereof, is not relevant. *See* Santobello v. New York, 404 U.S. 257 (1971).

B. Cooperation

1. "Queen for a Day"

A defendant will normally get some consideration from the court simply for pleading guilty—the federal sentencing guidelines call it "acceptance of responsibility." For the most part, however, he will obtain a significant reduction in sentence only if he is willing to cooperate and, again in the words of the guidelines, provides "substantial assistance" to the government in the investigation and prosecution of others who have likewise committed federal offenses.

Initiating cooperation is a bit tricky. The defendant does not want to confess and tell the prosecutor what he knows without some guarantee of immunity for the proffer session in case the deal falls through. The prosecutor, on the other hand, is not willing to immunize the defendant's proffer because, if there is no deal, the requirements of *Kastigar*[8] will make it next to impossible to prosecute the defendant. To solve this dilemma, the parties typically employ a compromise agreement, often (and oddly) called a "Queen for a Day" agreement or letter.

UNITED STATES v. LAUERSEN

2000 WL 1693538 (S.D.N.Y. Nov. 13, 2000)

PAULEY, District J.

. . . Presently before this Court is defendant Madga Binion's motion in limine to preclude the Government from introducing at trial statements she allegedly made to the Government under the terms of a Queen for a Day agreement. Binion argues that her proffer statements are not admissible because the Queen for a Day agreement governing the use of her statements is vague, overreaching and improperly interferes with her Sixth Amendment rights. . . .

Background

The facts giving rise to Binion's motion developed over a period of almost eleven months and are worth describing in moderate detail to give sufficient context to the legal arguments presented.

A. The May 12, 1998 Proffer Session

On May 12, 1998, Binion, a board certified anesthesiologist, and her attorney, Arthur Viviani, met with Government representatives in connection with the criminal investigation of the medical practice of Dr. Niels Lauersen, also a defendant in this

8. Kastigar v. United States, 406 U.S. 441 (1972), reprinted *supra* p. 482.

matter. . . . Days earlier, Binion had been informed that Dr. Neil Ratner, an anesthesiologist for whom Binion worked and who assisted Lauersen in his practice, had entered into a cooperation agreement with the Government and pled guilty.

The meeting among Binion, her attorney and the Government representatives was governed by the Queen for a Day agreement [a.k.a. "Proffer Agreement"] used in the Southern District of New York. . . .

Paragraph 1 of the Proffer Agreement states, in relevant part, that "[s]hould any prosecutions be brought against Client by this Office, the Government will not offer in evidence on its case-in-chief . . . any statements made by Client at the meeting."

Paragraph 2 of the Proffer Agreement enumerates two exceptions to the Government's promise in Paragraph 1 not to use statements made during the proffer in its case-in-chief. Paragraph 2(a) permits the Government to "use information derived directly or indirectly from the meeting for the purpose of obtaining leads to other evidence, which evidence may be used in any prosecution of Client by the Government." Paragraph 2(b) provides:

> Notwithstanding item (1) above: . . . (b) the Government may use statements made by Client at the meeting and all evidence obtained directly or indirectly therefrom for the purpose of cross-examination should Client testify, or to rebut any evidence or arguments offered by or on behalf of Client (including arguments made or issues raised sua sponte by the District Court) at any stage of the criminal prosecution (including bail, trial, and sentencing), should any prosecution of Client be undertaken. . . .

In addition, Paragraph 2(c) contains a waiver of the exclusionary rules for plea statements set forth in Rule 11(e)(6) of the Federal Rules of Criminal Procedure and Rule 410 of the Federal Rules of Evidence. The last line of Paragraph 2 reads: "It is the intent of this Agreement to waive all rights in the foregoing respects."

The subject of Binion's motion relates to the second clause of Paragraph 2(b) that describes the circumstances under which the Government may use her proffer statement to "rebut" evidence and arguments she presents at trial.

B. Binion's Understanding of the Terms of Her Proffer

In advance of the proffer session, Viviani, an experienced criminal defense attorney, explained to Binion what he believed to be the terms under which the session would take place. The Government did not provide the Proffer Agreement to Viviani in advance of the meeting. Thus, without the benefit of seeing the Proffer Agreement prior to the meeting, Viviani told Binion that she must be "truthful," that "she would not have what is known as derivative use immunity," and that "what she said could not be used against her unless she were to testify to a different version of the facts, at which time the government could use the statement to impeach her."

At the proffer session, when first presented with the Proffer Agreement, Viviani told Binion "that this is what we discussed about the Queen," and then she signed it. Viviani informs the Court that he did not have the understanding, nor did he explain to Binion, that the terms of the Proffer Agreement regarding rebuttal applied to "openings, cross-examination, and summation." Viviani further informs the Court that "[i]f the government has used those words (opening, cross, summations), I would have stepped out of the room with Dr. Binion and discussed whether we should go forward."

Binion, in an affidavit submitted to this Court, detailed an understanding of the Proffer Agreement consistent with Viviani's recollection. . . .

Special Agent Porzio, who attended the proffer session and prepared the Form FD-302 that purports to summarize what Binion related at the meeting, confirms the version of the facts set forth by Binion and Viviani. . . . [During the proffer session, Binion confessed to her participation in the crimes.] . . .

[Binion did not cooperate and trial is now scheduled.] In anticipation of the start of . . . trial, Binion moved . . . to preclude the Government from introducing the statements [she] made during the May 12, 1998 proffer session. . . . Binion sought a ruling from this Court clarifying "the specific range of cross-examination and argument that will and will not trigger admissibility of the proffer statements." . . .

In its initial opposition to Binion's motion, the Government set forth its position in . . . stark terms. . . . The Government contended that "Dr. Binion and her counsel knowingly and voluntarily gave up the ability to argue, or to present evidence (through direct testimony or cross-examination), that she is factually innocent, that she lacks the requisite criminal intent, that someone else committed the crimes charged, or that such crimes never occurred." The Government contends further that "any statements by Binion's counsel (including opening and closing remarks), or any evidence offered by Dr. Binion (through cross- or direct examination, or by way of documentary evidence), that is contradictory to her proffer statements, triggers the Government's right to admit such statements."

Binion [now] argues that the Proffer Agreement is vague, overreaching, and improperly interferes with her rights secured by the Sixth Amendment. Binion asserts principally that, given the ambiguities attendant to the scope of Paragraph 2(b), her waiver as to the exclusionary rules for plea statements was not knowing and voluntary under controlling Supreme Court and Second Circuit precedent. In addition, Binion asserts that her waiver, if effective, is not enforceable because it is tantamount to a waiver of the Sixth Amendment right to trial, as she will be forced to relinquish rights to cross-examination, to assertions of innocence by counsel during opening and summation, and to call witnesses on her behalf.

The Government takes issue with Binion's arguments, but challenges them from a different perspective. As expected, the Government argues that Binion's waiver was valid and enforceable. However, setting those issues aside, the Government submits that Binion's attorneys are precluded from adducing evidence of Binion's "actual innocence" by operation of the relevant rules governing attorney conduct. The Government contends that based on the substance of Binion's proffer statements, there is no good-faith basis to argue that Binion is factually innocent. . . . Still, the Government submits that Binion has available to her viable defenses at trial that do not trigger the Proffer Agreement. According to the Government, Binion may argue reasonable doubt, claim that the Government did not satisfy its burden of proof, and establish propositions not contradicted by her proffer statements. . . .

E. Discussion

Rule 11(e)(6) of the Federal Rules of Criminal Procedure and Rule 410 of the Federal Rules of Evidence contain substantively identical provisions that exclude from admission into evidence statements made by a criminal defendant during plea discussions. In *United States v. Mezzanatto*, the Supreme Court held that "absent some affirmative indication that the agreement was entered into unknowingly or involuntarily, an agreement to waive the exclusionary provisions of the plea statements Rules is valid and enforceable." The waiver at issue in *Mezzanatto* extended only to the use of the defendant's plea statements "to impeach any contradictory testimony he might give at trial if the case proceeded that far."

In applying a "knowing and voluntary" standard in determining whether a defendant has waived his rights under exclusionary rules for plea statements, the Supreme Court adopted the heightened standard reserved for waiver of rights essential to a fair trial and the reliability of the adjudicative process. . . .

In this regard, the Second Circuit has held that a waiver of such essential rights should be enforced only "if the record 'clearly demonstrates' that the waiver was both knowing (in the sense that the defendant fully understood the potential consequences of his waiver) and voluntary."

Apart from applying the knowing and voluntary standard, the Second Circuit has held that agreements containing waivers of essential rights, such as plea agreements, are to be construed narrowly because they "are unique contracts in which special due process concerns for fairness and the adequacy of procedural safeguards obtain." . . . First, courts are to construe such agreements "strictly against the Government," for the primary reason that the Government typically drafts the agreement and "the fact that the Government ordinarily has certain awesome advantages in bargaining power. Second, the agreements are to be construed "against a background understanding of legality." Third, courts may apply "general fairness principles" to invalidate particular terms of such agreements.

In this case, the Government has not demonstrated that Binion knowingly waived her rights as to the admissibility of statements made during her proffer for purposes beyond impeachment. Consequently, this Court holds that Binion's waiver is valid only to the extent it permits the Government to use her proffer statements for impeachment purposes should she testify. For all other purposes, Binion's waiver is invalid. . . .

Limiting Binion's waiver to allow her proffer statements to be used for impeachment purposes only affords the Government no more than what Supreme Court precedent permits. This Court notes, without deciding the issue, that a groundswell of doubt has been expressed in this Circuit concerning the enforceability of the waiver contained in the Proffer Agreement, "at least when the waiver extends beyond the use of the statements to impeach the defendant."

The decision to invalidate Binion's waiver for purposes other than impeachment does not settle the matter. This Court is duty bound to protect the integrity of the proceeding and to ensure that matters presented to the jury are grounded in good faith. Consequently, based on the substance of the statements made by Binion during the proffer session held on May 12, 1998, this Court will not permit Binion's counsel to elicit substantive (non-impeachment) testimony, either on cross-examination of witnesses called by the Government or from witnesses called to testify on her behalf, or to present arguments to the jury at any stage of the proceeding, including opening statements, that directly contradict specific factual statements made by Binion in the FBI-302 statement. . . .

SO ORDERED.

NOTES AND QUESTIONS

1. Some defense attorneys call the agreement the government tried to obtain in *Lauersen* a "Queen for a Day from Hell" letter. *See, e.g.*, Jon May, *Queen for a Day from Hell: How to Handle a Troubling Proffer Letter*, CHAMPION MAG., Sept.-Oct. 2006, at 16, available at http://www.nacdl.org/public.nsf/01c1e7698280d203852556d0b00789923/9e051282debec7d585257210005bd4d2?OpenDocument; *see also generally* Benjamin A. Naftalis, "*Queen for a Day" Agreements and the Proper Scope of Permissible Waiver of the Federal Plea-Statement Rules*, 37 COLUM. J.L. & SOC. PROBS. 1 (2003). The name fits, doesn't it?
2. A "Queen for a Day" letter is supposed to protect both the prosecutor *and the defendant* in case cooperation never comes about. A proffer is not supposed to be a confession. Does the "Queen for a Day from Hell" letter provide any protection for the defendant? If you were defense counsel, would you ever advise your client to sign one?
3. In any event, a defendant should not sign any "Queen for a Day" letter lightly. As one experienced defense attorney put it:

    > [H]ere is the bottom line. Barring unusual circumstances, you should only proffer if the following conditions are met: 1) indictment is a foregone conclusion absent a proffer; 2) a reasonably specific plea deal (or an immunity agreement) is contemplated by both sides if your proffer is truthful and covers the anticipated topics; 3) you and your attorney have decided that, all things considered, you definitely want the contemplated plea deal (or immunity agreement); 4) the prosecutor is totally trustworthy; 5) the prosecutor will not be undercut or overruled by his superiors; and 6) you are prepared to tell the whole truth at the proffer session and thereafter.

    Solomon L. Wisenberg, *Queen For A Day: The Dangerous Game of Proffers, Proffer Agreements and Proffer Letters*, Findlaw (2005), available at http://library.findlaw.com/2005/Feb/21/138691.html.
4. What about the ethical issue raised by the *Lauersen* court? Is there any way around it? Should there be?

2. Corporate Cooperation and Privilege Waiver

An area that has garnered a great deal of attention over the last couple of years is cooperation in the context of corporate defendants, particularly the impact such cooperation often has on the corporation's attorney-client privilege. Presented here are two opposing views on the matter.

MICHAEL L. SEIGEL, CORPORATE AMERICA FIGHTS BACK: THE BATTLE OVER WAIVER OF THE ATTORNEY-CLIENT PRIVILEGE

49 B.C. L. Rev. 1 (2008)

The federal government's efforts to ferret out and prosecute corporate criminals [after the Enron debacle and the bursting of the technology bubble in the stock market] were remarkably successful. Over the four-year period from 2002 to 2006, federal prosecutors brought charges against more than 200 chief executive officers, company presidents, and chief financial officers, and obtained over 1100 convictions or guilty pleas in white collar cases. These are staggering figures, particularly in light of the tremendous resources traditionally needed to investigate and prosecute complex fraud. DOJ's newfound success in this area, however, was not accidental. Rather, the Department had found a new and extremely powerful investigative tool: convincing corporations to cooperate by turning against their (often former) officers and employees.

Prior to 1998, DOJ had no set policy regarding the prosecution of corporations, and many prosecutors did not see the point of charging an entity that, as a mere legal fiction, could not be put in jail. A memorandum written by then-Deputy Attorney General Eric Holder in 1998, however, changed all this. For the first time in its history, the Department set out a list of criteria to guide prosecutors faced with deciding whether to indict a corporate (or other collective) entity. Among other factors, the memorandum mentioned the importance of a corporation's cooperation with the investigation. It further noted that such cooperation might require the corporation to waive its attorney-client privilege and work-product protection. The guidelines set forth in the Holder Memorandum were later reinforced in a memorandum written by Holder's successor, then-Deputy Attorney General Larry Thompson, in 2003. It did not take long before companies threatened with prosecution understood that the only realistic way of avoiding indictment was to cooperate fully.

It was the increase in cooperation by corporations faced with the danger of being indicted that enabled DOJ lawyers to wrap up so many cases in record time. . . .

Not surprisingly, DOJ's enhanced success was not well received within the corporate world. As high-profile corporate executives fell in domino-like fashion, corporations themselves bristled under the pressure to cooperate or face indictment. Soon, a backlash against white collar prosecutions began to take shape. The imperative to maintain a positive public image meant that Corporate America could not directly complain about governmental success in flushing out white collar criminality. So, instead, corporations took aim at the government's tactics. In particular, the business lobby, represented by the U.S. Chamber of Commerce and other groups, initiated a public campaign against DOJ's increasing insistence on the waiver of attorney-client privilege and work-product protection as part of an entity's cooperation. Joining forces with its attorneys, represented by the American Bar Association (the "ABA"), the Association of Corporate Counsel, and the National Association of Criminal Defense Attorneys, the business lobby complained that DOJ had created a "culture of waiver" that threatened the very existence of the time-honored attorney-client privilege. By framing the issue as one of the government intruding on fundamental rights, the business lobby was able to attract liberal groups such as the American Civil Liberties Union into its coalition, unimaginatively named the Coalition to Preserve the Attorney-Client Privilege (the "Coalition"). The battle over attorney-client privilege waiver was thus underway.

At first, the Department stood its ground. But the combination of business, lawyers, and civil rights groups proved too strong a force to resist. The Coalition took its case to Congress, prompting hearings at which the new Deputy Attorney General, Paul McNulty, found himself under sustained attack. Soon thereafter, Senator Arlen Specter introduced a bill that would prohibit government attorneys from asking a corporation to waive its attorney-client privilege or using its failure to waive as a factor in deciding whether to bring charges or determine its degree of cooperation. Reading the handwriting on the wall, on December 12, 2006, McNulty issued a revised memorandum on the subject to all DOJ attorneys. The McNulty Memorandum makes clear that (1) a corporation can cooperate without waiving its privilege if it can provide the necessary information through other means; (2) waiver requests should be made only if there is a "legitimate need"; and (3) waiver requests require high-level supervisory approval, which varies depending upon the sensitivity of the information sought.

The McNulty Memorandum failed in its bid to satisfy Coalition members. They stated that it did not go far enough and claimed that the proper resolution of the issue was a total ban on waiver requests. . . .

C. Public Benefits of Corporate Cooperation

1. Costs of Prosecuting White Collar Crime

The prosecution of white collar crime can be slow, resource-intensive work. There are numerous reasons for this. First, the crime itself is often very complex. Indeed, sophisticated white collar criminals frequently do all they can to add to the complexity of their crime by disguising what they did beneath layers of accounting tricks, false or fraudulent transactions, deleted records, and second sets of books. In a case of any significance, investigators might face hundreds of thousands—if not millions—of pages of documents, increasingly in electronic form, that they must sort through to unravel the criminal behavior. This work might take a team of investigative agents, at least some of whom are trained accountants, and one or more prosecutors years to carry out.

Second, white collar cases are often not open and shut. Many times, the key question will be whether the individual defendants, and thus the corporation, harbored the requisite criminal intent. The typical defendant will plead good faith or advice of counsel. Specifically, the defendant might claim that the action in question was a close accounting call, but that he was comfortable it fell on the right side of the law. Alternatively, the defendant will contend that he approved the transaction, or the manner in which it was recorded on the company's books and records, only after carefully consulting with the corporation's accountants and legal counsel. In cases in which the prosecution alleges that the defendant stole from the company, the defendant is very likely to claim that the compensation at issue was approved by the board of directors, or that some other corporate employee was the true culprit.

These kinds of defenses are unique to white collar crimes; a bank robber, for instance, cannot plead ignorance of the law or claim that the bank approved of his (illicit) withdrawal. Moreover, these defenses are difficult to overcome. At minimum, they require extensive interviews with the accountants, lawyers, and directors involved. If these individuals are not inclined to be cooperative, they must be subpoenaed to the grand jury and perhaps even granted immunity. This process can take months and even years. In addition, overcoming typical white collar defenses requires prosecutors to seek the advice of experts in the field and prepare the experts for possible testimony at trial.

Third, white collar defendants, especially major corporations and the individuals associated with them, usually have the resources to hire excellent attorneys who specialize in white collar criminal defense. These attorneys have the ability to slow down an investigation to a considerable extent if they so choose. They can object to subpoenas *duces tecum* on a whole host of grounds, forcing repeated hearings relating to subpoena enforcement. They can claim attorney-client privilege and work-product protection of the documents subject to a subpoena, requiring the establishment of a system to filter out challenged documents to obtain a ruling from the court before government agents may see them. Defense counsel can advise their clients not to give voluntary statements to government investigators and to exercise their Fifth Amendment right not to testify before the grand jury absent immunity. If they are coordinating their efforts through a joint defense agreement, counsel can ensure that this lack of cooperation is widespread, if not universal, forcing prosecutors to decide which potential witnesses to immunize in a situation of substantial uncertainty—something they are hesitant to do. Unless it is fueled by a whistleblower or other inside information, these tactics can slow an investigation to a snail's pace, and perhaps even cause it to stall altogether. . . .

If the cases are not settled through guilty pleas, each jury trial in a white collar case is likely to be time-consuming and expensive. Prosecutors almost inevitably must introduce a massive amount of documentary evidence, along with the testimony of dozens of witnesses, often including forensic accounting and other experts. Highly paid defense counsel will conduct extensive and often effective cross-examinations of the government's witnesses. After the government rests, the defense is very likely to put on a case of its own. In light of the fact that the defendant probably has no prior criminal record and may even be an upstanding citizen of the community (apart from the criminal conduct alleged in the case), she is free to take the witness stand to proffer her ignorance or good faith defense. Defense experts may be called to rebut the opinions of the prosecution experts. Sometimes, defense counsel will line up a parade of good character witnesses to testify to the defendant's honest, law-abiding nature. . . .

2. Benefits of Cooperation

. . . In light of the difficulties of waging war against uncooperative corporate targets, it should not be surprising that in recent years prosecutors have become increasingly aggressive in seeking out their cooperation. When a collective entity decides to be cooperative, the balance of power shifts dramatically. No longer foes, the corporation and the government can team up to unmask the individuals who were at the center of the criminal activity, thereby getting to the heart of the matter quickly and efficiently.

In the majority of cases, upon learning of possible criminal behavior in its midst, a corporation conducts an internal investigation to determine what happened and what to do about it. Upon reaching a conclusion, the investigators make a report—either orally or in writing—to the corporation's officers or board of directors or both. Those in charge then decide what remedial action, if any, to take.

In many cases, the internal investigation is substantially completed by the time government agents come knocking at the corporation's door. If so, the corporation is in an obvious position to be of significant help to prosecutors if it chooses to cooperate with them. The corporation has already isolated the critical documents and witnesses, compiled witness statements, and identified the likely culprits. If it willingly turns this information over to the government, a great deal of time can be shaved from the investigative phase of the criminal case. The corporation can do other things to help as well, such as provide background about the corporation, including its organizational structure and in-house policies.

With company cooperation, the successful completion of a complex white collar prosecution, including resolution of corporate as well as all individual charges, could very well be reduced from a matter of years to a matter of months. This huge efficiency gain represents a significant public good. Far more white collar criminal behavior can be attacked with the same amount of resources devoted to the effort.

The efficiency argument is equally strong even when prosecutors erroneously target an innocent company. The fastest way a company can convince government agents of its innocence is to share all pertinent information with them so that they can draw this conclusion themselves. . . .

II. Implicating the Attorney-Client Privilege

. . . [When a] corporation chooses to cooperate, much of the assistance it can offer will have no bearing on its attorney-client privilege. For example, the corporation can provide access to nonprivileged computer files and documents; including organizational charts, books and ledgers; policy manuals; and internal (nonlegal) memoranda. It can also make available for interviews and testimony officers and employees who are willing to speak. Corporate officers or counsel can explain to prosecutors how pieces of the puzzle fit together to form a coherent picture of the activity in question.

Sometimes, this degree of cooperation will be sufficient for prosecutors to decide either that no crimes took place or that certain of the corporation's employees merit indictment. It will also be a factor in determining whether, if criminality existed, the corporation should be charged separately as a legal entity. If cooperation short of waiver is sufficient, the case can be concluded without any impact on the corporation's attorney-client privilege. As the McNulty Memorandum indicates, this manner of resolution should be the prosecution's goal.

On other occasions, however, this level of corporate cooperation will be of more limited use. For example, the relevant corporate documents may have been devised at the request of in-house counsel acting as legal compliance officer. Such documents would thus be privileged and could not be shared with prosecutors absent privilege waiver. Alternatively, the corporation might have severed its relationship with the main culprits of the criminal activity, meaning that it would have no leverage to encourage them to provide statements or testimony. At the same time, however, the corporation may have in its possession the results of the internal investigation, conducted by counsel, which led it to fire the culprits and take other remedial action. As noted above, such materials would be protected by the privilege.

Even in cases of this latter kind, it is still possible that the corporation could provide substantial assistance to prosecutors without privilege waiver. If the case is small and the criminality focused, the corporation's sharing of nonprivileged information, combined with the federal government's ability to probe through its use of the grand jury and other investigatory techniques, may enable prosecutors to track down the responsible individuals in a fast and efficient manner. By requiring prosecutors to justify to their superiors why privilege waiver in any given situation is necessary, presumably the McNulty Memorandum protects the privilege in cases of this small, focused variety as well. Some white collar investigations, however, will involve criminality that spans years, implicates multiple individuals, and bleeds across a seemingly infinite array of documents. Worse yet for prosecutors, cases of this magnitude often involve extremely sophisticated schemes that are difficult for an outsider to understand, let alone unravel. In such cases, a corporation might point prosecutors in the right direction without waiving privilege, but this would be of only limited assistance. The investigation would still take years to run its course as prosecutors struggled to subpoena and interpret the right documents, immunize and debrief the correct witnesses, figure out whether a crime had been committed, and, if so, whether there was sufficient proof to bring charges. Only if the corporation short-circuited these extensive prosecutorial efforts by waiving privilege and sharing internal reports, documents, and witness statements that laid out the crime and the conduct of those responsible could it fairly claim to have rendered substantial assistance to the prosecution.

JULIE R. O'SULLIVAN, THE LAST STRAW: THE DEPARTMENT OF JUSTICE'S PRIVILEGE WAIVER POLICY AND THE DEATH OF ADVERSARIAL JUSTICE IN CRIMINAL INVESTIGATIONS OF CORPORATIONS

57 DePaul L. Rev. 329 (2008)

The white-collar criminal defense bar has never been reticent to complain about U.S. Department of Justice (DOJ) policies that threaten its clients or the viability of its practice. But nothing—at least in the author's twenty-plus years of involvement in white-collar issues—has consumed the bar as much as the threats posed to the corporate attorney-client privilege and work-product doctrine. While commentators have identified a variety of assaults on these protections, the bar is most vocally outraged by the DOJ policy, pursuant to which, it charges, federal prosecutors regularly insist that corporations waive these protections to secure cooperation credit, declination of criminal action against the corporate actor, and consideration at sentencing. For some time now, the defense objections to this particular policy have been unusually sustained, widespread, and passionate. Until recently, few outside the DOJ have questioned the bona fides of these objections. . . .

Why has this issue energized the corporate defense bar as never before and seemingly resonated with the judicial and political establishments? . . . There are, no doubt, a complex of factors, some of them self-interested, that contribute to this phenomenon. But, after numerous conferences, discussions, and informal talks with white-collar practitioners, my sense of the predominant "why" of this is difficult to footnote but very clear: these advocates are genuinely outraged by the feeling that the government has stepped over the line and made it virtually impossible for them to function as defenders of corporate clients in an adversarial confrontation with the government.

This Article's thesis turns on a circumstance that is rarely raised in this debate, but which is central to it: collective entities, such as corporations, cannot claim the Fifth Amendment right against self-incrimination. The attorney-client privilege and the work-product doctrine are critical, not because they encourage self-correction or candid communication between corporate client and counsel, but rather because they serve as a substitute for the Fifth Amendment in criminal investigations of corporations in two senses.

First, from a systemic point of view, the lack of a Fifth Amendment privilege strips a company of the only weapon it has in the preindictment stage to counterbalance the weighty advantages the government enjoys at that point: the power to refuse to provide evidence that will be a link in the chain to its own conviction. Second, and more concretely, these protections are the only means by which corporations, deprived of any privilege against self-incrimination, may shield from government scrutiny that which the government truly wants and often needs to make its case: the informed conclusions of counsel regarding what records are relevant and the witness statements to which counsel will be privy. Demands for this analytical and evidentiary material—in effect, in many cases, a roadmap for liability—force counsel not only to lay her client open for the government, but also to be the engineer of the case against it. Counsel's ultimate aim, of course, is to persuade the government that such extraordinary efforts warrant a declination of prosecution.

Practitioners do not analyze the waiver issue in these terms, but the general objections contained in some of their literature are entirely consistent with this thesis. In particular, two related themes emerge from a survey of practitioners' writings on this and related issues. First, practitioners seem to object to the pervasive presuppositions underlying the DOJ's policy—and the policies of a wide array of federal institutions—that corporations have duties not visited upon individuals to self-report potential wrongdoing within the company, cooperate fully with government investigators, remedy any damage, and act aggressively to prevent recurrence of the objectionable behavior. The assumption is that the proper role of corporations confronted with allegations of wrongdoing is, quite simply, to roll over. Individual defendants can fight like hell, but corporations should self-report, remediate harm, cooperate fully, and take whatever prosecutors and regulators believe they have coming. Zealous defense counsel find this assumption beyond galling.

The second theme resonating throughout the literature flows from the first. The bar argues that the waiver policy essentially "deputizes" corporate counsel in furtherance of this "crime-fighting partnership" between corporate America and the government. By definition, the reigning conception of what corporations ought to do when confronted with allegations of criminal wrongdoing means that counsel are no longer conceived of as the corporation's champions, poised to defend their clients in an adversarial joust. Rather, they are simply functionaries charged with exposing whatever wrongdoing has occurred, and advocates only in trying to convince the government to take the least-damaging avenue—such as regulatory sanction rather than criminal prosecution—in response to whatever is uncovered. In short, zealous advocates feel that they have become junior g-men, and they hate it.

What prevents corporate counsel and their clients from simply saying "no" to this new paradigm? The answer is that they would if they could, but a variety of circumstances make such choices exceedingly difficult. The same coercive forces that make the adversary system a myth in the context of corporate criminal liability also take away the bargaining leverage of corporations in attempting to resist DOJ privilege waiver "requests." These circumstances . . . include the malleable nature of the federal criminal code, the overbroad standards of corporate criminal liability, and the range and harshness of sanctions applicable upon conviction. The DOJ and other regulators could talk about "crime-fighting partnerships with corporate America" all they wish and could attempt to "deputize" defense counsel to work on their behalf, but, absent these circumstances, the defense could quite simply say "no" or "prove it," as is at least their hypothetical privilege in an adversary system. Given the existence of these coercive factors, however, counsel have few options in resisting government inquiries.

This Article provides some context for these themes and explains more completely why "requests" for waiver of a corporation's attorney-client privilege and work-product doctrine are viewed both as virtually irresistible and as the critical "tipping point" in both the balance of power between the government and the defense and the evisceration of defense counsel's role. To mix metaphors, the coercive factors mentioned above are the lever that DOJ prosecutors and other government agents have used to move the corporate boulder up to the precipice overlooking the Sea of Complete Capitulation. Once the "last straw" of privilege waivers is laid on, the lever sends the boulder over the cliff to be smothered in that Sea. . . .

The DOJ would argue that it can, and should, do everything possible to quickly and efficiently nip corporate crime in the bud and that corporate cooperation in this regard, through waivers of privilege and other means, is in the best interests of the public, as well as the entity and its shareholders. Prosecutors' positions are not irrational. Corporate crime can be exceedingly costly to society—whether that cost is assessed in financial terms, as collateral damage (for example, to the environment or to public safety), or by reference to public confidence in markets, financial institutions, and the like. Viewed from the perspective of punishing and deterring corporate crime through the most efficient and effective allocation of government resources, a "crime-fighting partnership" between the government and corporate America makes sense, as does enlistment of experienced corporate counsel as investigating arms of the government.

The only problem is that a similar balancing could be made for rapists, drug dealers, and murderers. Individual defendants' rights to resist the government to the bitter end are also costly and counterproductive measured by law enforcement imperatives. Yet the government has not structured its policies, at least as explicitly or comprehensively, with the clear expectation that individuals are wrong or irrational to stand on their rights. The assumption that corporations should engage in a "crime-fighting partnership" with the government, even if it means criminal prosecution and hefty penalties, is such a constant that its foundation is rarely, if ever, examined. But it does require justification, and I have not heard a convincing one.

The bulk of this Article lays a foundation for further conversations in which the central concern is not the symptom—the DOJ's waiver policy—but rather the underlying malady—the circumstances that conspire to rob organizational defendants of the benefits of the adversarial system—and the fallout from that reality. It is beyond the scope of this Article to contribute much to the debate over whether corporations, as "legal" rather than "natural" persons, should have abbreviated rights in criminal cases, but it will essay a few thoughts to start the conversation. As a preliminary matter, it is important to note that, if society truly believes that the adversary system is the best and fairest way to test criminal charges when individuals are in the government's cross-hairs, it is not at all clear why legal entities such as corporations should be denied its benefits. Further, society has obvious and significant—even if rarely articulated—interests in redressing the existing imbalance of power or at least providing corporations with some process by which to have prosecutorial theories and charges reviewed. As noted briefly in Part IV, regardless of how one conceptualizes corporations in terms of traditional models of justice, the status quo—in which organizational defendants have the protections of neither adversarial justice nor the bureaucratic safeguards of the inquisitorial system—is unacceptable, because not every theory of prosecution is valid and not every corporate subject deserves criminal sanction. That being the case, the DOJ could at least ameliorate the "justice" imbalance by reconsidering its "compelled-voluntary" waiver policy.

NOTES AND QUESTIONS

1. Who's got the better argument here? Should the government be able to "strong-arm" corporate defendants into cooperating and providing information against their employees? Is this legitimately maximizing the

resources brought to bear against corporate crime, as Seigel contends, or has it distorted the adversarial process, as O'Sullivan argues?

2. Others have agreed with O'Sullivan that the outrage over DOJ's new tactics in prosecuting corporate criminal law stems from corporate lawyers' feeling that they should not be made into "junior g-men." But their conclusion is the opposite of O'Sullivan's: They believe that corporate counsel should "get over it" and take on the roll of gatekeepers in the corporate environment, minimizing illegal activity. *See, e.g.*, Sung Hui Kim, *The Banality of Fraud: Re-Situating the Inside Counsel as Gatekeeper*, 74 FORDHAM L. REV. 983 (2005). Who's right about that?
3. O'Sullivan contends that, because corporations—in contrast to human beings—are not protected by the Fifth Amendment, they need the protection of the attorney-client privilege to balance things out. Here is Seigel's response to this claim:

> Some of the complaints about the Department's emphasis on corporate cooperation make it sound like the technique of "squeezing" or "coercing" cooperation from a putative defendant is unique to the white collar setting. This cannot be further from the truth: "Judicial leniency for cooperators traces its roots back hundreds of years to the common law practice of approvement, and American prosecutors have been striking deals with cooperators at least since the nineteenth century."
>
> Is the process of convincing a putative defendant to cooperate against others coercive? Of course it is. To facilitate cooperation, an individual defendant must waive his Fifth Amendment right against self-incrimination, along with his Seventh Amendment right to trial by jury, in addition to his right to appeal a guilty verdict. Also, going through the ordeal of admitting guilt, being debriefed, and possibly testifying against confederates in court is extremely unpleasant. Yet, many putative defendants choose to cooperate despite the cost because they judge that the benefit—a reduction in sentence—is worth the price. Their Hobson's choice is not caused by an unfair or overbearing government. Rather, it is the direct result of their prior criminal conduct. The same is true for a company faced with having to choose between cooperating [and waiving privilege] to minimize the damage done by corporate wrongdoing on the one hand, and fighting the charges on the other.

   Is this a convincing response? Why or why not?
4. The McNulty Memorandum appears to have shifted DOJ practice. Government attorneys are not starting off conversations about corporate cooperation with demands for privilege waiver; instead, they are approaching the subject as a last resort. This, combined with the defeat of Senator Arlen Specter in the Democratic primary to retain his seat and the change in presidential administrations in 2008, has caused this issue to move to the back burner, at least for now.
5. Recently, a growing number of corporations have chosen to cooperate with federal investigators and prosecutors in exchange for a "deferred prosecution agreement" or "DPA." *See* Candace Zierdt & Ellen S. Podgor, *Corporate*

Deferred Prosecutions Through the Looking Glass of Contract Policing, 96 KY. L.J. 1, 5-6 (2007-2008). In a DPA, the government promises not to indict the corporation as long as it lives up to certain terms and conditions for a specified period of time. These conditions traditionally include: (1) admission of wrongdoing; (2) purging of guilty executives; (3) not engaging in future criminal conduct; (4) cooperation with the ongoing investigation, including attorney-client privilege waiver, if necessary; (5) implementation of a tough compliance program, sometimes involving the appointment of an independent or government-selected director on the board; (6) restitution to victims; and (7) settlement of the related civil case.

Zierdt and Podgor argue that DPAs are problematic in that "the government is using its expansive power to secure agreement terms and this raises grave concerns regarding contractual fairness." *Id.* at 7.[9]

Do you agree with Zierdt and Podgor that the increasing use of DPAs in the corporate context is a "grave" development?

In the case that follows, the prosecution demanded more than simple waiver of attorney-client privilege as part of the defendant partnership's cooperation. The government pushed so hard that, as you will see, the court forcefully pushed back. The case received widespread media coverage and became "Exhibit A" for those fighting against DOJ's "abuse of power" in the white collar arena.

UNITED STATES v. STEIN

435 F. Supp. 2d 330 (2006)

KAPLAN, District Judge.

[The IRS and the Permanent Subcommittee on Investigations of the Senate Committee on Governmental Affairs began investigations into accounting firm KPMG's sales of an allegedly illegal tax shelter. Things were looking bad for KPMG.] Eugene O'Kelly, then KPMG chair, was concerned. . . . He retained Skadden Arps . . . , and particularly Robert S. Bennett, "to come up with a new cooperative approach." One aspect of that new approach was a decision to "clean house"—a determination to ask Jeffrey Stein, Richard Smith, and Jeffrey Eischeid, all senior KPMG partners . . . and all now defendants here—to leave the [the firm].

Given Mr. Stein's senior position and his relationship with Mr. O'Kelly, his departure was cushioned substantially. . . . He agreed to release the firm and all of its partners, principals, and employees from all claims. He and KPMG agreed also that Mr. Stein would be represented, at KPMG's expense, in any suits brought against KPMG or its personnel and himself, by counsel acceptable to both him and

9. *See also* John A. Gallagher, *Legislation is Necessary for Deferred Prosecution of Corporate Crime*, 43 SUFFOLK U. L. REV. 447 (2010); Lisa Kern Griffin, *Compelled Cooperation and the New Corporate Criminal Procedure*, 82 N.Y.U. L. REV. 311, 321 (2007); Benjamin M. Greenblum, *What Happens to a Prosecution Deferred? Judicial Oversight of Corporate Deferred Prosecution Agreements*, 105 COLUM. L. REV. 1863, 1864 (2005).

the firm or, if joint representation were inappropriate or if Mr. Stein were the only party to a proceeding, by counsel reasonably acceptable to Mr. Stein.

The agreement provided also that, "[n]otwithstanding any other provision of [the] Agreement," if Mr. Stein were named as a defendant in any action based on his activities with the firm, KPMG would indemnify him "(through its Professional Indemnity Insurance Program)," except as to "wilful or intentional unlawful acts," to the same extent it would have done had he remained with KPMG.

Despite KPMG's effort to stave off trouble by "cleaning house," much damage already had been done. In the early part of 2004, the IRS made a criminal referral to the Department of Justice ("DOJ"), which in turn passed it on to the United States Attorney's Office for this district ("USAO"). . . .

The Initial Discussion Between the USAO and Skadden

When the [IRS] referral reached the USAO on February 5, 2004, it came under the supervision of Shirah Neiman, who was chief counsel to the United States Attorney, the USAO's liaison to the IRS, a participant in the drafting of the Holder Memorandum, and a very experienced prosecutor. The USAO notified Skadden of the referral, and a meeting was scheduled for February 25, 2004.

In preparation for the meeting, Ms. Neiman, Assistant United States Attorneys ("AUSA") Weddle and Okula, and other members of the prosecution team conferred. They decided to ask Skadden whether KPMG was paying the legal fees of individuals under investigation. Accordingly, the government prepared a document headed "Skadden Meeting Points" setting forth matters that the government intended to discuss at the meeting. . . .

The meeting was attended by Mr. Bennett, Ms. Neiman, and many others on both sides. Mr. Weddle began by telling Skadden that the government was there to hear what Skadden had to say and that it had a few questions. Mr. Bennett explained that Skadden had been hired in view of Mr. O'Kelly's concern about the controversy with the IRS and the Senate hearings and that KPMG had decided to clean house and change the atmosphere at the firm. He reported that the firm had taken high-level personnel action already, that it would cooperate fully with the government's investigation, and that the object was to save KPMG, not to protect any individuals. In an obvious reference to the fate of Arthur Andersen,[9] he said that an indictment of KPMG would result in the firm going out of business.

After a discussion of the structure of KPMG and of potential conflicts of interest, Mr. Weddle "got to the subject of legal fees and asked whether KPMG was obligated to pay fees and what their plans were." Mr. Bennett tested the waters to see whether KPMG could adhere to its practice of paying its employees' legal expenses when litigation loomed. He asked for government's view on the subject. Ms. Neiman said that the government would take into account KPMG's legal obligations, if any, to advance legal expenses, but referred specifically to the Thompson Memorandum as a point that had to be considered. Mr. Weddle asked also for copies of KPMG's partnership agreement and by-laws.

10. [*See* Arthur Andersen LLP v. United States, 544 U.S. 696 (2005), *supra* p. 383.—Eds.]

At or about that point, Messrs. Bennett and Bialkin told the USAO that KPMG's "common practice" had been to pay legal fees. They added that the partnership agreement was vague and that Delaware law gave the company the right to do whatever it wished, but said that KPMG still was checking on its legal obligations. It would not, however, pay legal fees for employees who declined to cooperate with the government, or who took the Fifth Amendment, as long as it had discretion to take that position.

The conversation then shifted briefly to a discussion of the personnel changes that KPMG had made. Mr. Bennett reported that Messrs. Stein, Eischeid, and Smith had been asked to leave, but explained that neither KPMG nor Skadden had done an internal investigation to determine who were "bad guys" or whether any crime had been committed. Almost immediately, Mr. Weddle reverted to the subject of attorneys' fees, asking Mr. Bennett to determine KPMG's obligations in that regard. Ms. Neiman then said that "misconduct" should not or cannot "be rewarded" and referred to federal guidelines.

There is no dispute, and the Court finds, that this comment came immediately on the heels of a statement by Mr. Bennett relating to lawyers for KPMG partners. There are disputes, however, about precisely what Ms. Neiman said about "guidelines" and what she meant by it. The parties have focused in particular on whether Ms. Neiman intended her remark to be directed to the legal fee issue — i.e., to be a statement to the effect that payment by KPMG of employee legal fees could be viewed as rewarding misconduct — or to be directed instead at any severance arrangements between KPMG and Messrs. Stein, Eischeid, and Smith. Ms. Neiman testified that her intent was the latter. But the Court finds it unnecessary to decide Ms. Neiman's subjective purpose in making the remark because what is more important is how her comment was understood. . . .

KPMG Gets the Message

Shortly after the February 25, 2004 meeting, Mr. Bennett got back to Mr. Weddle on the legal fee issue. He reported that KPMG did not think it had any binding legal obligation to pay legal fees, but that "it would be a big problem" not to do so because the firm was a partnership. He said that KPMG was planning on putting a cap, or limit, on fees and conditioning their payment for any given partner or employee on that individual "cooperating fully with the company and the government." Apparently satisfied with the government's response, KPMG began to implement the policy. . . .

On March 11, 2004, the Skadden team had a conference call with the USAO. Mr. Bennett assured the USAO that KPMG would be "as cooperative as possible" so that the office would not exercise its discretion to indict the firm. Mr. Weddle urged that KPMG tell its people that they should be "totally open" with the USAO, "even if that [meant admitting] criminal wrongdoing." He commented that this would give him good material for cross-examination, a statement that strongly indicates that at least the lead line AUSA on the case expected, even at this stage, to prosecute individuals.

The actions of the USAO, coupled with the Thompson Memorandum, had the desired effect. On the same date, Skadden's Mr. Rauh wrote to the USAO, enclosing among other things a form letter that Skadden was sending to counsel for the KPMG Defendants then employed by KPMG who had received subject letters from the government or otherwise appeared to be under suspicion. The form letter stated that KPMG would pay an individual's legal fees and expenses, up to a maximum of $400,000, on the condition that the individual "cooperate with the government and . . . be prompt, complete, and truthful." Importantly, however, it went even further. It made clear that "*payment of . . . legal fees and expenses will cease immediately if . . . [the recipient] is charged by the government with criminal wrongdoing (emphasis added).*" . . .

The Government Presses Its Advantage

. . . From that point forward, the government took full advantage. It repeatedly notified Skadden when KPMG personnel failed to comply with government demands. In each case, Skadden promptly advised the attorney for the individual in question that the payment of legal fees would be terminated "[a]bsent an indication from the government within the next ten business days that your client no longer refuses to participate in an interview with the government." In some cases, the individuals in question relented under pressure of the threats from KPMG and submitted to interviews with the government. In others, they did not, whereupon KPMG terminated their employment and cut off the payment of legal fees.

The Conclusion of the Investigation, KPMG's Stein Problem and the Deferred Prosecution Agreement

. . . On August 4, 2004, the KPMG executives and lawyers met with Karen Seymour, then chief of the criminal division of the USAO, and other prosecutors. In the course of the meeting, Ms. Seymour said that the government had learned that KPMG had granted rich severance packages to certain executives and that this raised a "troubling issue under the 'Thompson Memo.'" Mr. Bennett deflected the issue, agreeing that severance packages were "high in one or two cases" but reiterating that KPMG's "expectation" was that legal fees of individuals would be paid only up to $400,000 and only on condition that recipients cooperated with the government. But the Stein severance agreement was not produced.

As time went by, KPMG came to view the Stein severance agreement as something of a ticking bomb. For one thing, KPMG had not adhered in Mr. Stein's case to the $400,000 pre-indictment legal fee cap that it had adopted in response to government pressure. It passed that figure by late October 2004, and so was at odds with its representation to the government. For another, it had known since August 2004 that the USAO was unhappy that rich severance packages had been given to senior executives. . . .

With the scene about to shift to Washington and a last-ditch effort to prevent an indictment by an appeal at the highest levels of the Justice Department, KPMG's objective was "to be able to say at the right time with the right audience, we're in full compliance with the Thompson Guidelines." It concluded that the Stein situation involved too great a risk. So on May 5, 2005, eight days before

KPMG was to meet with U.S. Deputy Attorney General James Comey to plead its case, KPMG unilaterally terminated the consulting services portion of the severance agreement and cut off payment of Mr. Stein's attorneys' fees. It did so, as Mr. Loonan candidly admitted, "because [KPMG] thought it would help [the firm] with the government." . . .

Having dealt, as best it could, with the Stein problem, KPMG turned to attempting to persuade Deputy Attorney General Comey not to indict the firm. The meeting took place on June 13, 2005. Once again, Mr. Bennett relied upon KPMG's cooperation with the government, in addition of course to other arguments. A Skadden memorandum of the meeting recounts some of his remarks as follows:

> "In addition, it [KPMG] had done something 'never heard of before'—conditioned the payment of attorney's fees on full cooperation with the investigation. 'We said we'd pressure—although we didn't use that word—our employees to cooperate. We told employees that attorney fees would not be paid unless they fully cooperated with the investigation.' He noted that whenever an individual indicated he or she would not cooperate, 'Justin [Weddle] or Stan [Okula] would tell us,' and KPMG took action. He went on to note that 'what played out' was that current or former personnel who otherwise would not have cooperated did cooperate, and those who did not had their fees cut off and, in two instances, were separated from the firm. This process exhibited 'a level of cooperation that is rarely done.'
>
> * * *
>
> "He noted that what was really 'precedent-setting' about the case was the conditioning of payment of legal fees on cooperation."

This time, KPMG was more successful.

The Deferred Prosecution Agreement and the Indictment in This Case

On August 29, 2005, KPMG and the government entered into a Deferred Prosecution Agreement ("DPA"). KPMG agreed, among other things, to waive indictment, to be charged in a one-count information, to admit extensive wrongdoing, to pay a $456 million fine, and to accept restrictions on its practice. The government agreed that it will seek dismissal of the information if KPMG complies with its obligations. In a nutshell, KPMG stands to avoid a criminal conviction if it lives up to its part of the bargain. . . .

At about the same time, the government filed the initial indictment in this case. True to its word, KPMG cut off payments to the defendants of legal fees and expenses.

The Present Motion

On January 19, 2006, the KPMG Defendants moved to dismiss the indictment or for other relief on the ground that the government had interfered improperly with the advancement of attorneys' fees by KPMG in violation of their [Fifth and Sixth Amendment] and other rights. . . .

The Supreme Court long has protected a defendant's right to fairness in the criminal process. It has grounded this protection primarily in the Due Process Clause as well as more specific provisions of the Bill of Rights, including the Confrontation and Assistance of Counsel Clauses of the Sixth Amendment. Whatever the textual source, however, the Court consistently has held that criminal defendants are entitled to be treated fairly throughout the process. In everyday language, they are entitled to a fair shake. . . .

One aspect of the required fairness protects the autonomy of the criminal defendant. It rests on the common-sense truth that, at the end of the day, it is the defendant "who suffers the consequences if the defense fails." So proper respect for the individual prevents the government from interfering with the manner in "which the individual wishes to present a defense." The underlying theme is that the government may not both prosecute a defendant and then seek to influence the manner in which he or she defends the case.

A defendant's right to control the manner and substance of the defense has several aspects. The defendant has the right to represent him- or herself, even if such a decision objectively may appear to be unwise. A defendant is guaranteed also "the right to be represented by an otherwise qualified attorney whom that defendant can afford to hire"—in other words, to use his or her own assets to defend the case, free of government regulation. Nor may the government interfere at will with a defendant's choice of counsel, as the Constitution "protect[s] . . . the defendant's free choice independent of concern for the objective fairness of the proceedings." Similarly, a defendant is generally free, within the procedural constraints that govern trials generally, to adduce evidence without unjustified restrictions and may choose which witnesses to present or cross-examine. In short, fairness in criminal proceedings requires that the defendant be firmly in the driver's seat, and that the prosecution not be a backseat driver. . . .

The Thompson Memorandum and the USAO pressure on KPMG to deny or cut off defendants' attorneys' fees necessarily impinge upon the KPMG Defendants' ability to defend themselves. . . .

The first difficulty is that the Thompson Memorandum does not say that payment of legal fees may cut in favor of indictment only if it is used as a means to obstruct an investigation. Indeed, the text strongly suggests that advancement of defenses costs weighs against an organization independent of whether there is any "circling of the wagons."

The USAO, possibly concerned with the breadth of the Thompson Memorandum, seeks to deal with this by asserting that, in practice, it considers the payment of legal fees as a negative factor only when payments are used to impede. Perhaps so. But whatever the government may do in the privacy of U.S. Attorneys' offices and in the DOJ's Criminal Division is not what defense lawyers see. They see the Thompson Memorandum. Few if any competent defense lawyers would advise a corporate client at risk of indictment that it should feel free to advance legal fees to individuals in the face of the language of the Thompson Memorandum itself. It would be irresponsible to take the chance that prosecutors might view it as "protecting . . . culpable employees and agents." As KPMG's new chief legal officer, former U.S. District Judge Sven Erik Holmes, testified, he thought it indispensable (as would any defense lawyer) "to be able to say at the right time with the right audience, we're in full compliance with the Thompson Memorandum."

The bottom line is plain enough. If the government means to take the payment of legal fees into account in making charging decisions only where the payments are part of an obstruction scheme—and thereby narrowly tailor its means to its ends—it would be easy enough to say so. But that is not what the Thompson Memorandum says.

The concerns do not end here. The argument that payment of legal fees to employees and former employees is relevant to gauging the extent of a company's cooperation also is problematic. There is no necessary inconsistency between an entity cooperating with the government and, at the same time, paying defense costs of individual employees and former employees. An entity may pay out of a judgment that extending this benefit will aid it in keeping and hiring competent and honest employees. It may pay in recognition that an employee caught up in an investigation, or even charged with a crime, because the employee did his or her job for the company has at least some claim to assistance, even in the absence of a legal right. In either case, however, a company may pay at the same time that it does its best to bare its corporate soul, stands at the government's beck and call to provide information and witnesses, and does a myriad of other things to aid the government and clean the corporate house. So it simply cannot be said that payment of legal fees for the benefit of employees and former employees necessarily or even usually is indicative of an unwillingness to cooperate fully. This is especially unlikely after employees have been indicted and fired, as is the situation here.

For these reasons, this aspect of the Thompson Memorandum is not narrowly tailored to achieve a compelling objective. It discourages and, as a practical matter, often prevents companies from providing employees and former employees with the financial means to exercise their constitutional rights to defend themselves. It does so in the face of state indemnification statutes that expressly permit businesses entities to provide those means because the states have determined that legitimate public interests may be served. It does so even where companies obstruct nothing and, to the contrary, do everything within their power to make a clean breast of the facts to the government and to take responsibility for any offenses they may have committed. It therefore burdens excessively the constitutional rights of the individuals whose ability to defend themselves it impairs and, accordingly, fails strict scrutiny. The legal fee advancement provision violates the Due Process Clause. . . .

The actions of the USAO in this case compounded the problem that the Thompson Memorandum created. . . .

Quite apart from the due process analysis, the KPMG Defendants argue that the Thompson Memorandum and its implementation by the government infringed their Sixth Amendment right to counsel. They are correct.

The Sixth Amendment provides that "[i]n all criminal prosecutions, the accused shall enjoy the right to . . . have the Assistance of Counsel for his defence." As already has been demonstrated, however, this guarantees more than the mere presence of a lawyer at a criminal trial. It protects, among other things, an individual's right to choose the lawyer or lawyers he or she desires and to use one's own funds to mount the defense that one wishes to present. . . .

The next question concerns the appropriate remedy for the violation of the KPMG Defendants' constitutional rights. Defendants ask the Court to dismiss the indictment or to order payment of their legal fees either by the government or by KPMG. The government argues that any relief should be limited to requiring KPMG to consider anew whether it wishes to advance expenses to the defendants, now free of the threat of government retaliation by virtue of the government's recent statement that it does not object to KPMG doing as it pleases. . . .

[Advancement by KPMG of defense costs to the KPMG defendants would be an appropriate remedy. T]there are at least two possibilities for resolving the issue of advancement of defense costs. KPMG, either on its own or at the government's urging or insistence, may advance the defense costs. Alternatively, the KPMG Defendants may succeed in obtaining an advancement order in a summary proceeding before this Court. In either event, the effect of the government's unconstitutional interference would have been remedied or, at least, mitigated substantially. Should that come to pass, the possibilities of dismissal of the indictment and other remedies likely would appear in a different light. In consequence, the Court declines to consider additional relief at this time, although it may do so in the future if KPMG does not, for one reason or another, advance defense costs. . . .

The motions of the KPMG Defendants to dismiss the indictment or for other relief are granted only to the extent that:

1. The Court declares that so much of the Thompson Memorandum and the activities of the USAO as threatened to take into account, in deciding whether to indict KPMG, whether KPMG would advance attorneys' fees to present or former employees in the event they were indicted for activities undertaken in the course of their employment interfered with the rights of such employees to a fair trial and to the effective assistance of counsel and therefore violated the Fifth and Sixth Amendments to the Constitution.
2. The government shall adhere to its representation that any payment by KPMG of the defense costs of the KPMG Defendants is acceptable to the government and will not be considered in determining whether KPMG has complied with the DPA or otherwise prejudice KPMG.
3. The Clerk shall open a civil docket number to accommodate the claims of the KPMG Defendants against KPMG for advancement of defense costs should they elect to pursue them. If they file a complaint within 14 days, the Clerk shall issue a summons to KPMG. The Court in that event will entertain the claims pursuant to its ancillary jurisdiction over this case. . . .

NOTES AND QUESTIONS

1. In a later ruling, Judge Kaplan dismissed the indictment against 13 of the 16 *Stein* defendants. United States v. Stein, 495 F. Supp. 2d 390 (2007) (holding that the government's behavior against then-current KPMG employees "shock[ed] the conscience in the constitutional sense").

2. Why was KPMG so scared of the government? Do you think that all collective entities facing the prospect of federal indictment react in the same way? Why or why not?
3. As noted in the introduction to the case, *Stein* came at the height of the "battle" over the corporate attorney-client privilege waiver. It added considerable fuel to the fire of those arguing that DOJ had gone too far in its zeal to prosecute white collar crime. However, even many who supported DOJ on the privilege issue thought that Judge Kaplan had decided this case correctly. What is it about the *Stein* case that makes the government's behavior so outrageous? Consider Judge Kaplan's description of the government's conduct in a later opinion in the same case:

   > The actions of the prosecutors with respect to legal fees may be considered also in light of their actions with respect to obtaining proffers from KPMG employees under suspicion, all of whom had a Fifth Amendment right to decline to speak to the government. The prosecutors knew that the Thompson Memorandum effectively compelled KPMG to make its personnel available for interviews by the government. They knew, as the government said at the fee hearing, that "there are two ways the company could get their people in. One is they could hold over their head their job. The other is they could cut off their legal fees." They therefore understood that KPMG would threaten to fire or cut off payment of legal fees for employees and former employees whom prosecutors reported were not cooperating—i.e., who were refusing to submit to interviews with the government. Yet the prosecutors identified such persons to KPMG anyway. These actions are significant not only in themselves, but also for the insight they provide into the prosecutors' actions with respect to payment of legal fees. For they demonstrate a willingness by the prosecutors to use their life and death power over KPMG to induce KPMG to coerce its personnel to bend to the government's wishes notwithstanding the fact that the Constitution barred the government from doing directly what it forced KPMG to do for it.

   United States v. Stein, 490 F. Supp. 2d 390, 413-414 (2007).
4. Note that, shortly after the *Stein* case, DOJ policy was amended specifically ceding to its holding: Prosecutors are now instructed *not to* take into account a firm's payment of its employees' attorneys' fees when evaluating its cooperation. *See* Memorandum from Paul J. McNulty, Deputy Attorney General, Dec. 12, 2006, available at http://www.justice.gov/dag/speeches/2006/mcnulty_memo.pdf.

chapter 13

Parallel Civil and Criminal Proceedings

I. INTRODUCTION

For a variety of reasons, prosecutions of street crime are rarely accompanied by a civil lawsuit. First, most street criminals have neither assets nor insurance, so suing them in tort is a waste of time and money. Second, given its non-economic nature, victims of street crime usually have no motivation to seek monetary restitution. Finally, the government has not seen fit to create an administrative agency with civil enforcement power to address violent crime. In the white collar context, however, all of these factors are reversed. There is often a "deep pocket," be it a corporation or wealthy individuals, or both, from whom injured parties can seek to recover monetary damages, and no shortage of plaintiffs' attorneys willing to take on worthwhile cases. At the same time, there is typically an administrative agency responsible for civil oversight and enforcement with respect to the activity in question. The same deep pockets available to pay plaintiffs are also available to pay civil fines and penalties, as well as restitution to victims who do not separately sue.

More often than not, civil and criminal white collar cases proceed simultaneously and are thus called "parallel proceedings." In many instances, the federal government is the instigator of both cases: Due process does not require that the government elect only one method of pursuing a purported bad actor.[1] Nevertheless, the existence of parallel proceedings creates special problems—and, occasionally, some benefits—for both white collar prosecutors and defendants. The cases in this chapter explore these various issues.

1. *See* United States v. Kordel, 397 U.S. 1 (1970).

II. CONSTITUTIONAL PARAMETERS OF PERMISSIBLE GOVERNMENT ACTION

UNITED STATES v. STRINGER

535 F.3d 929 (9th Cir. 2008)

SCHROEDER, Circuit Judge:

Prior to the criminal action that forms the basis of this appeal, the SEC began investigating the defendants, J. Kenneth Stringer, III, J. Mark Samper, and William N. Martin, and their company for possible civil securities fraud violations. The company was FLIR Systems, Inc. ("FLIR"), an Oregon corporation headquartered in Portland that sells infrared and heat-sensing cameras for military and industrial use. The SEC began the investigation on June 8, 2000. About two weeks later, the SEC held the first of a series of meetings with the Oregon United States Attorney's Office ("USAO") to coordinate the ongoing SEC investigation with a possible criminal investigation. An SEC Assistant Director and an SEC Staff Attorney met with the supervisor of the white collar crime section of the USAO to discuss the possibility of opening a criminal investigation. The meeting apparently convinced the USAO supervisor to investigate. Within days, the USAO and the Federal Bureau of Investigation ("FBI") opened a criminal investigation.

Federal securities laws authorize the SEC to transmit evidence it has gathered to the USAO to facilitate a criminal investigation by the USAO. *See* 15 U.S.C. §§77t(b), 78u(d). To gather evidence for its criminal investigation, the Oregon USAO in June of 2000 sent a letter to the SEC (the "Access Letter") requesting access to the SEC's non-public investigative files, and the SEC promptly granted access.

The civil and criminal investigations proceeded in tandem and the SEC continued to meet and communicate with the USAO and FBI. The SEC turned over documents the SEC collected through its civil investigation.

At the beginning of the criminal investigation, the USAO identified two of the three defendants, FLIR's former CEO, Stringer, and former CFO, Samper, as possible targets, and named them in the USAO's Access Letter to the SEC. . . . The district court concluded that the third defendant, Martin, former VP of Sales, was also an early potential target of the criminal investigation. . . .

Early in the criminal investigation, the USAO decided the investigation should remain confidential. At an October 2000 meeting between the SEC, USAO, and FBI, the AUSA advised that the evidence collected by the SEC might support criminal wire fraud charges. Nonetheless, an internal FBI memo issued in late October stated that the AUSA had concluded, based on the defendants' cooperation with the SEC at that point, that the SEC should investigate "without the assistance or inclusion of the FBI." At the January 2001 meeting between the SEC, FBI, and USAO, the SEC revealed that FLIR was cooperative and was providing evidence that was damaging to Stringer and Martin. . . .

The SEC facilitated the criminal investigation in a number of ways. The SEC offered to conduct the interviews of defendants so as to create "the best record possible" in support of "false statement cases" against them, and the AUSA instructed the SEC Staff Attorney on how best to do that. The AUSA asked the relevant SEC office, located in Los Angeles, to take the depositions in Oregon so that the Portland Office of the USAO would have venue over any false statements case that might arise from the depositions, and the SEC did so. Both the SEC and USAO wanted the existence of the criminal investigation kept confidential. The SEC Staff Attorney, at one of the Portland depositions, made a note that she wanted to "make sure [the] court reporters won't tell [FLIR's Attorney]" that there was an AUSA assigned to the case.

The SEC, however, did not hide from the defendants the possibility — even likelihood — of such an investigation. The SEC sent each of the defendants subpoenas in the summer of 2001, and attached to each was Form 1662, a form sent to all witnesses subpoenaed to testify before the SEC. Under the header "Routine Uses of Information," the four-page form states that "[t]he Commission often makes its files available to other governmental agencies, particularly the United States Attorneys and state prosecutors. There is a likelihood that information supplied by you will be made available to such agencies where appropriate."

Form 1662 also advises witnesses of their Fifth Amendment rights. After the heading "Fifth Amendment and Voluntary Testimony," the form states that:

> Information you give may be used against you in any federal . . . civil or criminal proceeding brought by the Commission of any other agency. You may refuse, in accordance with the rights guaranteed to you by the Fifth Amendment of the Constitution of the United States, to give any information that may tend to incriminate you or subject you to fine, penalty, or forfeiture.

None of the defendants invoked his right against self-incrimination during his deposition, and all proceeded to testify in compliance with the subpoena. Each of the defendants was represented by counsel when he testified.

During the course of Stringer's deposition, taken in Portland in October 2001, Stringer's attorney actually questioned the SEC Staff Attorney about the involvement of the USAO. In response to those questions, the SEC Staff Attorney answered as follows:

MR. MARTSON: My first question is whether Mr. Stringer is a target of any aspect of the investigation being conducted by the SEC.

STAFF ATTORNEY: The SEC does not have targets in this investigation.

MR. MARTSON: The other questions I have relate to whether or not, in connection with your investigation, the SEC is working in conjunction with any other department of the United States, such as the U.S. Attorney's Office in any jurisdiction, or the Department of Justice.

STAFF ATTORNEY: As laid out in the 1662 form, in the "routine use of" section there are routine uses of our investigation, and it is the agency's policy not to respond to questions like that, but instead, to direct you to the other agencies you mentioned.

MR. MARTSON: And which U.S. Attorney's Office might I inquire into?

STAFF ATTORNEY: That would be a matter up to your discretion.

The record does not show the SEC did anything to impede an inquiry, nor does it disclose that any inquiry was made. The record reflects that the government never furnished defendants with any false information concerning the existence of a criminal investigation.

In September 2002, a year before the criminal indictments, defendants Samper and Martin entered into consent decrees in the civil action, agreeing to pay penalties, disgorgement, and pre-judgment interest.

B. The "Swedish Drop Shipment" Evidence from the Attorney Jointly Representing Defendants

[At some point during the SEC investigation, attorney Lois Rosenbaum began representing both FLIR and Samper. Samper had waived any conflict.]

On June 30, 2000, the SEC sent Samper a subpoena with Form 1662 enclosed. It warned of possible dangers of joint representation. The form advised that "[y]ou may be represented by counsel who also represents other persons involved in the Commission's investigation. This multiple representation, however, presents a potential conflict of interest if one client's interests are or may be adverse to another's."

In July 2000, when the SEC learned that Rosenbaum was representing FLIR and its employees, it immediately sent her a letter warning of the specific dangers of this co-representation. "We are concerned that the broad range of interests possessed by your many clients cannot be adequately represented by a single attorney." The letter specifically pointed out the potential conflict of interest in representing a company under investigation by the SEC and upper level management who may have civil liability. The letter stated that, "Although it is far too early in the investigation for the SEC staff to identify people who may possess liability, we are troubled by the scope and breadth of your representation." Rosenbaum continued to represent both FLIR and Samper, among others.

One of the eventual charges in the indictment was that two of the involved defendants created the "Swedish Drop Shipment," an entry in FLIR's books that allegedly recognizes $4.6 million in revenue without substantiation. FLIR's Controller, David Meussle, first discovered the unsubstantiated entry. Meussle believed that Stringer and Samper made the entry. Rosenbaum represented Meussle, as well as Samper and FLIR.

The SEC civil complaint, filed on September 30, 2002, two years after the joint representation began, did not allege a charge relating to the "Swedish Drop Shipment." After Rosenbaum received a copy of the complaint, she called the SEC Staff Attorney, disclosed the existence of the "Swedish Drop Shipment," and facilitated SEC interviews with Meussle in order to enhance the level of FLIR's cooperation with the government. Rosenbaum also sent a memo to the SEC that contained possibly privileged communications she had with Samper about the transaction. The criminal indictment later charged that Stringer and Samper created the false entry. Thus Rosenbaum, while representing Meussle and FLIR, apparently in order to further the interests of FLIR, assisted the SEC's investigation. . . .

III. Discussion

A. The Parallel Investigations

The Supreme Court has held that the government may conduct parallel civil and criminal investigations without violating the due process clause, so long as it does not act in bad faith. *See* United States v. Kordel, 397 U.S. 1 (1970). In *Kordel*, the Supreme Court held that the government did not violate the due process rights of corporate executives when it used evidence it obtained from an FDA civil investigation to convict them of criminal misbranding. The Court explained that the FDA did not act in bad faith when it made a request for information, which ultimately was used in the criminal investigation, for the agency made similar requests as a matter of course in 75% of its civil investigations. The Court suggested that the government may act in bad faith if it brings a civil action solely for the purpose of obtaining evidence in a criminal prosecution and does not advise the defendant of the planned use of evidence in a criminal proceeding. The Court thus distinguished the *Kordel* investigation from bad faith cases where

> the [g]overnment has brought a civil action solely to obtain evidence for its criminal prosecution or has failed to advise the defendant in its civil proceeding that it contemplates his criminal prosecution; . . . [or] any other special circumstances . . . might suggest the unconstitutionality or even the impropriety of this criminal prosecution.

Id. at 12-13, 90 S. Ct. 763.

The Supreme Court has not had occasion to address such issues since *Kordel*, but lower courts have. In *SEC v. Dresser Industries, Inc.*, the D.C. Circuit applied the principles laid down in *Kordel* to a case involving parallel SEC civil and Department of Justice criminal investigations. *See* 628 F.2d 1368, 1376-77 (D.C. Cir. 1980) (en banc). The court emphatically upheld the propriety of such parallel investigations. "Effective enforcement of the securities laws requires that the SEC and Justice be able to investigate possible violations simultaneously." The court said it would refuse to bar such investigations absent unusual circumstances. It said courts should refuse to "block parallel investigations by these agencies in the absence of 'special circumstances' in which the nature of the proceedings demonstrably prejudices substantial rights of the investigated party or of the government."

District courts have occasionally suppressed evidence or dismissed indictments on due process grounds where the government made affirmative misrepresentations or conducted a civil investigation solely for purposes of advancing a criminal case. . . .

[On a related issue, t]he privilege against self-incrimination protects an individual from being forced to provide information that might establish a direct link in a chain of evidence leading to his conviction. Hoffman v. United States, 341 U.S. 479 (1951). It may be waived if it is not affirmatively invoked. In *Minnesota v. Murphy*, the Supreme Court stressed that the privilege is lost if not affirmatively invoked, even if the defendant did not make a knowing and intelligent waiver. 465 U.S. 420 (1984). . . .

The district court therefore erred in holding that defendants' waivers of the privilege were ineffective because they were not told of the U.S. Attorney's active involvement. The SEC Form 1662 used in this case alerts SEC investigative witnesses that the information can be used in a criminal proceeding. Defendants were on sufficient notice, and so were their attorneys. As one federal court has explained, all that was required was "sufficient notice . . . that any information could be used against [them] in a subsequent criminal proceeding." United States v. Teyibo, 877 F. Supp. 846, 855 (S.D.N.Y. 1995). That court emphasized that "SEC Form 1662 stated in no uncertain terms that the [g]overnment's request for information could be refused pursuant to the Fifth Amendment's protection against compelled self-incrimination." *Id.* We agree.

The SEC here went even further, warning each defendant at the beginning of each deposition that "the facts developed in this investigation might constitute violations of . . . criminal laws." Nonetheless, defendants proceeded to testify and failed to invoke their privilege against self-incrimination. Defendants have forfeited any claims that the use of their testimony against them in the criminal proceedings violates the privilege against self-incrimination.

The defendants next contend that the district court properly concluded that the government used the civil investigation solely to obtain evidence for a subsequent criminal prosecution, in violation of due process. . . . [T]he government argues that it did not violate defendants' due process rights because the civil investigation was not commenced solely to obtain evidence for a criminal prosecution. . . .

Our case is not remotely similar to [one in which due process was violated]. In this case the SEC's civil investigation was opened first, led to SEC sanctions and was conducted pursuant to the SEC's own civil enforcement jurisdiction. It was not a pretext for the USAO's criminal investigation of defendants. Congress has expressly authorized the SEC to share information with the Department of Justice to facilitate the investigation and prosecution of crimes. *See* 15 U.S.C. §§77t(b), 78u(d). We must conclude the SEC interviewed the defendants in support of a bona fide civil investigation. There was no violation of due process.

Defendant appellees finally contend that the district court properly concluded that dismissal or, in the alternative, suppression, was warranted because the government lulled the defendants into turning over incriminating evidence by engaging in "trickery and deceit." It was dispositive for the district court that the SEC staff attorney instructed court reporters to refrain from mentioning the AUSA's involvement and that the SEC gave evasive answers to questions about the imminence of a dual investigation. We have previously applied the Fourth Amendment's bar to unreasonable searches and seizures in the context of dual investigations by the civil and criminal branches of the IRS, where review of documentary evidence is inherent in the investigation. We have thus held that a search is unreasonable, even if consensual, if the consent is obtained by trickery or deceit. *See* United States v. Robson, 477 F.2d 13, 18 (9th Cir. 1973). While not every SEC and USAO dual investigation will necessarily involve a search and seizure, to the extent that the individual defendants may have been led through trickery or deceit to turn over documentary or physical evidence in their possession or to use their official authority to turn over evidence in the possession of the corporation, the defendants could state a claim under the Fourth Amendment.

A government official must not "affirmatively mislead" the subject of parallel civil and criminal investigations "into believing that the investigation is exclusively civil in nature and will not lead to criminal charges." However, "we have consistently held that the failure of an IRS agent . . . to warn a taxpayer that an audit may have potential criminal ramifications does not render the search unreasonable."

Other circuits have agreed that Fourth Amendment and possible due process limitations may be implicated in a dual investigation. Almost every other circuit has denied suppression, even when government agents did not disclose the possibility or existence of a criminal investigation, so long as they made no affirmative misrepresentations. . . .

In this case, the SEC made no affirmative misrepresentations. . . .

The defendant-appellees point to a number of collateral facts they argue demonstrate trickery or deliberate misleading. They argue the SEC Staff Attorney affirmatively misled Stringer's attorney when, in response to the attorney's question about other agency involvement, she directed him to the provision in Form 1662 that warned that the SEC would likely turn over to the USAO evidence it collected at the depositions. The Staff Attorney, during the deposition taken in Portland, declined to direct defense counsel to a specific U.S. Attorney's Office, which would have been the Portland Office, but there was nothing false or misleading in her response that it was up to the defendant to decide where to direct his inquiries.

The defendant-appellees also point to the Staff Attorney's request to the court reporters not to mention the AUSA in the presence of defendants' attorneys. While this indicates an intent to prevent disclosure to defendants of the actual criminal investigation, the possibility of criminal investigation should have been well known to both the defendants and their counsel. The request to the court reporters to, in effect, mind their own business did not mislead or misinform defendants about the existence of an investigation. Thus, to the extent that the Fourth Amendment may have been implicated by the dual investigation, the district court erred in concluding that the government's actions in this case constituted an unreasonable search or seizure.

B. Interference with Samper's Attorney-Client Relationship

The district court concluded that the government violated defendant Samper's due process rights when it obtained evidence about the "Swedish Drop Shipment" from Samper's attorney, knowing that she had a conflict of interest. The government argues that it did not deliberately intrude into Samper's attorney-client relationship because all that it did was receive information that Samper's attorney offered the government, wholly independent of any government conduct.

We have held that "government interference with a defendant's relationship with his attorney may render counsel's assistance so ineffective as to violate . . . his Fifth Amendment right to due process of law." United States v. Irwin, 612 F.2d 1182, 1185 (9th Cir. 1980). . . . A claim of government interference with the attorney-client relationship has three elements: (1) the government was objectively aware of an ongoing, personal attorney-client relationship; (2) the government deliberately intruded into that relationship; and (3) as a result, the defendant suffered actual and substantial prejudice.

Most cases finding deliberate intrusion into the attorney-client relationship involve government informants who somehow penetrate the attorney-client relationship to obtain confidential or privileged information, and then feed that information to the government. . . . In contrast, we have held that the government's asking a defendant's former attorney to turn over privileged information does not constitute deliberate intrusion on the part of the government when the attorney complies. *See* United States v. Rogers, 751 F.2d 1074, 1080 (9th Cir. 1985). "The fact that the attorney failed to assert the ethical obligation does not transform [the government's] investigation into governmental misconduct." *Id.*

For similar reasons, . . . [t]he government did not deliberately intrude into the relationship between Samper and Rosenbaum when it accepted potentially incriminating evidence from Rosenbaum, nor was Rosenbaum a government informant whom the government sought out. There was no impropriety on the government's part. . . .

Indeed, had the government contacted Samper directly to warn him about the conflict, bypassing his attorney, the government would have engaged in conduct that itself may have amounted to interference. *Cf.* Or. Rules of Prof'l Conduct R. 4.2; Model Rules of Prof'l Conduct R. 4.2. The government's receipt of evidence from counsel intended to assist one client, but that also tended to incriminate another, was not an intrusion or intentional interference with the attorney-client relationship and did not justify dismissal of the indictment or suppression of the evidence of the "Swedish Drop Shipment."

IV. Conclusion

For the foregoing reasons, we conclude that there was no deception or affirmative misconduct on the part of the government in the course of the SEC and U.S. Attorney investigations that warranted dismissal of the indictment or suppression of any of the evidence in question. In addition, defendants' Fifth Amendment rights were not violated.

The panel shall retain jurisdiction over any subsequent appeal in this matter.

The judgment of the district court dismissing the indictment is VACATED. The district court's suppression ruling is REVERSED. The case is REMANDED for further proceedings.

NOTES AND QUESTIONS

1. Why was it so important to the AUSA that the defendants not know about the criminal investigation?
2. The court appears correct that the government did not lie, but it is clear that the government, with the AUSA taking charge, was deliberately "sneaky" in eliciting incriminating evidence from the defendants in the civil case so as to use it in the criminal one. Does that offend your sensibilities, or do

you see it as good lawyering in the cause of justice? Does it comport with ABA Model Rule of Professional Conduct 4.1, "Truthfulness in Statements to Others"?

3. One could argue that the individuals who led the defendants to their slaughter were, in fact, the defense attorneys, specifically Martson and Rosenbaum. What did they do wrong? Was it unethical? Does it rise to the level of malpractice?
4. One would guess that the defense attorneys in the case were not *criminal* defense attorneys. One important reason to have taken this class, even if you do not end up practicing in the white collar criminal arena, is that it will help you know when it is time to call in the criminal specialists.
5. The existence of parallel proceedings sometimes places supplementary legal and ethical duties on prosecutors. For example, the prosecution may be required to turn over witness statements (or depositions) from the civil case during the discovery phase of the criminal one. Prosecutors who don't realize this obligation put their case and their bar license in peril. *See* United States v. Mahaffy, 2010 WL 2925952 (Jul. 21, 2010) (holding that prosecution's failure to turn over witness depositions generated during SEC enforcement action was not *Brady* violation because the depositions were not material, but expressing considerable frustration with the prosecutors). The *Mahaffy* court stated:

> I remain mystified by the government's failure to disclose the testimony of these various witnesses. I see no legitimate interest served by an approach that has the parties and the Court sifting through the transcripts of testimony taken by the SEC after the trial has already occurred—especially when the testimony was taken as part of the investigation that resulted in this very case.. . . . The disclosure obligations imposed by the federal rules, federal statutes and the Constitution are too important, and too easily complied with, to justify such an approach. Even if the prosecutors are not sufficiently motivated, as they should be, by the defendants' interest in a fair trial, one would think the government's selfish interest in the integrity and durability of the convictions it obtains would induce it to consider its disclosure obligations on an ongoing basis, and to err on the side of over-disclosure unless well-grounded concerns about particular witnesses or other investigations counsel otherwise.

As *Stringer* implies, an individual may invoke his Fifth Amendment privilege during civil proceedings to protect himself from self-incrimination in future criminal proceedings.[2] This leads to the next question: What are the ramifications of maintaining silence in a civil matter? The following case examines this issue.

2. *See also* Lefkowitz v. Turley, 414 U.S. 70, 77 (1973) ("The [Fifth] Amendment not only protects the individual against being involuntarily called as a witness against himself in a criminal prosecution but also privileges him not to answer official questions put to him in any other proceeding, civil or criminal, formal or informal, where the answers might incriminate him in future criminal proceedings.")

LASALLE BANK LAKE VIEW v. SEGUBAN

54 F.3d 387 (7th Cir. 1995)

Ilana Diamond Rovner, Circuit Judge.

LaSalle Bank Lake View has sued its former Assistant Teller Manager, Ellen Seguban, under the Racketeer Influenced and Corrupt Organizations Act ("RICO"), 18 U.S.C. §1962(c) & (d), asserting that she embezzled $940,000 from the bank during twelve years of her employment there. The action, which was filed on September 29, 1993, also named as a defendant Ellen's husband, Rafael Seguban, alleging that he accepted and used the funds with full knowledge of their illegal source. Along with its RICO claims, the bank brought supplemental state law claims for breach of fiduciary duty, conversion, and fraud.

In addition to this civil action, the Bank's allegations spawned a criminal investigation by the United States Attorney for the Northern District of Illinois. That investigation was underway on February 4, 1994, when the Bank moved for summary judgment in this action. The Segubans therefore asserted their Fifth Amendment privilege against self-incrimination in response to the Bank's motion and offered no evidence to rebut the Bank's statement of material facts. Finding that the Segubans had thereby failed to show the existence of a material factual dispute, the district court granted the Bank's motion and entered judgment against the Segubans in the amount of $2,820,000, three times the Bank's damages of $940,000, in accordance with RICO's trebling provision, 18 U.S.C. §1964(c). The Segubans now appeal, arguing that the district court improperly drew an inference of guilt based on their assertion of the Fifth Amendment privilege, and that without that inference the evidence did not entitle the bank to judgment as a matter of law. We reverse and remand for further proceedings.

I.

The Northern District of Illinois' Local Rule 12(M) requires that a movant for summary judgment file "a statement of material facts as to which the moving party contends there is no genuine issue and that entitle the moving party to a judgment as a matter of law. . . ." In response to that statement, Local Rule 12(N) requires the opposing party to file "a response to each numbered paragraph in the moving party's statement, including, in the case of any disagreement, specific references to the affidavits, parts of the record, and other supporting materials relied upon" and "a statement, consisting of short numbered paragraphs, of any additional facts that require the denial of summary judgment . . . ," also supported by record citations. Finally, Rule 12(N) admonishes that "[a]ll material facts set forth in the statement required of the moving party will be deemed to be admitted unless controverted by the statement of the opposing party." . . . The . . . question posed by this appeal is whether the normal operation of Rule 12(N) is precluded here because the Segubans' failure to file a 12(N) response was based on their assertion of the Fifth Amendment privilege.[2]

2. The Segubans did not move the district court to stay the Bank's civil action until the criminal investigation was concluded. We therefore need not consider the propriety of such a course, which is sometimes taken to avoid the dilemma faced by defendants like the Segubans.

The Fifth Amendment provides that "[n]o person . . . shall be compelled in any criminal case to be a witness against himself. . . ." In addition to direct compulsion, the Supreme Court has prohibited practices that are coercive in that they make the exercise of the privilege "costly." Spevack v. Klein, 385 U.S. 511, 515 (1967). Into that category the Court has placed sanctions with serious economic consequences, such as the loss of employment or state contracts.

In Baxter v. Palmigiano, 425 U.S. 308 (1976), the Court discussed whether the drawing of an adverse inference from Fifth Amendment silence in a civil proceeding imposed too high a cost on the exercise of the privilege. In that case, a prison inmate had been brought before a prison disciplinary board on charges of inciting a disturbance. Informed that state criminal charges might also be brought against him, the inmate was advised that he could remain silent at the disciplinary proceeding, but that his silence "would be held against him" in that forum. At the hearing, Palmigiano was confronted with incriminating evidence and remained silent. The board placed him in segregation for thirty days and downgraded his institutional status. The Court held that the rule it had articulated in the *Garrity-Lefkowitz* line of cases did not prohibit the drawing of an adverse inference from Fifth Amendment silence in a prison disciplinary proceeding when incriminating evidence had also been presented. Such an inference did not, in other words, impose an unconstitutional cost on the exercise of the privilege. The rule that adverse inferences may be drawn from Fifth Amendment silence in civil proceedings has been widely recognized by the circuit courts of appeals, including our own, in the two decades since *Baxter* was decided.

But while holding that factual inferences based on the assertion of the privilege do not place too high a cost on its exercise, the *Baxter* Court was just as clear that the rule of *Lefkowitz* and its predecessors would be violated if the failure to testify *alone* were taken as an admission of guilt, without regard to other evidence:

> [T]his case is very different from the circumstances before the Court in the *Garrity-Lefkowitz* decisions, where refusal to submit to interrogation and to waive the Fifth Amendment privilege, standing alone and without regard to the other evidence, resulted in loss of employment or opportunity to contract with the State. There, failure to respond to interrogation was treated as a final admission of guilt. Here, Palmigiano remained silent at the hearing in the face of evidence that incriminated him; and, as far as this record reveals, his silence was given no more evidentiary value than was warranted by the facts surrounding this case.

425 U.S. at 318. Thus, although "the Fifth Amendment does not forbid adverse inferences against parties to civil actions when they refuse to testify in response to probative evidence offered against them" (*id.*), an analysis of that evidence is nonetheless required. Silence is a relevant factor to be considered in light of the proffered evidence, but the direct inference of guilt from silence is forbidden. . . .

We further explored the constitutionally acceptable inference that could be drawn from the assertion of the Fifth Amendment privilege in National Acceptance Co. of America v. Bathalter, 705 F.2d 924 (7th Cir. 1983), when we held that the failure to answer the allegations of a civil complaint based on an assertion of the Fifth Amendment privilege could not be construed as an admission of those allegations even though FRCP 8(d) would otherwise require that result. . . .

II.

Here, the district court's summary judgment analysis consisted of the following:

> [I]n light of the facts adduced by the Bank in conjunction with the permissible negative inference drawn from the Segubans' assertion of their Fifth Amendment privilege, no reasonable trier of fact could find in favor of either of the Segubans. . . . The undisputed facts demonstrate that the Bank is entitled to a judgment as a matter of law on its claims under RICO and pendent state claims.

Because it fails to explain how the facts in the Bank's 12(M) statement entitle it to judgment as a matter of law on its civil RICO claim (not to mention its state law claims for breach of fiduciary duty, conversion and fraud), the district court's analysis is insufficient. Although the lack of an explanation alone would justify a remand and would certainly do so here in light of the constitutional implications, our concern in this instance is more than formal. Even assuming the facts contained in the Bank's Rule 12(M) statement to be true, it does not seem to us at all clear that the Bank was entitled to judgment as a matter of law.

III.

Without any explanation of why the Bank was entitled to judgment as a matter of law, we are helpless to review the district court's decision. But because the Bank's entitlement to judgment appears to us far from self-evident, we must conclude that the district court did draw an impermissible inference of liability based only on the Segubans' assertion of the Fifth Amendment privilege. If, even drawing those inferences from the Segubans' silence that are permissible, the facts do not entitle the Bank to judgment as a matter of law, then its motion for summary judgment must be denied regardless of the Segubans' failure to comply with Rule 12(N). The judgment of the district court is REVERSED and this case is REMANDED for further proceedings consistent with this opinion.

NOTES AND QUESTIONS

1. Is the *LaSalle Bank* holding a logical extension of the Supreme Court's *Baxter* decision? How much weight, exactly, should be given to a civil litigant's silence?
2. Do you think that the Seventh Circuit was influenced by the fact that, because it was a RICO case, plaintiff had been awarded treble damages based on defendants' assertion of their Fifth Amendment privilege? Should that matter?
3. For another case applying the doctrine outlined in *LaSalle Bank*, see Clancy v. Coyne, 244 F. Supp. 894 (N.D. Ill. 2002) (requiring defendant "to offer some evidence in responding to summary judgment where he bore burden of proof on issue was not coercive economic sanction.").

III. OBTAINING A STAY OR PROTECTIVE ORDER

MILTON POLLACK, SENIOR DISTRICT COURT JUDGE, PARALLEL CIVIL AND CRIMINAL PROCEEDINGS

129 F.R.D. 201 (1989)

The subject of parallel cases going on at the same time and the administration of the pre-trial proceedings in each has given rise to a whole body of jurisprudence which determines when and how a judge overseeing civil proceedings can best handle them so as to protect both the individual litigants' interests—constitutional and otherwise—as well as the public's interest in seeing the fast and efficient resolution of litigation.

Handling of the pretrial process in the civil cases has posed a balancing of the divergent interests in the parallel litigations; and, like most balancing processes, involves a number of factors which at first can seem confusing and complicated but which can be broken down to a couple of overriding themes.

In analyzing these factors, it is important to remember who is seeking relief in one or the other of the parallel cases. Let us first examine some of the questions from the viewpoint of the defendant in each case who is faced with the double barreled attack on him in the criminal and civil forums. Let us suppose that his pursuers seek to go forward in the civil pretrial arena that has been committed to the assigned multi-district judge.

My task is not so much to *educate* you as to *inform* you of some of the different approaches taken by various courts on this subject. I hope this . . . will serve to illumine some of the philosophy and treatment of the subject matter by different courts and how the problems have been resolved in the reported authorities.

When parallel civil and criminal actions arising from the same transactions or issues have been instituted, a court is faced with a dilemma. On the one hand, a parallel civil proceeding can vitiate the protections afforded the accused in the criminal proceeding if the prosecutor can use information obtained from him through civil discovery or testimony elicited in the civil litigation. This also may cause him to confront the prospect of divulging information which may incriminate him. On the other hand, the pendency of a parallel criminal proceeding can impede the search for truth in the civil proceeding if the accused resists disclosure and asserts his privilege against self-incrimination and thereby conceals important evidence. It may be that the Government seeks to withhold discovery which is §3500 material for the criminal trial and thereby deprives the defendant in the civil case of the means to defend fully therein.

Dicta from the leading case of Campbell v. Eastland, 307 F.2d 478, 487 (5th Cir. 1962) has led some to conclude that standard operating procedure entails *staying* civil proceedings altogether while a parallel criminal investigation or prosecution is being conducted. . . . However, there may be a substantial public interest to be conserved by proceeding promptly with the civil side. . . .

[T]he courts generally treat four factors as significant, if not dispositive, weights which can tip the balance either in favor of or against a stay of the plaintiff's quest for discovery. These four factors are: (1) the commonality of transactions or issues, (2) the timing of the motion, (3) judicial efficiency, and (4) the public interest.

First. The most important factor at the threshold is the degree to which the civil issues overlap with the criminal issues. Some civil issues are irrelevant to related criminal proceedings. For example, the issue of damages for wrongful death would not arise in most related criminal negligence prosecutions; in such a case, a stay of the civil proceedings on the issue of damages would rarely be appropriate.

Second. The current stage of the parallel criminal proceeding will often substantially affect the net balance of equities. Is resolution nearby or remote in time?

The strongest case for a stay of discovery in the civil case occurs during a criminal prosecution after an indictment is returned. The potential for self-incrimination is greatest during this stage, and the potential harm to civil litigants arising from delaying them is reduced due to the promise of a fairly quick resolution of the criminal case under the Speedy Trial Act.

The chances of the defendant's procuring a stay are less favorable (but still possible) if the government is conducting an active parallel criminal *investigation* in which an indictment or information has not yet been filed. . . .

If criminal proceedings are over or there is no substantial criminal exposure, the courts are most likely to deny a delay of plaintiff's discovery or other pre-trial relief. The accused's trial tactics have already been exposed, and the likelihood of self-incrimination may be diminished, particularly if the defendant has testified at trial. And, the appeal process is an uncertain, potentially long-ranging, process. Only unusual circumstances would justify an order staying a post-conviction civil proceeding. . . .

Third. Judicial efficiency is also a factor in the balancing analysis. Resolution of the criminal case may increase prospects for settlement of the civil case. Due to differences in the standards of proof between civil suits and criminal prosecutions, the possibility always exists for a collateral estoppel or res judicata effect on some or all of the overlapping issues. Conviction of a defendant in a parallel criminal case may effectively dispose of all common issues in a subsequent civil action, although the reverse is not true. . . .

Fourth. The effect of a stay of the civil case upon the "public interest" is perhaps the most important factor in the equation, albeit the one hardest to define. As I noted before, both plaintiffs and defendants have an interest in a timely judgment. In civil securities actions, the public has an interest in the maintenance of and preservation of the integrity of the securities market. These interests can be substantially prejudiced by stays imposing significant delays upon the civil proceeding. To this end it would behoove both the litigants and the court to tailor a stay at the instance of the defendant (if one is to be granted) to minimize any delays upon the process. . . .

With that said, let's turn to some specific examples of the grounds upon which a motion for a stay by a defendant or one at the request of the Department of Justice may properly be based and to cases which address the issue.

Criminal defendants who move for a stay of related civil proceedings against them usually do so on one of two grounds: they may assert their participation in civil proceedings jeopardizes their right against self-incrimination under the Fifth

Amendment, or, in civil cases in which the government is a party, they may contend the prosecution can circumvent strict criminal discovery guidelines or learn the basis of the defendant's criminal defense by receiving information gathered by another branch of the federal government in the civil case. . . .

We turn now to situations where it is the defendant who is seeking some sort of relief, such as documentary disclosure and depositions of particular witnesses, and the defendant is met by an attempt of the Government or by the plaintiff acting on request of the prosecutor to stay or defer the disclosure of the depositions, ostensibly to conserve the public interest in the prosecution of a related criminal case. Usually, this sort of request by the Government occurs when the Government is proceeding with both barrels blazing in the civil and criminal court, as when the SEC and Justice bring simultaneous actions. . . .

Although every discovery motion requires that the court, and I quote, must "balance the interests of the litigant[s]," Ross v. Bolton, 106 F.R.D. 23, 23 (S.D.N.Y. 1985), there is a strong presumption in favor of discovery that any party—the Government no less than any other litigant—must overcome if it seeks to withhold production or depositions.

Where district courts have stayed discovery most frequently in civil proceedings at the request of the Government, the stay questions have arisen in situations where the Government seeks to protect ongoing criminal *investigations* and pending *grand jury hearings*. . . .

Cases arise in which the Government no longer claims that any criminal *investigation* of movants will be placed in jeopardy by the discovery it is withholding; rather, the defendant has been indicted and Justice now asserts prejudice to its criminal *prosecution* of defendant and urges in opposition to a motion for pretrial disclosure in the civil suit that since the discovery in question is not at this time required from the *prosecution* under the rules of criminal procedure, it ought not be produced *by the SEC* or other parties or witnesses in the civil cases.

The question presented is whether the policy underlying the limited scope of *discovery under the criminal rules* justifies withholding legitimate discovery in these *civil* litigations. That policy is rooted in concerns about possible perjury, manufacture of *false evidence* and *intimidation* of confidential government informants.

As you can see, it is now the civil case *defendant* who asserts that the "public interest in the integrity of securities markets militates in favor [sic] of the efficient and expeditious prosecution of . . . civil litigations."

Allowing the Government to delay and ultimately prolong the conduct of the SEC action, and also the private litigations tagging along, would seem on the surface of things to oppose that public interest.

However, as well shall see, surface appearances are often deceiving. In Campbell v. Eastland, 307 F.2d at 487, to which I referred much earlier, the Department of Justice sought a stay of discovery in a civil suit brought by a taxpayer against the IRS on grounds that the civil discovery would give witness statements to the taxpayer that would not be available to the taxpayer in a criminal case. The Fifth Circuit indicated that, in exercising its discretion, the district court had to harmonize the differences between civil and criminal discovery rules: that a litigant should not be able to get through civil discovery what he could not get through criminal discovery. That suggestion was said to apply whether or not the taxpayer's civil suit was brought in good faith, because in either event the improper effect would be to nullify the Jencks Act. The District Court for the District of Columbia granted relief to the Government because it "is well established that a litigant should not be allowed to make use of the liberal [civil] discovery procedures . . . to avoid the restriction on criminal discovery." Founding Church of Scientology, Inc. v. Kelley, 77 F.R.D. 378, 380 (D.C. Cir. 1977). Similarly, a Southern District of New York case held that "where both civil and criminal proceedings arise out of the same or related transactions the government is ordinarily entitled to a stay of all discovery in the civil action until disposition of the criminal matter." United States v. One 1964 Cadillac Coupe DeVille, 41 F.R.D. 352, 353 (S.D.N.Y. 1966). . . .

However, while the Fifth Circuit in *Campbell* addressed the question of a complete stay of discovery, it also indicated in *dicta* that less drastic restraints on discovery were within the discretion of the district court to conserve all interests at stake. . . .

Let me summarize:

. . . Neither criminal nor civil procedure, in the Federal Rules, has a provision that explicitly addresses the problems of parallel proceedings. As a result, resort must be had to an *ad hoc* equitable remedy. As you have heard, some courts have stayed the civil proceeding, in whole or in part. Some courts have resorted to sealing or placing the records and proceedings under confidentiality protection. Still other courts have restrained civil discovery of designated specific areas as relates to specific documents and depositions pending developments in the criminal case. Still others have declined to provide any remedy. In all cases, the court must carefully balance the interests of the private litigants against those of the public.

In short, the courts in exercising their equitable powers have a wide range of responses when faced with motions seeking or opposing some form of restraint of discovery in the parallel civil and criminal proceedings and involving protection of the public interest or vindication or protection of the private interest.

Courts of Appeals have repeatedly observed that the decision lies within the informed, sound discretion of the trial court. Basically the avoidance of prejudice in the balancing of the equities is the goal to be set, no matter who is the moving or objecting party.

SEC v. DOODY

186 F. Supp. 2d 379 (S.D.N.Y. 2002)

KAPLAN, District Judge.

The United States moves to intervene in this civil action and to stay (a) production by the SEC of transcripts of prior witness depositions and interview notes, (b) initial disclosures of witness lists and related information under Rule 26(a)(i)(A), and (c) depositions, all pending completion of related criminal proceedings. Defendant Joseph F. Doody, one of three defendants in the civil case, but not a defendant in the related criminal case, resists the motion.

Facts

On November 8, 2001, a grand jury sitting in this district returned an indictment charging Joseph F. Doody, IV, with securities fraud. The charge, in substance, is that Doody traded on material inside information regarding an impending merger between BetzDearborn, Inc. and Hercules Incorporated which he obtained from his girlfriend, Diane Neiley.

On the same date, the SEC brought this civil action against Doody, his father, Joseph F. Doody ("Doody Sr."), and Neilly charging the same insider trading scheme. Doody is alleged to have tipped Doody Sr. on the basis of the tips he received from Neilly, and Doody Sr. is alleged to have traded on that information as well. The SEC seeks an injunction and other relief.

The trial of the criminal case now is set for March 8, 2002 before Judge Scheindlin. In the meantime, Doody Sr. has commenced an ambitious discovery program in this action, seeking answers to interrogatories from and production of documents by the SEC which, the government says, would result in premature disclosure of the evidence upon which it hopes to rely in the criminal case. In addition, Doody Sr. has noticed Neilly's deposition, and the government apprehends that he will seek to depose individuals who are likely to be witnesses in the criminal trial, thus further tipping the government's hand and, in effect, giving Doody an extra opportunity to cross-examine the government's witnesses.

Discussion

The government has made a persuasive case that its interest in protecting its criminal case justifies its intervention here, and Doody makes no serious argument to the contrary. Accordingly, the government will be permitted to intervene for the purpose of seeking relief against discovery in this case pending the completion of the criminal trial. The question is whether it is entitled to that relief.

Once an indictment has been returned, the government often moves for and frequently obtains relief preventing a criminal defendant from using parallel civil proceedings to gain premature access to evidence and information pertinent to the criminal case. In granting such relief, courts must weigh competing interests, including "the interests of the defendants, the interests of the plaintiffs in proceeding with the litigation, the public interest, and the interests of the courts and of third parties."

Doody Sr. argues that the abundance of authority is not controlling or, arguably, even pertinent here because he is not a defendant in the criminal case and, moreover, has a compelling need to proceed expeditiously in the civil case. The need is said to stem from the fact that he is employed by Enron, is likely soon to be out of a job and, absent speedy disposition of the civil case, would have difficulty finding employment with the stigma from the SEC's charges against him hanging over his head.

To be sure, most cases involving stays of civil actions pending the completion of parallel criminal proceedings have involved common defendants. This case therefore is different to the extent that it is Doody Sr. who is leading the charge toward discovery in this civil case. But the Court would have to be unimaginably naïve to suppose that Doody Sr. is not a stalking horse for Doody himself. Whether Doody Sr. discovers the government's case against his son or his son's attorneys do it by exercising their right, as counsel to a co-defendant in the civil case, to participate in discovery here is immaterial. The fact is that discovery here that would afford Doody access to information to which he would not be entitled in his defense of the criminal case almost surely would occur absent some relief.

Doody Sr. is at least arguably right also in saying that this case is unusual in that he would be subjected to some prejudice by a delay of civil discovery different than anything that might be claimed by one who is a defendant in both cases. But he has failed to demonstrate that he will suffer prejudice that outweighs the government's interest in obtaining a stay. Perhaps he will lose his job, and perhaps he will have some difficulty finding new employment while this action is pending. But the fact is that he has not lost it yet and may not lose it. Even if he does, the criminal case is scheduled for trial in approximately four weeks. Doody Sr. has provided no information concerning his financial situation, so there is no basis whatever to suppose that a delay of discovery in this case for, say, six weeks would mean the difference between his putting food on the table and starvation. Thus, Doody Sr.'s position is based on unfounded assumptions and inappropriate exaggerations. But he is not alone in having overstated his case.

The relief the government seeks is virtually a blanket stay of all disclosure in this case. Perhaps no discovery could be provided here without implicating its legitimate concerns in the criminal case, but that is not self evident. In consequence, the Court is left guessing as to just what protection the government legitimately requires. After having weighed the competing interests of the various parties, it therefore must make the best judgments it can in the circumstances.

Conclusion

The government's motion for leave to intervene and for a stay of certain discovery is granted to the following extent:

(a) Intervention is granted for the purpose set forth above.

(b) The following discovery is stayed until the earliest of (i) the entry of a plea of guilty, (ii) the completion of the trial of the criminal case, and (iii) March 20, 2002:

   (1) Rule 26(a)(i)(A) discovery.

   (2) Production of transcripts of SEC testimony and notes of interviews of any person whom the United States Attorney's Office certifies may be called as a witness in the criminal case.

   (3) Depositions of any person whom the United States Attorney's office certifies may be called as a witness in the criminal case.

The motion is otherwise denied, albeit without prejudice to further application by the government for relief upon a specific showing that the particular discovery sought would threaten to prejudice the criminal prosecution.

SO ORDERED.

NOTES AND QUESTIONS

1. After reading Judge Pollack's article, can you articulate the various factors that should be considered when:

   a. The defendant in a parallel civil action requests a stay?
   b. A third-party plaintiff in a parallel civil action requests a stay?
   c. The government as plaintiff in a parallel civil action requests a stay?

2. A related issue that frequently arises in parallel proceedings is what to do when a grand jury issues a subpoena for material covered by an existing civil protective order. The Supreme Court has yet to address this question. The weight of authority holds that there is a presumption in favor of enforcing a grand jury subpoena that can be overcome only by a showing of compelling circumstances. *See, e.g.*, In re Grand Jury Subpoena,138 F.3d 442 (1st Cir. 1998); In re Grand Jury Subpoena Served on Meserve, Mumper & Hughes, 62 F.2d 1222 (9th Cir. 1998); In re Grand Jury (Williams), 995 F.2d 1013 (11th Cir. 1993); In re Grand Jury Subpoena, 836 F.2d 1468 (4th Cir.), *cert. denied*, 487 U.S. 1240 (1988). *But see* Martindell v. ITT, 594 F.2d 291, 296 (2d Cir. 1979) (holding that to enforce a grand jury subpoena and gain access to civil discovery protected by a protective order, the Government must demonstrate either "improvidence in the grant of a Rule (6(c) protective order or some extraordinary circumstance or compelling need").

IV. USE OF GRAND JURY MATERIALS IN CIVIL CASES

UNITED STATES v. JOHN DOE, INC. I
481 U.S. 102 (1987)

Justice STEVENS delivered the opinion of the Court.

In United States v. Sells Engineering, Inc., 463 U.S. 418 (1983), we held that attorneys for the Civil Division of the Justice Department may not automatically obtain disclosure of grand jury materials for use in a civil suit, but must instead seek a court order of disclosure, available upon a showing of "particularized need." We explicitly left open the "issue concerning continued use of grand jury materials, in the civil phase of a dispute, by an attorney who himself conducted the criminal prosecution." Today, we decide that open question. In addition, for the first time, we review a concrete application of the "particularized need" standard to a request for disclosure to Government attorneys.

I.

In March 1982, attorneys in the Antitrust Division of the Department of Justice were authorized to conduct a grand jury investigation of three American corporations suspected of conspiring to fix the price of tallow being sold to a foreign government and financed by the Department of State's Agency for International Development. After subpoenaing thousands of documents from the three corporate respondents, and taking the testimony of numerous witnesses, including the five individual respondents, the Department of Justice conferred with some of respondents' attorneys and concluded that although respondents had violated §1 of the Sherman Act, 15 U.S.C. §1, criminal prosecution was not warranted under the circumstances. In early June 1984, the grand jury was discharged without returning any indictments. . . .

After further investigation, the Antitrust Division attorneys came to the tentative conclusion that respondents had violated the False Claims Act, 31 U.S.C. §§3729-3731, and the Foreign Assistance Act, 22 U.S.C. §§2151-2429, as well as the Sherman Act. Because the Civil Division of the Department of Justice has primary responsibility for enforcing the False Claims Act, the Antitrust Division deemed it appropriate to consult with lawyers in the Civil Division before initiating a civil action. Additionally, because of the venue of the contemplated civil action, the Antitrust Division felt it necessary to consult with the United States Attorney for the Southern District of New York. Accordingly, the Antitrust Division lawyers filed a motion in the District Court for the Southern District of New York requesting an order under Federal Rule of Criminal Procedure 6(e) allowing them to disclose grand jury material to six named Government attorneys and such associates as those attorneys might designate. After an *ex parte* hearing, the District Court granted the motion, based on its finding that the Government's interest in coordinating fair and efficient enforcement of the False Claims Act, and obtaining the Civil Division's and United States Attorney's expert consultation, constituted a particularized need for the requested disclosure.

After expedited consideration, the Court of Appeals reversed both aspects of the District Court's order. We granted certiorari, and now reverse.

II.

The "General Rule of Secrecy" set forth in Federal Rule of Criminal Procedure 6(e) provides that certain persons, including attorneys for the Government, "shall not disclose matters occurring before the grand jury, except as otherwise provided for in these rules." Unlike our previous decisions in this area, which have primarily involved exceptions to the general rule, this case involves a more preliminary question: what constitutes disclosure? The Court of Appeals acknowledged that "to characterize [attorneys'] continued access in the civil phase to the materials to which they had access in the criminal phase as disclosure within the meaning of rule 6(e) seems fictional at first glance." But the Court of Appeals reasoned that the attorneys could not possibly remember all the details of the grand jury investigation and therefore the use of grand jury materials "to refresh their recollection as to documents or testimony to which they had access in the grand jury proceeding is tantamount to a further disclosure."

Contrary to the Court of Appeals' conclusion, it seems plain to us that Rule 6(e) prohibits those with information about the workings of the grand jury from revealing such information to other persons who are not authorized to have access to it under the Rule. The Rule does not contain a prohibition against the continued use of information by attorneys who legitimately obtained access to the information through the grand jury investigation. The Court of Appeals' reasoning is unpersuasive because it stretches the plain meaning of the Rule's language much too far. It is indeed fictional—and not just "at first glance"—to interpret the word "disclose" to embrace a solitary reexamination of material in the privacy of an attorney's office. . . . As the Court of Appeals for the Eighth Circuit recently concluded, "[f]or there to be a disclosure, grand jury matters must be disclosed to *someone*."

. . . Without addressing the very different matter of an attorney's disclosing grand jury information to others, inadvertently or purposefully, in the course of a civil proceeding, we hold that Rule 6(e) does not require the attorney to obtain a court order before refamiliarizing himself or herself with the details of a grand jury investigation.

III.

The Department of Justice properly recognized that under our holding in *Sells* it could not disclose information to previously uninvolved attorneys from the Civil Division or the United States Attorney's office without a court order pursuant to Rule 6(e)(3)(C)(i). Upon the Department's motion, the District Court granted an order, finding a "particularized need for disclosure" pursuant to the considerations described in *Sells.* The District Court accepted the Government's argument that consultation and coordination between the Civil Division, the United States Attorney, and the Antitrust Division was necessary to ensure consistent enforcement of the False Claims Act and "the fair and evenhanded administration of justice." The Court of Appeals reversed on this point, however, concluding that disclosure was unnecessary because the same information could eventually have been obtained through civil discovery.

In *Sells* we noted that Rule 6(e) itself does not prescribe the substantive standard governing the issuance of an order pursuant to Rule 6(e)(3)(C)(i) and that the case law that had developed in response to requests for disclosure by private parties had consistently required "a strong showing of particularized need" before disclosure is permitted. S*ee generally* Douglas Oil Co. v. Northwest Petrol Stops Northwest, 441 U.S. 211, 222-23 (1979).[8] Although we held that this same standard applies where a court is asked to order disclosure to a government attorney, we made it clear that the concerns that underlie the policy of grand jury secrecy are implicated to a much lesser extent when the disclosure merely involves Government attorneys.

In this case, the disclosures were requested to enable the Antitrust Division lawyers who had conducted the grand jury investigation to obtain the full benefit of the experience and expertise of the Civil Division lawyers who regularly handle

8. In *Douglas Oil*, we described the standard as follows:

> "Parties seeking grand jury transcripts under Rule 6(e) must show that the material they seek is needed to avoid a possible injustice in another judicial proceeding, that the need for disclosure is greater than the need for continued secrecy, and that their request is structured to cover only material so needed. . . ." 441 U.S., at 222.

litigation under the False Claims Act, and of the local United States Attorney who is regularly consulted before actions are filed in his or her district. The public purposes served by the disclosure—efficient, effective, and evenhanded enforcement of federal statutes—are certainly valid. . . . To be sure, as we recognized in *Sells*, not every instance of "saving time and expense" justifies disclosure. The question that must be asked is whether the public benefits of the disclosure in this case outweigh the dangers created by the limited disclosure requested.

In *Sells* we recognized three types of dangers involved in disclosure of grand jury information to Government attorneys for use related to civil proceedings. First, we stated that disclosure not only increases the "number of persons to whom the information is available (thereby increasing the risk of inadvertent or illegal release to others), but also it renders considerably more concrete the threat to the willingness of witnesses to come forward and to testify fully and candidly." Neither of these fears is well founded with respect to the narrow disclosure involved in this case. The disclosure of a summary of a portion of the grand jury record to named attorneys for purposes of consultation does not pose the same risk of a wide breach of grand jury secrecy as would allowing unlimited use of the material to all attorneys in another division—the disclosure involved in *Sells*. Moreover, the fact that the grand jury had already terminated mitigates the damage of a possible inadvertent disclosure. Finally, because the disclosure authorized in this case would not directly result in any witness' testimony being used against him or her in a civil proceeding, there is little fear that the disclosure will have any effect on future grand jury testimony.

The second concern identified in *Sells* is the threat to the integrity of the grand jury itself. We explained that if "prosecutors in a given case knew that their colleagues would be free to use the materials generated by the grand jury for a civil case, they might be tempted to manipulate the grand jury's powerful investigative tools to root out additional evidence useful in the civil suit, or even to start or continue a grand jury inquiry where no criminal prosecution seemed likely." The discussion of this concern in *Sells* dealt with whether the Civil Division should be given unfettered access to grand jury materials. We think the concern is far less worrisome when the attorneys seeking disclosure must go before a court and demonstrate a particularized need prior to any disclosure, and when, as part of that inquiry, the district court may properly consider whether the circumstances disclose any evidence of grand jury abuse. In this case, for example, one of the Government attorneys involved in the criminal investigation submitted an affidavit attesting to the Department's good faith in conducting the grand jury investigation and there has been no evidence or allegation to the contrary. The fact that a court is involved in this manner lessens some of the usual difficulty in detecting grand jury abuse. Moreover, we think the fear of abuse is minimal when the civil use contemplated is simply consultation with various Government lawyers about the prudence of proceeding with a civil action.

The final concern discussed in *Sells* is that "use of grand jury materials by Government agencies in civil or administrative settings threatens to subvert the limitations applied outside the grand jury context on the Government's powers of discovery and investigation." We continue to believe that this is an important concern, but it is not seriously implicated when the Government simply wishes to use the material for consultation. Of course, when the Government requests disclosure for use in an actual adversarial proceeding, this factor (as well as the others) may require a stronger showing of necessity. . . .

While the possibility of obtaining information from alternative sources is certainly an important factor, we believe that the Court of Appeals exaggerated its significance in this case. Even if we assume that all of the relevant material could have been obtained through the civil discovery tools available to the Government, our precedents do not establish a *per se* rule against disclosure. Rather, we have repeatedly stressed that wide discretion must be afforded to district court judges in evaluating whether disclosure is appropriate. The threat to grand jury secrecy was minimal in this context, and under the circumstances, the District Court properly considered the strong "public interests served" through disclosure. As we noted in *Sells*, the governing standard is "a highly flexible one, adaptable to different circumstances and sensitive to the fact that the requirements of secrecy are greater in some situations than in others." The District Court correctly examined the relevant factors and we cannot say that it abused its discretion in determining that the equities leaned in favor of disclosure.

The judgment of the Court of Appeals is
Reversed.

NOTES AND QUESTIONS

1. Although the Court discusses a variety of reasons for Rule 6(e)'s prohibition on the use of grand jury materials for non-criminal purposes, its overarching concern seems to be that government lawyers would otherwise be tempted to manipulate or abuse the grand jury process to benefit civil cases. Given the extraordinary power of the grand jury to compel testimony and the production of documents, this concern is legitimate. In light of the low threshold needed to overcome 6(e)'s presumption of secrecy set out in *Doe, Inc.*, does the process of obtaining a court order provide sufficient protection against abuse? Can a court effectively judge the motivation of prosecutors in an ex parte hearing?
2. *Douglas Oil* sets out the standard that must be met by a non-governmental third party who seeks access to grand jury material. (If you missed it, the standard is referenced in footnote 8 of the opinion, *supra* p. 603) The *Doe, Inc.* Court says that its holding is simply an extension of *Douglas Oil.* Is that true, or would it be fairer to say that the standard is entirely different for government attorneys? Should it be?
3. The U.S. Attorneys' Manual instructs federal prosecutors as follows:

> "**Disclosure of Matters Occurring before the Grand Jury to Department of Justice attorneys or use in civil case:** Disclosure of matters covered by Rule 6(e) to Department of Justice attorneys for use in a civil suit is permissible only pursuant to a court order under Rule 6(e)(3)(C)(i). United States v. Sells Engineering, Inc., 463 U.S. 418 (1983).
>
> When disclosure is authorized by court order under Rule 6(e)(3)(C)(i), of the Federal Rules of Criminal Procedure, for use in

> civil proceedings, there is a danger of misuse, or the appearance thereof, when such disclosure is made during the pendency of the grand jury investigation. There is no rule of law that would require a civil disclosure within the Department to be deferred until the relevant criminal investigation has been completed. Unless there is a genuine need for disclosure during the pendency of the grand jury investigation, however, it is the better practice to forestall the disclosure until the criminal investigation is completed."

9 U.S. ATTORNEYS' MANUAL, CRIMINAL RESOURCE MANUAL §156(C), available at http://www.justice.gov/usao/eousa/foia_reading_room/usam/title9/crm00156.htm (last visited Feb. 1, 2011).

It is rare that DOJ advises prosecutors to refrain from exercising power specifically granted to them by the courts. It appears to do so here out of the fear that obtaining a Rule 6(e)(3)(C)(i) order during the pendency of the grand jury proceeding creates a heightened danger of grand jury abuse, or at least the appearance thereof. Why is the timing so important?

V. CASES INVOLVING FRAUD AGAINST THE GOVERNMENT

UNITED STATES ATTORNEYS' MANUAL, COORDINATION OF CRIMINAL AND CIVIL FRAUD AGAINST THE GOVERNMENT CASES

§9-42.010

A. The United States has both statutory (e.g., the False Claims Act, 31 U.S.C. §§3729-3733) and common law rights of action arising from fraud against the government and from the corruption of its officials. Every report of fraud or official corruption should be analyzed for its civil potential before the file is closed. In the first instance, this review should be conducted by an Assistant United States Attorney or Departmental Trial Attorney assigned to the initial referral. Claims of fraud against the government involving more than $1,000,000 in single damages plus civil penalties also should be referred to the Civil Division's Commercial Litigation Branch.

B. The Federal Bureau of Investigation has been directed to furnish both the Fraud Section of the Criminal Division and the Commercial Litigation Branch of the Civil Division with copies of all reports in all matters involving fraud against the government, or bribery or conflict of interest involving a public employee. Other federal investigative agencies are required to forward similar reports of investigation to the Branch Director or appropriate United States Attorney.

C. Cases pursued criminally must also be analyzed for civil potential. This analysis should be conducted at the earliest possible stage. Criminal dispositions by plea bargain should not waive or release the government's civil interests, except in return for adequate consideration, as measured by the Department's standards for civil settlements generally. Proposed civil dispositions involving over $1,000,000 in single damages plus civil penalties must be referred to the Commercial Litigation Branch for approval.

D. As to cases referred to it, the Commercial Litigation Branch notifies the appropriate United States Attorney and other interested offices within the Department of Justice of potential civil actions that come to the Branch's attention. The Branch coordinates its cases with the appropriate United States Attorney to ensure the pursuit of both civil and criminal redress. Cases are similarly coordinated within the United States Attorneys' offices. This coordination may include the simultaneous initiation of civil and criminal proceedings in cases in which the monetary recovery to the government and the deterrent effect will be enhanced, giving due consideration to the risks to the criminal case and the availability of protective orders and stays.

E. The attorney from the Commercial Litigation Branch or Assistant United States Attorney assigned to the matter follows the investigation as it develops and, where necessary, requests, in coordination with other interested offices of the Department of Justice, that an investigation be conducted relating to areas such as damages, which are particularly pertinent to civil actions. It is the policy of the Department to coordinate jointly the investigation of criminal and civil actions. Pursuant to this policy, an Attorney General memorandum to the United States Attorneys dated July 16, 1986 states that "where possible, documents should be obtained by methods other than grand jury subpoenas." This Attorney General memorandum encourages the use of Inspector General subpoenas as an alternative to grand jury subpoenas in those cases where an Inspector General has determined that such usage is appropriate.

F. The Branch attorney or AUSA assigned to the matter, should give consideration at the earliest possible date to the initiation of civil action and advise other interested offices in the Department or United States Attorneys' offices of any contemplated civil action. Absent a specific, detailed statement that there is a strong likelihood that institution of a civil action would materially prejudice contemplated criminal prosecution of specific subjects, the decision to institute civil action is governed solely by the standards specified in 38 Op. Att'y Gen. 98 (1934). That is, the suit is instituted unless there is doubt as to collectability or doubt as to the facts or law. . . .

I. Inquiries should be directed to: Director, Commercial Litigation Branch, Civil Division, and Chief, Fraud Section, Criminal Division.

J. Each United States Attorney's Office has an Affirmative Civil Enforcement (ACE) coordinator, who should be consulted on issues arising from parallel criminal and civil cases.

UNITED STATES ATTORNEYS' MANUAL, MULTI-DISTRICT (GLOBAL) AGREEMENT REQUESTS

§9-27.641

A. No district or division shall make any agreement, including any agreement not to prosecute, which purports to bind any other district(s) or division without the express written approval of the United States Attorney(s) in each affected district and/or the Assistant Attorney General of the Criminal Division.

The requesting district/division shall make known to each affected district/division the following information:

1. The specific crimes allegedly committed in the affected district(s) as disclosed by the defendant. (No agreement should be made as to any crime(s) not disclosed by the defendant.)
2. Identification of victims of crimes committed by the defendant in any affected district, insofar as possible.
3. The proposed agreement to be made with the defendant and the applicable Sentencing Guideline range.

RICHARD MARMARO & JOHN W. CRUMPACKER, GOVERNMENT PROCUREMENT: THE EVER-EXPANDING SCOPE OF LIABILITY AND METHODS OF DAMAGE CONTROL

161 PLI/CRIM. 371 (1991)

1. Prior to entering into settlement discussions, counsel must identify and prioritize the contractor's goals. "Global settlements" are almost always the ultimate goal. Although generally difficult to obtain, such settlements allow the contractor to conclusively limit liability, secure finality and, hopefully, resume its normal business activities. The alternative—a multi-front defense of parallel proceedings—can be completely unmanageable. To increase the likelihood of securing a global agreement (or something close to it), counsel must consider both the legal and practical limitations involved.
2. The primary limitation—general prosecutorial reluctance to enter into global settlements binding agencies other than their own—is founded in both legal and practical concerns. As a practical matter, government officials try to avoid "stepping on the feet" of their compatriots and fear having to justify their existence subsequent to "giving a case away." As a legal matter, prosecutors involved in "global settlements" have a legitimate concern of later being charged with improper conduct and abuse of the criminal process based on allegations that the criminal case was used to extract a civil settlement.

* * *

4. There may be additional practical limitations on the acquisition of a global settlement as a result of political pressures in high profile cases and prior "settlement precedent" with respect to factually similar cases. Thus, counsel should be armed with supporting "comparables" prior to the commencement of formal negotiations. Because the identification of a proposed settlement which is palatable to the government and which provides the contractor with maximum benefit is a highly fact specific process, there is no substitute for a thorough review of recent dispositions within the district, the circuit and the industry as a whole.

5. Fortunately, global settlements are often in the government's best interest as well. All inclusive agreements potentially allow the government to: (a) obtain a guilty plea from the responsible party without a protracted trial and the risk of high profile defeat; (b) recover restitution resulting from improper conduct and assess penalties; (c) purge corrupt employees from both the corporation and the government; (d) change the contractor's "improper" methods of doing business; and (e) avoid a multi-front battle which could result from litigating parallel proceedings. Ultimately, the probability of "selling" a global settlement to the government may be dependent on counsel's ability to effectively and unambiguously communicate a fair proposal to all relevant officials.

NOTES AND QUESTIONS

1. Quoting an old Attorney General Memorandum, §9-42.010(E) of the U.S. Attorneys' Manual directs that, when parallel proceedings are contemplated, "documents should be obtained by methods other than grand jury subpoenas [if possible]." Why is this so?
2. Thirty years ago, it was nearly impossible for a U.S. Attorney's Office to obtain approval to enter into a global settlement with a group of defendants. Today, these settlements have become more or less routine. Other than attitudes, what has changed in the intervening years?

chapter **14**

Sentencing in Federal White Collar Cases

I. PROLOGUE

Modern-day sentencing practices in the United States stem from the mid-nineteenth century. Long sentences, combined with rapid population growth and increasingly sophisticated police practices, had culminated in a crushing prison overcrowding problem, particularly in big cities. This predicament refocused sentencing from the harsh retributivist ideal prevalent in early colonial America to an approach based on the principle of rehabilitation. The sentencing judge acquired greater discretion in formulating a sentence, and newly created parole boards made the ultimate determination as to when a prisoner had been sufficiently "cured" to warrant release (called "parole"). In 1870, New York became the first state to adopt a comprehensive open-ended—or "indeterminate"—sentencing system. By 1922, the federal government and all but four states employed either an indeterminate or similar parole-based sentencing system. Every state had an indeterminate system by the 1960s.

The rehabilitative ideal began to decline in the face of ever-increasing crime rates experienced in U.S. urban centers during the 1970s and '80s. While those in favor of rehabilitation continued to see offenders as victims of social injustice who needed education, training, and a second chance, others began to question whether rehabilitation failed to deter criminal activity and to achieve justice by not adequately punishing the guilty. As a result, throughout the 1970s, many states changed their sentencing laws. California, a state that previously had been at the forefront of the rehabilitative movement, replaced its indeterminate sentencing system with a determinate one in 1976. The new California law abolished parole and required judges to impose specific sentences for major felonies, allowing for a higher or lower sentence only if adequate aggravating or mitigating circumstances were present.

Eventually, Congress also became disillusioned with the perceived inadequacies of the indeterminate sentencing regime. It had grown tired of a system that led to huge disparities in sentences among those who committed the same crime based upon their personal characteristics or, worse yet, the random proclivities of the federal judges involved. In addition, the indeterminate system appeared to be downright dishonest: For example, most offenders served only one-third of their sentence, and "life imprisonment" typically meant only ten years behind bars (both due to the availability of parole). Thus, in 1984, Congress established the U.S. Sentencing Commission[1] and directed it to draft a set of mandatory sentencing guidelines.

To calculate a sentence under the U.S. Sentencing Guidelines, one must first consult the index to find the guideline corresponding to the offense in question. From this, one can discern the crime's "base offense level." This guideline also delineates specific offense characteristics that may add or subtract levels to the base. For example, fraud crimes start out at a base offense level of 6 or 7, depending upon the particular crime.[2] The offense level is then increased according to the amount of money lost by the scheme's victims. For frauds involving between $5,000 and $9,999, two offense levels are added; for frauds involving more than $400,000,000, the additional number of offense levels is 30.[3] The Guidelines mandate other offense-specific adjustments for fraud crimes based on criteria such as whether (1) the offense involved multiple victims;[4] (2) the offense involved theft of a trade secret;[5] (3) the fraudulent scheme was relocated to a new jurisdiction to avoid law enforcement detection;[6] or (4) the offense involved "sophisticated means."[7] In addition to offense-specific adjustments, the Guidelines also call for across-the-board adjustments to be taken into account. These include a possible increase in offense levels if the defendant attempted to obstruct justice and a decrease if, once caught, he accepted responsibility for his conduct.[8] The Guidelines also feature rules on aggregation for multi-count indictments.[9]

1. The Commission is an independent entity within the judicial branch of government. *See* 28 U.S.C. §991(a). It has seven members, including no more than three federal judges, appointed by the President with the advice and consent of the Senate. The Attorney General and Chief of the Parole Commission are non-voting ex-officio members.

2. §2B1.1.

3. It should therefore come as no surprise that a key issue during the sentencing phase of many white collar cases is calculating the correct amount of loss for guideline purposes. *See, e.g.*, United States v. Turk, 626 F.3d 743 (2d Cir. 2010) (calculating loss where fraud involved deceit about the position of mortgages and determining that the correct starting point is the amount of the principal balance of the loans, not an expectation of the future value of the collateral); United States v. Mancini, 624 F.3d 879, 881-82 (8th Cir. 2010) (agreeing with the First, Third, Seventh, and Eleventh Circuits that "loss resulting from a mortgage fraud includes loss to the mortgage insurer"); United States v. Ebbers, 458 F.3d 110 (2d Cir. 2006) (holding that in securities fraud case, losses from market forces must be deducted from losses caused by defendant's conduct); United States v. Mallory, 709 F. Supp. 2d 455 (E.D. Va. 2010) (same as *Mancini*).

4. §2B1.1(2).

5. §2B1.1(5).

6. §2B1.1(9)(A).

7. §2B1.1(9)(C).

8. *See* Guidelines, Ch. 3.

9. *Id.*

After the defendant's offense level is determined, attention shifts to his criminal history. Up to one prior conviction will place the defendant in criminal history category "I"; two or three convictions, category II; four, five, or six convictions, category III; and progressively up to category VI.[10] Once the criminal history category is calculated, the defendant's sentencing range is computed using the Sentencing Table, which is a grid that places offense levels down a vertical axis and criminal history categories horizontally across the top. The box where the two intersect contains the sentencing range for this defendant, expressed in months. The lower and higher ends of the range differ by no more than fourteen months.

In general, the Sentencing Commission calculated the base offense level for individual crimes by calculating the national average of judge's pre-Guidelines sentences. One of the goals of the new system, however, "was to eliminate the two-tier system of justice in which white collar criminals received lenient treatment for acts of theft and fraud that would merit lengthy prison terms if committed on the street."[11] As a result, the Guidelines' enactment caused an immediate and substantial increase in jail time for white collar offenders. No longer could they make pleas for mercy based upon, among other things, their philanthropy, service on corporate or community boards, or the argument that they had already suffered enough. The party, so to speak, was over.

The system's treatment of white collar defendants became even more harsh as time went on, typically in response to a huge scandal or economic meltdown:

> In recent years, sentences have increased for many white collar crimes. The . . . Sentencing Commission . . . attributes two factors to the increased rate of imprisonment in the fraud/theft category. First is the fact that 'statutory and guideline penalties increased for many fraud offenses as a result of the [Sentencing] Commission's Economic Crime Package of 2001, the 2002 Sarbanes-Oxley Act and other recent legislation. Second is the increased number of prosecutions.[12]

Consequently, a white collar defendant who, back in 1985, could expect a probationary sentence could today face incarceration of five, ten, or even 25 years, depending primarily on the magnitude of the economic harm caused by his illicit activity.

When the Federal Sentencing Guidelines were originally adopted, the imposition of a guidelines sentence was mandatory. This, of course, severely diminished the range of possible sentences a judge could impose in any given case. In limited circumstances, the court could depart upward or downward from the guideline range, but it was required to state specific reasons for doing so. Even more constraining, departures were only permissible if "there exist[ed] an aggravating or mitigating circumstance of a kind, or to a degree, not adequately taken into consideration by the Sentencing Commission in formulating the guidelines."[13] Judges quickly found that there was very little that the Commission had not taken into account.

10. *See* Guidelines, Ch. 4.

11. Senator Edward M. Kennedy, *Address Before the U.S. Sentencing Commission Symposium on Corporate Crime*, Sept. 12, 1995.

12. Ellen S. Podgor, *The Challenge of White Collar Sentencing*, 97 J. CRIM. L. & CRIMINOLOGY 731, 752 (2007).

13. Guidelines, §5K2.0; 18 U.S.C. § 3553(b)(1).

The Commission's agenda was even more focused. It had designed the Guidelines to encourage routine downward departures in only one scenario: when a defendant "switched sides"; that is, when he confessed and cooperated with authorities. Under §5K1.1, a court is empowered to depart downward without limitation (other than a statutory mandatory minimum) if it finds that the defendant has provided the government with "substantial assistance in the investigation or prosecution of another person who has committed an offense." Prosecutors, not defense counsel, have unfettered discretion to determine whether to file a §5K1.1. This feature of the Guidelines undoubtedly helps federal prosecutors take down large conspiracies,[14] but many participants and observers question the cost. To a large extent, federal prosecution is an edifice built on the testimony of turncoats.[15]

The Guidelines were also designed to punish the full scope of a defendant's criminal activity, regardless of the specific charges leveled against him. This is known as "real offense" (as opposed to "charge-based") sentencing, and it requires the sentencing judge to take into account all of the defendant's "relevant conduct."[16] This includes conduct for which the defendant has been acquitted by the jury, as long as the judge finds that the defendant engaged in such conduct by a preponderance of the evidence. Defendants' attacks on this practice as being in violation of the Double Jeopardy Clause were twice rejected by the Supreme Court.[17]

Persistent defense assaults on the constitutionality of the Guidelines finally began to yield fruit around the turn of the century. By this time, many federal judges had become receptive audiences because they resented the Guidelines for stripping them of their discretion and converting sentencing into a mathematical operation.[18] In Apprendi v. New Jersey, 530 U.S. 466 (2000), the Supreme Court considered whether, pursuant to the Due Process Clause of the Fourteenth Amendment, a factual determination authorizing an increase in a prison sentence must be made by the jury on the basis of proof beyond a reasonable doubt. Apprendi had been charged with possession of a firearm for an unlawful purpose, a second-degree offense punishable by imprisonment for between five and ten years. A separate New Jersey hate crime statute provided that, if the trial judge found by a preponderance of the evidence that the defendant's conduct met the definition of a hate crime, the judge could extend the term of imprisonment by an additional ten to 20 years, a power exercised in Apprendi's case. The Supreme Court held that, other

14. *See* United States v. Mateos, 623 F.3d 1350, 1367 (11th Cir. 2010) (affirming sentencing disparities between co-conspirators when some defendants substantially assist the government, even if those co-conspirators are more highly involved in the fraudulent scheme); United States v. Bras, 483 F.3d 103, 114 (D.C. Cir. 2007) (agreeing with the trial court that the substantial assistance in the investigation by co-conspirators brought to light the extent of the fraudulent scheme).

15. *See, e.g.*, United States v. Gallegos, 480 F.3d 856, 859 (8th Cir. 2007) (holding substantially lower sentence for co-defendant was not unwarranted since the co-defendant cooperated with law enforcement by placing calls to defendant, assisting in surveillance, and leading agents to other co-conspirators' residences).

16. §1B1.3.

17. *See* United States v. Watts, 519 U.S. 148 (1997); United States v. Witte, 515 U.S. 389 (1995).

18. *See* Sandra D. Jordan, *Have We Come Full Circle? Judicial Sentencing Discretion Revived in* Booker *and* Fanfan, 33 Pepp. L. Rev. 615, 624-626 (2006).

than the fact of a prior conviction, any fact that could potentially increase the sentence for a crime beyond the statutory maximum must be decided by the jury and proved by the State beyond a reasonable doubt.

Apprendi involved a statutory scheme—rather than sentencing guidelines, which at the time many saw as a significant distinction. Presumably, guidelines would be insulated from an *Apprendi*-type challenge because guideline sentences are capped by the crime's maximum statutory sentence. To the Supreme Court, however, this distinction turned out to be immaterial.

II. THE PARTIAL DEMISE OF THE SENTENCING GUIDELINES

BLAKELY v. WASHINGTON

524 U.S. 296 (2004)

Justice Scalia delivered the opinion of the Court.[19]

Petitioner Ralph Howard Blakely, Jr., pleaded guilty to the kidnapping of his estranged wife. The facts admitted in his plea, standing alone, supported a maximum sentence of 53 months. Pursuant to state law, the court imposed an "exceptional" sentence of 90 months after making a judicial determination that he had acted with "deliberate cruelty." We consider whether this violated petitioner's Sixth Amendment right to trial by jury.

I.

Petitioner married his wife Yolanda in 1973. He was evidently a difficult man to live with, having been diagnosed at various times with psychological and personality disorders including paranoid schizophrenia. His wife ultimately filed for divorce. In 1998, he abducted her from their orchard home in Grant County, Washington, binding her with duct tape and forcing her at knifepoint into a wooden box in the bed of his pickup truck. In the process, he implored her to dismiss the divorce suit and related trust proceedings.

When the couple's 13-year-old son Ralphy returned home from school, petitioner ordered him to follow in another car, threatening to harm Yolanda with a shotgun if he did not do so. Ralphy escaped and sought help when they stopped at a gas station, but petitioner continued on with Yolanda to a friend's house in Montana. He was finally arrested after the friend called the police.

The State charged petitioner with first-degree kidnapping. Upon reaching a plea agreement, however, it reduced the charge to second-degree kidnapping involving domestic violence and use of a firearm. Petitioner entered a guilty plea admitting the elements of second-degree kidnapping and the domestic-violence and firearm allegations, but no other relevant facts.

19. [Stevens, Souter, Thomas, and Ginsberg, JJ., joined.—Eds.]

The case then proceeded to sentencing. In Washington, second-degree kidnapping is a class B felony. State law provides that "[n]o person convicted of a [class B] felony shall be punished by confinement . . . exceeding . . . a term of ten years." Other provisions of state law, however, further limit the range of sentences a judge may impose. Washington's Sentencing Reform Act specifies, for petitioner's offense of second-degree kidnapping with a firearm, a "standard range" of 49 to 53 months. A judge may impose a sentence above the standard range if he finds "substantial and compelling reasons justifying an exceptional sentence." . . . Pursuant to the plea agreement, the State recommended a sentence within the standard range of 49 to 53 months. After hearing Yolanda's description of the kidnapping, however, the judge rejected the State's recommendation and imposed an exceptional sentence of 90 months—37 months beyond the standard maximum. He justified the sentence on the ground that petitioner had acted with "deliberate cruelty," a statutorily enumerated ground for departure in domestic-violence cases. . . .

Petitioner appealed, arguing that this sentencing procedure deprived him of his federal constitutional right to have a jury determine beyond a reasonable doubt all facts legally essential to his sentence. The State Court of Appeals affirmed, The Washington Supreme Court denied discretionary review. We granted certiorari.

II.

This case requires us to apply the rule we expressed in Apprendi v. New Jersey, 530 U.S. 466, 490 (2000): "Other than the fact of a prior conviction, any fact that increases the penalty for a crime beyond the prescribed statutory maximum must be submitted to a jury, and proved beyond a reasonable doubt." This rule reflects two longstanding tenets of common-law criminal jurisprudence: that the "truth of every accusation" against a defendant "should afterwards be confirmed by the unanimous suffrage of twelve of his equals and neighbours," 4 W. Blackstone, Commentaries on the Laws of England 343 (1769), and that "an accusation which lacks any particular fact which the law makes essential to the punishment is . . . no accusation within the requirements of the common law, and it is no accusation in reason," 1 J. Bishop, Criminal Procedure §87, p. 55 (2d ed. 1872). These principles have been acknowledged by courts and treatises since the earliest days of graduated sentencing; we compiled the relevant authorities in *Apprendi* and need not repeat them here. . . .

In this case, petitioner was sentenced to more than three years above the 53-month statutory maximum of the standard range because he had acted with "deliberate cruelty." The facts supporting that finding were neither admitted by petitioner nor found by a jury. The State nevertheless contends that there was no *Apprendi* violation because the relevant "statutory maximum" is not 53 months, but the 10-year maximum for class B felonies. It observes that no exceptional sentence may exceed that limit. Our precedents make clear, however, that the "statutory maximum" for *Apprendi* purposes is the maximum sentence a judge may impose *solely on the basis of the facts reflected in the jury verdict or admitted by the defendant.* In other words, the relevant "statutory maximum" is not the maximum sentence a judge may impose after finding additional facts, but the maximum he may impose *without* any additional findings. When a judge inflicts punishment that the jury's verdict alone does not allow, the jury has not found all the facts "which the law makes essential to the punishment," and the judge exceeds his proper authority. . . .

Because the State's sentencing procedure did not comply with the Sixth Amendment, petitioner's sentence is invalid.

III.

Our commitment to *Apprendi* in this context reflects not just respect for longstanding precedent, but the need to give intelligible content to the right of jury trial. That right is no mere procedural formality, but a fundamental reservation of power in our constitutional structure. Just as suffrage ensures the people's ultimate control in the legislative and executive branches, jury trial is meant to ensure their control in the judiciary. *Apprendi* carries out this design by ensuring that the judge's authority to sentence derives wholly from the jury's verdict. Without that restriction, the jury would not exercise the control that the Framers intended.

Those who would reject *Apprendi* are resigned to one of two alternatives. The first is that the jury need only find whatever facts the legislature chooses to label elements of the crime, and that those it labels sentencing factors — no matter how much they may increase the punishment — may be found by the judge. This would mean, for example, that a judge could sentence a man for committing murder even if the jury convicted him only of illegally possessing the firearm used to commit it — or of making an illegal lane change while fleeing the death scene. Not even *Apprendi*'s critics would advocate this absurd result. The jury could not function as circuitbreaker in the State's machinery of justice if it were relegated to making a determination that the defendant at some point did something wrong, a mere preliminary to a judicial inquisition into the facts of the crime the State *actually* seeks to punish.

The second alternative is that legislatures may establish legally essential sentencing factors *within limits* — limits crossed when, perhaps, the sentencing factor is a "tail which wags the dog of the substantive offense." What this means in operation is that the law must not go *too far* — it must not exceed the judicial estimation of the proper role of the judge.

The subjectivity of this standard is obvious. Petitioner argued below that second-degree kidnapping with deliberate cruelty was essentially the same as first-degree kidnapping, the very charge he had avoided by pleading to a lesser offense. The court conceded this might be so but held it irrelevant. Petitioner's 90-month sentence exceeded the 53-month standard maximum by almost 70%; the Washington Supreme Court in other cases has upheld exceptional sentences 15 times the standard maximum. Did the court go *too far* in any of these cases? There is no answer that legal analysis can provide. With *too far* as the yardstick, it is always possible to disagree with such judgments and never to refute them.

Whether the Sixth Amendment incorporates this manipulable standard rather than *Apprendi*'s bright-line rule depends on the plausibility of the claim that the Framers would have left definition of the scope of jury power up to judges' intuitive sense of how far is *too far*. We think that claim not plausible at all, because the very reason the Framers put a jury-trial guarantee in the Constitution is that they were unwilling to trust government to mark out the role of the jury.

IV.

. . . Justice O'Connor argues that, because determinate-sentencing schemes involving judicial factfinding entail less judicial discretion than indeterminate schemes, the constitutionality of the latter implies the constitutionality of the former. This argument is flawed on a number of levels. First, the Sixth Amendment by its terms is not a limitation on judicial power, but a reservation of jury power. It limits judicial power only to the extent that the claimed judicial power infringes on the province of the jury. Indeterminate sentencing does not do so. It increases judicial discretion, to be sure, but not at the expense of the jury's traditional function of finding the facts essential to lawful imposition of the penalty. Of course indeterminate schemes involve judicial factfinding, in that a judge (like a parole board) may implicitly rule on those facts he deems important to the exercise of his sentencing discretion. But the facts do not pertain to whether the defendant has a legal *right* to a lesser sentence—and that makes all the difference insofar as judicial impingement upon the traditional role of the jury is concerned. In a system that says the judge may punish burglary with 10 to 40 years, every burglar knows he is risking 40 years in jail. In a system that punishes burglary with a 10-year sentence, with another 30 added for use of a gun, the burglar who enters a home unarmed is *entitled* to no more than a 10-year sentence—and by reason of the Sixth Amendment the facts bearing upon that entitlement must be found by a jury.

But even assuming that restraint of judicial power unrelated to the jury's role is a Sixth Amendment objective, it is far from clear that *Apprendi* disserves that goal. Determinate judicial-factfinding schemes entail less judicial power than indeterminate schemes, but more judicial power than determinate *jury*-factfinding schemes. Whether *Apprendi* increases judicial power overall depends on what States with determinate judicial-factfinding schemes would do, given the choice between the two alternatives. Justice O'Connor simply assumes that the net effect will favor judges, but she has no empirical basis for that prediction. Indeed, what evidence we have points exactly the other way: When the Kansas Supreme Court found *Apprendi* infirmities in that State's determinate-sentencing regime in State v. Gould, 271 Kan. 394, 404-14 (2001), the legislature responded not by reestablishing indeterminate sentencing but by applying *Apprendi*'s requirements to its current regime. The result was less, not more, judicial power. . . .

The judgment of the Washington Court of Appeals is reversed, and the case is remanded for further proceedings not inconsistent with this opinion.

It is so ordered.

Justice O'Connor, dissenting.

The legacy of today's opinion, whether intended or not, will be the consolidation of sentencing power in the State and Federal Judiciaries. The Court says to Congress and state legislatures: If you want to constrain the sentencing discretion of judges and bring some uniformity to sentencing, it will cost you—dearly. Congress and States, faced with the burdens imposed by the extension of *Apprendi* to the present context, will either trim or eliminate altogether their sentencing guidelines schemes and, with them, 20 years of sentencing reform. It is thus of little moment that the majority does not expressly declare guidelines schemes unconstitutional, for, as residents of "*Apprendi*-land" are fond of saying, "the relevant inquiry is one not of form, but of effect." The "effect" of today's decision will be greater judicial discretion and less uniformity in sentencing. Because I find it implausible that the Framers would have considered such a result to be required by the Due Process Clause or the Sixth Amendment, and because the practical consequences of today's decision may be disastrous, I respectfully dissent. . . .

II.

Far from disregarding principles of due process and the jury trial right, as the majority today suggests, Washington's reform has served them. Before passage of the Act, a defendant charged with second degree kidnapping, like petitioner, had no idea whether he would receive a 10-year sentence or probation. The ultimate sentencing determination could turn as much on the idiosyncrasies of a particular judge as on the specifics of the defendant's crime or background. A defendant did not know what facts, if any, about his offense or his history would be considered relevant by the sentencing judge or by the parole board. After passage of the Act, a defendant charged with second degree kidnapping knows what his presumptive sentence will be; he has a good idea of the types of factors that a sentencing judge can and will consider when deciding whether to sentence him outside that range; he is guaranteed meaningful appellate review to protect against an arbitrary sentence. Criminal defendants still face the same statutory maximum sentences, but they now at least know, much more than before, the real consequences of their actions. . . .

The majority does not, because it cannot, disagree that determinate sentencing schemes, like Washington's, serve important constitutional values. Thus, the majority says: "This case is not about whether determinate sentencing is constitutional, only about how it can be implemented in a way that respects the Sixth Amendment." But extension of *Apprendi* to the present context will impose significant costs on a legislature's determination that a particular fact, not historically an element, warrants a higher sentence. While not a constitutional prohibition on guidelines schemes, the majority's decision today exacts a substantial constitutional tax.

The costs are substantial and real. Under the majority's approach, any fact that increases the upper bound on a judge's sentencing discretion is an element of the offense. Thus, facts that historically have been taken into account by sentencing judges to assess a sentence within a broad range—such as drug quantity, role in the offense, risk of bodily harm—all must now be charged in an indictment and submitted to a jury simply because it is the legislature, rather than the judge, that constrains the extent to which such facts may be used to impose a sentence within a pre-existing statutory range. . . .

Some facts that bear on sentencing either will not be discovered, or are not discoverable, prior to trial. For instance, a legislature might desire that defendants who act in an obstructive manner during trial or post-trial proceedings receive a greater sentence than defendants who do not. In such cases, the violation arises too late for the State to provide notice to the defendant or to argue the facts to the jury. A State wanting to make such facts relevant at sentencing must now either vest sufficient discretion in the judge to account for them *or* bring a separate criminal prosecution for obstruction of justice or perjury. And, the latter option is available only to the extent that a defendant's obstructive behavior is so severe as to constitute an already-existing separate offense, unless the legislature is willing to undertake the unlikely expense of criminalizing relatively minor obstructive behavior. . . .

The majority may be correct that States and the Federal Government will be willing to bear some of these costs. But simple economics dictate that they will not, and cannot, bear them all. To the extent that they do not, there will be an inevitable increase in judicial discretion with all of its attendant failings. . . .

IV.

A.

The consequences of today's decision will be as far reaching as they are disturbing. Washington's sentencing system is by no means unique. Numerous other States have enacted guidelines systems, as has the Federal Government. Today's decision casts constitutional doubt over them all and, in so doing, threatens an untold number of criminal judgments. Every sentence imposed under such guidelines in cases currently pending on direct appeal is in jeopardy. . . .[2]

The practical consequences for trial courts, starting today, will be equally unsettling: How are courts to mete out guidelines sentences? Do courts apply the guidelines as to mitigating factors, but not as to aggravating factors? Do they jettison the guidelines altogether? The Court ignores the havoc it is about to wreak on trial courts across the country. . . .

Justice BREYER, dissenting.

. . . The majority ignores the adverse consequences inherent in its conclusion. As a result of the majority's rule, sentencing must now take one of three forms, each of which risks either impracticality, unfairness, or harm to the jury trial right the majority purports to strengthen. This circumstance shows that the majority's Sixth Amendment interpretation cannot be right.

A.

A first option for legislators is to create a simple, pure or nearly pure "charge offense" or "determinate" sentencing system. In such a system, an indictment would charge a few facts which, taken together, constitute a crime, such as robbery. Robbery would

2. The numbers available from the federal system alone are staggering. On March 31, 2004, there were 8,320 federal criminal appeals pending in which the defendant's sentence was at issue. Between June 27, 2000, when *Apprendi* was decided, and March 31, 2004, there have been 272,191 defendants sentenced in federal court. Given that nearly all federal sentences are governed by the Federal Sentencing Guidelines, the vast majority of these cases are Guidelines cases.

carry a single sentence, say, five years' imprisonment. And every person convicted of robbery would receive that sentence—just as, centuries ago, everyone convicted of almost any serious crime was sentenced to death.

Such a system assures uniformity, but at intolerable costs. First, simple determinate sentencing systems impose identical punishments on people who committed their crimes in very different ways. When dramatically different conduct ends up being punished the same way, an injustice has taken place. Simple determinate sentencing has the virtue of treating like cases alike, but it simultaneously fails to treat different cases differently. . . .

B.

A second option for legislators is to return to a system of indeterminate sentencing, such as California had before the recent sentencing reform movement. Under indeterminate systems, the length of the sentence is entirely or almost entirely within the discretion of the judge or of the parole board, which typically has broad power to decide when to release a prisoner.

When such systems were in vogue, they were criticized, and rightly so, for producing unfair disparities, including race-based disparities, in the punishment of similarly situated defendants. The length of time a person spent in prison appeared to depend on "what the judge ate for breakfast" on the day of sentencing, on which judge you got, or on other factors that should not have made a difference to the length of the sentence. And under such a system, the judge could vary the sentence greatly based upon his findings about how the defendant had committed the crime—findings that might not have been made by a "preponderance of the evidence," much less "beyond a reasonable doubt."

Returning to such a system would diminish the "'reason'" the majority claims it is trying to uphold. It also would do little to "ensur[e] [the] control" of what the majority calls "the peopl[e,]" *i.e.*, the jury, "in the judiciary," since "the peopl[e]" would only decide the defendant's guilt, a finding with no effect on the duration of the sentence. While "the judge's authority to sentence" would formally derive from the jury's verdict, the jury would exercise little or no control over the sentence itself. It is difficult to see how such an outcome protects the structural safeguards the majority claims to be defending.

C.

A third option is that which the Court seems to believe legislators will in fact take. That is the option of retaining structured schemes that attempt to punish similar conduct similarly and different conduct differently, but modifying them to conform to *Apprendi*'s dictates. Judges would be able to depart *downward* from presumptive sentences upon finding that mitigating factors were present, but would not be able to depart *upward* unless the prosecutor charged the aggravating fact to a jury and proved it beyond a reasonable doubt. The majority argues, based on the single example of Kansas, that most legislatures will enact amendments along these lines in the face of the oncoming *Apprendi* train. It is therefore worth exploring how this option could work in practice, as well as the assumptions on which it depends.

1.

This option can be implemented in one of two ways. The first way would be for legislatures to subdivide each crime into a list of complex crimes, each of which would be defined to include commonly found sentencing factors such as drug quantity, type of victim, presence of violence, degree of injury, use of gun, and so on. A legislature, for example, might enact a robbery statute, modeled on robbery sentencing guidelines, that increases punishment depending upon (1) the nature of the institution robbed, (2) the (a) presence of, (b) brandishing of, (c) other use of, a firearm, (3) making of a death threat, (4) presence of (a) ordinary, (b) serious, (c) permanent or life threatening, bodily injury, (5) abduction, (6) physical restraint, (7) taking of a firearm, (8) taking of drugs, (9) value of property loss, etc.

This possibility is, of course, merely a highly calibrated form of the "pure charge" system discussed in Part I-A, *supra.* And it suffers from some of the same defects. The prosecutor, through control of the precise charge, controls the punishment, thereby marching the sentencing system directly away from, not toward, one important guideline goal: rough uniformity of punishment for those who engage in roughly the same *real* criminal conduct. The artificial (and consequently unfair) nature of the resulting sentence is aggravated by the fact that prosecutors must charge all relevant facts about the way the crime was committed before a presentence investigation examines the criminal conduct, perhaps before the trial itself, *i.e.*, before many of the facts relevant to punishment are known.

This "complex charge offense" system also prejudices defendants who seek trial, for it can put them in the untenable position of contesting material aggravating facts in the guilt phases of their trials. . . .

2.

The second way to make sentencing guidelines *Apprendi*-compliant would be to require at least two juries for each defendant whenever aggravating facts are present: one jury to determine guilt of the crime charged, and an additional jury to try the disputed facts that, if found, would aggravate the sentence. Our experience with bifurcated trials in the capital punishment context suggests that requiring them for run-of-the-mill sentences would be costly, both in money and in judicial time and resources. In the context of noncapital crimes, the potential need for a second indictment alleging aggravating facts, the likely need for formal evidentiary rules to prevent prejudice, and the increased difficulty of obtaining relevant sentencing information, all will mean greater complexity, added cost, and further delay. Indeed, cost and delay could lead legislatures to revert to the complex charge offense system described in Part I-C-1, *supra*. . . .

D.

Is there a fourth option? Perhaps. Congress and state legislatures might, for example, rewrite their criminal codes, attaching astronomically high sentences to each crime, followed by long lists of mitigating facts, which, for the most part, would consist of the absence of aggravating facts. But political impediments to legislative action make such rewrites difficult to achieve; and it is difficult to see why the Sixth Amendment would require legislatures to undertake them.

It may also prove possible to find combinations of, or variations upon, my first three options. But I am unaware of any variation that does not involve (a) the shift of power to the prosecutor (weakening the connection between real conduct and real punishment) inherent in any charge offense system, (b) the lack of uniformity inherent in any system of pure judicial discretion, or (c) the complexity, expense, and increased reliance on plea bargains involved in a "two-jury" system. The simple fact is that the design of any fair sentencing system must involve efforts to make practical compromises among competing goals. The majority's reading of the Sixth Amendment makes the effort to find those compromises—already difficult—virtually impossible. . . .

[The dissenting opinion of Kennedy, J. is omitted.]

NOTES AND QUESTIONS

1. In the days of indeterminate sentencing, a judge could take into account any facts she wanted when fashioning a defendant's sentence, as long as the sentence did not exceed the statutory maximum prescribed for the crime of conviction. The jury did not need to find these facts. Indeed, the judge was not even required to articulate what they were, meaning that they could be completely unrelated to the crime charged (e.g., the defendant's educational history or his experiences as a child). If judicially found facts under a guideline system must be decided by the jury, it would seem that the same should hold true for the facts used by a judge in the indeterminate setting as well, no? But Justice Scalia says that indeterminate sentencing is perfectly constitutional. How does he pull that rabbit out of his hat? Is his argument convincing?
2. Justices O'Connor and Breyer both focus on the practical consequences of the *Blakely* holding. Indeed, Justice Breyer very specifically relates a parade of horrible alternatives to a determinate guideline system. Is he convincing? Are there any alternatives he leaves out?
3. Justice Breyer had more than a passing interest in the Federal Sentencing Guidelines. From 1985 to 1989, while a judge on the U.S. Court of Appeals for the First Circuit, he served as a member of the U.S. Sentencing Commission. He played a key role in reforming federal criminal sentencing procedures and producing the very first version of the Federal Sentencing Guidelines. Thus, in some sense, he was fighting in these cases to save his own creation.
4. For a classic defense-oriented critique of guideline sentences for white collar criminals, see Ellen S. Podgor, *The Challenge of White Collar Sentencing*, 97 J. Crim. L. & Criminology 731 (2007).

The *Blakely* decision created pandemonium in both federal and state courts. It called into question hundreds of thousands of sentences handed down pursuant to mandatory guideline systems. States, it seemed, had no option but to comply.

However, the Department of Justice held out hope that, somehow, the federal sentencing guidelines would survive an *Apprendi* challenge. In the meantime, federal prosecutors had no idea how to charge new cases in the vacuum left by *Blakely's* wake. Recognizing the chaotic situation it had caused, the Supreme Court agreed to consolidate and review the next sentencing cases on an expedited basis. Argument was heard during the first week of the 2004 Term and the opinion came down a few months later.

UNITED STATES v. BOOKER
UNITED STATES v. FANFAN

543 U.S. 220 (2005)

Justice STEVENS delivered the opinion of the Court in part.*

The question presented in each of these cases is whether an application of the Federal Sentencing Guidelines violated the Sixth Amendment. In each case, the courts below held that binding rules set forth in the Guidelines limited the severity of the sentence that the judge could lawfully impose on the defendant based on the facts found by the jury at his trial. . . . We hold that both courts correctly concluded that the Sixth Amendment as construed in *Blakely* does apply to the Sentencing Guidelines. In a separate opinion authored by Justice Breyer, the Court concludes that in light of this holding, two provisions of the Sentencing Reform Act of 1984 (SRA) that have the effect of making the Guidelines mandatory must be invalidated in order to allow the statute to operate in a manner consistent with congressional intent.

I.

Respondent Booker was charged with possession with intent to distribute at least 50 grams of cocaine base (crack). Having heard evidence that he had 92.5 grams in his duffel bag, the jury found him guilty of violating 21 U.S.C. §841(a)(1). That statute prescribes a minimum sentence of 10 years in prison and a maximum sentence of life for that offense. §841(b)(1)(A)(iii).

Based upon Booker's criminal history and the quantity of drugs found by the jury, the Sentencing Guidelines required the District Court Judge to select a "base" sentence of not less than 210 nor more than 262 months in prison. See United States Sentencing Commission, Guidelines Manual §§2D1.1(c)(4), 4A1.1 (Nov. 2003) (USSG). The judge, however, held a post-trial sentencing proceeding and concluded by a preponderance of the evidence that Booker had possessed an additional 566 grams of crack and that he was guilty of obstructing justice. Those findings mandated that the judge select a sentence between 360 months and life imprisonment; the judge imposed a sentence at the low end of the range. Thus, instead of the sentence of 21 years and 10 months that the judge could have imposed on the basis of the facts proved to the jury beyond a reasonable doubt, Booker received a 30-year sentence. . . .

*Justice Scalia, Justice Souter, Justice Thomas, and Justice Ginsburg join this opinion.

Respondent Fanfan was charged with conspiracy to distribute and to possess with intent to distribute at least 500 grams of cocaine in violation of 21 U.S.C. §§846, 841(a)(1), and 841(b)(1)(B)(ii). He was convicted by the jury after it answered "Yes" to the question "Was the amount of cocaine 500 or more grams?" Under the Guidelines, without additional findings of fact, the maximum sentence authorized by the jury verdict was imprisonment for 78 months.

A few days after our decision in *Blakely*, the trial judge conducted a sentencing hearing at which he found additional facts that, under the Guidelines, would have authorized a sentence in the 188-to-235-month range. Specifically, he found that respondent Fanfan was responsible for 2.5 kilograms of cocaine powder, and 261.6 grams of crack. He also concluded that respondent had been an organizer, leader, manager, or supervisor in the criminal activity. Both findings were made by a preponderance of the evidence. Under the Guidelines, these additional findings would have required an enhanced sentence of 15 or 16 years instead of the 5 or 6 years authorized by the jury verdict alone. Relying not only on the majority opinion in *Blakely*, but also on the categorical statements in the dissenting opinions and in the Solicitor General's brief in *Blakely*, the judge concluded that he could not follow the particular provisions of the Sentencing Guidelines "which involve drug quantity and role enhancement," *id.*, at 11a. Expressly refusing to make "any blanket decision about the federal guidelines," he followed the provisions of the Guidelines that did not implicate the Sixth Amendment by imposing a sentence on respondent "based solely upon the jury verdict in this case."

Following the denial of its motion to correct the sentence in Fanfan's case, the Government filed a notice of appeal in the Court of Appeals for the First Circuit, and a petition in this Court for a writ of certiorari before judgment. Because of the importance of the questions presented, we granted that petition, as well as a similar petition filed by the Government in Booker's case. In both petitions, the Government asks us to determine whether our *Apprendi* line of cases applies to the Sentencing Guidelines, and if so, what portions of the Guidelines remain in effect.

In this opinion, we explain why we agree with the lower courts' answer to the first question. In a separate opinion for the Court, Justice Breyer explains the Court's answer to the second question.

II.

. . . As the dissenting opinions in *Blakely* recognized, there is no distinction of constitutional significance between the Federal Sentencing Guidelines and the Washington procedures at issue in that case. This conclusion rests on the premise, common to both systems, that the relevant sentencing rules are mandatory and impose binding requirements on all sentencing judges.

If the Guidelines as currently written could be read as merely advisory provisions that recommended, rather than required, the selection of particular sentences in response to differing sets of facts, their use would not implicate the Sixth Amendment. We have never doubted the authority of a judge to exercise broad discretion in imposing a sentence within a statutory range. *See Apprendi*, 530 U.S. at 481. Indeed, everyone agrees that the constitutional issues presented by these cases would have been avoided entirely if Congress had omitted from the SRA the provisions that make the Guidelines binding on district judges; it is that circumstance that makes the Court's answer to the second question presented possible. For when a trial judge exercises his discretion to select a specific sentence within a defined range, the defendant has no right to a jury determination of the facts that the judge deems relevant.

The Guidelines as written, however, are not advisory; they are mandatory and binding on all judges. While subsection (a) of §3553 of the sentencing statute lists the Sentencing Guidelines as one factor to be considered in imposing a sentence, subsection (b) directs that the court "*shall* impose a sentence of the kind, and within the range" established by the Guidelines, subject to departures in specific, limited cases. (Emphasis added.) Because they are binding on judges, we have consistently held that the Guidelines have the force and effect of laws..

The availability of a departure in specified circumstances does not avoid the constitutional issue, just as it did not in *Blakely* itself. The Guidelines permit departures from the prescribed sentencing range in cases in which the judge "finds that there exists an aggravating or mitigating circumstance of a kind, or to a degree, not adequately taken into consideration by the Sentencing Commission in formulating the guidelines that should result in a sentence different from that described." 18 U.S.C. §3553(b)(1). At first glance, one might believe that the ability of a district judge to depart from the Guidelines means that she is bound only by the statutory maximum. Were this the case, there would be no *Apprendi* problem. Importantly, however, departures are not available in every case, and in fact are unavailable in most. In most cases, as a matter of law, the Commission will have adequately taken all relevant factors into account, and no departure will be legally permissible. In those instances, the judge is bound to impose a sentence within the Guidelines range. It was for this reason that we rejected a similar argument in *Blakely*, holding that although the Washington statute allowed the judge to impose a sentence outside the sentencing range for "'substantial and compelling reasons,'" that exception was not available for Blakely himself. The sentencing judge would have been reversed had he invoked the departure section to justify the sentence.

Booker's case illustrates the mandatory nature of the Guidelines. The jury convicted him of possessing at least 50 grams of crack in violation of 21 U.S.C. §841(b)(1)(A)(iii) based on evidence that he had 92.5 grams of crack in his duffel bag. Under these facts, the Guidelines specified an offense level of 32, which, given the defendant's criminal history category, authorized a sentence of 210-to-262 months. See USSG §2D1.1(c)(4). Booker's is a run-of-the-mill drug case, and does not present any factors that were inadequately considered by the Commission. The sentencing judge would therefore have been reversed had he not imposed a sentence within the level 32 Guidelines range.

Booker's actual sentence, however, was 360 months, almost 10 years longer than the Guidelines range supported by the jury verdict alone. To reach this sentence, the judge found facts beyond those found by the jury: namely, that Booker possessed 566 grams of crack in addition to the 92.5 grams in his duffel bag. The jury never heard any evidence of the additional drug quantity, and the judge found it true by a preponderance of the evidence. Thus, just as in *Blakely*, "the jury's verdict alone does not authorize the sentence. The judge acquires that authority only upon finding some additional fact." There is no relevant distinction between the sentence imposed pursuant to the Washington statutes in *Blakely* and the sentences imposed pursuant to the Federal Sentencing Guidelines in these cases. . . .

III.

The Government advances three arguments in support of its submission that we should not apply our reasoning in *Blakely* to the Federal Sentencing Guidelines. It contends that *Blakely* is distinguishable because the Guidelines were promulgated by a Commission rather than the Legislature; that principles of *stare decisis* require us to follow four earlier decisions that are arguably inconsistent with *Blakely*; and that the application of *Blakely* to the Guidelines would conflict with separation-of-powers principles. . . . These arguments are unpersuasive. . . .

IV.

. . . Accordingly, we reaffirm our holding in *Apprendi*: Any fact (other than a prior conviction) which is necessary to support a sentence exceeding the maximum authorized by the facts established by a plea of guilty or a jury verdict must be admitted by the defendant or proved to a jury beyond a reasonable doubt.

Justice BREYER delivered the opinion of the Court in part.*

. . . We here turn to the second question presented, a question that concerns the remedy. We must decide whether or to what extent, "as a matter of severability analysis," the Guidelines "as a whole" are "inapplicable . . . such that the sentencing court must exercise its discretion to sentence the defendant within the maximum and minimum set by statute for the offense of conviction."

We answer the question of remedy by finding the provision of the federal sentencing statute that makes the Guidelines mandatory, 18 U.S.C. §3553(b)(1), incompatible with today's constitutional holding. We conclude that this provision must be severed and excised, as must one other statutory section, §3742(e), which depends upon the Guidelines' mandatory nature. So modified, the federal sentencing statute, 18 U.S.C. §3551 *et seq.*, 28 U.S.C. §991 *et seq.*, makes the Guidelines effectively advisory. It requires a sentencing court to consider Guidelines ranges, see 18 U.S.C.A. §3553(a)(4), but it permits the court to tailor the sentence in light of other statutory concerns as well, see §3553(a).

I.

We answer the remedial question by looking to legislative intent. We seek to determine what "Congress would have intended" in light of the Court's constitutional holding. In this instance, we must determine which of the two following remedial approaches is the more compatible with the Legislature's intent as embodied in the 1984 Sentencing Act.

*The Chief Justice, Justice O'Connor, Justice Kennedy, and Justice Ginsburg join this opinion.

One approach, that of Justice Stevens' dissent, would retain the Sentencing Act (and the Guidelines) as written, but would engraft onto the existing system today's Sixth Amendment "jury trial" requirement. The addition would change the Guidelines by preventing the sentencing court from increasing a sentence on the basis of a fact that the jury did not find (or that the offender did not admit).

The other approach, which we now adopt, would (through severance and excision of two provisions) make the Guidelines system advisory while maintaining a strong connection between the sentence imposed and the offender's real conduct—a connection important to the increased uniformity of sentencing that Congress intended its Guidelines system to achieve.

Both approaches would significantly alter the system that Congress designed. But today's constitutional holding means that it is no longer possible to maintain the judicial factfinding that Congress thought would underpin the mandatory Guidelines system that it sought to create and that Congress wrote into the Act. Hence we must decide whether we would deviate less radically from Congress' intended system (1) by superimposing the constitutional requirement announced today or (2) through elimination of some provisions of the statute. . . .

II.

Several considerations convince us that, were the Court's constitutional requirement added onto the Sentencing Act as currently written, the requirement would so transform the scheme that Congress created that Congress likely would not have intended the Act as so modified to stand. First, the statute's text states that "[t]he court" when sentencing will consider "the nature and circumstances of the offense and the history and characteristics of the defendant." 18 U.S.C. §3553(a)(1). In context, the words "the court" mean "the judge without the jury," not "the judge working together with the jury." . . .

This provision makes it difficult to justify Justice Stevens' approach, for that approach requires reading the words "the court" as if they meant "the judge working together with the jury." Unlike Justice Stevens, we do not believe we can interpret the statute's language to save its constitutionality because we believe that any such reinterpretation, even if limited to instances in which a Sixth Amendment problem arises would be "plainly contrary to the intent of Congress." Without some such reinterpretation, however, this provision of the statute, along with those inextricably connected to it, are constitutionally invalid, and fall outside of Congress' power to enact. . . .

Second, Congress' basic statutory goal—a system that diminishes sentencing disparity—depends for its success upon judicial efforts to determine, and to base punishment upon, the *real conduct* that underlies the crime of conviction. That determination is particularly important in the federal system where crimes defined as, for example, "obstruct[ing], delay[ing], or affect[ing] commerce or the movement of any article or commodity in commerce, by . . . extortion," 18 U.S.C. §1951(a), or, say, using the mail "for the purpose of executing" a "scheme or artifice to defraud," §1341, can encompass a vast range of very different kinds of underlying conduct. But it is also important even in respect to ordinary crimes, such as robbery, where an act that meets the statutory definition can be committed in a host of different ways. Judges have long looked to real conduct when sentencing. Federal judges have long relied upon a presentence report, prepared by a probation officer, for information (often unavailable until *after* the trial) relevant to the manner in which the convicted offender committed the crime of conviction. . . .

To engraft the Court's constitutional requirement onto the sentencing statutes . . . would destroy the system. It would prevent a judge from relying upon a presentence report for factual information, relevant to sentencing, uncovered after the trial. In doing so, it would, even compared to pre-Guidelines sentencing, weaken the tie between a sentence and an offender's real conduct. It would thereby undermine the sentencing statute's basic aim of ensuring similar sentences for those who have committed similar crimes in similar ways. . . .

The Court's constitutional jury trial requirement . . . if patched onto the present Sentencing Act, would [also] move the system backwards *in respect both to tried and to plea-bargained cases. In respect to tried cases,* it would effectively deprive the judge of the ability to use post-verdict-acquired real-conduct information; it would prohibit the judge from basing a sentence upon any conduct other than the conduct the prosecutor chose to charge; and it would put a defendant to a set of difficult strategic choices as to which prosecutorial claims he would contest. The sentence that would emerge in a case tried under such a system would likely reflect real conduct less completely, less accurately, and less often than did a pre-Guidelines, as well as a Guidelines, trial.

Because plea bargaining inevitably reflects estimates of what would happen at trial, plea bargaining too under such a system would move in the wrong direction. That is to say, in a sentencing system modified by the Court's constitutional requirement, plea bargaining would likely lead to sentences that gave greater weight not to real conduct, but rather to the skill of counsel, the policies of the prosecutor, the caseload, and other factors that vary from place to place, defendant to defendant, and crime to crime. Compared to pre-Guidelines plea bargaining, plea bargaining of this kind would necessarily move federal sentencing in the direction of diminished, not increased, uniformity in sentencing. It would tend to defeat, not to further, Congress' basic statutory goal.

Such a system would have particularly troubling consequences with respect to prosecutorial power. Until now, sentencing factors have come before the judge in the presentence report. But in a sentencing system with the Court's constitutional requirement engrafted onto it, any factor that a prosecutor chose not to charge at the plea negotiation would be placed beyond the reach of the judge entirely. Prosecutors would thus exercise a power the Sentencing Act vested in judges: the power to decide, based on relevant information about the offense and the offender, which defendants merit heavier punishment. . . .

Fifth, Congress would not have enacted sentencing statutes that make it more difficult to adjust sentences *upward* than to adjust them *downward.* As several United States Senators have written in an *amicus* brief, "the Congress that enacted the 1984 Act did not conceive of—much less establish—a sentencing guidelines system in which sentencing judges were free to consider facts or circumstances not found by a jury or admitted in a plea agreement for the purpose of adjusting a base-offense level *down*, but not *up*, within the applicable guidelines range. Such a one-way lever would be grossly at odds with Congress's intent." Yet that is the system that the dissenters' remedy would create.

For all these reasons, Congress, had it been faced with the constitutional jury trial requirement, likely would not have passed the same Sentencing Act. It likely would have found the requirement incompatible with the Act as written. Hence the Act cannot remain valid in its entirety. Severance and excision are necessary.

III.

We now turn to the question of *which* portions of the sentencing statute we must sever and excise as inconsistent with the Court's constitutional requirement. Although, as we have explained, we believe that Congress would have preferred the total invalidation of the statute to the dissenters' remedial approach, we nevertheless do not believe that the entire statute must be invalidated. Most of the statute is perfectly valid. And we must "refrain from invalidating more of the statute than is necessary." Indeed, we must retain those portions of the Act that are (1) constitutionally valid, (2) capable of "functioning independently," and (3) consistent with Congress' basic objectives in enacting the statute.

Application of these criteria indicates that we must sever and excise two specific statutory provisions: the provision that requires sentencing courts to impose a sentence within the applicable Guidelines range (in the absence of circumstances that justify a departure), *see* 18 U.S.C. §3553(b)(1), and the provision that sets forth standards of review on appeal, including *de novo* review of departures from the applicable Guidelines range, *see* §3742(e). With these two sections excised (and statutory cross-references to the two sections consequently invalidated), the remainder of the Act satisfies the Court's constitutional requirements. . . .

The remainder of the Act "function[s] independently." Without the "mandatory" provision, the Act nonetheless requires judges to take account of the Guidelines together with other sentencing goals. *See* 18 U.S.C. §3553(a). The Act nonetheless requires judges to consider the Guidelines "sentencing range established for . . . the applicable category of offense committed by the applicable category of defendant," §3553(a)(4)(A), the pertinent Sentencing Commission policy statements, the need to avoid unwarranted sentencing disparities, and the need to provide restitution to victims, §§3553(a)(1), (3), (5)-(7). And the Act nonetheless requires judges to impose sentences that reflect the seriousness of the offense, promote respect for the law, provide just punishment, afford adequate deterrence, protect the public, and effectively provide the defendant with needed educational or vocational training and medical care. §3553(a)(2).

Moreover, despite the absence of §3553(b)(1), the Act continues to provide for appeals from sentencing decisions (irrespective of whether the trial judge sentences within or outside the Guidelines range in the exercise of his discretionary power under §3553(a)). *See* §3742(a) (appeal by defendant); §3742(b) (appeal by Government). We concede that the excision of §3553(b)(1) requires the excision of a different, appeals-related section, namely, §3742(e), which sets forth standards of review on appeal. That section contains critical cross-references to the (now-excised) §3553(b)(1) and consequently must be severed and excised for similar reasons.

Excision of §3742(e), however, does not pose a critical problem for the handling of appeals. That is because, as we have previously held, a statute that does not *explicitly* set forth a standard of review may nonetheless do so *implicitly.* We infer appropriate review standards from related statutory language, the structure of the statute, and the "'sound administration of justice.'" And in this instance those factors, in addition to the past two decades of appellate practice in cases involving departures, imply a practical standard of review already familiar to appellate courts: review for "unreasonable[ness]." 18 U.S.C. §3742(e)(3). . . .

As we have said, the Sentencing Commission remains in place, writing Guidelines, collecting information about actual district court sentencing decisions, undertaking research, and revising the Guidelines accordingly. The district courts, while not bound to apply the Guidelines, must consult those Guidelines and take them into account when sentencing. The courts of appeals review sentencing decisions for unreasonableness. These features of the remaining system, while not the system Congress enacted, nonetheless continue to move sentencing in Congress' preferred direction, helping to avoid excessive sentencing disparities while maintaining flexibility sufficient to individualize sentences where necessary. We can find no feature of the remaining system that tends to hinder, rather than to further, these basic objectives. Under these circumstances, why would Congress not have preferred excision of the "mandatory" provision to a system that engrafts today's constitutional requirement onto the unchanged pre-existing statute—a system that, in terms of Congress' basic objectives, is counterproductive?

We do not doubt that Congress, when it wrote the Sentencing Act, intended to create a form of mandatory Guidelines system. But, we repeat, given today's constitutional holding, that is not a choice that remains open. Hence we have examined the statute in depth to determine Congress' likely intent *in light of today's holding.* And we have concluded that today's holding is fundamentally inconsistent with the judge-based sentencing system that Congress enacted into law. In our view, it is more consistent with Congress' likely intent in enacting the Sentencing Reform Act (1) to preserve important elements of that system while severing and excising two provisions (§§3553(b)(1) and 3742(e)) than (2) to maintain all provisions of the Act and engraft today's constitutional requirement onto that statutory scheme.

Ours, of course, is not the last word: The ball now lies in Congress' court. The National Legislature is equipped to devise and install, long term, the sentencing system, compatible with the Constitution, that Congress judges best for the federal system of justice. . . .

It is so ordered.

[The dissenting opinions of Justices Stevens, Scalia, Thomas, and Breyer are omitted.]

NOTES AND QUESTIONS

1. If Justice Scalia pulled a rabbit out of his hat in fashioning the *Blakely* opinion, Justice Breyer pulled a lion out of his by achieving this outcome in *Booker.* Through two different majorities, the Court held that judicial fact-finding

during a determinate sentencing (i.e., mandatory guideline) process is unconstitutional, but it is perfectly constitutional when done as part of an indeterminate (i.e., advisory guideline) system. By making the Guidelines advisory, Justice Breyer rescued them just as they appeared bound for oblivion.

2. How does this outcome strike you from a practical point of view? Many would say it is the best of both worlds. The Guidelines are still carefully calculated in every case to give an "objective" measure of the appropriate sentence. In theory, the Guidelines provide an anchor (see Note 3, below), reducing arbitrary variation in sentences across defendants. Nevertheless, because they are advisory only, a trial court can still fashion a different sentence if such action is necessary to fit a particular defendant's personal situation.
3. Social scientific study strongly supports the proposition that providing individuals with an "anchor value" subconsciously causes them to make a later decision based on a deviation from the anchor rather than by starting from some other point. The first and still classic study demonstrating this phenomenon was conducted by psychologists Amos Tversky and Daniel Kahneman. *See* Amos Tversky & Daniel Kahneman, *Judgment Under Uncertainty: Heuristics and Biases*, 185 Sci. 1124, 1128 (1974). (In 1996, Kahneman won the Nobel Prize for Economics, in which Tversky would have shared had he still been alive.) Thus, one can postulate that even advisory guidelines have a significant—though, sometimes subconscious—impact on sentences meted out by judges.
4. How does the *Booker* outcome strike you as a matter of constitutional interpretation? Which justice switched majorities to cause it?
5. Which players in the criminal justice system would you expect to be happy with the outcome in *Booker*? Are there any that you would expect to be unhappy?

III. CURRENT SENTENCING PROCEDURE

GALL v. UNITED STATES
552 U.S. 38 (2007)

Justice Stevens delivered the opinion of the Court.

In two cases argued on the same day last Term we considered the standard that courts of appeals should apply when reviewing the reasonableness of sentences imposed by district judges. The first, Rita v. United States, 551 U.S. 338 (2007), involved a sentence *within* the range recommended by the Federal Sentencing Guidelines; we held that when a district judge's discretionary decision in a particular case accords with the sentence the United States Sentencing Commission deems appropriate "in the mine run of cases," the court of appeals may presume that the sentence is reasonable.

The second case, Claiborne v. United States, 549 U.S. 1016 (2007), involved a sentence *below* the range recommended by the Guidelines, and raised the converse question whether a court of appeals may apply a "proportionality test," and require that a sentence that constitutes a substantial variance from the Guidelines be justified by extraordinary circumstances. We did not have the opportunity to answer this question because the case was mooted by Claiborne's untimely death. We granted certiorari in the case before us today in order to reach that question, left unanswered last Term. We now hold that, while the extent of the difference between a particular sentence and the recommended Guidelines range is surely relevant, courts of appeals must review all sentences—whether inside, just outside, or significantly outside the Guidelines range—under a deferential abuse-of-discretion standard. We also hold that the sentence imposed by the experienced District Judge in this case was reasonable.

I.

In February or March 2000, petitioner Brian Gall, a second-year college student at the University of Iowa, was invited by Luke Rinderknecht to join an ongoing enterprise distributing a controlled substance popularly known as "ecstasy." Gall—who was then a user of ecstasy, cocaine, and marijuana—accepted the invitation. During the ensuing seven months, Gall delivered ecstasy pills, which he received from Rinderknecht, to other conspirators, who then sold them to consumers. He netted over $30,000.

A month or two after joining the conspiracy, Gall stopped using ecstasy. A few months after that, in September 2000, he advised Rinderknecht and other co-conspirators that he was withdrawing from the conspiracy. He has not sold illegal drugs of any kind since. He has, in the words of the District Court, "self-rehabilitated." He graduated from the University of Iowa in 2002, and moved first to Arizona, where he obtained a job in the construction industry, and later to Colorado, where he earned $18 per hour as a master carpenter. He has not used any illegal drugs since graduating from college.

After Gall moved to Arizona, he was approached by federal law enforcement agents who questioned him about his involvement in the ecstasy distribution conspiracy. Gall admitted his limited participation in the distribution of ecstasy, and the agents took no further action at that time. On April 28, 2004—approximately a year and a half after this initial interview, and three and a half years after Gall withdrew from the conspiracy—an indictment was returned in the Southern District of Iowa charging him and seven other defendants with participating in a conspiracy to distribute ecstasy, cocaine, and marijuana, that began in or about May 1996 and continued through October 30, 2002. The Government has never questioned the truthfulness of any of Gall's earlier statements or contended that he played any role in, or had any knowledge of, other aspects of the conspiracy described in the indictment. When he received notice of the indictment, Gall moved back to Iowa and surrendered to the authorities. While free on his own recognizance, Gall started his own business in the construction industry, primarily engaged in subcontracting for the installation of windows and doors. In his first year, his profits were over $2,000 per month.

Gall entered into a plea agreement with the Government, stipulating that he was "responsible for, but did not necessarily distribute himself, at least 2,500 grams of [ecstasy], or the equivalent of at least 87.5 kilograms of marijuana." In the agreement, the Government acknowledged that by "on or about September of 2000," Gall had communicated his intent to stop distributing ecstasy to Rinderknecht and other members of the conspiracy. The agreement further provided that recent changes in the Guidelines that enhanced the recommended punishment for distributing ecstasy were not applicable to Gall because he had withdrawn from the conspiracy prior to the effective date of those changes.

In her presentence report, the probation officer concluded that Gall had no significant criminal history; that he was not an organizer, leader, or manager; and that his offense did not involve the use of any weapons. The report stated that Gall had truthfully provided the Government with all of the evidence he had concerning the alleged offenses, but that his evidence was not useful because he provided no new information to the agents. The report also described Gall's substantial use of drugs prior to his offense and the absence of any such use in recent years. The report recommended a sentencing range of 30 to 37 months of imprisonment.

The record of the sentencing hearing held on May 27, 2005, includes a "small flood" of letters from Gall's parents and other relatives, his fiancé, neighbors, and representatives of firms doing business with him, uniformly praising his character and work ethic. The transcript includes the testimony of several witnesses and the District Judge's colloquy with the Assistant United States Attorney (AUSA) and with Gall. The AUSA did not contest any of the evidence concerning Gall's law-abiding life during the preceding five years, but urged that "the Guidelines are appropriate and should be followed," and requested that the court impose a prison sentence within the Guidelines range. He mentioned that two of Gall's co-conspirators had been sentenced to 30 and 35 months, respectively, but upon further questioning by the District Court, he acknowledged that neither of them had voluntarily withdrawn from the conspiracy.

The District Judge sentenced Gall to probation for a term of 36 months. In addition to making a lengthy statement on the record, the judge filed a detailed sentencing memorandum explaining his decision, and provided the following statement of reasons in his written judgment:

> The Court determined that, considering all the factors under 18 U.S.C. 3553(a), the Defendant's explicit withdrawal from the conspiracy almost four years before the filing of the Indictment, the Defendant's post-offense conduct, especially obtaining a college degree and the start of his own successful business, the support of family and friends, lack of criminal history, and his age at the time of the offense conduct, all warrant the sentence imposed, which was sufficient, but not greater than necessary to serve the purposes of sentencing.

At the end of both the sentencing hearing and the sentencing memorandum, the District Judge reminded Gall that probation, rather than "an act of leniency," is a "substantial restriction of freedom." In the memorandum, he emphasized:

> [Gall] will have to comply with strict reporting conditions along with a three-year regime of alcohol and drug testing. He will not be able to change or make decisions about significant circumstances in his life, such as where to live or work, which

> are prized liberty interests, without first seeking authorization from his Probation Officer or, perhaps, even the Court. Of course, the Defendant always faces the harsh consequences that await if he violates the conditions of his probationary term.

Finally, the District Judge explained why he had concluded that the sentence of probation reflected the seriousness of Gall's offense and that no term of imprisonment was necessary:

> Any term of imprisonment in this case would be countereffective by depriving society of the contributions of the Defendant who, the Court has found, understands the consequences of his criminal conduct and is doing everything in his power to forge a new life. The Defendant's post-offense conduct indicates neither that he will return to criminal behavior nor that the Defendant is a danger to society. In fact, the Defendant's post-offense conduct was not motivated by a desire to please the Court or any other governmental agency, but was the pre-Indictment product of the Defendant's own desire to lead a better life.

II.

The Court of Appeals reversed and remanded for resentencing. Relying on its earlier opinion in United States v. Claiborne, 439 F.3d 479 (CA8 2006), it held that a sentence outside of the Guidelines range must be supported by a justification that "is proportional to the extent of the difference between the advisory range and the sentence imposed." Characterizing the difference between a sentence of probation and the bottom of Gall's advisory Guidelines range of 30 months as "extraordinary" because it amounted to "a 100% downward variance," the Court of Appeals held that such a variance must be—and here was not—supported by extraordinary circumstances.

Rather than making an attempt to quantify the value of the justifications provided by the District Judge, the Court of Appeals identified what it regarded as five separate errors in the District Judge's reasoning: (1) He gave "too much weight to Gall's withdrawal from the conspiracy"; (2) given that Gall was 21 at the time of his offense, the District Judge erroneously gave "significant weight" to studies showing impetuous behavior by persons under the age of 18; (3) he did not "properly weigh" the seriousness of Gall's offense; (4) he failed to consider whether a sentence of probation would result in "unwarranted" disparities; and (5) he placed "too much emphasis on Gall's post-offense rehabilitation." As we shall explain, we are not persuaded that these factors, whether viewed separately or in the aggregate, are sufficient to support the conclusion that the District Judge abused his discretion. As a preface to our discussion of these particulars, however, we shall explain why the Court of Appeals' rule requiring "proportional" justifications for departures from the Guidelines range is not consistent with our remedial opinion in United States v. Booker, 543 U.S. 220 (2005).

III.

Our explanation of "reasonableness" review in the *Booker* opinion made it pellucidly clear that the familiar abuse-of-discretion standard of review now applies to appellate review of sentencing decisions.

It is also clear that a district judge must give serious consideration to the extent of any departure from the Guidelines and must explain his conclusion that an unusually lenient or an unusually harsh sentence is appropriate in a particular case with sufficient justifications. For even though the Guidelines are advisory rather than mandatory, they are, as we pointed out in *Rita*, the product of careful study based on extensive empirical evidence derived from the review of thousands of individual sentencing decisions.

In reviewing the reasonableness of a sentence outside the Guidelines range, appellate courts may therefore take the degree of variance into account and consider the extent of a deviation from the Guidelines. We reject, however, an appellate rule that requires "extraordinary" circumstances to justify a sentence outside the Guidelines range. We also reject the use of a rigid mathematical formula that uses the percentage of a departure as the standard for determining the strength of the justifications required for a specific sentence.

As an initial matter, the approaches we reject come too close to creating an impermissible presumption of unreasonableness for sentences outside the Guidelines range. Even the Government has acknowledged that such a presumption would not be consistent with *Booker.*

The mathematical approach also suffers from infirmities of application. On one side of the equation, deviations from the Guidelines range will always appear more extreme — in percentage terms — when the range itself is low, and a sentence of probation will always be a 100% departure regardless of whether the Guidelines range is 1 month or 100 years. Moreover, quantifying the variance as a certain percentage of the maximum, minimum, or median prison sentence recommended by the Guidelines gives no weight to the "substantial restriction of freedom" involved in a term of supervised release or probation. . . .

On the other side of the equation, the mathematical approach assumes the existence of some ascertainable method of assigning percentages to various justifications. Does withdrawal from a conspiracy justify more or less than, say, a 30% reduction? Does it matter that the withdrawal occurred several years ago? Is it relevant that the withdrawal was motivated by a decision to discontinue the use of drugs and to lead a better life? What percentage, if any, should be assigned to evidence that a defendant poses no future threat to society, or to evidence that innocent third parties are dependent on him? The formula is a classic example of attempting to measure an inventory of apples by counting oranges.

Most importantly, both the exceptional circumstances requirement and the rigid mathematical formulation reflect a practice — common among courts that have adopted "proportional review" — of applying a heightened standard of review to sentences outside the Guidelines range. This is inconsistent with the rule that the abuse-of-discretion standard of review applies to appellate review of all sentencing decisions — whether inside or outside the Guidelines range.

As we explained in *Rita*, a district court should begin all sentencing proceedings by correctly calculating the applicable Guidelines range. As a matter of administration and to secure nationwide consistency, the Guidelines should be the starting point and the initial benchmark. The Guidelines are not the only consideration, however. Accordingly, after giving both parties an opportunity to argue for whatever sentence they deem appropriate, the district judge should then consider all of the §3553(a) factors to determine whether they support the sentence requested by a party.[6] In so doing, he may not presume that the Guidelines range is reasonable. He must make an individualized assessment based on the facts presented. If he decides that an outside-Guidelines sentence is warranted, he must consider the extent of the deviation and ensure that the justification is sufficiently compelling to support the degree of the variance. We find it uncontroversial that a major departure should be supported by a more significant justification than a minor one. After settling on the appropriate sentence, he must adequately explain the chosen sentence to allow for meaningful appellate review and to promote the perception of fair sentencing.

Regardless of whether the sentence imposed is inside or outside the Guidelines range, the appellate court must review the sentence under an abuse-of-discretion standard. It must first ensure that the district court committed no significant procedural error, such as failing to calculate (or improperly calculating) the Guidelines range, treating the Guidelines as mandatory, failing to consider the §3553(a) factors, selecting a sentence based on clearly erroneous facts, or failing to adequately explain the chosen sentence—including an explanation for any deviation from the Guidelines range. Assuming that the district court's sentencing decision is procedurally sound, the appellate court should then consider the substantive reasonableness of the sentence imposed under an abuse-of-discretion standard. When conducting this review, the court will, of course, take into account the totality of the circumstances, including the extent of any variance from the Guidelines range. If the sentence is within the Guidelines range, the appellate court may, but is not required to, apply a presumption of reasonableness. But if the sentence is outside

6. Section 3553(a) lists seven factors that a sentencing court must consider. The first factor is a broad command to consider "the nature and circumstances of the offense and the history and characteristics of the defendant." 18 U.S.C. §3553(a)(1). The second factor requires the consideration of the general purposes of sentencing, including:

> "the need for the sentence imposed—
> "(A) to reflect the seriousness of the offense, to promote respect for the law, and to provide just punishment for the offense;
> "(B) to afford adequate deterrence to criminal conduct;
> "(C) to protect the public from further crimes of the defendant; and
> "(D) to provide the defendant with needed educational or vocational training, medical care, or other correctional treatment in the most effective manner." §3553(a)(2).

The third factor pertains to "the kinds of sentences available," §3553(a)(3); the fourth to the Sentencing Guidelines; the fifth to any relevant policy statement issued by the Sentencing Commission; the sixth to "the need to avoid unwarranted sentence disparities," §3553(a)(6); and the seventh to "the need to provide restitution to any victim," §3553(a)(7). Preceding this list is a general directive to "impose a sentence sufficient, but not greater than necessary, to comply with the purposes" of sentencing described in the second factor. §3553(a). The fact that §3553(a) explicitly directs sentencing courts to consider the Guidelines supports the premise that district courts must begin their analysis with the Guidelines and remain cognizant of them throughout the sentencing process.

the Guidelines range, the court may not apply a presumption of unreasonableness. It may consider the extent of the deviation, but must give due deference to the district court's decision that the §3553(a) factors, on a whole, justify the extent of the variance. The fact that the appellate court might reasonably have concluded that a different sentence was appropriate is insufficient to justify reversal of the district court.

Practical considerations also underlie this legal principle. "The sentencing judge is in a superior position to find facts and judge their import under §3553(a) in the individual case. The judge sees and hears the evidence, makes credibility determinations, has full knowledge of the facts and gains insights not conveyed by the record." "The sentencing judge has access to, and greater familiarity with, the individual case and the individual defendant before him than the Commission or the appeals court." *Rita*, 551 U.S., at 357-58. Moreover, "[d]istrict courts have an institutional advantage over appellate courts in making these sorts of determinations, especially as they see so many more Guidelines sentences than appellate courts do." Koon v. United States, 518 U.S. 81, 98 (1996).

"It has been uniform and constant in the federal judicial tradition for the sentencing judge to consider every convicted person as an individual and every case as a unique study in the human failings that sometimes mitigate, sometimes magnify, the crime and the punishment to ensue." The uniqueness of the individual case, however, does not change the deferential abuse-of-discretion standard of review that applies to all sentencing decisions. . . . [T]he opinion of the Court of Appeals in this case does not reflect the requisite deference and does not support the conclusion that the District Court abused its discretion. . . .

V.

. . . The Court of Appeals clearly disagreed with the District Judge's conclusion that consideration of the §3553(a) factors justified a sentence of probation; it believed that the circumstances presented here were insufficient to sustain such a marked deviation from the Guidelines range. But it is not for the Court of Appeals to decide *de novo* whether the justification for a variance is sufficient or the sentence reasonable. On abuse-of-discretion review, the Court of Appeals should have given due deference to the District Court's reasoned and reasonable decision that the §3553(a) factors, on the whole, justified the sentence. Accordingly, the judgment of the Court of Appeals is reversed.

It is so ordered.

NOTES AND QUESTIONS

1. Are the Court's reasons for according trial judges so much deference in sentencing decisions convincing? Should trial judges have so much power when it comes to depriving convicted defendants of their liberty?
2. One of the tangible accomplishments of mandatory sentencing guidelines was achieving relative uniformity in sentences for similar crimes. (Guidelines

champions' motto was, "Same crime, same time.") Any discretion accorded trial judges in the new advisory setting necessarily erodes this uniformity. On the other hand, judicial discretion furthers the cause of justice by individualizing punishment. Do you think *Gall* strikes the right balance between these two goals?

3. Test your understanding: Explain the post-*Booker* sentencing procedure in federal court, step-by-step, including the standards of review.

Table of Cases

Principal cases indicated by italics.

Table of Statutes

INDEX